ASHES TO ASHES

ASHES TO ASHES: THE SONGS OF DAVID BOWIE, 1976-2016

CHRIS O'LEARY

Published by Repeater Books

An imprint of Watkins Media Ltd

Unit 11 Shepperton House
89-93 Shepperton Road
London
N1 3DF

A Repeater Books paperback original 2019
3

Distributed in the United States by Random House, Inc., New York.

Cover design: Johnny Bull
Typography and typesetting: Frederik Jehle
Typefaces: Meridien LT Std, Bebas Neue, Raleway, EB Garamond, Gill Sans

ISBN: 9781912248308
Ebook ISBN: 9781912248360

Printed and bound in the United Kingdom by TJ International Ltd

CONTENTS

"Trust nothing but your own experience."
David Bowie, 2004

INTRODUCTION

The response to the death of David Bowie in January 2016 may be among the last unified moments in global civilization. Or at least it felt that way, for about a week. His timing, as often, was spot-on. His death kicked off a year that would see his home country and his adopted one upturned by December. Along with the death of Prince that April, it signaled that the twentieth century was well and truly over, and that we were in a new world.

That week in January, some who didn't know Bowie's albums after, say, *Never Let Me Down* discovered the full breadth of his work — fifty-two years' worth of recordings (with a few gaps, of course). Maybe they heard for the first time *The Buddha of Suburbia* or *Heathen* or his wonderfully odd debut from 1967, and learned there was far more to him than the "Let's Dance" celebrity or Ziggy Stardust.

I began writing about Bowie because I was in a similar state: I'd never heard a good chunk of his music. In July 2009, I started a blog called "Pushing Ahead of the Dame" (I came up with the title — a pun on a line from Bowie's "Queen Bitch" and his nickname in some quarters of the British music press — in about ten minutes. It's a silly name and I've regretted it over the years). It was a writing exercise, intended as a contrast to a sprawling blog that I'd done in the 2000s that had covered all genres of music from the twentieth century. No more! Now it would be just one artist, just one song at a time, in chronological order. Easily done, I thought. Listen to a Bowie song at breakfast, do a spot of research, write a couple of paragraphs, hit "publish," and that would be that. And here we are ten years later, with the second of two books derived from that blog. (The first, *Rebel Rebel*, which covers "Liza Jane" to "Station to Station," was published in 2015.) The length of this book proves that John Lennon was right when he said life's what happens to you while you're busy making other plans.

I owe this change of fortune to a few in particular — my editor Tariq Goddard, for instance (see Acknowledgements) — but more to the fact that people wanted to read and talk about Bowie's music in depth. The blog soon attracted a strong readership, many of whom had insights into Bowie's work that surpassed my own — the musician Momus became a fixture of the comment sections. This was, again, a matter of good timing. The blog's peak years (when I was writing at least an entry a week — a rate of production that astonishes my creaky self today) of 2010-2013 coincided with the growing realization that Bowie had possibly retired. He hadn't put out an album since 2003, hadn't toured in nearly a decade. It was unusual to even see a new photograph of him by this point. He'd begun to be missed.

So nearly two-thirds of "Pushing Ahead of the Dame" (Bowie's return with "Where Are We Now?" coincided with the last *Buddha of Suburbia* entries) was written about an artist who wasn't quite there anymore. Bowie's public absence seeped into the writing. I framed entries in a past tense, describing the music of someone who'd departed. And then he came back.

In 2013, the blog suddenly found itself covering a vital contemporary artist who was releasing new music at a pace to shame musicians two generations younger than him. Everything changed. Opinions needed to be reconsidered. Themes no longer fit. Narratives no longer worked. There was so much possibility. Being a Bowie fan from January 2013 to the first week of 2016 was to follow a revived serial whose plots regularly surprised you (he's writing a play! he's doing jazz!). Recall that one weekend in January 2016 when *Blackstar* had just come out, *Lazarus* was on stage, and David Bowie was still alive.

When his death was announced, it felt as if the whole point of the blog was for it to be there on that day, as one place for Bowie fans to speak and to mourn. Nothing was quite right again afterward. Already exhausted from writing about Bowie for so long, I now had nothing to say about him. I took about six months off and when I returned, to start the *Blackstar* entries, I found it to be truly unhappy labor and in autumn 2017, I stopped writing the blog with five entries left to go (to be fair, this coincided with doing the major revisions in this book). I hope that in *Ashes to Ashes* I've improved some later pieces, which were as much a processing of information about a song as a criticism of it. The five "unreleased" blog entries— "No Plan," "Killing a Little Time," "Dollar Days," "I Can't Give Everything Away," and the title track— are found in the *Blackstar* chapter.

My status as a Bowie critic is still rather a mystery to me. I was never a true fan: never had Bowie posters on my wall, never paid that much attention to his music in my teenage years. I had considered him to be roughly on par with George Harrison or Mick Jagger — an older musician who still got on the radio. I saw him once in concert, in Hartford in 1990, and I bought most of his Seventies albums on their Rykodisc reissues around that time, with *The Man Who Sold the World* and *Low* hitting me the hardest. But for quite a while, roughly post-*Earthling*, I lost touch with what he was doing, to the point where in 2002 he played a gig at Queens College, a quick subway ride from my apartment in Sunnyside, and I had no idea he was there.

This "objectivity" (or "ignorance," if you'd like) naturally informed my writing on his music. So did being of a certain age (too young for Ziggy Stardust, just a smidgen too old for *Labyrinth*) and being American. See *Rebel Rebel*, where I wrote that "Britain" won the World Cup in 1966. An Englishman complains about that to me every six months or so. With hope, there are fewer cultural errors this time around.

Being a critical study of Bowie's music, this book relies greatly on the work of others: concert tapers and compilers, interviewers, documentarians, photographers, biographers. The labors of Kevin Cann and Nicholas Pegg can't be praised enough, and the websites *Teenage Wildlife* and *Bowie Wonderworld* provide a miraculous day-by-day chronology of Bowie's doings from 1997 on. The "David Bowie Tin Machine" YouTube account, a thorough collection of Bowie live footage and TV/radio interviews, is also an essential source.

When revising what were, in some cases, essays written eight or more years ago, I had to walk the line between preserving the tone of the original piece and improving it with new information, fresher quotes, a sharper interpretation, and being less flippant and caustic — a flaw of the blog's early years. Some pieces were trimmed, others fattened up. I tried to avoid making the book too "posthumous" but sometimes this proved unavoidable: finality was given its due.

I wanted from the start of the blog to treat each period, each album and each tour, with as much thoroughness as any other. To acknowledge nostalgia but not let it color my interpretations, to ground the songs in the time of their creation but also note how they were heard in later years. I greatly disliked some songs (you'll soon see that) but tried to give them a fair shake. I devoted more space to the music — its creation, production, and performances — than to lyrical analysis, as the latter is too often the ruling party in rock criticism.

My books are an early draft of history. There's some educated guesswork in them as to how songs were written and recorded. One day, perhaps, the Bowie estate will allow a researcher (someone else, please) to document and annotate all of his lyric drafts, outtakes, demos, studio logs, etc., and thus create a fuller analysis of his music. Until then, what follows is my best effort: a decade's labor, now done. I hope that you enjoy it.

A BRIEF GUIDE TO THIS BOOK

Songs are listed in the rough order of their creation, with exceptions for narrative purposes (e.g., "Bring Me the Disco King," first recorded in 1992, is in the *Reality* chapter; "Jewel," a 1997 recording, was moved to 1999 to serve as an "end of an era" piece). A song merits an entry if a) Bowie wrote it and/or b) he produced, sang, or played on it, whether in the studio or on stage. All versions of a song are addressed in its earliest appearance, chronologically — so "China Girl" is in *The Idiot*'s chapter, for example. A brief appendix lists songs that reportedly exist but haven't been bootlegged.

First release means when the song was first made available. If it came out in the UK before the US (often the case), the UK date is listed, and vice versa (for the sake of clarity and simplicity, dates are either for the UK or US, although there are cases when an album came out in some European countries earlier (e.g., *Earthling* and *The Next Day*)). For *'hours...'*, the date is when the album was released on the internet, weeks before it was in stores. Note: the specific date listed is the agreed-upon date by a variety of sources, backed up by my research (typically trade magazines like *Billboard* and *Cash Box* and the weekly UK music papers of the period), that appears to be the most likely, given available information. Especially for singles, before the SoundScan era (pre-1991), there is little verifiable data on the actual date that releases hit stores. Further, release dates were far from universally honored by retailers: if they got an album in a week early, they'd put it in the racks. So while I've gone with the date with the most sources to back it up, there's often no definitive proof that a particular date is the "right" one.

All songs were written by David Bowie unless otherwise specified in the text.

Broadcast is any performance done specifically for TV or radio. This includes awards ceremonies primarily intended for broadcast (the MTV

Awards, for example), and excludes live performances that were also shown on TV or the internet (Bowie's fiftieth birthday concert, for example). The date given is the date of taping, not when the performance aired, which was sometimes months afterward; in some cases, these performances were never aired.

Recording dates have been verified to the best of my abilities. I particularly thank Reeves Gabrels for vastly improving my information about the recording of Bowie's Nineties albums, and Nicholas Pegg for *Next Day* and *Blackstar* session information. For many albums it remains difficult to determine specific days or weeks of recording — "circa" carries a lot of weight. For greater clarity, I've eliminated listing most demos and remixes. Musician credits come from liner notes, interviews, and supposition. When there's a question mark after someone, it means "it's possibly him or her, based on available evidence." If there's one after an instrument, it means "either this person or the other person(s) with a "?" played this instrument, but no one remembers who" (e.g., Tony Visconti and Bowie on tambourine for "Heroes.")

Given the length of this book, its notes section had to become an online supplement, much to my regret. Here is where you will find credits, sources for quotes, and a host of details cut from the final edit of the book: **https://bowiesongs.wordpress.com/ashes/notes**.

THE STORY SO FAR

Ashes to Ashes begins in 1976, with the recording of *The Idiot* and *Low*. If you're interested in Bowie's earlier music, I suggest you read *Rebel Rebel*, my earlier book. But if you've picked up only *this* book, have no fear. Here's where things stand at this juncture in his life.

He was born David Robert Jones, on 8 January 1947, the only son of Haywood "John" Stenton Jones and Margaret "Peggy" Burns. Growing up in Bromley, he left school in 1963 and spent the Sixties trying to become a pop star, changing his name, burning through bands and labels, with little to show for it but flop singles and a poorly-selling album, *David Bowie* (Deram, 1967).

Bowie got a hit at last in late 1969 with "Space Oddity." He was at risk of being considered a one-hit-wonder, and a period of eccentric floundering ensued. But by 1971, the pieces were in place, including a capable, if cutthroat manager (Tony Defries), an ambitious spouse and de facto co-manager (Angela Bowie), a brilliant guitarist/arranger (Mick Ronson), and a deal with RCA Records, which gave him time to develop his compositions and to plan a campaign that would win over the press and get him on the charts.

The Rise and Fall of Ziggy Stardust and the Spiders from Mars (1972) made him a bonafide British pop star. What followed were four years of constant reinvention — killing off his Ziggy Stardust character in 1973, swiftly moving to dark theatrical rock with *Diamond Dogs* (1974), even more swiftly moving to dark theatrical "plastic soul" in *Young Americans* (1975). The latter broke him in America, with "Fame" topping the *Billboard* Hot 100.

By mid-to-late 1975, when he was starring in *The Man Who Fell to Earth* and making *Station to Station*, he was isolated in Los Angeles. Reeling from a costly breakup with Defries and having become a cocaine addict, he obsessed over such interests as Nazism and the Kabbalah while trying, and failing, to complete the film's soundtrack. Given the state of his finances, touring was one of the few reliable means of income for him, so off he went in early 1976. This was the Thin White Duke period, where a skeletal Bowie, commanding one of the finest bands of his life, made his escape from America. He left Los Angeles, vowing never to return, and took a friend along for the tour. His name was Iggy Pop.

CHAPTER
ONE:

NEW
PEOPLE

(1976-1977)

What was I when I left — all but out of my mind! I knew nothing then and know still less now. I'm in need of good people.
— Fyodor Dostoevsky, *The Idiot*

The horrible speed of life at the present day, and the distracting influences upon the nervous system, must eventually result in reaction.
— Edmund Shaftesbury, "The New Race"

A sign of our nervous, precipitate age… we are all, each and every one of us, attuned to aphoristic, terse and catchy tunes.
— Ernst von Wolzogen, founder of Berlin's first cabaret

I want to travel in Europe, Alyosha, I shall set off from here. I know that I am only going to a graveyard, but it's a most precious graveyard.
— Dostoevsky, *The Brothers Karamazov*

We're pioneers — new people — you can trust us.
— Banner at a Young Pioneer camp, USSR, shown in Vertov's *Kino-Eye*, 1924

Sister Midnight

(Bowie, Pop, Alomar.) **Recorded**: *(backing tracks, vocals) ca. 5 June-early July 1976, Château d'Hérouville, Hérouville, Val d'Oise, France; (vocals, overdubs) ca. late July-early August 1976, Musicland Studios, Arabella-Hochhaus, Arabellastraße 5, Munich; (overdubs, mixing) ca. 21-28 August 1976, Hansa Tonstudio 1, 8-9 Nestorstraße, Berlin. Iggy Pop: lead vocal; David Bowie: piano, Baldwin electric piano, guitar, harmony vocals; Phil Palmer: lead guitar; Carlos Alomar: rhythm guitar; George Murray: bass; Dennis Davis: drums, tambourine. Produced: Bowie; engineered: Laurent Thibault.*

First release: *18 March 1977,* **The Idiot** *(RCA PL 12275/APL1-2275, UK #30, US #72).* **Broadcast**: *(Pop and Bowie) 15 April 1977, Dinah!* **Live**: *(Pop and Bowie) 1977; (Pop) 1977, 1979-1980, 1986-1987, 1996-1997, 2014-2016, 2018; (Bowie) 1976, 2003-2004.*

We should start with Iggy.

James Newell Osterberg Jr., born in 1947, was an only child who lived in a trailer park and dreamed about becoming "Jim Bowie, as tall as a big oak tree. I can do anything and I have to be out there on the edge." Gregarious and quick-witted, he flourished in his environment: mid-century Michigan at its most prosperous and class-fluid. His public school system was flush with Cold War and automaker money; his classmates were the children of Ford and University of Michigan executives. He was friends with the Wrigley's Gum heiresses and the godson of Secretary of Defense Robert McNamara; he dated the city administrator's daughter. In his button-down shirts, slacks, and loafers, Osterberg was at ease in the homes of the rich, which would serve him well later in life.

He would rewrite his youth, make it more hardscrabble, calling himself a trailer-park hoodlum (this was how David Bowie first knew him, as a scuzzy "Jean Genie"). In 1965 he grew his hair, started tripping on his asthma medicine. He drummed in a band called the Iguanas, slashing at a ride cymbal studded with rivets. He went to the University of Michigan to study anthropology but soon dropped out and joined the Prime Movers, a band with ties to the growing student activist scene. They teased him for his greaser rock 'n' roll past, calling him "Iggy" (a shortened "Iguana"). He stuck around because "I sort of smelled out that there was a bunch of leftists around campus who knew about all sorts of stuff I didn't know about," he recalled decades later. "That was a whole lot more interesting than trying to write garage songs." He was looking for a scene to dominate. Playing drums for a blues musician in Chicago, Osterberg saw that, as with the upper crust of Ann Arbor, he was second-rate compared to the naturals. "These guys were way over my head," he said of the bluesmen. "I thought, what you gotta do is play your own simple blues."

So he fashioned a stage persona. In high school, he'd played talent shows as "Hyacinth," a poet and dancer. Now he became Iggy Pop, an overgrown child (in 1980, he recalled that "I used to work off the age of one and two... Now I go back to age six or eight"), full of animal spirits — you can't imagine Iggy ever catching a cold. He was a violent boy who wouldn't leave you alone until you responded. He'd cut himself, smear peanut butter on his chest, jackknife into crowds; he welcomed the tossed bottles and middle fingers. And he kept it up for decades. In Dublin in 2002, he hurled his mike and spat at members of the Corrs when he saw them chatting in their stageside box during his set.

Then there was his voice. By the time he co-founded the Stooges in 1967, he had a bluesy, nasally rasp ("*NAHN*-teen-six-ty-*NAHN*"), keeping to a small range, his phrasings full of long, heavy drags, as if he was testing how much weight a single note could bear. "I hear words musically," he said. *Last year I was twenny-**ONE**/I didn't have a lot of **FUUN**. All **NIIIIGHT** till I **BLOW** uh-**WAY**. I took a **RAAAAAAH-CORD** of pretty **MYOOSSIC**.* There was violence in his syllables: Jo-***han***-uh, JO-***HAN***-UH.

"I was the worker in the band," he said of the Stooges. Rock was "a 24-hour, 365-day-a-year job." In his autobiography, he proposed a rock musician's union to pay him a standard wage for working six days a week. "We're the hardest-working band — who *cares* if we're not the best," he said on stage at a Stooges gig in 1973. Even when he had to be roused from a stupor before he took the stage, Pop and the Stooges were always on, remorseless. "We could never afford to turn down even one job," Pop said at the time. "'Cause our backs were always against the wall."

He was once seen far offshore an LA beach, slamming into waves as if at war with the sea. Even at his most down-and-out, his post-Stooges years in LA in the mid-Seventies, he kept hustling. He got into rock 'n' roll "because I wanted to live a one-piece life"; he felt umbilically tied to his guitarists and their backline, "the proximity of the electric hum in the background and just the tremendous feeling of buoyancy and power. When guitars are played properly, hitting the same sound at the same time... you are dangerously abandoned. It is the most honest experience I have ever encountered."

Or as his guitarist Ron Asheton told him, "you really need the freedom, don't you, Iggy?"

Escapees

When they first met, in New York in September 1971, Pop charmed Bowie, who would produce him (*Raw Power*), and Bowie's manager, who signed him. "Bowie wanted to tap into the rock 'n' roll reality that Iggy lived," the photographer Leee Black Childers said. After the fall of the Stooges, Bowie and Pop lost touch, reconnecting in Los Angeles in spring 1975. By then Pop, a heroin user, had spent time in the UCLA Neuropsychiatric Institute (that or jail, the LAPD said), while Bowie was at the summit of his cocaine addiction. Demo sessions yielded half-finished songs, including "Turn Blue," completed on *Lust for Life* (see Ch. Two).

Then Pop tagged onto Bowie's tour at its LA stop in February 1976. "We both escaped from LA," he recalled fifteen years later. Bowie "was on top of the heap of LA and it was ruining him, and I was on the bottom of it, the other end of the circle from him. We were so far apart we were together. If he walked out his door, they wanted to bend over and kiss his butt... And I was the most reviled street-scum in Hollywood of no fixed address."

He joined the tour looking for distractions to stay clean, but he was also enticed by Bowie's offer of a song he'd written with his guitarist Carlos Alomar, proposing that Pop record it. Every night, Pop stood in the wings "watching Bowie doing exactly what he craved to be doing himself," Nick Kent wrote in 1977. "He never showed bad form," Pop said of Bowie, who wouldn't break character even in nightclubs at 3am. "All the shit I know, that's let me take care of myself, basically I learned travelling with Bowie on the *Station to Station* tour."

By the end of the tour, Bowie and Pop had a mind-meld; they were always in each other's company and planned to move to Berlin together. Pop encouraged Bowie's darker impulses to prevail over his all-around entertainer instincts ("I think that was liberating for him"). Ironically, Bowie considered Pop an all-around entertainer, if one in the rough ("[he] stands a very good chance of becoming one of the most important young actors in America," Bowie opined on tour in 1976). He also found rehabilitating Pop a challenge, a way to trump peers Lou Reed (who had called Pop "very sweet but very stupid") and Ian Hunter ("Iggy has all the attributes of stardom except that he doesn't deliver on any level"). Pop hadn't performed live in a year and had no chance of getting a record deal unless Bowie backed him.

Pop played the American roughneck to Bowie's cracked European aristocrat, but it's easy to over-simplify their relationship. Bowie was just as tempestuous, while Pop discarded his wild man persona at will: touring musicians would sometimes find a glasses-wearing Pop at breakfast, drinking coffee and reading European newspapers.

Sound and Fury

Bowie first thought to produce a Pop "Sister Midnight" single in Munich when the tour was over (introducing "Sister Midnight" at a Toronto gig, he told the audience he'd written the song "for a friend of mine, Iggy Pop... it's for you tonight"). But after visiting the Château d'Hérouville, a studio located within an eighteenth-century château (where he'd cut *Pin Ups* in 1973), he decided to record an entire Pop album there and, optimistically, have his label RCA fund it. This wasn't quite the case, as Bowie fought for royalty advances throughout its making.

He liked the studio's manager, Laurent Thibault, former bassist of the French prog group Magma, and its equipment ("this is a great rock 'n' roll studio"). In the first days of June 1976, Bowie and Pop arrived with a Baldwin electric piano, a Dan Armstrong Plexiglas guitar and an ARP Axxe synthesizer. Though he'd done some cassette demos, singing wordless vocal lines while playing chords on the Baldwin, Bowie wasn't inspired to finish his sketches. He'd been in a compositional drought and used the guise of making an Iggy Pop record to reduce himself, to work less deliberately. ("Poor Jim," Bowie said. "I didn't have the material at the time and I didn't feel like writing at all.") He had Thibault recruit a French drummer, Michel Santangeli, whom Bowie conducted with hand signals — he wouldn't even let Santangeli tune his drums. Listening to playback, Bowie sat without saying a word until yelling "suivons!" when he thought a track was done.

It was the stage-clearing he'd done on *Diamond Dogs*, now in another voice ("Jimmy's album," as he called it). He foreshadowed his plan during a tour interview, in which he said "the crack-up of artists... is a fundamental of rock 'n' roll... Not seeing superheroes. Watching the process of a person learning how to come to terms with what he really is. Suddenly seeing an artist recognize his own failings. The emphasis is not on watching somebody who's invulnerable and godlike."

He'd already considered producing a hard-rock album for his LA friend, Deep Purple's Glenn Hughes ("he kept telling me, 'you've got to keep changing — cut your hair, don't write the same songs,'" Hughes later said). Now Pop's album became a laboratory for Bowie's crack-up. He made murky, sloppy mixes, had Thibault come up with basslines and was content with Santangeli's thudding drums, which Santangeli regretted upon hearing the album. Bowie relied on his glam survival instincts — cloak instruments in fresh disguises, favor the rehearsal take over the polished one.

As for Pop, he roamed the Château grounds on the hot afternoons, went to Paris for a disastrous reunion with his former lover Nico, and started a new affair with a fellow studio guest (see "China Girl"). He'd sit in the control room listening to backing tracks, scribbling lyrics and improvising vocals. "I was a guinea pig," Pop said decades later. "If [Bowie] had a new idea and wasn't sure how to approach it, he would write or arrange something in a similar manner for one of my projects... he worked with personnel and engineers with me first, until he got the lay of the land."

Bowie chose the album's title, honoring Fyodor Dostoevsky's novel about an impoverished aristocrat who crashes into nineteenth-century Saint Petersburg, his purity and naïve honesty set against corrupt high society. "He'd always marvel at what a dick I was — how awkward I was in social situations and in all the things that you can do to make your career go better," Pop said. "Finally he said, 'look, we're going to call this album *The Idiot*.' I took it as a challenge: OK, I'll show you... He's the kind of guy who had obviously read *The Idiot* by Dostoevsky, which I hadn't, and he probably saw all the resonance of the term and its possibilities. But I think his basic thrust, when he suggested it, was just to insult me: 'You fucking idiot'." (In 2002, Bowie mused "can one write assuredly from the point of view of an idiot? Is it true that the fool knows more than the complicated or sophisticated man?")

Yet *The Idiot* was as much a Bowie album as a Pop one. (In late 1977, he wondered whether "it was probably a little too much of me than was necessary on *The Idiot*. That was more because Iggy was still feeling his way again after a considerable absence from things."). He co-wrote all songs, played all the piano and synthesizer parts, sketched guitar lines and produced it (rather chaotically, needing Tony Visconti and Eduard Meyer to salvage the over-modulated tapes). The true "Berlin" trilogy is *The Idiot*, *Low* and *"Heroes,"* with Pop's *Lust for Life* a supplement and *Lodger* an epilogue.

"I Love Noises"

"Sister Midnight" started as Bowie and Alomar's sequel to "Fame" — another one-chord vamp (G7) with a sidestepping guitar riff. Beefing up his gear to compete with Earl Slick on *Station to Station*, Alomar got an Olympic Maverick guitar and a custom-made 12" subwoofer ("a gigantic system built at Olympic in LA"). Demoed either during *The Man Who Fell to Earth* soundtrack sessions in Los Angeles in December 1975 or, more likely, in pre-tour rehearsals in Jamaica the following month, "Sister Midnight" "came from this Olympic guitar, which gave me sounds I was fascinated with," Alomar said.

The Bowie "Sister Midnight" is the sound of a post-*Station to Station* LP had he remained in Los Angeles — icy funk with lots of soloing. The occult influences of *Station to Station* were still there, with Bowie possibly referencing Peter Mays' *Sister Midnight*, a hallucinatory experimental film that premiered at the Fox Venice in LA in 1975. As performed during the first two months of Bowie's tour, it had a stomping groove built on Dennis Davis' rapid-fire kick drum and a popped George Murray bassline, colored by Tony Kaye's synthetic hisses and whirrs. Its two verses had a handful of lines, one of which referred to Bowie's as-yet released film ("you've got me falling to Earth"). Much of it was place-filler syllables.

Bowie was working through what he was hearing on Kraftwerk's *Radio-Activity*, which he played in his limo for Pop during drives between tour stops. The half-written "Sister Midnight" became the ward of his 1976 touring band. After both verses repeated, with Bowie singing the last up an octave, "Sister Midnight" typically ended with a guitar duel, closing with a harmonized run by Alomar and Stacy Heydon. Bowie prowled the lip of the stage, scatting, groaning, making eye contact only to slide away.

For the *Idiot* revision of "Sister Midnight," Pop pumped fresh blood into

25

the song. His new lines were daggers: "you put a beggar in my heart," "what can I do about my dreams?" "This record is bent," he said in 1977. "I've never succeeded before in making a record that was quite as bent-sounding as I am." In a new verse, Pop sleeps with his mother, dodges his father's six-gun blasts. He said it came from a dream (another Pop dream had inspired Bowie's "TVC 15"), though he'd free-versed about his mother in Stooges shows.

Encouraged by Bowie to develop his lower registers, Pop starts in his bass voice, making two slow ascents for each phrase. Bowie doubles him well over an octave, his voice a piping halo. In the third verse, Pop finally moves to his "rock" register and his stress phrasing: "Can you HEAR ME *CALLLL*? Can you hear ME *WAIIIIL*," with his ultimate "can you hear *meeeeeeee — ataaaaaaaaaall*" pulled through three bars and expiring down an octave. He sometimes nearly blew out the microphone pre-amp.

On "Sister Midnight," the piano barely sounds like one — it's Bowie playing a Yamaha piano miked into a Harrison console, equalized and distorted. Guitars (Alomar, Phil Palmer, likely Bowie) were run through effects pedals and a Leslie speaker: see the snappy riff at 0:35 or the shearing two-chord riff in the last verse. The deadened drum tone is thanks to a severely dampened kit. As the musician Bradley Banks noted, whenever Davis hits his crash cymbal, there's no reverberation. The sound just dies, as if someone grabbed the cymbal each time he struck it. There was a precedent: Bowie's mix of *Raw Power*, for which he used a Cooper Time Cube for echo effects, gave Pop's vocals massive reverb and added a second, out-of-phase drum track to "Penetration" (on *The Idiot*, the drum tracks are often a blend of Davis and Santangeli takes). *The Idiot* also had its share of happy accidents. While Bowie was cutting a piano track, Thibault hit an equalizing button on the console, making a "bip" sound (at 1:05). Hearing the "bip" during playback, Bowie said "it's nice! We'll keep it. I love noises." In the final mix, a burst of feedback answers it.

It was a summoning. In 1979 Bowie turned the song into "Red Money," using the same backing tracks as his Pop recording. "Sister Midnight," the first "Berlin" song written, leads off *The Idiot* and its regeneration is the last song on *Lodger*. A period that begins with calling down spirits ends in a panic, with an aborted liftoff.

FUNTIME

*(Bowie, Pop.) **Recorded**: (backing tracks, vocals) ca. 5 June-early July 1976, Château d'Hérouville; (lead vocals, guitar overdubs) early-mid August 1976, Musicland; (overdubs, mixing) ca. 21-28 August 1976, Hansa 1. Pop: lead and backing vocal; Bowie: treated Yamaha piano, ARP Axxe, guitar?, backing vocal; Palmer: guitar; Thibault and/or Murray: bass; Michel Santangeli: drums. Produced: Bowie; engineered: Thibault.*

***First release**: 18 March 1977, **The Idiot**. **Broadcast**: (Pop and Bowie) 15 April 1977, Dinah! **Live**: (Pop and Bowie) 1977; (Pop) 1977-1983, 2015-2016, 2018.*

"Funtime" is fascist goodtime rock 'n' roll. Its "fun!" interjections, straight from Sly and the Family Stone, are bouncers' orders; its lyric is Little Richard's "Rip It Up" as sung by a sociopath ("I just do what I want to do"). Originally titled "Fun Fun Fun," it opens with what sounds like Iggy Pop holding back a sob.

Boys are on the town, looking for action, a night on the tiles that could end in a morgue. "Can I have some *fun time*? Might get *killed*!" Pop yelled to kick off the song on stage in 1977. The perspective blurs from singular to plural, a man as a mob, while the vocal harmonies are a street fight. References flick from William S. Burroughs (*The Ticket That Exploded*: "we want flesh — we want junk — we want power"; Iggy: "we *want* some, we *want some*") to a line about Dracula that would work in Bobby "Boris" Pickett's "Monster Mash." "My love song," as Pop called "Funtime" in 1977.

Bowie told Pop to sing like Mae West, to play the bawd, not the john ("like a bitch who wants to make money," Pop said). Pop kept to the span of a fourth in the verses, making his plays in emphases — take how many lascivious ways he sings "we like your lips." It wound up being "a little bit gay," he said. "The vocals there became more menacing as a result of that suggestion." It spins like a carnival ride — four-bar verses into four-bar refrains, each verse punched open with a chanted "fun!" (marrying the Velvet Underground's "White Light/White Heat" with Neu!s "Lila Engel"). As with "Sister Midnight," the verse keeps on one chord (D5), while the refrain progression is a creep rightward on the keyboard: B-flat ("allll ah-"), C major ("-boooard for"), punctuated by two white keys that form the D5 ("FUN-TIME"). The slashed two-chord guitar solo in the E major bridge is met by the drums' deadened assault, with processed cymbal hits as accents, their airless tone owed to Tony Visconti using an Eventide Harmonizer during mixing (see "Breaking Glass"). Piano and bass drone; guitar overdubs gauze the track, including a "Satisfaction" riff, while the scrappy left-mixed rhythm guitar could be Bowie's work. Pop closes with a Tarzan yell.

BABY

(Bowie, Pop.) **Recorded**: *(backing tracks) ca. 5 June-early July 1976, Château d'Hérouville; (lead vocals, guitar overdubs) early-mid August 1976, Musicland; (overdubs, mixing) ca. 21-28 August 1976, Hansa 1. Pop: lead and harmony vocal; Bowie: treated Yamaha piano, Baldwin electric piano?, ARP Axxe, backing vocal, guitar?; Palmer: guitar; Thibault: bass; Santangeli: drums. Produced: Bowie; engineered: Thibault.*

First release: *18 March 1977,* **The Idiot.** **Live**: *(Pop) 2016.*

While Bowie did sonic experiments on *The Idiot*, Iggy Pop wrote about wanting sex, companionship, but also control, wanting his girls to stay young and "clean" despite whatever he does (see "Tiny Girls"). In "Baby," he warns a girl of the world's bad intentions and gives his broken self as an example, or at least an alternative ("I've *already* cried"): he's the devil she knows. "The story of a man who's torn apart in his heart between his need for egotism and animalism and desire to be human, but when he indulges in human things, he's consistently disappointed," Pop said in 1977.

"Baby" alternates eight-bar verses, where Pop sings the intro's synthesizer lullaby melody over a grudging bassline (doubled by treated piano), and two-part bridges ("walking *down*/the street of *chance...*" "baby there's *nothing* to see"). The latter, carried by tentative drums, briefly break open the song, offering a key change, keyboard flourishes and open steals from the Kinks, whose "Dead End Street" is in the top melody and whose "Sunny Afternoon" is in the descending progression of piano and bass. Never performed live until 2016, "Baby" has a hangover of a mix that leaves in a snippet of studio chatter (0:46).

TINY GIRLS

(Bowie, Pop.) **Recorded**: *(backing tracks) ca. 5 June-early July 1976, Château d'Hérouville (lead vocals, guitar overdubs); early-mid August 1976, Musicland; (overdubs, mixing) ca. 21-28 August 1976, Hansa 1. Pop: lead vocal; Bowie: tenor saxophone, organ, treated Yamaha piano, ARP Axxe?, rhythm guitar?; Palmer?, Michel Marie?: guitar; Thibault: bass; Santangeli: drums. Produced: Bowie; engineered: Thibault.*

First release: *18 March 1977,* **The Idiot**.

"Tiny Girls" is Bowie using his "Rock 'n' Roll Suicide" formula, setting the vocal line of a chanson (here, Jacques Brel's "Ne Me Quitte Pas") to the 12/8 rhythm of a Fifties doo-wop song. He encircled verses with two-chorus saxophone solos. Among his lengthiest on record, Bowie doused his saxophone generously in reverb, particularly on his high notes. He was dismissive of his playing, said he'd wanted to play like Gerry Mulligan but lacked technique. He'd hire pros to redo performances he considered under par, as he did with lead guitar parts on *The Idiot*. For the intro, he stays within the confines of the melody and indulges in leaps of fancy only towards the fade.

In verses that change key as if out of spite, mostly keeping to Brel's melody, Pop sang a lyric that's blunt even by his standards (and true to life, as he'd had a fourteen-year-old girlfriend when he was in his early twenties). His girl is giving him trouble, so he wants a younger, less jaded girl without "tricks." But when he gets *her*, she's just as poisoned by life, so on he goes to the next model (see "Mass Production"). His songs viewed women as a collective poison, as alluring "young banshees" like the woman who'd inspired the Stooges' "Johanna" ("she destroyed me, man, just drove me out of my mind," Pop told Nick Kent). The prospect of finding the right one was a guiding star for him, though sampling "all the little girls in Berlin," as he reminisced in 1980, proved fruitless.

Dum Dum Boys

(Bowie, Pop.) **Recorded**: *(backing tracks) ca. 5 June-early July 1976, Château d'Hérouville; (lead vocals, guitar overdubs) early-mid August 1976, Musicland; (overdubs, mixing) ca. 21-28 August 1976, Hansa 1. Pop: lead vocal; Bowie: treated Yamaha piano, ARP Axxe, lead guitar, backing vocal; Palmer: lead guitar; Thibault and/or Murray: bass; Santangeli and/or Davis: drums. Produced: Bowie; engineered: Thibault.*

First release: *18 March 1977,* **The Idiot**. *Live: (Pop) 1981, 1983, 1990, 2015.*

At the piano in Château d'Hérouville, Pop sounded the same notes again and again, at a loss about where to go. Bowie said he should write about the Stooges ("do a song about your broken-up group, Jim"), giving him a working title: "Dum Dum Days."

Rock 'n' roll runs on self-mythology, from the Barbarians' "Moulty" to AC/DC's "It's a Long Way to the Top." These songs end in the triumphant present — the band's made it at last. But by the time of "Dum Dum Boys," the Stooges were over, their records falling out of print, most members trying to shake addictions. "Dum Dum Boys" opens with a casualty list. Zeke Zettner, a bassist who overdosed on heroin in 1973, and original bassist Dave Alexander, who died in 1975 of a pulmonary edema after contracting pancreatitis. Scott Asheton, detoxing home in Ann Arbor, and James Williamson, who's "gone straight."

As he sang, Pop first met the future Stooges when they were standing on a street (in front of Discount Records, where the then-James Osterberg worked). They were wild boys, Ann Arbor's own Droogs. The Asheton brothers: Ron, with his Nazi memorabilia, and Scott, who looked like a Roger Corman biker thug. Alexander, roped in and strung out. A few years later, Williamson, the Brutalist guitarist who usurped Ron, demoting him to the bassist of the band Asheton had co-founded.

Iggy "felt he was an outcast, but Ronnie, Scotty and I, we *were* outcasts," former Stooge Bill Cheatham told Paul Trynka. Pop called the Stooges "basic Archie Bunker juniors — all of 'em real spuds." He gave them ambition, they grounded him. The Stooges began as a performance art project, a free jazz trio where Pop played vacuum cleaner, blender, and a Hawaiian guitar whose strings were all tuned to E. In 1968, they were signed by Elektra as the junior-league version of their friends the MC5. The Stooges made stronger, harder records. Living in utter disorder, they managed to stave off their inevitable collapse for years. At their last concerts in the Midwest in early 1974, after their label had dumped them, they were nearly all strung out on heroin and were under siege by dwindling, hostile audiences — the last campaign of some battered brigade. "We were sort of the wandering lost tribe of rock 'n' roll," Pop reminisced in 2009.

"Dum Dum Boys" is Pop's "Ziggy Stardust," its perspective that of a Ziggy wondering whatever became of the Spiders, whom he'd abandoned. "I felt almost like a sociologist looking back, but I still feel the same about it," he said. It has a Shangri-Las intro, complete with finger snaps, and melodic and lyrical callbacks to Dylan's "A Hard Rain's a-Gonna Fall" ("where are you now my *dum dum boys*?"). The song sways between seventh chords, from a tonic D7 ("I can't seem") to a subdominant G7 ("…laaanguaage").

Much of what Pop called the track's "Angry Young Guitar" started as Bowie's work: "He struggles…when he plays [guitar]… His fingers start cramping after a while and we have to stop halfway through, and he's yelling, 'I don't know why the fuck I'm doing this for you, you jerk!'" Bowie had Phil Palmer, a guitarist recruited for overdub sessions in Munich, play "that guitar arpeggio that metal groups love today," as Pop said. Palmer followed Bowie's lead lines note for note, with Bowie demanding dozens of takes, each with exacting instructions like "bend that note more."

Sequenced to lead off *The Idiot*'s second side, "Dum Dum Boys" was the ruin of the past answered by the no-future of side-closer "Mass Production." A lost boys' requiem, "Dum Dum Boys" is the album's bruised heart. "I just know for a fact that if anyone's going to be the next to go it'll be me," Pop predicted in 1975. But like Keith Richards, he was fated to survive where so many of his friends fell, ending up a weathered monument to excess.

CHINA GIRL

(Bowie, Pop.) **Recorded: (Pop)** *(backing tracks) ca. 5 June-early July 1976, Château d'Hérouville; (lead vocals, guitar overdubs) early-mid August 1976, Musicland; (overdubs, mixing) ca. 21-28 August 1976, Hansa 1. Pop: lead vocal; Bowie: treated Yamaha piano, alto saxophone, toy piano, rhythm guitar, ARP Axxe, backing vocal; Palmer: lead guitar; Thibault: bass; Santangeli: drums, tambourine.*

Produced: Bowie; engineered: Thibault; **(Bowie)** *ca. 4-20 January 1983, The Power Station, 441 West 53rd Street, New York. Bowie: lead vocal; Stevie Ray Vaughan: lead guitar; Nile Rodgers: rhythm guitar; Rob Sabino: keyboards, Prophet-5?; Carmine Rojas: bass; Omar Hakim: drums; Sammy Figueroa: percussion; Frank Simms, George Simms, David Spinner: backing vocals. Produced: Rodgers, Bowie; engineered: Bob Clearmountain.*

First release*: (Pop) 18 March 1977,* **The Idiot***; (Bowie) 14 April 1983,* **Let's Dance** *(EMI America AML 3029, UK #1, US #4).* **Broadcast***: (Bowie) 3 March 1997, The Rosie O'Donnell Show (as "Rosie Girl"); 23 August 1999, VH1 Storytellers; 8 October 1999, TFI Friday; 20 October 1999, Nulle parte ailleurs; 25 October 1999, Saturday Music Show; 17 November 1999, The Rosie O'Donnell Show; 15 June 2002, A&E Live By Request.* **Live***: (Pop and Bowie) 1977, 1985; (Pop) 1977, 1979-1983, 1986, 1987, 1990-1994, 1998, 2016, 2018; (Bowie) 1983, 1987, 1990, 1996, 1999, 2000, 2002-2004.*

It began when Pop and Bowie were drunk one summer night. "Politely drunk, after-dinner drunk," Pop recalled. A glass of wine too many. They stumbled into a room at the Château d'Hérouville. Pop sat down at Bowie's son's starter drum kit, Bowie at a toy piano. They hit upon a groove, calling the piece – barely a riff – "Borderline."

Pop was infatuated at the time with another guest at the castle, Kuelan Nguyen, the girlfriend of French actor/singer Jacques Higelin. Nguyen spoke no English, Pop no French, so they communicated in gestures, expressions and pidgin attempts at each other's language. Pop would grow frustrated trying to get through to Nguyen in sign language and barbarian French; she once put a finger to his lips to shush him.

"Borderline" became "China Girl" (although Nguyen was Vietnamese). Pop improvised much of the lyric at the mike, with Bowie watching in admiration. As with "Dum Dum Boys," Pop was working in a pop tradition. Here, a song in which language hinders lovers, such as the Beatles' "Michelle" or Chuck Berry's "La Juanda," where Berry asks a Mexican girl to dance but neither understands the other, or pretends not to — she may be a prostitute, he may be negotiating.

"It's about a very blundering, blustering rock 'n' roll hero who has big plans and Western habits [and] who becomes enchanted and subdued by a Chinese girl," Pop said. He cast Nguyen as the mysterious, sensual Orient and himself ("Jimmy") as unwilling agent of the corrupt West. He moves from natural elements in the first verses – falling stars, heartbeats as "loud as thunder," which he sings softly, letting spaces fall in between each note – to modern effluence: Marlon Brando, swastikas (another Eastern symbol perverted by the West), television, cosmetics. "I'll ruin everything you are." Yet he can't avoid it — his passion's too addicting. She's poisoning his dreams, and he rakes through memories of them for impurities. Hence the wordplay of the title — "China" as pure heroin as well as the girl's fragility (though she seems more together than Iggy is).

As with many tracks on *The Idiot*, "China Girl" fits its vocal, a twisted nerve of a performance, into a distorted backdrop and minimal structure. Built on E minor progressions, it's a series of eruptions. Pop lurches into view a beat into the song, his voice submerged in the mix, only clearing at the moment he goes mad, building to the scream of "whiiiiiiiiiiite of my eyes!" Bowie overlaid stabs of Phil Palmer's guitar (a four-note lead hook, a grinding rhythm track mixed right, with ska-style fills in the bridges), buttressed by his own distorted Baldwin piano. He made the ARP a string section, while cutting multiple overdubs of saxophone for the last verses. The chirping riff that Bowie played on toy piano is still prominent in the final mix.

Just You Shut Your Mouth

For much of the world, "China Girl" is a David Bowie song. He made Pop's "China Girl" into a successor. The song's original recording now sounds like a remake, a sonic vandalism done to a Bowie hit.

"China Girl" was one of Bowie's trio of MTV-fueled singles in 1983, his glossy new testament. Where "Let's Dance" was a call to the floor and "Modern Love" a paranoid jive, "China Girl" was a slick anomie. Its sonic perfection sharpened its ironies, its invocation of Asian stereotypes, from Nile Rodgers' "Asian" guitar riff to Bowie mocking how the girl says "mouth", to its designer video, where Bowie, dressed as an Old Etonian, pats the head of his pajama-clad "Chinese" girl (Geeling Ng — again, not Chinese but a New Zealander) as if he's bagged her on safari, then makes a visual play on Eddie Adams' 1968 "Execution of a Vietcong Prisoner" photograph. Ng has dragon lady fingernails; Bowie courts her by slanting his eyes. Filmed in Sydney's Chinatown district, he dramatically hurls a bowl of rice into the air.

Bowie cut "China Girl" to help Pop, who was broke in the early Eighties. But his recycling of Pop collaborations, his increased reliance on covers in general, was a hedge against the decline in his songwriting in the Eighties. With "China Girl," Bowie's commercial instincts were on point: he saw in it a potential smash that he'd obscured on *The Idiot* (he originally intended "China Girl" as the lead-off single from *Let's Dance*). Even his and Pop's live performances of it in 1977 had been catchier, with frenetic drumming and Bowie's organ playing — more "96 Tears" than would-be Krautrock drone.

Where Pop sang in frenzy, Bowie's vocal is assured, playful (the lilting run of high notes on "wake up in the mor-ning," the repetition of "she says..."), while his build up to the "whites of my eyes" bridge is a cool demonstration of power. Everything has its place, from Carmine Rojas' bass lagging the beat (moving to a staccato sequence in the last verses—he was trying to play the marimba line of the Rolling Stones' "Under My Thumb" from memory), to the drum fills imbued with ambient sound, to placid washes of synthesizers and keyboards that carpet the track. Bowie and Rodgers layered in hooks: the "oh-oh-oh-OH-oh-oh" intro and Rodgers' guitar riff, doubled on keyboards. (While Rodgers feared that he was "putting some bubblegum over some great artistic heavy record," Bowie loved the riff.) Stevie Ray Vaughan's guitar solos close it out. Vaughan misjudged the length of his first solo, playing longer than his allotted bars and closing on a note he hadn't intended. He said he'd fix the blunder, but a delighted Bowie said it should remain.

Did Bowie's remake desecrate Pop's desperation by turning it into MTV pop? Or did it come closer, with its mandarin disco sound, to what Pop had been fumbling at? Performing "China Girl" at the end of the last century, Bowie said it was about "invasion and exploitation." Earlier, he said the song captured "the colonialist imperialist feeling in the Englishman towards people from other races. It's fairly angry but it's loving." (After his death, Nguyen revealed that Bowie had also made a play for her that summer at the Château, "that I was afraid of him, of me, of what was happening to us.") He was the more adept exploiter, the more elegant racist; his perspective was wider, his self-loathing deeper. Pop was too much in his own shadow. Bowie was in the sun: he saw the rot, making a cross-border love into a soft imperialism, a cultural toxin. He shone it up, he sold it well.

MASS PRODUCTION

(Bowie, Pop.) **Recorded**: *(backing tracks) ca. 5 June-30 July 1976, Château d'Hérouville (lead vocals, guitar overdubs) early-mid August 1976, Musicland (overdubs, mixing) ca. 21-28 August 1976, Hansa 1. Pop: lead vocal; Bowie: treated Yamaha piano, Baldwin electric piano, ARP Axxe, backing vocal, drum machine; Palmer: lead guitar; Thibault: sound effects; Murray and/or Thibault: bass; Davis and/or Santangeli: drums. Produced: Bowie; engineered: Thibault.*

First release: *18 March 1977,* **The Idiot**. **Live**: *(Pop) 1983, 2009-2010, 2015-2018.*

"Mass Production," the eight-minute industrial horror movie that finishes off *The Idiot*, starts with a synthesizer fading in, as if drawing breath. The sound is held to the right channel, its foghorn drone answered by four notes of mechanical birdsong. A drum fill jolts the track into a semblance of life. Iggy Pop sounds like an android holding a hostage: "Do me a *fav*-errr... Give me a *num*-berrrr..." He builds to a groaning run of lines that he inflicts with his usual stress phrasings: "*THERRRE* in the *MIRRRR*-OR."

Underlying the track was a loop of "overloaded industrial noises" that Laurent Thibault had pieced together, making a master tape of his smaller loops. He recalled Bowie sitting and watching the tape spool around "like a child transfixed by a train set." The idea may have come from the 1975 Pop/Bowie demo sessions in LA, at which Bowie was reported being "enveloped by a hideous groundswell of distorted sound emanating from the monitors [while] remarking in zombie deadpan, 'noise is what the earth is all about.'"

Bowie offered scenarios when Pop was stumped for lyrics, and here pushed him to do something with his memories of industrial Detroit, of seeing a machine press at Ford's River Rouge plant pound out a new fender every minute, of "how much I admired the beauty of the American industrial culture that was rotting away where I grew up... the beautiful smokestacks and factories — whole cities devoted to factories," Pop said. In "Mass Production," even machinery's cold promise is a lie. Its visual analogue is David Lynch's street sets for *Eraserhead*: a city purged of human beings.

Four verses keep on a single chord (F7), harried by a riff on guitar and synthesizer, both likely played by Bowie. Two twelve-bar bridges have Phil Palmer guitar arpeggios and the release of a chord change. An organizing influence is Neu!'s "Seeland." Pop's endless need for a fresh girl has become a type of factory labor; salvation lies in reprogramming. The instrumental verse is detuned synthesizers playing mocking singsong patterns. The track ends as it began, with foghorn and birdsong, industry and industrialized. ("I get a lot of my influence from the electric shaver," Pop once told Dinah Shore.) "Mass Production" was the future: Joy Division, among others, starts here.

NIGHTCLUBBING

(Bowie, Pop.) **Recorded***: (lead vocals, guitar, synthesizer, drum machine) mid-August 1976, Musicland; (overdubs, mixing) ca. 21-28 August 1976, Hansa 1. Pop: lead vocal; Bowie: treated Yamaha piano, guitar?, synthesizer, backing vocal, drum machine; Palmer: lead guitar; Thibault and/or Murray: bass; Davis: drums? Produced: Bowie; engineered: Thibault.*

First release*: 18 March 1977,* **The Idiot***.* **Live***: (Pop) 1977, 1980-1983, 1986-1987, 1997, 2009, 2014-2017.*

The last track recorded for *The Idiot*, "Nightclubbing," foreshadows Bowie's imminent *Low*, with its fragmented lyric, minimal chord structure, and sense of being a frustrated instrumental — Pop appears after the song's been underway for over a minute (see "Sound and Vision"). Cobbled together from drum machine, bass, piano and synthesizer, with the occasional guitar jab, the track emerged at the end of overdub sessions in Munich. With most of the gear packed up, Bowie was sitting at a piano playing "some old Hoagy Carmichael stuff," Pop recalled. Pop wrote a two-verse lyric and they quickly recorded a take using what Pop described as "a lousy drum machine."

They would overdub Laurent Thibault and possibly George Murray on bass, Phil Palmer's guitar and some reverb-laden synthesizer overdubs, but when Bowie said they should redo the drum track with Dennis Davis, Pop balked. "He thought 'that doesn't sound professional enough'," [and I said]... it's good enough for me, it's only Iggy Fucking Pop," he said in 2004. (That said, Bradley Banks argues for acoustic drums, though heavily processed, in the final mix.) The drum machine was the pulsebeat of Pop's dragging vocal, which creeps back and forth stepwise and ends phrases by trailing off. The harmony vocals on the second verse offer melodic variety, if sounding deranged. (It's also the messiest of *Idiot* mixes, with an audible count-in and Pop vocals that sound off-balance at times.)

In "Nightclubbing," debauchery has predictable rhythms, on/off cycles. "It's about the incredible coldness and deathly feeling you have after you've done something like that and how much you enjoy it," Pop said in 1977. A Valiumed take on the rhythms of Neu! and Harmonia, which Bowie would further attempt on his next albums, it's also decayed glam rock, its beat a slowed-down version of the hook of Gary Glitter's "Rock and Roll Part 2" (which the Human League noted, performing a medley of the songs).

Bowie and Pop were readying for West Berlin but didn't move there until fall 1976. The clubland of "Nightclubbing" is anticipatory, its sounds and imagery imported. Pop said of the song, "it could be about LA or Paris or New York"; he and Bowie told Palmer to craft his guitar solo by imagining walking down Wardour Street in London, hearing music blasting from different clubs.

WHAT IN THE WORLD

Recorded: (backing tracks) ca. 1-20 September 1976, Château d'Hérouville; (overdubs) early October-18 November 1976, Hansa Tonstudio 2, 38 Köthener Straße, Berlin. Bowie: lead and harmony vocal; Ricky Gardiner: lead guitar; Alomar: rhythm guitar; Roy Young: Farfisa organ, piano; Brian Eno: ARP 2600? ARP Axxe? ("Report ARP"), EMS Synthi AKS ("Rimmer E.M.I."); Murray: bass; Davis: drums; Pop: backing vocal. Produced: Bowie, Visconti; engineered: Thibault, Meyer, Visconti.

*First release: 14 January 1977, **Low** (RCA PL 12030/CPL1 2030, UK #2, US #11). **Broadcast:** 30 May 1978, Musikladen Extra. **Live:** 1978, 1983, 1995, 2002.*

What Bowie began recording at Château d'Hérouville in the first week of September 1976, days after finishing *The Idiot*, had no initial design. The story of *Low* is that of a depressed, worn-down man seeing if he could write songs again, and half-wondering whether he wanted to. He would run an experimental session with Brian Eno and started by having his rhythm section —Carlos Alomar, George Murray and Dennis Davis — jam in the studio to his loose directions.

At least one song was possibly slated for *The Idiot*. "What in the World" sounds crafted for Iggy Pop's voice (Pop is audible on the track, particularly on "wait until the *crowd goes*!") and its little girl with grey eyes is another in *The Idiot*'s gallery of vulnerable women ("China Girl," "Baby," "Tiny Girls"). But now the verse ends in fifteen seconds, the first refrain in twenty-five. Were it not for its lengthy outro, "What in the World" would be done in a minute and a half. Performing it on stage, Bowie had to double its length: first doing a reggae version, then breaking into a sprint to do the whole song again at twice the tempo.

For his vocal, Bowie moves from his lower registers, staggering up an octave ("*talking* through the gloom") only to run aground on the title phrase, which he sings flatly, drawing the blood out of the words. In the second refrain he changes it to "what in the world can *I* do," using the biting "ay" phoneme to unsettle an already-erratic song. The track's heart is a funk piece driven by Alomar's in-the-pocket rhythm, his guitar reduced to its high tones. Each verse bar downshifts from F major to E-flat, Alomar holding a barre chord shape and sliding between two frets; the refrain does the same, the chords now moving between D and C major.

Tony Visconti's mix is invigorating — nothing's fore-grounded, each instrument fights for space. Davis' Harmonized snare (see "Breaking Glass") is so dynamic that when he shifts to toms he all but vanishes — it's as if the track's lost gravity. Players move in and out of focus. Ricky Gardiner, whose guitar's brittle tone came from a borrowed, trebly Fender amp (he hadn't wanted to bring his custom-made Lombardi on the plane to France), takes a four-bar solo and blithely keeps going. Visconti spotlights each player at the right moment — Gardiner's scraping lines in the first verse; Roy Young's Farfisa organ, making a warm bed for the second refrain; Eno's EMS Synthi AKS "suitcase" synthesizer, whose bubbling saturates the first verse and persists, off and on, like the sound of a party upstairs.

On *Low*, Bowie's lyrics read like telegrams. Here he breaks off a seduction with "never mind — say something!" Ghosts of old songs flit in and out: "I'm In the Mood For Love," the Doors' "You're Lost Little Girl," Syd Barrett's "Golden Hair" ("talking through the gloom"), the Who's "The Real Me" (muttered in the outro) and the Yardbirds' "For Your Love." In the latter, Keith Relf had rocketed the last word of the title ("for-your-*LOVE*!"). Now Bowie places an equal weight on each word, as if singing phonetically: "FOR–YOUR–LOVE." This disconnect suits a song that was originally titled

"Isolation." It's a shut-in's attempt to connect with another: the grey-eyed girl who never leaves her room, just as Bowie locks himself away in "Sound and Vision." He's talking to a part of himself that he's hidden away, his muse or his anima, his feminine unconscious (another grey-eyed girl was the goddess of wisdom, Athena), trying to coax it out of hiding, half-fearing it will come out.

SPEED OF LIFE

Recorded: (backing tracks) ca. 1-20 September 1976, Château d'Hérouville; (overdubs) ca. early October-18 November 1976, Hansa Tonstudio 2. Bowie: Chamberlin M1, ARP 2600?, ARP Solina?, ARP Axxe? ("arp. tape horn and brass — synthetic strings"); Alomar: rhythm guitar; Young: piano; Murray: bass; Davis: drums. Produced: Bowie, Visconti; engineered: Thibault, Meyer, Visconti.

*First release: 14 January 1977, **Low**. Live: 1978, 2002.*

Low opens underway, its first track faded up to establish its parameters. There's a sixteen-bar verse in E-flat (declamatory guitar riff, expiring synthesizer line), a five-bar bridge that shifts to the relative minor, and a two-chord refrain with duetting synthesizers, soprano Chamberlin and tenor ARP—a synthetic take on the piccolo-baritone saxophone pairing in "Moonage Daydream."

As with its LP-side bookend "A New Career in a New Town," "Speed of Life" was intended to have lyrics but as the synthesizer/guitar lines were enough of a melodic hook, Bowie kept it an instrumental. It became an overture, a cast of characters tumbling out on stage — Carlos Alomar, drawing from his deep bag of riffs; Dennis Davis' treated drums; George Murray's thickly-intoned bass notes (in verses, he's advancing up the scale while the rest of the band follows a descending progression; in refrains, he's the quiet backup to the synths). The synthesizer line's a Bowie trademark, the latest reincarnation of "The Laughing Gnome" bassoon line, heard here tromping down over an octave.

It's the closest we have to hearing how the first *Low* sessions sounded, when Bowie let his band set the pace. Take how Davis varies his snare fills, or how the synthesizer line twists around in the final refrain. It possibly came out of "What in the World," with Bowie promoting one of the latter's battling chords, E-flat, to be the tonic of the new piece, while again using a dueling pair of chords (D-flat and C major) for the refrain.

The title, a play on "speed of light," is also a twist on "tree of Life," the Kabbalist image that Bowie had been obsessed with while making *Station to Station*. It's one of many hints that *Low* is Bowie sending up his Dark Magus image. As detached as *Low* can be, it has a sense of play, from the wry liner notes (note how many fake synthesizers Eno and Bowie are credited with playing) to the punning "Low profile" cover photo, to how, in "Speed of Life," the guitar and synthesizer all but play the refrain of the Fortunes' "Here Comes That Rainy Day Feeling Again."

A New Career in a New Town

Recorded: (backing tracks) ca. 1-20 September 1976, Château d'Hérouville; (overdubs) early October-18 November 1976, Hansa Tonstudio 2. Bowie: harmonica, ARP 2600? ("tape sax section"), Chamberlin M1, piano; Gardiner: lead guitar; Alomar: rhythm guitar; Young: piano; Eno: EMS Synthi AKS, ARP 2600? ("all synthetics"), piano; Murray: bass; Davis: drums. Produced: Bowie, Visconti; Engineered: Thibault, Meyer, Visconti.

First release: 14 January 1977, **Low**. **Live**: 2002-2004.

"A New Career in a New Town," footbridge between the "rock" and "instrumental" sides of *Low*, begins as an electronic piece whose metronomic pulse recalls Kraftwerk's "Geiger Counter," its harmonized synthesizers their "Radioactivity," its structure that of La Düsseldorf's "Silver Cloud." The drum track (disco 4/4, with a fill on the sixth bar) is Dennis Davis' kick, possibly treated by Brian Eno's EMS Synthi AKS. Four synthesizers pan across the mix. A right-mixed Chamberlin is an exosphere, rising and falling over a tone. The two left-mixed ARPs take turns playing the top melodic line, the center-mixed EMS moves downward.

After a bar's suspense, in pile Davis' drums, George Murray's bass, a crackling dialogue of Carlos Alomar (left, twisting) and Ricky Gardiner (right, harsh chords), and at least two piano tracks, all running through a C major chord progression. Instead of a vocal, it's Bowie's harmonica, its first appearance on record since "Jean Genie." It grounds the section in the past. The harmonica, in Sixties British pop, meant the North, earthiness, an allegiance with blues or folk, or at least Bob Dylan. John Lennon's harmonica was key to the early Beatles sound, as were Mick Jagger and Keith Relf's blues harps for the Stones and Yardbirds. Bowie's harmonica melody was an open steal from the 1970 British instrumental hit "Groovin' With Mr. Bloe." During the filming of *The Hunger*, Bowie put "Mr. Bloe" on the jukebox, and when the musician David J summoned up the courage to say it sounded like "New Career," Bowie put a finger to his lips and smiled.

The track's sections are also America (imagined) and Europe (intended): the future (sampled-sounding drums; synthesizers; rhythmic loops) and the past (the studio set-up of a Beatles record from 1963, with the Beatles' old Hamburg pal Roy Young on piano). For Bowie, which was the "new town"? It's reconciled by his players and Eno's treatments: the yearning synthesizers sound more "human" than the processed guitars and drums. A repeat of the "electronic" section alters course, with a different lead melody and shorter length; the return of the "rock" section is all but identical until bass and synthesizer (the latter faded up in the last thirty seconds) slide away in the coda.

Bowie named the track while finishing *Low* in West Berlin. Among his most self-referential titles, "A New Career in a New Town" had Bowie drafting his Berlin adventures before he lived them (true to form). It was one of his essential messages to his audience: *if you don't like where you are, move.*

ALWAYS CRASHING IN THE SAME CAR

Recorded: (backing tracks) ca. 1-20 September 1976, Château d'Hérouville; (vocals, overdubs) early October-18 November 1976, Hansa Tonstudio 2. Bowie: lead and harmony vocal, ARP 2600? ARP Axxe? Chamberlin M1 ("tape cellos"); Gardiner: lead guitar; Alomar: rhythm guitar; Young: piano, Farfisa organ; Eno: guitar treatments, EMS ("E.M.I.") Synthi AKS; Murray: bass; Davis: drums. Produced: Bowie, Visconti; Engineered: Thibault, Meyer, Visconti.

*First release: 14 January 1977, **Low**. Broadcast: 5 September 1997, CKZZ; 8 September 1997, Breakfast Show (KNDD), Morning Mountain Show (KMTT); 9 September 1997, Johnny Steele Breakfast Show (KITS); 10 September 1997, Tammy*

Bruce Show (KROQ); 16 September 1997, KFOG; 26 September 1997, CFNY; 30 September 1997, WBCN; 2 October 1997, World Café (WXPN); 16 October 1997, WXRT; 7 November 1997, Rock & Pop; 23 August 1999, VH1 Storytellers; 22 November 1999, MusiquePlus; 27 June 2000, Bowie at the BBC Radio Theatre. **Live**: *1997, 1999-2000, 2002-2004.*

A last meditation on Los Angeles, "Always Crashing in the Same Car" allegedly references Bowie ramming his car into that of a drug dealer who'd ripped him off. Alternately, it was a drunk Bowie tearing around a West Berlin parking garage, half-trying to kill himself. Both stories seem a touch suspect, particularly the idea of Bowie as an avenging Sonny Corleone type. But he had indeed crashed his Mercedes, which a cash-strapped Bowie was trying to offload to a French garage while recording *The Idiot*. "Always Crashing in the Same Car," the depression in the middle of *Low*'s manic side, is an atonement for something.

As with its origin stories, each verse has different scenarios — Bowie speeding on the street or in a hotel garage ("touching close to ninety-four"). There's a Buddhist sensibility, with Bowie's LA life as a period of *saṃsāra*, a cyclic period of suffering and no advancement. A pointless life, the equivalent of getting into a different car crash every day, but in the same car. As he later described his mid-Seventies, "it was like being a car where the steering had gone out of control and you were going towards the edge of a cliff and whatever you did with the wheel, it was inevitable that you were going over the edge... I'd almost resigned myself."

In line with the vagueness of key (mostly in E minor, the harmonic murkiness finally resolved with a closing Em chord), Dennis Davis' drums are treated, his hi-hat sixteenths processed to sound like a synthesizer line. Bowie's Chamberlin has the main hook, a waltzing "cello" pattern that's truncated to a two-note motif, while Eno does a theremin imitation on his EMS Synthi AKS. The second verse is rattled by a Davis tom fill while Bowie arbitrarily lengthens his vocal line, moving into bars he'd left vacant in the previous verse. Carlos Alomar later called the track "the hardest one to get right. It had this kind of gloomy thing to it... but it also had this chordal thing I was trying to get. The chorus is a bit different to the verse, and I felt it was a little disjointed."

It took until the end of mixing in West Berlin before Bowie had a lyric (stumped for ideas, he sang a verse imitating Bob Dylan's voice — Tony

Visconti described it as "spooky, not funny"). After straining to write two verses by raiding Syd Barrett's "No Good Trying" ("you're spinning around and around in a car with electric lights flashing very fast"), Bowie handed the last over to Ricky Gardiner, humming three notes to start him off on his solo and letting him get on with the rest.

SOUND AND VISION

Recorded: (backing tracks) ca. 1-20 September 1976, Château d'Hérouville; (vocals, overdubs) October-18 November 1976, Hansa Tonstudio 2. Bowie: lead and harmony vocal, Chamberlin M1 and/or ARP Solina ("synthetic strings"), baritone saxophone; Gardiner: lead guitar; Alomar: rhythm guitar; Young: piano; Eno: backing vocal; Murray: bass; Davis: drums; Mary Hopkin: lead and backing vocal. Produced: Bowie, Visconti; Engineered: Thibault, Meyer, Visconti.

First release: 14 January 1977, Low. Broadcast: 2 June 2002, Top of the Pops 2; 15 June 2002, A&E Live by Request. Live: 1978, 1990, 2002-2004.

Some time ago, my marriage fell apart. A salve for personal catastrophe is routine. Life is reduced to minor actions. Today I will arrange the bookcase. Tomorrow I will go to the store. Tonight I'll listen to this record. But what to listen to? Bob Dylan's *Blood on the Tracks* was a war correspondence, as was Richard and Linda Thompson's *Shoot Out the Lights*. Those records had too much pain, and I'd had enough already. What I played, over and over, was *Low*, and what I played on *Low*, most of all, was "Sound and Vision."

The small pleasures of an unexpected solitude. Bowie called "Sound and Vision" his "ultimate retreat song." "It was wanting to be put in a little cold room with omnipotent blue on the walls and blinds on the windows," he said. ("Deep blue was the color that I took to every dwelling," he wrote in an autobiographical fragment in 1975). On the set of *The Man Who Fell to Earth*, he sat alone in the desert sands for hours, listening to records on a hand-cranked gramophone. *Low*, he said in 1977:

[...] was a reaction to having gone through... that dull greenie-grey limelight of America... and its repercussions; pulling myself out of it and getting to Europe and saying, For God's sake re-evaluate why you wanted

43

to get into this in the first place? Did you really do it just to clown around in LA? Retire. What you need is to look at yourself a bit more accurately. Find some people you don't understand and a place you don't want to be and just put yourself into it. Force yourself to buy your own groceries.

"Sound and Vision" opens in a locked room. Everything is in its place, a clockwork song. Two guitars, panned to either channel; piano; exuberant bass; Harmonized drums and whooshing percussion (a processed snare) that sounds like a radiator coming to life. Then a descending synthesizer line, and sighs of delight. A song is assembling itself: rhythm section, then "strings" (ARP Solina), then backing vocals, then brass, until its composer appears, as if called to the stage to take a bow.

Bowie started by giving a simple descending-by-fifths G major progression to his band, and singing a few melodies, offering a few bassline and drumline ideas. Dennis Davis "thought it sounded like a Crusaders tune" (possibly "Stomp and Buck Dance"), while George Murray heard Bo Diddley. The band cut the backing tracks with their usual economy; a few takes, done.

It's shot through with little moments of joy. Mary Hopkin's cameo appearance, for which the whole piece has been waiting; Bowie's baritone saxophone, an old friend showing up unexpectedly; Davis' drum fills as a string of firecrackers; Bowie's opening phrase, a sleepy rise and fall over an octave ("don't-you-won-der some tiiii-i-ii-i-ii-i-i-i-iimes"), as if he's been listening along and started singing, carried away by what he'd set in motion. There's a precision to his vocal, of having to plot his course exactly, keeping to his lower register and doubled at the octave. He underscores flights of fancy (the long-held ooooos) with glum, nearly-spoken phrases ("nothing to say").

While Brian Eno mainly has walk-on roles on *Low*'s first side, he suggested the structure of "Sound and Vision," telling Bowie to hold off from singing until things were underway (1:30, the halfway mark), to confound listener expectations. As the side starts and ends with instrumentals, "Sound and Vision," parked midway in the sequence, appears to be another one at first. Eno had used a similar trick on his "Here Come the Warm Jets" — the singer who doesn't show up until the song's almost done. (Eno, a pornography connoisseur, also may have suggested Bowie listen to Linda and the Lollipops' single "Theme from Deep Throat," which has a similar sighing motif.)

"Sound and Vision" is the breaking of a dry spell. "The thing that was most exciting about it... I found that without drugs I was still writing very well," Bowie said in 1993. "Realizing it was possible to survive all that and not become a casualty." Unlike other *Low* tracks, where he'd struggled to come up with lyrics, he wrote a long set here, then pared them down. Invoking a muse is older than poetry, and "Sound and Vision" is a humble wish to sit down and wait for the gift. No grand gestures, just a man at a piano, hoping that the notes come, some words appear. He's wondering aloud if he could ever write a "Life on Mars?" again and isn't troubled if he can't. He's content to have come this far, grateful for what's left to him. "Sound and Vision" fades out long before one wishes it gone.

BE MY WIFE

Recorded: (backing tracks) ca. 1-20 September 1976, Château d'Hérouville; (lead vocal, overdubs) October-18 November, Hansa Tonstudio 2. Bowie: lead and harmony vocal, guitar, ARP 2600? ("pump bass"); Gardiner: lead guitar; Alomar: rhythm guitar; Young; piano, Farfisa organ; Murray: bass; Davis: drums. Produced: Bowie, Visconti; engineered: Thibault, Meyer, Visconti.

First release: 14 January 1977, **Low**. **Broadcast**: 27 June 2002, Friday Night with Ross & Bowie. **Live**: 1978, 1990, 2002-2004.

RCA, Bowie's bewildered label, issued "Be My Wife" as a single six months after *Low*'s release. It would be the first newly-issued Bowie single since 1971 not to chart in Britain. Its promo film, as the musician Momus described it in 2004, is:

A mime sketch of a rock star making a rock video, yet too comically glum and sulky to go through the required hoops and lacking the necessary gung-ho conviction... the character (because it isn't really Bowie, it's a fellow, a sad sack, a thin-lipped melancholic) makes to play his guitar and gives up halfway through the phrase. He just can't be bothered.

When Bowie sings the refrain of "Be My Wife" for the first time, he cocks his head and stares into the camera. He has no readable expression — he could be suppressing a smile, or about to scream. As the image fades, the life drains from his face. It's as if a marionette is professing love to you and, worse, that the marionette may not really mean it.

Staying in a five-note range, Bowie sings his brief lyric (four verse lines, four refrain lines) in the East End accent of his first album, falling by either a fourth ("sometimes you get so lone-ly") or a fifth ("sometimes you get no-where"), the latter frustrated by the band not shifting to the expected F major chord. The players try to force a resolution as Bowie stands still. When he moves, it's grudgingly. Leaving the A minor verse to the C major refrains, everyone — drums, bass, Roy Young's Farfisa organ — pushes to the dominant G major chord. But Bowie only moves up one on note ("be"), then collapses to sing "my wife."

"I've lived all over the world," he sings. A sentiment heard in everything from Ricky Nelson's "Travelin' Man" to Deep Purple's "Woman from Tokyo": a singer talking up life on the road. It's a set-up line, meant to lead to *but I've never met someone like you* or *but I'm with you tonight*. Instead Bowie follows with a meek "I've left every place." That's the end of it. The verse shrugs off. Another begins, but it's an instrumental. Bowie sings a line ("sometimes you get so lonely"), then stops, as if the effort's not worth it. "That's enough of those depressing songs, this one's merely *sad*," he said, introducing "Be My Wife" on stage in 2004.

"Be My Wife" could be a plea from Bowie to his wife, Angela, written as his marriage was dying (in 1978, he said the lyric was "genuinely anguished, I think" but also that "it could have been about anybody"). An offer to be alone together, to pretend to be spouses for once, its first verse is dominated by Bowie, the second by Ricky Gardiner's guitar solo. After the refrain, the third verse is their union — Bowie sings two bars, Gardiner solos for two, and so on. But Bowie doesn't change a word of what he sang before, with Gardiner breaking up Bowie's cold repetitions. Each remains in his own world. It's a divorce settlement.

BREAKING GLASS

(Bowie, Davis, Murray.) **Recorded**: *(backing tracks) ca. 1-20 September 1976, Château d'Hérouville; (lead vocal, overdubs) October-18 November 1976, Hansa Tonstudio 2. Bowie: lead and harmony vocals; Gardiner: rhythm guitar; Alomar:*

lead, rhythm guitar; Eno: ("splinter") Minimoog; Murray: bass; Davis: drums.
Produced: Bowie, Visconti; engineered: Thibault, Meyer, Visconti.

First release: *14 January 1977,* **Low**. *Live: 1978, 1983, 1995-1996, 2002-2004.*

Interviewed two decades after he made *Low*, Bowie disputed its influences. Some critics had called it Bowie's reaction to punk, though it was mixed before the Sex Pistols released their first single. By the Nineties there was, in Bowie's view, an overemphasis on Kraftwerk's influence over the black and Latino American musicians — Dennis Davis, Carlos Alomar and George Murray — who were the album's backbone. "Kraftwerk's percussion sound was produced electronically, rigid in tempo, unmoving. Ours was the mangled treatment of a powerfully emotive drummer, Dennis Davis," he said in 1999. "The tempo not only 'moved' but also was expressed in more than 'human' fashion. Kraftwerk supported that unyielding machinelike beat with all synthetic sound-generating sources. We used an R&B band."

Bowie liked to use Kraftwerk as foils (see "V-2 Schneider") but he was right: there's little of Kraftwerk in *Low* (it's more Bowie recreating the sound of Neu! ("aggressive guitar drone") with a funk drummer). Alomar, Davis, and Murray (plus the English keyboardist Roy Young and the Scottish guitarist Ricky Gardiner) worked in the studio for two weeks with a laconic Bowie giving them chord progressions, a few melodies and tempos. Then they packed off, leaving Bowie and Brian Eno to scribble over the tracks. The latter's contribution to "Breaking Glass" is a descending three-note bleat on "splintered" Minimoog, panned right-to-left, then left-to-right, as if he was doing a stereo placement test.

Credited to Bowie, Murray, and Davis, "Breaking Glass" is Murray holding a track together with his fingers, supporting Davis' drum fills in the intro/refrain, playing a rolling root-heavy line in the verses, becoming the lead melodist in the last verse. Alomar's lead guitar (he also plays rhythm, a scratchy counterpart he said was meant to sound like a jaw harp) is a vocalist. His opening riffs, feasting on F# and D# notes and with Mick Ronson-style bends on the G string, offer more melody and range than Bowie's vocal. "When the vocal starts, I hit one A note but I slam the shit out of it and keep droning it hard until the signature line begins again," Alomar later said.

On "Breaking Glass," Davis plays beats that had never been on a Bowie record before, let alone any British rock record. (It's as if he was asked to outplay the synthetic drums on Cluster's "Caramel".) The trick was Tony Visconti's use of the Eventide H910 Harmonizer, an effects processor that Visconti boasted to Bowie and Eno "fucks with the fabric of time." On *Low*, Visconti sent a feed from the snare drum mike into the Harmonizer. Then he dropped the pitch by a semitone and "added the feedback of this tone to itself." So when Davis hit his snare, he heard in his headphones the "crack" while the subsequent "thud" only deepened in tone. It sounded, Visconti said, like a man struck in the stomach. "We soon discovered that the rate of the Harmonizer's drop off was controlled by an envelope at its input. So now that Dennis could hear the effect as he played, he was able to control the sound by how hard he hit his snare."

In the opening seconds of "Breaking Glass," you hear Davis play against his echo like a game of racquetball, varying the power and duration of his snare hits: one! two! one-two! one-two! Davis described what he heard in his headphones as being "like a floor tom with snares on the bottom! That's a really fine thing to do if you are playing some really hard backbeat rock 'n' roll... you get a sound as big as a house." The engineer Eduard Meyer recalled that while Hansa Studios also had a Harmonizer, they'd never thought to use it "in such an eccentric and listenable form as in Bowie's case." As it happened, Davis and Visconti helped create the massive gated drum sound of Eighties pop (see "Let's Dance").

By contrast to Davis' exuberance, Bowie took what could have been a groove piece like "Golden Years" and whittled it down to a fragment. Inspiration came when his wife Angela and her current boyfriend arrived for a visit at the Château, which upset the communal mood — Visconti said he had to break up a fight between Bowie and Angela's lover, while the band heard the goings-on. Soon afterward, Bowie asked for a new track. "He wanted just like angry, just like very punky," Alomar recalled, "punk without the fuzz, the white noise. It has this thin, thin, veiled harshness." Upon hearing the lyric, Davis figured that Bowie "probably did that shit yesterday in somebody's room! David's writing some shit about *life* here!"

Bowie's phrasing sounds random — *I've... **been**... break-ing-glass inyour**room**again* — but he's following Murray's bassline, often moving from dominant note ("don't look") to root note ("carpet"). There's a tie to "Sound and Vision": the first verse ends with *listen!*, the second with *see?* What passes for a refrain is a line that doesn't rhyme, doesn't scan, and ends with an octave jump: "Oh-oh-OH-OH!" like Iggy Pop's last howls on

"Funtime."

"Breaking Glass" is a purging: two chords, a lyric of thirty-five common words. The Kabbalist Tree of Life, so mysterious in "Station to Station," is a squiggle on a carpet. The sudden fade doesn't feel as if the song's been cut short: it has nowhere else to go, so it ends. It was another Eno suggestion. Don't build the song out. "Leave it abnormal. Leave it strange. Don't normalize it," Eno said. Bowie had to do just that, however, when he sang "Breaking Glass" live: repeating verses and adding a coda, with the band chanting, "I'll never touch you!" over kick-drum hits. Performing it at a Milton Keynes Bowl concert in 1983, he tried to keep the song from dissipating in the summer air and came off as someone reading a homicidal diary entry on a Jumbotron screen.

SUBTERRANEANS

Recorded: (backing tracks) ca. December 1975, Cherokee Studios, 751 North Fairfax Avenue, Los Angeles; ca. 20-30 September 1976, Château d'Hérouville; (overdubs) early October-18 November 1976, Hansa Tonstudio 2. Bowie: lead vocal, tenor saxophone, piano, Chamberlin M1, Fender Rhodes, guitar?; Paul Buckmaster: piano, keyboards; J. Peter Robinson: Fender Rhodes, ARP Odyssey, ARP Solina; Alomar: guitar; Eno?: EMS Synthi AKS?; Murray: bass. Produced: Bowie, Visconti; engineered: David Hines, Thibault, Meyer, Visconti.

First release: 14 January 1977, **Low**. Live: 1995, 2002.

Upon *Low*'s release in January 1977, the journalist Wesley Strick asked an RCA "operative" what he thought of its second, mostly-instrumental side. "It's avant-garde. It's ambitious. Frankly, I think it needs more work," he said. How about the LP closer, "Subterraneans"? "Religious," he sighed. (It remains unclear whether and to what degree RCA rejected an earlier version of *Low*—Bowie always maintained that they had, and Reeves Gabrels recalled seeing the framed rejection letter from RCA at Bowie's house in 1988.)

Low's working title was *New Music: Night and Day*, its sequencing the reverse of *Neu! 75*, which also had two distinct sides — Side A, a sequence by the original two-man Neu!, the other side a thrashing set recorded with a different line up (drummer Klaus Dinger switched to guitar, two drummers

49

were added). *Low*'s "day" side had "seven quite manic disco numbers, like *Station to Station* carried with gritted teeth," as Eno described it at the time. "They're all really short and they've got interesting shapes." While the "night" side was "soundtrack music."

It's how the musicians at the Château d'Hérouville heard it as well. Roy Young recalled that after the backing tracks for the Side A pieces were done, Bowie took everyone into the control room "to play the music that he wanted to put on the B-side. It was so far away from the music we had just finished recording, we all looked at each other in surprise that he wanted to pursue it," Young said. "It really wasn't a style that was going to work with us; hence he brought in Eno." Eno already had been doing soundtrack work, which he'd collect on *Music for Films*.

The most pertinent film score predecessor was Bowie's never-completed *Man Who Fell to Earth* soundtrack, which he credited with teaching him how to write instrumentals. Though Bowie later said he'd only taken the "reverse bass part" directly from the tapes, "Subterraneans" was in great part an instrumental he had recorded for the soundtrack at the end of 1975. Paul Buckmaster, who collaborated with Bowie on the soundtrack, said the "Subterraneans" on *Low* was "identical to what David, [J. Peter Robinson] and I recorded. I recall being there when the reel was turned over for the 'backwards' sounds and… for each keyboard overdub, which was David, Peter, and me." Added at later sessions were vocals, tenor saxophone and "volume-controlled electric guitar."

Bowie had a renewed interest in painting, which "helped me get back into music again," he said in 1978. He'd spend his Berlin years working on canvases as much as he did making records, attempting an "expressionist realist" style. Mostly-instrumental tracks like "Subterraneans" were diverted paintings. He was thinking along the same lines as Kraftwerk, who described their work as "audio-visual music."

He gave *Low*'s instrumental pieces a theme: a tour of an imaginary Eastern Europe by the isolate, paranoiac character of *Low*'s manic side. Bowie called "Subterraneans" a portrait of those left in East Berlin after the Wall was built, "the faint jazz saxophones representing the memory of what it was." Those behind the Wall were a preterite — the souls who hadn't made the cut for heaven. They lived in the West's dream of the communist East: newspapers of official lies; cramped apartments; tapped phones; bread queues; classical music on the radio. The Second World, one of chess masters, secret poets, and gymnasts. Narnia under the White Witch.

"Subterraneans" came from Jack Kerouac's 1958 novella *The Subterraneans* and its characters, of whom Kerouac wrote "they are hip without being slick, they are intellectual as hell… they are very quiet, they are very Christlike," like Bowie's Tibetans, wild-eyed boys, and supermen. Bowie closed his isolation record by dreaming a city of the abandoned. The track ends with the creak of a chair in the studio, breaking the spell like the phone ringing at the end of "Life on Mars?"

As with other *Low* instrumentals, "Subterraneans" has a discernible structure: here, seven repetitions of a sixteen-bar "refrain" with fluid time signatures. A five-note rising bassline (B-C#-D-E-F#) keeps the ear grounded. It appears twice in each section, at the start and midpoint. If you get lost, the next bassline puts you back on the map. Chants start with the third refrain, Bowie's saxophone kicks off the fifth, a vocal "chorus" (Bowie harmonizing with himself in thirds) is the sixth:

Share bride faaail-
ling soooo
Care-line **Care-**line
Careline
Careline *ride-ing-me*
ShirleysurelyShirley onnn
Share-bride fai-ii-ling sta-arrr

"The point of using phonetics was to get rid of the language element," Eno said in 1977. "If you want to have music that's got a 'drifting' aspect to it, it's very hard to make lyrics that will fit." It's sung by someone whose grasp of language has slipped away upon waking one morning. Words uprooted from meaning, vowels and consonants reduced in rank, of no more significance than the notes that Bowie sounds from his saxophone bell.

ARPs are the string section, playing an obscure repertoire: among the melodic lines are the refrain of Bowie's 1967 "She's Got Medals," Anthony Newley's "The Party's Over" and Edward Elgar's "Nimrod," from the *Enigma Variations*. The backdrop is reversed tapes (guitar, Bowie's Rhodes electric piano, *Man Who Fell to Earth* keyboards); dense synthesizer tones are percussive figures. Bowie plays two elegiac, broken solos on saxophone. "Religious," as the RCA operative said.

ART DECADE

Recorded: *(establishing tracks) ca. 20-30 September 1976, Château d'Hérouville; (overdubs) October-18 November 1976, Hansa Tonstudio 2. Bowie: piano, Chamberlin M1, ARP Solina? ARP Pro Soloist? ("synthetic strings"), backing vocal, drum machine ("prearranged percussion"), guitar; Eno: piano, Minimoog, Chamberlin M1, EMS ("E.M.I.") Synthi AKS; Meyer: cello. Produced: Bowie, Visconti; engineered: Thibault, Meyer, Visconti.*

First release: *14 January 1977,* **Low***.* *Live: 1978, 2002.*

Brian Eno was born in 1948, in Woodbridge, Suffolk. The son of a Flemish woman and a Woodbridge postman, he had a music-tinkerer pedigree (his grandfather played saxophone and bassoon, built music boxes and hurdy-gurdies) and attended the Ipswich School of Art, where he was taught by Roy Ascott (Pete Townshend was one of Ascott's former pupils at Ealing Art School), performing "aversion exercises" — actions counter-intuitive to one's nature, so Eno played a servant — and acquiring a taste for abusing tape recorders. By 1968, he owned thirty, only one of which worked properly.

The following year, he was in London, living in an art cooperative in Camberwell and playing in the Scratch Orchestra, a group of enthusiast non-musicians. At the same time, Bowie was running an Arts Lab in Beckenham. The two attended a 10 March 1971 Philip Glass performance of *Music with Changing Parts* at the Royal College of Art. "One of the most extraordinary musical experiences of my life," Eno recalled of the concert. "Sound made completely physical and as dense as concrete by sheer volume and repetition. For me it was like a viscous bath of pure, thick energy... all intricacy and exotic harmonics."

Known in London as a sound boffin, Eno recorded demos for a band, Roxy Music, whose members included an acquaintance, Andy Mackay, and Newcastle University graduate Bryan Ferry. Working in the back of the room in early Roxy gigs, Eno sang harmony vocals while distorting the band's guitars and keyboards via his EMS VCS 3 synthesizer. ("You can hear the songs from the first [Roxy Music] album in the background and over the top is this complete blitz of synthesizer nonsense," he said of a Roxy BBC performance). It soon made sense to move Eno onstage and, given the needs of his and Ferry's gear, they set up at opposing ends of the stage. A divide owed to stage logistics soon became symbolic. Eno, wearing animal-skin prints and feathers, was Roxy Music's font of impractical ideas. Ferry became more formalist and suppressed his deadpan humor in interviews. The break was inevitable. Jumping before he was pushed, Eno left Roxy Music in July 1973.

What followed was an outrageously fecund period, with Roxy's label EG footing Eno's studio bills. Between August 1973 and September 1976, Eno recorded three solo vocal albums and two singles, cut four instrumental albums, distorted and/or performed on more than a dozen other albums, played with the Portsmouth Sinfonia, toured with the Winkies and the 801, played with John Cale, Nico and Kevin Ayers, produced demos for the band Television, and started a record label. In his spare time he devised theoretical projects (Luana and the Lizard Girls, the Pan Am International Steel Band). He kept up this pace even when laid up after being struck by a taxi in London. He once referred to himself as "more of a technologist, manipulating studios and musicians in a funny way."

One musician he wanted to manipulate was Bowie, who was eager for the treatment. They made tentative plans to work together after meeting backstage at one of Bowie's Wembley shows in May 1976, phoning each other during the summer. They were in similar positions. Bowie was exhausted from touring and with songwriting. Eno had found each solo record increasingly harder to make — now he was sifting through the hundreds of tracks that would become *Before and After Science*. He was done with live performance as well.

Eno had mostly worked with an insular group of London-based art rockers — now here was someone with multiple #1 albums and who'd made the cover of *People* and *Rolling Stone*. Recognizing in Eno a fellow chancer, Bowie was bemused by his occasional spotlight grabs, such as getting into studio photographs to be shot working the console. Even today, some journalists will still credit Eno with co-producing the "Berlin" albums, though he didn't record a single one of them (to be fair, Eno never claimed this). Eno had stronger ties to contemporary German music, having met Popol Vuh and having spent late summer 1976 living with Harmonia in their commune. "After Roxy Music, [Eno] was searching for a new way, and in Germany he found something," Dieter Moebius later said.

Bowie was already using Eno's methods on *The Idiot* — a "collective plural" as a lyrical tense; downplaying lead vocals in favor of sonic landscapes, and basing tracks on number counts instead of bar structures. He admired *Discreet Music* and *Another Green World*, considering using the latter's sequence of intertwining vocal and instrumental tracks on *Low* (though in the end he'd segregate them to different LP sides). Bowie wanted stage direction, to be an Iggy Pop to Eno's Bowie. Eno wasn't "in rock but [was] associated with rock," Bowie said. "I needed somebody to work with [who I could] relate to if I was going to discover for myself how I was going write in the future... I needed some help. I couldn't do it myself, because I couldn't look at myself properly at the time, and I think I was very fortunate in deciding on such an empathetic git as Eno to work with."

Music for Four Hands

"Art Decade" is greatly influenced by Eno and for a time was co-credited to him (as of the most recent *Low* and *Stage* reissues, songwriting credit is restored to solely Bowie). The synthetic percussion is close to that of *Another Green World* (especially "The Big Ship") while an "elephant trumpeting" sound (first heard at 0:39) is similar to Robert Fripp's processed guitar riff on "Sky Saw."

It began as a piano composition for four hands, which Bowie thought didn't work and put in the discard pile. Left to his own devices in the studio when Bowie was away on legal business, Eno revived the piece and added layers, using Bowie's collection of ARPs and Chamberlin (responsible for the percussion), a Minimoog, and his own "suitcase" EMS Synthi AKS. Further layers were applied at overdub sessions at Hansa in Berlin, including a cello line to underscore the bassline (particularly from 1:05-1:25), played eight times by Hansa engineer Eduard Meyer, who sat in the center of Hansa's Studio 2.

Eno suggested that rather than bringing in Dennis Davis for a drum track, they should record a metronome clicking a specified number of times while Tony Visconti, on another track, called out each click number in sequence. This provided a compositional map (so, for example, a spoken "33" would cue the cello entrance) to free Bowie and Eno from strictures: no time signatures, chord progressions, bars. Yet "Art Decade" had a recognizable structure, confirming Eno's instinct that random systems tend towards a "natural" order, or that Bowie's pop instincts were hard to suppress.

After a brief percussive opening, "Art Decade" unfolds as two alternating sections, much the same structure as "A New Career in a New Town." There's a nine-bar (or, if you'd like, 36-metronome-click) main theme. Over a progression from E-flat to D major to E major, a descending four-note line is severed to a two-note phrase, then a whole note. Repetitions of this decayed melody make up the other section — alternating patterns of notes descending a whole step (F#-E) and rising a half-step (D#-E).

During his time at Harmonia's studio/commune in rural Forst, Germany, Eno and the group recorded some pieces before he went to France to work on *Low*. The tapes from the "Harmonia '76'" sessions, which weren't released until 1997, bear similarities to *Low* instrumentals: the interlocking patterns of "By the Riverside," for example. Yet such tracks as "Aubade," "Welcome" and "Sometimes in Autumn" are freer in tempo and construction — the pieces move, sometimes rhythmically, sometimes melodically, in unpredictable designs. They have the lightness of indulged thoughts. "Art Decade" feels claustrophobic, its beauties funereal, a walk through a city "cut off from its world, art and culture, dying with no hope of retribution," as Bowie said.

WARSZAWA

(Bowie, Eno.) **Recorded**: *(piano, establishing tracks, vocals?) ca. 20-30 September 1976, Château d'Hérouville; (overdubs) October-18 November 1976, Hansa Tonstudio 2. Bowie: lead and harmony vocal, ARP Solina? ARP Pro Soloist?; Eno: piano, Chamberlin M1, EMS Synthi AKS, Minimoog. Produced: Bowie, Visconti; engineered: Thibault, Meyer, Visconti.*

First release: *14 January 1977*, **Low**. **Live**: *1978, 2002.*

When he recorded "Warszawa," Bowie had been in its namesake city once in his life, for a few hours. He'd gone through Poland in 1973, en route from Moscow, but hadn't left his train. Then in April 1976, Bowie and Iggy Pop took a train from Zurich to Moscow, again via Poland. As Pop described it to his biographer, Paul Trynka, "they saw towns still pockmarked with bullet holes and a landscape scarred by unrepaired bomb craters; drawing alongside a goods train in Warsaw, they witnessed a worker unloading coal piece by piece in the gray, freezing sleet."

In Warsaw, their train was held at Dworzec Gdański (Gdansk Station). Here the tale becomes legend. Generations of Polish Bowie fans maintain that Bowie went for a walk in Warsaw's Żoliborz district, in what was then called Plac Komuny Paryskiej (since rechristened Plac Wilsona). There, Bowie stopped at a record shop and bought LPs by the folk song and dance ensemble Śląsk, one of which had Stanisław Hadyna's composition "Helokanie."

Of these scant impressions Bowie made a world, or at least a city. He named the hymn that opens *Low*'s "night" side not after Moscow, a city he'd visited, nor his soon-to-be home Berlin, but Warsaw, a city he'd glimpsed. Something about it resonated during his brief walk. He'd left Los Angeles, a city of professional dreams. He'd made his art out of fabrications — plastic rock stars, comic-book dystopias. Warsaw had none of this. It had the iron residue of history. It had been nearly leveled during the war, a great part of its population murdered in death camps, failed uprisings, reprisals. For Bowie, it was a fallen city, a conquered city, one left to the spies and the winter.

The song he named after Warsaw begins with a slow tolling: the sound of a funeral bell as played by a child at a piano.

Invisible City

Brian Eno was working alone for a few days at Château d'Hérouville, towards the end of September 1976. Bowie, who had gone to Paris for a contentious meeting with an ex-manager, told Eno he wanted "to compose a really slow piece of music, but I want a very emotive, almost religious feel to it." It was in line with what Eno described as the terms of their collaboration: "I would set up sonic scenarios for him and he would react to them."

Eno also was using studio time to work on pieces for his slowly-gestating next album. "I had all the time I needed to do this very tedious job of building up a big-sounding thing from single notes," he said in 1976, with his instrumental piece "Sparrowfall" as one possible starting point. But he heard Tony Visconti's four-year-old son on the studio piano, pressing three consecutive white keys: A, B and C. He sat down next to the boy and played along, finishing the melody. This would become the main "Warszawa" theme, with Eno entwining it into a larger structure. He'd done the same on *Another Green World*, building songs out of initial one- or two-fingered piano melodies.

As with "Art Decade," Eno set the piece to a series of metronomic clicks (in this case 430), each click numbered on another track, so he could peg a chord change or a bassline to a randomly-chosen number. And again, the song's layout is discernable and even traditional. It's in four distinct sections (generally in 4/4 time): an opening twenty-four-bar "overture" (0:00 to 1:17), a forty-eight-bar "theme" (1:18 to 3:46), a thirty-two-bar "chorus" (Bowie's vocal, 3:47 to 5:25) and a sixteen-bar repeat of the theme.

The pianist Jason Lindner, who played on *Blackstar*, wrote how Bowie and Eno "strategically placed harmonic tones against key melody notes to bring them out. Otherwise it's very sparse, melody against bass." "Warszawa" is built on root notes instead of chords. It begins with eight bars of tolling, treated piano (four consecutive A notes played together); a first fragmented melody played on ARP is a horizontal movement (a progress from A to E) against a vertical stasis (the root note remains A). After another round of A octaves, the melody started by Visconti's son appears, played on (most likely) an ARP Solina — A, B, C (each note played in four octaves). Again, the movement of notes freezes while the root note octaves intone, until the theme section. Over a slow progression of chords up to C# major, the three-note pattern returns to blossom into an arcing melody whose expiration is a slow fall into sleep. After a repeat, there's a new movement, a stepwise dance up an octave. The clean simplicity of these lines suggests Erik Satie's *First Gymnopédie*; the slow coagulation of sound, the opening movement of Shostakovich's Eleventh Symphony.

The instruments were the synthesizers Bowie and Eno had brought to the sessions — Eno's EMS Synthi AKS, a Minimoog, Bowie's Chamberlin and small collection of ARPs (and possibly treated guitars). Both synthesizers and piano play the tolling octaves underneath much of the piece; the Chamberlin doubles for a wind section. The theme section ends, a new root note of E establishes itself, a cello muses, voices appear.

Bowie returned from Paris drained and wanting to move operations to Berlin. Yet when he heard Eno's music, he quickly came up with a lyric. He had Poland on the brain — he'd intended the "emotive" piece that he asked Eno to write to be "a musical picture of the countryside in Poland," describing his initial aim as even "quite positive ideas." Yet in 1997, talking to a Polish journalist, he said, "I attempted to capture and render musically the anguish which I had heard in these Polish folk songs... I know that my music doesn't portray Warsaw the city, but for me it was a kind of a symbol, a catchphrase which carried content that was very important for me." Bowie told Visconti the piece reminded him of "a Polish choir he'd heard as a child" (i.e., the Śląsk records he'd just picked up in Warsaw) and said he wanted a similar sound for his vocals, some of which sound like the "helo helo" chorus of "Helokanie."

Su-la-vee mi-leh-ho
*So-lo-veee mi **leh**-ho*
*Cheli venco **dey**-ho*
Cheli venco dey — heyeey — oh
Mah-li-ohhh
***HE**-libo SEY-YO-maaan...*

It's like a dialect of Esperanto. The lines aren't nonsense words but a series of phonetics, with a rich internal rhyme scheme and common rhythmic base (six syllables for each phrase except "malio"). "A phonetic language that doesn't exist," Bowie said in 1977, whose aim was to "capture the feeling between East and West, between West Germany and Poland, the different kinds of tensions." His words are easy to sing, a fusion of melodious Romance tongues — Italian, French, Spanish and Portuguese — with a pinch of Slavic. (The "East" is there as well, with the chanted "om"s of the bassline). It's a public tongue, with richness and warmth: the long vowels, the easy lift of the mild consonants ("nice-sounding words," as Eno called them). The beauty of Bowie's phrasing, the little downward dash he makes with "so-lo-vie." It's the lost language of a common Europe, an alternate blessed continent that escaped the wars. A tone poem from a world that wasn't.

As the music of "Warszawa" is the work of a synthetic orchestra, its vocals are a choir of a man's manipulated voice. Bowie sings his first lines in his regular baritone. Then, beginning with "cheli venco," Bowie sang onto a tape Visconti had slowed down two semitones: played back at normal speed, his voice had become a child's. His final lines seemed sung by a dervish.

Low's first side was brief messages from a shattered man, its second side interior landscapes. Warsaw, which Bowie had walked through one afternoon, was the album's center. A broken man as a city. "Warszawa" resounded for years: it was the original name of Joy Division (Ian Curtis was obsessed with the song), while Scott Walker's "The Electrician" has its tolling opening.

How was it heard in Warsaw itself? Polish punk groups drew on other influences than Bowie. But the song was a touchstone for the Polish poet Andrzej Sosnowski, who used "Warszawa" as a hidden reference in his work. Sosnowski's Warszawa "is always filtered through Bowie's Warszawa, meaning there's a mythical, concrete, bleak Warszawa that Bowie had in mind, that only partially is the real Warsaw," the writer Agata Pyzik told me:

> The image that has been prolonged in Western minds is very much like this, but you may also say that Bowie immortalized a certain image of the city, his inner Warsaw. I thought it always one of the most solemn, uncanny Bowie songs, and a proper homage to my city, which is until this day quite sinister.

SOME ARE

(Bowie, Eno.) **Recorded**: *ca. late September 1976, Château d'Hérouville?, October-18 November 1976, Hansa Tonstudio 2?; (overdubs) ca. 1988-early 1991, Mountain Studios, Montreux. Bowie: lead vocal, ARP 2600, piano?, additional synthesizers; Eno: piano? EMS Synthi AKS? Produced: Bowie, Visconti; mixed, 1991: Bowie, David Richards.*

First release: *27 August 1991, **Low** (Ryko reissue, CDEMD 1027/RCD 101042).*

Are there lost *Low* tracks? An apocryphal claim that "dozens of bittersweet songs" were left over from the album sessions was one font of this speculation. And a rumor during Bowie's "lost" years was that he and Visconti were working on a deluxe reissue of *Low*, a release that would presumably include some lost bittersweet songs. This wasn't the case, as Visconti's energies went into assembling *The Gouster* and remixing *Lodger,* and there are no indications as of this writing that Bowie approved any sort of "bootleg series" edition of *Low*. There are still only two official outtakes from *Low*, first included on its 1991 reissue by Rykodisc, who received the bonus tracks directly from Bowie. The key outtake is "Some Are," canonical enough for Philip Glass to make it part of his *Low* symphony in 1993.

A Bowie and Brian Eno collaboration, "Some Are" bears a resemblance to "Warszawa," particularly its pounded piano octaves (the tolling continues throughout in the right channel), but it's a fool's errand to assert when it was written. As Bowie sings the synthesizer melody almost note-for-note, it's possible he did a scratch vocal with an improvised lyric and decided to keep it (a very Eno move), while its long instrumental development section, with synthesizers stacked in modal harmony, suggests a slow accumulation of overdubs over years, if not a decade.

Unlike the phonetics of "Subterraneans" and "Warszawa," Bowie's lyric is recognizable English but his phrasing is shaded enough and his words have enough homonyms that his lines lack definition. Is it "summer bound to fade" or "some are bound to fail"? "Some are winter sun" or "summer-winter sun"? There's a free-associative wintry logic to these blurred images, with Bowie getting "coal" from "cinder," and moving from "koala bears on ice" to "winter." It's as close as he got to writing a Christmas song.

Writing on "Some Are" twenty years later ("a quiet little piece Brian Eno and I wrote in the Seventies"), Bowie tweaked anyone who'd tried to make sense of him. The song concerned "the failed Napoleonic force stumbling back through Smolensk. Finding the unburied corpses of their comrades left from their original advance on Moscow... The cries of wolves in the background are sounds that you might not pick up on immediately. Unless you're a wolf." Or then again, maybe the song was about "a snowman with a carrot for a nose; a crumpled Crystal Palace Football Club admission ticket at his feet. A *Weltschmerz* [world weariness] indeed. Send in your own images, children, and we'll show the best of them next week."

ALL SAINTS

(Bowie, Eno.) **Recorded***: ca. late September 1976, Château d'Hérouville?, October-November 1976, Hansa Tonstudio 2?; Mountain Studios, Montreux, ca. 1-15 September 1978? (overdubs) ca. 1988-early 1991, Mountain Studios. Bowie: treated guitar, ARP 2600, Chamberlin? additional synthesizers; Eno: EMS Synthi AKS? Produced: Bowie, Richards; mixed, 1991: Bowie, Richards.*

First release*: 27 August 1991,* **Low** *(Ryko reissue).*

The other official *Low* outtake, "All Saints" may not hail from the sessions at all. At best, "All Saints" is made up of fragments from some Berlin-era recording (possibly as late as *Lodger*) that were diced up and blended by Bowie a decade later. Tony Visconti has no memory of the track, adding that its use of electronic loops was anachronistic. As was its title: a tribute to Eno's Nineties record label, founded in the year the outtake was released. "All Saints" centers on a synth bassline while washes of sound come and go: a battery of distorted guitar riffs (leftover from "Weeping Wall"?), a secondary bassline, and percussive loops. It builds in intensity until faded out at an arbitrary moment. "Some Are" is essential; this is a dubious addition.

WEEPING WALL

Recorded: late October-18 November 1976, Hansa Tonstudio 2. Bowie: xylophone, vibraphone, Chamberlin M1, ARP Pro Soloist, ARP Odyssey? ARP Solina?, piano, lead guitar, vocal. Produced: Bowie, Visconti; engineered: Meyer, Visconti.

First release: 14 January 1977, **Low**. **Live**: 2002.

The last song composed and recorded for *Low*, "Weeping Wall" was made entirely by Bowie at Hansa in West Berlin. "He works it out in his head," Eduard Meyer told Tobias Rüther. "He didn't have any score, just definite ideas as to how he wanted a number." Inspired work by a gifted student, "Weeping Wall" is in debt to the composer Steve Reich's "Music for Mallet Instruments, Voices and Organ" (1973) and, to a lesser extent, "Music for 18 Musicians," whose European premiere, at West Berlin's Metamusik Festival in early October 1976, Bowie allegedly attended.

Reich had studied under serialist composers like Luciano Berio, whose works had "no regular beat. There was a simultaneous move to have no sense of key, cadence, or resting point in the music," Reich said in 1996, whereas he "had come from Bach, Stravinsky and jazz (particularly John Coltrane), all of which shared a very clear, demarcated pulse. I realized that if I were going to do anything that had the least emotional resonance for myself, I had to reinstate the pulse, front and center."

His innovation was phasing, which he called a technological update of the medieval canon. It started as tape manipulations. On his "It's Gonna Rain" and "Come Out," Reich isolated a few seconds of a spoken recording, looped it, then ran an identical loop in sync, then slowly out of sync, with the original loop. "What you hear is, first the unison, then this kind of reverberation, then an irrational relationship that you can't pin down." It made painting seem played-out, as Eno once said of Reich's music. By the time he wrote "Mallet Instruments," Reich had moved away from tape pieces towards live performance, scoring works for an ensemble. "Mallet Instruments" began by building up a duplicate of a "preexisting repeating marimba or glockenspiel pattern, with the duplicate being one or more beats out of phase with the original." This in turn triggered voices and organs into doubling, then doubling again, their notes.

Bowie began by dubbing overlapping sets of vibraphone and xylophone lines as a rhythmic base, a loose affiliation of tones soon firmed up by a sequenced eighth-note synthesizer line. Then he introduced melodic figures, generally center-mixed, where his percussive lines were left- or right-scoped. In sequence there comes what's likely an ARP Pro Soloist (playing the first notes of "Scarborough Fair" or "We Three Kings," soon echoed by Bowie's voice and Chamberlin), treated electric guitar — his gnarliest lines since *Diamond Dogs* — and finally his wordless vocal, accompanied by a sung bassline and a staggered choir of ARPs and Chamberlin, with a low-frequency oscillator on the ARP to create a theremin-like sound (esp. around 2:25). "An accumulative piece," as he later described it.

These melodies are so dominant that they obscure the rhythmic interplay for large stretches of the track. In "Mallet Instruments," Reich wanted his voices and electric organ to fuse into one sound, producing "a new timbre that is both instrumental and vocal at the same time," with marimbas and glockenspiels moving in unison for the climax. In "Weeping Wall" Bowie's xylophone/vibes lines never range far out of phase. Their development is stunted, their prominence in the mix owed to Bowie pushing up a fader at a designated metronome click.

Of the four *Low* instrumentals, "Weeping Wall" is the most derivative, its influences too fresh to fully absorb. Lacking his backing band, Bowie held back from rhythmic development in favor of sonic novelty. Reich's works slowly build, waver and crystallize; "Weeping Wall" moves briskly, with striking textures, but as a whole it feels tentative. Bowie would be more assured when he returned to Hansa in July 1977 to make *"Heroes."* Before then, however, there was a city to live in.

CHAPTER TWO:

BERLINERS
(1977)

Goodbye from tomorrow, arrival yesterday
That's the German dream.
— Thomas Brasch

A spirit possessed of such vitality that it can be happy, even in Berlin.
— Christopher Isherwood, *Goodbye to Berlin*

The future of Germany is being tentatively anticipated by Berlin. The man
who wants to gather hope should look there.
— Heinrich Mann, 1921

I asked them what they thought of Bowie's interpretation. They said it was
not rock 'n' roll. It was cabaret. Behind my shades I can imagine him. There
in Berlin. In the abandoned section. I imagine him stumbling through old
boxes and props in the street. I imagine him in love with the whole world or
totally dead.
— Patti Smith, "Heroes: A Communique"

Sometimes he saw his real face
And sometimes a stranger at his place.
— Kraftwerk, "The Hall of Mirrors"

One average, stupid, representative case: Johnny Yen… His immortality
depends on the mortality of others — the same is true of all addicts.
— William S. Burroughs, *The Ticket That Exploded*

TURN BLUE

(Bowie, Lacey, Peace, Pop.) **Recorded***: ca. 4-18 June 1977, Hansa Tonstudio 3, 38 Köthener Straße, Berlin. Pop: lead vocal; Bowie: organ, ARP 2600? ARP Solina?, backing vocal; Ricky Gardiner: lead guitar; Carlos Alomar: rhythm guitar?; Tony Sales: bass, backing vocal; Hunt Sales: drums, backing vocal. Produced: Bowie, Pop, Colin Thurston ("Bewlay Bros."); engineered: Thurston, Eduard Meyer.*

First release*: 29 August 1977,* **Lust for Life** *(RCA PL-12488/AFL1-2488, UK #28, US #120).* **Live***: (Pop and Bowie) 1977.*

Why Berlin? It was cheap, and Bowie needed to scrimp. And it was off the radar. When Bowie and Iggy Pop moved there in autumn 1976, with Bowie's assistant Coco Schwab getting them an apartment at 155 Hauptstraße in the Schöneberg neighborhood (a short bike ride from the Wall), it took the British press months to find out where Bowie was. He'd found a city to get lost in. Fans had hounded him in Paris; in London he was a notorious celebrity. But in West Berlin, "they care not a sot for anyone in the music business," he said in late 1977. "I became a person again."

He'd first visited West Berlin in October 1969, for a television appearance. It was a guided tour — staying at the Plaza Hotel on the Kurfürstendamm, a snapshot trip to the Wall, stops at nightclubs that had been paid by the TV show's producer so that upon arriving "one of David's records would blare out from the jukebox and all eyes turned toward him," his manager Kenneth Pitt wrote.

In 1973, after a train trip through the USSR and Poland, Bowie and his friend Geoff MacCormack, as the latter wrote in his memoir, encountered at the East German border

> soldiers [who] were like film extras directed to act like they were the most intimidating SS officers on parade. Instead of simply opening the door to the washroom and looking inside, one made a great show of kicking the door open with the shiny toe of his boot and brandishing the muzzle of his machine gun left and right.

When he and Bowie pulled into West Berlin, met on the platform by fans in makeup and feather boas, "everything felt normal again, familiar even.

David pulled the window down and stuck his head out. I don't know if he wanted to see what was going on or if he needed some fresh air to blow away the memory of the stiflingly depressing scenes we'd just traveled through… We were home."

And West Berlin became his home after another visit in May 1976, during which Bowie met nightclub owner and his soon-to-be lover Romy Haag. But Bowie wanted to live in his fictional ideal of Berlin: a city of Expressionist films, Christopher Isherwood novels, and *Cabaret*. ("Berlin had to live up to the Isherwood myth," said Timothy Garton Ash, a British expatriate in Berlin in the same era.) As the writer Tobias Rüther noted, Bowie derived his Berlin period look from Bob Fosse's film *Cabaret*, even sporting its lead actor Michael York's side-part haircut.

"Bowie in Berlin" was an off-stage performance. He had a moustache or beard, allegedly washed his own clothes, took his breakfast of coffee and Gitanes at the Anderes Ufer down the street. And it was a short-lived one. Given his touring, promotions and travel, Bowie spent barely more than a year all told living in Berlin. "Berlin was just a temporary stop off," the Hansa engineer Eduard Meyer said. Bowie's altbau flat had mattresses, canvases, books, a roll of writing paper, recording equipment and little else; it was a bohemian hotel suite.

Living in West Berlin made Bowie "feel uneasy, very claustrophobic. I work best under those sort of conditions." Berlin was the surrealist cage, in which only those inside were free, the composer György Ligeti said. "You always remembered that you were confined here, a prisoner on an island of luxury, culture and pleasure," David Byrne wrote, while the German musician Michael Rother described Berlin as being "cut off from the outside world. Everyone was working in total isolation." ("We were cut off from the world by this heavy purple curtain — if you opened it, there were the gunners on the Wall," as Carlos Alomar described recording *"Heroes"* at Hansa Studios.)

Its industries left in ruins after the war, West Berlin lived by the grace of greater powers. By the Seventies, 40% of the city's budget came from the West German government, which threw housing subsidies and tax write-offs at anyone willing to live there. In Berlin, Bowie would rebuke his public infatuations with Nazi and fascist imagery, in part from social embarrassment. Haag introduced him to artists and leftists, some of whose fathers had been Nazis, and he was living in a city that had been leveled and severed. "That was a good way to be woken up out of that particular dilemma," he said in 1980.

Johnny Yen's Big Break

Iggy Pop would bathe in German ponds to wash the American out of him. He liked West Berlin because it was simple. You slept in, you ate sausage, you fucked, you went to clubs, you made records. The city was populated by "grumpy, snotty students smoking hash and hating everything, superimposed over a working class neighborhood with just enough commerce to sustain life," he recalled. "There are just a few children… it's mostly young people and old people and very little in between." Small town life in an empty city. Even the cops were alright. When Pop fell down drunk in the street, they would drop him off at his doorstep to let him sleep it off.

Lust for Life, the exuberant album he cut in West Berlin, is more his record than *The Idiot*, with Bowie relegated to a supporting role (as on Pop's spring 1977 tour, where he played keyboards, sang backup, and declined interviews). Bowie wasn't a lesser presence on *Lust for Life* for want of effort — he co-composed most of the songs. But Pop was tired of his control-freak tendencies. Bowie had kept the masters of *The Idiot* and had RCA release *Low* before it (so that Pop's record looked like a response to *Low* instead of being, in truth, its predecessor). "Rockism was starting to set in, and I was starting to revert," Pop told Paul Trynka. "[Bowie] was sick of the whole thing at that point and just wanted to get the damn thing over with. But he did well."

On *Lust for Life*, Pop "realized I had to be quicker than [Bowie] or whose album was it gonna be? I was working to be one jump ahead of them for the next day." He rejected some of Bowie's arrangements and melodies (see "Success"), pushing to work from scratch. He had allies in the studio now, with the second coming of the Stooges for a rhythm section: the brothers Hunt and Tony Sales. Along with guitarist Ricky Gardiner, Bowie and the Saleses supported Pop during his cross-Atlantic tour in March-April 1977. Honed over all-night rehearsals in a screening room in the former UFA Studios, Pop's set was nine Stooges songs, three from *The Idiot* and three destined for *Lust for Life*. At the British shows (held at sites of past Bowie triumphs, the Friars Club and the Rainbow Theatre), the punk vanguard paid homage. Milling backstage were Billy Idol, the Sex Pistols' Glen Matlock, the Damned's Brian James and the Buzzcocks' Howard Devoto, who gave Pop a copy of *Spiral Scratch*, saying "I've got all of your records, now you've got all of mine."

Bowie, whose agency booked the tour, was playing an older brother role in Berlin — doling out to Pop his 10 DM per diems, warning off a cabbie who was delivering Pop heroin. He tried to do the same on the tour but was defeated ("the drug use was *unbelievable* and I knew it was killing me," Bowie said in 1993). The tour was Pop's first-ever billing as a solo artist and he drove his band hard, with any detoxing achieved in Berlin going by the board.

The British press was unsure. Nick Kent blamed Bowie for the enervated sound, for playing "an almost tinker-toy two-note organ motif" on opener "Raw Power." The punks wanted the wild boy of their imaginations, not the semi-professional entertainer they saw (Johnny Thunders feared Bowie had made Pop go cabaret), though Ian Moss, singer of Manchester's the Hamsters, was impressed at how Iggy was "disciplined and tight [with] no excess of any kind." Where British audiences clumped along Bowie's side of the stage, the American shows were full of Stooges die-hards — bootlegs of gigs like Detroit document a frenzied crowd.

Bowie's de facto manager Pat Gibbons thought the tour ill-advised. He wasn't promoting *Low* in the press, and now he was playing backup for Iggy Pop in small clubs? There was a parallel to Bowie's folk trio Feathers in 1968, another commercially marginal group he used to escape his obligations (he'd do the same with Tin Machine a decade later). For Bowie, Pop's tour was a way to ease back into public life. He was "definitely playing second fiddle to Iggy and enjoying it," Friars Club promoter David Stopps recalled, with Bowie quietly reading backstage while Pop worked himself into his stage madman routine.

Jesus? This Is Iggy

In London and New York, Pop got a taste of punk rock which, to his ears, was the sound of the Stooges marketed under a new label. Interviewed in March 1977, he called punk rock "a word used by dilettantes and heartless manipulators... a term based on contempt." Hearing the likes of the Damned rewrite him (and covering the Stooges' "1970" as "I Feel Alright") lit a competitive fire. He went back to Berlin, got a cold-water flat in Bowie's building (the first lease he'd ever signed in his name) and in about ten days in June 1977 he made *Lust for Life* at Hansa Studios.

A fixture of his 1977 tour, "Turn Blue" was the album's oldest composition, dating to Pop and Bowie's attempt to record in Los Angeles in May 1975. Its music co-written by Bowie and MacCormack, its lyric was written by Pop and the LA-based artist Walter Lacey, apparently before Pop went to Europe. While on stage "Turn Blue" sounded improvised, it hardly changed in performance, nor in its studio take. It moves from Pop spying a girl in an El Dorado ("Christ, *she's beautiful!*") to a check-in with God, from tales of junkie camaraderie to an aside where Pop envies how "the blacks... get off on you so sexually," squeezing out the last word. His voice is a junk-box — nasal rants, murmured asides, bass rumblings, comic bits (a stop-time "Jesus? This is Iggy," which Pop sang on stage gazing into a spotlight), a bit he sings as if he's doubled up on the studio floor.

Built on kick drum, bass, and arpeggiated guitar, with Bowie playing organ and ARP synthesizers as if to invoke the organist Jimmy McGriff's 1965 instrumental of the same name, "Turn Blue" rambles from verse to verse, with Pop's bruising phrasing: "I shot myself *down*!" "*step-ping-on-our-hearts*!" "Don't re-*ject* me! Don't for-*get* me!" Shifting to double time (4:59), the song builds in crescendo, with Bowie and the Saleses closing in on Pop, making him commit to his degradation. It ends with a hard cut — Pop shooting up with a needle or a gun. On stage in Detroit, he yelled, "I killed myself!" as the band lurched to a close.

SOME WEIRD SIN

(Bowie, Pop.) **Recorded**: ca. 4-18 June 1977, Hansa Tonstudio 3. Pop: lead vocal, handclaps?; Bowie: backing vocal, organ, ARP 2600?; Gardiner: lead guitar; Alomar: rhythm guitar; T. Sales: bass, backing vocal; H. Sales: drums, cowbell, backing vocal. Produced: Pop, Bowie, Thurston; engineered: Thurston, Meyer.

First release: 29 August 1977, **Lust for Life**. Live: (Pop and Bowie) 1977, (Pop) 1977, 1981, 1983, 1986-1988, 2015-2018.

Debuted in Pop's spring 1977 tour, "Some Weird Sin" is eager to do away with itself — Ricky Gardiner's guitar solo seems to last as long as one of Hunt Sales' cowbell fills. Sharp edits (1:04 and 2:12) further a sense that the song can't move fast enough for its makers, with the tail-end of one guitar solo lopped off. Hunt shuts it down with a smeared cymbal crash, like the close of "John, I'm Only Dancing."

Pop keeps mainly to his higher registers, with Bowie echoing him in verses, doubling him in refrains — in the last descending "some weird sin," he's almost two octaves up from Pop. The chord sequence, a G# minor verse brightening to B major in refrains, seems like Bowie's work. The lyric, derived from "an angry poem written in Berlin," is Pop's outsider credo: "I never got my license to live" (a reference to the hassle of getting a West Berlin residence permit); "when things get too straight, I can't bear it." Longing for a stable life can't match the fun of a new abasement. The guitars, from the intro's multi-tracked Gardiner to Carlos Alomar's elbows-out riffs, back his play.

Tonight

(Bowie, Pop.) **Recorded**: *ca. 4-18 June 1977, Hansa Tonstudio 3. Pop: lead vocal; Bowie: ARP 2600?, piano, backing vocal; Gardiner: lead guitar; Alomar: rhythm guitar; T. Sales: bass, backing vocal; H. Sales: drums, backing vocal. Produced: Pop, Bowie, Thurston; engineered: Thurston, Meyer;* **(Bowie remake)** *ca. May-June 1984, Le Studio, 201 Rue Perry, Morin Heights, Quebec, Canada. Bowie: lead vocal; Tina Turner: lead vocal; Alomar: guitar; Derek Bramble: synthesizer, guitar, bass; Carmine Rojas: bass; Omar Hakim: drums; Sammy Figueroa: percussion; Guy St. Onge: marimba; Curtis King, George Simms, Robin Clark: backing vocals. Produced: Bowie, Hugh Padgham, Bramble; engineered: Padgham.*

First release: *29 August 1977,* **Lust for Life**; *(remake) 24 September 1984,* **Tonight** *(EMI America EL 2402271/R-144418, UK #1, US #11).* **Live**: *(Pop and Bowie) 1977; (Pop) 1977, 2016, 2018; (Bowie and Tina Turner) 1985.*

Spun from a stray line in "Turn Blue," "Tonight" debuted as the climactic number of the *Idiot* tour. It verged on the ridiculous, from Pop's opening line ("this is a song about my girlfriend who's *dead!*," answered by audience cheers) to Bowie and the Saleses' wailing wall of harmonies. But there was heartbreak in Pop's singing: he sold the song. In Detroit, as Pop began, Hunt Sales yelled "hey!" as if just hearing the news. The refrain, a slow advance from D major, has the loveliest melody on *Lust for Life*: a slowly descending phrase ("no one moves/no one talks...") that comes to a rest on the dominant chord, A major (the last "night"). Opening in shock, with Pop discovering his girlfriend's corpse, "Tonight" becomes an ode to death, although as he sings that he'll love the girl to the end (which is now), it's also a breakup song.

On *Lust for Life* Bowie's roles were keyboardist (he played all piano and synthesizer parts, like the shaky ARP lines here) and backing singer, often a distantly-mixed, octave-higher echo of Pop's baritone. Bowie kept Pop's bad dreams company. On "Tonight" he and the Saleses stay at a distance, offering no consolation, only witnessing.

Bowie's cover of "Tonight" in 1984 titled the album he released that year. If any single recording demonstrates his decline in judgment and taste in the mid-Eighties, it was here, when Bowie turned a junkie's lament into a light reggae cocktail-lounge duet with Tina Turner. Cleaned up at the height of Thatcher and Reagan, Bowie disposes of a dead girl's body while turning her eulogy into a desiccated come-on.

Interviewed at the time by Charles Shaar Murray, Bowie all but called his remake a travesty. As Pop's original was "such an idiosyncratic thing of Jimmy's that it seemed not part of my vocabulary," Bowie instead "changed the whole sentiment around" while trying to retain a "barren feeling." He cut the prelude because he thought Turner would have balked at singing it. She was of built of sterner stuff: *Private Dancer* has her take on Paul Brady's "Steel Claw," with lines like "sometimes I'm contemplating suicide." More notably, she also took on Bowie's "1984," singing about breaking craniums and shooting up. No matter, as Bowie's "Tonight" somehow manages to make Turner superfluous. Where Bowie and the Saleses are competing airwave signals, howling over Pop's baritone, Bowie sings his remake in a soft croon, leaving Turner no entry point. Despite the intimacy of its recording, made with Bowie and Turner facing each other in the studio, she wound up having to sing over him.

Pop's "Tonight" sounds like the band is holding it together by luck and will; Ricky Gardiner's guitar runs are moments of grace. Bowie replaced Gardiner's solo with a marimba reverie. Even Carlos Alomar, the sole holdover from the original recording, is a whisper of his old self. It was Bowie baldly reusing the "China Girl" formula of cleaning up a weird Iggy Pop song to get an MTV hit, but "Tonight" stiffed, ending his commercial resurgence in the US. In the summer of "When Doves Cry" or Turner's "What's Love Got to Do With It," it just sounded old.

NEIGHBORHOOD THREAT

(Bowie, Gardiner, Pop.) **Recorded**: *ca. 4-18 June 1977, Hansa Tonstudio 3. Pop: lead vocal; Bowie: ARP 2600, piano, backing vocals; Gardiner: lead guitar; Alomar: rhythm guitar; T. Sales: bass, backing vocals; H. Sales: drums, tambourine, backing vocals. Produced: Pop, Bowie, Thurston; engineered: Thurston, Meyer.* **(Bowie remake)** *ca. May-June 1984, Le Studio. Bowie: lead vocal; Alomar: guitar; Arif Mardin: synthesizer; Bramble: synthesizer, bass?; Rojas: bass?; Hakim: drums; Figueroa: percussion; King, Simms, Clark: backing vocals. Produced: Bowie, Padgham, Bramble; engineered: Padgham.*

First release: *29 August 1977,* **Lust for Life;** *24 September 1984,* **Tonight.** *Live: (Pop) 1977, 1982, 2015-2016.*

"Neighborhood Threat" is Iggy Pop social commentary ("somewhere a mother's needing"), if still centered on his street-walking cheetah persona. It's a jostle of voices over a two-chord A minor progression — Ricky Gardiner's arpeggios and lead lines (at first piercing, later a churning figure sawing through a muddy mix), Hunt Sales' tympani-sounding tom fills and cheerful abuse of his ride cymbal, Carlos Alomar's tugging rhythm guitar, Bowie's shuddering ARP lines and his and the Saleses' eerie vocal counterpoint.

Where Bowie's dismal remake of "Tonight" had a commercial logic to it, covering "Neighborhood Threat" on the same album seems arbitrary. Kitted up with gated drum cannonades, backing singers who sound recruited from Off-Broadway auditions, and staccato synthesizers, it casts Alomar in the role of flashy lead player (a foreshadowing of his bid for center stage in the Glass Spider tour). A grotesque recording, as Bowie admitted in 1987 ("it went totally wrong"), his "Neighborhood Threat" sounds as if he was aiming for a pinball machine soundtrack take on it. He woke up halfway through the performance, with some lively phrasing in the last refrains, boring into the title line at 2:59. The vocals in the bridge, described by Thomas Inskeep as sounding like "Oompa Loompas on drugs," add to the luridness. It's enough to make the case that it's Bowie's version being blasted on a thug's boombox in Alan Moore and Dave Gibbons' *Watchmen*.

LUST FOR LIFE

(Bowie, Pop.) **Recorded**: *ca. 4-18 June 1977, Hansa Tonstudio 3. Pop: lead vocal; Bowie: piano; Gardiner: lead guitar; Alomar: rhythm guitar; T. Sales: bass, backing vocals; H. Sales: drums, tambourine, shaker, backing vocals. Produced: Bowie, Pop, Thurston; engineered: Thurston, Meyer.*

First release: *29 August 1977,* **Lust for Life. Live**: *(Pop) 1977-1978, 1980-1981, 1986-1987, 1989-1994, 1996-2003, 2008-2009, 2015-2018; (Bowie) 1996.*

Bowie and Pop would watch American television shows on the Armed Forces Network (AFN), especially *Starsky & Hutch*. The station ident of the AFN was a radio conning tower making a staccato BEEP-beep-beep, BEEP-BEEP-be-BEEP. One night, Bowie took his son's ukulele and played the AFN riff on it. He and Pop started building up a song. "Call this one 'Lust for Life'," he said.

They moved the riff from guitar to drums. Pop was a drummer at heart and he worked out his songs as percussion. "Lust for Life" starts with a thirty-bar intro, Hunt Sales playing open-tuned toms, soon shadowed by Tony Sales' bassline. (It's the riff in its primal form — Pop sings much of the second verse over it.) Hunt's drum figure mixed the AFN hook and the bassline of "You Can't Hurry Love," and had the cymbal-dense sound of the jazz drummer Shelly Manne. Hunt was the king of the track — New Order's Stephen Morris would later describe "Lust for Life" and "The Passenger" as having "the loudest cymbals known to man!" The drum riff converts the other players. Carlos Alomar and Ricky Gardiner soon fall subservient, as does Bowie's low-mixed R&B piano ("you can't play a counter-rhythm to that. You just had to follow," Alomar told Paul Trynka). Shakers and handclaps fatten the beat, as does Pop, often keeping to a single note. He sings "lust-for-LIFE" like three raps on a snare.

Over a pounding all-major-chord vamp in A, Pop improvised much of his lyric at the mike, drawing on LA memories and William S. Burroughs novels — from the latter, flesh machines and love being like hypnotizing chickens. Johnny Yen is the ambisexual gigolo of Burroughs' Nova Trilogy, doing stripteases, getting wrecked on booze and cocaine, getting his ear stabbed with a scalpel. Pop's improvised lines are better than some composers' catalogs ("I'm worth a million in *prizes*!" and he sings "bought the gimmick" like "bought the gimp"). It's Pop casting himself as Burroughs' gigolo and, as in "Success," wanting off the minstrel circuit. "No more beatin' my brains," he mutters. "I'm through with *sleepin'* on the *sidewalk*." The title homages Pop's appetite for drugs and self-destruction and the 1956 Vincente Minnelli film about Vincent van Gogh, another tortured artist who didn't sell and who'd also had it in the ear before ("that's a common expression in the Midwest," Pop said in 2011. "To give it to him right in the ear means to fuck somebody over.") It was Andrew Kent's photograph used for the LP cover: a beaming Iggy, shot in a dressing room during his UK tour, looking like a confidence man close to a score.

After Elvis Presley died in August 1977, RCA made the Elvis catalog their priority, tying up pressing plants. So *Lust for Life* became hard to find once its first printing sold out, even though it hit #28 in the UK. Pop didn't help. He locked himself in the Schloßhotel Gehrhus with a "small mountain of cocaine," staring at the album sleeve, deciding he hated the cover photo, thought it was all crap. During a chaotic tour to promote the album, Pop fired the Sales brothers. He ran out his RCA contract by issuing a bootleg, then began another comeback on another label.

"Lust for Life" had too much life in its bones to stay underground for long. In the mid-Nineties, an edit used in *Trainspotting* finally gave it a mass audience. It was released as a single in 1996 and sounded fresher than much of the Britpop on the charts. A decade later came the farcical epilogue. Chopped down to its opening drum riff and Pop's Johnny Yen line, "Lust for Life" soundtracked Royal Caribbean cruise line ads. A junkie gluttony rant sold family vacations, with lines from Pop and Burroughs singing through millions of TV sets.

Success

(Bowie, Pop, Gardiner.) **Recorded***: ca. 4-18 June 1977, Hansa Tonstudio 3. Pop: lead vocal; Bowie: electric piano; Gardiner: lead guitar; Alomar: rhythm guitar; T. Sales: bass, backing vocals; H. Sales: drums, backing vocals. Produced: Bowie, Pop, Thurston; engineered: Thurston, Meyer.*

First release*: 29 August 1977,* **Lust for Life***. Live: (Pop) 1977, 2016, 2018.*

Iggy Pop rejected much of Bowie's proposed arrangement for "Success," including a top melody he disparaged as "some damn crooning thing" (it sings in the lead guitar lines). He honed it to a three-chord shuffle in D major, alternating eight-bar refrains with guitar retorts. His main phrasing was a one-note, four-beat line, putting weight, as usual, on the last syllable ("here-comes-suck-*sess*"). For contrast, Pop used a six-beat descending line, triggered by the dominant A major chord ("here-comes-my *Chi-nese-rug*"). His metallic-sounding vocal owes to a whim: Hansa engineer Edu Meyer plugged Pop's mike into a Music Man guitar amp, and Pop liked what he heard.

The Sales brothers allegedly cut their backing vocals in a single take without hearing Pop's lead track (they'd done a similar routine on tour versions of "No Fun"). Starting off as a cheering section, hollering Pop's lines back at him, the brothers grow progressively unhinged. In the third refrain, Pop drops out while they keep going; they whisper a line ahead of time, as if prompting him on stage. Pop starts trying to get them to crack up on mike ("I'm-gonna-go-out-on-the-street-n-do-anything-I-want!"), while the Saleses lob a grumbled line back at him at full force: "OH SHIT!"

In the late Sixties, Randy Newman wrote "Lonely at the Top" for Frank Sinatra, who never sang it. On stage, Newman, a cult act, sang wearily about all the money he's made, all the women he's loved. "Success" is a similar joke, Pop poking fun at his professional rehabilitation, mocking his plan to, as Johnny Thunders feared, go cabaret. But he really *had* bought a Chinese rug for his Berlin apartment ("I'd advise anybody to put their money in rugs... you can sit on 'em; best of all, you can always pawn 'em"). He thought he was going to be a rock star, that he'd finally reached the zone of comfort Bowie lived in (though his finances were erratic, Bowie always kept up appearances). That said, there's also a drug joke — "here comes the Zoo!!," with Pop and the Saleses cheering the U-Bahn stop where you could score.

While Pop sidelined Bowie (he was only the piano player here), the latter was as watchful as ever. With its droning propulsion and knockabout dialogue of guitars, drums, and singers, the sound of "Success" was that of *"Heroes,"* recorded a month later.

THE PASSENGER
SIXTEEN

(Pop ["Sixteen"], Pop, Gardiner ["Passenger"].) **Recorded**: ca. 4-18 June 1977, *Hansa Tonstudio 3. Pop: lead vocal; Bowie: piano, electric organ ("Sixteen"), backing vocals; Gardiner: lead guitar; Alomar: rhythm guitar; T. Sales: bass, backing vocals; H. Sales: drums, tambourine, shaker, cowbell, backing vocals. Produced: Bowie, Pop, Thurston; engineered: Thurston, Meyer.*

First release: *29 August 1977,* **Lust for Life**. *Live: ("Sixteen") 1977, 1982-1983, 1987-1989, 1996-2000, 2002-2003, 2009, 2015-2018; ("Passenger") 1977, 1981, 1983, 1986-1989, 1991-1994, 1996-2003, 2009-2010, 2012-2013, 2015-2018.*

The *Lust for Life* tracks without Bowie co-writes are staples of Pop's live act well into the twenty-first century. "Sixteen" is what one would expect from a Pop solo credit: lust for underage girls, a fixation on details (leather boots here), a barely-there melody, a percussive riff flashing from organ to guitar, a refrain as the cut-off to a ranting verse.

"The Passenger" is the gravity well of *Lust for Life*, with co-writer Ricky Gardiner's riff (he came up with it while playing guitar in a bucolic English garden) a slashing base rhythm, Carlos Alomar as needling counterpoint and Hunt Sales' drums as lead instrument, each crash cymbal hit landing like an uppercut, each snare fill like a hard tumble downstairs. Inspired by Jim Morrison's "The Lords" (which Pop plundered for lines, e.g. "ripped backsides"), Pop reversed his typical *Lust for Life* persona of a man consuming whatever he comes across. The passenger is passive, maybe a captive; the city's a narcotic he craves but might be denied. Perspective blurs from first to third person as Pop moves up an octave: it's the scenario of "Nightclubbing" and "Funtime" — dirty boys on the town — turned nightmare, with Bowie acidly singing the "la la la"s that are strung like wire through the refrains.

FALL IN LOVE WITH ME

(Bowie, Pop, T. Sales, H. Sales.) **Recorded**: *ca. 4-18 June 1977, Hansa Tonstudio 3. Pop: lead vocal; Bowie: organ, electric piano; Alomar: lead guitar; T. Sales: rhythm guitar; H. Sales: bass; Gardiner: drums. Produced: Pop, Bowie, Thurston; engineered: Thurston, Meyer.*

First release: *29 August 1977,* **Lust for Life.** *Live: (Pop) 1977, 1982, 2016.*

During a lull in the *Lust for Life* sessions, everyone swapped roles for a laugh. Ricky Gardiner sat behind the drum kit, Hunt Sales took his brother's bass and Tony played guitar. They fell into a loose groove. Gardiner and Hunt played cloddish disco, Tony some blues licks. Carlos Alomar was the ringer, staying on guitar to keep things from fraying too much, while Bowie played an organ hook and abridgements of his "Laughing Gnome"/"Speed of Life" descending line. Iggy Pop free-associated a lyric. Cut to six and a half minutes, "Fall in Love with Me" became the album closer, honoring the minor rock 'n' roll tradition of padding out an LP with a studio jam.

The album would be the lesser without it. Pop's lines are as cutting ("you're younger than you look") as they're touching ("when you're tumbling down, you just look finer"). He's singing to the same girl as in "Baby" and "Sixteen" and "Tiny Girls": it's *always* the same girl for him — young, pure, broken. What's absent here is his need for control. It's a carefree seduction, in a few details — plastic raincoat, white wine, a table made of wood. The latter was Pop's symbol of Berlin: solid, unpretentious, practical.

Struck by how Pop could get a song out of a whim, Bowie saw a working method for his next album (he'd also use some of "Fall in Love with Me" in his cover of "Criminal World" years later). It marked the temporary end of the partnership of Pop and Bowie, which ended as well as it could have, with a vamp cooked up over an afternoon in West Berlin. Loose talk, tall tales, idle confessions, shot-glass epiphanies. Someone looks at the clock, excuses are made, goodbyes exchanged, the party breaks up.

SONS OF THE SILENT AGE

Recorded: 11 July-5 August 1977, Hansa Tonstudio 2. Bowie: lead and harmony vocal, Chamberlin M1, ARP Solina?, tenor saxophone; Eno: EMS Synthi AKS, guitar treatments; Alomar: guitar; George Murray: bass; Dennis Davis: drums, tambourine; Tony Visconti: harmony vocal. Produced: Bowie, Visconti; engineered: Visconti, Thurston.

First release: 14 October 1977, *"Heroes"* (RCA PL 12522/AFL1-2522, UK #3, US #35). *Live*: 1987.

The only song Bowie wrote before recording *"Heroes,"* "Sons of the Silent Age" is the odd man out on the record. It keeps outside, an ambassador of his past. Its characters, part *homo superior*/part Bewlay Brothers, wander through a Bowie urban dreamscape, which is a Jacques Brel dreamscape, a surreal take on Brel's "Amsterdam." Bowie honored Brel by taking his title and song structure from Brel's "Fils de" ("Sons of") and lines ("old folks never die/they just put down their heads and go to sleep one day") from Brel's "Les Vieux."

Brel's Sons are equal under God ("sons of the great, or sons unknown/ all were children like your own"), while his Old are leveled by weakness, sitting around or lying in bed (not coming, like Bowie's Sons do), waiting for death, marked by time. Bowie mixes Brel's pairs — his Sons are old wraiths and rent boys ("pick up in bars and cry only once"), they stand on train platforms and in platform shoes; their gods are the pop stars Sam Therapy and King Dice; they war like old Supermen and expire in a Gnostic way, with sleep instead of death.

Compositionally "Sons of the Silent Age" feels like a refugee from the *Hunky Dory* era, with a cloudy tonality and ambiguous pitch class in the melody: its G major verses and oddly-made E-flat major/A-flat major refrains could be different songs. A mirror-image chromatic saxophone progression links them — rising in the intro, falling in passages between verse and refrains. (It's also a harmonic reverse of "What in the World" — like the latter, "Sons of the Silent Age" has a verse that moves between chords a whole step apart, but the modulation for its refrain is a whole step down, whereas "World" vaulted a whole step up.) Bowie has two voices for the two sections, singing his verses (shuttling between two augmented chords) in an "East End" accent to bless the rhyme scheme ("*sy*-lunt *ay*dj"), then belts the refrains in his "epic" register, a taxing enough performance that, for the song's revival on the Glass Spider tour, Peter Frampton sang them while Bowie did a dance routine.

Sequenced as a break between the colossal title track and side-closer onslaught "Blackout," its verses have a swirl of saxophone, treated arpeggiated guitar and crash cymbal punctuation, with a Chamberlin backdrop. The refrains are cushioned by four-part harmonies and a musing Alomar counterpart, in service of a lead vocal that sounds as if it's been recorded via satellite.

BEAUTY AND THE BEAST

Recorded: 11 July-5 August 1977, Hansa Tonstudio 2. Bowie: lead and harmony vocal, piano; Robert Fripp: lead guitar; Alomar: rhythm guitar; Eno: EMS Synthi AKS, guitar treatments; Murray: bass; Davis: drums; Antonia Maaß, Visconti: harmony vocals. Produced: Bowie, Visconti; engineered: Visconti, Thurston.

First release: 14 October 1977, *"Heroes."* **Broadcast**: 30 May 1978, Musikladen Extra. **Live**: 1978.

Inspired by how quickly *Lust for Life* was cut, Bowie wanted to improvise an album, using Hansa as a workshop (a week or so after finishing *Lust*, he'd visited the studio of artist Victor Vasarely in France), writing and recording "live." Apart from "Sons of the Silent Age," no songs existed beyond a chord sequence. "The whole thing... evolved on the spot in the studio," Brian Eno said soon after the album's release. "It was all done in a very casual kind of way. We'd sort of say 'Let's do this then' — and we'd do it, and then someone would say 'stop' and that would be it, the length of the piece. It seemed completely arbitrary to me."

The rhythm section arrived but their gear hadn't made it to Hansa Studios yet. No matter — Bowie had them set up with whatever they found lying around ("They had this weird amp that I used. I don't know what it was," George Murray said in 1978, while Dennis Davis cobbled together a drum kit (see "Blackout")). Most backing tracks were rehearsals, often first takes, cut in about three days. Tony Visconti recalled Bowie ad-libbing whole songs, singing at the top of his lungs. Bowie was constantly "up" during *"Heroes,"* doing Goon Show voices in the studio, arranging tours of Berlin clubs in evenings. "It was the best, most positive album that we made together... there were no bad scenes... [David] was very upbeat. He had a life!" Visconti said. The jazz singer Antonia Maaß, who was recording in an adjacent studio and was recruited for harmony vocals, described the period as being "like a ray of light."

"This song is somewhat schizophrenic in nature," Bowie quipped before going into "Beauty and the Beast" on German TV in 1978. Staying mainly on one chord (an A7, though the track sounds sped up a semitone to B-flat), it opens like Roxy Music's "The Thrill of It All" or his "Station to Station," with Bowie playing a simple pattern on the bass end of a piano: a two-note "dyad" chord (mainly E-G) with a single note retort (usually A). A nudge of Robert Fripp's treated guitar appears. Murray's bass and repeating octaves on piano build until Bowie's entrance, an "oooooh!" glissando to tumble into the opening verse. It's a man in broken movements, Bowie exploiting his lower register, running lines together, becoming hysteric (the brief refrain). His lyrics are non-sequiturs and in-jokes: Visconti's exasperated curse during the sessions — "someone fuck a priest!" — became a refrain line. "Those lyrics come from a nook in the unconscious," Bowie said in 2001. "Still a lot of housecleaning going on, I feel."

Patti Smith's essay on *"Heroes"* for *Hit Parader* in 1978 quoted some nameless German teenagers who called Bowie cabaret, not rock 'n' roll, and "Beauty and the Beast" makes their case: it's cabaret disco, with Maaß swooning out "liebling!" The counterweight is Alomar, who plays a funk riff under Fripp's lead lines, while his sly rhythm after "liebling" nearly takes over the song.

Fripp was a latecomer to *"Heroes."* Bowie had planned to use Michael Rother (Neu!, Harmonia). They had talked earlier in the summer, with Rother recommending Can's Jaki Liebezeit on drums. For whatever reason, Rother was told not to come to Berlin, whether due to label pressure for a "name" guitarist or miscommunication. (Only when exchanging emails in 2001 did Bowie and Rother realize that each believed the other had stood them up.) Fripp had played with Eno for years and could work quickly, with little guidance. Upon flying in, he sat down at Hansa, plugged his guitar into Eno's EMS Synthi AKS and cut lead lines to tracks he'd never heard before, not knowing the keys, and getting oblique advice from Bowie, who'd yet to write lyrics or top melodies. His work completed in about three days, Fripp said he left Berlin without time for a drink or to find someone to sleep with, describing his lead work on tracks like "Beauty and the Beast" as extravagant sexual frustration.

BLACKOUT

Recorded: 11 July-5 August 1977, Hansa Tonstudio 2. Bowie: lead and backing vocal, piano; Fripp: lead guitar; Alomar: rhythm guitar; Eno: EMS Synthi AKS, guitar treatments; Murray: bass; Davis: drums, percussion. Produced: Bowie, Visconti; engineered: Visconti, Thurston.

First release: 14 October 1977, *"Heroes." Live*: 1978.

Where Dennis Davis' drumming, as shaped by Tony Visconti's Harmonizer, rules *Low*, Visconti used the Harmonizer sparingly on *"Heroes,"* and only at the mixing stage. So *"Heroes"* is the sound of Davis playing to the room.

It was a grand room: Hansa Tonstudio 2 could house a one-hundred-and-fifty-person orchestra. Davis set up on a riser that, in a past life, had been used for choirs. At one end of the room, sitting five feet off the floor, Davis could see George Murray to his right (when Davis used his kick drum, Murray felt like he was being hit in the face), Carlos Alomar to his left and Bowie, on piano, in front of him. At the other end Visconti placed a microphone to pick up Davis' aftershocks. Davis conducted the band with his wrists and feet. His "most abstract set of drums you could imagine," including tympani and two congas as floor toms, is best heard on "Blackout," where Davis is a percussive orchestra, his fills like spins of a clock's second hand. A human jazz metronome, as Visconti later called him.

As abrasive as *"Heroes"* gets, "Blackout" has punch-up verses and refrains as referee breaks. Robert Fripp's guitar has dog-whistle frequencies. Eno's EMS burbles in the right channel. Alomar (mixed left, as if isolated from the contagion) plays a riff that marries "Suffragette City" to "Bony Moronie," while the refrain reworks "Stay." Bowie sings meandering phrases that he severs with shouts and groans. His 1978 tour pianist Sean Mayes described the song as "built on two structures over which the vocals create three distinct sections... [Bowie] has a way of producing vocal lines which spring from the roots of the music... varying the vocal line as if the songs were alive and growing." It's one of his most bizarre vocals, from a ranted "I'm-under-Jap-a-nese-influence and my honor's at *stake*!" to would-be New Yorkese ("skin expozyuh"). Momus wrote of "the Expressionist way the words tumble out... the confident articulation of doubt. It's an Ernst Kirchner painting come to life." Bowie falters while singing "kiss me in the rain," as if he's so spent he can't form the words in his mouth.

The lyric was a live-at-the mike improv, with Bowie using scraps of cut-up lyrics (he got one line by mashing "wine from your" and "cut hands"). Inspired by disasters domestic (disturbed by his wife, he was hospitalized briefly in late 1976) and international (the New York City power outage of July 1977 — the song was "a reflection on America from a bit of a distance," he said), it's an urban song, flush with crowd paranoia. "My God! There's angst in the air!" as Bowie said of Berlin at the time. Though he sings for someone to get him on the streets, he's been there all along — the guitars, effects and drums are a heavy traffic, his voice another signal in an overloaded frequency. Singing "Blackout" on stage the following year, he kept at the song, altering his phrasing, ad libbing, never letting it rest.

JOE THE LION

Recorded: 11 July-5 August 1977, Hansa Tonstudio 2. Bowie: lead and harmony vocal, ARP?, piano; Fripp: lead guitar; Alomar: rhythm guitar; Eno: EMS Synthi AKS, guitar treatments; Murray: bass; Davis: drums; Visconti: harmony vocal, guitar treatments. Produced: Bowie, Visconti; engineered: Visconti, Thurston.

First release: 14 October 1977, *"Heroes." Live*: 1983, 1995.

The American artist Chris Burden was once bolted with copper bands to a gallery floor between buckets of water, each with a live electric line submerged within it, so that someone could kick over a bucket and electrocute him (*Prelude to 220, or 110*, 1971). Mock-crucified on the hood of a Volkswagen Bug (*Trans-Fixed*, 1974), shot in the arm with a .22 rifle (*Shoot*, 1971), Burden was body art as adolescent provocation, though "I am not Alice Cooper," he told the *New York Times* in 1973, for an article illustrated with a photograph of Burden in a ski mask. "Art doesn't have a purpose,"

83

Burden said. "It's a free spot in society, where you can do anything." As C. Carr wrote, Burden "took his risks in the manner of a scientist — one who decides he must test a new serum on himself alone, who later declares he always knew it would work."

In a 1979 radio interview, Bowie claimed making art allowed him to "take dangerous risks that you wouldn't do in real life... and so you can use it for an experimental area for trying out new lifestyles without having to take the consequences." He wanted to put himself into "dangerous situations," though this greatly consisted of living in a comfortable West Berlin neighborhood. A middle-class Englishman at heart, a redactor by habit, Bowie was fascinated by a Burden or an Iggy Pop, all the wild men raving on stage. Stooges performances were like Burden exhibits: Pop once fell on glasses and cut his chest, singing as blood squirted out of him. "It was horrible, like a Roman arena," Wayne County recalled, while Scott Thurston described Iggy's performance that night as being "like a protest against himself."

Also in the song was John Lennon ("Jooooohn the Lennon!" was allegedly an early version of the vocal hook), another figure of power and decadence, who Bowie recently had caught up with in Hong Kong. (Tony Visconti recounted a night in New York where he, Bowie and Lennon consumed a "Matterhorn" of cocaine). "Made of *iron*!" Bowie sang with admiration. "Joe the Lion" was his tribute to them all, and a character he was trying out in the Berlin nights in summer 1977 — drinking himself to oblivion with half-liters of König Pilsener (at Joe's Beer House, another possible reference in the lyric), snarling at fans who tried to talk to him, sporting a leather jacket and boots like a modern-day Teddy Boy. "Virtually any time I saw him in Berlin he was drunk, or working on *getting* drunk," Angela Bowie wrote in her memoir.

But he couldn't keep up the wild man act for long. "When I started with the characters, I would put myself through terrible experiences and positions," he said. "Eno put it more into focus for me, that you could do all the experimentation in the actual creating of the music and not have to put your body through the same kind of risks." "Joe the Lion" was music as self-torture, a clashing set of D-flat, E-flat, B-flat and G-flat chords cued by George Murray's bass, over which Robert Fripp and Carlos Alomar's guitars tore at each other, distorted by Eno (live) and Visconti (later). Bowie's only guidance to Fripp was to play in a bluesy style, like Albert King, possibly an impetus for Fripp's three-note hook. Dennis Davis chafes to go off on his own rounds.

Taken by Pop's improvisations on *Lust for Life*, Bowie went into the booth without a lyric, came up with a line or two, got them onto tape. It was a transcript of his mind at work: "couple of drinks" becomes "couple of dreams," then "get up and sleep." Bowie bellows the title phrase in a smear of vowels ("JOOOOOEtheLIII-ON"); he leaves bars empty, then jams in so many words he can barely sound them all. The "interlude" break has some of his most brilliant phrasing, a news announcer's deadpan "it's Monday" (the day he was cutting his vocal) that becomes a tumbling run of words that avalanche into the hoarsely-sung "your DREEEEEEEEEEEEEAMS tonight!" A phenomenal track, one of the high peaks of Bowie's late Seventies.

"Heroes"

(Bowie, Eno.) **Recorded**: *11 July-5 August 1977, Hansa Tonstudio 2. Bowie: lead and harmony vocal, piano, ARP Solina, Chamberlin, tambourine?; Fripp: lead guitar; Alomar: rhythm guitar; Eno: EMS Synthi AKS, guitar treatments; Murray: bass; Davis: drums; Visconti: metal canister, tambourine?, backing vocal. Produced: Bowie, Visconti; engineered: Visconti, Thurston; (vocal overdubs for "Héros" and "Helden": late August 1977, Mountain Studios).*

First release: *23 September 1977 (RCA PB 1121, UK #24), "Héros" (RCA PB 9167), "Helden" (RCA PB 9168).* **Broadcast:** *7 September 1977, Marc; 11 September 1977, Bing Crosby's Merrie Olde Christmas; 1 October 1977, Odeon; 13 October 1977, TopPop; 16 October 1977, Le Rendezvous du Dimanche; 19 October 1977, Top of the Pops; 30 May 1978, Musikladen Extra; 27 June 2000, Bowie at the BBC Radio Theatre, 15 June 2002, A&E Live by Request.* **Live**: *1978, 1983, 1985, 1987, 1990, 1992, 1996-1997, 2000-2004.*

Reports

Berlin, Bowie observes, reflecting upon the environments in which he has produced his last two albums, is a city made up of bars for sad disillusioned people to get drunk in. "...It's hard to sing 'Let's all think of peace and love...' No, David, why

did you say that? That is a stupid remark. Because that's exactly where you should arrive... You arrive at a sense of compassion. The title track of "Heroes" is about facing that kind of reality and standing up to it. The only heroic act one can fucking well pull out of the bag in a situation like that is to get on with life from the very simple pleasure of remaining alive, despite every attempt being made to kill you."
— Allan Jones, "Goodbye to Ziggy and All That," *Melody Maker*, 29 October 1977

Regions

In the United States, and to a lesser extent in Britain, "Heroes" was a flop single. It didn't crack the *Billboard* Hot 100; some Americans were unaware of it until Bowie's performance at Live Aid. "Heroes" would of course become a global Bowie standard, his consensus masterpiece, but it was also a later addition to the canon. In the US at least, "Heroes" was the Bowie song famous somewhere else.

That was Europe. Bowie said the song had a special resonance there, and he pushed the single in that market, cutting German and French vocals. Maybe his declamatory singing was more familiar to the European ear, or maybe "Heroes" tapped into something. In 1977, Europe's fate was the property of others. The continent's flash point, Berlin, was irrelevant. If there was to be a war, West Berlin would fall to the Soviets in a day and be annihilated. The decadence in West Berlin, the parades and drills in East Berlin, were stage shows.

There's a lassitude, a faded grandeur, in "Heroes": its dragging beat; its backdrop of squalls and radio signals; its lyric, staged at the continent's scarred heart; Bowie's metal-edged vocal; Robert Fripp's feedback ostinatos. "Heroes" is Bowie at his most empathic and desperate, a wish-chant that offers a tiny regency for the spirit. Bowie, who once filled his songs with starmen and supermen, is reduced to a minor scale, despite his talk of kings and queens. Any hope "Heroes" has is meager: *we can be better than we are.* And only sometimes, and not for long.

Reductions

Interviewer: I remember one lyric: "all the nobody people, all the somebody people. I need them."

*Bowie: Yes, well, that character definitely did, 'cause the world was exploding… That **was** definitely a character. That was Ziggy Stardust. He was the archetype needing-people rock star.*
— Amsterdam press conference, 15 October 1977

Around 1975, the writer Greil Marcus noticed the rise of "survivors." He heard the word on TV shows, bestowed upon middle-aged actors promoting a new film, in politics ("Reagan was a survivor," as per Lou Cannon's biography), in films, and particularly on the radio: "Soul Survivor," *Street Survivors*, "Survival" (O'Jays single and Bob Marley album), "I Will Survive," even a band called Survivor. As Marcus wrote at the decade's end, "it seemed to me to speak for everything empty, tawdry, and stupid about the Seventies, to stand for every cheat, for every failure of nerve." "Survivor" once meant someone who had endured trauma — a concentration camp survivor, a plane crash survivor, someone who has been assaulted. Now it was applied to anyone competent at living.

The prominence in the media of "survivors," of people being called "heroes" for the mildest of reasons, was as if, in the decades after the war, the common person had wanted too much, had attempted to reach too great a height. Now they were being herded down, their ambitions being reduced to maintenance. Going to work, paying your bills, raising your children, hitting thirty, managing a chronic disease — these became "heroic" acts. Everyone alive became a survivor. Common life, as its radical prospects diminished, was exalted.

Bowie's "Heroes" can seem part of this reduction, the forefather of "Wind Beneath My Wings" and Mariah Carey's "Hero," and it's certainly been interpreted as such: see the *X-Factor* finalists getting a UK #1 with a cover of it in 2010. What keeps Bowie's recording from sentimentality is its coldness, its being compromised at the start. We can be kings, we can be heroes, nothing will hurt us, he sings, but he'll settle for much less. *We can be **us***, hissing the last syllable: could we even venture that?

When he'd first seen the lovers who allegedly inspired his last verse, sitting on a bench by the Berlin Wall, he'd wondered why they'd chosen so grim a place to meet. Did they feel shame at what they were doing? Was it where they assumed no one would see them? Or were they just looking for kicks, pawns playing at being rooks? "I assumed their motive was guilt, thus the act of heroism in facing it," Bowie said in 1977. "Of course, it could just be my wonderful imagination. Probably their offices were nearby." West Berlin was where you played at life but also where you became human. Wim Wenders' films in which angels become mortals take place in Bowie's Berlin.

"Heroes" is best known in its single edit, which lops off about two minutes and starts with its third verse. This edit was used for Stanley Dorfman's promo film, appears on most compilations, and is how Bowie mostly performed it on stage. The cuts weaken the song. The buildup to the last verses is too short (Bowie's "heroic" vocal starts at 1:23 in the single edit, nearly two minutes before it does on the album) and the lyric is diminished as well. The full "Heroes" opens with a claim — "I, I will be king" — in the formal voice of the Sixties pop tragedy "I (Who Have Nothing)." In the second verse, the artifice falls away: *And you, you can be mean/And I, I'll drink all the time.*

The intimacy of these lines, which Bowie sings close to the mike (and slightly obscured, so the first line sounds like "you could be me") gives a reality: lovers seeing no way out, facing each other across a table, reading each other's faces. Bowie sings "that is that" as a settled fact in a settled life. It's the contrast to the histrionics of the later verses, where Bowie can barely keep his fantasies from collapsing, screaming that nothing will drive them away. But who are "them"?

Until its last verse, "Heroes" is abstract, its setting could be anywhere, like the empty backdrop used in Bowie's promo film. Then the lovers are revealed to be by the Wall, the guns firing above them, as Bowie sings in a sustained scream. Are the guards shooting at them, or are they so insignificant the guards don't notice them while trying to pick off a Wall jumper? (And which side of the Wall is the shame on?) The Wall verse is as much a fantasy as being a king for a day or swimming like dolphins. It's the dream of someone wishing his empty days and tawdry love affair had nobility, looking for dignity under tyranny.

Recognitions

Iggy Pop had scrapped his proposed music for "Success," so Bowie was considering using a G-C-D chord sequence for himself, working on it with Brian Eno in rehearsals. Eno wanted to call it "Heroes," as the song, even in embryo, had a rousing feel, much like Neu!'s "Hero," and so complementing Bowie's Kraftwerk tribute "V-2 Schneider." It began as a backing track with Bowie on piano, Eno on EMS Synthi AKS "making these beautiful spatial noises" (as per Tony Visconti) and the core set of Carlos Alomar on rhythm guitar, George Murray on bass and Dennis Davis on drums.

The track was "a combination of Brian's piano technique and [mine] which are both dastardly, and ended up sounding like the Velvet Underground," Bowie later said: it was another reworking of "I'm Waiting for the Man," a song he'd been obsessed with for a decade (Eno and Bowie considered German bands like Neu! to be the VU's proper heirs, and John Cale later praised the percussive piano and "horizontal groove" of "Heroes.") Murray's bass was sent through a flanger; Eno's EMS Synthi plays throughout, its oscillators at a low frequency rate (Visconti estimated five cycles per second) and using a noise filter; Bowie added high-pitched lines on ARP Solina. This created the "shuddering, chattering effect [that] slowly builds up and gets more and more obvious towards the end," Visconti said. Alomar came up with riffs as underlying hooks, like a twining three-part figure that plays against lines like "nothing will keep us together."

"Heroes" is five verses, some expanded with a six-bar tag, and an outro that works as a long-held-back refrain. In D major, the verses (and intro/solo sections) move between D and G major, with the arrival of C major ("nothing will keep us together") and a two-bar foray into A minor and E minor (on "beat them" and "forever"), briefly disrupting the pattern. The song is in the D mixolydian mode — Bowie replaces what would be the song's dominant (V) chord, A major, with A minor, swapping chords from the parallel minor, D minor, then shuttling back to the tonic chord, D major.

Robert Fripp played while the song was still inchoate, with no lyrics or top melodies yet. While on "Joe the Lion," Fripp's guitar came in like a thunderclap, on "Heroes," he's there at the start, singing in the upper atmosphere. While guitarists who played "Heroes" on stage often used an EBow to get Fripp's sound, Fripp worked out his feedback patterns on foot. Standing in Studio 2, his guitar routed through Eno's EMS, Fripp marked with tape places on the studio floor where he could get a feedback loop on any given note. So four feet from his amp was an A, three feet away was a G. He stepped and swayed through the song: his sound owed to a simple cartography.

Fripp cut three takes, each with a different tone (further treated by Eno), moving in different directions, not synchronized — Visconti bounced them to a single track, creating what he called "a dreamy, wailing quality." He also emphasized the drone by burying the kick drum and elevating the bassline (Murray's bass and one of Alomar's guitar tracks), creating a propulsion furthered by Fripp's guitar and Eno's low-oscillating synthesizer.

Much of "Heroes" was owed to expediency. An intended horn part (at the start of the second verse) was replaced by a three-note "brass" line played on Bowie's Chamberlin ("it sounds more like a weedy little violin patch," Visconti said), while basslines took the place of what could have been string parts. When overdubbing percussion, Bowie and Visconti even made do without a cowbell, using an empty tape canister Visconti thwacked with a drumstick (first heard at 2:55). The other percussion is a tambourine that starts in the final verse (at 3:56) and shakes, not quite in time, through the rest of the track.

Reverberations

After the backing tracks were done, "David lived with it for quite a while before he identified where he would write the verses and where he would write the choruses, but before that happened we blissfully started overdubbing synthesizers and other guitar parts," Visconti recalled in 2014. "Fripp's guitar part was overdubbed before the melody was conceived... when you're at a master level like David, you can 'jam' a song into existence." Listening to playback in his headphones, Bowie wrote a line or two and sang them. Visconti rewound to where he'd left off; Bowie would record another line. It's why his phrasing is a series of dramatic pauses and sudden movements.

Visconti planned to tape Bowie's vocal as if he thought he only had one shot at capturing it. He set up three Neumann microphones, placing the first, a valve U47, nine inches from Bowie's face (using "fairly heavy compression, because I knew beforehand that he really was going to shout").

The second, a U87, was set up around twenty feet away from Bowie, and the third, another U87, was at the end of the room, some fifty feet away. The latter mikes had electronic gates: they would be turned off until being triggered by Bowie hitting a certain volume. Once on, the mikes captured the sound of Hansa's Meistersaal ringing with Bowie's voice. And it meant that Bowie, once he'd opened the other mikes, had to go full blast to keep them on.

Like Fripp's solo, Bowie's vocal was done in three takes (most of the released vocal is from the last take, with punch-ins for stray notes). Bowie immediately moved to making two tracks of backing vocals with Visconti (hence the Brooklyn accent you hear on "I remember" and "wall"), harmonizing in thirds and fifths below the lead vocal. The backing chorus is the song's last essential ingredient. Until now Bowie's been alone in his fantasies — having another voice back him up adds reassurance at last. From the first line that he sang to his last punch-in edit, it took about five hours.

Redactions

Where he'd made "Station to Station" from his inventory of obsessions at the time, Bowie's words in "Heroes" are fewer, simpler, precisely chosen and, sometimes, stolen. ("I will be king, you will be queen" is from the English folk song "Lavender's Blue" which Bowie would sing onstage sometimes to prelude "Heroes.") There are some later-noted sources. "A Grave for a Dolphin," by the Italian aristocrat Alberto Denti Di Pirajno, details a doomed affair between an Italian sailor and a Somalian girl in the years before World War II (and so allegedly inspired the "dolphins can swim" verse). And a 1916 Otto Mueller painting hanging at the Brücke-Museum: *Liebespaar Zwischen Gartenmauern* ("Lovers Between Garden Walls"). Bowie transplanted Mueller's image of two lovers embracing by a high stone wall, placing them before the Wall he saw from Hansa's control room window.

As legend now has it, Bowie was looking out that very window when he spied Visconti (married at the time to Mary Hopkin) and Antonia Maaß kissing by the Wall. Lovers standing before a concrete madness of governments, though it was a shabby act, a man cheating on his wife. Yet Tobias Rüther interviewed Maaß, who said the lines couldn't have been about her and Visconti, as "Heroes" had been completed before their affair started, and that Bowie couldn't have seen them there anyhow. It's the male gaze, the male protagonist, and the woman who claims the story isn't true.

Another story recently came to light thanks to the Italian Bowie website *Blackstar*. The artist Clare Shenstone, who met Bowie in 1969, visited him in West Berlin during that *"Heroes"* summer. She'd first known him when he was mourning his father's death, and during one depressive period in Berlin, Bowie called and asked her to come. He played her *Low,* and they spent a day walking by the Wall, later going through Checkpoint Charlie to East Berlin. The day started, she said, "with David asking me if I dreamed about him because he dreamed about me. I told him I had just had a beautiful dream about swimming with dolphins."

If this is the "true" story of "Heroes," it shows how Bowie wove museum references and a sea of other red herrings to obscure its humble inspiration — a lost young man asking his friend (or more, Shenstone was discreet about their relationship) to spend a day with him in the divided city he'd come to live in. But all other interpretations are as valid — Visconti is convinced of his role in the story, and who's to deny him? An epic rarely has a single author. "Heroes," with its peaks and removes, its rages and absences, is a glass for anyone to find themselves in. It's crafted to be dispersed, to be carried in the air, to be used by whoever hears it.

Reputations

I just can't express the feeling of freedom I felt [in Berlin]. Tony, Brian and I created a powerful, anguished, sometimes euphoric language of sounds. In some ways, sadly, they captured, unlike anything else in that time, a sense of yearning for a future that we all knew would never come to pass.
— Bowie, 2001.

In 1977, Bowie promoted "Heroes" across two continents, talking to any interviewer who would have him. He would tailor the song for grand moments — his Live Aid set, his tributes to Freddie Mercury and to the dead of 9/11. The song was also used to sell mobile phones, cars, software, digital film, life insurance, Coke, football matches, HBO's Latin American programming, hockey, and rock star video games. It promoted a comic book TV series and a cover of it was used in a *Godzilla* remake.

None of it tainted "Heroes," Bowie's holy song for a secular world. "I believe in a God beyond God, in a heaven beyond heaven," he once said. "Temporary heroes. I think the heroes are the people that we never get to meet, people who under the most extraordinary circumstances *continue to live.*"

THE SECRET LIFE OF ARABIA

(Bowie, Eno, Alomar.) **Recorded***: 11 July-5 August 1977, Hansa Tonstudio 2. Bowie: lead and harmony vocal, piano; Alomar: guitar; Eno: EMS Synthi AKS, guitar treatments; Murray: bass; Davis: drums, congas; Maaß, Visconti?: harmony vocals. Produced: Bowie, Visconti; engineered: Visconti, Thurston.*

First release*: 14 October 1977, **"Heroes."***

Album closer "The Secret Life of Arabia" is a tonal shift from the rest of *"Heroes"* and in particular its otherwise mostly-instrumental second side. Consider it a trailer for the next LP ("David Bowie Will Return... In *Lodger*"). For some at the time, it was a mood-killer; for others, it was a relief from the album's abrasiveness and somberness.

It's a throwback to the funk workouts of *Young Americans* and *Station to Station*, with Carlos Alomar's only songwriting credit on the record. The two guitar riffs, a hard-strummed opening and one that makes the refrains swing, are classic Alomar: concise, melodic, rhythmically incisive. George Murray's also in inspired form: the Clash's "The Call Up" runs on a sped-up variation of his bassline. A D minor vamp built on a set of refrains, its bridge oases find Bowie in desert gear, making asides to his audience: "I walk through a desert song when the heroine dies." He's a disco-era Lawrence of Arabia, his title playing on *The Secret Lives of Lawrence of Arabia*, a 1969 biography that delved into Lawrence's alleged homosexuality and masochism. Bowie's vocal is a checklist of past affectations, from mock-Cockney "uh-RY-bee-uh" to the calisthenics of his opening lines, stringing the title phrase through an octave jump ("see-*cret*") and fall. There's a goony joy in it, with Antonia Maaß getting into the camp spirit. The outro has one of Bowie's sunniest grooves, with a touch of Andrea True Connection's "More More More."

V-2 Schneider

Recorded: *11 July-5 August 1977, Hansa Tonstudio 2. Bowie: tenor saxophone, vocal, piano, synthesizer; Alomar: guitar; Eno: EMS Synthi AKS; Murray: bass; Davis: drums. Produced: Bowie, Visconti; engineered: Visconti, Thurston.*

First release: *23 September 1977, "Heroes" (RCA PB 1121).* **Live**: *1997.*

"V-2 Schneider" honors Kraftwerk co-founder Florian Schneider, with Bowie using Schneider's nickname (Kraftwerk's other co-founder, Ralf Hütter, was called "Der Doktor"). But this was insider knowledge. Many of Bowie's British listeners at least would have assumed "V-2" to reference one of Hitler's last gambles, the Nazi rockets that struck London in 1944-45. After all, Bowie's thoughts on Kraftwerk in the press were a mingle of admiration and darker projections. "I think that there are two bands now who come close to a neo-Nazi kind of thing: Roxy Music and Kraftwerk," he said in 1976. "It's not Nazism so much as nationalism. I think it may be too clichéd to use the Nazi thing; it's more nationalistic." This was at the height of his fascist-sympathizing, cocaine-addled incarnation and gave the British music press free reign to call Kraftwerk Nazis.

He liked to contrast Kraftwerk with his take on German music. Kraftwerk was rigid, pristine, a sealed room. "They're like craftsmen... they're gonna make this particular wooden chair that they designed, and each one will be very beautifully made, but it will be the same chair." Whereas he made music with a human element. "Much has been made of [their] influence on our Berlin albums, most of it lazy analyses, I believe," he said in 2001,

> Kraftwerk's approach to music had in itself little place in my scheme. Theirs was a controlled robotic extremely measured series of compositions, almost a parody of minimalism. One had the feeling Florian and Ralf were completely in charge of their environment... My work tended to expressionist mood pieces, the protagonist (myself) abandoning himself to the Zeitgeist... with little or no control over his own life. The music was spontaneous for the most part.

With their dress suits and investment bankers' haircuts, deadpan expressions and literal lyrics, Kraftwerk courted being called automatons;

they eventually had robots play their music on stage. Growing up in the postwar Düsseldorf that also produced the painter Anselm Kiefer, Schneider and Hütter were of the generation that, as Werner Herzog said, "had no fathers, only grandfathers," growing up in a country whose past had been erased by general consent. "After the war, German entertainment was destroyed," Hütter said,

> Our parents were bombed out of their homes. Their main interest was to reconstruct a life for themselves. They became obsessed with material things and went over the top... We are the first generation born after the war to shake this off, and know where to feel American music, and where to feel ourselves... Music didn't exist and we had to make it up.

Where Kiefer would photograph and paint himself giving the Nazi salute in front of scenic German landscapes, Kraftwerk fetishized what Richard Witts called "the shiny, new everyday objects of the Nazi period — its cars, the motorways, its short-range radios... and like Kiefer, present[ed] them in a utopian glow... The provocation is that of a society projected as though it is not yet defeated." Kraftwerk took the pre-Nazi utopianism of the Bauhaus movement (permissible, as this era was now the "acceptable" German past) and put it into contact with now-*verboten* Nazi aesthetics to ironically comment on how West Germany became capitalism's favorite child. They sang about the Autobahn, a Nazi-era construction, and the Trans-Europe Express, the descendant of Deutsche Reichsbahn, a train meant to roll across a borderless Europe that was one cleansed Reich.

Bowie had discovered Kraftwerk in Los Angeles in 1975, keeping *Autobahn* on repeat in his limo. He wanted them to open his 1976 tour — when that didn't work out, Bowie used Kraftwerk as pre-show music. The car-ignition opening of "Autobahn" inspired "Station to Station," with its slow assemblage of train sounds. ("I suppose we influenced Bowie. At least that's what he told us," Hütter later said.) Yet Bowie was already making distinctions, using an "analog" device (a sound effects LP) where Kraftwerk used synthesizers. He liked to play up his British amateur's take on electronic music ("playing rather dotty old synthesizers, Chamberlins... quite kind of doodly, weeble sounds"). Kraftwerk's *Trans-Europe Express*, recorded around the time that Bowie cut *Low*, was their answer record to "Station to Station." In their title track Kraftwerk reclaims the train. It's cleaned up, humming along contentedly. To top it off, they name-checked Bowie and Iggy Pop.

They all had met in April 1976 at the Paris stop of Bowie's tour — when Schneider and Hütter walked into the nightclub, Bowie and Pop led their party in a standing ovation. Bowie visited Kraftwerk's headquarters in Düsseldorf to discuss producing what would become *Trans-Europe Express*, though "in the end, finally they decided against co-productions, and they have their reasons," as Kraftwerk percussionist Wolfgang Flür recalled decades later. Kraftwerk was flattered, however, considering Bowie's praise high validation — in 1977, Hütter told a journalist that Bowie's support "was reassuring. We have been going for nearly ten years and have been constantly attacked by German critics." He praised Bowie's music. "There's a spiritual transparency and honesty I find in his work."

"V-2 Schneider" is an odd tribute, however, as the only Kraftwerk homages are Dennis Davis' snare fills, treated to sound like synthetic percussion, and the title phrase, which coheres near the fade after being murky vowel sounds for most of the track. Though inspired by the vocoder on Kraftwerk's *Radio-Activity* ("part of our music is derived from the feeling of our language," Schneider said. "Our method of speaking is interrupted, hard-edged... a lot of consonants and noises... 'pzzt, pzzt, pzzt'"), Bowie was too impatient to wait for one to be shipped to Hansa, so instead he used "a cheap little synthesizer in the studio" on which he "found sounds that had a vowel shape that resembled: Vee-Too-Schnei-Der," as Tony Visconti wrote. "The idea was to use those four separate patches for each note and David would supply just the consonants with his voice filtered electronically (all the 'body' taken out), i.e.: V-T-Sch_D... and it kind of worked."

It opens with incoming waves of airplanes and distorted saxophone hooks, while it's held together by George Murray's quivering muscle of a bassline. Bowie started off-beat on his saxophone overdub, having missed his cue, but recalling an Eno Oblique Strategies card about honoring your mistakes, he kept the take ("you get this extraordinary intro where it's all the wrong way round...[it's] impossible to write that," he said in 1978). Compared with other *"Heroes"* instrumentals, "V-2 Schneider" is conventionally structured (four-bar saxophone/guitar passages, eight-bar "refrains") and more of a band track. Kraftwerk returned the favor with an incisive portrait of Bowie, "The Hall of Mirrors," in which even the greatest star loses himself in the mirror.

ABDULMAJID

(Bowie, Eno.) **Recorded**: *(backing tracks) ca. 11 July-5 August 1977, Hansa; (later overdubs) ca. 1990-1991, Mountain Studios. Bowie: piano, Chamberlin, Korg M1?, Roland CR-78?; Eno: treatments, EMS Synthi AKS; Erdal Kızılçay?: synthesizer? Produced: Bowie, Visconti; engineered (overdubs): David Richards.*

First release: *27 August 1991, "Heroes" (Ryko reissue, RCD 10143).*

Purportedly an outtake from *"Heroes,"* "Abdulmajid" first appeared on its 1991 Ryko CD reissue. If it indeed started as instrumental scraps that Eno and Bowie cut while recording *"Heroes,"* it was reworked over a decade later in Switzerland, with Bowie sneaking a newly-made track onto a *"Heroes"* reissue in the guise of being an outtake. What gives the game away is that some of the synthesizers used on the track are almost certainly post-Seventies models, such as what sounds like a Korg M1 (1988) playing the lead melody. Like "All Saints," its title is anachronistic, honoring Bowie's second wife, Iman Mohamed Abdulmajid, whom he married in 1992. Tony Visconti told Nicholas Pegg the track was a forgotten *"Heroes"* piece that became "a heavily-remixed, worked-on Nineties creation." With a bass ostinato reminiscent of the Walker Brothers' "Fat Mama Kick," "Abdulmajid" develops into a dancing melody on synthesizer, lovely enough for Philip Glass to make it one of his *"Heroes"* symphony movements. Its textures — overlapping basslines, "hoots," clacking percussive patterns — are overgrown variations on the "tropical" miniatures of Eno's *Another Green World*.

SENSE OF DOUBT

Recorded: *ca. late July-5 August 1977, Hansa Tonstudio 2; (possible overdubs) ca. August 1977, Mountain Studios. Bowie: piano, Chamberlin M1, Mellotron?; Eno: treatments, EMS Synthi AKS. Produced: Bowie, Visconti; engineered: Visconti, Thurston.*

First release: *14 October 1977, "Heroes."* **Broadcast:** *1 October 1977, Odeon.* **Live**: *1978.*

Before they began what would become "Sense of Doubt," Bowie and Brian Eno drew cards from the latter's Oblique Strategies deck. Devised by Eno and Peter Schmidt, these cards were part-fortune cookie, part-*Monopoly* "Chance" cards, meant to spur random creative acts. Bowie, who spent the late Seventies trying to write in "a new language," welcomed another way to shake up his songwriting. While Eno used Oblique cards prominently in the *Lodger* sessions, during *"Heroes"* he kept the deck to the latter stages, when he and Bowie were devising instrumentals.

Bowie and Eno agreed not to reveal their cards until they finished the track. As Bowie's read "emphasize differences" and Eno's "try to make everything as similar as possible," they went to work unknowingly at odds. "It was like a game. We took turns working on it; he'd do one overdub and I'd do the next, and he'd do the next... I was trying to smooth it out and make it into one continuum [while] he was trying to do the opposite," Eno said in 1978.

"Sense of Doubt" was a sound-picture of this conflict. Mixed left was a descending four-note piano passage (C-B-Bb-A, at the bass end), a reoccurring movement set against appearances of synthetic winds, waves, moans and rattles. An influence was Kraftwerk's "Midnight," which pitted a repeated descending piano line against whirrs, violin and stark percussion. Among the variables on "Sense of Doubt" are a Chamberlin, possibly a Mellotron, and Eno's EMS Synthi, locked into cycles until the patterns mutate — chords are clipped short, while a stunning faded-in sequence (1:43) is a way out. Bowie in 1978 described the track as pitting an "organic sound" against a false one, but the "artificial" provides the only glimpses of sunlight.

In the liner notes for his *Music for Airports*, Eno wrote "whereas conventional background music is produced by stripping away all sense of doubt and uncertainty (and thus all genuine interest) from the music, Ambient Music retains these qualities." He wrote this a year after he made "Sense of Doubt," which seems an early go at this scenario — "uncertain" background music in which a doomsday piano pattern snuffs out whatever flashes of hope have appeared since it turned up last.

MOSS GARDEN

(Bowie, Eno.) **Recorded**: *ca. late July-5 August 1977, Hansa Tonstudio 2; (possible overdubs) August 1977, Mountain Studios. Bowie: koto, ARP Solina?, ARP Pro Soloist?, Chamberlin M1; Eno: EMS Synthi AKS. Produced: Bowie, Visconti; engineered: Visconti, Thurston.*

First release: *14 October 1977,* **"Heroes."**

With Bowie and Eno again playing Oblique Strategies and not revealing their cards, "Moss Garden" was another clash of intentions. Bowie drew chaos (a card that read "destroy everything"), Eno, order ("change nothing and continue with immaculate consistency"). The piece was a soundscape of Saihō-ji, a Zen Buddhist temple in Kyoto, Japan, which Bowie had visited while on tour (its garden has a hundred varieties of moss). He'd acquired a koto, a thirteen-string traditional Japanese instrument, which he used as the voice of "Moss Garden," playing with an amateur's restraint, repeating a few harshly-plucked scale patterns (see "Brilliant Adventure").

Hanging between F-sharp and G-sharp, "Moss Garden" partners West and East, with synthesized airplane drones over the koto's musings. His template was Edgar Froese's "Epsilon in Malaysian Pale" (1975), which opens with "jungle" noises overlapped by synthetic jet sounds. (Another livelier ancestor was Eno's "Burning Airlines Give You So Much More," with its China-bound jet liner ruffling the beard of a meditating sage in some placid moss garden.) The eye of *"Heroes,"* "Moss Garden" has a quiet dynamism, with accents on Bowie's koto patterns and a crescendo of synthesizers for its final minute, capped with the appearance (4:40) of a synthetic bark whose timbre is accurate enough to prick a dog's ears.

NEUKÖLN

(Bowie, Eno.) **Recorded**: *ca. late July-5 August 1977, Hansa Tonstudio 2; (possible overdubs) August 1977, Mountain Studios. Bowie: tenor saxophone, loops, ARP Solina?, ARP Pro Soloist? Chamberlin M1, guitar?; Fripp: guitar?; Eno: treatments, loops, EMS Synthi AKS. Produced: Bowie, Visconti; engineered: Visconti, Thurston.*

First release: 14 October 1977, *"Heroes."*

Bowie began as a saxophone player but never mastered the instrument. "I found I didn't have a very good relationship with the sax and that lasted right the way through," he said in 1983. "We're sort of pretty embittered with each other… I really have to go through traumas to get anything out of it that has anything to do with what I want it to say. So it's not a steady relationship; it's not a good one." But it carried an emotional weight (one thing he didn't allow displayed in the *David Bowie Is* exhibit was his first saxophone, an acrylic Grafton that his father had bought him), and he made it a blunt voice in his music.

He played what he called "melodic saxophone," emulating R&B players like King Curtis and the fat-toned Earl Bostic. His saxophone lines were the nostalgic element of his early Seventies records, meant to invoke Little Richard's brass section: "I would play baritone, tenor and alto [and create] a thick wedge of sound… and I would compress them very tightly." In Berlin he tried a "Turkish modal thing" against loops of synthesizer and guitar; his saxophone as the track's "humorous aspect."

"Neuköln," the last instrumental sequenced on *"Heroes,"* opens with Bowie as wailing counterpoint to his and Eno's synthesizers (reminiscent of the latter's "The Big Ship"), droning organ tones, and three-note guitar and Chamberlin loops. At 2:45, he rumbles into a solo that runs for the rest of the track, playing variations on earlier lines, building to shrieking runs. He closes alone, with two descending (and treated) lines, the last starting with a stumble needed to take a breath. The limits of his technique hem him in — he's "avant-garde" in a predictable way, veering off where one would expect him to veer off.

He titled the piece "Neuköln" (dropping an "l", whether by design or accident) after a West Berlin neighborhood adjacent to the Wall, greatly populated by Turkish *Gastarbeiters*. This spawned a persistent myth that he lived there. Some have found in "Neuköln" the isolation of Turkish immigrants in a city that used them for labor and denied them citizenship, or a musing about Islam's place in the West (the sax seems to imitate a muezzin call), or a study of someone lost in the cradle of the Cold War. But if Bowie had called the track "Tiergarten," would it be considered a rumination on Nazi persecutions, a eulogy for murdered radical Rosa Luxemburg? A word creates worlds.

CHAPTER THREE: SOMEBODY ELSE'S HORIZON

(1977-1979)

Where are you going when you leave Berlin? Far away? Yes, you're a bird of passage. When I was young I longed to travel, to swallow the whole wide world. Well, it's damn well happened.
— Vladimir Nabokov, *Mary*

I'm going away; and wherever I go, I'll still be the same wild and rather frightened little man. I'm not scared of anybody. I'm just scared of myself. I'm like a traveller. I shed a skin at this place, leave my little message… and move on to another red blot on the map.
— Ray Gosling, *Sum Total*

It always seemed that she'd taken it upon herself to be at home everywhere and a stranger everywhere, at home and a stranger in the same instant.
— Christa Wolf, *The Quest for Christa T*

The poetry of motion! The real way to travel! The only way to travel! Here today — in next week tomorrow! Villages skipped, towns and cities jumped — always somebody else's horizon! O bliss! O poop-poop!
— Kenneth Grahame, *The Wind in the Willows*

The Thin White Duke was an isolationist, very much on his own, with no commitment to any society.
— Bowie, 1978

MADMAN
SITTING NEXT TO YOU

(Bowie, Bolan.) **Recorded**: *("Madman", unreleased) ca. 4-7 March 1977?, 142 Upper Richmond Road West, East Sheen, London. David Bowie: lead vocal, rhythm guitar; Marc Bolan: lead guitar, backing vocal; ("Sitting Next to You") 7 September 1977, Granada Studios, Quay Street, Manchester. Bowie: vocal, guitar; Bolan: guitar; Dino Dines: keyboards; Herbie Flowers: bass; Tony Newman: drums. Produced: Muriel Young.*

Broadcast: *("Sitting Next to You") 7 September 1977, Marc.*

They met in the summer of 1964. He was still David Jones then, while Mark Feld already had discarded one pseudonym and would soon acquire another. They were prospects of the promoter Leslie Conn, who put them to work painting an office (Conn returned to find them gone, with only half of the walls painted). Born within nine months of each other, Marc Bolan and David Bowie were fast friends, going through discard bins on Carnaby Street for clothes, living on crumbs from the banquet that was mid-Sixties London.

As the decade waned, they made their move. Bowie hit first in 1969 with "Space Oddity," but Bolan soon swept past him. Ditching the mummery and twenty-word titles of his earlier albums, Bolan became the first pop idol of the Seventies. His success in T. Rex rattled Bowie, who aped Bolan's singing voice on "Black Country Rock," had him play lead guitar on "The Prettiest Star," and in "Lady Stardust" tried to make him a predecessor to his Ziggy Stardust. "I never had any competition. Except Marc Bolan, back in England," Bowie told the journalist Lisa Robinson in 1976,

> I had to find somebody I would have friction with, somebody I could compete with, just to get me off the ground. Someone that would give me motivation to do the thing in the first place. So Marc was perfect; a friend, [who] gets there before me. I fought like a madman to beat him. Knowing theoretically there was no race. But wanting passionately to do it.

In 1972 and 1973, they were on top together — glitter-spackled planet queens of pop. Paupers in the Sixties, they had come into their inheritances.

But when glam faded, Bolan was like a drunken host trying to revive a dying party. An attempt at futuristic R&B, *Zinc Alloy and the Hidden Riders of Tomorrow — A Creamed Cage in August* (a bad sign that the elephantine titles were back), was the first of several weak-charting albums. He'd alienated his producer Tony Visconti; a taste for brandy and cocaine bloated him. Meanwhile Bowie broke America, where Bolan remained a one-hit wonder.

Their friendship endured. When Bowie came to London for Iggy Pop's tour in March 1977, he stayed at Bolan's flat. He offered to co-write a song, and what resulted, a grungy piece called "Madman," had promise. Built on a one-chord riff that presages the Gang of Four, the best surviving demo of "Madman" has Bolan shredding and Bowie snarling "when a man is a *man* he's destructive/ when a man is a *man* he's seductive." Bolan played the tape for friends, saying he'd cut it for his next album.

He'd cleaned up by summer 1977, having recently become a father. The punks revered him and he was out and about in London. Landing a teatime music variety show with Granada TV, Bolan hosted the Jam, Hawkwind, the Boomtown Rats, and Generation X. For the final episode he got Bowie, who was in Britain to promote *"Heroes."*

The taping started well, Bowie catching up with the studio band, who included his former drummer Tony Newman and bassist Herbie Flowers. Bowie and Bolan rehearsed a piece to close out the show. It wasn't much, a twelve-bar blues with a guitar line close to the riff of "Lady Madonna" (as it didn't have a title, its bootleg name came from a refrain vocal during rehearsals: "what can I do?/sitting next to yoo-hoo"). Then Bowie ran the band through "Heroes," concentrating on getting feedback for his pre-taping backing track, and it soon became clear there was no place for Bolan in the song. Bolan went to his dressing room while Bowie's security men and assistants took over the taping, preventing journalists, Bolan's PR man and even show staffers from entering the studio. Caught up with recording a usable take of "Heroes," Bowie hadn't noticed.

By the time Bolan and Bowie taped their closing song, the mood was tense. Mustering himself for the cameras, Bolan introduced a "new song" that Bowie kicked off on guitar. For a minute, they were Leslie Conn's scruffs again, playing blues, making faces, calling each other out. Bowie missed his cue (he'd struggled with timing during the rehearsal), having to lunge towards the mike to yell "what can I do?" while Bolan, going to strike a guitar hero pose, fell off the stage. The crew, fed up with the afternoon's shenanigans and under union rules, refused to shoot a retake. The great reunion ended with a flump.

About a week later, Bolan and his girlfriend Gloria Jones went out for the night. At five in the morning, Jones crashed Bolan's Mini GT into a steel-reinforced concrete fence post on Barnes Common. He died within seconds. A heartbroken Bowie went to his funeral and quietly supported Jones and Bolan's son for decades. He'd lost a friend, a rival, and someone who'd known him when all he had was ambition.

PEACE ON EARTH/LITTLE DRUMMER BOY

(Kohan, Fraser, Grossman ["Peace"], Simeone, Onorati, Davis ["Drummer"].) **Recorded**: *11 September 1977, Elstree [ATV] Studios, Clarendon Road, Borehamwood, Hertfordshire. Bowie: lead vocal; Bing Crosby: lead vocal; uncredited musicians: piano, bass, drums, strings. Produced: Frank Konigsberg.*

First release: *19 November 1982, BOW 12/ PB 13400 (UK #3).* **Broadcast**: *11 September 1977, Bing Crosby's Merrie Olde Christmas.*

Where he'd done little to sell *Low*, Bowie agreed to do promotions for *"Heroes"* in autumn 1977. Days after the Marc Bolan taping, Bowie appeared on a Bing Crosby Christmas special. Its premise had Crosby, in Britain for Christmas, encountering a few stars like Twiggy and Ron Moody. Landing Bowie gave the show a shot in the arm ("Bing was no idiot," said Ian Fraser, who co-wrote music for the special. "If he didn't know [who Bowie was] his kids sure did.") Bowie would get to plug *"Heroes"* in exchange for singing a Christmas carol with Crosby.

But he balked at the selection, "Little Drummer Boy." "I hate that song," he reportedly said, though scriptwriter Buz Kohan said Bowie's biggest complaint was that "Little Drummer Boy" wasn't a good showcase for his voice. Kohan, Fraser, and his co-composer Larry Grossman dashed out a counterpoint song in little over an hour on a piano in a studio storage room. "Peace on Earth," with its mawkish totalitarian sentiments ("every child must be **made** aware/every child must be **made** to care") at least gave Bowie the soaring melody he wanted.

At the time, Bowie said he'd been charmed by Crosby, who died that

October after suffering a heart attack on a Madrid golf course (it was a strange period where everyone who Bowie appeared with on television died soon afterward). "He was *fantastic*," Bowie said in 1978. "That old man knew everything about everything. He knew rock and roll backwards, even if he didn't know the music... I'm glad I met him." His memories had soured by 1999, however, when he described Crosby as "look[ing] like a little old orange sitting on a stool... there was just nobody home at all, you know? It was the most bizarre experience. I didn't know anything about him. I just knew my mother liked him." A worse-for-wear Crosby, squatting in a mansion, gets a visit from a freeloading hip neighbor (Bowie namedrops Harry Nilsson). They duet on a pair of Christmas songs and it sounds beautiful. The magic of television.

There was no plan to release "Peace on Earth" ("we never expected to hear about it again," Kohan said), so the sixteen-track master tape was erased — for its issue as a single in 1982, RCA had to use the on-line mix, in which Bowie and Crosby's vocals were picked up by a boom mike. A Christmas hit in Britain in 1982, the duet had a second life in America thanks to MTV, which ran the Bowie/Crosby performance throughout the holidays. It looked like your grandfather meeting Han Solo. The internet canonized it, culminating in a word-for-word parody by Will Ferrell and John C. Reilly in 2010. What had been one-off TV fodder is now a Christmas tradition: one day soon, if not already, kids in holiday pageants will play the Bing and Bowie roles.

PETER AND THE WOLF

(Prokofiev.) **Recorded**: *(music) 8 October 1975, Scottish Rite Temple, 150 North Broad St., Philadelphia; (narration) 17 and 19 November 1977, RCA Studios, 110 W. 44th St., New York. Bowie: narration; Philadelphia Orchestra: flute, oboe, clarinet, bassoon, horns (3), trumpet, trombone, tympani, drum, violin (2), viola, celli, basses (conducted: Eugene Ormandy). Produced: Jay David Saks; engineered: Paul Goodman.*

First release: *7 April 1978, **David Bowie Narrates Prokofiev's Peter and the Wolf** (RCA Red Seal RL-12743/ARL1-2743, US #136).*

The last Bowie "all-round entertainer" appearance in 1977 was to narrate Sergei Prokofiev's *Peter and the Wolf* for RCA. He did it for his son and to burnish his tarnished standing at his label by doing a prestige recording. He soon learned he was RCA's third choice for the job, after Peter Ustinov and Alec Guinness (the latter in demand post-*Star Wars*) had turned them down. Conductor Eugene Ormandy "quite frankly didn't know who Bowie was, and when he found out he was a rock star he was a little concerned, to say the least," the album's producer Jay David Saks said in 1983.

Commissioned by the Central Children's Theatre in Moscow to write a symphony to develop musical taste in children, Prokofiev wrote *Peter and the Wolf* (Op. 67) in a week and premiered it at the theatre on 2 May 1936, to lukewarm reception. It was in keeping with Soviet art of the Thirties which, during the peak of Stalin's terror, devoted itself to fairy tales, national legends (see Eisenstein's *Alexander Nevsky*), and promotion of the family, with Stalin as national paterfamilias. During the war *Peter and the Wolf* went West, its place in the classical repertoire assured after Walt Disney's animated short in 1946. Classical labels hired any actor with a spare afternoon to record narration. There have been over four hundred recordings of *Peter and the Wolf*, narrated by Basil Rathbone, Boris Karloff, William F. Buckley Jr., Paul Hogan, Eleanor Roosevelt, Sirs John Gielgud, Ralph Richardson and Sean Connery, Dame Edna Everage, and Sharon Stone. (Even Brian Eno's on a 1975 recording, with Viv Stanshall as narrator and Phil Collins on drums and vibraphone.) "The classical music equivalent of *The Vagina Monologues*," as Cynthia Kaplan wrote.

With a lively performance by the Philadelphia Orchestra (recorded two years before, at the now-demolished Scottish Rite Temple), Bowie's narration is charming, if his voice is mixed low. He always approached children's material with wit and grace, avoiding condescension. His best role is the pissy-sounding cat: "is it worth climbing up so *high*? By the time I get there the bird will have *flown away*!" After hearing "Kooks," Bowie's producer Ken Scott said he'd wished Bowie would do an album of kid's songs. Along with *Labyrinth*, this is as close as he ever came.

THE REVOLUTIONARY SONG

*(Bowie, Fishman.) **Recorded**: (Bowie vocal, piano) 6 December 1977, Hansa; (further vocals, overdubs) ca. early 1978, West Berlin and/or London (Olympic and/or CBS Studios). Bowie: vocal, piano; uncredited musicians: vocals, guitar, piano?, violin, bass, drums. Produced: Jack Fishman; engineered: Keith Grant.*

***First release**: (as "The Rebels") ca. 23 February 1979, **Just a Gigolo** (Schöner Gigolo — Armer Gigolo) OST (Jambo JAM1).*

Bowie's second feature film was 1978's *Just a Gigolo* (its official title was *Schöner Gigolo, Armer Gigolo*, in the tongue of its producer), one of the last postwar multi-national extravaganzas, the sort of film that sank a small fortune yet managed to look cheap, with a few aging stars for the marquee. Boasting the largest budget ($19 million, inflation-adjusted) for a German film since the war, *Gigolo* died at the German box office and was cut repeatedly until limping into a British release nearly a year later. Bowie washed his hands of the film, calling it all of his Elvis movies in one.

Gigolo was the curious vanity project of British actor David Hemmings, best known for starring in *Blow-up*. Hemmings wooed Bowie for the lead (he was a hard-drinking rakish storyteller, a type Bowie found irresistible) by stressing convenience, as the West Berlin shoot would wrap by the start of Bowie's 1978 tour, and by hiring legendary actresses, including Kim Novak and (the clincher) Marlene Dietrich. As Dietrich refused to travel to West Germany, where she'd never felt welcome, Bowie's "face to face" scene with her was shot with Dietrich on a Paris soundstage and Bowie acting to a chair in West Berlin.

Bowie took the role because his dream project, starring in a biopic of the Expressionist painter Egon Schiele (provisionally titled *Wally*), faced continual delays in scripting and production; the film would finally collapse in 1979. In *Gigolo*, Bowie plays Paul, a scion of the German officer class, bred to serve the Fatherland by dying valiantly on the battlefield. When he returns home from the Great War to find a broken republic, he has no idea what to do. Bowie is purely reactive: his character (he often looks like his "Be My Wife" promo film mime) has no inner life. "I feel like a puppet!" he complains, and he's manhandled throughout the picture. "The whole point about that character is that he is a sponge — he is supposed to be cold and somewhat thick," Hemmings said years later.

In *Gigolo*, the fall of Weimar Germany is played for dark laughs. Bowie's like Jayne Mansfield in *The Girl Can't Help It* — the beautiful, oblivious object of desire for the rest of the cast. There's a slapstick gunfight at a funeral, a Nazi rally out of *Blazing Saddles*, a Christmas scene where characters fail to kill a struggling goose. Bowie is shot in the street by accident and becomes a Nazi martyr: it's *Horst Wessel Fell to Earth*, with the last shot of Bowie in a coffin in Nazi uniform coming off as a trolling of the press and a ridiculous end to his fascist affectations.

As they had a rock star for a lead, the film's producers wanted something from Bowie on the soundtrack. They got the paltriest thing he recorded in the Seventies: "The Revolutionary Song," Brecht/Weill mixed with *Fiddler on the Roof*. The composer Jack Fishman tarted up a doodle Bowie had sung during filming, a "la-la-la-la-la-la-la-LA-la-la" melody possibly derived from his unreleased 1970 song "Miss Peculiar." Like Bowie and Dietrich's scene in the film, "Revolutionary Song" was an edit of two incongruous sessions — a Bowie vocal, likely cut as a demo; and a full-band rendition with session singers.

ALABAMA SONG

(Brecht, Weill.) **Recorded: (live)** *either 29 April 1978, Spectrum Arena, Philadelphia, 5 May 1978, Civic Center, Providence, RI, or 6 May 1978, Boston Garden, Boston. Bowie: lead vocal; Adrian Belew: lead guitar; Alomar: rhythm guitar, backing vocal; Simon House: electric violin; Sean Mayes: piano, backing vocal; Roger Powell: ARP Odyssey, ARP Solina, Prophet-5; Murray: bass, backing vocal; Davis: drums;* **(studio)** *2 July 1978, Good Earth Studios, 59 Dean Street, London. Bowie: lead and backing vocals; Belew: lead guitar, backing vocal; Alomar: rhythm guitar, backing vocal; House: electric violin; Mayes; piano, backing vocal; Powell: Prophet-5; Murray: bass, backing vocal; Davis: lead drums; Visconti: backing vocal. Produced: Bowie, Visconti.*

First release: *(studio) 15 February 1980, RCA BOW 5 (UK #23); (live): 11 May 1992,* **Stage** *(Ryko RCD 10144/10145).* **Broadcast:** *30 May 1978, Musikladen Extra; 18 September 2002, Live and Exclusive (BBC Radio 2).* **Live**: *1978, 1990, 2002.*

"I'm going out as myself this time. No more costumes, no more masks. This time it's the real thing," Bowie said of his 1978 tour of North America, Britain, Europe, Australasia, and Japan. He would flesh out *Low* and *"Heroes"* tracks for an audience that hadn't bought them on record, hoping to get Robert Fripp as lead guitarist and Brian Eno on keyboards and treatments, but both turned him down. So he broke "Fripp" into the electric violinist Simon House, a UK progressive rock veteran, and Adrian Belew, a young guitarist nabbed from Frank Zappa's touring band. "Eno" became keyboardists Roger Powell (avant) and Sean Mayes (garde).

Where Bowie knew House and Mayes from the British touring circuit (Mayes' revival rock band Fumble had opened for the Spiders from Mars), the ninteen-year-old Belew was an unknown quantity. As was Powell, a brilliant programmer ("a musician seduced into computer programming," as he later described himself) who built a hand-held controller for a self-rigged sequencer stack and who would create one of the first MIDI sequencers for the Apple II. Bowie said he wanted "to try and play my same music with a band which is not built for it quite the same way." Mayes wrote that "David had chosen us for our individual abilities and didn't really interfere with us much." The bandleader was Carlos Alomar, who ran rehearsals, set tempos, and conducted the band onstage during curtain-raiser performances of "Warszawa."

His setlists (which hardly varied over five months) were a compromise. Shows opened with an hour of mostly new material, including some "Berlin" instrumentals. After intermission, Bowie returned with a condensed *Ziggy Stardust* ("Five Years" was greeted by screams), a Berlin entr'acte ("Art Decade," "Alabama Song"), and closed with *Station to Station*'s monster songs and a "Rebel Rebel" capper.

With the exception of a reggae "What in the World" (which came out of the band fooling around in rehearsals), the songs were kept close to their studio arrangements, though Powell (who played the ARP Odyssey and Solina, the RMI KC-II, and an early version of the Prophet-5) added a web of textures, entwining synthesizer figures with House's violin. The 1978 tour was the last great showing of the glam fans, sitting with lightning bolts painted on their faces while Bowie played "Sense of Doubt."

The tour's document was *Stage*, a double LP that compiled performances from the Philadelphia, Boston, and Providence dates. With Tony Visconti committed to cutting an "100% live album" compared to the heavily-doctored *David Live*, *Stage* has strong performances of "Warszawa," "Stay," and "Station to Station." It's Bowie's band adapting the *Low* and *"Heroes"* songs for the stage and creating *Lodger* in the process. But many uptempo songs pale when compared to their studio originals, in particular those from *Ziggy Stardust*. The album's original sequencing was also strange. With Bowie's approval, Visconti arranged the songs in order of original release, so that the LP began with "Hang Onto Yourself," had a nearly all-instrumental side, and ended with "Beauty and the Beast." A 2005 reissue thankfully changed the sequencing to that of a typical 1978 show.

The Next Little Dollar

A few weeks into the US leg of the tour, Bowie started putting Bertolt Brecht and Kurt Weill's "Alabama Song" in sets, replacing the larynx-scraping "Rock 'n' Roll Suicide." While negotiations to star in a *Threepenny Opera* film directed by Rainer Werner Fassbinder may have inspired him, it was also the theme of his ongoing Berlin adventures (in 2002, he said he'd sung "Alabama Song" at breakfast every morning there). It disclosed the ancestry of some recent songs: compare its phrasing ("FOR–IF–we-don't-FIND — the-next WHIS-KEY bar") to his vocals in "What in the World" and "Breaking Glass." "A pretty strident piece of music," as he called "Alabama Song" at the time.

  With a melody suited to Brecht's flint-box of a voice, "Alabama Song" was a typical Brecht ballad: "nothing more than a notation of [Brecht's] speech-rhythm and completely useless as music," Kurt Weill said. Where Brecht had compressed the start of the refrain, "O moon of Alabama," into two bars, Weill extended the line over five — making "O" a whole note and having "Alabama" descend an octave. It was their partnership in miniature: Brecht's depiction of man as a scavenging animal set to a bouncing Weill tune. "Alabama Song" was in their *Mahagonny-Songspiel* (1927) and its operatic reworking three years later, *The Rise and Fall of the City of Mahagonny*. Sung by a prostitute and her gang on the road to the fabled city of Mahagonny (Manhattan, though it predicts Las Vegas), "Alabama Song" was "performed by a priestess in the cult of money," as the critic Daniel Albright wrote. When Lotte Lenya first sang it for Brecht, he told her "'not so Egyptian,' turning my palms upward, extending my arms," she recalled. For his 1978 tour version, Bowie went back to Weimar, singing verses with a blank expression, flattening and deadening his tone, sometimes smoking a cigarette. Then he'd swoon into the refrains, closing his eyes, his band chanting behind him.

Pleased with how "Alabama Song" worked on stage, Bowie brought his touring band into Visconti's Good Earth Studios in London on the day after his final Earl's Court show to cut a prospective single. Bowie wanted a fresh arrangement, telling Dennis Davis to play a track-length drum solo. As Davis kept throwing off the band in rehearsals, Visconti started by recording a backing track of Mayes' piano and Murray's bass. Davis, freed to play "lead drums" in overdubs, opens with a rumbling run on toms and cymbals, and then makes a stammering off-beat commentary on the refrains. "David wanted that to sound more like a circus," Alomar recalled in 2017. The final mix was a patchwork, with Mayes writing that "David had us record several verses and choruses, which he edited together later in the order he felt worked best." Bowie issued "Alabama Song" as his first single of the Eighties, an ode to sex and dollars for a new decade.

MOVE ON

Recorded: (backing tracks) ca. late August-15 September 1978, Mountain Recording Studios, Casino Barrière de Montreux, Rue du Théâtre 9, Montreux, Switzerland; (vocals, overdubs) ca. early March 1979, The Record Plant, Studio D, 321 West 44th St., New York. Bowie: lead and backing vocal; Belew: rhythm guitar; Alomar: rhythm guitar; Mayes: piano; Murray: bass; Davis: drums; Visconti: backing vocal, rhythm guitar. Produced: Bowie, Visconti; engineered: Visconti, David Richards, Rod O'Brien.

First release: 18 May 1979, **Lodger** (RCA BOW LP1/ AFL1-2488, UK #4, US #20).

"I don't live anywhere, really. I travel 100% of the time." It was Bowie's credo of the late Seventies, starting in early 1977 when he took airplanes for the first time in five years. He was bowing to tour logistics — booked to play Japan and Australasia, he could no longer indulge lost weeks of taking an ocean liner to Yokohama. He found that he enjoyed flying again, apart from the take-offs and landings. It let him zip in and out of countries, exploring places he may never have gone to otherwise. In particular Kenya, which he visited in late 1977 and again in early 1978.

He created a new public image: the traveler. "I have never got around to getting myself a piece of land, putting up a house on it, and saying, 'this is mine, this is home'." (Barring his house in Switzerland, that is.) A stateless figure without personal ties. "The more I travel, the less sure I am about exactly which political philosophies are commendable," he said in 1977. "All my traveling is done on the basis of wanting to get my ideas for writing from real events rather than from going back to a system from whence it came." He was open to fresh experience, like a clean piece of blotting paper. Ziggy Stardust, though he'd appeared to come from Aldebaran, was a product of Sixties suburban Britain. Even the Thin White Duke was a British spin on continental decadence. Now he was transitional. A man who'd once feared airplanes now spent days in them. Bowie of the *Let's Dance* era would be another variation: the international businessman counterpart to the bohemian backpacker. In each case, he cast himself as someone moving alone in the world.

Calling his new album *Lodger* symbolized this attitude — he was just staying week-to-week. As always, there were other forces at play. He was inspired by Roman Polanski's 1976 film *The Tenant*, which he paid homage to with a cover image where a sprawled, battered-looking Bowie looks as if he's pressed under glass. In his film, Polanski plays a lodger who becomes convinced he's being turned into his room's former occupant, a woman who attempted suicide by jumping from a window: a fate Polanski's character ultimately reenacts. The *Lodger* cover suggested that Bowie would also wind up, like the Tenant, broken and bandaged from his fall, smushed like a bug on a windshield.

Planned Accidents

Lodger is "a certified nonclassic," as Robert Christgau once wrote. Bowie and Tony Visconti later regretted its production (with Visconti finally remixing it in 2017), and his label and fans didn't think much of it at the time, as it was one of his poorest-selling records of the decade.

Its inclusion in a trilogy with *Low* and *"Heroes"* didn't help its reputation, as *Lodger* wound up as the *Godfather Part III* of the set. It was recorded in a cramped, overheated studio in Switzerland and a second-rate room in New York, a step down from a haunted French château or "Hansa by the Wall." Where *"Heroes"* and *Low* were each finished in about two months, *Lodger* was a more leisurely affair. Backing tracks were cut in August-September 1978, but Bowie didn't cut vocals until March of the following year, and the disjunction shows — at times he's doing avant-garde karaoke over muddy-sounding instrumentals. "There was absolutely no mixing equipment there, maybe two limiters, and we were on a tight deadline. It was make or break. We had to do it; we had no choice," as Visconti recalled of the overdub sessions at the Record Plant.

Yet it was a record dense with ideas (*"Lodger* was the sketchpad of all of them," Bowie said), with a what-the-hell feel of adventure — "African Night Flight" and "Yassassin" remain some of the strangest things he ever recorded. It was, as Jon Savage called *Lodger,* "self-plagiarism," with Bowie rewriting lines, recasting players. To return to Polanski, as *The Tenant* is Polanski's cover version of Alfred Hitchcock's *The Lodger,* so *Lodger* is of *The Tenant* — a misreading upon misreading. A working title for one song was "Emphasis on Repetition," drawing on Søren Kierkegaard's concept of "repetition" as retracing one's steps in the hope of finding the new.

"Move On" began when Bowie was listening to tapes on a Revox and accidentally played "All the Young Dudes" backwards. Struck by the resulting strangled melody, he had Carlos Alomar write out the inverted chord progression. He crafted a vocal to dip and push against the new flow, while for backing vocals he and Visconti sang Mott the Hoople's refrain. "David and I flipped the new version's tape over and played it backwards and sang the melody of "All the Young Dudes" forwards... and that became 'Move On,'" Visconti wrote.

A travelogue inspired by recent trips to Kenya, Japan, and Australia, "Move On" (its title recycled from an unfinished Iggy Pop/Bowie collaboration) is a self-assessment by a man who discards friends and lovers as he would an old coat. "He does know the meaning of the words 'move on'," the pianist Mike Garson once said of Bowie. "Feeling like a shadow, drifting like a leaf," Bowie sings, like an actor unsure as to how to play his part, falling back on old stage habits, sounding in shock, then pushing into fervid phrasing. He's alienated from his own words, devolving into a blur of backwards voices (the 2017 remix all but drowns Bowie's lead vocal in a maelstrom of them). The track's earlier titles included "Someone's Calling Me" and

"The Tangled Web We Weave."

In "Move On," sex holds as much interest as modes of transportation: "Might take a train (a lift from Wilbert Harrison's "Kansas City")... might take a girl..." Bowie idly imagines who might live in the squares and rectangles on a globe he's spinning. "Pick a country. Touch a pin to the map," as he described his travels. "Cyprus... when the going's rough" is an in-joke — home island of his soon-to-be-ex-wife and where he'd once gotten into a head-on collision while driving.

In D major, its opening verse works more as a refrain that never repeats while the rest of the song alternates between bridges (one of which is the reversed "Dudes" progression). Dennis Davis rumbles on toms; Sean Mayes, as per Bowie's instructions, plays "something like Dvořák." George Murray, parked low in the mix, is a secret melodist.

AFRICAN NIGHT FLIGHT

(Bowie, Eno.) **Recorded**: *(backing tracks) late August-15 September 1978, Mountain Studios; (vocals, overdubs) ca. early March 1979, Record Plant. Bowie: lead and backing vocal, guitar?; Alomar: guitar; Mayes: piano; Murray: bass; Davis: drums, percussion; Eno: backing vocal, prepared piano, EMS Synthi AKS, "cricket menace" (Roland CR-78?). Produced: Bowie, Visconti; engineered: Visconti, Richards, O'Brien.*

First release: *18 May 1979,* **Lodger**.

On Bowie's "Berlin" records, Brian Eno played "fifth business," a phrase the novelist Robertson Davies coined to describe a stage role that wasn't a lead part but "[was] nonetheless essential to bring about the recognition or the denouement." Eno would push a track off-kilter by treating guitars or suggest that Bowie leave spaces blank by delaying or erasing a vocal. Only on the instrumental sides was he a full collaborator, writing progressions and melodies and crafting arrangements.

This changed for *Lodger*, where Eno was more creatively aggressive — it has the most Bowie/Eno co-compositions of the trilogy — to the point where Bowie said he'd had to "wrestle back" the album during mixing. (Tony Visconti's remix of *Lodger* made it even more "Eno," with once-marginalized clutter now prominent in the stereo picture — the original mix now appears to be an effort to foreground Bowie's vocals, an ill-fated attempt to make the album more commercial.) Where Eno came to earlier Bowie sessions after stays in the German countryside, he arrived for *Lodger* after a spell in New York City, where he was the toast of young bands (there was "Eno Is God" graffiti on Lower East Side walls) and the press, and he'd found in David Byrne an ideal disciple. Doing another Bowie album was a bit old hat for Eno, who'd just recorded No Wave bands like Mars and Teenage Jesus and the Jerks.

He began by challenging the process Bowie had used since *Young Americans*: give his band chords and instructions, have them jam in the studio, get rhythm tracks down, piece together songs, cut vocals last. Finding this predictable, and believing studio improvs inevitably became dreary blues jams, Eno suggested making chord changes at random, writing eight chords on a chalkboard and having everyone play whichever one he hit with a pointer. This sort of thing was especially irritating because the band was Bowie's touring group, who'd forged a working relationship on the road and was now being deconstructed by a man who called himself a non-musician. While Bowie supported Eno's "art pranks," he later admitted they were alienating. It didn't help that in Mountain Studios the control room was on another floor, with Bowie, Eno and Visconti monitoring players via closed-circuit TV cameras and giving directions via intercom. It made the musicians feel like laboratory animals.

Peak *Lodger* Eno is "African Night Flight" ("[it's] almost all Brian," Visconti told Mark Paytress in 2017), which started life with the band jamming on Dale Hawkins' "Susie Q." Eno promoted as lead instrument a clanging John Cage-esque prepared piano on whose strings he placed scissors and other metal objects. There were also blasts of "cricket menace" — "little crickety sounds that Brian produced from a combination of my drum machine [described by Visconti as a "Roland beatbox," likely the recently-released CR-78] and his 'briefcase' synth," Bowie said in 2001 — and other noises, with one inspiration "Broken Head," a track Eno had cut with Cluster. "The backing track for "African Night Flight," with all those looped African chants and animal noises, was originally made by editing, like, six pieces of tape together. It was a terrible way to mix a track," Visconti later said.

Over this backdrop Bowie devised an Africa inspired by his trips to Kenya, where along with spending a few hours with the Maasai tribe, he'd found some expatriate German pilots drinking in Mombasa bars while still wearing their pilot's gear. They flew their Cessnas into the bush to smuggle contraband or arm rebels, spending the rest of the time drunk and "always talking about when they are going to leave," he said.

It was an Africa cooked up in a Swiss hotel and a midtown New York studio, an imaginary continent aligned with experimental novels like Walter Abish's *Alphabetical Africa* and Michel Leiris' *L'Afrique Fantôme*—an English boy's colonial landscape, scorching under the equatorial sun ("Burning Eyes" was a working title), with stuffed rhinos and wise orangutans, lost pilots (Antoine de Saint-Exupéry flies overhead), mercenaries, and missionaries. A guiding spirit for his herky-jerky, word-choked phrasings are the patter songs of Noël Coward, in particular the colonialist barb "Mad Dogs and Englishmen." See the chant refrain: "*a*santi habari habari/*a*santi nabana nabana," mostly taken from Swahili ("habari," a common greeting) and Lingala ("na bana," basically "your kids," though Bowie apparently intended the latter to be Swahili for "goodbye"). Harping on a single note (usually F) until he makes looping runs across two octaves, with flatted notes for emphases, Bowie cut overdubs that shriek-doubled his lead and gave murmuring undercurrents of distress. As far as he went on this line, "African Night Flight" was more a preview of Eno and Talking Heads' *Remain in Light* and Eno and Byrne's *My Life in the Bush of Ghosts*.

Yassassin

Recorded: (backing tracks) ca. late August-15 September 1978, Mountain Studios; (vocals, overdubs) ca. early March 1979, Record Plant. Bowie: lead and backing vocal, synthesizer; Alomar: rhythm guitar, backing vocal; Visconti: acoustic guitar, backing vocal; House: violin, backing vocal; Murray: bass, backing vocal; Davis: drums, tambourine, backing vocal. Produced: Bowie, Visconti; engineered: Visconti, Richards, O'Brien.

First release: 18 May 1979, Lodger.

Another studio motley, "Yassassin" combines reggae and ersatz Turkish folk into a base of down-mixed funk. The latter was courtesy of George Murray, who front-loads each measure with notes, letting the singers (everyone in the studio) fill out the rest of the bar. (The chords, a shuffle between E7 and F7, are a sparse framework, similar to "Fame.") The reggae took longer, as Murray, Carlos Alomar, and Dennis Davis allegedly weren't familiar with the style, at the time more popular with white Brits than black Americans. Tony Visconti claimed he played "Jamaican 'up-chop' rhythm guitar" on the off-beats while asking Davis to play kick drum, rather than snare, on backbeats.

The song's "Turkish" strands include Alomar's game attempt to imitate a bouzouki on his guitar's high strings and Simon House's roving violin — filling in spaces, given the outro to play out. The latter's work on Hawkwind's "Hassan I Sahba" is similar in tone and phrasing, to the point where it's conceivable "Yassassin" started by Bowie having his band spoof the Hawkwind track.

As on "Neuköln," Bowie was inspired by Turkish immigrants who'd lived in Berlin since the Sixties ("the kind of character you'd find in coffee bars in Turkey"). He'd seen *yaşasın* scrawled on a wall and, intrigued, called the Turkish embassy for a translation (good thing it meant "long live," though it's used more like "hooray" in English). Bowie plays a migrant Turk in a Western city that needs his labor but despises him. Walking "proud and lustful," the refrain shifts between 2/4 and 4/4 and opens with an octave jump ("yas-SASS-in") that detumesces in repeats to seventh and fifth intervals.

Allegedly influenced by Arabic singers (he tries to ululate on "resonant world" in the first verse and the 2017 mix restored some groaning lines in the outro), Bowie sang hard-edged ranting runs of syllables graced by the occasional rhythmic color, like the undertows of the third verse ("if there's someone in *charrge*, then listen to *meeee*") deepened by House's long notes. A thick genre-muck, "Yassassin" is more akin to Bowie's "Revolutionary Song" than any type of Turkish music. "It was pretty transparent that it was me trying to relate to that particular culture," he said in 1980 of his various "ethnic" songs. "Not in my wildest dreams would I think I was trying to represent them."

RED SAILS

(Bowie, Eno.) **Recorded***: (backing tracks) ca. late August-15 September 1978, Mountain Studios; (vocals, overdubs) ca. early March 1979, Record Plant. Bowie: lead and backing vocal; Belew: lead guitar; Alomar: rhythm guitar; House: violin; Mayes: piano; Murray: bass; Davis: drums; Eno: EMS Synthi AKS, guitar treatments, backing vocal; Visconti: backing vocal; Stan Harrison: saxophone. Produced: Bowie, Visconti; engineered: Visconti, Richards, O'Brien.*

First release*: 18 May 1979,* **Lodger***.* **Live***: 1983.*

Sequenced to close *Lodger*'s "travel" side, "Red Sails" followed the wandering rock star of "Move On" and expatriate pilots of "African Night Flight" with English mercenaries ("cum swashbuckling Errol Flynn") foundering in the China Sea (with the jazz standard "Red Sails in the Sunset" spurring the title). Bowie played with fragments — red sails, action, thunder ocean, getting around — racking and scrambling them like Scrabble tiles. "We have a lovely cross reference of cultures. I honestly don't know what it's about," he said in 1979.

It was a crackpot homage to Neu! and Harmonia, with Bowie and Eno having their musicians replicate Klaus Dinger's motorik drumbeat and Michael Rother's delay-tinged guitar and soft synthesizer lines, winding up with a near-plagiarism of Harmonia's 1975 "Monza (Rauf und Runter)." It was American and English cut-ups having a go at being Serious German Musicians.

As usual, Carlos Alomar, George Murray and Dennis Davis execute the manifests, with Davis doing a credible take on Dinger (rolling tom fills, a crash cymbal every four bars). The original mix was a fog (a synthesizer wash, starting at 1:47, blends into violin and saxophone), as if the band had been taped by a bootlegger — in the outro Davis sounds as if he's on paper drums.

Gone is Bowie's commanding baritone of "Station to Station" or the octave-leaping nerviness of "Life on Mars?" In "Red Sails," with its shaky trellises of disjunct melodies, he hits notes that sound chosen at random for him, then layers in squawks, screams, mutters, and Beatle shouts (see the "oooooh!" at 1:35). He'd originally thought to do it as a pseudo-Maoist propaganda song. The second verse finds him spiking to a run of high As and Cs; a juddering series of fourths ("RED-sail-AC-tion") is answered by hazy "red sail" repetitions, with vocals shifting in and out of phase. The stunts keep coming: Bowie sings "sailor can't dance like yoooo-oooo" (see Lou Reed's "Sally Can't Dance") by sinking two octaves in a breath and capping it off with a scream. There's the calm of "life... stands... still... and... stares," all half or whole notes, very Eno in phrasing. "The HINTER-land" chant — Bowie, Visconti, and Eno as colonial troops pushing upcountry. At last, the song collapses — "it's a far-far fa-fa da-da da da da-da-DAH," as if the English language has been infected. Bowie starts counting in, spits out "three four!" (a callback to Philip Glass' *Einstein on the Beach*) and ends with a last Beatle scream.

As with Robert Fripp on *"Heroes,"* Bowie and Visconti didn't let Adrian Belew hear any backing tracks before he soloed, then spliced together his solos from multiple takes. Belew tore through three takes apiece, cut off just as he grew familiar with each song. On "Red Sails," Bowie wanted Belew's take on Michael Rother, a guitarist who Belew had never heard before, "I didn't know what was coming, so I started with a long sustained tremolo D. Once I heard a bit of the track I bent things around until I was in the same key," Belew said. His tremolo-laden skronk on "Red Sails" was an inspired ending: waves of thought voiced on bent strings.

REPETITION

Recorded: (backing tracks) ca. late August-15 September 1978, Mountain Studios; (vocals, overdubs) ca. early March 1979, Record Plant. Bowie: lead and backing vocal; Belew: lead guitar; Alomar: rhythm guitar; House: violin; Mayes: piano; Powell: Prophet-5; Murray: bass; Davis: drums. Produced: Bowie, Visconti; engineered: Visconti, Richards, O'Brien.

First release: 18 May 1979, Lodger. Broadcast: ca. 6 January 1997, ChangesNowBowie; 20 October 1999, Nulle part ailleurs; 25 October 1999, Mark Radcliffe Show. Live: 1997, 1999.

Though fascinated by identity and power, Bowie had avoided direct commentary on "society" (barring the very occasional likes of "God Knows I'm Good"). So "Repetition," a song about domestic violence, was something new under the sun for him. In interviews, he sounded incredulous to have discovered that men beat women, which he once claimed was an American phenomenon. It suggested his imaginative reserves were growing depleted, forcing him to live off a land he didn't recognize.

In typical *Lodger* fashion, his lyric was a double reference. Its title is from Søren Kierkegaard's 1843 philosophical novel, in which a Young Man regrets making a marriage proposal, as while love is heaven, marriage can be hell. Yet Bowie's setting and characters are those of a Fifties Northern drama, with his lead character Johnny suggesting John Osborne's protagonist Jimmy Porter in *Look Back in Anger*, a man who terrorizes his wife and sleeps with her friend.

"Repetition" is a piece of confinement, a man pacing in a room. The verses shift between A major and B major chords. George Murray worries root notes, Dennis Davis is relentless except in gaps between verses (Simon House's violin patches one hole). A key change to A minor after the last verse dims things further. "There's a numbness to the whole rhythm section that I try to duplicate with a deadpan vocal, as though I'm reading a report rather than witnessing the event," Bowie said in 1979. He held on a single note and kept a taut rhythm — usually a short phrase for the B major bar ("I guess the"), a longer one for the A major ("bruises won't show"). There's the occasional aside: the mocking way he sings "blue silk blouse" as a descending sweep of notes.

He breaks character for a near-spoken "don't hit her" between Johnny arriving home and beating his wife off-stage. It's a response to Lou Reed's deadpan "you better hit her" in the Velvet Underground's "There She Goes Again." Another response came in 1981, when the post-punk band the Au Pairs recorded the song. Lesley Woods keeps a similar reserve as Bowie, but her disgust and anger builds as she sifts through the evidence (she sneers "Johnny is a maaan"). The Au Pairs give an indictment pegged on basslines, harried by violin. Bowie's revision of "Repetition" in 1997, stripping it down to an acoustic guitar figure, was in the shadow of one of the few artists who bettered him on his own song.

D.J.

(Bowie, Eno, Alomar.) **Recorded**: *(backing tracks) ca. late August-15 September 1978, Mountain Studios; (vocals, overdubs) ca. early March 1979, Record Plant. Bowie: lead and backing vocal, piano?, Chamberlin; Belew: lead guitar; Alomar: rhythm guitar; House: violin; Murray: bass; Davis: drums; Eno: EMS Synthi AKS?; Visconti: backing vocal? Produced: Bowie, Visconti; engineered: Visconti, Richards, O'Brien.*

First release: *18 May 1979,* **Lodger**. **Live**: *1995-1996.*

The disc jockey created rock 'n' roll, or so it seemed to the kids. He'd unearthed it and cast it into the air. Rock 'n' rollers celebrated and courted DJs, labels were content to bribe them. In "Roll Over Beethoven," Chuck Berry mails a request, opening his song with a percussive phrase that releases its accumulating tension on the holy word "deejay." In "Having a Party," politely making hip requests, Sam Cooke acknowledges the DJ as king of his party. DJs were friends, confidants, liberators.

Not quite the case in Britain. The BBC barely played rock 'n' roll until the mid-Sixties. After the Wilson government shuttered pirate radio stations in 1967, a few pirate DJs were scooped up for the newly-formed Radio One, where John Peel was the house oddball. By the late Seventies, a similar shift was underway in America, with "free form" FM stations hardening into "album-oriented-rock" formats. The DJ became a stooge and a philistine. Elvis Costello's "Radio Radio" was a prosecutor's brief: the DJ is a bought man, his playlists as sterile as he wants to make your life. By the century's end, industry consolidation and the internet finished DJs off, reducing them to interchangeable cogs, voices to break up an algorithm-generated playlist.

Bowie's "D.J." is the voice of an unemployed shut-in whose girl's left him but who still has listeners. His last power lies in the occasional disco gig, where he can make people move to his commands: seeing his former boss on the floor, the DJ turns him into "a puppet dancer" by playing Bee Gees singles. (The song was originally titled "I Bit You Back.") The writer Ian Mathers called the song "a horror story about a human being reduced to nothing more than work," and in a 1979 radio interview, Bowie backed up this reading, saying the DJ's work had become an ulcer-generating job driven by the war against "dead air." "If you have thirty seconds' silence, your whole career is over," he said. He begins "D.J." with an acute impersonation of Talking Heads' David Byrne, whose muses were work and systems ("I'm home! Lost my job!").

There's also the sense that the singer's a sociopath, regarding others as objects to play with. Its video intercuts shots of Bowie as studio exile with those of him walking down Earl's Court Road in London. Men and women kiss him, he dances with strangers: there's an electricity, even menace in the shots (one man looks like he's demanding his wallet). After John Lennon's shooting, Bowie would never let himself be so openly exposed to the public again. The video ends with him pulling down the blinds of his cave (a tribute to David Lean's *Great Expectations*) while the Bowie in the crowd makes his face a mask.

An A minor composition with a neurotic compulsion to move to the parallel major, it was issued as *Lodger*'s second UK single. While George Murray enforced disco, playing a swinging bassline with popped notes (Blur's "Girls and Boys" starts here), he's sunk in the mix along with Dennis Davis' drums and Carlos Alomar, his guitar shrouded via an Envelope phaser (the 2017 remix, one of Visconti's best on the reissue, restores Davis and Alomar to center stage). Simon House's violin mimics Bowie's vocal in the first verse, then gets run through Eno's EMS, sometimes replaced by synthesizer altogether (cost-cutting in action). The track peaks with another of Adrian Belew's forced improvisations (see "Red Sails"). As he later said, it sounds like you're scanning the radio and grabbing bits of guitar solos here and there along the dial.

Like other *Lodger* tracks, "D.J." has a nervous breakdown in its long coda — the collapse of the DJ into dead air, dragging out "time flies when you're having fun" over four bars and reduced to chanting "I've got believers." At the fade, backing singers call back: *leave us, leave us*.

FANTASTIC VOYAGE

(Bowie, Eno.) **Recorded**: *(backing tracks) ca. late August-15 September 1978, Mountain Studios; (vocals, overdubs) ca. early March 1979, Record Plant. Bowie: lead and backing vocal, piano; Belew: mandolin; Alomar: rhythm guitar; House: violin, mandolin; Mayes: piano; Murray: bass; Davis: drums; Eno: "ambient drone" (EMS Synthi AKS?); Visconti: mandolin, backing vocal. Produced: Bowie,*

Visconti; engineered: Visconti, Richards, O'Brien.

First release: *27 April 1979, RCA BOW 2 (UK #7).* **Live**: *2003-2004, 2006.*

One of the last songs Bowie ever performed on stage, in 2006, was "Fantastic Voyage," *Lodger*'s lead-off track and cranky humanist manifesto. On record it starts in a daze, as if in a recovery ward, with airy piano and Bowie in mid-thought: "In the event... that this fantastic voyage... should turn to erosion...," with the formality of a Google translation. Bowie chops words up ("val-you-uh-bul"), flattens them out. A clue is in the middle of the song: *the wrong words make you listen*. He doesn't want you to hum along — he's setting speed bumps to slow you down. "It's an anxious song, *pretending* to be a jaunty, poppy thing," as Rick Moody wrote.

"So many things are out of our own control," Bowie said in 1979. "It's just this infuriating thing that you don't want to have [leaders'] depression ruling your life." He'd once reveled in the apocalypse, believing it had the potential for transformation. By the time of "Fantastic Voyage," he had a peasant realism — we are governed by killers and fools, and our lives hang on their arbitrary mercies. To the novelist Yukio Mishima, who wrote of the samurai "there is dignity in clenched teeth and flashing eyes," Bowie responds cryptically: "Dignity is valuable, but our lives are valuable, too" (see "Heat"). Should survival take precedence? Should it countenance disgraceful acts and submission to power? A resigned "we'll get by, I suppose" is the only answer he's got.

It was a premonition, a response to a renewal of Cold War tensions. "I have no doubt that Europe will be the first target in any nuclear strike, because of its comparative poverty and loosening ties with America," Bowie said in 1977. As usual, he was up on the reading, including Paul Erdman's *The Crash of '79* (predicting a Middle East war, financial panic and energy crisis) and *The Third World War: August 1985*, a novel by a former NATO general where West Germany is invaded and Birmingham annihilated in a Soviet nuclear strike. Far more would come in the early Reagan/Thatcher years. What "Final Day" or "99 Luftballons" or *War Games* share with "Fantastic Voyage" is fatalism and absurdity — knowing that the apocalypse could come thanks to a wrongly identified blip on a radar screen (as nearly happened a few times).

Sharing the D major key and chord progression of "Boys Keep Swinging," the verses of "Fantastic Voyage" barely scan and rhyme; its refrains disintegrate. Bowie argues until there's a snap to attention — piano, bass and drums build in crescendo while he makes a slow ascent of nearly an octave, drenching his last notes with extravagant vibrato. Held together by eighth-note patterns on piano and bass, the band becomes waves and sweeps of sound, with Brian Eno providing an "ambient drone" to smoke-shroud them. Hearing similarities between Bowie's vocal melody and "Love Me Tender," Visconti scrapped a plan to use strings and wrote lines for mandolin (inspired by a childhood memory of Jackie Gleason's twenty-mandolin orchestra on his 1955 album *Lonesome Echo*). Bowie's driver had to go around Montreux to rent mandolins. Played by Visconti, Simon House, and Adrian Belew, the mandolins were each tracked three times and then, perversely, buried in the original mix; Visconti's *Lodger* remix rectified this at last.

Look Back in Anger

(Bowie, Eno.) **Recorded**: *(backing tracks) ca. late August-15 September 1978, Mountain Studios; (vocals, overdubs) ca. early March 1979, Record Plant. Bowie: lead and backing vocal; Alomar: "lead" rhythm guitar; Mayes: piano; Murray: bass; Davis: drums; Eno: EMS Synthi AKS, "horse trumpet," French horn ("Eroica horn"); Visconti: backing vocal. Produced: Bowie, Visconti; engineered: Visconti, Richards, O'Brien;* **(remake)** *ca. June 1988, Mountain Studios. Bowie: lead and backing vocal, synthesizer; Reeves Gabrels: lead guitar; Kevin Armstrong: rhythm guitar; Erdal Kızılçay: synthesizer, bass, drum programming. Produced: Bowie, Richards; engineered: Richards.*

First release: *18 May 1979,* **Lodger**; *(remake) 27 August 1991,* **Lodger** *(reissue) RCD 10146.* **Broadcast**: *18 September 2002, Live and Exclusive; 20 September 2002, Later with Jools Holland.* **Live**: *1983, 1988, 1995-1997, 2002.*

Robert Fripp said in 1979, describing an older cultural thought process, "Why doesn't God put it right? Where are these angels descending from the heavens... these angels to put the world right?" His answer was that all we have for saviors are ourselves: "Here we are. It's up to us." Around the same time, Bowie was reading Julian Jaynes' *The Origin of Consciousness in the*

Breakdown of the Bicameral Mind, which theorized humanity once had a split consciousness in which we heard our thoughts, emanating from the right hemisphere of our brains, as the voices of gods. To Jaynes, the emergence of angels in Middle Eastern cultures around 1,000 BC was the first sign of a breakdown in this mind-division — angels were hybrids, intermediaries between man and the gods.

Bowie's "Look Back in Anger," a dialogue between a "tatty Angel of Death" and his intended, is an internal conversation, a parry between mental selves. *You **know** who I am, he said.* Its refrain is a statement, placed within quotation marks on the LP lyric sheet. But who gets the line? Is it an angel's order to the doomed, or the words of someone who's been hoping for death since birth? It's fitting that the refrain's a duet. First Tony Visconti's backing vocals are heard: plaintive, narrow in range, treated to sound like John Lennon's varisped voice on *Sgt. Pepper* tracks like "She's Leaving Home." Then in the refrain's fourth bar, Bowie sweeps in; nearly an octave higher, as he'd first appeared on "Space Oddity." It's Ground Control talking to Major Tom in space again.

He furthered the split-personality angle in David Mallet's promo film for the song. In an artist's loft, Bowie paints a self-portrait as an angel until he, reverse-*Dorian Gray* style, transforms into a grotesque with encrusted skin. (The song's original title was "Fury.") The video refers to *The Image*, a 1967 short film in which a man paints his doppelganger (Bowie) who comes to life, along with the schizophrenia and role-playing in Polanski's *The Tenant*. In the last shot, Bowie crawls under his bed: he's been made leprous by his art.

The lyric's narrative ends abruptly, with no more verses after the bridge. In the final refrain Bowie breaks his descending vocal pattern for a push upward — "feel it in my VOICE!" — with his last words a slow surrender. It's also a comic portrait — take the gravelly way he phrases lines, sounding like a bored Yahweh. He said his inspiration was the shabby Angel of Death being stood up by a soon-to-be deceased man, so he had to kill time instead in a cafe, reading a magazine.

The rhythm section makes "Look Back in Anger" *Lodger*'s most invigorating track. Sean Mayes pounds the bass end of his piano, Carlos Alomar's guitar darts and weaves around Dennis Davis' drums. Kicking off a beat ahead of the band, Davis rings the bell on his ride cymbal, plays a rolling fill under Bowie's runs of words, works in constant response on hi-hat, snare, and toms. Visconti's remix turned him into the rightful king of the song.

When Bowie asked for a guitar break to fill a refrain, Alomar thought, "if I am going to take a solo, I'm going to take a rhythm-guitar solo," as he told David Buckley. Inspired by John Lennon's rhythm work on Beatles' records, Alomar's solo also challenges Nile Rodgers, dominating the charts with Chic at the time. Alomar and Rodgers had been friends as teenagers in New York, both had cut their teeth in session work, and had similar styles — riffing with syncopated chords with shortened tones. On "Look Back in Anger," the snappy moves between chords, making melodic hooks out of strum patterns, was among Alomar's greatest moments on a Bowie record.

Other pieces of the track were found randomly. Going through Mountain Studios' brass collection, Eno discovered a huntsman's horn (called "horse trumpet" on the LP sleeve) and a French horn he dubbed the "Eroica horn," a reference to its prominence in Beethoven's 3rd Symphony. Barely able to play either, Eno processed the horns until they became distorted washes of sound. There's also a wail after the final refrain ends.

One of Bowie's strongest songs of the late Seventies, "Look Back in Anger" was released as a single only in the US and Canada, neither of which took to it. A decade later, he overhauled it for a dance routine with the La La La Human Steps troupe. An innovative reworking, varying and extending the song's rhythmic centers while keeping the top melody intact, it was the connective tissue between *Never Let Me Down* and what was soon to come with Tin Machine, whose utility player Kevin Armstrong plays supple rhythm lines. In his debut on a Bowie recording, Reeves Gabrels crashes in with a ferocious run of notes. The pairing works so well — Armstrong keeping the dancers moving, Gabrels tearing up the stage behind them — that it's a shame their interplay wasn't more prominent in the band Bowie would soon assemble.

BOYS KEEP SWINGING

*(Bowie, Eno.) **Recorded**: (backing tracks) ca. late August-15 September 1978, Mountain Studios; (vocals, overdubs) ca. early March 1979, Record Plant. Bowie: lead and backing vocal, guitar, piano, Chamberlin?; Belew: lead guitar; Eno: piano, EMS Synthi AKS; House: violin; Visconti: bass, backing vocal; Alomar: drums. Produced: Bowie, Visconti; engineered: Visconti, Richards, O'Brien.*

First release: 27 April 1979, RCA BOW 2. *Broadcast*: 23 April 1979, *The Kenny Everett Video Show*; 15 December 1979, *Saturday Night Live*; 14 December 1995, *The White Room*. *Live*: 1995-1996.

"Boys Keep Swinging" takes on the Village People, with double-entendres worthy of "In the Navy": a lustily chanted refrain and a delight in the cartoon masculine. Like Bowie's Sixties "childhood" songs, it's a boy's idea of manhood as being like joining a Scout troop. *Uncage the colors! Unfurl the flag!* A bisexual man imagining a gay fantasy of straight life. Masculinity as a pose, an absurdity, an act. A club you can join if you swing the right way. A club you can sneak into if you'd like. A song of violent camaraderie, its backing singers dominate on refrains while lead and backing vocals jostle on lines like "you'll get your share!" "The glory in that song was ironic," Bowie said in 2000. "I do not feel that there is anything remotely glorious about being either male or female. I was merely playing on the idea of the colonization of a gender."

Using the same chord progression as "Fantastic Voyage" ("Boys" has more tension, its returns to the home chord packing more of a wallop), it has roughly the same structure — two verses and two refrains, the latter extended by stalling on an A major chord. The sawing background drone, led by Simon House's violin, is yet another return to the Velvet Underground's "Waiting for the Man." During early takes, Bowie was frustrated by how well his band was playing. He wanted them to sound like "young kids in the basement [who were] just discovering their instruments," Carlos Alomar said. So he had them switch instruments, a trick used on *Lust for Life*'s "Fall in Love With Me." Alomar competently played drums and Dennis Davis not-so-competently bass, requiring Tony Visconti to cut a new bassline during mixing. (He took the opportunity to play a hyperactive line like his work on *The Man Who Sold the World*, with a touch of the Beach Boys' "You're So Good to Me"). George Murray, assigned to keyboards, apparently was wiped from the final mix, as only Bowie and Eno are credited.

Its last ninety seconds are an Adrian Belew guitar solo, again pasted together by Visconti and Bowie from three different takes (the only clue they gave Belew was that Alomar was on drums), with possible additions by Bowie himself: the feedback tone and use of tremolo alters towards the fade. Belew was fresh from Kentucky and had an aw-shucks quality to him that Bowie liked. He kept trying to imitate Belew's bluegrass accent, which is basically the accent Bowie attempted in the *Twin Peaks* movie. "Boys Keep Swinging" was inspired by Belew, Bowie told him, because he thought Belew was a "world's your oyster type of guy." All the opportunities laid out in front of some young rock guitarist — a platter to feast on. You can do it all. Buy a home of your own, learn to drive and everything.

The "Berlin" albums are chaste: love and sex are compromised, alienated acts. Then there's "Boys Keep Swinging." It's an end to Bowie's glam years and a look at the Eighties we could have had, not the one we got from him. In David Mallet's promo film, over Belew's closing solo, shrieking in its manically phallic way, Bowie does a drag show as his backing singers. It's the best mime acting of his life — each of his women is her own character: a brassy Sixties belter, an elegant dowager (modeled on Marlene Dietrich), a skeletal high-society vampire. Taking a cue from his lover Romy Haag, at peak moments in Belew's solo Bowie tears off his wig and smears lipstick across his face with the back of his hand. The dedicated work of hours of gender preparation, erased in a disdainful, magnificent moment.

RED MONEY

(Bowie, Alomar.) **Recorded**: *(backing tracks) ca. 5 June-early July 1976, Château d'Hérouville; (vocals, overdubs) ca. early March 1979, Record Plant. Bowie: lead and backing vocal, guitar; Belew: lead guitar; Powell: Prophet-5; Alomar: rhythm guitar; Murray: bass; Davis: drums; Visconti: backing vocal. Produced: Bowie, Visconti; engineered: Laurent Thibault, Visconti, O'Brien.*

First release: *18 May 1979,* **Lodger**.

The last track on Bowie's last record of the Seventies, "Red Money" is freighted with symbolism, closing out the Eno, Iggy Pop, and Berlin era by coming full circle and recycling backing tracks from "Sister Midnight," the opening track of Pop's *The Idiot*. "Project cancelled!" is a refrain hook. Asked in 2001 whether it was him drawing the curtain on "the Eno triptych," Bowie replied, "Not at all. Mere whimsy."

Never underestimate how many of Bowie's apparently calculated moves were mere whimsy. Still, "Red Money" elaborates themes Bowie had developed on *Lodger*: repetition, oblique influence (a provisional album title was *Despite Straight Lines*), absence, impending obsolescence, weariness with songwriting and performing, a broadening of perspective beyond the repertory theater of the mind. "Red Money" is a palimpsest of a track, with Iggy Pop erased from a song that Bowie gave him. Pop had invoked a muse, raged into an Oedipal nightmare. Bowie processes information: Jackie Wilson and Bob Dylan songs; some recent paintings — see the "small red box" ("must not dropit-stopit-takeit*away*!"), an image that kept cropping up in his art and signified "responsibility" to him. Travelers are stranded in diseased landscapes, collecting blood money, aborting missions — there's a possible reference to Skylab, the space station that crashed to Earth in 1979 to commemorate the shoddy end of the space age: "it will tumble from the sky" (falling Skylab returns in an early version of "Up the Hill Backwards").

As the Alomar/Murray/Davis band didn't re-record their performances, this suggests that Bowie came up with the idea of rewriting "Sister Midnight" during the mixing/overdub sessions of March 1979. Bowie and Adrian Belew cut new abrasive guitar parts and Roger Powell added Prophet-generated noise and clattering electronic percussion. "Red Money" is Bowie reclaiming a property, his melody more adventurous than Pop's, marked by octave leaps and falls in a single bar ("see *it* in the *sky*"), his phrasings working against the verses' harmonic movement. The vocal arrangement peaks with Bowie singing the title line in stereo-panned four-part harmony with himself. Despite his closing line that "it's up to you and me," he's alone again in his head.

I PRAY, OLÉ

Recorded: (backing tracks?) ca. late August-15 September 1978, Mountain Studios?, ca. early March 1979, Record Plant?; (backing tracks, overdubs, vocals) ca. 1988-1991, Mountain Studios. Bowie: lead and backing vocal, lead guitar? rhythm guitar? Korg M1?; Belew: lead guitar? drums?; House: violin?; Eno: synthesizer?; Murray: bass?; Kızılçay?: Korg, guitar, bass, drums? Produced: Bowie; engineered: Richards.

First release: 27 August 1991, **Lodger** (Ryko reissue, RCD 10146).

Like other "Berlin" outtakes, little of "I Pray, Olé" hails from its alleged era. Mixed and released during Bowie's Tin Machine years, its lyric is very Machine ("it's a god eat god world") while its guitars suggest Reeves Gabrels, though the wailing towards the fade seems more Adrian Belew's style. The drumming is almost certainly not Dennis Davis, despite him getting liner-note credit. Candidates are Belew (who started out as a drummer and who reportedly drummed on some March 1979 *Lodger* overdub sessions) and, far more likely, Bowie's Eighties studio hand Erdal Kızılçay.

Played the track by Nicholas Pegg, Tony Visconti didn't recognize "I Pray, Olé," saying he'd "definitely rule it out of the *Lodger/ Scary Monsters* sessions... the mixing is not my style," and guessing it could have started in early 1980 at Mountain Studios with David Richards. Despite its sonic affinities with *Tin Machine II*, Tin Machine's producer Tim Palmer also had no memory of recording the track. It's likely that "I Pray, Olé" started with Bowie's 1988 remake of "Look Back in Anger," and that while revising the latter, Bowie listened to *Lodger* tapes and retrieved a few things — a Simon House violin line, an Eno keyboard (Eno's credited on synthesizer in the Ryko CD liners) — to mix into the foundation of an otherwise brand-new track. In 2011, Palmer said "it was no coincidence that David was re-working 'Look Back in Anger' during the Tin Machine days. I think he missed the excitement of that style of recording." Whatever Bowie's motive, he made a cuckoo's egg: the official outtake of an album it had nothing to do with. Fittingly, "I Pray, Olé" is only found today on the long out-of-print Ryko *Lodger*. Fabricating a lost song is a very Bowie conceit, foreshadowing his mischief in the Nineties, where he helped to devise the biography of a nonexistent painter.

PLAY IT SAFE

(Bowie, Pop.) **Recorded***: ca. late August-September 1979, Studio 1, Rockfield Studios, Amberley Court, Monmouth, Gwent, Wales. Iggy Pop: lead vocal; Steve New: lead guitar; Ivan Kral: lead and rhythm guitar; Barry Andrews: keyboards, synthesizer; Glen Matlock: bass, backing vocal?; Klaus Kruger: drums; Bowie, Jim Kerr, Charlie Burchill? Mick MacNeil? Brian McGee? Derek Forbes?: backing vocals. Produced: James Williamson (uncredited), Pat Moran; engineered: Peter Haden.*

First release: 8 February 1980, **Soldier** (Arista SPART 1117/AB 4259, US #125).
Live: (Pop) 1979-1980.

Iggy Pop ended his RCA contract with a quickie live album and used an advance from his new Arista deal to spend the latter half of 1978 writing songs. It was domestic life in West Berlin with his girlfriend, the photographer Esther Friedman. He released a fine record in April 1979, *New Values*, a minor success in Britain. Arista believed the next album could be his commercial breakthrough at last and gave Pop a New Wave supergroup: former Sex Pistol Glen Matlock, former Rich Kid Steve New, and Barry Andrews, whose organ playing was a primary color of the first XTC albums. Pop also brought back former Stooge James Williamson, who'd produced *New Values*. For a studio, Pop chose Rockfield, a converted farmhouse in southeast Wales (Queen had recorded *Sheer Heart Attack* there).

Having toured for a good chunk of 1979, Pop had to come up with songs in a month's time. He'd lost Scott Thurston, who'd helped craft *New Values*, and was relying on Matlock to fill the gap. The sessions alternated between inertia and paranoia. Williamson demanded constant retakes while trying to rig up a forty-eight-track console and chiding Pop whenever he got too outrageous in the vocal booth. Then Bowie arrived, reportedly dressed like the Scarlet Pimpernel in an all-red outfit, "complete with cape," as per Paul Trynka. Realizing that the studio atmosphere was toxic, Bowie acted as an "Eno" figure, trying to generate fresh ideas. He began spinning tales of London lowlife, particularly the notorious John Bindon, a gangster turned actor (*Get Carter*, *Performance*) who had run security for Led Zeppelin and was renowned for having an enormous penis that, Bowie reportedly said, was greatly appreciated by Princess Margaret.

This was enough for Pop, who improvised an obscene rap about Bindon and the Princess. Being a criminal was like being a rock star, it was *better* than being a rock star: the safest thing to be is a criminal. *I'm gonna play it safe!* Iggy beamed. The band worked up a groove driven by Andrews' keyboards and Klaus Kruger's drums. Bowie encouraged Pop to get wilder. Williamson, believing Bowie was trying to usurp him and still sore about Bowie's mix of the Stooges' *Raw Power*, allegedly retaliated by sending a dose of feedback into Bowie's headphones. Bowie and Williamson soon departed, leaving the album rudderless — it was pieced together months later in London.

Bowie considered "Play It Safe" as a studio exercise to lead Pop to write better songs, so hearing that it could make the album, he feared Pop would run afoul of British libel laws by slandering the royals. Meeting Pop and Ivan Kral in New York in December 1979, Bowie urged them to axe the track. Instead, Pop reworked "Play It Safe," cutting the Princess Margaret verses and most of New's guitar lines — the two were now on the outs. Even bowdlerized, "Play It Safe" stood out on Pop's album *Soldier*. The keyboard drone is a base for a pub singalong refrain (hollered by Bowie and most of Simple Minds, who had been working in the adjacent studio). Pop starts with Dwight Eisenhower and ends with the Son of Sam, Jim Jones, and Bobby Darin's "Splish Splash" (singing it live in late 1979, he swapped in fresh characters: "Judas played it safe! Tokyo Rose played it safe! Fulgencio Batista! Lucky Luciano — he never got a jaywalking ticket!!") There's poignancy in how he sings the title line; it's the voice of a man trapped in a diminishing legend.

VELVET COUCH
PIANO-LA (PIANOLA)

(Bowie, Cale.) **Recorded***: (unreleased) ca. 5-15 October 1979, Ciarbis Studios (sic), New York. Bowie: vocal; John Cale: piano, vocal.*

John Cale first heard of David Bowie during the former's tenure as "weirdo music" A&R man for Warner Records in the early Seventies. Cale loved *Hunky Dory*, which he saw as the heir to Lionel Bart and Anthony Newley, but he knew Warner wouldn't offer Bowie a record deal, as so happened. The two finally met later in the decade, in New York. Bowie was hanging around the underground scene while Cale was playing riotous shows at CBGB (Greil Marcus, on one gig: "from the way Cale took and held the stage, you would have thought war had been declared").

On April Fool's Day 1979, Bowie and Cale performed together at a Philip Glass and Steve Reich benefit show promoted as "The First Concert of the Eighties." Bowie, in a black kimono, attempted to play viola for the first time in his life for Cale's "Sabotage." A reviewer noted that "Bowie was unheard in the mix, which was just as well, since he seemed to have no command of the instrument." That October, when Bowie was back in New

York, he "picked me up to go to the Mudd Club and I was in the studio, and we started working, throwing things around," Cale later wrote. Two demos were later bootlegged. "He could improvise songs very well, which was what that bootleg was all about," Cale said in 2008,

> When we did that bootleg, it was like the good old bad old days. We were partying very hard. It was exciting working with him, as there were a lot of possibilities and everything, but we were our own worst enemies at that point... Did I ever want to produce Bowie? After spending time with him, I realized the answer was no. The way we were then would have made it too dangerous.

"Piano-la," or "Pianola," has a barely-audible Bowie singing place-filler notes over Cale's piano. "Velvet Couch" is more realized, with Bowie tracing together a melody, singing lines like "we won't do things like that anymore," "we'll be as we are" and "they never sleep and they never play guitar." Having little in common with Bowie's work on *Lodger* and *Scary Monsters*, they're more in line with Cale pieces like "Chorale." Was Bowie considering a partnership with Cale for the Eighties, with Cale as his new Eno? All that remains are these shadows of songs.

CHAPTER FOUR:

A SOCIETY OF ONE

(1980-1981)

Like everyone in New York except the intellectuals, I have led several lives and I still lead some of them.
— Renata Adler, *Speedboat*

Knowing what game you are playing does not, ipso facto, make it possible for you to change.
— Thomas Harris, *I'm OK—You're OK*

His terror of us all comes from having been held at arm's length from society.
— Bernard Pomerance, *The Elephant Man*

So I open the door
It's the "friend" that I'd left in the hallway
— Gary Numan, "Are 'Friends' Electric?"

I don't know any hallways.
— Bowie, "Teenage Wildlife"

It's No Game (Part 1)
It's No Game (Part 2)

Recorded: (backing tracks, vocals ["Pt. 2"]) ca. 15 February-early March 1980, The Power Station, 441 West 53rd St., New York; (vocals, overdubs) ca. mid-April-early June 1980, Good Earth Studios. David Bowie: lead and backing vocal, piano; Robert Fripp: lead guitar ("Pt. 1"); Carlos Alomar: rhythm guitar; George Murray: bass; Dennis Davis: drums, ratchet ("Pt. 1"); Michi Hirota: lead vocal ("Pt. 1"); Tony Visconti: backing vocal. Produced: Bowie, Visconti; engineered: Larry Alexander, Jeff Hendrickson, Visconti.

First release: 12 September 1980, Scary Monsters (BOW LP 2/RCA AQL1-3647, UK #1, US #12).

Scary Monsters was "Bowie's decision to take his work in rock and roll seriously," Robert Fripp said soon after its making. "Anyone who goes to New York takes his work seriously — the city certainly has that effect." Wanting a richer sound and a livelier mix than *Lodger*, Tony Visconti booked the state-of-the-art Power Station for rhythm tracks ("the most glossy studio in New York") and used his own Good Earth Studios in London for vocals and overdubs. Bowie cut back on vocal-booth improvisation: once backing tracks were down, he spent over two months working up lyrics. "I try not to write as immediately as I once used to," he said at the time.

Though Bowie still seemed aligned with Brian Eno, telling a radio interviewer that "there are an awful lot of mistakes that I went with, rather than cut them out," there weren't many planned accidents now. *Scary Monsters* was his most chart-minded record since *Young Americans*, "the first real attempt at making a truly commercial album and to stop the experimenting," Visconti said. Chuck Hammer, recruited to provide "guitarchitecture" (see "Ashes to Ashes"), recalled an intense mood at the Power Station, with Bowie ticking off items on a clipboard while Visconti, distracting himself from a failing marriage, assembled the record as if supervising the building of an ocean liner.

In Britain, the album restored Bowie's fortunes, giving him his first #1 single in five years and his first #1 LP since *Diamond Dogs* (it didn't sell as well in the US, which had only taken to disco Bowie). *Scary Monsters* has a consistent, exuberant anger ("the music is grinding and intense, totally *present*," wrote Charles Shaar Murray and Roy Carr). If wildly front-loaded, it's weathered the past forty years as well as anything of its time: it still sounds like Bowie's "modern" album — he could have called it *2019*.

Its freshness was a confidence trick. Like the Rolling Stones' contemporaneous *Tattoo You*, *Scary Monsters* refurbished older, abandoned songs: nearly half of its ten tracks derive from early- and mid-Seventies Bowie pieces. It's a rummage through an estate sale, with callbacks to everything from "Space Oddity" to "Heroes" to "The Laughing Gnome," while Edward Bell's album cover has a Berlin Bowie retrospective — *Low*'s Man Who Fell to Earth, the Egon Schiele tribute of *"Heroes,"* the stricken *Lodger* (attached to Aladdin Sane's body) — with the characters blurred, shrunken, distorted. It's a touring company disbanding, reflecting what was soon to come. Roy Bittan and Robert Fripp never worked with Bowie again, nor did George Murray and Dennis Davis, and *Scary Monsters* would be the last Visconti-produced Bowie album of the twentieth century. Bowie's cover role as a clown was a nod to his time "in the circus" with the mime Lindsay Kemp in the late Sixties — his costume was designed by Natasha Korniloff, who worked with him and Kemp in those years. But there are two clowns on the album cover: the dignified one who looks straight at you; and the disheveled one who hides behind him, casting a long shadow.

Konagona Ni Kudake

Two versions of "It's No Game" open and close *Scary Monsters*, with the tracks in turn bookended by the sounds of a twenty-four-track Lyrec TR532 tape machine. The album begins with Visconti rewinding and pressing play, and ends with the tape spooling out.

Woken by noise in the street, Bowie clicks through TV channels — brownshirts, protesters aflame, deposed dictators, new presidents for life, films of refugees, a dish-soap advertisement. A world in flickers, in silhouettes and shadows; an existence comprehensible only through private jokes: a pun on Eddie Cochran's "Three Steps to Heaven," a Noël Coward-esque "to be *insulted* by these *fascists* — it's so *degrading*." A declamatory "I really don't understand — the *SITUATION*" is the axis of the song. He's as estranged from political life as from an emotional one. ("I hear the Clash and I don't react," he wrote in a draft of "Ashes to Ashes.") Decades later, in his play *Lazarus*, Bowie made "It's No Game" an absurdist set piece. The extraterrestrial Thomas Jerome Newton, holed up in his apartment, shaken by a montage of death and chaos on his television, hallucinates being hurled around his room by a female samurai.

"It's No Game Pt. 2" was the song's first version, and the only track completed during the Power Station sessions of February 1980. (Its development paralleled that of the Beatles' "Revolution," first recorded as an acoustic track (the *White Album* version) and months later as a distorted rocker.) With its close-range vocal, mid-tempo beat, and restrained guitars (Carlos Alomar, doubling Murray's bassline and driving the harmonic rhythms, playing D6 and E major diminished chords to clear the way for the A minor change ("heaven or hearth"), "Pt. 2" is a sanctioned protest. As Bowie said in 1980,

> what happens when a protest or angry statement is thrown against the wall so many times is that the speaker finds that he has no energy to give any impact anymore. It comes over in that very lilting, very melodic kind of superficial level. The sentiment is exactly the same as in the first part [of the song] but the ambiance has changed, with a gentle, almost nostalgic quality to it, rather than being an angry vehement statement.

The bridge uses the melody and lines from "Tired of My Life," a song dating to Bowie's youth, in which the singer's wearied by life in the way only a barely-grown man could be. It furthers the lassitude of "Pt. 2," in which a shift up to E major for Alomar's solo soon pales, tumbling back via snare crashes to D major for the last verse. The song ends unchanged; the tape runs out.

Double Fantasy

A world away, or at least a side, is its vehement "Pt. 1" revision, the sinister clown to the sad one. Davis counts in the band by waving a ratchet over his head. For the first time since *Low*, Visconti used the Eventide H910 Harmonizer in force, even dosing the ratchet with it. The fresh ingredient is the Power Station, whose room ambiance, mikes, and consoles midwifed the drum sound of the Eighties ("Visconti would sometimes have me turn the drum mikes down, boost the room mikes, and then flange the combined sound electronically," engineer Larry Alexander said, while Bowie said Studio A reminded him of a Swiss chalet).

First we hear the voice of Japanese actress Michi Hirota, snapping "shiruetto ya kage ga!" ("silhouettes and shadows"). She'd come to an overdub session in London to help Bowie voice a Japanese translation of his lyric: he'd intended to sing the lines himself. But she struggled to make the translation fit his vocal melody (the former was near-literal, with too many syllables), so Bowie asked her to recite the lyric in an aggressive, "masculine" manner. Japanese has a severe gender separation in which men and women use different words, tenses, and phrasings. In Japan, should a woman speak as Hirota does on "It's No Game," it would still be considered startling, as it's a tone you'd only hear women use while playing a hard game of soccer, for instance. Hirota uses "ore," the equivalent of the "I" pronoun typically reserved for an older Japanese man, and her verb endings are more direct than those a woman "should" use. She has an exaggerated masculine tone: she speaks how a boastful Japanese teenage boy would.

Bowie wanted Hirota as the song's revolutionary, "to break down a particular type of sexist attitude about women," he said.

I thought the [idea of] the "Japanese girl" typifies it, where everyone pictures them as a geisha girl, very sweet, demure and non-thinking, when in fact that's the absolute opposite of what women are like. They think an awful lot! With quite as much strength as any man. I wanted to caricature that attitude by having a very forceful Japanese voice on it. So I had [Hirota] come out with a very samurai kind of thing.

Having used John Lennon's *Plastic Ono Band* as the premise for his 1979 remake of "Space Oddity," Bowie's shrieked and bellowed lines in "Pt. 1" was his take on the primal scream catharsis of Lennon's "God," which Bowie quoted in a 1980 TV interview ("I don't believe in Beatles," he said with a smile). His admiration was couched in vicious parody: "Pt. 1" is sung by a raving, histrionic Englishman who's undercut by an aggressive Japanese woman. Hirota's first barrage triggers Bowie. He sounds blown out by rage, leaping and falling octaves, playing hell with his vocal cords while screaming "HEAVVVEN." He's acting out the "Western" equivalent to Hirota's performance, and it's so brutal that the "Tired of My Life" harmonies in the bridge are an island of stability for the ear. In barges Robert Fripp, whom Bowie asked to imagine trying to outplay B.B. King in a guitar duel. His riffs throughout the track, built on odd chord shapes, often moving between minor and major thirds, at times playing a Lydian modal figure, and using a cryptic syncopation, now culminate in an eight-bar solo, fired by the key change and barbed with tritones. Fripp pushes the track to the verge of collapse until Davis' fills restore order, then gets off a last round in the coda, locked in a looping figure until Bowie howls for him to shut up.

"Put a bullet in my brain, and it makes all the papers." It's one of the oldest lines in the song, taken from "Tired of My Life," written at a time when Bowie was living in Beckenham, walking the streets unnoticed except when he wore dresses. In "Pt. 2," Bowie sings the line in a melancholy descending phrase; in "Pt. 1," a double-tracked Bowie sneers, biting on the "s" in "papers." A beat later Hirota lacerates him.

On the night of 8 December 1980, Lennon was shot in front of his home by a man who allegedly had Bowie on his list of targets, and he died in the back seat of a police car driving him to the hospital. In his Chelsea apartment, Bowie watched television coverage of Lennon's murder until dawn, screaming, "What the fuck is going on in this world!" He really didn't understand the situation.

BECAUSE YOU'RE YOUNG

Recorded: (backing tracks) ca. 15 February-early March 1980, Power Station; (vocals, overdubs) ca. mid-April-early June 1980, Good Earth. Bowie: lead and backing vocal; Pete Townshend: lead guitar; Alomar: rhythm guitar; Andy Clark: Minimoog, Yamaha CS-80; Murray: bass; Davis: drums. Produced: Bowie, Visconti; engineered: Alexander, Hendrickson, Visconti.

First release: 12 September 1980, Scary Monsters.

Bowie and Pete Townshend had first met in 1965, in a minor humiliation for Bowie. Townshend watched Bowie sing "You've Got a Habit of Leaving," then remarked that it sounded like one of his songs (it did). Townshend went off to help write the Sixties. Fifteen years later, he was balancing solo work and keeping the Who going after Keith Moon's death, like a family business he was reluctant to shutter but knew was bankrupt. "We were pretending to be a rock 'n' roll band, we were pretending to be musicians and it was all *absurd*," he recalled in 1989. "The punk thing was happening in the UK and the Who had completely and utterly lost the plot... [so] much energy and craftsmanship and effort and money and sweat went into producing such limpid and pretentious crap."

He wanted the punks to push him into the grave. "This is something real," he said of punk in 1977. "I felt I was spending all my time behind a desk and the Sex Pistols were out enjoying the dream." "Who Are You," inspired by a self-flagellating night with half of the Sex Pistols, was a hungover man berating the mirror. "I got depressed and was just hitting out at everybody." By the time Bowie asked him to play on *Scary Monsters*, Townshend had fallen into an abyss: full-blown alcoholism (drinking four bottles of brandy during one Who gig at the Rainbow); heroin and cocaine addictions; being separated from his wife and children; nearly going broke. The crash ended in early 1982, when Townshend checked himself into a rehabilitation clinic. His guest spots on Bowie's "Because You're Young" and Elton John's "Ball and Chain" were interludes in a hard season. "I'd become the personification of my own worst fears, and I really wanted to be beaten for it."

Townshend showed up at the Power Station in a "foul, laconic" mood, alleviated by downing some red wine ("on a recording session, one of the nice things is I can drink half a bottle of brandy and spend a couple hours experimenting," he said around this time. "If I set out to do something safe, I can't pull it off.") He couldn't relate to Bowie and Visconti, who were acting like old men, in Visconti's words: "we just talk about the planets and religious subjects... and [Townshend] was ready for a right rave-up." After small talk, there was nothing else to do but record. When Townshend asked him what he wanted, Bowie replied "chords," a nebulous statement that Visconti clarified: Pete Townshend chords. "Townshend shrugged, 'oh, windmills,' and did a perfect windmill on his guitar," as if auditioning for a musical adaptation of his life. His jolting between E minor and C major (with his usual trick of leaving out the third note in each chord: "it's almost like using a chord as a drone") has his recognizable sting, though downplayed in the mix.

In "Because You're Young," an older man watches young lovers make mistakes and longs for the freedom to be as foolish (Bowie got the title from Duane Eddy's 1960 hit, "Because They're Young," written on a page of lyric ideas for the album). It was an awkward song: verses built on stop-start bass and drum patterns and barrages of octave-leaping vocal phrases, a refrain whose chord progression was like following a pinball's progress, and a lengthy pre-chorus to weld them together. A late decision to replace a piano track, which had been a steady harmonic foundation, with Andy Clark's synthesizer chords and arpeggios gave a crowded song less room.

An earlier vocal take had Bowie using John Lennon-esque phrasing, particularly on the half-written pre-chorus (it sounds like "Mind Games" at times), while his lyric had a first-person teenager POV, the title line being "because I'm young." His revision was a vocal whose perspective was one of "a sort of old roué... looking down on these two young mad things and knowing that it's all gonna fizzle out," Bowie said. "God, I'm a depressive person!" The rewrite suited Townshend's role, as the latter would tell interviewers that "I've felt old all my life."

KINGDOM COME

(Verlaine.) **Recorded**: *(backing tracks) ca. 15 February-early March 1980, Power Station; (vocals, overdubs) ca. mid-April-early June 1980, Good Earth. Bowie: lead and backing vocal, synthesizer?; Fripp: lead guitar; Alomar: rhythm guitar; Murray: bass; Davis: drums; Visconti, Lynn Maitland, Chris Porter: backing vocals. Produced: Bowie, Visconti; engineered: Alexander, Hendrickson, Visconti.*

First release: *12 September 1980,* **Scary Monsters**.

The great New York band Television broke up in the summer of 1978. A perfectionist streak and label wrangles meant that while among the first of the CBGB groups to form, Television were among the last to release an album. Poor promotion of their second record and tensions between guitarists Richard Lloyd and Tom Verlaine finished them off. Bowie was a fan, having seen Television in New York in 1974, and he called Verlaine one of "New York's finest new writers... I wish he had a bigger audience." He also had an eye on the guitarist's downtown style, once wearing his hair in little bangs that he told members of Blondie was his Tom Verlaine look.

Verlaine, born Thomas Miller, started out as a poet and his songs had casual epiphanies, words like runs of notes on his Fender Jazzmaster.

Broadway looked so medieval. I'm uncertain when beauty meets abuse. Puts on her boxing gloves and went to sleep. The standout on his 1979 solo debut, *Tom Verlaine*, was the purgatorial "Kingdom Come," where life is a chain gang routine: breaking rocks and cutting hay while watched from a guard tower.

Carlos Alomar suggested doing "Kingdom Come," which would be the first cover on a Bowie album since *Station to Station*. "It was simply the most appealing [track] on his album," Bowie said. "It just happens to fit into the scattered scheme of things, that's all." Maybe the lyric spoke to a man starting another cycle of record-promo-tour. During the New York sessions, Bowie asked Verlaine to play lead guitar on the track. Tony Visconti recalled Verlaine showing up at the Power Station looking "a little down on his luck and lugubrious." Saying he needed to get the right sound, Verlaine tried out every amp in the studio while Visconti and Bowie ate, watched TV, and ultimately left him alone, still auditioning amps. "I don't think we ever used a note of his playing, if we even recorded him," Visconti wrote. Robert Fripp instead got the lead lines. (Verlaine would only grow more exacting — on stage, he'd spend long minutes tuning before going into the next song.)

Bowie's "Kingdom Come" aims for grandeur, though staying in Verlaine's E major key, with layers of guitars and call-and-response vocal lines by an impromptu chorus: Visconti, a British friend Lynn Maitland, and engineer Chris Porter. Some changes were inspired, like moving a drum hook to George Murray's bass, which freed Dennis Davis to play fills and reduce the song's monotonous tendencies. Others were sloppy ("the face of doom" became the "voice of doom," but Bowie kept the following line about the voice "shining"), or baffling, like pulling the title hook from the refrain and not using it until nearly the fade.

His vibrato-heavy lead vocal was a late choice, as an earlier take has a more restrained performance. Where Verlaine had a penitential tone, Bowie savaged lines, ending phrases by beating them to death ("waw-haw-haw-*alked*... ray-hay-hay-*hain*"). The agonizing bridge finds him barely in tune while trying to sing like Ronnie Spector. A bewildering performance, "Kingdom Come" portends his future interpretive disaster "God Only Knows."

Up the Hill Backwards

Recorded: (backing tracks) ca. 15 February-early March 1980, Power Station; (vocals, overdubs) ca. mid-April-early June 1980, Good Earth. Bowie: vocal, organ?; Maitland, Porter: vocal; Fripp: lead guitar; Visconti: acoustic guitar, vocal; Roy Bittan: piano; Alomar: rhythm guitar; Murray: bass; Davis: drums, claves? Produced: Bowie, Visconti; engineered: Alexander, Hendrickson, Visconti.

First release: 12 September 1980, **Scary Monsters**. *Live*: 1987.

"Up the Hill Backwards" is a stoic self-help manual, with Bowie mocking the Seventies lifestyle guide *I'm OK—You're OK*. Accept that you have no control, that life has little to do with your actions. There's a poem for children that begins: "He walked up the hill backwards/So as not to see how high it was." That's how we make do, stumbling up towards a future that we won't imagine, our eyes on ground already crossed. A cyclical chord structure adds to the effect: marches away from the tonic chord, A major; returns home at every turn, even on the "arrival of freedom." Asked by Angus MacKinnon whether the song was "implying that there's bugger all you or I or anybody can do about the state of things," Bowie said he didn't agree with that viewpoint, that "music itself carries its own message."

There was another message. Nicholas Pegg discovered that much of the first verse was lifted, nearly word for word, from Hans Richter's 1964 *Dada: Art and Anti-Art*. Richter, a Dadaist painter and filmmaker, contrasted Zurich Dada, "in placid Switzerland [which] preserved a psychic equilibrium," with Berlin Dada, which had the symptoms of a cultural neurosis, making Berlin Dadaists "intoxicated with their own power in a way that had no relation to the real world at all." The collapse of Imperial Germany in 1919 led to a "vacuum created by the sudden arrival of freedom and the endless possibilities it seemed to offer if one could grasp them firmly enough."

One of Bowie's greatest steals, cutting and pasting lines from an art history into a pop lyric, it also shows where his thoughts were in 1980. The contrast of placid Switzerland (his legal home) to manic Berlin, which he was leaving behind. The neurotic intensity of avant-garde artists like the Dadaists compared to his own "long chain with a ball of middle-classness at the end of it." How long could he keep going? What "new" was left for him? "Ever since the Dadaists pronounced art is dead, it's very hard to get more radical than that," he said. "Since 1924 it's been dead, so what the hell can we do with it from there on? One tries to [at] least keep readdressing the thing and looking at it from a very different point of view."

So: a different point of view. In "Up the Hill Backwards" Bowie is heard in unison with Tony Visconti, Chris Porter, and Lynn Maitland. Submerging his voice in the collective, with Maitland taking the high end of the harmonies (the idea perhaps came from Eno's "Tina and the Typing Pool" chorus for Talking Heads' "The Good Thing"), he wanted to make the song "very MOR voiced," to sound like "the epitome of indifference." The quartet instead gives strength and reassurance, cheerleading ("yeah! yeah!") in the title refrain.

Starting life as "Cameras in Brooklyn," its draft lyric was close to its final version (he originally sang "Skylabs are falling"). George Murray's fluid bass lines in the verses extend the vocal harmonies (as does the bed provided by the organ), while his lines in the outro counter Robert Fripp's soloing. Dennis Davis drives the verses like a drill sergeant, with calls to order on his snare. He's the center of an intricate percussion arrangement — claves in the intro, what sound like steam whistles (Harmonized cymbals?) in the refrains. Chuck Hammer's synthetic guitar lines, however, didn't make the final mix: "too bad, [as they were] perhaps the most exploratory of all the tracks recorded," he recalled decades later.

The track's bookended with what Bowie called "a high-energy Fripp quasi-Bo Diddley thing": guitar breaks in 7/4 time (Visconti, playing acoustic guitar, gritted his teeth and counted "1&2&3&4&5&6&7" through takes). Fripp's closing solo, which he described as "a system of echo repeats, fairly fast, on the guitar," is melodically constrained — the aggression's in his tone. The guitar breaks "give ["Backwards"] another kind of switch: it has far more power than it would first seem," Bowie said. "It has a very strong commitment, but it's disguised in indifference."

SCREAM LIKE A BABY

Recorded: (backing tracks) ca. 15 February-early March 1980, Power Station; (vocals, overdubs) ca. mid-April-early June 1980, Good Earth. Bowie: lead and backing vocals; Alomar: guitar; Clark: synthesizer; Murray: bass; Davis: drums. Produced: Bowie, Visconti; engineered: Alexander, Hendrickson, Visconti.

First release: 12 September 1980, **Scary Monsters**.

Over a discursive interview in August 1980, Bowie remembered the future. He regretted he hadn't been able to do a *Diamond Dogs* film and still thought his concept of feral punks roller-skating through ruined cities was a more likely future than what was being proffered by Gary Numan or the Human League, a future of sentient cars and robot men, of dreams of wires. "The kleen-machine future," the interviewer Angus MacKinnon called it. A false future, Bowie replied, perpetuated by television, politicians, and advertisers. "I don't believe in this hi-tech society at all," he said later that year. "I don't believe it exists: I think it's a great myth... one foresees [the future] becoming more terrifyingly *real*, *anti*-tech. The old symbolic street fighting thing probably won't be as symbolic as it was, but will become a reality. One can foresee it in the dreadful Eighties."

Bowie's Buddhist leanings led him to regard history as being cyclical, not progressive. His futures were collapses: war, neo-fascists, Big Brothers, nuclear holocausts. Finding himself in 1980, a year he'd half-expected never to come, he wrote "Scream Like a Baby," a song he could have written for *The Man Who Sold the World*. It's a sequel to "All the Madmen," the narrator again institutionalized and civilized by force. The backdrop of gays and other "undesirables" being clubbed off the streets, sent into reeducation camps, drugged, brainwashed, and liquidated, is the fascist Britain of Alan Moore's *V for Vendetta*, and the United States of Brother D with Collective Effort's "How We Gonna Make the Black Nation Rise," which warns of racial genocide ("the ovens may be hot by the break of dawn").

Decades later, Mark Fisher would shed light upon the late Seventies and early Eighties as the time when the future — the idea of perpetual progress and newness — started being dismantled. The kleen-machine future, in which humanity would exponentially improve, receded into the distance, never to be arrived at (see Donald Fagen's "I.G.Y.," which, with loving irony, wrapped the Fifties' idea of 1982, all jetpacks and undersea rail, into the year as it was lived). In the future's place came "a culture of retrospection and pastiche," Fisher wrote, in which "neoliberal capitalism's destruction of solidarity and security [had] brought about a compensatory hungering for the well-established and the familiar."

In "Scream Like a Baby" nothing has changed. The future remains the bad dream of the past. Adding to the future retro, the song was Bowie's rewrite of "I Am a Lazer," written in 1973 for his "soul" trio, the Astronettes, and which he'd cut (but hadn't used) for *Young Americans*. "Lazer" had a booming, hook-filled refrain, but here Bowie cluttered it, hanging its key between C minor (verses) and E-flat major (refrains), linked by a descending "Laughing Gnome" keyboard line and spanned by a bridge of augmented and diminished chords. In the bridge, starting at 2:39, two vocal tracks, singing the same lines and split across stereo channels, separate as Visconti speeds up one while slowing the other. It's a schizophrenic breakdown, with "Sam" the splintered piece of the singer's mind being snuffed out. The rousing Astronettes refrain is Bowie idealizing himself.

The time of "Are 'Friends' Electric?", *Scary Monsters*, and *V for Vendetta* is as far away from us as World War II had been for Numan, Bowie, and Moore. Maybe 2019 is Numan's future after all, with its blurred lines between virtual and "actual" reality, the omnipresence of soft machines. Yet Bowie's un-future, a world of street fighting, repression, and brute force, still lies beneath it, about to surface.

Is There Life After Marriage?

Recorded: (unreleased) ca. 15 February-early March 1980, Power Station. Alomar: rhythm guitar; Murray: bass; Davis: drums, cowbell. Produced: Bowie, Visconti; engineered: Alexander, Hendrickson, Visconti.

For *Scary Monsters*, Bowie planned to cover Cream's "I Feel Free," a song he'd performed with the Spiders from Mars in 1972, but a backing track cut at the Power Station was as far as it went. Twelve years later he finally recorded it for *Black Tie White Noise*, using a similar chord structure, guitar line, and tempo as the *Scary Monsters* take (see "I Feel Free".) What remains is the backing track, a demonstration by Carlos Alomar, Dennis Davis, and George Murray of what Bowie owed them. Alomar is spidery rhythm, Murray melodic steadiness; Davis cuts loose when he spots an opportunity. Bootleggers mistakenly gave the track the working title of another *Scary Monsters* piece (allegedly an unreleased song), the title being a joke by the just-divorced Bowie that he may have picked up from a Quentin Crisp revue.

SCARY MONSTERS (AND SUPER CREEPS)

Recorded: *(backing tracks) ca. 15 February-early March 1980, Power Station;*
(vocals, overdubs) ca. mid-April-early June 1980, Good Earth. Bowie: lead and
backing vocals; Fripp: lead guitar; Visconti: acoustic guitar, EDP Wasp, backing
vocal; Alomar: rhythm guitar; Murray: bass; Davis: drums, cowbell? Produced:
Bowie, Visconti; engineered: Alexander, Hendrickson, Visconti.

First release: *12 September 1980,* **Scary Monsters**. *Broadcast*: *8 February 1997,*
Saturday Night Live; 17 February 1997, Nulle part ailleurs; 3 March 1997, The
Rosie O'Donnell Show; 8 April 1997, 99X Breakfast Show (WNNX), WBCN; 18
April 1997, The Jack Docherty Show; 8 September 1997, Breakfast Show (KNDD),
The Mountain Morning Show (KMTT); 9 September 1997, Johnny Steele Breakfast
Show (KITS); 10 September 1997, Tammy Bruce Show (KROQ); 16 September
1997, KFOG; 25 September 1997, Live from Studio One; 30 September 1997,
WBCN; 2 October 1997, World Café (WXPN); 16 October 1997, WXRT. **Live**:
1983, 1987, 1995-1997.

"Scary Monsters (and Super Creeps)" was "a piece of Londonism," one
narrated by a Martin Amis-style "criminal with a conscience who talks about
how he corrupted a fine young mind." Bowie sang in one of "those terrible
Cockney accents" (as he wrote in a list of vocal/lyric ideas), giving an East
End flavor to his tale: "she 'ad an 'orror of rooms." As always dedicated to
his whims, he'd keep the accent for most live performances of the song.

It was a reclamation effort on an album full of them — some of it dated
to around 1975, a song called "Running Scared" that Bowie had offered Iggy
Pop in Los Angeles. "He was playing it on the guitar and wanted to know if
I could do something with it. I couldn't. He kept it and worked it up," Pop
said in 2016. (There's also a touch of the Big Bopper's "Chantilly Lace" in it,
showing that Bowie had Fifties songs on the brain: see "Ashes to Ashes".)

At the Power Station, "Scary Monsters" began as a mid-tempo all-major-
chord piece with lines like "too many people, too many teeth." Bowie
and Tony Visconti pushed the rhythm section until, in the latter's words,
"Manhattan-based funk musicians... play[ed] like a British punk group."
And not just any punk band. The distorted cowbell (via a guitar fuzz pedal)
is a tell that Bowie used Joy Division's "She's Lost Control" as a guide, with
the cowbell in a similar role as the synth-drum on the Joy Division track.

As Momus noted, Dennis Davis "is playing suspiciously Stephen Morris-like snare fills, as though someone has just played him the first Joy Division album right there at the Power Station." (On a lyric sketch page for *Scary Monsters*, Bowie wrote "Joy Div.")

Where "She's Lost Control" concerned an epileptic, the woman here is out on the street talking to herself, chased by demons. "Scary Monsters (and Super Creeps)" — Bowie said he nabbed the title from a Kellogg's Corn Flakes box offering "scary monsters and superheroes" prizes — has its corrupter corrupted, a contemporary Clarissa and Lovelace. After playing havoc with her, inciting her fears, making her dependent on him, the singer becomes obsessed with her.

The mix of "Scary Monsters" is full of collisions — Robert Fripp's ferocious guitar; the intro's descending dog-bark bassline, via the EDP Wasp synthesizer; the acoustic guitar strumming that holds everything together; the sibilance of Bowie's lead vocal (*"she's stupid in the street and she can't socialize"*); Davis' tom fills punctuating phrases; Bowie's quiver of backing vocals. It was one of Visconti's last analog masterpieces. After isolating a snare hit or guitar note, usually via razor blade, he "rearranged the faders, added special effects and equalization changes," then spliced the piece of tape back into the primary mix tape. He used the Wasp to have instruments trigger others — so Davis' kick drum eighth notes triggered George Murray's bass, which Visconti made "pulsate" by routing it through a Kepex noise gate. "Sometimes the kick drum and tom-toms that bled into the snare drum track also triggered the sequence."

The variable was Fripp, who soloed by playing "wrong" notes on his Les Paul Custom — he worked with the pre-chorus chords rather than the E major verse, worrying "D" and "B" notes in sonic tribute to his collaborator. The dynamism of its arrangement, Bowie's scraping vocal, and the pop rush of its refrains helped "Scary Monsters" create alternative rock: when Frank Black and Trent Reznor sang it with Bowie in the mid-Nineties, they were honoring their birthmother.

TEENAGE WILDLIFE

Recorded: (backing tracks) ca. 15 February-early March 1980, Power Station; (vocals, overdubs) ca. mid-April-early June 1980, Good Earth. Bowie: lead

151

and backing vocal; Fripp: lead guitar; Chuck Hammer: Roland GR-500 guitar synthesizer; Bittan: piano; Alomar: rhythm guitar; Murray: bass; Davis: drums; Porter, Maitland, Visconti: backing vocals. Produced: Bowie, Visconti; engineered: Alexander, Hendrickson, Visconti.

First release: *12 September 1980*, **Scary Monsters**. **Live**: *1995-1996*.

Around 1976, London clubs began having "Bowie nights," where DJs played Bowie records and clubgoers came dressed as an edition of him. For some, it was the pupal stage before they became punks. Others kept at it. By 1978, the big Bowie night was at Billy's in Soho, where Rusty Egan was the DJ and Steve Strange worked the door. By the turn of the Eighties, the scene had shifted to the Blitz Club in Covent Garden, where Bowie nights became competitive pose-offs. Doing a variation on Bowie was *work*. In summer 1980, Jon Savage saw a group whose lead singer, "banging around in a Lurex mini-dress, was drawing entirely from a vocabulary invented by Bowie. And people stood and took it." Egan and Strange formed Visage, later described by Simon Reynolds as "a confederacy of punk failures looking for a second shot at stardom" (so, very Bowie).

Bowie recognized his heirs, visiting the Blitz (he was sneaked in and ensconced in an upper room, like slumming royalty) and using Strange and other Blitz kids as mourners in his video for "Ashes to Ashes." Each party had few illusions about the other. Strange regarded Bowie as a skilled operator, someone "allowed to get his ideas across quicker than up-and-coming bands. He's always in the right place at the right time, checking out ideas. When he was in London he was always at the Blitz or at Hell." And Bowie bottled his thoughts into "Teenage Wildlife," his early midlife crisis song.

There was a tart individualism in Britain in the late Seventies, a taste of Thatcher's reign to come, and Bowie nights were part of it. Robert Elms recalled being a Billy's kid, walking through Soho streets piled with trash during the Winter of Discontent in 1978-1979. "Little peacock clusters, our plumage an affront to a still judgmental town," he wrote. "Billy's was like a do-it-yourself teenage version of a Neue Sachlichkeit painting, *Cabaret* on a student grant." Strange said "the Blitz was an escape route. When the kids were dressing up at night they were living the fantasies. The kids wanted somewhere to go to look good. They do go out to be noticed." In his autobiography, his memories were grander: "350 of the most creative, individualistic people in London would cram into the club." The Billy's and Blitz kids lived in performance, competing for status. As Elms wrote, "I had no idea what I was supposed to look like, but we all knew you had to *look* and make people look."

Bowie, who constantly altered his appearance, who had no ties to anyone — no longer a wife, no longer a country — fit this mood better than any other rock star of the time. Being Bowie had been a way of life for British teenagers since his *Top of the Pops* appearance in 1972. But "his example of self-creation was serious and playful," Simon Frith wrote in 1981. "His tastes, the selves he created, were impeccably suburban... Bowie was youth culture not as collective hedonism but as an individual grace that showed up everyone else as clods."

Now the game was more serious — there were as many press photographers at the club door as actual Blitz kids, and the scene was full of fashion reporters and label executives "calculating the commercial possibilities of a national Blitz culture." Touring in 1978, sampling scenes in London and New York, Bowie could see he was becoming an industry (the first-ever Bowie convention was held in Chicago while he cut *Scary Monsters*), being disassembled and used for parts. The Cuddly Toys took *Ziggy Stardust*, as did Bauhaus, who also raided *The Man Who Sold the World*. Duran Duran feasted on *Young Americans*, while Gary Numan built an altar to *Low*. Numan particularly irritated Bowie, to the point where Numan alleged Bowie had him kicked out of a TV show on which they were both slated to appear. Numan argued that "image is to be copied. That's the essential reason I created mine," that he "never claimed to be original," and that his success was owed to him filling a role for younger fans that Bowie had abandoned.

Bowie's public thoughts on "Teenage Wildlife" were that "ironically, the lyric is something about taking a short view of life, not looking too far ahead and not predicting the oncoming hard knocks," he wrote in 2008, where nearly thirty years before he'd said of the song "I guess it would be addressed to a mythical teenage brother if I had one, or maybe my latter-day adolescent self, trying to correct those things one thinks one's done wrong." The lyric's starting point was a word-pile of resentment and paranoia from which he quarried ideas for "Ashes to Ashes," "Teenage Wildlife," and "Because You're Young." On this page of densely-written text (part of the *David Bowie Is* exhibit), Bowie wrote "let's write about society and events of international import… who's going to lead the working clash? It ain't me buddy." Over the page Bowie keeps circling back to the idea of an impending crisis ("won't stop with Iran"). "There's going to be war… there's going to be chaos… you're not gonna turn away. Pricks will write songs about it and tell you 'it's the truth'." A few lines down, he becomes the prick: "it's not strange it happens every day… It's the truth." The working title of "Teenage Wildlife" was "It Happens Every Day."

The kids shouldn't look to him for answers. "Teenage Wildlife" is another take on John Lennon's "God," a bloody denial of past selves. "Don't ask me," Bowie sings, after breaking the fourth wall and referring to himself as "David." *I feel like a group of one*. The title is a play on adolescent abandon and teenagers as beasts. Pop and fashion are hard commerce, glam reborn as malicious ambition. ("The Conservative radicals were sounding really sharp," Peter York wrote in 1980, where ABC's Martin Fry later said that Britain in the early Eighties "wanted a strong figure. They wanted individuals. They wanted heroes.") A kid with squeaky-clean eyes becomes an ugly teenage millionaire. Pop stars are a succession of Lady Jane Greys, queens crowned and dethroned in a week. As Pete Townshend would say in 1989, "all pop music is a service industry."

The longest track on *Scary Monsters*, "Teenage Wildlife" is a series of hard demands on the listener, even with its Ronettes vocal hooks and the comforting piano of Roy Bittan, recruited from Bruce Springsteen's *The River* sessions in another Power Station studio (it took Visconti years to "warm up to this track"). As if leaving space for last-minute agitations, the song has no refrain: its verses end only when punctuated by the title phrase and a Robert Fripp guitar break. Yet it was meticulously constructed. Chuck Hammer, who provided synthesized guitar textures, recalled that the song "had a complex arrangement with a number of different sections, each requiring a different structure," and that Visconti patiently led him through the song's chord chart.

There's an ecstatic isolationism in Bowie's vocal — a performance that none of his imitators could have matched, let alone conceived. It's peacocking: he wrings out each phrase, swooping upward, haranguing syllables, unraveling as he sings, making flapping banners of words ("teenyage mill-yuuuun-aaaaaiiire") summoning new personalities on a dime (he sounds like Richard Butler of the Psychedelic Furs on the first bridge), placing stresses on words as if to break them, forcing and suppressing rhymes, closing out by singing "wiiild-liiife" at the frayed high end of his range. A vocal chorus runs beside him, sometimes in support, sometimes to translate, sometimes left in their own world to hum.

He wanted the guitars to be "a splintery little duel" between Fripp and Carlos Alomar, while Hammer's guitar synthesizer (used to greater effect in "Ashes to Ashes") adds an eerie choral tone. In his most glorious appearance on *Scary Monsters*, Fripp rewrites his work on "Heroes" — his yearning leads are the answer Bowie's kabuki of a vocal won't provide. If "Teenage Wildlife" was Bowie's bequest to his successors, it's a poisoned transfer of power. The future can't live up to him: the ambitious kid can't pass the test. Bowie considered it a central work of the period, writing that he was "still enamoured of this song and would give you two 'Modern Loves' for it any time," in one of his last public statements.

ASHES TO ASHES

Recorded: (backing tracks) ca. 15 February-early March 1980, Power Station; (vocals, overdubs) ca. mid-April-early June 1980, Good Earth. Bowie: lead and backing vocal; Hammer: Roland GR-500 guitar synthesizer; Bittan: flanged piano; Clark: Minimoog, Yamaha CS-80; Alomar: rhythm guitar; Murray: bass; Davis: drums; Visconti: shaker, other percussion. Produced: Bowie, Visconti; engineered: Alexander, Hendrickson, Visconti.

First release: 1 August 1980, RCA BOW 6 (UK #1, US #101). Broadcast: 5 September 1980, The Tonight Show; 22 November 1999, MusiquePlus; 29 November 1999, Later with Jools Holland; 27 June 2000, Bowie at the BBC Radio Theatre; 2 June 2002, Top of the Pops 2; 15 June 2002, A&E Live by Request. Live: 1983, 1990, 1999-2000, 2002-2004.

Scary Monsters for me has always been some kind of purge. It was me eradicating the feelings within myself that I was uncomfortable with... You have to accommodate your pasts within your persona. You have to understand why you went through them. That's the major thing. You cannot just ignore them or put them out of your mind or pretend they didn't happen or just say "Oh I was different then."
— Bowie, 1990

Two nuns, a priest, a girl in a party dress, and a sad clown walk abreast in a funeral procession. A sexton drives a bulldozer behind them. There's no burial, for there's no body (but there will be a grave). The clergy slap the ground as they walk, as if consecrating the beach. The clown, half-smiling, clasps his hands in prayer. His mother arrives late, nags at him as he dutifully walks along the strand with her. For a hymn, the mourners chant a children's bogeyman song. *My mother said, I never should/Play with the gypsies in the wood.*

This is the dream of a man in a padded room. He once was someone else. There's a monochrome memory, framed like a Fifties coffee commercial: he sits at breakfast, wearing his spacesuit, ready for his commute. *She packed my bags last night, pre-flight.* Protein pills, helmet on. The memory catches fire. The mourners from the beach appear in periphery. He's still in space, floating alone in the deep. He came home only to be stowed away in a basement. The papery visions of an old junkie. Dreams nested within dreams, like matryoshka dolls.

Somewhere in Ground Control, in a room visited only by custodians and lost interns, an ancient Telex machine rumbles to life. I'M HAPPY HOPE YOU'RE HAPPY TOO. A pause, as if it draws a breath. I'VE LOVED ALL I'VE NEEDED LOVE SORDID DETAILS FOLLOWING. But nothing else follows.

Action Man

On 6 February 1969, on a Greenwich soundstage, David Bowie dressed up as an astronaut. He was making a promotional film for a song that no one knew. The crew snickered at his costume (the film was a vanity project funded by his manager, in the hopes of reviving a stalled career), but when they heard "Space Oddity" in playback, stagehands began humming lines. As Bowie walked off the set, a crew member called him Major Tom. Bowie was delighted: he'd finally become someone else.

"Space Oddity" opens Bowie's tale, expanding it into space; "Ashes to Ashes" closes it, collapsing upon itself, sounding like a store's worth of music boxes opened at once. "Space Oddity" took Bowie's idea of the all-American GI and set it against the sublime, letting him fall into the deep. "Here we had the great blast of American technological know-how shoving this guy up into space, but once he gets there he's not quite sure why he's there.

And that's where I left him," Bowie recalled in 1980, when he brought Major Tom home.

He'd revised "Space Oddity" in 1979, stripping it down, showing the folk song that lay beneath its space-age trappings. The original "Space Oddity" was a theater piece, with its instruments (nasally Stylophone, parade-ground snare, soaring Mellotron) characters in a revue. Now Bowie clarified it, reducing it to a vocal melody, a twelve-string guitar, and a spartan rhythm section of piano-bass-drums. Instead of a countdown, seconds of silence. Instead of the back-and-forth of Major Tom and Ground Control, a solitary vocal.

Released as a B-side in early 1980, the "Space Oddity" remake led Bowie to consider doing a sequel. In New York, his band had cut backing tracks for a song called "People Are Turning to Gold." Compiling lyric ideas for it on a sketch page, Bowie wrote "It's not all Music that spacemen listen to/ Doesn't mean they don't pay back debts/Space talk is cheap — lightweight/ Gravity of the situation." In a retrospective mood, he knew the timing was right for a sequel: the start of a new decade, one that would be the funhouse mirror of the Sixties.

He said he'd wanted to see what had become of Major Tom in the Seventies, which had opened with moon landings and ended with Skylab crashing. "The complete dissolution of the great dream that was being propounded when they shot him into space," he said.

> We come to him 10 years later and find the whole thing has soured, because there was no reason for putting him up there... [So] the most disastrous thing I could think of is that he finds solace in some kind of heroin-type drug, actually cosmic space feeding him: an addiction. He wants to return to the womb from whence he came.

Valuable Friends

Rock 'n' roll was an overnight fad — you moved quick to cash in on whatever sold. "Johnny B. Goode" led to "Bye Bye Johnny," "The Twist" spawned "Let's Twist Again." Buddy Holly's "Peggy Sue Got Married," his sequel to "Peggy Sue," has a wry self-consciousness. It opens with Holly asking if you recall his older hit ("such an *early* song"). He equivocates — he's heard something, he could be wrong, he's only the messenger. "I just heard a *rumor* from a friend," he teases ("I heard a rumor from Ground Control"). There are vocal tics, oohs, moans, stagy interjections: "I don't *say*... that it's *true*," ("oh no, not again!"). Rock 'n' roll sequels expire in respectability. Johnny B. Goode leaves for Hollywood to make bad movies. Louie Louie goes back to his wife. Wild, irresistible Peggy Sue gets married, moves to a prefab house, has kids. Where else for Major Tom to go but back to Earth?

It's not only "Peggy Sue Got Married" that's heard in "Ashes to Ashes," as the latter is riddled through with other songs — Bowie called it a "1980s nursery rhyme." The moves between F and E-flat in Bowie's childhood favorite "Inchworm" are there, with slides from F to Eb to close verses (like Danny Kaye singing "Inchworm," Bowie rises and falls against a wavering choral counter-melody). The refrain is a children's chant for "the awful Eighties," Bowie said — it sounds like an old horror bricked up in rhymes — but it's also from Anthony Newley. "Typically English," a song in Newley's *Stop the World — I Want to Get Off*, starts with a "my mother said/I never should..." rhyme. The play is about a mime figure, Littlechap, who goes through life wanting more than he has. He finally realizes he's ignored his good fortune and makes a sacrificial bargain with death.

Day Flights

"Space Oddity" was built in stages. Its structure, its staggered arrangements, made it a one-way flight. It kept going up. "Ashes to Ashes" came together in pieces. There's a density in its mix — percussion (shaker, a stick hit off-beat), layers of keyboards, a synthesizer choir, a synthesized guitar solo, Dennis Davis' intricate hi-hat work, muttered backing vocals. The noises that are heard only once or twice: a sprinkle of piano notes; Bowie's groans during an instrumental break; piercing guitar chords.

First, the "People Are Turning to Gold" backing track: Carlos Alomar, playing opaque reggae, George Murray popping his bass throughout, and Davis, having to fulfil Bowie's charge to play "an old ska beat." Davis struggled through a session until Bowie drummed the pattern he wanted on a chair and cardboard box. Davis practiced all night, got it down the next day.

Roy Bittan played the main keyboard riff on a falsified Wurlitzer. A stereo

Wurlitzer had arrived at the Power Station with only one side working, and "even then not very well," Visconti wrote. So instead Bittan played a grand piano that was run through an Eventide Instant Flanger until Visconti "got a decent moving stereo image to emulate a Wurlitzer." The riff is an arpeggio figure which, instead of repeating every three bars as it first appears to do, has a "missing" bar that interrupts its progress, creating a disorienting sense of being in 3/4 against a 4/4 backdrop. The riff's odd structure works in tandem with the chord progression of intro and outro, an intrusion of B-flat minor into an A-flat major key.

Chuck Hammer's guitar synthesizer treatments (which he called "guitarchitecture") were another element. Hammer, who had toured with Lou Reed, sent Bowie cassettes to demonstrate his technique, for which he used a Roland synthesizer to get "infinite" sustain on his guitar notes. Bowie was intrigued and had Hammer come in once he and Visconti determined which tracks had the most potential for Hammer's sound. For "Ashes," Hammer layered four multi-track guitar textures, which Visconti recorded in a Power Station stairwell for greater reverb. Hammer played "various chord inversions for each chorus section," with each multi-track given a unique timbre via the Eventide Harmonizer and other texture effects. Hammer was the song's last mourner, ushering it out with Andy Clark's synthesizer, a high pitch in the chorus.

The resulting track seems built by a surrealist watchmaker, from the scuffles and shrieks in its margins to the warm chords that support its verses and bridges. One of Bowie's greatest studio moments, no live performance came close to it.

Dips and Swoops

Bowie wrote an extravagant melody (live, he often brought it down an octave) that, like the piano riff, often lands on contrasting beats ("funk" on the downbeat, "fun-ky" on off-beats) or singing through bars ("Major To-om's") and shifts between melodic arcs to near-conversational phrasings. It's as if the conductor of an orchestra is also the lead tenor. The first verse starts with Bowie swooping from a high A-flat to an A-flat deeper in his range ("re-*mem*-ber-a-guy that's-*been*"). After more octave falls comes a line with a shorter range, with Bowie as a newscaster breaking into the song ("oh no..."). Again, this is Buddy Holly. As Theodore Gracyk wrote, "Holly's dips and swoops embroider the beat and thus bind rhythm and melody together, dissolving the typical division between vocal and rhythm section... exploiting the peculiarities of his own voice." The second verse has the same structure, even if its falls are less severe.

By contrast, the two bridges are a series of arcs, with Bowie starting low in his range, rising to a high note and descending in the same breath. A menacing rumble in the first bridge, the voices grow more distinct in the second, delay-echoing the lead vocal — a deadpan voice repeats Bowie's "who-oh-oh." And in the refrain, Bowie again sings a series of falls: the last line is a descending sequence (Eb-Db-C) ending, appropriately, on "low." The song expires with its kid's chant, each line ending in a three-note descent. Major Tom, returned to the cruel world of children, is consumed by them.

Do Astronauts Have Electric Dreams?

"Ashes to Ashes" was Bowie's second UK #1 single (the first, appropriately, was a reissued "Space Oddity"). It was a surprise return to commercial form, as many, including his label, had written him off as a hitmaker. The promo film, directed by David Mallet to Bowie's script and set designs, merged the past (Bowie wore a Pierrot costume designed by his old collaborator/lover Natasha Korniloff) with the present (the Blitz kids as mourners). The video created the language of MTV as it disposed of Bowie's past selves, auctioning them off in images.

It's easy, perhaps intentionally so, to read Bowie's career into the lines of "Ashes to Ashes." The cold self-assessment of having done nothing spontaneously. The recovering addict trying to keep clean. The Nietzschean images of wanting to crack open the ice and free himself. Or how he'd described the legacy of glam rock in a 1979 interview: "In the beginning of the Seventies when it was sort of a bit dull, there was the idea of creating a flash of some kind. And the flash was created, but nobody was really found holding the smoking pistol. So [rock] sort of went off at tangents after that."

There's something sublime and eerie in "Ashes to Ashes," a song that lives in the nerves. As Tom Ewing wrote, it was as if "Major Tom thought he was starring in an Arthur C. Clarke story and found himself in a Philip K. Dick one by mistake, and the result is oddly magnificent." *Ziggy Stardust* had helped end the Sixties, but Bowie, moving from face to face, had remained, in his way, a believer, a child of the summer's end. Now he could taste winter. *It's the end, but the moment has been prepared for*, as Tom Baker, another Sixties remnant, said in his last words in *Doctor Who*, not long after "Ashes to Ashes" hit #1.

Bowie had far more years to run; there were far more songs to come and far more farewells. But "Ashes to Ashes" is his *last* song, the closing chapter that comes midway through the book. Bowie sings himself offstage with a children's rhyme: eternally falling, eternally young.

FASHION

Recorded: (backing tracks) ca. 15 February-early March 1980, Power Station; (vocals, overdubs) ca. mid-April-early June 1980, Good Earth. Bowie: lead and backing vocal; Fripp: lead guitar; Andy Clark: Minimoog, Yamaha CS-80; Alomar: rhythm guitar; Murray: bass; Davis: drums. Produced: Bowie, Visconti; engineered: Alexander, Hendrickson, Visconti.

First release: 12 September 1980, **Scary Monsters**. **Broadcast**: 24 October 1996, VH1 Fashion Awards; 27 June 2002, Friday Night with Ross & Bowie; 4 September 2003, Trafic.musique. **Live**: 1983, 1987, 1990, 1997, 2002-2004.

A dance song with bad intentions, "Fashion" was the last track completed on *Scary Monsters*. Bowie claimed it wasn't about politics, though "we are the goon squad" and "turn to the left, turn to the right," and how he sings the title as a near-homophone of "fascism," suggest otherwise. The draft lyric was more violent, with a scrapped verse that went "hell up ahead, burn a flag/shake a fist, start a fight/if you're covered in blood, you're doing it right," while the goon squad threatens to "break every bone."

He'd intended to update the Kinks' "Dedicated Follower of Fashion" (and his own Sixties satires "Join the Gang" and "Maid of Bond Street") for 1980, with hipness as an occupation, another not-so-subtle dig at the Blitz Kids (see "Teenage Wildlife"). "When I first started going to discos in New York in the early Seventies, there was a very high-powered enthusiasm and [the scene] had a natural course about it," he said. "[It] seems now to be replaced by an insidious grim determination to be fashionable, as though it's actually a vocation. There's some kind of strange aura about it." The video followed in this line, with its older would-be Blitz Kids doing a repertoire of flailing dance moves.

It began as a reggae spoof (the clicking of Andy Clark's sequencer as guitar upstroke) with a hook of "Jahhh-*mai*-ca!" Bowie was going to scrap the track until Visconti implored him to write a lyric. The next day, Bowie turned up with his lines (using the title of a song he'd written for the Astronettes in 1973, "People from Bad Homes," and a "beep-beep" hook from his goofball 1971 outtake "Rupert the Riley"), cut his vocals at his usual speed. Mixing started that evening.

Built on a few augmented chords (G7 and Fadd9 in the verse, B-flat7 in the refrain), "Fashion" was Bowie's best dance track since "Golden Years," with which it had structural similarities. Unlike the wide-spanning ranges of other *Scary Monsters* vocals, Bowie keeps to a comfortable three-note span for the verse. His phrasings are dance steps: opening with three descending notes, then a longer descending line. Even what sounds like a misstep in the second verse, with Bowie having too few syllables to fit the phrase ("dancing on *the-uuh* dance floor"), was there on his lyric draft sheet (written as "the-er"). The "misstep" is a miniature performance: Bowie puts weight on "the," drags it up an octave and extends it, conveying the sense of trying to foot his way onto a crowded dance floor.

Robert Fripp takes two eight-bar solos and some shriek-breaks, like the eruption starting at 2:43. The single edit neutered him, cutting an entire solo. Fripp called his performance "blues-rock played with a contemporary grammar": it's a run of dissonant tones that occasionally threaten to cohere into melodies. He was recorded across the studio room (the cavernous sound of the opening), then closer-miked with a flanger applied. Fripp cut his solos one morning in London after a night's drive from Leeds. "There's nothing you feel less like in the world than turning out a burning solo — fiery rock and roll at 10:30 in the morning — just out of a truck," he said.

Along with being Fripp's last bow on a Bowie track, "Fashion" is the end for George Murray, who previews the "fash-ion" two-note hook before Bowie sings it, and Dennis Davis, with his hissing disco hi-hat. Davis played to a drum machine pattern for the first time in his work with Bowie, and he was so tight in sync with it that Visconti kept both Davis and the drum machine in the mix at times ("I treated it with digital effects to make it more techno"). Bowie's concept for the track was "loud stamping dance sounds

— take out some instruments," but instead "people started overdubbing stuff onto it," Visconti said. "It grew into a monster."

CRYSTAL JAPAN

Recorded: ca. 15 February-early March 1980, Power Station; ca. mid-April-early June 1980, Good Earth? Bowie: Chamberlin? ARP?, synthesized bass? drum machine?; Visconti: synthesizers, vocal. Produced: Bowie, Visconti.

First release: ca. summer-fall 1980, "Crystal Japan" (RCA SS-3270).

The all-seeing internet has exposed the practice of celebrities doing TV ads in foreign countries for everything from whiskey to banks to furniture. (Sofia Coppola's *Lost in Translation* captures the end of the pre-YouTube era, when selling out overseas was a discreet, lucrative, and anomic business.) In March 1980, between *Scary Monsters* backing and vocal sessions, Bowie shot an ad for a Japanese liquor manufacturer, Crystal Jun Rock, filming a spot at a Kyoto temple and providing an instrumental called "Fuji Moto San" for the soundtrack. "The money is a useful thing," he said, adding that he got more airplay via TV ads then he was from radio at the time.

Allegedly considered for the album's closer, the retitled "Crystal Japan" was entirely the work of Bowie and Tony Visconti (who sang the treated falsetto vocal line). Only available as a Japanese single until it appeared a year later as the B-side of "Up the Hill Backwards," "Crystal Japan" has some of Bowie's most gorgeous melodies packed into its three-minute length: a Romantic motif that begins at 0:25; a subsequent choral melody and development; a resolution, with a gong-like synthesized bass; three-note patterns, in slight debt to John Williams' *Close Encounters* theme, that sparkle before the curtain falls. His finest miniature.

CAT PEOPLE (PUTTING OUT FIRE)
THE MYTH

(Bowie, Moroder; ["The Myth"] Moroder.) **Recorded: (soundtrack)** *(music) ca. early 1981, "Carla Ridge Camp," 1720 Carla Ridge, Beverly Hills, CA; (vocal) ca. July 1981, Mountain Studios. Bowie: lead vocal; Giorgio Moroder: guitar, bass, Minimoog, Polymoog; Michael Landau, Tim May: guitar; Sylvester Levay: Wurlitzer, Fender Rhodes; Brian Banks: Synclavier II; Charles Judge: Prophet-5, Jupiter-8; Leland Sklar: bass; Keith Forsey: drums, percussion; Craig Huxley: Blaster Beam; Alexandra ("Alex") Brown, Paulette McWilliams, Stephanie Spruill: backing vocals;* **(remake, "Cat People")** *ca. 10-20 January 1983, Power Station. Bowie: lead vocal; Stevie Ray Vaughan: lead guitar; Nile Rodgers: rhythm guitar; Rob Sabino: keyboards; Carmine Rojas: bass; Tony Thompson: drums; Sammy Figueroa: woodblocks; George Simms, Frank Simms, David Spinner: backing vocals. Produced:* **(soundtrack)** *Moroder;* **(remake)** *Bowie, Rodgers; engineered:* **(soundtrack)** *Brian Reeves, David Richards;* **(remake)** *Bob Clearmountain.*

First release: (soundtrack) *12 March 1982, MCAT 770 (UK #26);* **(remake)** *14 March 1983, "Let's Dance" (EMI America EA 152).* **Live:** *1983.*

1981 should have been a busy year. Bowie was considering making a new album, planning an exhibit of his acrylic paintings and experimental videos, and said that he'd tour in the autumn. John Lennon's murder put paid to that. A justifiably paranoid Bowie left New York in early spring 1981 to go home to Switzerland. There he hired an ex-Navy SEAL for a bodyguard and took classes in self-defense, learning to identify potential stalkers (he was advised to move, as fans knew his address). He skied, doted on his son, lived in well-apportioned exile. Oona O'Neill, Charlie Chaplin's widow, was one of the few who saw him. "He doesn't speak French very well, he doesn't know many people around here, and he really is quite lonely. So I'm his friend," she said.

At some point in 1981, he decided he didn't want to record, either. He was angry with RCA for poorly promoting his recent albums while flooding the market with repackages like *Changestwobowie*. He was also waiting out contractual obligations to his former manager Tony Defries — after October 1982, Defries would no longer get a percentage of royalties from his new recordings.

So instead Bowie acted in films and did the occasional one-off music project, like a song for the director Paul Schrader's garish remake of *Cat People*. The original *Cat People* (1942) is a subtle exploration of sexual repression and xenophobia: an all-American guy marries a "foreign" girl with a lethal past. Schrader's remake is a gory fashion spread. Though he wanted "to make a film about what Cocteau called 'the sacred monsters,' the things that have galloped through man's dreams since time immemorial," he was also infatuated with his lead actress, Nastassja Kinski, and his cameras leered at her through the film.

In July 1981, Bowie met with Giorgio Moroder at Mountain Studios. Moroder, who was doing the film's soundtrack, played him a C minor piece he'd recorded for the title theme, a slow builder that would have Bowie sing the opening verses in his lower register, then vault up for the refrain. Moroder's soundtrack was similar to what he'd done for Schrader's *American Gigolo* — a pop single as centerpiece; variations on it for incidental music (for *Gigolo*, it was Blondie's "Call Me"). *Cat People* opened with a brooding instrumental version of the title song, called "The Myth," with some Bowie humming. The actual song didn't appear until the end credits.

Bowie's lyric suited the film's pretensions (Kinski and Malcolm McDowell's would-be incestuous relationship was Schrader's homage to Dante and Beatrice, if the latter had transformed into panthers), with lines of burning, pulsing, lusting, and references to William Blake and Vachel Lindsay. "It works on a dream state, it feels like the kind of thing you go through at night," Bowie said of Schrader's film. "That's the way I took it lyrically." Moroder's soundstage gave Bowie license to go over the top. His sepulchral croon in the opening verses, channeling Iggy Pop and Jim Morrison ("I said 'Jim,' after hearing three notes," said the latter's widow, the writer Patricia Kennealy-Morrison. "Man, this sounds like an outtake from *The Soft Parade*"), works against minimalist percussion — a repeated cymbal pattern, clattered sticks — and yearning Prophet and Jupiter-8 synthesizer lines. The octave-leaping vault of *"gas-oh-LIIIIIIIIIIIIIIINE!"* that triggers the band's entrance is a magnificent moment, giving Bowie such punch in the mix that everything camp about the song falls away.

In its nearly seven-minute full version, "Cat People" goes on too long, with a coda that begs to be faded down, but its power was waiting to be tapped. A young Quentin Tarantino was amazed that Schrader had wasted such a song, using it a quarter-century later in his *Inglourious Basterds* for a sequence that unveils the scheme of the Jewish avenger Shosanna Dreyfus (Mélanie Laurent) to slaughter a cinema full of Nazis. Lines like "you wouldn't believe what I've *been through*" or "a judgment made can never bend" now acquired righteous purpose. Tarantino made "Cat People" seem as if it had been written for Laurent, who was born two years after its recording.

Bowie was unhappy with the Moroder track, telling Nile Rodgers he wanted to remake it for *Let's Dance* (it also meant one less song to write). "The way 'Cat People' came out on the soundtrack really bothered him," Rodgers said in 1984. "He didn't like it at all. He played me his original demo and I said, 'Wow, *that's* the way 'Cat People' goes?" Rodgers made it cut-time "but kept the same tempo so [Bowie] could sing the vocal the same way and the band could keep the pocket." The remake was more aggressive, with its verses halved, its intro rolled by Rodgers' guitar and snare fills, its backing vocals given a brittle, trebly sound by being routed through an Eventide Harmonizer and having their pitch raised a minor third. "I took the instruments away," Bowie claimed in 1983. "They don't weave quite such a magic spell over the construction of the lyrics... they get the chords right and that's about all I wanted to do." Stevie Ray Vaughan's guitar solo, full of glissandi and bends on his upper strings, greatly improved on the colorless solo in the original version, but Bowie's hoarse vocal and rushed phrasing was inferior: he even defuses the power of the "gasoline!" break, as if grand dramatics were now beneath him.

COOL CAT
UNDER PRESSURE

(Bowie, Queen; ["Cool Cat"] Mercury, Deacon.) **Recorded**: *ca. July 1981, Mountain Studios; (overdubs) ca. August 1981, Power Station ["Cool Cat" with Bowie vocals, unreleased]. Freddie Mercury: lead vocal, piano, organ, handclaps, finger snaps; Bowie: lead vocal, piano, synthesizer, handclaps?, finger snaps?; Brian May: guitar; John Deacon: bass, handclaps, finger snaps; Roger Taylor: drums, backing vocal, handclaps, finger snaps; David Richards: synthesizer? organ? Produced: Bowie, Queen; engineered: Richards, Reinhold Mack.*

First release: 26 October 1981, EMI 5250/E-47235 (UK #1, US #29). **Broadcast**: *(Bowie) 14 December 1995, The White Room; 26 January 1996, Taratata; 29*

January 1996, Karel; 19 February 1996, Brit Awards. **Live:** *(Queen) 1981-1982, 1984-1986; (Bowie) 1992, 1995-1997, 2000, 2003-2004.*

The comic book *Marvel Team-Up* followed a simple formula. In each issue, Spider-Man met another superhero, often fought him or her by mistake, then joined his co-star to defeat whatever villain turned up. While generally a make-work program for third-string Marvel characters, once in a moon *Team-Up* had an above-the-marquee pairing like Spider-Man and Wolverine.

"Under Pressure" is the *Marvel Team-Up* of Bowie songs: Bowie sharing the mike with Freddie Mercury in a duet that Tom Ewing compared to an exhibition match: "Sir Fred's mighty 'Why can't we give ourselves one more chance?' is the song's most ridiculous, glorious moment: a stunning strike from the Queen frontman whose over-the-top goal celebration ('give love, give love, give love') just prolongs the joy."

It began as a courtesy jam in the summer of 1981. Queen had booked Mountain Studios to record the album that would become *Hot Space*, while Bowie had settled into one of his personae for the decade —a tourist attraction for visiting bands. Queen "turned up in Montreux, which is not far from where I live in Switzerland. Needless to say, when groups come to record, they find out where I live... so this is how I tend to see a lot of bands — under the influence of Switzerland," he said in 1983.

David Richards, Mountain's engineer, called Bowie to let him know Queen was in town. Bowie turned up to chat, mainly about record advances — he was shopping for a label and wanted to know about Queen's label EMI. "You could see his one good eye gleam when Freddie [Mercury] used the words artistic control," an engineer at Mountain told Bowie biographer Christopher Sandford. "After that, David was all over him for details. Were the advances prompt? Who paid what?"

Bowie cut backing vocals and a spoken middle eight for a track called "Cool Cat," a song so dire that he asked for his vocals to be removed upon learning it would be on *Hot Space*. (The Bowie version was eventually bootlegged: he was correct.) After more than a few bottles were emptied, Bowie and Queen "started one of those inevitable jams," Bowie recalled. "I think the process was we were all drunk and... we were playing all sorts of old songs... whatever came into our heads," Roger Taylor said. "And I think David said, 'why don't we write our own? We don't have to play other people's stuff'." In 1982, Bowie said that "jams always come about when I haven't been writing much — I get a bit twitchy."

He was sounding out ideas on the piano ("the song was written from the ground up on the night I visited their studio" he said in 2004), though the kernel of the song was an unassuming instrumental track, provisionally titled "Feel Like," that Queen had been working on. The "skeleton of a song," as Bowie called it, "was quite a nice tune, so we finished it off... It was a rush thing, one of those things that took place over 24 hours. I think it stands up better as a demo." First called "People on Streets" and ultimately "Under Pressure," it remains a studio jam: Brian May's opening guitar line is little more than the arpeggiated pattern of "Feel Like," "a little tinkling guitar riff on top of John's bass riff" that Bowie was "adamant" he recut on twelve-string. There are several places where a performance would normally be touched up or redone — take the distortion on Mercury's mike and his stray flat notes, or Taylor's hesitations during double time sections. It was a minimal song structure. Keeping within D major, "Under Pressure" is just two verses and two bridges, the second of the latter extended to be the song's climax.

Bowie was the first to realize something was coming together. It reminded him of "Fame," "like what happened when I invited Lennon down to the sessions... this song appears," Bowie recalled in 1993. He bored down ("My God, it's caught fire!" he said at one point), with May recalling him saying "we should just press on instinctively: something will happen." Bowie suggested to Mercury that they go in the vocal booth without telling the other what they planned and sing whatever came into their heads. So Mercury's early scatted lines are him working out phrases he assumed he'd fill in later, and never did. "That's why the words are so curious, some of them anyway," May said. "There was a point where somebody had to take control... David took the reins and decided he wanted to rationalize the lyrics and then say what he felt they should say." After rough vocals were cut, Bowie employed a variation on his cut-up method — he assembled the best lines he and Mercury had sung, making "a kind of compilation 'best-of' vocal track, which would then be used as the template for the final vocals," May said.

A few motifs are heard throughout — a two-note synth line that sounds like a French horn (intro, verses, and outro) and a two-note piano quote. The rhythms build, with the piano (Bowie or Mercury) moving to vamping in the verses. Taylor shifts from hi-hat in the intro to his snare in verses to playing a crescendo for Mercury's bird-of-prey howls in the bridge, Bowie yelling "no! no! no!" as if an air raid's underway. May played a "heavy riff in D" that had Pete Townshend qualities ("it won't sound like the Who by the time we're finished," Bowie said at the time — he later called the song "*West Side Story* meets Queen").

Bowie was even apparently responsible for John Deacon's two-note bassline — six D notes, then an A; repeat, with minor variations. Twice in interviews in the Eighties, Deacon said that Bowie came up with the line, though May and Taylor have argued otherwise, that Deacon first played the hook and Bowie reminded him of it after a dinner break by singing the notes to him, even stopping him from fretting until he had the pattern down (all agree the bassline on the single is an overdub, done in New York). Set against the bare-bones percussion of the intro (claps, finger snaps, hi-hat: all mainly on the same track), the bass riff acts as a pedal tone, obstinately unchanging despite the underlying chord. It's so relentless (the "Ice Ice Baby" bassline swings a touch more, with an added sixteenth note jump back to D at the end of every other bar) that it makes the ear disregard any harmonic conflict — the song works in service to its bassline.

The last battles came while mixing at the Power Station a month later. Irritated by Bowie's power plays, May didn't take part, so it was Bowie against Mercury, Taylor, and the engineer Reinhold Mack. At some point the desk broke down, forcing Bowie and Queen to release a monitor mix as the single. It had copious reverb, particularly on the drum tracks, while sections of the mix (the bridges, for example) were bluntly given emphasis by suddenly removing modulation effects. "Under Pressure" came out in late 1981. The single sleeve had no photographs, its video was cobbled together by David Mallet from stock footage, Queen and Bowie barely promoted it at the time. And it hit #1.

People on Streets

The once-David Jones and the once-Farrokh Bulsara met in the late Sixties, when Bowie was an obscure folkie and Mercury was selling clothes in a Kensington Market stall. A decade later, Bowie and Mercury were the last glam superstars standing. Meeting by chance at the start of the Eighties, the two were compelled to deliver some pronouncement, a state-of-the-union address.

A problem with rock star "social commentaries" is that the star, isolated by money and sycophants, speaks in generalities, as though fearful of alienating constituencies with an inappropriate detail. So we get things like: *Feed the world. We are the world. People need to be free. The children are our future.* "Under Pressure" is a case in point. *People on streets*, Mercury and Bowie sing — so abstract a line it lacks definite articles. "Pressure" itself is so ill-defined that it's both a material force — burning buildings down — and a spiritual blight, causing divorce and homelessness. The brutal syntax of Bowie's "insanity laughs, under pressure we're breaking" doesn't help, while the song builds to the flattery of Mercury, offering unearned forgiveness for indeterminate sins.

Nick Lowe wrote "(What's So Funny 'Bout) Peace, Love and Understanding," which Elvis Costello covered five years later. Lowe's song is a sad hippie lost in a cruel world and wondering where the good times have gone — there's a touch of cruelty in it. But Costello took the lyric seriously, and the song, warming to its interpreter, became heartbreaking. "Where are the *strong*? and who are the *trusted*?" became indictments. Something similar happens in "Under Pressure," which is a sad hippie song beneath its arias and cannonades ("it's quite simply about love, which is the most un-cool, un-hip thing," Taylor once said), and it's owed to its singers.

Bowie and Mercury simply will "Under Pressure" into being far better than it deserves to be. Take how Mercury sings the cliché "it never rains but it pours," in an impossibly light falsetto or how he soars to the diva high note that even Annie Lennox would struggle to hit. It's a man carving his own monument. The ferocity of Bowie's appearance on the first bridge dispels some vagaries of his verse. Then there's his performance in the second bridge. It's a melody he's held back like an ace of trumps, the staircase-climb of "*love*'s such... an old-fashioned *word... dares* you to *care* for..." It's Bowie at his most humanist, his mirrors gone, his defenses down, making the claim that all that matters in the end is how much we love one another. It was his new hymn for the young dudes, and the most Christian moment of his artistic life — he closed it with the Lord's Prayer when performing "Under Pressure" at the late Mercury's tribute in 1992. Watching a rehearsal performance, George Michael started singing along in awe.

"Under Pressure" is a day's indulgence by two men moving past their prime, and who were entering a decade that would diminish them. Mercury had only ten years left. There's a sadness in their bravado, a loss in their heroics. Something is going away, going away for good, and they see it, if only in shadow.

BAAL'S HYMN

(Brecht, Muldowney.) **Recorded**: *(TV performance) 12 August 1981, BBC Television Centre, Studio One, Wood Lane, Shepherd's Bush, London; (EP) ca. mid-September 1981, Hansa Tonstudio 2. Bowie: lead vocal; uncredited musician: banjo (TV perf.); Erwin Milzkott: flute; Axel-Glenn Müller: clarinet; René Waintz: trumpet; Ralf Armbruster: trombone; Michael Bucher: tuba; Eckehard Scholl: piano; Uwe Weniger: viola; Rolf Becker: cello; Ingo Cramer: guitar; Bernd Machus: bandoneon; Ulrich Berggold: contrabass; Thomas Hoffmann: drums; Dominic Muldowney: arranger, conductor. Produced: Bowie, Visconti; engineered: Eduard Meyer.*

First release: *2 March 1982*, **David Bowie in Bertolt Brecht's Baal** *(BOW 11/ CPL1-4346, UK #29).* **Broadcast**: *2 March 1982, Baal.*

Starring in a BBC production of Bertolt Brecht's first full-length play, *Baal*, is considered a cul-de-sac in Bowie's career, a time-filling ploy whilst waiting out contracts. Only two Bowie biographies give *Baal* more than a scant mention. But *Baal*'s soundtrack EP is one of his best-achieved records of the decade — a farewell to the performer he once was and a glimpse of the artist he could have been and sometimes wanted to be.

In early 1981, the director Alan Clarke proposed reviving *Baal* for the BBC. Working with producer Louis Marks and writer/translator John Willett, Clarke would convey Brecht's "alienation" effect by using split-screen (actors, images, or intertitles would comment on actions shown in the other half of the screen). Bowie was a consensus choice for the lead, as Clarke and Marks noted his recent success on stage in *The Elephant Man*. After visiting him in Switzerland, they offered him the role, for which he received the standard BBC scale. Marks and Willett were surprised to find their rock star lead knew as much about early-twentieth-century Germany as they did, and Willett had edited the definitive collection of Brecht's poems.

Bowie considered *Baal*, like *The Elephant Man*, as a step to prepare for a life beyond rock 'n' roll. "I remember him saying that there was a limit to how long he could go on doing tours," Marks said. "There comes a point when you actually have to quit... He had one more tour he had to do at that point, [then] he wanted to embark on a career of acting."

Enough Sky When He's Dead

Before he was a playwright, director, theorist, or undesirable (having to flee both Nazi Germany and the postwar US), Bertolt Brecht was a poet. Inspired by cabaret performers in his native Bavaria, Brecht wrote verses whose rhythms are guitar down-strums; his poems are a kind of plainsong, as his interpreter David Bowie once said. While Brecht drew on classic German literature and narrative ballads, he also loved mass-produced pop culture, especially trashy sentimental popular songs. He preferred the latter to the *Volkslieder* ("pure" German folk music) in vogue after German unification, part of a revival of Germanic folklore and mythology (this didn't end well). For Brecht, *Volkslieder* was fossil-music that offered nothing to the working class of Berlin and Munich. As he later said, working people have no wish to be Folk.

Baal is the fruit of his youth in Augsburg and Munich, where he was a fitful student, walking around town and in the woods, writing on scraps of paper he kept in his pockets. Brecht's friends recalled *Baal* as a communal effort, a play that Brecht pulped from the lives of young artists who hung around his loft. It had a wayward path to production. Brecht revised the play several times after its initial 1918 version, cutting scenes, discarding and inserting songs. Performed sporadically in the Twenties, *Baal* wasn't part of the modern theater repertoire (one of its few notable productions was a 1969 West German TV play directed by Volker Schlöndorff and starring Rainer Werner Fassbinder).

It's an episodic portrait of a drunk, poet, moocher, singer, guitarist, seducer, murderer, and general agent of chaos. Brecht once called the character "the antisocial man," while Marks described Baal as a "quintessential amoral artist... a totally uncontrollable and dynamic and creative person." For Bowie, Baal was a contemporary artist, one "resigned to the fact that the human race is going to topple itself. In any given situation that he can concoct, the people in that situation will let the situation down and will ruin everything, and he expects that and wants that."

Brecht used *Baal* to rebuke the provincial, bourgeois, "enterprising," arts-loving Wilhelmine Germany of his youth, using barely-disguised episodes from the lives of the poets François Villon and Paul Verlaine (in 1926, Brecht, setting the play in line with current political leanings, invented a working-class inspiration, one "Josef K.," a washerwoman's bastard who died in the Black Forest). While Baal is monstrous, seducing and abandoning women and stabbing a friend to death, he's also without hypocrisy: "any vice for Baal has got its useful side/it's the men who practice it he can't abide." He's all ravenous life, as fearless of death as an animal.

Bowie's take on Baal drew on this, but he also played the character as a prototype rock star, a Wilhelmine Ziggy Stardust who consumes everything he sees, from the women he tumbles into bed to the clouds in the forest sky. It's tempting to call it a self-portrait of a faded self, a take on the Bowie of a decade before, who had absorbed as much of the world as he could while burning through friends and lovers. Baal is the righteous, devouring voice of Bowie's 1969 "Cygnet Committee," now encased in a stage performance, preserved as a keepsake.

The Quest for Fun

"Baal's Hymn" (more accurately translated as "Chorale of the Great Baal") is *Baal*'s fourteen-stanza prologue. As in the BBC production, the poem is often broken up in performance, its stanzas distributed throughout as between-scene commentary. Clarke and Willett reduced the hymn by two stanzas and occasionally jumbled their order, with the final stanza as epilogue.

Bowie had the benefit of Willett's strong translation, which kept the drive of Brecht's German, set to a pentameter with a hard weight on the last rhyming syllable. The BBC "Baal's Hymn" is only Bowie and banjo (a chord usually struck on each line's first and last beat), its appearances serving as set-changers and commentary on performances or intertitles shown in split-screen. It was murder to record — Bowie had to sing twelve Brecht quatrains (the banjo played by an off-screen accompanist), with takes repeatedly spoiled by construction noise elsewhere in the BBC studios.

For the "Baal's Hymn" that Bowie recorded in West Berlin a month after the TV play was filmed, the arranger Dominic Muldowney and Bowie had to rework the song as a unified performance, to let it build, rather than being, as in the BBC version, a set of a dozen similarly-sung verses. Bowie convened Muldowney, Tony Visconti, and Eduard Meyer to record the five *Baal* songs at Hansa Studios in September 1981. He told Visconti the session was a souvenir, that he was recording the songs for posterity and allegedly footing the studio bill (*Baal* was a kiss-off to RCA, a label Bowie had grown to hate: if they'd thought *Low* wasn't commercial enough, good luck selling this one). There was a more cynical motive, Willett speculated, wondering if Bowie recorded the songs in the studio to reduce the appeal of bootlegs made from the TV broadcast recordings. Whatever its inspiration, the *Baal* EP, released to coincide with the BBC broadcast in 1982, was a farewell to Berlin, where Bowie never recorded again, and to Visconti, with whom he wouldn't work again for nearly twenty years.

Muldowney scored the *Baal* songs for a fifteen-person band — one musician per instrument, to get the German pit orchestra sound, Visconti said. The group, all West Berlin pros, was the orchestra of percussionist "Sherry" Bertram. Muldowney was startled to hear Visconti's mixing, as he compressed and flanged instruments until "four strings sounded like four tanks." Bowie had wanted to sing live with the band, but he showed up late, having overslept. As these were German union musicians, the session began and ended on time. It was a beneficial tardiness, as listening to the musicians gave Bowie a chance to mentally rehearse his vocals, Visconti said.

Using as its basis an uncredited piece in Brecht's 1927 *Die Hauspostille* (a refrain in G major whose melody rises an octave, moving up in thirds for the first three lines, descending a third for the last), the studio "Baal's Hymn" had the most intricate arrangement of the sessions, while deviating the most from Bowie's BBC performance. After a flute and strings intro, Bowie sings over dramatically-chorded piano for three verses, followed by a strings and brass interlude. The remainder of the piece varies between this arrangement and one in which Bowie sings in a bouncing meter over tramping accompaniment. The effect was of Bowie doing a take on Scott Walker's late-Sixties covers of Jacques Brel, complete with florid asides to end phrases ("vul-chur SOUP!"). The operatic phrasing of "marr-vel-ous!" in the last verse would soon reappear on "Let's Dance."

For Bowie's vocal, Visconti and Meyer used the "Heroes" rig-up of having three mikes placed around Hansa's Meistersaal to capture Bowie's voice at different levels, imbuing the louder-sung passages with room ambiance. After cutting all his vocals in a few hours, Bowie took Muldowney on a guided tour of Berlin low-life, hitting transvestite bars and New Wave clubs. It was a night out with a Baal who became a global pop star instead of expiring in the Black Forest.

REMEMBERING MARIE A.

(Brecht, arr. trad.) **Recorded**: *(TV performance) 8-11 August 1981, BBC Television Centre; (EP) ca. mid-September 1981, Hansa Tonstudio 2. Bowie: lead vocal; uncredited musician: banjo (TV perf.); Milzkott: flute; Müller: clarinet; Waintz: trumpet; Armbruster: trombone; Bucher: tuba; Scholl: piano; Weniger: viola; Becker: cello; Cramer: guitar; Machus: bandoneon; Berggold: contrabass; Hoffmann: drums; Muldowney: arranger, conductor. Produced: Bowie, Visconti; engineered: Meyer.*

First release: *2 March 1982,* **Baal**. **Broadcast**: *2 March 1982, Baal.*

Brecht wrote "Sentimental Song No. 1004" on a train to Berlin in February 1920. Allegedly inspired by Marie Rosa Amann, an Augsburg girl whom he'd met in an ice-cream parlor, Brecht set his poem (retitled "Erinnerung an die Marie A") to the tune of "Verlorenes Glück," described by the playwright Carl Zuckmayer as "a vulgar hit tune well known towards the end of the war." After publication in 1924, the poem was sung on stage, recorded several times and, though not intended for *Baal*, it was reportedly used in its 1926 Brecht-directed production.

In the BBC *Baal*, "Remembering Marie A." replaced an ode to the latrine ("a place that teaches you be humble, for you can't hold on to things"). The setting is a tavern in an evening when Baal's humiliating Emily, a society woman he's recently seduced, while trying to seduce a young woman. Swapping in "Marie A." for the toilet song elevated the atmosphere for a moment, a dramatic pause furthered by Bowie's performance, in which he sang, strummed his banjo, and paced the length of the set, back and forth, against a tableau of tavern-goers.

In "Remembering Marie A.," the narrator recalls a late-summer day in his youth. As the three-stanza verse proceeds, the memory fades. He claims the girl means nothing to him now; he can't recall what it was like to kiss her. All he remembers is a cloud he'd spied for a moment on that lost afternoon, which dissipated as he watched it pass. Dominic Muldowney began with Brecht and Franz Bruinier's original music for "Marie A.," whose soaring melody lofted the disillusioned lyric. Bowie's vocal is a series of steady and aborted climbs, topping out at the climax of each verse on a high D: e.g., "it was quite *white*." The broadcast performance is briskly-paced, with Bowie in an acerbic voice (see the viciously garbled note on the last "moments"). The studio version, whose arrangement builds from piano to clusters of strings and woodwinds, finds Bowie more reflective and occasionally purple — one of his more Anthony Newley moments of the decade.

THE DROWNED GIRL

(Brecht, Weill.) **Recorded**: *(TV performance) 12 August 1981, BBC Television Centre; (EP) ca. mid-September 1981, Hansa Tonstudio 2. Bowie: lead vocal; uncredited musician: banjo (TV perf.); Milzkott: flute; Müller: clarinet; Waintz: trumpet; Armbruster: trombone; Bucher: tuba; Scholl: piano; Weniger: viola; Becker: cello; Cramer: acoustic guitar; Machus: bandoneon; Berggold: contrabass; Muldowney: arranger, conductor. Produced: Bowie, Visconti; engineered: Meyer.*

First release: *2 March 1982*, **Baal**. **Broadcast**: *2 March 1982, Baal.*

The playwright Carl Zuckmayer saw Bertolt Brecht at a party in Munich, in October 1923. When Brecht reached for his guitar, conversations died, tango dancers halted, and "everyone sat on the floor around him caught up in his magic spell." With a "raw and cutting" voice, clasping his guitar to his gut as if stanching a wound, Brecht sang "Remembering Marie A.," "Ballad of the Pirates" and "Ballad of the Drowned Girl." Zuckmayer felt hypnotized, his mind reeling. Brecht "had become an almost totally irresistible seductive force," John Fuegi wrote. "He could now usually impose his own will on virtually anybody."

Though inspired by the murder of Marxist revolutionary Rosa Luxemburg during the Berlin uprising in January 1919 (a provisional title was "On the Girl Beaten to Death" — Luxemburg was clubbed and shot by Freikorps soldiers, her corpse hurled into the Landwehr Canal), "The Drowned Girl" wasn't a keep-the-faith revolutionary memorial. It's in the gauzy realm of Rimbaud's poem "Ophélie," with Brecht detailing the slow decomposition of a girl's body as she floats down a river, her body burdened with seaweed, consumed by fish, washed clean even of a name, until she's reached such a state that even God forgets her.

Brecht included "Drowned Girl" in his later revisions of *Baal*. While tramping in the Black Forest, Baal hears that Johanna, a girl whom he seduced, has killed herself. "The Drowned Girl" is an amoral man expiating his guilt by taking cold delight in the business of death. Kurt Weill set the poem to music in 1928 for *Das Berliner Requiem*, a cantata intended for radio broadcast, which aimed to express what "urban man of our era has to say about the phenomenon of death," as he wrote.

Retaining Weill's music (an A minor lament that brightens to E major in its last lines), Dominic Muldowney's arrangement for the *Baal* studio take has a bassoon play a counter-melody, a guitar establish chords, strings provide a discreet backdrop and brass players (particularly a trumpet) only emerge in the last bars. Bowie's vocal didn't vary much from his TV performance, which he'd recorded on the last day of shooting. For both versions, Bowie took Lotte Lenya's recording as a guide (Weill originally scored the song for a male chorus), using her phrasings on lines like "through her limbs the cold-blooded fishes played," and his wrangling of the final notes is close to her own.

His main alteration was to sing the first stanza of "Drowned Girl" nearly staccato at times, which John Willett found a strange choice. He keeps low in his baritone range as the girl's corpse slides through the waters, then disperses the haziness of "when the sky that same evening grew dark as smoke" with the sharply-sung "k" in "smoke," which starts a rapid climb up the octave (a very Sinatra move, Muldowney said). The intimacy of the first stanzas is gone, with Bowie's voice resounding upon his triggering of two distantly positioned microphones in the studio, as he'd done on "Heroes." Muldowney called the performance "an absolute tutorial in how to paint a text": it was one of Bowie's finest vocals of the era.

DIRTY SONG

(Brecht, Muldowney.) **Recorded**: *(TV performance) ca. 8-11 August 1981, BBC Television Centre; (EP) ca. mid-September 1981, Hansa Tonstudio 2. Bowie: lead vocal; Milzkott: flute; Müller: clarinet; Waintz: trumpet; Armbruster: trombone; Bucher: tuba; Scholl: piano; Weniger: viola; Becker: cello; Cramer: guitar; Machus:*

bandoneon; Berggold: contrabass; Hoffmann: drums; Muldowney: arranger, conductor. Produced: Bowie, Visconti; engineered: Meyer.

First release: 2 March 1982, **Baal**. **Broadcast**: 2 March 1982, Baal.

Looking for a song for a performance scene (the 1926 Baal, the basis of the BBC production, doesn't note what Baal sings), Alan Clarke and John Willett retrieved a poem from the play's original version. Co-written with his friend Ludwig Prestel, Brecht's poem, known as "Baal's Song" or "If a Woman's Hips are Ample," dates to July 1918. The scene in question finds Baal performing for drunks at a seedy nightclub. He haggles over his contractual brandy rations, then sings an ode to screwing, grabbing his current fling from her seat so that he can hump her on stage. Afterward, Baal flees to the toilet with his banjo and crawls through the window to run into the woods. It's the end of his professional career.

Barely forty seconds long, "Dirty Song" was the shortest Bowie track since 1969's "Don't Sit Down." It varied little from the TV performance, which had Bowie singing to snare-and-brass backing. The EP's stage-Cockney vocal and woodwind/horn arrangement could've been from his debut album. Three nasty verses and it's over with a plop.

BALLAD OF THE ADVENTURERS

(Brecht, Muldowney.) **Recorded**: (TV performance) 8-11 August 1981, BBC Television Centre; (EP) ca. mid-September 1981, Hansa Tonstudio 2. Bowie: lead vocal; uncredited musician: banjo (TV perf.); Milzkott: flute; Müller: clarinet; Waintz: trumpet; Armbruster: trombone; Bucher: tuba; Scholl: piano; Weniger: viola; Becker: cello; Cramer: guitar; Machus: bandoneon; Berggold: contrabass; Hoffmann: drums; Muldowney: arranger, conductor. Produced: Bowie, Visconti; engineered: Meyer.

First release: 2 March 1982, **Baal**. **Broadcast**: 2 March 1982, Baal.

"Ballad of the Adventurers" is the last song performed in Baal, apart from the final stanzas of "Baal's Hymn." Unlike his other boisterous tavern performances, "Ballad of the Adventurers" is Baal singing to a few drunk friends, and he won't play until the lights are turned down. It's the end of his run: he's older, shabbier, a once-charismatic artist who's become a relic. He's been living out in the woods for years. Returning to civilization, he finds that the spaces he once burrowed within it have been filled in.

The song, a four-stanza poem included in most *Baal* productions, is interrupted after every stanza — Baal's banjo goes out of tune, his former lover Emily calls for the lights to be turned up, his friend Ekart yells for him to go on (Baal stabs Ekart to death when the song's over). It's a farewell to rebellion — a song to honor conquistadors, seafarers, and marauders, those whose only peace was in their mother's womb. The song ends with a glimpse of empty blue sky: Baal's only conception of eternity. Compared to the BBC performance, the studio take is a full-bore assault in Bowie's stagiest voice, his most "formal" vocal on the EP. "Ballad of the Adventurers" is Bowie's version of Tennyson's "Ulysses": a waning creative power who vows to keep hounding at life until it's finally rid of him.

Bowie's Eighties would be a decade of multi-platinum albums, pop musicals, TV commercials, world tours. *Baal* seems in retrospect a path declined, a doorway into an alternate life in which he settled into the commercial avant-garde. Collaborating with Robert Wilson, Jean-Michel Basquiat, or Laurie Anderson. Scoring or starring in Jim Jarmusch or Wim Wenders films. Making soundscape records for Nonesuch, performing Brecht on the London stage. Instead *Baal*, as with so many Bowie artifacts, became a boundary marker.

CHAPTER FIVE:

THE STRIKE PRICE

(1982-1985)

The price at which you have the right to buy or sell the stock... By itself, the strike price has no value. You could say it is like a series of steps on a staircase.
— Michael Sincere, *Understanding Options*

He got what he wanted but he lost what he had!
— Little Richard

Here comes my Chinese rug!
— Iggy Pop, "Success"

It's not that I've got anything against money. It's just what you have to do to get it.
— Colin (Eddie O'Connell), *Absolute Beginners*

I could not concentrate at Chess, draw one and lost one of three games by simply forgetting to look at the board. Once I am sure I have won, I lose interest... I should like to hand over the game to a secretary to finish off for me.
— Aleister Crowley, *Magical Diaries*, 1923

Here in Mahagonny, life is lovely.
— Scene title in Brecht/Weill's *Mahagonny-Songspiel*, 1927

LET'S DANCE

Recorded: (demo) 19 December 1982, Mountain Studios, Montreux; *(album)* ca. 3-20 January 1983, Power Station, New York. David Bowie: lead vocal; Stevie Ray Vaughan: lead guitar; Nile Rodgers: rhythm guitar; Rob Sabino: Hammond organ, keyboards, bass synthesizer?; Erdal Kızılçay: bass (demo); Carmine Rojas: bass; Omar Hakim: drums; Sammy Figueroa: woodblocks, congas, tambourine; Mac Gollehon: trumpet; Robert Aaron, Stan Harrison: tenor saxophone; Steve Elson: baritone saxophone; George Simms, Frank Simms, David Spinner: backing vocals. Produced: Bowie, Rodgers; engineered: Bob Clearmountain.

First release: 14 March 1983 (EA 152, UK/US #1); (demo) 8 January 2018 (download). *Broadcast*: 27 June 2000, Bowie at the BBC Radio Theatre; 15 June 2002, A&E Live by Request. *Live*: 1983, 1985, 1987, 1990, 1996, 2000, 2002-2004.

It begins in hysteria. A mass of singers surge upward by thirds — aaaah, *aaaah*, **aaaah**, AAAAAAH. A guitarist plays a chord, slides down the neck to invert it, does it again. Drums, bass, trumpet, saxophones convulse. It's an explosion you've heard before — the climax of the Beatles' "Twist and Shout," a rave-up to drive audiences wild. For "Let's Dance," it's the *intro*.

"Let's Dance" was bred to conquer. The producer Nile Rodgers and engineer Bob Clearmountain crafted it to pop when heard on the radio ("it's got a hard cut, very high on treble — it *sears* through," Bowie said at the time) but still heavy enough to hold the dance floor. The seven-minutes-thirty version on the LP and 12" single is a series of set pieces (trumpet solo, guitar solo, percussion solo, saxophone solo), as if a DJ's shuffling through dance instruction records. The single edit is pure economy, with Stevie Ray Vaughan's first appearance truncated to a single note.

It starts mid-leap, stays in the air. (Bowie said it was his response to American television: a show had to hook you in its first thirty seconds or you switched channels.) Verse and refrain are fused together, while the bridge works as another refrain, building to the peak: Bowie, over the "Twist and Shout" crescendo, makes two halted attempts to move up — "if you should fall... into my arms" — and finally summits with a fifth-spanning, wildly-mannered "trem-ble-like-a *flowwwww-er*!" ("ripped, Expressionist, semi-Japanese," as Momus described his phrasing), as if still in character from Brecht's *Baal*. It's the watermark on his mega pop hit, daring his imitators to use it.

There's a severity in "Let's Dance," in its refrains, in its imperial vocal, in how each of its instruments is penned in its own cage. Listening to "Let's Dance" is like spinning past rows of iron sculptures. Yet it's the most *popular* Bowie song, more than "Changes," more than "Young Americans" or "Rebel Rebel" or "Space Oddity." A bar of it announces Bowie's cameo appearance in *Zoolander*; it's his oeuvre in a ringtone. The biggest single of his life, "Let's Dance" hit #1 in the UK, #1 in the US, #1 in Canada, Ireland, Holland, Switzerland, New Zealand, Norway. It made him, at last, the colossal celebrity that he had pretended to be.

It was coronation music for Bowie's new incarnation, the hip CEO figure found on stage throughout 1983, starring in a run of hit videos — the blond bouffant, the monochrome suits with dangling, unknotted neckties, the golf gloves, the modest dancing. It was Bowie as "an avatar of pure fame," a logo like the Nike swoosh. The Man Who Sold Himself to the World, which bought him.

A Brief Aside on Money

Before he made *Let's Dance*, Bowie hunted for a new record deal. His contract was up with RCA, which was foundering: it had lost $14.5 million in 1981 alone, thanks to an industry-wide slump in record sales, while a bet on manufacturing videodiscs was proving disastrous with the rise of VCRs. In 1985, General Electric would buy the label, then sell it off within a year to Bertelsmann. So in its last years of independence, RCA didn't have the capital to satisfy Bowie, who was their Bob Dylan: great press and prestige, mediocre sales. Bowie wanted Michael Jackson or Fleetwood Mac-level money, but he sold nowhere in their range, particularly in America.

As of 1982, few of his albums had gone platinum: only the compilation *Changesonebowie* in the US and four albums in the UK. He reportedly had only sold ten million albums between 1972 and 1982 — by contrast, eleven million copies of *Frampton Comes Alive* sold in a single year. And where most of his mid-Seventies albums had gone gold, the "Berlin" albums had been relative duds — *Lodger* had reportedly moved only 153,000 units four years after its release. Bowie was so commercially marginal in the US that K-Tel declined to acquire the North American rights to issue the compilation *Best of Bowie*. George Lukan, a K-Tel executive, said that because his label would have needed to spend $500,000 on US promotion, they would have had to sell 700,000 copies to break even "and we didn't feel we'd be able to do that in the US with Bowie."

If he'd still had to share earnings with his former manager Tony Defries, perhaps Bowie would have been content to remain a top-tier cult artist. But the agreement expired in 1982. Bowie could now keep every penny he earned. He'd make radio-friendly tracks and hype them — press conferences in London, New York, and Tokyo; interviews with everyone from *Modern Recording & Music* to *Penthouse*. Quick to realize the potential of music video, he would be at the core of the early MTV universe, as iconic a character as Boy George or Annie Lennox, but one with a history that new fans could discover in back issues.

After negotiating with four labels, he chose EMI, with which he signed a three-album deal reportedly worth $17 million (about $36 million, inflation-adjusted). At a press conference at the Carlyle Hotel to announce the deal, Bowie, wearing a natty tweed suit, looked as if he'd acquired EMI in a takeover bid.

Non-Uptight Music

One night in autumn 1982, in the drafty VIP section of the New York club The Continental, a drunk Billy Idol was babbling to Nile Rodgers. Rodgers, escaping, spied Bowie sitting alone. "He was dressed almost as though he was the manager of the club," Rodgers recalled. "All he wanted to do was talk about jazz — he knew so much and was really into some pretty out-there, avant stuff." Soon afterward, Bowie asked Rodgers to produce his next album, thus dumping Tony Visconti, who had already penciled in three months to record.

Visconti's ousting seems inevitable in retrospect, as Bowie had determined to clean house. On set for *Merry Christmas Mr. Lawrence* a few months before, Bowie told an interviewer that he wanted to work with new people. Even Carlos Alomar was gone after being refused his customary request for a raise and offered a lowball fee.

In Rodgers, Bowie saw a proven hitmaker. Rodgers was hungry. Chic had suffered from the disco backlash and Rodgers' development of a post-disco minimalist sound on his *Adventures in the Land of the Good Groove* (a record built on bass synthesizer, guitar, and Linn Drum) had gone nowhere. Rodgers saw Bowie as a way into art rock; he thought he'd be producing a *Dark Side of the Moon* for the Eighties. Instead "David's directive was clear," Rodgers said, recalling that Bowie said "I want you to make *hits*. That's what you do best. You make *hits*... It's a fact."

Promoting *Let's Dance*, Bowie rolled out catchphrases for the album — simplicity, directness, warmth, "organic." No synthesizers!, as if he was an honorary member of Queen (who were using synthesizers by this point). No more experimentation. "I don't have the urge to play around with musical ideas. At the moment."

Working with Nagisa Oshima on *Merry Christmas Mr. Lawrence*, Bowie, who always kept an eye on his directors, saw that Oshima shot in sequence, with no dailies. When a reel was finished, it was mailed off. "Two takes and it was done," Bowie marveled. "For the first time, I was caught up in the momentum of making a film... You only get one shot at it... It was a bit like making old rock 'n' roll records, when James Brown and his band would do it just once." Upon his return to Japan, Oshima had a rough print of the film in four days. Making *Let's Dance*, Bowie and Rodgers worked at a similar pace — most songs needed one or two takes to nail the backing tracks; Bowie cut his vocals with the usual dispatch; there were no outtakes; recording and mixing was completed in roughly seventeen days.

Isolated on Rarotonga in the Cook Islands while filming *Mr. Lawrence*, Bowie had for company a selection of records from his collection — mostly Forties and Fifties R&B, jazz, jump blues, early rock 'n' roll. The Alan Freed Rock 'n' Roll Orchestra. The saxophonist Red Prysock. Bandleaders Stan Kenton and Johnny Otis. Blues guitarists Buddy Guy and Albert King. Nothing under twenty years old. "I wanted to find stuff I could play over and over again... I asked myself: why have I chosen this music? What is it about it that makes me play it over and over again?" Bowie concluded it was "non-uptight music. It comes from a sense of pleasure and happiness."

The immediacy of these records, their insistence, their stark emotional highs and depths, countered what Bowie considered a "vacuousness" in contemporary pop. *Let's Dance*, its title spelled out in dance step instructions, has a cover photo of Bowie in the boxing ring, ready to take on all comers to the title. If his "Berlin" albums had been Expressionist, now came his *Neue Sachlichkeit* — the Weimar German art movement which had rejected

Expressionism for more realist works. When he first heard Little Richard as a boy, Bowie said he thought, "This is my paint and canvas... this is the pliable stuff that I can use." Here were his pliable materials, new music with "that quality of necessity."

Make It Dance

In December 1982, Rodgers flew to Bowie's home in Lausanne, Switzerland. Bowie sat down with his twelve-string acoustic guitar (Rodgers noted it only had six strings) and ran through songs: chords, top melodies, a refrain or two. Before he started one, Bowie said he thought *this* was the hit. It sounded like a folk song, its verse/refrains in bleak B-flat minor, with fleeting escapes to Gb major (its bridge is centered on the brighter Ab major). "I was like, 'that's not happening, man,'" Rodgers recalled to Paul Trynka. "It totally threw me. It was not a song you could dance to."

How could you have a song called "Let's Dance" that "sounded like Donovan meets [Anthony] Newley, and I don't mean that as a compliment," as Rodgers later wrote? For Rodgers, this paradox was white privilege. Black artists, he said, have to work more literally — if a black band has a song called "Let's Dance," it's a dance song, end of story. "It's not because there isn't interesting intellectual subject matter for black artists to delve into, it's the fact that you won't get played," he told David Buckley.

Hired to make hits, for a first test Rodgers was given an alleged hit song in which he "could only hear what was missing." He started by making the song less tentative in feel, replacing "the strummy chords... and the moving voice... with staccato stabs and a strict harmonic interpretation." He filled it with brief silences, making a groove out of contrasts, reducing melodic movement, and plotting a series of spotlight turns. For Rodgers' guitar part in the verse, which he'd first played as a "chucking" syncopated pattern, he pared it down to four quickly-played chords every other bar. "I was so afraid of 'disco sucks' that I didn't want to chuck anymore," he said. The rhythm came more from the delay effects. (On its demo, Rodgers "chucks" on guitar far more—it's basically Bowie singing over a Chic demo.)

Every piece of "Let's Dance" was pared, cut, altered. Rodgers made a studio demo with "some Swiss cats," including future Bowie collaborator Erdal Kızılçay. When Kızılçay tried out a florid, Jaco Pastorius-inspired bassline,

Rodgers reportedly said, "don't play that shit — it's not your solo album, it's David Bowie's." The final bassline was two alternating hooks: a four-note stepwise descent and a five-note pattern that falls a step or holds on the same note (first heard at 0:15 and 0:11, respectively). (Despite Bowie's "no synthesizer" claims, Carmine Rojas' Fender bass sounds blended with Rob Sabino's bass synthesizer, a Rodgers trick to expand the bass' dynamic range.)

Then there were the drums. Omar Hakim's intricate kick pattern, which only repeats every eight bars (Duran Duran soon nicked it for "Union of the Snake"), is just one piece of a crushing gated-snare drum track. This sound had been developed at the Power Station by engineers like Clearmountain, and at London's Townhouse for Phil Collins' drum tracks on Peter Gabriel's 1980 album (besotted with the gated snare, Collins would devote the decade to its worship.) Engineers always wanted to improve the "snap" of a snare drum: it was a thankless task, as tape never captures the sound of a snare head being struck live. Using a reverb-heavy room meant that mikes picked up echoes of the snare hit, and so muddied it.

Clearmountain and Townhouse engineer Hugh Padgham found similar solutions: place a mike right on the snare to record the hit, and rig stereo ambiance mikes above the kit, equipped with noise gates. These mikes would capture the reverb from a stick hitting the snare for a half-second, then switch off. On tape was the hard snap of the hit and a dose of explosive reverb that abruptly stops: the snare hit became a block of pure force. (Drummers needed to avoid using cymbals, Padgham later said. "If there are cymbals at the same time it sounds like somebody hitting a giant dustbin. It completely annihilates the drums.")

This inhuman precision, an acoustic instrument made into a synthetic giant, defines "Let's Dance," a track on which Sammy Figueroa's woodblocks sound like a mechanical rattlesnake. Rodgers altered saxophone and trumpet lines by recording a rhythm guitar track, then using a Kepex processor "to overlay the guitar rhythm on the horns. It sounds almost unnaturally tight. The attacks come from out of nowhere. There's no pre-attack breathing. The horns just come in, 'pop pop,' and then decay out fast" (especially from 3:30-4:00). The use of echo returns was again triggered by the Kepex. "The echoes would move about, depending on what the rhythm section was doing," Rodgers said. Heard in isolation, the vocal tracks sound as if they were recorded in a canyon.

Past Perfect

First in New York and later in Switzerland, Bowie kept playing Rodgers records and showing him things he was interested in: jazz album sleeves, paintings, photographs. Rodgers said it was like "a snapshot of Bowie's brain," and he flashed on what Bowie wanted when he saw Bowie's photo of a bouffanted Little Richard getting into a space-age Cadillac. "This picture still looked like the future," Rodgers said. "He wanted me to make a record that sounded like the future, but still sounded like the essence of rock 'n' roll and R&B, but would be timeless."

"Let's Dance" is how Rodgers fulfilled the brief: it's an Eighties MTV pop hit shuffled together from Fifties and Sixties records. Its title is that of a Chris Montez song Bowie had played with his first band; there's the "Twist and Shout" rave-up and a melodic steal from "She Loves You" in the bridge; the brass riffs were lifted from Henry Mancini's *Peter Gunn* soundtrack. Stevie Ray Vaughan, after taping his guitar solo, admitted he was straight-out playing Albert King licks. "Let's Dance" was a sampler of American music, a catalog in jump-cuts: electric blues, funk, Hollywood jazz, R&B, rock 'n' roll, Latin (Figueroa's congas and woodblocks) and even a dueling tenor saxophone break that sounds more like the World Saxophone Quartet than a contemporary R&B horn section.

Prised out of the casing Rodgers devised for it, "Let's Dance" is fragile, regretful, and ominous (Bowie would heighten this mood when he rearranged the song for his last tours: let's dance, for tomorrow we may die ("this is our last dance," he'd sung not long before)). An apparent inspiration was Aleister Crowley's "Lyric of Love to Leah," with its call to dance "to the moon and Sirius." *Put on your red shoes and dance* is a triple reference. The medieval "St. Vitus dance" outbreak in Strasbourg where hundreds of people fanatically danced for days, until falling unconscious or dying — the mad dancers "cured" at last by having their bloody, bruised feet put into red shoes and then made to circle a statue of St. Vitus. Then there's Hans Christian Andersen's tale, in which a poor girl wears red shoes that she can't take off, and which make her dance without stopping until she has her feet chopped off. And the 1948 Powell & Pressburger film *The Red Shoes*, in which a ballerina performing an adaptation of Andersen's story hurls herself off a balcony.

In all these cases, dancing spreads like a plague. There's desperation in

Bowie's imperious tone, his croaking phrases. The whole song is conditional — *let's dance, let's sway; if you say run, I'll run; if you should fall.* Nothing actually happens. No matter: it carried on a broad wavelength, a song for a crowd, its emphasis on the plural: "they're" playing music on the radio. Go back to that day in Switzerland, when Bowie played his doomy ballad to Rodgers. He knew Rodgers was alchemist enough to turn it into a hit. "Let's Dance" finally made Bowie. What would it make of him?

Modern Love

Recorded: ca. 3-20 January 1983, Power Station. Bowie: lead vocal; Rodgers: rhythm guitar; Sabino: piano; Rojas: bass; Hakim: drums; Gollehon: trumpet; Aaron, Harrison: tenor saxophone; Elson: baritone saxophone; George Simms, Frank Simms, Spinner: backing vocals. Produced: Bowie, Rodgers; engineered: Clearmountain.

*First release: 14 April 1983, **Let's Dance** (EMI America AML 3029/SO-517093, UK #1, US #4). **Broadcast**: 4 September 2003, Trafic.musique; 11 September 2003, Friday Night with Jonathan Ross; 18 September 2003, The Today Show. **Live**: 1983, 1985, 1987, 1990, 2003-2004.*

Released in September 1983 as *Let's Dance*'s clean-up hit, "Modern Love" in video form was a recapitulation of triumphs: shots of Bowie working a crowd in Philadelphia, his preferred city for live footage. It was a rock video as tour commercial — don't miss the giant inflated crescent moon! The horn section in pith helmets! Coming to your town next!

The song itself, its backing tracks cut on the first day of the *Let's Dance* sessions in January 1983, was stranger: a cultural doom-piece like "Five Years" recast as a boogie, nihilism in the high key of Little Richard, who inspired its call-and-response vocal arrangement ("it all comes from Little Richard," Bowie said) and its drumline, a gated descendant of Charles Connor's barrage on "Keep a Knockin'." Rob Sabino's piano, the track's prime mover, is a dancing homage to players like Johnnie Johnson; the saxophone solos (swaggering baritone break, soaring tenor coda) are in the line of Fifties R&B honker Earl Bostic.

The Kinks' "Come Dancing," released right before *Let's Dance* was recorded, has affinities. Ray Davies sings of how rock 'n' roll killed off big band jazz, how the liberated Sixties buried the Forties, for good or ill. In "Modern Love," rock 'n' roll is the endangered music, coasting on glories. Whatever transcendence it offered is gone, leaving colors and noise, consolations of memory. The first verse opens with Bowie buying a newspaper that tells him there's no news. The refrain progression runs through the key of C major like a shuttle train (C, D, Em, Fmaj7), while its lyric is a flowchart, moving from modern love to "church on time" to "God and man" and back again (paralleled harmonically by a return to the tonic chord, C major, upon each disappointment). It's an uptempo take on John Lennon's "God," with Bowie checking off everything that's failed him — religion, confessions, marriage, love. He ends where he started, on "modern love," most glamourous of false gods. "It's answering the questions of chaos with chaos," he once said of the song.

His spoken opening lines are the song's only decisive force: "I know when to go out. I know when to stay in: get things done." A shareholder letter, the words of a counterfeiter for a debased time, a man clean of vices and ready to work. He never doubts himself, despite what he encounters; he'll sell you through it. The Simms brothers and David Spinner, who sound like a demented glee club on most of *Let's Dance*, are put to good use as audience surrogates, chanting back what Bowie feeds them, being whipped along before him.

"Modern Love" was Bowie's usual encore closer for his 1983 and 1987 tours, where he burned through the song. The studio version is a slower build, opening (in 6/8 time) with Nile Rodgers' stuttering guitar riff, like someone trying to tug a motor into life, that's soon met by Omar Hakim's drums (it's the reverse of the opening of "Lust for Life"). Carmine Rojas' bass holds the low end, with murmured commentaries to tie off verses, while the penned-up saxophones are raring to go as the second verse ends. Bowie holds back until, having gone through his circle of disappointment again, he accepts the inevitable — when there's nothing of value left, one must accept nothing, and work at it. "MODERN LOVE!" he cries, caught up in it. Everyone's borne along: frantic singers, frantic horns, cymbal-happy drummer. The fade comes while everyone's dancing in a circle. The communal joy of "Modern Love" is that of a life in which work is the last religion standing. A song pressed for its times.

SHAKE IT

Recorded: ca. 10-20 January 1983, Power Station. Bowie: lead vocal; Vaughan: lead guitar; Rodgers: rhythm guitar; Sabino: keyboards, organ, Prophet-5; Rojas: bass; Tony Thompson: drums; Figueroa: woodblocks, congas; Gollehon: trumpet; Aaron, Harrison: tenor saxophone; Elson: baritone saxophone; George Simms, Frank Simms, Spinner: backing vocals. Produced: Bowie, Rodgers; engineered: Clearmountain.

First release: 14 April 1983, **Let's Dance**.

At the time he recorded *Let's Dance*, Bowie was more an actor than a musician. He hadn't toured since 1978 and hadn't been in the studio since May 1980, barring one-off sessions. Instead he'd made two films, a teleplay, and starred in a Broadway production. He talked of writing a screenplay with Mick Jagger, and had considered the role in *Brimstone and Treacle* that went to Sting. And he made *Let's Dance* as if he was in his dressing room (the Power Station lounge, in this case) until being called to the set. "I don't play a damned thing. This was a singer's album," he said. It was laziness as an oblique strategy. He'd reached the limit with his late-Seventies band, who could guess his moves in advance. He wanted new people at the console, new people in the studio, to whom he'd respond in the vocal booth, an actor working to a scenario suggested by his director. "Every time he would come in and listen, he would have fresh ears," Rodgers recalled in 2018. The problem came when there was nothing for anyone to build on.

Rodgers and Bowie went into the *Let's Dance* sessions with a handful of songs — "Let's Dance," what became "Ricochet," and three covers/remakes Bowie planned to sing ("China Girl" was dispatched early in the sessions, while "Cat People" and "Criminal World" were done towards the end). This left a few "thumbnails," as Rodgers called them — chord progressions, riffs, melodic and lyrical ideas — that had to be fleshed out in the studio. At its worst, this process resulted in "Shake It," the work of an out-to-lunch composer whose producer gamely tried to guess what Bowie wanted when he said he wanted "hits."

"Shake It" embodies Bowie's bad habits in the Eighties: an indifference to quality; broadly playing to a public of his imagination; getting pop wrong. Whenever Bowie tried to slum with a dance song, he stumbled. "There'll always be something spiky about my stuff," he said at the time. "Shake It," with its twerpy two-chord keyboard hook and chorus vocals ("what's my liiiiiiiiine!": a game show theme from hell), clumps along. Rodgers does what he can with some chuck riffs, Carmine Rojas dives down an octave on bass to juice each bar, but it's a queasy song built on restless changes — see G ("on the sea") to Gb ("it's a brand new") to F ("day"). Its banal lyric, with Brian Wilson and John Lennon references ("'Til I Die" and "Mind Games," respectively), is mild anomie: talking to faceless girls; a lover who's better than money. "I feel like a sailboat, adrift on the sea" is an honest report: he's content to let the tides take him where they will.

RICOCHET

Recorded: ca. 10-20 January 1983, Power Station. Bowie: lead vocal; Vaughan: lead guitar; Rodgers: rhythm guitar; Sabino: keyboards; Rojas: bass; Thompson: drums; Figueroa: congas; Gollehon: trumpet; Aaron, Harrison: tenor saxophone; Elson: baritone saxophone; George Simms, Frank Simms, Spinner: backing vocals. Produced: Bowie, Rodgers; engineered: Clearmountain.

First release: 14 April 1983, **Let's Dance**.

As Genesis evolved from a progressive rock troupe into Phil Collins' off-year stadium band, there was small recompense for older fans: each new album, no matter how many Top 40 bids it had, would still have at least one "prog" track for old times' sake. A similar obligation is in "Ricochet," the only song on *Let's Dance* to suggest Bowie's art rock past. It's a "previously on" recap: "Hi, I'm David Bowie. Do you remember me? I wrote 'Joe the Lion' and 'Subterraneans'."

Though it was one of his favorite songs on the album, Bowie regretted turning over "Ricochet" to Nile Rodgers. "The beat wasn't quite right. It didn't roll the way it should have, the syncopation was wrong. It had an ungainly gait; it should have flowed," he said in 1987. The idea was to try to do a variation on a Ghanaian highlife beat. That Rodgers, a man who likely blows his nose in perfect time, was flummoxed by "Ricochet" shows how awkward a piece it is: two D major verses, whose bassline often plays median notes, bridged by a long refrain that sways between G major and A minor, and whose biggest hook is a trudging three-note descending phrase ("march-of-flowers").

Bowie was right about the beat. While Carmine Rojas varies his basslines, the drumline keeps in rigid formation: snare on downbeat, two kick drum hits on the third beat, triplets on hi-hat, crash cymbal every other bar. The use of gated mikes didn't help, as the kick drum is barely distinguishable from the gated snare. The arrangement is both overworked (backing vocals range from Soviet choral harmonies in the last refrains to the "*ri*-co-chet it's-not-the-end-of-the-*world*" tag — Frank Simms said it was the most difficult song to master) yet has a sense of Rodgers tossing things against the wall to see what sticks. He once said of the song, "Bowie just threw it together and I went out and wrote the horn arrangement, the dit-dit-dit, all that stuff." Saxophones wander in from a jazz-fusion session; congas enliven a verse; Stevie Ray Vaughan ducks in at the fade.

Originally titled "Shame, Shame (It's Not the End of the World)," for its lyric Bowie raided W.H. Auden's "Night Mail," a poem written for a documentary honoring a London-to-Scotland postal train. His clunking phrasing tries to replicate Auden's juddering tetrameter to convey a train pushing uphill, while some Auden lines appear barely altered: his "men long for news" becomes Bowie's "men wait for news" and the closing line of both song and poem is "who [himself] can bear to be forgotten?" Auden's poem honors community, the mail train tethering each city it rolls through. "Ricochet" is a Thatcherite sequel — no community, just beaten-down individuals, each trying to persevere, dreaming of lost jobs: "pieces of machinery, mine shafts, things like that" — the latter line spoken by Bowie in a Welsh accent, for whatever reason. It's surplus men, weeds to be cleared, collateral damage of late capitalism — after all, a ricochet is often when something misses a target.

CRIMINAL WORLD

(Browne, Godwin, Lyons.) **Recorded**: *ca. 10-20 January 1983, Power Station. Bowie: lead vocal; Vaughan: lead guitar; Rodgers: rhythm guitar; Sabino: keyboards; Rojas: bass; Thompson: drums; George Simms, Frank Simms, Spinner: backing vocals. Produced: Bowie, Rodgers; engineered: Clearmountain.*

First release: *14 April 1983,* ***Let's Dance***.

I'm gay and always have been, even when I was David Jones.
— Bowie, *Melody Maker*, 22 January 1972.

By the early Eighties, a generation of rock musicians were downplaying or denying their bisexuality and homosexuality. Lou Reed had a song whose refrain was "I love women/ We all love women." Freddie Mercury and Rob Halford kept to their closets. Elton John even married a woman. Then there was Bowie, who, in a May 1983 *Rolling Stone* interview (cover line: "David Bowie Straight"), said "the biggest mistake I ever made was telling that *Melody Maker* writer that I was bisexual. Christ, I was so *young* then. I was *experimenting*." He said the same to *Time* soon afterward, calling his admission a miscalculation, "an image." It was the end of Queer David. "The years have wiped away the androgyny," noted a sympathetic *Playboy* profile of July 1983. "For the first time, he seems at ease with himself as a man."

It came at a cruel time. By 1983, AIDS, wreaking hell through gay communities, was the subject of vile false rumors: that you could get AIDS from doorknobs and toilet seats, that HIV-positive waiters were spitting into your food, that homosexuality was inseparable from filth and disease. Someone who had told a cross-dressing kid "hey babe, your hair's alright" seemed to repudiate a culture that had revered him, at its darkest hour. He'd once sung "oh no, love, you're not alone!" Now, it seemed: I'm sorry, you are.

Bowie wasn't gay, but a bisexual who primarily chose women for long-term relationships. Now he no longer defined himself as bisexual. What did he owe? He had trafficked in gay culture, he'd claimed to be gay, and gays were some of his oldest and most loyal fans. Had he always just been an opportunist — and being gay in 1983 was something to be avoided?

Bowie's "biggest mistake" quote came after he'd downed a few cans of Foster's on the "Let's Dance" video shoot in Australia — it was the only reference he made to his bisexuality to the interviewer, Kurt Loder. But Loder and *Rolling Stone* knew a scoop when they saw one, and placed the quote high in the article, which was unsubtly titled "Straight Time." Still, Bowie, the son of a PR man, knew how the quote would play, and he kept underlining it. A few months later, he spoke to Lisa Robinson, whom he'd known since the Ziggy Stardust days. He said in the Seventies, his whole life had been experimentation, with his bisexuality a rough equivalent of his youthful Nietzscheanism. "I threw myself through a test of absorbing every possible experience that I could while I was young, with no real realization of what happens later in life… It was one vast experiment. I've learned a lot from it."

Yet calling his bisexuality admission a mistake was also a hard-nosed, commercially-minded decision. He felt he was regarded in America as a bisexual first, artist second (for example, in 1977, the *York* [Pennsylvania] *Daily Record* ran a syndicated gossip column headlined "Bianca Jetsetting with Bisexual Bowie.") "It just became like a banner over me, for such a long time," he told the writer Robert Palmer,

> That's the reason, the *only* reason, I regret it. I've never regretted it because I *was* a bisexual, but it was used like it was *damning* or something. It put people off my work for such a long time, it was such a hurdle to get over. My work meant nothing to a great majority of people for a number of years because they couldn't see past that.

Speaking to Chet Flippo for his *Serious Moonlight* tour book, Bowie was blunt about the larger audiences he now drew: "It's given me people who, before, would have said, oh he's that red-haired faggot, you know, we don't want that, we can't see that creep. Now it's changing. Now they like it. That's terrific." Looking back in 2002, Bowie said "America is a very puritanical place, and I think [being known as a bisexual] stood in the way of so much I wanted to do… I had no inclination to hold any banners or be a representative of any group of people."

He feared being defined by association with any community, that his individual acts would be used to represent a group, that working for the whole would mean lesser work. He'd used a similar reasoning for why he couldn't stand his Arts Lab in the Sixties. Some considered Bowie's 1983 statements to be queer erasure, suggesting that one's homosexuality or bisexuality could be discarded when convenient. The cabaret performer Justin Vivian Bond told Marc Spitz that "[Bowie] decided he was going to cash in on his white, male privilege and put a distance between him and his stigmatized fans, and by doing that, he basically said, 'Okay, I am the dick that you love hating. I am Rod Stewart'." Who was David Bowie Straight? A man straightening his past's crooked lines, swapping ambiguity for clarity, and knowing, as he sang, when to stay in, not go out. In 1980, Jon Savage wrote that "the spice in [Bowie's] image was gayness." Now he was a less savory dish.

In his *Melody Maker* "coming out" interview Bowie said he "doesn't have much time for Gay Liberation." He'd play the role and he'd abandon it when he wanted to. No one was asking him why he wasn't doing Philadelphia Soul anymore (well, RCA had been). His demand to not be seen as bisexual any more was in line with this — he never wanted to lead a movement, so movements shouldn't rely on him.

In later interviews, he looked to the future, hoping that boundaries between gay and straight would be less severe, that there would be more border crossings. "There is a sort of radical right view that you are only a hetero or only a gay," he said in 1995. "The idea that you actually vacillate between all forms of sexuality doesn't seem to be in there. And I still think, am I the only fucking person that knows this?"

"When I was actually declaring my bisexual status, I realized it had a kind of weight. Now it seems almost commonplace," Bowie said to *Details* that year,

I did not want everything that I was doing to be purely colored by my sexuality. I was dealing in a very primitive way with a very new area of public perception... Whatever I do, wherever I go, someone somewhere feels betrayed. I'm not singing this song. I'm not wearing these kinds of clothes, my sexuality seems to now be polarized towards heterosexuality. But it's what I am, it's why I am... I think we live in a fully hybridized world where there is no such thing as an absolute... I do not and refuse to have a station in life. I go from station to station. (laughs)

Amidst all this, tucked away on the second side of *Let's Dance*, was Bowie's cover of a bi-themed song from 1976, Metro's "Criminal World," which the BBC allegedly had banned at the time for bisexual overtones. Was it a secret message, a "psst — I'm still here" note? Another twist of the knife?

Its inclusion on *Let's Dance* is Bowie sneaking a transgressive song onto a platinum record that grandmothers bought. But it wasn't the same song. Bowie cut half the first verse: "I'm not the queen so there's no need to bow... I'll take your dress and we can truck on out" and inserted new phrases of his own, and rather telling ones: "I guess I recognize your destination."

More ridiculously, in the second verse he changed "I saw you kneeling at my brother's door" to "you caught me kneeling at your sister's door." The composer of "Velvet Goldmine" and "John, I'm Only Dancing" had bowdlerized a vaguely-bi obscurity, removing any lines a journalist could quote to suggest that his sexuality was still ambiguous. Why? He never said, no one apparently asked him. Perhaps he thought the lines needed improving. Or was he trying to reconcile his newfound public heterosexuality with his queer past? His "Criminal World" had a slinking menace to it, and he did keep the lines about the boys being like baby-faced girls.

"Criminal World" was a strong cover. Nile Rodgers plays a variation on his "China Girl" riff, a bouncing movement on his high strings, and after the refrain the stomping riff of the Hollies' "Long Cool Woman in a Black Dress" rumbles in. Stevie Ray Vaughan takes two exuberant solos, if staid compared with the guitar on Metro's original. It's the best track on its side. But why is it even there? As with "Ricochet," it's Bowie offering watered-down takes on his past work for his all-ages record. A once-fearless man hedges his bets in a quietly disgraceful act.

WITHOUT YOU

Recorded: ca. 10-20 January 1983, Power Station. Bowie: lead vocal; Vaughan: lead guitar; Rodgers: rhythm guitar; Sabino: Prophet-5, keyboards; Bernard Edwards: bass; Thompson: drums; Figueroa: congas; George Simms, Frank Simms, Spinner: backing vocals. Produced: Bowie, Rodgers; engineered: Clearmountain.

First release: 14 April 1983, **Let's Dance**.

Nile Rodgers once said every Chic record tells the same story. "We're the opening act for a really big star, and we're unknown. No one has ever heard of us, we're brand new, and we're a live band coming out on stage to tell everybody who we are." The sound of Chic was *this is us*. Rodgers muting his strings as much as he sounded notes. Bernard Edwards on bass: a duke of melody. Tony Thompson, the battery house. Norma Jean Wright, Alfa Anderson, Luci Martin: elegant narrators. They played heavy enough that Marvin Gaye, hearing them one night from backstage, thought an earthquake was happening.

When he hired Rodgers to produce, Bowie assumed he'd get the rest of Chic in the bargain. But the band was in hard shape by late 1982, partying enough to become unreliable. Rodgers said he couldn't take the chance that Edwards in particular would bail on a session for which Bowie was paying the bills and "watching every penny like a hawk." Only in the last days of *Let's Dance*, when most songs had been tracked, did he call in both of his bandmates. David Bowie and Chic were only heard on one track — the B-flat ballad "Without You."

"Without You" is a conversation between Rodgers and his old partners — Thompson, who hit his snare with so much strength he dimmed the Power Station's lights, and Edwards, who "was pissed off that I hadn't called him for the rest of the album, but he knew I was proud to show off his genius," as Rodgers wrote. Edwards came in for a bassline that Carmine Rojas had found difficult. He sat down, scanned the chord sheet, cut a take in under fifteen minutes. Edwards played a taut opening hook, serving as a net for Bowie's high-wire phrasing (tolling one root note per bar as Bowie skies up for "the best things in life... *are gone*"), and moved to roaming lines under Stevie Ray Vaughan's solos. Thompson gives fluttering pushes on his kick drum and plays snare hits on twos and threes, in sync with how Bowie avoids downbeats and pushes through bars (the quick cross-set fill at 1:54 is his only showcase moment).

Bowie played the star that Chic was supposed to support on stage, his lyric in the service of a theatrically exhaustive phrasing. The fragile falsetto, the coolly-sung fills, the swoops down an octave as though he can barely stand up at the mike: it all suggests Bryan Ferry, on whose world-worn persona Bowie would do variations throughout the Eighties (see "As the World Falls Down").

WAIATA

Recorded: 23 November 1983, Takapūwāhia Marae, Porirua, New Zealand. Bowie, George Simms, Frank Simms: harmony vocals.

Broadcast: 22 November 2008, "Bowie's Waiata," Radio New Zealand.

EMI's contract with Bowie was a good bet, as *Let's Dance* repaid their advance within the year, moving some six million copies (reportedly the label's fastest seller since *Sgt. Pepper's Lonely Hearts Club Band*), hitting #1 in the UK and #4 in the US, spawning three global hit singles. Then Bowie went on tour for eight months.

At first, promoters thought Bowie would play to an established fanbase (an "older well-dressed audience") in theaters. The reception he got at the US Festival upended that idea, and when the initial run of indoor shows were announced, there were 250,000 requests for 44,000 tickets. He was moved up to stadiums — working the same circuit as Bruce Springsteen and the Police — and had to connect with a faceless mass on a nightly basis, playing to video screens that broadcast him to the nosebleed seats. His mime training came in handy, as did, the writer Robert Palmer suspected, "some reading in the literature of crowd psychology." Bowie worked in broad gestures, shadow boxing during "Let's Dance," rising from a chair like a bored king in "Golden Years."

Carlos Alomar, bandleader of the 1983 tour, described it as "David Bowie does David Bowie. He's singing about the guy who wrote about these people." Setlists were more adventurous than one might expect — the less-canonical Seventies albums were represented, from *Pin Ups* ("I Can't Explain," "Sorrow") to *Lodger* ("Red Sails"), while some warhorses were stabled: no "Changes," no "Ziggy Stardust" or "Suffragette City." Some critics, particularly the British, knocked the tour for being "family entertainment, and all the family is buying" (*Melody Maker*), "the rewards of mediocrity" (*NME*), "fish and chips" fare (*Sounds*). Older fans were surprised to see the types normally found at a Dire Straits gig singing along to "Jean Genie."

He made a mint out of it, earning nearly $1 million for three concerts in Chicago, $1.2 million for a single Edmonton show. He commissioned a private Boeing 707. The crew and musicians drank and dined like emperors. Despite expenses, Bowie reportedly netted between $25 million to $35 million for the tour; once royalties were added, he possibly cleared at least $50 million in 1983, at comfortable Swiss tax rates. The former Beckenham oddity now had a net worth comparable to a lesser Windsor (Charles Shaar Murray: "I saw the footage of Bowie in Singapore. And I suddenly thought, he's turned into Prince Charles. In a suit, with an old-fashioned haircut like a lemon meringue on his head, talking in this posh accent").

Bowie's look on the tour — bleached blond hair, Oxford shirts, regimental ties, light gabardine suits to accent his hair and features — inspired similar "colonial" looks for the band. The brass section wore safari gear, the singers were Edwardian music hall performers, Alomar was a sheik or as "a very dapper Nehru," keyboardist Dave LeBolt dressed like a "coolie." Much of it came from *Merry Christmas Mr. Lawrence*, where Bowie had played a beautiful blond soldier with whom his Japanese captor is obsessed. As in his "China Girl" video, Bowie was an embodiment of whiteness, a British royal on a goodwill tour of Japan, Australia, Singapore, Hong Kong, and Bangkok. (The strange tour film *Ricochet* documents these shows, with Bowie as a David Attenborough figure exploring the mysterious cultures of Southeast Asia, getting spat in the face during one Bangkok ceremony.)

On 23 November 1983, before playing Wellington, New Zealand, Bowie was invited to Takapūwāhia Marae in nearby Porirua. He was the first rock musician officially welcomed into a Māori marae, the centerpiece of a Māori community. For the occasion, he and the Simms brothers wrote a three-part harmony, four-line vocal piece to perform — "Waiata," a greeting and salutation to his Māori hosts. He and the Simmses sang cross-legged on the ground at the marae: "We ran to the ocean and pledged far to go/to land in New Zealand and sing you our songs/we're happy and honored to be here with you/we thank you for sharing the way that you do." It was the gracious entertainer who'd played the Malta International Song Festival in summer 1969, where he'd written lyrics for a Maltese song for an informal competition. No longer an alternative candidate, he held executive office.

IMAGINE

(Lennon, Ono.) **Live**: *(unreleased) 8 December 1983, Hong Kong Coliseum, 9 Cheong Wan Road, Hung Hom, Hong Kong. Bowie: lead vocal; Earl Slick: lead guitar; Carlos Alomar: rhythm guitar; Dave LeBolt: keyboards; Rojas: bass; Thompson: drums; Lenny Pickett, Harrison: tenor saxophone; Elson: baritone saxophone; George Simms, Frank Simms: backing vocals.*

John Lennon's murder horrified Bowie, whose public image in the Eighties — a polite distance, a determination to mean *less* to people, to defang his cult — was a response to that December night. Lennon had been vulnerable, walking the streets without bodyguards, his home address common knowledge. He'd spent the Seventies humanizing himself, promoting his new record by telling fans it was time to move on. "We were the hip ones in the Sixties," Lennon said in his last interviews. "But the world is not like the Sixties. The whole world's changed... Produce your own dream... It's quite possible to do anything... The unknown is what it is. And to be frightened of it is what sends everybody scurrying around chasing dreams, illusions." A cruel legacy of his murder was that his open commitment to the future was lost when he was made a trademark of a glorious past.

Considering the self-righteous rocker as the "true" Lennon, as many critics did, ignored that he was also a sentimentalist who filled his last record with odes to his family. He'd meant "Imagine" to be schlocky, calling it a sugar-coated nihilist-utopian message that Robert Goulet could sing. (Lennon would have been delighted when the artless naïf David Archuleta sang it on *American Idol*.) On the third anniversary of Lennon's murder, for the last song of the last show of his tour, Bowie sang "Imagine" to a Hong Kong audience (Earl Slick had suggested they perform "Across the Universe," to which Bowie replied, "if we're gonna do it, we might as well do 'Imagine.'") The performance, which borders on Vegas schmaltz — saxophone fanfare, the Simms brothers emoting, Bowie sounding like he's auditioning for *Beatlemania* — honored it well.

TUMBLE AND TWIRL

(Bowie, Pop.) **Recorded**: *ca. 1 May-10 June 1984, Le Studio, Morin Heights. Bowie: lead vocal; Alomar: rhythm guitar, cuatro guitar; Derek Bramble: keyboards, guitar?, bass; Rojas: bass; Hakim: drums; Figueroa: woodblocks, congas; Guy St. Onge: marimba; Mark Pender: trumpet; Pickett: tenor saxophone; Harrison: alto saxophone; Elson: baritone saxophone; Robin Clark, Curtis King, George Simms: backing vocals. Produced: Bowie, Bramble, Hugh Padgham; engineered: Padgham.*

First release: *24 September 1984,* **Tonight**.

The first thought was a live record: call it *Serious Moonlight*. Take a breath, sell a souvenir of a bank-breaking tour, recharge (it would finally appear in 2018). Instead, five months after leaving the stage, Bowie was in Canada making a dreadful album.

Tonight is among the least-loved #1 records of its era. Front-loaded in orders and certified platinum in two months, its sales slumped once people heard it: an immaculately rancid scrap-bag in which a hit single was stuffed into a pile of covers. It was a Bowie album as a software upgrade or a next-generation coffee maker. Deep in Rod Stewart territory, Bowie was following a blazed path — grind out a record, get a hit, make a flashy video, get on the cover of *Rolling Stone*; confess your sins in later interviews. At the time, Carlos Alomar noted that Bowie "gets the new EMI deal, they say, 'we want you to deliver.' He does deliver, and now he delivers again."

The question is why he made the album at all, as he told Charles Shaar Murray in 1984 that he hadn't been able to write on the road. "It's the only record I've ever done to try and prove something to other people, and it was a huge mistake," Bowie said in 1987. "It was the exuberance of having had such a huge success... I was pressured to go back into the studio on the tail end of that. It was a scantily-dressed album, three good songs and the rest was really desperate." *Tonight*'s producer Hugh Padgham agreed: "It was too soon to record it. It was really badly thought out." EMI was happy to have a new album in the shops for autumn 1984 but Bowie, one of their top-selling artists, held a strong hand. He could have pushed a release to the following year if he didn't have the songs.

But he *did* have the songs, or so he thought. "I want to go further, much further, with the next one," Bowie said in 1983, talking of what he wanted to make after *Let's Dance*. He wanted a bluesy, contemporary R&B/funk/reggae album, extending the *Let's Dance* line. To this end, he asked around for hot young producers and found a twenty-two-year-old British musician named Derek Bramble. "I had no idea, he just came searching for me," Bramble said. (Nile Rodgers wasn't an option. More than one article had described *Let's Dance* as Rodgers making Bowie relevant again. "It seemed to be a conscious effort to distance himself from me," Rodgers said.)

Bramble was fresh and ambitious (the former bassist of Heatwave, he'd just started looking for writing and production work). Bowie used the same formula as he had with Rodgers — he invited Bramble to Switzerland to demo songs and "program" him as to what he wanted to make. (Bowie emphasized reggae, to the point of making up stories about living in Brixton where "a black guy upstairs was always pumping out this reggae and ska," as Bramble recalled.) He got Bramble into Mountain Studios with a few Swiss musicians and cut what some at the *Tonight* sessions said were tremendous demos — funky, raw, full of promise.

For a drum sound and as insurance, which he'd need to use, Bowie hired Hugh Padgham as engineer, who had just produced the Police's *Synchronicity*, while Carlos Alomar was back in his role of bandleader and fix-it man (Alomar was stunned that Bowie had made ten demos — the most prep work he'd ever done). "I feel David had a pretty good idea of how he wanted [the album] to turn out," Padgham said. "It was just a question of having a listen to the demo and then going in and doing it." Not wanting to record at the same Bahamas studio as Mick Jagger, Bowie decided to cut the album at Le Studio in Canada. Here his troubles began.

Le Studio was a tranquil manse in the Laurentian Mountains of Québec, some ninety minutes away from Montréal. Its amenities were beauty, seclusion, and being near ski slopes. Unfortunately, as Padgham noted, "this was May, just after the snow had gone." There was little for Bowie and his musicians to do but watch television, take walks or, in Bowie's case, womanize beyond his usual capacity. As with *Let's Dance*, he let his producers and musicians arrange backing tracks, showing up for vocals or throw the I Ching to determine whether a mix was finished. He grew restless and bored, particularly as the sessions dragged on for weeks with little to show for it. Bramble kept asking for retakes (especially irritating for Bowie, master of the one-take vocal). Alomar was blunt when interviewed by David Buckley, saying that Bramble "was a really nice guy, but he didn't know jack-shit about producing."

After a break in the sessions, Padgham was now running the show. By then, Bowie had given up on the album, no longer interested in working off the demos, instead shifting his focus to covers. Padgham thought the success of *Let's Dance* had gone to Bowie's head: "to be a big star was probably on his mind more... it was sort of epitomized by the fact that there were some great songs that he couldn't be bothered to finish because he wanted to get the record out." It was a salvage strategy — make *Tonight* a half-covers album with a Sixties throwback feel, complete with sequencing "slow" and "dance" LP sides.

It was his "violent" sequel to his Seventies cover album *Pin Ups*, he later claimed. Talking to a Hong Kong journalist in late 1983, Bowie said *Pin Ups* had given him breathing space after he'd ended his Ziggy Stardust character. The same applied now — he thought he needed a new album to keep label and fans happy. He kept much of the *Let's Dance* crew for continuity: one Simms brother, a reconstituted "Borneo Horns," and the rhythm section of Carmine Rojas, Omar Hakim, and Sammy Figueroa. *Tonight* would buy time "so that I could prepare myself for something else."

Movie Night in Java

Of the handful of songs written for *Tonight,* "Tumble and Twirl" was a collaboration between Bowie and Iggy Pop, their first in five years. Cut loose from Arista (see "Play It Safe"), Pop had turned to the road, working the club circuit and eventually winding up in Haiti, where Pop antagonized a local voodoo priest and lost all of his money, causing his girlfriend Esther Friedman to work as a back-alley dentist's assistant. They got in a car crash; menacing strangers kept showing up at their house.

Then in 1983, the cash started coming in. Bowie's "China Girl" earned six-figure royalties for Pop, who also started to get paid for the Sex Pistols' cover of "No Fun" and Grace Jones' version of "Nightclubbing." Bowie's excessive covering of Pop songs on *Tonight* (five of nine tracks are co-compositions or covers) was an extension of a generous line of credit. At the end of the year, Pop and Bowie vacationed in Indonesia with Coco Schwab and Pop's new girlfriend and future wife, Suchi Asano. "We both share the same affection for solitude in foreign climes," Bowie said.

"Tumble and Twirl" was their jaundiced take on first-class third-world tourism. Bowie and Pop had visited an oil magnate in Java whose colonial-style mansion had an open drain system through which raw sewage spewed onto the beaches. The magnate would show movies projected on bedsheets hung in his garden. "It felt so bizarre to sit there in the jungle watching movies... through monsoon weather with rain pouring down. Images of Brooke Shields," Bowie said.

Pop wrote much of the lyric (almost certainly he was the one who rhymed "dusky mulatto" with "nylons and tattoos") — natives in Playboy, Bob Marley, and Baby Doc Duvalier t-shirts; Coke bottles full of "hot juice" (a possible reference to a Haitian "cocktail" where pharmacists would fill empty Coke bottles with paregoric, the camphorated tincture of opium); movie nights in a rich man's garden, when the monsoons have washed out the roads. The singer, in his airplane seat flying back to the free world, reads a book on Borneo to learn what he's seen. It's Bowie's *Lodger* as a clueless tourist, returning to his safe European home.

The music — the verses a series of wide stand-offs in E minor, refrains a rapid-fire four-chord shuffle — has a similarly absurdist quality. There's an "island" arrangement with interruptions from the Rainbow Room: a Manhattan Transfer-style "Bor-nee-oh" vocal tag; badgering brass. Supper-club singers on the bridge sing about sewage treatment, with Bowie showing up eight bars in, as if he'd been in the john. As often on *Tonight*, the line between satire and self-contempt is blurry. "I felt that I didn't want whatever it was I'd sort of earned for myself," as Bowie recalled a decade later. Only the Alomar-led rhythm section (he was charged with loosening up the song's "frantic complex swing" and played some lines on a gut-string *cuatro* guitar from Puerto Rico) comes through with dignity.

DON'T LOOK DOWN

(Pop, Williamson.) **Recorded**: *ca. 1 May-10 June 1984, Le Studio. Bowie: lead vocal; Alomar: rhythm guitar; Bramble: guitar, piano, Jupiter-8, Oberheim OB-Xa, PPG, Yamaha DX7, bass; Rojas: bass?; Hakim: drums; Figueroa: woodblocks; Pender: trumpet; Pickett: tenor saxophone; Harrison: alto saxophone; Elson: baritone saxophone; Clark, King, Simms: backing vocals. Produced: Bowie, Bramble, Padgham; engineered: Padgham.*

First release: *24 September 1984,* **Tonight**.

Tonight is a wearying listen, with its overcrowded mixes, its cokey treble. It's like a revue in which everyone is hamming it up, even the stagehands. An exception is Bowie's cover of Iggy Pop's "Don't Look Down," which has a luxurious low end, giving the basslines a deep snap. Sammy Figueroa crisply accents beats on woodblocks; each breath the trumpeter Mark Pender draws is captured in the net.

"Don't Look Down" was a brooding, weird track on Pop's *New Values*. Pop mutters a survivalist's advice: *don't look down, because you're standing over a pit.* The Alfono sisters are sympathetic sirens; the saxophonist's looking for a way out. Bowie struggled to interpret the song, futzing with a drum machine to attempt jazz and rock versions until settling on a nightcrawling Donald Fagen imitation over a mild reggae beat. Having Derek Bramble in the studio, who could play "proper reggae basslines," was an inspiration. Bowie said that "taking energy away from the musical side of things reinforced the lyrics and gave them their own energy." In translation, this meant draining the song of power and tidying up its squalor (even replacing some Pop lines with the grisly likes of "don't know who else came to kneel/on this empty battlefield"). It was cocktail hour pantomime: the quasi-Jamaican phrasing of lines like "Central Park to shanty town"; the cheery lounge band sign-off in the last bar. Vampiric music, and not in a good way.

BLUE JEAN

Recorded: ca. 1 May- 10 June 1984, Le Studio. Bowie: lead vocal; Alomar: rhythm guitar; Bramble: guitar, bass; Rojas: bass; Hakim: drums; St. Onge: marimba; Pender: trumpet; Pickett: tenor saxophone; Harrison: alto saxophone; Elson: baritone saxophone; King, Simms: backing vocals. Produced: Bowie, Bramble, Padgham; engineered: Padgham.

First release: ca. 3 September 1984, EA 181 (UK #6, US #8). *Broadcast*: 14 September 1984, MTV Awards. *Live*: 1987, 1990, 2004.

Bowie wrote off "Blue Jean" as a cheap score. He didn't think much of it — it got him on the radio, let him do a fun video. Bit of a sexist rock 'n' roll thing, he said. Music for picking up girls. Hugh Padgham regretted that of the demos he'd heard, "Blue Jean" was one of the few Bowie developed in the studio, as it was Padgham's least favorite. He'd always wanted to work with Bowie. Fate assigned him *Tonight*, like a lifelong Alfred Hitchcock fan collaborating on *Topaz*.

It's easy to see why Bowie chose "Blue Jean," as it's the "Let's Dance" formula: another uptempo throwback with Fifties and Sixties flavors — Eddie Cochran's "Something Else" in particular. Its title vixen is out of a Frankie Laine or Tom Jones song (she's got "Latin roots"). There's also Sam Cooke ("somebody send me") and Elvis asides; Bowie's low-pitched word-tumbling vocal in the verses goofs on Jacques Dutronc; the alto saxophonist sounds like a Georgie Fame player who's had some benzedrine. Removing Robin Clark from the vocal chorus makes the backing singers more conspiratorial.

Where "Let's Dance" got something fresh from its compost of the past, "Blue Jean" stayed in the pastiche lane, which suited Bowie's mood. In his twenty-minute *Jazzin' for Blue Jean* video, directed by Julien Temple, he got to play at being part of London again (he soon had a role in Temple's *Absolute Beginners*.) Missing the Mod Sixties, the smartness in dress, the dominance of youth, Bowie found in Thatcherite London a simulacrum of it. After all, there was money, fashion, swinging parties, respectable drugs. Sixties London got its flavor from working-class life and provincial imports, where aspirational Eighties London was an after-hours playground for young professionals.

Welded to D major, (verses shift between D major and a D suspended fourth; refrains strut between mediant (F# minor) and dominant (A) chords), "Blue Jean" spins like a top: two verses, three refrains, no bridges or solos except a four-bar riff break. Its graces are its supporting players: Omar Hakim varying fills at the end of each verse — hard on snare, quick on bass drum; Carlos Alomar's rhythm lines, lagging the beat midway through verses; the marimba player Guy St. Onge, who accents the guitars, falls in with the drumline, and plays counter-melodies in refrains. Clever (Bowie's going to write a poem in a letter if he can only "get that faculty together"), catchy, and flash, "Blue Jean" was one of his best second-rate hits.

I KEEP FORGETTIN'

(Leiber, Stoller.) **Recorded***: ca. 1 May-10 June 1984, Le Studio. Bowie: lead vocal; Alomar: guitar; Bramble: guitar, bass?; Rojas: bass?; Hakim: drums; Figueroa: tambourine; St. Onge: marimba; Pender: trumpet; Pickett: tenor saxophone; Harrison: alto saxophone; Elson: baritone saxophone; Clark, King, Simms: backing vocals. Produced: Bowie, Bramble, Padgham; engineered: Padgham.*

First release*: 24 September 1984, **Tonight**.*

In 1962, Smokey Robinson told Chuck Jackson the latter's new single, "I Keep Forgettin'," was too ahead of its time to be a hit. He was right. Produced by Jerry Leiber and Mike Stoller, the single's first half is Jackson's baritone set against a small orchestra of percussive instruments (marimba, tambourine, shakers, toms, tuned timbales — piano and guitar also play percussive roles), with only touches of harmonic ones: brief tuba grunts, barely-there strings, dashes of accordion. Leiber's lyric has Jackson being led around by his feet and fists; he's a set of motor functions. Stoller varied his tempo and meter (bars of 2/4 slam into cut-time 4/4 bars), gave the song a wrong-way round construction, with the refrain backing into the verse. Leiber was so delighted that he danced around his office after cutting the record.

It became a favorite among Sixties R&B fanatics, including young David Jones of Bromley. Covers abounded: the Artwoods used an organ instead of accordion; Topmost (from Finland!) was defeated by the tempo. Phil Spector produced a Sonny Charles take that sounds as if waxed from molasses. Bowie had wanted to cover "I Keep Forgettin'" for years (he said it was on the list of a possible *Pin Ups 2* in a 1982 interview). With a versatile crew on hand at Le Studio — Guy St. Onge on marimba, Sammy Figueroa on percussion, Omar Hakim on drums — it seemed like the ideal opportunity, but the percussion was mostly St. Onge and gated tom fills, while a horn break was replaced by a generic guitar solo. Bowie sounds as if he's getting his voice in shape to sing "Blue Jean." An antic bore, the *Tonight* "I Keep Forgettin'" is a party song as performed by your parents.

LOVING THE ALIEN

Recorded: ca. 1 May-10 June 1984, Le Studio. Bowie: lead vocal; Alomar: guitar; Bramble: guitar, keyboards, Oberheim OB-Xa, Yamaha DX7, Jupiter-8, bass; Rob Yale: Fairlight CMI; Rojas: bass; Hakim: drums; Figueroa: woodblock, congas; St. Onge: marimba; Pender: trumpet; Pickett: tenor saxophone; Harrison: alto saxophone; Elson: baritone saxophone; Clark, King, Simms: backing vocals; uncredited musicians: violins, violas, celli, double bass (arranger: Arif Mardin). Produced: Bowie, Bramble, Padgham; engineered: Padgham.

First release: 24 September 1984, **Tonight**. *Live*: 1987, 2003-2004.

"Loving the Alien" meant a great deal to its composer, who honed it throughout the *Tonight* sessions, led off the album with it, and spent his most substantive interview in 1984 trying to make sense of it. It was a would-be masterpiece that aimed for the heights of "Station to Station" and missed.

Demoed by Bowie and Derek Bramble in Switzerland before the sessions (known as "Demo No. 1"), "Loving the Alien" became a focal point in the studio, as the song needed to be the album's Epic Bowie Song as well as a likely single. Arif Mardin wrote a string arrangement while Bramble went through Le Studio's collection of synthesizers (the opening "ah ah ah" bed was likely played on a Fairlight, used similarly by Thomas Dolby on Prefab Sprout's *Steve McQueen*).

Bowie said he wrote it out of anger. While he'd worn a crucifix since his Los Angeles days and believed it held some beneficial power over him, he considered organized religion a sham, built on sand, the work of countless mistranslations. It was the idea of the Church ruling over the dreams of generations, its teachings based on lies. Research meant another deep dive into crackpot "hidden history" books, of the sort that had fueled "Station to Station." Here it was Hugh Schonfield's *The Passover Plot*, Michael Baigent, Richard Leigh, and Henry Lincoln's *The Holy Blood and the Holy Grail*, and Donovan Joyce's *The Jesus Scroll*. Their common thread (from which Dan Brown cherry-picked conspiracies for his *Da Vinci Code*) is that the Christian Gospel is a cover-up, as Jesus Christ didn't die on the cross but faked his own death for political reasons (Schonfield), in truth dying at Masada at age eighty (Joyce), with his descendants marrying into a French royal dynasty (Baigent *et al*).

He set his lyric in the Holy Land, with Crusaders and Saracens and their counterparts in Israel and Palestine a millennium later, battling over land that may not be holy at all (he mentioned the Lebanese historian Kamal Salibi, who very questionably argued the historical kingdom of Israel was in today's Saudi Arabia, so that the Hebrews were Arabian immigrants). If the verses are a historical trap, actors stuck in reruns, the refrain is escape: salvation by delusion. In Bowie's best line of the song, if you pray, all your sins are hooked upon the sky. Even a false god can do the job: he hadn't ditched the crucifix, after all.

Carlos Alomar thought the song "had to do with Major Tom." While Bowie said nothing to suggest this, Alomar hit home indirectly. "Loving the Alien" is an apocryphal sequel to Bowie's astronaut songs and *The Man Who Fell to Earth*: a transformed man or an extraterrestrial (a Major Tom come home) who's misinterpreted as a savior. Perhaps that's the only escape for mankind: finding a Starman who fell to Earth. As the physicist Paul Davies wrote in *God and the New Physics* (another possible influence on

"Loving the Alien"), extraterrestrial intelligences would shatter "completely the traditional perspective on God's relationship with man," as one could imagine "a host of alien Christs systematically visiting every inhabited planet in the physical form of the local creatures."

"Loving the Alien" imposes its dream-speculative scheme upon a real political situation, especially in its weak second verse, which addressed the Middle East of 1984, with the Lebanese Civil War raging and "Palestine a modern problem." Bringing his muddled thoughts out into the sharp air, they expire — Bowie's speculations seem trite, his viewpoint that of a man on safari watching the convulsions of an anthill.

"For better or for worse, the information is inherent in the *song*, not in the writer or his intentions or even in the lyrics," he said in 1984. Dressed as an epic, "Loving the Alien" had some of his cloudiest harmonic colors of the period, its key blurring between G major verses and C minor refrains, paralleling the lyrical shift from Earth to heaven. He begins verses with hopeful slight ascents, only to drop in tone when he hits reality, whether Saracen or telegram. He lowers his high note upon each repetition of "pray" or "prayer" in the refrain, dialing down celestial expectations (so where he starts out hitting a high G on the first "pray," it's down a fifth to C by "a-lien"). Guy St. Onge takes the opening riff on marimba (suggesting the Psychedelic Furs' "Love My Way") and the song coalesces around guitar arpeggios working over the bassline, which has a similar descending hook as "Let's Dance." Mardin's strings are tasteful by the standards of *Tonight*, as is the vocal chorus, often a catastrophic force on the album. But there's a strain in the song's construction: the pre-chorus feels like a stage crew struggling to change a set, with three bars of upward jolts to link up to the refrain.

For a 2003 Tibet House benefit, Bowie performed "Loving the Alien" for the first time since the Glass Spider tour, with Gerry Leonard's guitar his sole accompaniment. He went back into the song as if trying to catch sight of its inspiration, while Leonard provided a grace that its studio recording never managed.

GOD ONLY KNOWS

*(Wilson, Asher.) **Recorded**: ca. 1 May-10 June 1984, Le Studio. Bowie: lead vocal; Alomar: rhythm guitar; Bramble: keyboards, bass?; Yale: Fairlight CMI; Rojas: bass; Hakim: drums; Figueroa: woodblock, congas; St. Onge: marimba; Pender: trumpet; Pickett: tenor saxophone; Harrison: alto saxophone; Elson: baritone saxophone; Clark, King, Simms: backing vocals; uncredited musicians: violins, violas, celli, double bass; Mardin: arrangement. Produced: Bowie, Bramble, Padgham; engineered: Padgham.*

***First release**: 24 September 1984, **Tonight**.*

Talking in 2011 about the latest salvage of the Beach Boys' *Smile*, Brian Wilson called the album "a teen's expression of joy and amazement. It's unrestrained. We thought of ourselves as teens then, even though we were in our twenties." Odd Victorians — butterfly collectors, mathematicians, heretical parsons — had idealized children. In the Sixties, in California, that cult was overturned in favor of the teen, the beautiful corrupted child. Adolescence became the peak of life. Catalogs of songs were made in its honor. Adulthood should be put off as long as it could. Wilson permanently put it off — he's a seventy-five-year-old who still sings about being a teenager.

Recorded in March-April 1966, when Wilson was twenty-three, "God Only Knows" was a prayer as a love song. Nothing new: soul singers had long taken expressions and phrasings used to praise God and put them in the service of lust and love. What was different about "God Only Knows" was its awkwardness. Tony Asher's lyric is an adolescent's thoughts: whip-fast revisions, bristling defensiveness. "I may not always love you," Carl Wilson sings. The bluntness of this line shows how ambiguous "God Only Knows" is — an eternal pledge of devotion by someone with a weak grasp on eternity. The second verse opens with bluster — every line in the verse ends with "me," its only rhyme. Brian Wilson's music adds to this, with blurs in tonality (a sway between E major, the key of the verse, and A major, the apparent key of the refrain) and instrumentation. The opening melody is a fusion of accordion, French horn, and strings; the staccato quarter-note chords that undergird the track are played by blends of sleigh bells, pizzicato strings, organ, harpsichord and slap-echoed piano and bass.

The instrumental bridge sends the song off into a new world. The extended coda, with its perpetual rounds, is a suddenly-imaginable bliss.

The sweet teenage holiness of the Beach Boys' records was exotic to British musicians. A cult formed around Wilson. "I *believe* you, Mr. Wilson," John Cale sang in 1975. "I believe you *anyway*." By then Wilson was padding about in a bathrobe, writing songs about Johnny Carson while his California mythland had gone to seed. "When I listen to your music, you're still thousands of miles away," Cale sang about being a nobody in Wales when he first heard Wilson's Californian exotica, and on Wilson's own distance from the promises his music made. Wilson was a dreamer who could never fall asleep, so he doled out his dreams to others.

Bowie heard a soul song in "God Only Knows," which is how he first covered it, with his "soul trio" the Astronettes in 1973. Ava Cherry sang it with fervor while keeping a happy bewilderment. Bowie's arrangement, with mandolin in the verses and a garrulous saxophone solo, was an ill omen, however. A decade later, he'd lost his tactical intelligence as a singer, his way of reconciling styles within himself. Deciding to cover "God Only Knows" on *Tonight*, he sounded like a man lost in a cathedral who begins to deface the walls in panic.

"When you do covers, you have to do them equally as well as the original — or better," Hugh Padgham said in 1984. But Bowie was defensive about "God Only Knows," wincing when Charles Shaar Murray mentioned he didn't like his version ("it might be a bit saccharine, I suppose," he said). A charitable reading is that Bowie interpreted the song as a pop singer of the Sixties would have — in particular Andy Williams. In his cover of "God Only Knows," Williams was respectful, cool: he takes his time with the melody, and when he moves towards the grandiose, he checks himself with awed, quiet phrasings of the title refrain.

As even the rare defender of Bowie's "God Only Knows" would admit, this was not Bowie's interpretation. He's restrained enough in the opening verse, though his croaking soon grates. His major alteration was to open the song with its second verse to heighten its possessiveness. So Bowie doesn't begin by saying he may not always love you. Instead he's already threatening *if you should ever leave me*. This theatrical jealousy takes root in his phrasing, which gets progressively more stylized: he handles "starrrrs" like he's gargling, and gets snagged on "sure," rolling it around on his tongue.

Strings become offensive weapons, followed by the horns. One saxophone gets a solo phrase that's hateful in its insipidness. The singers come in, up to no good. But the worst crimes are left to the artiste, who carries the coda by himself. Bowie sours the pleasures of the title's long vowels — the way "*ohn*-lee" and "knows" are warm sisters, a communal reassurance after the hard, short vowel in "God." Instead he puts his weight on "God" and rushes the rest of the phrase, letting it expire with a sickly gasp on "with-out yeeeeeww." The last repeat, in which he brutalizes each word, wringing whatever he can from each syllable, caps a performance that's astonishing in its tastelessness. The worst recording he ever made, but a fascinating one.

DANCING WITH THE BIG BOYS

(Bowie, Pop, Alomar.) **Recorded**: *ca. early June 1984, Le Studio. Bowie: lead vocal; Iggy Pop: lead vocal; Alomar: lead, rhythm guitar; Bramble: keyboards, Oberheim OB-Xa, Yamaha DX7, Jupiter-8; Rojas: bass; Hakim: drums; Figueroa: congas; Pender: trumpet; Pickett: tenor saxophone; Harrison: alto saxophone; Elson: baritone saxophone; Clark, King, Simms: backing vocals. Produced: Bowie, Bramble, Padgham; engineered: Padgham.*

First release: *ca. 3 September 1984, "Blue Jean".* **Live**: *1987.*

Iggy Pop was at the *Tonight* sessions for about a week. Not enough time, Hugh Padgham regretted, as Pop's presence shook Bowie's indifference. Along with witnessing the embalming of some of his songs, Pop wrote new pieces with Bowie, few of which were developed at the time. After a day's recording, around ten at night, Pop and Bowie went into the vocal booth with bottles of beer and "bellowed anything that came into their heads," Padgham said. "And I just recorded it all."

The result was "Dancing with the Big Boys," as close as *Tonight* ventured to spontaneity: Bowie and Pop trading lines over an A major-based rhythm track that was mostly Carlos Alomar's doing, earning him a songwriting credit. It was "the last thing we did, that was just thrown out there," Alomar said at the time. The obvious precedent was "Fall in Love with Me," another album closer/filler owed to vocal booth improvisations. But "Dancing with the Big Boys" was loaded with effects: discordant brass (the saxophonists and trumpeter were playing the wrong score), synthesizer punctuation (a bass-deepening distortion effect, as on Yello's "Oh Yeah"), the backing singers rooting for Bowie and Pop to knock each other out. Arthur Baker's 12" single remix (the first proper Bowie dance remix) went the whole hog, bringing in a truckload of booms, clatters, and shrieks.

Pop and Bowie had a scenario ("a takeoff on corporate structures and the way they crush the little guy," Pop said), but were mostly recalling lines from old notebooks. The best lines were Pop's: "this dot marks your location" was from a poem written at the Gramercy Park Hotel; "your family is a football team" was about immigrant families running bodegas in New York ("where they don't have too many resources in a capitalist society, they just get the whole family to work together for survival," Pop said). Bowie altered a Pop line, "too many people, too little belief," changing it to "too *much* belief" to reflect his current thoughts on religion (see "Loving the Alien"). It had some of the best, weirdest lines on the album — "death to the trees," "nothing is embarrassing" — and a spunk the rest of *Tonight* lacked. Bowie realized it, saying in 1984 that while he'd tried to "write musically and develop things" (to compose like his idea of a Fifties songwriter), he was done with that now. An improvised stomp like "Dancing with the Big Boys" was more what he was looking for, adding "I'd like to try maybe one more set of pieces like that."

THIS IS NOT AMERICA

(Bowie, Mays, Metheny.) **Recorded**: *(demo, backing tracks? overdubs) ca. September 1984, Odyssey Studios, 23-25 Castlereagh St., London; EMI Studios, 3 Abbey Road, St. John's Wood, London; (vocals, backing tracks, overdubs) ca. September-October 1984, Mountain Studios. Bowie: lead and backing vocal; Pat Metheny: guitar, Roland GR-300 guitar synthesizer, Synclavier; Lyle Mays: Oberheim, Prophet-5, Rhodes Chroma, Kurzweil, marimba; Steve Rodby: bass; Paul Wertico: drums. Produced: Bowie, Metheny; engineered: Marcellus Frank, David Richards.*

First release: *ca. 5 February 1985, EMI America 190/8251 (UK #14, US #32).*
Broadcast: *27 June 2000, Bowie at the BBC Radio Theatre. **Live**: 2000.*

Upon finishing *Tonight*, Bowie regretted having made it. He all but apologized for the record in the few interviews he gave to promote it, and had no intention of touring it. In a trough, he started doing soundtracks, composing and performing songs for four films (two of which he acted in). He found inspiration in contract work. Give him a plotline, a lyrical cue, an incidental requirement, and he was free from his inertia.

The first of these songs, "This Is Not America," recorded with the Pat Metheny Group in autumn 1984, was written for John Schlesinger's *The Falcon and the Snowman*, the true story of two upper-middle-class kids from California who committed espionage. Christopher Boyce (Timothy Hutton), a CIA contractor, began passing on secrets to the Soviets, with his go-between his boyhood friend Andrew Daulton Lee (Sean Penn), a dope dealer who found treason an effective way of arranging financing. They were arrested and jailed in 1977. Schlesinger's film was an anomaly at the height of the Reagan years, when movies were refighting Vietnam, equating the Grenada invasion with the Korean War, and killing Soviets and terrorists wholesale. *Falcon* refuses to have a sympathetic point-of-view character: Hutton's Boyce is callous, Penn's Lee a wretched user. It's Schlesinger's last thoughts on the Sixties, a story of minor players discarded by all sides, their actions touching no one in power. Theirs is a treason of boredom and nihilism. "I freely chose my response to this absurd world," Hutton's Boyce says upon confessing. "If given the opportunity, I would have been more vigorous."

The jazz guitarist Pat Metheny was hired for the soundtrack and spent time in Mexico City in early 1984 during filming. There he came up with an instrumental piece called "Chris," which would be Boyce's theme in the film. Attending soundtrack recording that summer, Schlesinger proposed that Metheny get Bowie to help turn "Chris" into a full-length song. Given Schlesinger's reputation in Sixties Britain (he'd directed *Darling* and *Billy Liar*), it's easy to see why Bowie was enticed.

Bowie turned up in London for a screening and took notes throughout for lyric and title ideas (Metheny recalled that Bowie had thirty good candidates by the last reel). They agreed that one line, "this is not America," (a retort from a Mexican cop who's arresting Lee, as the latter's whining about being an American citizen), had good potential. Bowie returned to Switzerland with Metheny's demo, to which he added "an additional vocal line on top of the 'A' section," Metheny said. He and his group went to Montreux a month later to cut the track with Bowie. After asking if anyone could sing (they couldn't), Bowie cut all backing vocals, transforming into different characters for each harmony track, Metheny recalled.

"This Is Not America" was hardly a jazz piece, as it has no improvisational sections. Metheny plays rhythm guitar throughout, not soloing even in the long outro. It's built on a repeating four-chord G minor sequence with Lyle Mays' synthesizer motifs, including a fanfare and a "French horn" counter-melody in the second verse, as well as a marimba line. The need to reference the film's title meant Bowie had some clunky lines about the falcon spiraling and the snowman melting "from the inside," along with the creaky identical rhyme of "piece"/"peace" and "America"/"miracle."

Bowie opens by reinforcing the declarations of his backing lines, then twists and reshapes his phrasing of "America"; his descending phrases match lyrical depictions of decay (blossoms failing to bloom, falcons falling). His vocals on the bridge are a highlight — the fragile octave leap on "was a TIME," the peak run of high Gs and As on "blew so pure," a touch of Donald Fagen on "faintest idea." He deftly handles the key change after the first bridge (to G-sharp minor), which puts a bite into the song, giving tension to the repeat of the first verse. Performing it live in 2000, Bowie held back the modulation to give the climax more of a wallop.

It was a quiet warning for the mid-Eighties — *this is not America*, whispering on a mall PA system, playing in an airport lounge. The best of its later interpreters was Charlie Haden, whose Liberation Music Orchestra made the song a raucous collaboration, as if to disprove its title.

CHILLY DOWN

Recorded: (studio demo ("Wild Things"), unreleased) ca. April 1985; (vocals, backing tracks) ca. June-July 1985, EMI Studios; (overdubs) ca. late October-early November 1985, Atlantic Studios, 1841 Broadway, New York. Charles Augins, Richard Bodkin-Martin, Kevin Clash, Danny John-Jules: lead vocals; Bowie: lead vocal (demo), backing vocal (soundtrack); Clare Hirst: backing vocal (demo); Kevin Armstrong: lead guitar, rhythm guitar; Nick Plytas: keyboards; Matthew Seligman: bass; Neil Conti: drums. Produced: Bowie; engineered: Tony Clark.

First release: 23 June 1986, **Labyrinth** (EMI America AML 3104/SV-17206, UK #38, US #68).

Here we intersect with a parallel world: the cult of *Labyrinth*, the 1986 Jim Henson film in which Bowie starred as the Goblin King, Jareth, and for which he wrote five songs. The average Bowie fan may regard *Labyrinth* as a footnote; the average *Labyrinth* fan may consider Bowie's portrayal of Jareth the best thing he ever did. (In a 2012 *Digital Spy* reader survey of the best Bowie songs of all time, "Magic Dance" made the Top 10.)

Henson began writing *Labyrinth* while promoting his first foray into "adult" fantasy, *The Dark Crystal*. As that all-puppet film had mixed reviews and performed weakly at the box office, "this time I want *people* in the film," Henson told the illustrator Brian Froud. The new film started with Froud's sketches of a maze and a baby surrounded by goblins. Henson did script treatments with Dennis Lee, a Canadian poet who wrote a ninety-page novella for his draft, and Monty Python's Terry Jones, who ignored this novella to write a script based on Froud's drawings. The plot concerned a goblin king who steals a baby to "lure a new challenger into the labyrinth," as per a 1984 Henson memo.

Henson first thought of Jareth as a puppet but soon realized the character would fare better if portrayed by an actor who could sing. Bowie quickly came to mind (other candidates were Michael Jackson, Sting, and David Lee Roth). After first meeting in New York in June 1984, Henson offered Bowie the role the following February. As Bowie liked Froud's sketches and the "inane insanity" of Jones' script, he was game. "I could see the potential of making that kind of movie with humans, with songs, with more of a lighter comedy script," he said.

He conceived the role of Jareth as a guy stuck ruling a backwater goblin kingdom when all he wanted was to hang out in a nightclub, and as something of a spoof on Iggy Pop. "Jareth at worst is a spoiled child, vain and temperamental, kind of like a rock 'n' roll star," Bowie said. Jareth's obsession with the heroine Sarah (Jennifer Connelly) was because "she's strong, wild and pure," like any girl in any Iggy song. His outfits are burlesques of a rock star's garb. He's a Ziggy Stardust who never got out of the provinces: well-hung, with a snow-white tan.

So from June to August 1985, Bowie spent weeks in Elstree Studios making a film in which his co-stars were an infant, puppets (the first days of his shoot were mostly a loss, as he kept looking off-camera whenever a puppeteer spoke), and a teenage actress with whom he had the best screen chemistry of his career ("I was just this side of getting it. Getting who David

Bowie was," Connelly said years later).

For the *Labyrinth* songs, "Jim gave me a complete free hand," Bowie said. "He allowed me to write the things I wanted." Henson's son Brian recalled that while his father expected Bowie to make piano-and-vocal demos to use for principal photography, Bowie instead showed up with "these gorgeous, virtually finished tracks" (including a version of "Underground" that already had choir vocals). The composer Trevor Jones wrote the film score after hearing Bowie's songs, incorporating pieces of them.

Bowie's *Labyrinth* songs are him in his scrapper mode, taking bits he'd considered for a "proper" album and repurposing them for a fantasy movie. Take "Chilly Down," a *Tonight*-style reggae piece given to jabbering puppets called the Fireys, whose heads float off and plop down, sometimes on different necks. They rip out their eyeballs, play croquet with their limbs, possibly attempt to kill Sarah — it's a badly-cut and shot sequence in which poor Connelly wanders around in front of a bluescreen, decapitating puppets. "It wasn't a nightmare but it was confusing," said Charles Augins, who choreographed the scene (and sang on "Chilly Down"), while Brian Henson later said the bluescreen use was "too early... I've often been tempted to go back in and re-do that whole sequence."

For the scene, shot in May 1985, Henson used a studio demo that Bowie had supervised the month before at EMI Studios. Originally called "Wild Things," the demo had a lead vocal by Bowie, coaching the Fireys quartet of Augins, Danny John-Jules, Kevin Clash, and Richard Bodkin-Martin ("he's very hands-on with his songs," Clash said). Like other *Labyrinth* tracks, it went through a few different sessions — rhythm tracks were cut at Abbey Road in summer 1985 while overdubs were finished that autumn in New York. "Chilly Down" is of mild interest: you can hear Bowie toying with what became the refrain melody of "Absolute Beginners" (there's a similar descending piano line) while his lyric is puppet Iggy Pop ("strut your nasty stuff, wiggle in the middle yeah").

MAGIC DANCE

Recorded: (film and album versions) ca. July 1985, EMI; ca. late October-early November 1985, Atlantic. Bowie: lead, backing vocal; Dann Huff: lead guitar; Robbie Buchanan: synthesizers, programming, guitars, keyboards; Will Lee;

bass; Steve Ferrone: drums; Lee, Diva Gray, Fonzi Thornton: backing vocals. Produced: Bowie, Mardin, Jones; engineered: Lew Hahn.

First release: *23 June 1986,* **Labyrinth**.

In the summer of 1986, EMI's vice president of A&R, Neil Portnow, spoke at an industry panel about the soundtrack album boom. *Footloose, Flashdance, Beverly Hills Cop, Top Gun* had spawned #1 hits and ruled the album charts, suggesting that films were supplanting radio as a primary way to hear new music. This had its downsides. Too many soundtrack appearances and an artist risked overexposure. Portnow singled out Bowie. "In the past he was an anonymous, mystical character, out of the public eye." Appearing in *Absolute Beginners* and *Labyrinth* back-to-back and the star of each film's soundtrack LP, he'd made things "difficult from a record industry standpoint, because it conflicts with the mystical [persona]." Portnow knocked *Labyrinth* in particular: "The lyrics were about puppy dogs and goblins — not relevant to Bowie's career from the mystical standpoint.*"*

Cut to a castle room. A man with a great shock of hair and clad in tight pants dances a jig around nearly fifty gyrating puppets. He grabs a baby and hurls him in the air, all the while singing "dance, magic dance! Dance, magic dance!"

Already wary of Bowie as global pop star, some older fans recoiled at his latest incarnation: a Goblin King who looked like he'd perform an ice-skating routine at some point in the picture. Portnow's complaints showed that EMI was also bewildered by their marquee artist. Where was the next album? What was this *Dark Fraggle Rock* nonsense? They all missed what Bowie was doing — winning a new generation of fans, and becoming even more of a Goth icon than he already was.

"Magic Dance" is "The Laughing Gnome" for the Eighties: both clever songs for kids, both pure products of their time ("Gnome," woodwind-happy 1967; "Magic Dance," synthesizer-mad 1985), both having more going on than first appears. Take the opening "you remind me of the babe. What babe?" routine, which Bowie lifted almost verbatim from a gag between Cary Grant and Shirley Temple in *The Bachelor and the Bobby-Soxer*, a film which, like *Labyrinth*, has a young woman attracted to an older, charismatic figure. Or how Bowie's opening lines parody Iggy Pop finding his dead junkie girlfriend in "Tonight." The refrain's closing line, "slap that baby — make him free!" is more whimsy-wisdom. When would you slap a baby? To make it breathe at birth. In a film about leaving childhood behind, here once a child gets slapped into life, she's free to go off on a journey of her own.

And apart from the goblin babe intro, "Magic Dance" has nothing to do with *Labyrinth* — it's Bowie dusting off the old pop theme of using black magic to get love. "Magic Dance" doesn't warm to its D major key until its refrains, while in the verses Bowie is modest in range until midway through he leaps an octave — "bay-bee-**blue!** No-**bo-dy**-knew!" — an astonishing bit of singing, as he moves from his chest voice to his head voice in a few beats. There's a crafty call-and-response vocal arrangement in the refrain, where the backing singers take the lead while Bowie waits until the third beat of each bar to counter them.

For its soundtrack re-recording, "Magic Dance" grew to over five minutes (there was even a seven-minute dance mix). Where the in-film track has Bowie playing against the voices of *Labyrinth* puppeteers, the soundtrack is a Bowie-dominated chorus, with Bowie even doing the baby gurgles (the intended vocalist, singer Diva Gray's baby, kept quiet whenever the mike was on). The soundtrack also gets a flashy guitar solo by Dann Huff. Mick Ronson had "Width of a Circle," Earl Slick had "Station to Station," Robert Fripp had "Heroes." Huff, drawing a pair of deuces, got "Magic Dance." He does what he can.

AS THE WORLD FALLS DOWN

Recorded: (film and soundtrack versions) ca. June-July 1985, EMI; ca. late October-early November 1985, Atlantic. Bowie: lead, backing vocal; Nicky Moroch: lead guitar; Jeff Mironov: lead, rhythm guitar; Buchanan: synthesizers, programming, guitars, keyboards, arranger; Lee; bass; Ferrone: drums; Robin Beck: backing vocals. Produced: Bowie, Mardin; engineered: Hahn.

First release: 23 June 1986, **Labyrinth**.

A thematically schizophrenic film, *Labyrinth* is torn between its rite-of-passage metaphor for teenage girls and its kid's games, with puppet dances, farting swamps, and Monty Python absurdity. Henson had intended the film to be the "heroine's journey" of an adolescent (his daughter Heather was exactly Jennifer Connelly's age). "A magical world that was the creation *of* and the creation *for* a young girl," recalled Mira Velimirovic, his creative designer in the mid-Eighties. But the influence of Terry Jones, who amped up the gags and didn't give a toss about Joseph Campbell-style mythology, muddied this idea. Trying to hook eight-year-olds and their adolescent sisters, the film has awkward tonal shifts and ends in an odd compromise. It didn't help that the script went through over twenty drafts, including those by George Lucas and Elaine May.

Central to the rite-of-passage concept was Bowie's Jareth as a sexually alluring adult figure, complete with legendarily tight pants. "Jareth has the tight pants because he is many, many things that a teenage girl relates to," said Brian Froud, who designed Bowie's costume. "He is a leather jacket guy... He's Heathcliff and also a ballet dancer... He's an amalgam of the inner fantasies of this girl." In early character sketches, Henson described Jareth as a "Hollywood talent scout" type, a sleaze on the make, looking to entice a young woman (Bowie would use this scenario in his own "Beat of Your Drum"). It's fair to say *Labyrinth* pulled this off, as a great number of people who were Eighties teenagers have testified that seeing Bowie in this film was a sexual awakening — there have been Facebook groups and websites devoted to Jareth's pants.

At roughly the midpoint of the film, Connelly's Sarah, having eaten a drugged peach, falls into a dream. At a masked ball, she dances with Jareth: the two of them gaze at each other. She's come to Jareth's world as a champion of childhood, looking to win back her infant brother, but now adulthood with all its temptations is laid out before her. The scene is set to Bowie's lush ballad "As the World Falls Down." ("Jim wanted something that was fairly old-fashioned in its sentiments," he said.)

Keeping with the film's mood swings, Bowie's *Labyrinth* pieces move from puppet singalongs in early scenes ("Chilly Down," "Magic Dance") to more emotionally-fraught pieces in the later reels, which Jareth sings alone. "As the World Falls Down," the first temptation of Sarah, "tells Sarah to stay in the dream where she can have anything she wants," as per an early script revision. "And oh, how she wants to forget it all, all her restrictions."

Glazed in High Eighties production by Arif Mardin, "As the World Falls Down" has a graceful melody where early upward pushes in the verse ("sad love," "pale *jewel*") lead to longer rising phrases ("within your *eyes*") until a tumble downward for the closing phrase. The refrain ends with Bowie lightly soaring up a fifth to close on the dominant note ("down"). It suggests he'd been checking in on Bryan Ferry, as Jareth's sophistication borders on ennui: "ev'ry *thrill* has gone, wasn't too much fun at *all*" is pure jaded Ferry.

Hooked on an eleventh-spanning Will Lee bassline, the soundtrack version of "As the World Falls Down" has a guitar solo to briefly pull it out of A major. Bowie's lyric is greeting-card copy ("I'll place the moon within your heart") but it fits the scene: Sarah's never been attracted to anyone before and has to start somewhere, with standard romantic lines for incomprehensible emotions. It ends in melancholy, Bowie murmuring "falling in love" to himself until the fade.

Slated as a Christmas 1986 single to coincide with *Labyrinth*'s British premiere, "As the World Falls Down" had a video shot by Steve Barron (the lead actors are a puppet and a fax machine) but the release was scrapped. Nicholas Pegg's speculation that Bowie was clearing the decks for his soon-to-come "hard rock" album seems right. Had it been released, "As the World Falls Down" might have been a hit, Bowie's own "Lady in Red" or "Careless Whisper." Whether he would have wanted one is another question.

WITHIN YOU

Recorded: (film and soundtrack versions) ca. June-July 1985, EMI; ca. late October-early November 1985, Atlantic. Bowie: lead and backing vocal; Buchanan: synthesizers, programming, guitars, keyboards; Brian Gascoigne, David Lawson, Simon Lloyd: keyboards; Lee; bass; Ferrone: drums. Produced: Bowie, Mardin; engineered: Hahn.

*First release: 23 June 1986, **Labyrinth**.*

Labyrinth's climactic song is a histrionic recitative that jolts from 3/4 to 4/4 to 6/4 time and barely has a melody, its refrain a wailing three-line expiration. "I had to write something that sounded like stone walls and crumbling power," Bowie said. Jennifer Connelly's Sarah reaches the heart of the labyrinth: an M.C. Escher-inspired set of gravity-defying staircases. (Like many bright teenagers in the Eighties, she has Escher's *Relativity* on her bedroom wall — another clue the Labyrinth world is in her mind.) Jareth demands that she love him and stay with him forever, that he'll be her slave in exchange for her bondage; she chooses to sacrifice herself to save her brother and is freed, whether to become an adult or to stay within childhood as long as she can, leaving on her terms.

As *Labyrinth* retreats into boisterous adventure upon encountering adolescent sexuality, Sarah and Jareth's last confrontation needs to derive its emotional power from one previous scene, the ballroom hallucination of "As the World Falls Down." So where Jareth has mostly come off as a dickish chessmaster, now he offers Sarah an all-consuming passion, merging her childhood fantasy life with her adolescent one. Well, in theory: in the scene as shot, she spends most of the time running up and down stairs, as if playing a level of *Dragon's Lair*. (It could have been worse: the original idea was for Sarah and Jareth to have a sword duel.)

Recorded as a demo before the Escher staircase scene was storyboarded (artist Martin Asbury had "a little audiocassette" with Bowie's song, and he "drew the panels in time with the beats"), "Within You" has an octave-spanning bass synthesizer motif paralleled by Bowie's opening phrases. Higher-pitched lines ("your *eyes* can be so *cruel*", peaking on a high G in each phrase) lead to collapse: the song packs off with a four-bar "I — iiiiii-i can't live within you," as Jareth gives up the game before the last moves are made. Four keyboardists vie to be the most over-the-top, as if Arif Mardin had offered a prize at the end of the session.

UNDERGROUND

Recorded: (soundtrack versions) ca. late October-early November 1985, Atlantic. Bowie: lead and backing vocal; Albert Collins: lead guitar; Moroch: rhythm guitar; Buchanan: synthesizers, programming, guitars, keyboards; Andy Thomas: programming; Richard Tee: piano, Hammond B-3; Bob Gay: alto saxophone; Lee: bass; Ferrone: drums, drum effects; Luther Vandross, Chaka Kahn, Cissy Houston, Fonzi Thornton, Eunice Peterson, Renelle Stafford, Daphne Rubin-Vega, A. Marie Foster, Beverly Ferguson, Garcia Alston, James Glenn, Marc Stevens, Marcus Miller, Mary Davis Canty: backing vocals. Produced: Bowie, Mardin; engineered: Michael O'Reilly.

First release: ca. 9 June 1986, EMI America EA 216/B-8323 (UK #21).

"Underground" has royalty for its backing singers: Luther Vandross, Chaka Khan, Cissy Houston, Fonzi Thornton (Chic, Roxy Music), Eunice Peterson (a session singer often working with Dionne Warwick), Renelle Stafford (another legend — she's on Paul Simon's "Mother and Child Reunion"), Daphne Rubin-Vega (future star of *Rent*), and members of the Radio Choir of the New Hope Baptist Church. Its lead guitarist is the master bluesman Albert Collins.

This cast, mostly recruited by Arif Mardin for a session at Atlantic Studios in New York, is the great squandered opportunity of Bowie's career. *This* is the only return of Luther Vandross, now an R&B superstar, into Bowie's orbit? *This* is the only time Chaka Khan appeared on a Bowie record? *This* is how you use Collins — put him low in one stereo channel, have him noodle against a wall of synthesizers, then let him take a solo in the coda where he struggles to be heard? Principal players in the final mix are keyboardist Robbie Buchanan and Bob Gay on alto saxophone. It's a wonder that Bowie and Mardin didn't hire Miles Davis and replace his trumpet lines with Fairlight dubs.

"Underground" flopped in the US, not cracking the *Billboard* Hot 100, and had a mediocre charting in the UK. Bowie never performed it on stage, and his only promotional effort was Steve Barron's video, which had puppets, animation sequences (budgets for these apparently went up after A-ha's "Take on Me"), and a *Doctor Who* regeneration style-montage of past Bowie incarnations. There's little mystery why "Underground" failed: it's a draggy song that squanders its resources, taking forever get to the payoff — the call-and-response refrain. After unveiling his choir, Bowie trudges back to the start and runs through the entire song again: sax solo, another verse, another pre-chorus, another bridge. It's almost two minutes before another refrain.

Kicking off with a key change to C major, the refrain has Bowie in good, rough voice and Richard Tee on romping piano, but it doesn't quite land its punch. The choir is a faceless blob; when Bowie's parries against and rallies them, their responses are muted. There's no real dialogue. "Gospel pop" was on trend in the mid-Eighties, with choirs carted in for Foreigner's "I Want to Know What Love Is" and U2's "I Still Haven't Found What I'm Looking For" from *Rattle and Hum*. There, the choir was a community to welcome the solitary, questing singer. Bowie's choir sings about a delusory world, a purgatory or hell, and supports him in his madness. He's tempted to disappear into a world of fantasy or could be contemplating suicide — hence the occasional screams for help, dutifully repeated by the choir. As if to atone for an atrocious lyric ("too much rejection/no love injection"; was this outsourced to Sammy Hagar?), Bowie was dedicated to keeping his song on the tracks, going falsetto at times to goose things up.

That's Motivation

Recorded: (backing tracks) ca. late June 1985, EMI Studios; (vocals, overdubs) ca. late August 1985, West Side Studios, Olaf Centre, 10 Olaf Street, Shepherd's Bush. Bowie: lead vocal; Armstrong: guitar; Steve Nieve: piano, keyboards; Don Weller: tenor saxophone; Seligman: bass; Conti: drums; Luis Jardim: percussion. Gil Evans: horn arrangement. Produced: Clive Langer, Alan Winstanley; engineered: Mark Saunders?

First release: 24 March 1986, **Absolute Beginners (Songs from the Original Motion Picture)** (Virgin V 2386/EMI America SV 17182, UK #19).

In the summer of 1985 Bowie was acting in two films in London back to back and recording songs for their soundtracks, while rehearsing for Live Aid. Like *Labyrinth*, Bowie's role in the other film, Julien Temple's *Absolute Beginners*, was a charismatic villain, another adult corrupter of pure youth. Only this time he wasn't dressed like a ballet dancer.

Bowie had taken a shine to Temple, who would replace David Mallet as his favorite video director for a time. Temple was young, flashy, ambitious; Bowie liked his energy, his aim to be part of a movement to invigorate British film. They hung out in London and indulged each other's nostalgia — Bowie's, for Swinging London; Temple's, for the punk summer of 1976.

When Temple brought Colin MacInnes' *Absolute Beginners* to the screen, Bowie wanted in on it. A British response to *The Catcher in the Rye*, MacInnes' 1959 novel was one of the first celebrations of the teenager. A prophet of youth culture (though he was forty-five when the novel was published), MacInnes had been an outsider his whole life, a bisexual whose allegiances lay with society's misfits and outcasts, and whose novels sing of polyglot London, with MacInnes regarding African and West Indian immigrants as Britain's saviors, the New Britons with style and soul. He would not be the last white hipster to praise blacks for their "realness" and "spontaneity," setting them against white Britons, who were "sexless sparrows in their suburban love-nest... outside their tiny world of consecrated mediocrity, nothing exists whatever." At the end of *Absolute Beginners*, the narrator, ready to emigrate, stops in his tracks upon seeing African immigrants disembarking an airplane. "I shouted out above the engines, 'Welcome to London! Greetings from England! Meet your first teenager!'"

While he ended his film with a *West Side Story*-style take on the Notting Hill race riots of 1958, Temple was more interested in showing the scaffolding of Modernity Britain being assembled. Asked to do a theme song, Bowie told Temple he'd do it if he could play a role as well. He was cast as Vendice Partners, a Satanic ad man with a shaky American accent, driving an E-type Jaguar, wearing streamlined Italian suits (it was the world of Terry Burns, Bowie's elder half-brother). Bowie's performance (his scenes were shot in August 1985, ending by the 20th) was his long-stewed revenge on the ad industry, where he'd worked briefly as a teenager ("It seemed an abuse of art. I was very high-falooting then"), and a winking acknowledgment that youth culture had been sold out in the cradle. Bowie "is, in a sense, the pied piper who leads successive movements," Temple later said. "I liked the idea of him playing a kind of devil. He has always been a manipulator of sorts."

Intended as a small-scale picture, a tribute to the dawn of the Sixties (Ray Davies also had a role), the film was crushed by expectations. *Absolute Beginners* was supposed to revive the British film industry, reinvent the musical, and launch a new generation of stars. Naturally, the British press hated it before principal photography was done. London's rain-plagued summer meant that location shots kept being postponed, and the budget ballooned ("we were a million pounds over budget before we started," Temple recalled). The film was cut by three editors working separately and not talking to each other. When *Absolute Beginners* finally premiered in March 1986, it had been knocked around for so long that it was old news. Reviewed modestly, performing dismally (it only opened in four theaters in the US), the film's failure led Temple to move to America. (In LA, he got a call from Michael Jackson, who invited Temple over to watch him and his sister Janet perform the *Absolute Beginners* dances.)

"That's Motivation" was Vendice Partners' set piece, "a real big number in the old tradition," Bowie said. It's Partners seducing the teenage Colin with a philosophy summed up by Alan Sinfield, writing of MacInnes' novel:

"if you listen to jazz, dress snappily and stay cool, then the rest of it needn't bother you." Its horn-driven sound is a mélange of "Heat Wave" and "The Name Game." Bowie's lyric has a few Sixties references (the Julie Christie version of *Far from the Madding Crowd*) and reuses imagery — the bloody skies of "This Is Not America" are back. Having to be lengthy enough to accommodate various set-pieces (a dance on a giant typewriter, a Seven Deadly Sins roll call), "That's Motivation" feels interminable, particularly when stuck in one of its amelodic bridges.

VOLARE (NEL BLU DIPINTO DI BLU)

(Migliacci, Modugno.) **Recorded**: *ca. spring-summer 1985, Mountain Studios. Bowie: lead and backing vocal; Erdal Kızılçay: lead guitar, rhythm guitar, marimba, bongos, keyboards, bass, drums, handclaps. Produced: Bowie, Kızılçay.*

First release: *24 March 1986,* **Absolute Beginners: The Official Motion Picture Soundtrack** *(Virgin VD 2514).*

The world of *Absolute Beginners* was the peak of Italy's influence on postwar British youth (the Italians were the inept junior partners in the Axis, so no hard feelings about air raids). Italy provided blueprints for what became Mod, with a vogue for coffee bars, Vespa and Lambretta scooters, winklepicker shoes, Anita Ekberg and Sophia Loren films, and Italian pop music. Among the latter was Domenico Modugno's "Volare" (officially "Nel Blu Dipinto di Blu"), Italy's entrant for the 1958 Eurovision Song Contest. It became a worldwide hit, with Dean Martin's version charting simultaneously in the UK and US. After suggesting that "Volare" should be heard in the film (it's background music in a few scenes), Bowie said he'd make his own version. In Switzerland, he popped round to Mountain Studios to cut "Volare" with his now-regular studio hand, Erdal Kızılçay. It sounds cheap and sprightly, with a bongos/marimba/handclaps rhythm base and a "period" guitar solo. Singing in credible Italian, Bowie retained the strange opening verse in which he recalls a dream where he painted his flesh blue and soared into the sky.

ABSOLUTE BEGINNERS

Recorded: *(backing tracks) ca. late June 1985, EMI; (vocals, overdubs) ca. late August 1985, West Side Studios; (piano overdubs) ca. autumn 1985, unknown studio. Bowie: lead vocal; Armstrong: guitar; Nieve: piano, keyboards; Rick Wakeman: piano; Don Weller: baritone saxophone (solo); Andy Macintosh, Gordon Murphy: baritone saxophone; Gary Barnacle, Paul Weimar, Willie Garnett: tenor saxophone; Seligman: bass; Conti: drums; Luis Jardim: percussion; Janet Armstrong: backing vocal. Produced: Bowie, Langer, Winstanley; engineered: Saunders.*

First release: *3 March 1986, Virgin VS 838/EMI America B-8308 (UK #2, US #53).* *Broadcast*: *23 June 2000, TFI Friday; 27 June 2000, Bowie at the BBC Radio Theatre; 2 June 2002, Top of the Pops 2.* *Live*: *1987, 2000, 2002.*

I once read of a DJ who was taken by the response when they played "Absolute Beginners," especially at the end of an evening. It's the Bowie song that people forget they love, they said. Nearly a UK #1 (held off by Diana Ross' "Chain Reaction" and a Cliff Richard/Young Ones duet), "Absolute Beginners" ends Bowie's reign on the singles charts, as he'd only have one more solo appearance in the UK Top 10 for the rest of the century. While some of its success was owed to the hype surrounding *Absolute Beginners* (the single died in the US, where the film barely existed), it was also one of his broadest, most heartfelt-seeming pop songs, even sounding like Neil Diamond in refrains.

On the radio in the late Seventies and early Eighties were songs about adulthood — fraying commitments, missed chances, regrets, sacrifices, sneaking around, feeling used up but still going at it. Some were saccharine, self-deceiving, some were home truths: "Still the One," "Reminiscing," "Against All Odds," "Secret Lovers," "Oh Sherrie," "Glory Days," "Hard to Say I'm Sorry." By the turn of the century, country music had annexed much of this territory, with today's pop charts ruthlessly dedicated to youth's pleasures and complaints. As a kid, I hated whenever a ballad about being lost in middle-aged love knocked off an important song like "Rock Me Amadeus" in the charts. But those songs were an undercurrent, warning that life in years ahead would have different concerns, different fears; it was the last time the pop charts were a generational dialogue.

"Absolute Beginners" is in this line of world-worn pop — it's not a song for the young, though Bowie casts himself as a beginner in love. His lyric, full of slant rhymes ("ocean"/"reason," "offer"/"beginner"), is a desperate equivocation, perhaps influenced by his recent cover of "God Only Knows." A heartbroken man has been down so long that it feels like it's the first time again, but he can't pretend it's so — his eyes are open, his feet are on the ground, he's sane. There's wariness even in the soaring refrains, despite the flying over mountains and laughing at oceans (not love per se but its commercial vehicles — songs and films). Where the first refrain finds Bowie saying there's no reason to fear the past, by the repeat he admits there is: falling in love is daring to make a mistake again. He's playing with the word "absolute": it means unconditional, as in a pledge of absolute love, but it also means to be complete. Two absolute beginners may be unfortunate lovers.

Bowie was doing a session for "That's Motivation," using a band assembled by Andy Ferguson, Thomas Dolby's manager, who worked for EMI at the time. It included the Attractions' keyboardist Steve Nieve, Prefab Sprout drummer Neil Conti, and Dolby associates bassist Matthew Seligman and guitarist Kevin Armstrong. Each musician was told they were supporting a "Mr. X" at Abbey Road, though most knew who "X" was before they arrived (Conti was tipped off that the artist "had a glass eye.")

Quickly getting through "That's Motivation," with which "Absolute Beginners" shares an opening guitar line, Bowie and the band had some time left, so they started working on something he was fleshing out for the film's theme song. Fueled by cigarettes, strong coffee, and allegedly cocaine (musicians at the session have differing memories), Bowie sketched chord progressions and lyric phrases, leading the band through the song as he wrote it, moving eight bars at a time, scribbling the lyric in bursts. Bowie was open to suggestions — a key change; an exuberant bassline by a beside-himself Seligman — and gave his own, like "think green" or "think Brazilian."

Solidly in D major (with shifts for tension, like using an A major 7th for the dominant chord, or an F# chord on "nervous"), "Absolute Beginners" is structurally close to "Underground," also slowly moving towards its payoff refrain like a plane taxiing on a runway. Its verses are each forty bars, over a minute in length, with languid phrasings — Bowie often extends a three-beat line over four bars. Even on the single edit, the refrain doesn't appear until two minutes in. But "Absolute Beginners" doesn't drag, either — it feels pliable. Able to be lengthened "Let's Dance" style (saxophone solo, percussion breakdown) or shortened to a single verse/refrain without sacrificing its feel, it works as a five-minute single edit, an eight-minute track on the soundtrack LP, a two-minute cut for the *Absolute Beginners'* opening credits, and a six-minute cut for its end titles.

Its refrain has one of the great Bowie melodies, worthy of comparison to "Lady Grinning Soul" and the second bridge on "Under Pressure." When Clive Langer and Alan Winstanley, who were producing the soundtrack, heard the rough take of "Absolute Beginners," they didn't know how to improve it. "We've just been given this one on a plate," Langer recalled telling his partner in the elevator afterwards. Their biggest contribution was to fulfill Bowie's request for a backing singer "who sounds like a shopgirl." The twenty-two-year-old Janet Armstrong's (Kevin's sister) performance on "Absolute Beginners" was her first-ever major-label studio session. It was another play on the title, with Bowie duetting with a newcomer.

The recording is a group triumph: Nieve's keyboards, which swell like an accordion; Seligman's musing lines on bass, taking advantage of the gaps between Bowie's phrases; Rick Wakeman's ABBA-esque flourishes on piano (though he claimed he was doing Rachmaninoff), embellishing on the vocal melody in refrains; the baritone-heavy saxophone section, which takes up the "bom-bom-bah-*oooh*!" vocal hook (a cousin of the vocal hook on "The Prettiest Star") and Don Weller's baritone sax solo, full of plump notes, as a wagging counterpart to the conga break; Bowie and Armstrong's last "true," which they hold aloft as long as they can, then descend together hand in hand. Gorgeous and valedictory, "Absolute Beginners" is Bowie's last time in the center.

DANCING IN THE STREET

(Gaye, Hunter, Stevenson.) **Recorded**: *(backing tracks, vocals) ca. 29-30 June 1985, EMI Studios; (overdubs) ca. early July 1985, Power Station, Atlantic Studios. Bowie: lead vocal; Mick Jagger: lead vocal; Armstrong, Earl Slick, G.E. Smith: guitar; Nieve: keyboards; Seligman, John "Skinny" Regan: bass; Conti: drums; Jimmy Maelen, Pedro Ortiz: percussion; Gollehon: trumpet; Pickett: tenor saxophone, baritone saxophone; Harrison: alto saxophone, tenor saxophone; Helena Springs, Tessa Niles: backing vocals. Produced: Langer, Winstanley; engineered: Mark Saunders, Bob Clearmountain, Stephen Benben.*

First release: 12 August 1985, EMI America EA 204/B-8288 (UK #1, US #7).
Live: 1986.

This single was made for charity and, as it sold well, it made a good amount of money, and some of that money, after the bankers, grifters, politicians, and warlords were compensated, helped to feed and clothe indigent people. That's a noble thing and should be commended. It was only meant as a Live Aid souvenir, a by-popular-demand release. Recorded on the fly, its backing tracks and vocals done in under four hours (it shows), its video shot later the same night (it shows), this ramshackle throwaway isn't one of the worst rock 'n' roll singles of all time, as a few have claimed.

That said, Bowie and Mick Jagger's "Dancing in the Street" is still a rotten record for which everyone involved should be embarrassed. Most likely they are, or have bravely embraced its absurdity. Bowie, late in life, was a fan of the "music-less" version of the video on YouTube, whose soundtrack is shuffles, groans, grunts, and burps. That "Dancing in the Street" would be his last UK #1 single and last Top 10 US hit is terrible but unsurprising. Chuck Berry went out on the charts with "My Ding-a-Ling."

Jagger and Bowie had been friendly rivals for years. "I maintained a very healthy relationship with Mick," Bowie said in 1983. "We sort of sparred around each other over the years, but I think what we have is a very good relationship compared to most." For Live Aid, they planned to sing a cross-Atlantic duet on stage — Bowie in London, Jagger in Philadelphia — but there was an insurmountable issue. Due to satellite signal delays, they'd be a second behind or ahead of each other (Bowie also allegedly suggested that one of them could go up in the Space Shuttle to duet, while in orbit, with the other back on earth). So instead they decided to make a video that would air during the concert. Though the original plan was to do Bob Marley's "One Love" (just imagine that for a moment), they chose Martha and the Vandellas' "Dancing in the Street."

Backing tracks and vocals were cut at Abbey Road at the close of June 1985, with the same band Bowie was using for the *Absolute Beginners* soundtrack, bolstered by percussionists and backing singers. Jagger brought the tapes to New York in early July, larding the mix with more vocals, percussion, horns, and guitar tracks by G.E. Smith and Earl Slick.

The Abbey Road session began with the band slogging through takes. Having learned the song by listening to a tape on a boombox, the band sounded "fucking awful... like a cabaret band," as producer Alan Winstanley recalled to David Buckley ("I had my head in my hands, thinking, what the fuck is this?"). Jagger's arrival got everyone down to business, with lead vocals done quickly — Jagger, Bowie, and the backing singers at first all sang together, which caused bleeding between mikes, so Jagger and Bowie re-recorded their lead vocals separately, with Bowie going it through line-by-line for one complete take. Drummer Neil Conti recalled Jagger being on an ego trip, strutting around, establishing his alpha credentials to the tea boys, and convulsing in the vocal booth, as per engineer Mark Saunders, "like he was performing to a packed Madison Square Garden," even breaking into a dance whenever backing tracks were played. Bowie gave Jagger the reins (Conti recalled him smiling "sphinxlike... while Jagger snarled at the engineer"; bassist Matthew Seligman said "Mick was much more vocal, mouthy — more rockist. David was the smiling, indulgent one"), an imbalance of power that extends to its video, where Bowie plays Robin to Jagger's louche Batman, and to its only live performance at the 1986 Prince's Trust concert, which Jagger dominates, in part thanks to Bowie having a wonky mike.

At the time, Jagger was trying to establish himself as a solo artist. The Rolling Stones were a mess: he and Keith Richards were barely speaking, Bill Wyman had his eye on the door, Ron Wood was in an orbit of celebrity parties and recording sessions, poor Charlie Watts was using heroin. Jagger admired Bowie's commercial intuition, to the point where for his solo album *She's the Boss* it seemed as if he'd sent a copy of *Let's Dance* to his label with a note attached: "How does one go about getting one of these?" Jagger used Nile Rodgers, Carlos Alomar and other Bowie collaborators: fair play, given how much Bowie had stolen from him over the years.

On "Dancing in the Street," both parties looked to affirm their A-1 celebrity status. A pernicious effect of the Live Aid/Farm Aid/Band Aid spectacles was to cement a rock hierarchy where "legend" acts stood at the top, with a lower tier of anointed successors (Tom Petty, Sting, Dire Straits, U2). It was the dawn of the Boomer Counter-Reformation, in which young musicians were eclipsed by the returns of Crosby, Stills, Nash & Young, a slumming George Harrison, an adult-contemporary Pink Floyd, Robbie Robertson pretending he was Peter Gabriel (a version who couldn't sing), an all-star Yes, a Zeppelin-sampling Robert Plant, and the Stones of *Steel Wheels*, reincorporated into a multinational.

Worse, Bowie and Jagger desecrated a song that kept every promise rock 'n' roll ever made. Martha Reeves' "Dancing in the Street" was as bright as the sun, with drum fills and breakneck turnarounds, carnival horns and Vandellas. It was global in aspiration, local in intention — Reeves singles out Washington and Detroit; it was dancing as collective liberation, committed to the present and the future. Few records are so gloriously *public*. Towards the fade, when Reeves sings, "let's form a big strong line," its political reading is unmistakable.

Van Halen had turned "Dancing in the Street" into pop-metal disco; *The Big Chill* had already spoiled Motown. But there's something uniquely awful in Bowie and Jagger's take: it's two men selling off their youth at cut rates. Its greatest legacy was its video, now lovingly reenacted on YouTube by kids born twenty years after its release. Jagger's dancing verified Truman Capote's snark that the former's stage act was "as sexy as a pissing toad." The choreography works best if you imagine that each man is pretending to duet with Tina Turner (choreographer Charles Augins' job consisted of telling Bowie and Jagger they had eight bars to move to the next mark). Bowie looks like a gawky fan who won an MTV contest to co-star with Jagger, with hand twirls, flailing judo kicks, and swaying his hips and clasping himself as he lip-syncs "streets of Brah-zil!" in one of the more ludicrous moments of his performing life. It ends with a freeze-framed synchronized ass-waggle. Hating this camp disaster takes too much effort and Bowie's death even made it poignant.

Do They Know It's Christmas?

(Geldof, Ure.) **Live**: *13 July 1985, Wembley Stadium, London. Bowie, Bob Geldof, George Michael, Paul Weller, Bono, Sting, Paul McCartney, et al: vocals.*

Bowie managed to avoid singing on the "Band Aid" 1984 Christmas charity single, though he contributed a spoken bit for its B-side. At the close of the Wembley half of the Live Aid concert, he led off the group singalong finale of "Do They Know It's Christmas?," taking the opening lines that Paul Young had done on the single. The Live Aid performance was a happy shambles, with Geldof singing Boy George's part as a Bill the Cat imitation, Paul McCartney sounding like he's in the last minutes of "Hey Jude," and

Freddie Mercury, fresh from one of the legendary Queen performances, not even given the mike. As soon as his part is over, Bowie deftly hands George Michael the mike and slips into the back rows to clap along and smile with the likes of Andrew Ridgeley.

"WHEN THE FIRES BROKE OUT ON THE RIO GRANDE"

Recorded: (unreleased) 18 August 1985, West Side Studios. Bowie: lead vocal (musicians same as "Absolute Beginners"). Produced: Langer, Winstanley; engineered: Saunders.

In January 1986, a television tribute to the fiftieth anniversary of *Looney Tunes* aired. Bowie took part. Filmed in the lobby of what looks like a Trump property, Bowie at first denies knowing Bugs Bunny, then admits he's a friend, then confesses he might work on an album with Bugs. With outrage, he says that Bugs once stole his girlfriend.

Ten years before, Bowie, at the peak of his coke-wraith image, made *The Man Who Fell to Earth* look like a documentary. Now he was starring in a Jim Henson movie, selling Pepsi, doing skits about Bugs Bunny. His persona was an elegant man making light of the fact he'd once been cool or strange. Though Bowie reportedly told friends that he was miserable during this time, in public he carried himself lightly. Being a rock star is inherently ridiculous; he was letting you in on the joke. In *Jazzin' for Blue Jean*, he played both the pompous rock artiste and the doofus in the audience. As Vendice Partners, he was an agent of Mod gentrification; on "Dancing in the Street," he honored the "Dame" nickname that *Smash Hits'* Tom Hibbert had given him. Asked to play the villain in *A View to a Kill*, he could have stepped in for Roger Moore, with a similar sense of camp and of having comfortably-large accounts in Swiss banks.

He was always irreverent in the studio. While making *Blackstar*, Bowie busted the chops of Donny McCaslin and Tim Lefebvre between takes. And one legendary joke tape came from a vocal session for "Absolute Beginners" in August 1985 that, a few days after Bowie's death, the session's engineer Mark Saunders played on his radio show.

In six minutes, over the backing tracks of "Absolute Beginners" one night in London, Bowie roasted his contemporaries, singing the same ridiculous refrain, whose last lines were (generally): "When the fires broke out on the Rio Grande/left nothin' standin' but the *smell* of the land/and the hubcaps that *burnt* through the skin of *your hand*/nothin' left at *all* but the *sound* of a *rock 'n' roll baaaaaand*." He sang it as Bruce Springsteen: groaning out the last phrase as if Clarence Clemons had him in a headlock. He imitated Marc Bolan, complete with bleating noises; a dusty theatrical Tom Waits; a deadpan Lou Reed (after a while, Bowie gives up: "no, no, no: it's real hard, Lou"); a regional circuit Anthony Newley; a shaky Iggy Pop ("difficult: he's somewhere between all of them"); a wan Neil Young. It's telling that apart from Waits, Bowie's impressions were of friends, collaborators, and influences. He was the laughing gnome on the margins again, doing *Mystery Science Theater 3000* riff tracks on rock 'n' roll. May the Bowie vaults be filled with hours of jokes.

CHAPTER SIX:

THE MAN ON THE SPIDER

(1986-1987)

I had all these thwarted dreams of what I'd tried to do with rock 'n' roll in the early Seventies, and I was trying to do all that a bit late.
— David Bowie, 1991

David never makes minor errors, only fundamental ones.
— Charles Shaar Murray, 1977

I found myself forced to impersonate a false character, to resemble the man they imagined I still was.
— André Gide, *The Immoralist*

I am the shipwreck of my own wanderings.
— Fernando Pessoa, *The Book of Disquiet*

SHADES

(Pop, Bowie.) **Recorded**: *ca. late April-early May 1986, Mountain Studios, Montreux. Iggy Pop: lead vocal; Kevin Armstrong: lead guitar, backing vocal; Erdal Kızılçay: bass, drums, organ, Yamaha DX7, E-mu Emax?, E-mu Emulator II?, Akai S900 sampler, backing vocal; David Bowie: backing vocal; David Richards: Linn drum programming. Produced: Bowie, Richards; engineered: Richards.*

First release: *6 October 1986,* **Blah-Blah-Blah** *(A&M AMA/SP 5145, UK #43, US #75).* **Live**: *(Pop) 1986-1987, 2017.*

David Bowie's last act of goodwill for Iggy Pop was to make him a hit record. He selected some demos, wrote other songs with Pop, and recorded the lot over roughly three weeks with a two-man crew. Kevin Armstrong played guitar and Erdal Kızılçay the rest: bass, synthesizers, keyboards, drums, strings. Both sang backing vocals, as did Bowie, though uncredited. Co-producer David Richards programmed a Linn drum, on loan from Queen's Roger Taylor. Bowie and Pop were the roadies, hauling gear into the studio.

Blah-Blah-Blah was crafted to be Pop's *Let's Dance* — quickly-made, contemporary-sounding, with a sure-fire single (here, a cover of Johnny O'Keefe's "Real Wild Child"). Pop was a willing partner in his rehabilitation. "I wanted to write stuff people would hum," he said in 1986. "[The album] sounds real good and I know it. It sounds good enough to be played on the radio." Shopped around to labels, it "was almost like a David Bowie record that, as a record company, you wished you'd had but never got," said Nancy Jeffries, talent head at the time for A&M. The latter got the album for around $500,000, including a producer's fee (Bowie wasn't *that* altruistic). A&M's promotion staff, in savvy counter-Christmas programming, pushed "Real Wild Child" in Britain in December 1986. It hit #10, the best singles chart performance of Pop's life.

Pop would occasionally grouse about *Blah-Blah-Blah* ("it's not my favorite album, but it got me some hits, so maybe it should be") and its none-more-1986 sound, particularly the Yamaha DX7-heavy arrangements. But the album was Pop in strong voice, dedicated to melody in a way he'd never been before. For once, there are no half-assed covers, no sloppy improvisations. It's a document of a hard-won early middle age. And some of Bowie's co-compositions rank among his best songs of the decade. As with his soundtrack work, he liked having someone else's name on the label — the challenge of making Pop commercial shook him out of his torpor. He went on a writing binge, piling up a stack of songs for an album of his own, which he wanted to make as briskly as he'd done *Blah-Blah-Blah*.

The Reformed Guy

After a turbulent early Eighties (drugs, voodoo), Pop was living with his wife Suchi Asano in a small Greenwich Village apartment. He spent his days "staying very straight": taking acting classes (landing a cameo in Martin Scorsese's *The Color of Money*), working out, reading, doing chores. He clipped newspaper articles for cut-up verses, brought his portable typewriter to Washington Square Park.

To an interviewer in 1987, Pop said that Bowie "sees me as a character. Probably an American beatnik who survived, Kerouac thirty years later. And I see him as one of the only representatives of the enfranchised world that understands me or that I can stand." Bowie was set to produce Pop's next album — a December 1984 *People* profile noted that Pop "waits for the signal [from Bowie] to start work" — but his movie-heavy schedule made Pop restless. He got in touch with former Sex Pistols guitarist Steve Jones, with whom he wrote two dozen songs and demoed nine, including "Cry for Love," "Fire Girl," and "Winners and Losers." Pop was considering cutting an album with Jones in LA. "David and I had talked for a couple of years... but why should he have to come up with the sound and the songs and the musicians?" he said. "I wanted to do this myself, and in fact he had to nearly twist my arm to let him produce once I was done with demos."

The two reconnected in November 1985, when Bowie was in New York finishing the *Labyrinth* soundtrack. Having assumed Pop "was in California doing Stooges retreads," he was surprised to hear a collection of solid songs whose only flaw was that they were all mid-tempo. Bowie would elaborate on the very "basic guitar, drums and vocal" Pop and Jones demos ("I was looking for someone who could color the music," Pop said) and had more cachet than Jones — he'd be a producer, PR man, and means to land a record deal.

Over three comfortable months, including trips to Mustique and Gstaad, Pop and Bowie wrote the rest of *Blah-Blah-Blah*. To reduce Bowie's compositional influence, Pop mandated that new songs would be demoed as his and Jones' had been. Bowie went to Manny's Music on West 48th St. to buy a four-track recorder, Ovation guitars, a Roland drum machine, a Casio synthesizer, and a Boss digital sampler. He brought the haul to their rehearsal space, where he and Pop spent hours reading manuals to figure out how the gear worked. Once recording began at Mountain Studios in Montreux, Bowie smoked packs of Gauloises, drank espressos, walked around holding a clipboard with each day's recording schedule, checking off takes. "There was a certain dynamic that evolved... that made the project both intense and ordered," he said in 1987.

Of the six Bowie/Pop collaborations, "Shades" was greatly Bowie's: he wrote the music (building off of the riff of Jones/Pop's "Cry for Love") and much of the lyric. Inspired by seeing Pop give a present to his wife, "Shades" is Bowie writing in the voice of a domesticated Iggy. "One of those 'reformed guy' kinda songs," Pop called it ("Shades" was sequenced as a response to "Real Wild Child"). "I think David saw it as a commentary on the kind of personal growth I've been having in the last few years."

With a pair of verses to gently usher in a refrain where Pop's baritone is tracked over an octave by the backing singers, the track is mostly Kızılçay — a bubbling synthesizer entwined with the bassline; an organ riff that slowly gains prominence; a tuba-like synthesizer line in refrains; a wildly-compressed drum intro and scattered fills throughout the track. Pop took his time with the melody, building confidently to peak with the refrains. He'd had to rewrite some of Bowie's lyric, whose refrain originally began "I know what kind of man I am/I'm not Saint Francis of Assisi or Baudelaire's son." Bowie "tends to be a little grand in his allusions," Pop said.

BABY, IT CAN'T FALL

(Pop, Bowie.) **Recorded**: *ca. late April-early May 1986, Mountain. Pop: lead vocal; Armstrong: lead and rhythm guitar, backing vocal; Kızılçay: bass, drums, congas, organ, E-mu Emax? E-mu Emulator II?, Akai S900, Yamaha DX7, backing vocal; Richards: Linn programming. Produced: Bowie, Richards; engineered: Richards.*

First release: *6 October 1986,* **Blah-Blah-Blah**. **Live**: *(Pop) 1986.*

Before recording *Blah-Blah-Blah*, Bowie, Iggy Pop, and David Richards went through contemporary albums. They liked the drum sound on Bruce Springsteen's *Born in the USA* and Bill Laswell's gargantuan production of Public Image Ltd.'s *Album* (or *Cassette* or *Compact Disc*, depending on its medium). *Album* was a vicious corporate rock record, a faceless board of directors issuing songs about torture and capitalism-as-narcotic. Laswell mixed the drums (some by Tony Williams and Ginger Baker) to sound like sustained aerial bombardment. But where Laswell had top players on call in New York's premier studios, Bowie and Pop were making a record on the cheap in Switzerland (as Pop didn't have a record deal, *Blah* was self-funded), reusing chips on Roger Taylor's Linn, and leaning on Erdal Kızılçay to do the work of ten players.

Born in Turkey, Kızılçay had gone to Istanbul's equivalent of the Julliard School (as per Bowie's description in 1987), where he'd had to learn nearly every instrument in the standard orchestra. So he could play viola and French horn, oboe, vibes, and drums; he'd swap instruments mid-song in his Swiss nightclub gigs. For Bowie, he was a godsend — a one-man band who let him cut full studio demos without the bother of shipping in players. Using Kızılçay as a substitute for a band on a proper album, however, had its downsides.

Case in point: "Baby, It Can't Fall," a song for which Bowie wrote the music, and which sounds like a victim of budget cuts. Its mix, with yo-yoing vocals, synthetic horn fills and whooshes, clutters up Pop's pledges of love and declaration of war against death. Its cheery keyboard hook is all but lifted from Huey Lewis and the News' "Heart and Soul." Relief comes via Kevin Armstrong's rhythm guitar, while his solo sounds as if it was played on baling wire. Recordings from Pop's 1986 tour, where "Baby, It Can't Fall" was recast as a sparring match between guitar and organ (expanding on a too-brief interchange between Armstrong and Kızılçay), vastly improve on the studio version.

LITTLE MISS EMPEROR

(Pop, Bowie.) **Recorded**: *ca. late April-early May 1986, Mountain. Pop: lead vocal; Armstrong: guitar, backing vocal; Kızılçay: bass, drums, organ, E-mu Emax? E-mu Emulator II?, Akai S900, Yamaha DX7, backing vocal; Bowie: backing vocal;*

Richards: Linn programming. Produced: Bowie, Richards; engineered: Richards.

*First release: 6 October 1986, **Blah-Blah-Blah**. Live: (Pop) 1986.*

One seeming ambition of *Blah-Blah-Blah* was to beat Billy Idol at his own game, a game for which Iggy Pop had designed the board and written the rules. "Cry for Love" and "Real Wild Child" were the best Idol singles of 1986, while the latter's B-side, "Little Miss Emperor," also claimed Idol territory (it was included on the CD and the British cassette.) Erdal Kızılçay, whose thunder-thudding bassline locks in with the Linn drum, plays a sparse piano line for transitions, staccato strings for the coda, and panned synth washes at the fade. With lines like "your open arms they flinch/Joan Crawford style" and a steal from Allen Ginsberg's "Howl," it's Iggy lusting after yet another imperious heartbreaker.

REAL WILD CHILD (WILD ONE)
FIRE GIRL
CRY FOR LOVE
WINNERS AND LOSERS

*(O'Keefe, Greenan, Owens ["Real Wild Child (Wild One)"]; Pop, Jones ["Fire Girl," "Cry For Love," "Winners and Losers"].) **Recorded**: ca. late April-early May 1986, Mountain Studios. Pop: lead vocal; Armstrong: lead guitar, backing vocal; Steve Jones: guitar; Kızılçay: bass, drums, organ, E-mu Emax?, Akai S900, Yamaha DX7, violin, backing vocal; Bowie: backing vocal; Richards: Linn drum programming. Produced: Bowie, Richards; engineered: Richards.*

*First release: 6 October 1986, **Blah-Blah-Blah**. Live: (Pop) ["Fire Girl," "Cry for Love"] 1986-1987; ["Winners"] 1986-1989, 1992; ["Real Wild Child"] 1986-1994, 1996-2004, 2015-2018.*

The songs that Pop and Steve Jones wrote in summer 1985 which made the cut for *Blah-Blah-Blah* were among its poppiest tracks — "Fire Girl" and "Cry For Love" in particular sound like lost Top 40 hits of the era. (A demo version of "Fire Girl," with prominent Bowie backing vocals, was an untitled bonus on a 2009 Pop beat-the-bootleggers box set, *Where the Faces*

Shine.) And the album's leadoff track, Pop's straight-faced cover of Johnny O'Keefe's "Real Wild Child," was a UK Top 10 hit and became a *de rigueur* soundtrack choice for movies about bratty kids (*Problem Child, Adventures In Babysitting,* etc.).

ISOLATION

*(Pop, Bowie.) **Recorded**: ca. late April-early May 1986, Mountain. Pop: lead vocal; Armstrong: guitar, backing vocal; Kızılçay: bass, drums, percussion, organ, piano, E-mu E-max?, E-mu Emulator II?, Akai S900, Yamaha DX7, backing vocal; Bowie: backing vocal, saxophone?; Richards: Linn programming. Produced: Bowie, Richards; engineered: Richards.*

***First release**: 6 October 1986, **Blah-Blah-Blah**. Live: (Pop) 1986.*

During his time in Greenwich Village (it was a cover version of Bowie's dry-out period in Berlin, down to Pop touting the joys of buying groceries and cleaning the house), Pop wanted to "work up my sense of melody," something he'd neglected on earlier albums. "The reason I had been singing in a monotone over the chord patterns in my songs was that I never practiced doing melodies," he said. "I thought that if I practiced doing melodies for a year or so at home, I would learn to think melodically." And Bowie wanted to make Pop "better aware of the qualities of his own voice," to know that "he didn't have to be so histrionic in what he was doing physically or with sound, and still have the same kind of weight as a performer and artist." He pushed Pop to sustain notes longer, extend phrases, expand his range.

The fruit was "Isolation," for which Pop gave his strongest vocal on the record. When Bowie tried to recruit Pop for a festival he was curating in 2002, he said Pop should sing "Isolation," "as it was a damn good song." Its recording was an ornate wall of keyboards, from a piano underline up through tiers of synthesizers and organ, while the song's creation was more spontaneous — emerging out of what Pop called "let's go down to the basement and play some music."

Its melody (similar to the harmonica line in "New Career in a New Town") and dumb-brilliant lyric ("I need some lovin'/like a fastball needs control") were greatly Pop's work, as was possibly the no-frills C major progression.

Bowie arranged the harmony vocals, whose ranks audibly include him. The staggered, shorter-held chorus responses push against Pop's longer-held phrases, then strengthen his build to the refrain (was Thom Yorke listening? "Isolation" is in the refrains of Radiohead's "Let Down"). While the saxophone, which crops up in the refrain and later trades phrases with Pop, is uncredited, its tone marks it as likely being Bowie's work. Title aside, "Isolation" is Bowie and Pop's tightest collaboration on *Blah-Blah-Blah*.

HIDEAWAY

*(Pop, Bowie.) **Recorded**: ca. late April-early May 1986, Mountain Studios. Pop: lead vocal; Armstrong: lead and rhythm guitar, backing vocal; Kızılçay: bass, drums, organ, E-mu Emax? E-mu Emulator II?, Akai S900, Yamaha DX7, backing vocal; Richards: Linn programming. Produced: Bowie, Richards; engineered: Richards.*

First release: *6 October 1986, **Blah-Blah-Blah**. **Live**: (Pop) 1986.*

Another of *Blah-Blah-Blah*'s pleas for commitment and refuge (northwest Mexico, here), "Hideaway" hangs on the frail hope that love can hide you from the world oozing in through the television set (see "Blah-Blah-Blah"). Iggy Pop moves from an opening complaint about how "big industry" has fouled the Earth to admitting his complicity in the ruin — in his last verse, which he sings over a circling synth line and Linn drum, he pledges he won't waste his last resource. With Kevin Armstrong playing high on his frets, building to a solo with a metallic taste of Roy Orbison's "Running Scared," the song has a bone-bare canyon for a refrain melody — only eight sung notes in twelve bars. Its philosophy is a Pop aphorism: "They say, 'So what?'/I say, 'So this'"; its only misstep is a bridge where Pop's touched by hearing children's voices.

BLAH-BLAH-BLAH

*(Pop, Bowie.) **Recorded**: ca. late April-early May 1986, Mountain Studios. Pop: lead vocal; Armstrong: lead guitar, backing vocal; Kızılçay: bass, drums, organ, E-mu Emax? E-mu Emulator II?, Akai S900, Yamaha DX7, backing vocal;*

Bowie: backing vocal; Richards: Linn programming. Produced: Bowie, Richards; engineered: Richards.

First release: 6 October 1986, **Blah-Blah-Blah**. *Live: (Pop) 1986-1987.*

Iggy Pop had yelled at the television all his life; *Blah-Blah-Blah* was no different. "Bad TV that insults me freely" ("Cry for Love"), "raw greed and king TV" ("Hideaway"), "I have no time to watch TV" ("Fire Girl"). His title track was a stream of vitriol at the set, with Pop pacing around the room, hurling abuse at whoever's face appears in the box — designers, celebrities, politicians (Israeli foreign minister Shimon Peres; "Senator Rambo," which Pop sings like "Rimbaud"), and frozen food manufacturers. "A way of saying that I disrespect the things that the media and the world in general are saying to me. It's a very polite way of saying 'fuck you'," as he explained the song's title.

He'd started painting as a way of creating a "reverse TV." "Blah-Blah-Blah" is a complaint by a minority shareholder on the state of the whole rotten enterprise. Rock music as another subsidiary, another detergent brand. "That phrase, 'rock and roll,' doesn't mean anything to me now," Pop said in 1987,

All the governments have gotten behind it, all the corporations are behind it. In America, they use Fifties rock songs to sell Corn Flakes and baby diapers... I could see a day when rock music could be used during civil riots just to keep people quiet. *Boom-boom chick. Citizens: surrender now. Boom-boom chick.*

This was only two years before the Panama invasion, when the US Army besieged the Vatican embassy where dictator Manuel Noriega was holed up, blasting the likes of "Welcome to the Jungle," "We're Not Gonna Take It," "I Fought the Law," and "Let's Dance" at deafening volume for days.

Who's "Iggy Pop" anyway? An accredited provider of "danger." "In our daydreams, we all think we're Superman," he said. "Rock singers are nothing but low-grade forms of Superman... a bunch of trash Supermen." At the center of it all was the media, the urine stream of "information," which has made us a fundamentally unserious people who deserve whatever we get. "The most spoiled brats on God's green Earth," Pop mumbles towards the fade. Built along the lines of Bowie and Pop's "Dancing with the Big Boys," "Blah-Blah-Blah" is cluttered with whatever geegaws were on hand. Pop's voice is echoed, delayed, sped-up; it claws for room against synthesized dog-barks, Kevin Armstrong's guitar lines — full of hammerings, feedback groans and little barbed riffs — and Erdal Kızılçay's garage-band organ.

For its co-composer, "Blah-Blah Blah" was what Bowie would attempt for the rest of the decade: "topical" protest songs, rants, barrages, abuses, self-purges, finger-pointing. He never did it as well as Pop did in three minutes here.

The End of the Affair

We have drifted away from each other, and in a way I understand why. I've never talked to him about this… I think there was a moment where Jim decided that he couldn't do a fucking article without my name being mentioned, and I don't think that's a very comfortable feeling. I completely understand — I really, really do. Unfortunately, I think Jim took it personally, and that's a shame because I would have liked to remain closer to him.
— Bowie, 1999

Is he still pals with Bowie? No. When did he last see him? I can't remember. I spoke with him on the phone about seven years ago, he got my number and we caught up, had a very cordial, nice conversation. He's living a certain life, I'm living a certain life, there's not a cross there right now.
— Pop, 2010

After *Blah-Blah-Blah*, Pop and Bowie never collaborated again. The break was mainly Pop's doing. He was tired of being David Bowie's reclamation project. *Brick by Brick*, his Bowie-less but commercially successful 1990 album, was a vindication. Their friendship waned gradually, as many do — like the slow clouding-over of an afternoon. They worked some festivals together in 1996 and spent a few days touring Greece. They'd occasionally talk, mainly about work: Bowie wanted him to play Meltdown Festival (and sign to his independent label). If Bowie's 2004 summer tour hadn't ended abruptly, he and Pop would've played the same festival in Spain.

But whatever uses they'd had for each other, whatever roles they'd once played, were done. One of the people Bowie was talking to in "Where Are We Now?" was his old Berlin friend. "You never knew that: that I could *do that*," he sang, still playing the straight man to Pop's wild boy. After Bowie died, Pop described their relationship to the press as "this guy salvaged me from certain professional and maybe personal annihilation — simple as that," and that he considered Bowie "more of a benefactor than a friend, in a way most people think of friendship." Yet the first thing that he said publicly upon hearing the news was that "David's friendship was the light of my life."

WHEN THE WIND BLOWS

(Bowie, Kızılçay.) *Recorded*: ca. spring-summer 1986, Mountain Studios. Bowie: lead and backing vocal; Kızılçay: guitar, Yamaha DX7, E-mu Emax, Akai S900, keyboards, bass, drums, drum programming, congas, strings, horns (arranged: Kızılçay). Produced: Bowie, Richards; engineered: Richards.

First release: 27 October 1986, **When the Wind Blows: Original Motion Picture Soundtrack** (Virgin V2406/7 90599-1).

Bowie's last Eighties soundtrack piece was for Jimmy Murakami's *When the Wind Blows*, an animated adaptation of the graphic novel by Raymond Briggs. He intended it to be one of several songs he'd do for Murakami's film, but needing to focus on his own record, he pulled back from the project, with Roger Waters filling in.

Born in 1934, Briggs was a lower-middle-class London suburbanite. He attended art college, became a freelance illustrator and cartoonist, got renown as a children's author, especially for *Father Christmas* (1973) and *The Snowman* (1978). One of a bilious generation of British illustrators, his peers were Ralph Steadman, chronicler of *Fear and Loathing in Las Vegas*, and Gerald Scarfe, who did the artwork and animation for Pink Floyd's *The Wall*. Briggs was radicalized in the Eighties, joining the Committee for Nuclear Disarmament after researching the effects of nuclear war for *When the Wind Blows*. His 1984 *The Tin-Pot Foreign General and the Old Iron Woman* vilified both sides of the Falklands War, depicting Thatcher and the Argentine junta alike as murderous iron monsters.

In *When the Wind Blows*, an old couple learns of imminent war and set about making do in the Blitz spirit (Bowie's theme song has a melodic suggestion in the verses of Vera Lynn's wartime standard "We'll Meet Again"): following government pamphlets to create a lean-to shelter from wooden doors. After the nukes fall, they're as helpless as children, going through the motions of their old life (teatime, sweeping up their shattered house) until coming down with radiation sickness. The film ends with them dying in agony while still trying to Keep Calm and Carry On. As the *Bulletin of the Atomic Scientists* wrote in its review of Briggs' book, "following government safety guidelines is of course useless; common sense is useless; good cheer is useless; optimism and bravery are mere self-delusion."

While he'd struggle on his next album to write about the state of "urban life," Bowie was adept at writing about cataclysms — it was a stage large enough for his concerns. In *When the Wind Blows*, the slow expiration of one middle-class English home stands for the inhumanity of the Cold War, with its mutual death pacts and militarization of nature. Bowie caught this idea in his song, using imagery associated with comfort and calm, then poisoning it. His refrain is a repetition of "when the wind blows," which he sings mournfully and chillingly: it's a death sentence, as the wind carries fallout. By far the best of the brief collaboration of Bowie and Erdal Kızılçay (see "Girls" and "Too Dizzy"), "When the Wind Blows" is Bowie singing over a demo that Kızılçay had made. He'd asked Kızılçay to turn the demo "into a big classical explosion," and "that's what I did, obviously," the latter said in 2018. "I remember playing 32 tracks of this song at Mountain Studio."

GIRLS

(Bowie, Kızılçay.) **Recorded: (Tina Turner)** *ca. late 1985-early 1986, Mayfair Studios, Studio Grande Armée. Turner: lead vocal; Terry Britten: guitar, bass; Nick Glennie-Smith: keyboards; Phil Collins: drums; Gary Kattell: percussion. Produced: Britten; engineered: John Hudson.* **(Bowie)** *(backing tracks, vocals) ca. September-November 1986, Mountain Studios; (overdubs) ca. November 1986, Power Station. Bowie: lead and backing vocal, keyboards; Peter Frampton: lead guitar; Carlos Alomar: rhythm guitar; Philippe Saisse: piano; Kızılçay: bass, drums, keyboards, Yamaha DX7, E-mu Emax, Akai S900; Crusher Bennett: percussion; Earl Gardner: trumpet; Stan Harrison: alto saxophone; Steve Elson: baritone saxophone; Lenny*

Pickett: tenor saxophone; Robin Clark, Loni Groves, Diva Gray, Gordon Grodie: backing vocals. Produced: Bowie, Richards; engineered: Richards, Malcolm Pollack.

*First release: (Turner) 23 September 1986, **Break Every Rule** (Capitol EST 2018/PJ 512530); (Bowie) 29 June 1987, "Time Will Crawl" (EA 237/B 43020, UK #33); (Japanese vocal version) 18 April 1987, **Never Let Me Down** (EA CP32-5398). **Live**: (Turner) 1987-1988.*

Tina Turner credited Bowie with helping revive her fortunes, as he'd recommended that EMI sign her. If only their collaborations were kept to label politics. Following a somnolent duet on "Tonight," Bowie and Turner paired up again for "Girls," which Bowie co-wrote (with Erdal Kızılçay) for the follow-up to Turner's massive *Private Dancer*. She summoned everyone on the charts to take part. Bowie, Rupert Hine, Bryan Adams, Mark Knopfler, and Paul Brady contributed songs; musicians included Steve Winwood, Phil Collins, and Eric Clapton; Steve Lillywhite and Bob Clearmountain were among the horde who put it together. *Break Every Rule* went platinum, spawned eight singles targeted to regional markets, and was soon forgotten.

"Girls" wasn't a retread of the *Private Dancer* sound, as Terry Britten and Graham Lyle's "Typical Male" was. Bowie had a fresh urge to write a Jacques Brel-style *chanson*. With a theatrical verse patched to a set of bludgeoning climaxes, "Girls" has Turner brooding about the caprices of "girls" while jumping through hoops (take the dead stop at 2:28). She was a gifted interpreter — knowing just where a song would crack, as on "Proud Mary" — while her later work has a scorched-earth quality. In "Girls," she's mostly trying to get a handle on the song.

Bowie cut his version of "Girls" during the *Never Let Me Down* sessions (maybe as a hedge — had Turner's take been a hit, he could've ridden in its slipstream). It was issued as a B-side in summer 1987, with Bowie singing a Japanese vocal version as well. Though "Girls" starts in the cabaret vein of "Time" and "My Death," once the refrains get underway, with backing singers and merciless saxophone, the song slips away from Bowie as it had Turner. The arrangement sounds as if Bowie and Kızılçay rummaged through a junk drawer: some "China Girl" in the rhythm guitar; the bassline of "Criminal World"; a touch of Rita Coolidge's Bond theme "All Time High." Bowie even used the same *Blade Runner* line ("like tears in the rain") he'd quoted on a note he'd sent to his half-brother's funeral in 1985 (see "Jump They Say").

By the four-minute mark, "Girls" is ready to expire of exhaustion (the single edit mercifully ended here), but its "extended edit" had two minutes more to go, including a guitar solo so devoted to wankery that whoever played it deserved a repetitive strain injury. An ambitious composition smothered in the making, "Girls" symbolizes the album for which it didn't make the cut (though it was included on reissues).

DAY-IN DAY-OUT

Recorded: (backing tracks, vocal) ca. September-November 1986, Mountain Studios; (overdubs) ca. November 1986, Power Station. Bowie: lead and backing vocal, keyboards; Sid McGinnis: lead guitar; Alomar: rhythm guitar; Saisse: piano; Kızılçay: bass, drums, keyboards, Yamaha DX7, E-mu Emax, Akai S900; Bennett: percussion; Gardner: trumpet; Harrison: alto saxophone; Elson: baritone saxophone; Pickett: tenor saxophone; Clark, Groves, Gray, Grodie: backing vocals. Produced: Bowie, Richards; engineered: Richards, Pollack.

First release: 23 March 1987, EMI America EA 320/B-8380 (UK #17, US #21). Live: 1987.

In the heart of the Eighties, a mime-trained theatrical musician released an album. It had the artist engaged with the world, refining contemporary life through a baroque imagination. With its mastery of the synthesizer, the intricacy of its compositions, its brilliant sequencing, its interlinked videos, the album was a masterpiece. The ambitious young have stolen from it for over thirty years.

David Bowie was alive and well in the mid-Eighties. Her name was Kate Bush.

The Prologue, in Switzerland

"When I'm not working, I lead a quiet existence," Bowie said at a press conference in 1987. "I'm self-contained. I can go for months without wanting to see anyone... I live in the mountains and I'm an obsessive skier." He always said his work was colored by where it was made. So we have Bowie's London years, his Los Angeles period, his Berlin albums, his last New York

City albums. But there are no Switzerland albums, no "Switzerland trilogy," though Bowie wrote, demoed, and recorded parts of seven albums there, for over a decade.

The Switzerland albums are a disparate bunch — there's little to unite *Never Let Me Down*, *The Buddha of Suburbia*, *Tin Machine*, *Black Tie White Noise*, and *1. Outside*, and there was little romance in their making. It's the work of a millionaire living in a fourteen-room Belle Époque château in the hills above Lausanne — "it's just a regular house," he'd protest, though from photographs it looks like the sort of place where a severely-bowed cello is heard in an upper room and whose cellar has vintages older than many democracies. During sessions, he drove to work each morning like a bank chairman: east on the A9, paralleling the Lake Geneva shoreline, with Mont Pèlerin looming on the left, then down to the lakeside Mountain Studios in Montreux.

After looking at street photos of Lausanne and Montreux, Momus wrote:

I understand Bowie's lost years better. In such a beautiful landscape, rolling with natural reverb, things may well sound better — more dignified — than they would elsewhere. Bad ideas might sound like good ones... vague social commentary about homelessness might well sound edgy and incisive. Time might well crawl up here, and musical trends might well seem adequately summarized by a talented multi-instrumentalist discovered in a local restaurant.

The sound of the Switzerland albums is that of efficiency, of economy and adaptation, of discipline and production. Erdal Kızılçay described the making of *Never Let Me Down* as running on a loose swing shift — start at 10am, end by dinner at eight. Listen to the composer's multi-tracked demos, read his lyrics, cut the tracks with little fuss.

"I live in the quietest of countries," Bowie said in 1987. "The Swiss are a mountain people... very insular... very contained into themselves." He could have been describing his own time there, a period when, as he said nearly a decade later, "I lost the trade winds and found myself in the creative doldrums." In 1986, a year mostly spent in Lausanne, Bowie worked constantly, writing and demoing songs. This became *Never Let Me Down*, his truest "Swiss" album, the work of a cossetted exile trying to write about the dirty world beyond the Alps.

The Failure

Never Let Me Down lies in the valley of the "worst-evers," often regarded as Bowie's equivalent to *Ishtar*, *Gigli*, the Microsoft Zune. In 1995, Bowie called it his "nadir... such an awful album... I really shouldn't have even bothered going into the studio to record it. In fact, when I play it, I wonder if I did sometimes." He was still harsh a few years later, telling Charlie Rose "I was writing crap and nothing was going right, artistically, for me."

Yet its critical savaging was gradual. Some early reviews were even glowing: Glenn O'Brien in *Spin* praised the album as "an inspired and brilliantly crafted work." It was framed as that deathless critical cliché, the "return to form," with Bowie going back to his roots, back to rock 'n' roll, back to *real* music, not the poncing pop stuff (*Washington Post*: "it could turn out to be something of a comeback album"). It was what his fans supposedly craved: a hard rock record from a refreshed Bowie, who was addressing Important Issues like prostitution, homelessness, drug abuse, and environmental degradation. Its timing was acute. As Baby Boomer revivalism got underway, *Never Let Me Down* was awash in Sixties nostalgia, flavored with the sounds of John Lennon, Smokey Robinson, and Neil Young. And unlike his previous two albums, there was no lack of new material. Bowie even played some guitar solos.

The backlash started in Britain, where *Never Let Me Down* was dying in the shops: its lead-off single peaked at #17 and the album at #6, the worst performance of a Bowie record in the UK since 1971. The cross-Atlantic promotional junket ("club" shows-cum-press conferences in nine cities) didn't help things. The whole enterprise — album, global mega-tour, the latest edition of Bowie with his half-moon haircut — seemed like an extravagant product launch for second-rate goods. Tom Hibbert, who had been baiting Bowie for years in *Smash Hits*, saw him stumbling and went in for the kill. "If Dame David is such a bleeding chameleon, why, pray, can't he change into something more entrancing than the skin of an ageing rock plodder?"

Though Bowie wrote off *Never Let Me Down* as early as the Tin Machine days (he never performed anything from it after 1987), he was proud of it at the time: it was his renewed commitment to craft after years of indolence. Peter Frampton recalled arriving in Switzerland and having Bowie show off "the lyrics he was so proud of. He'd got a new baby and he wanted to share it." "I am really happy with the songs I've written," Bowie said at one press conference. "He praised it until the minute the reviews came in," Kızılçay recalled in 2018. "Then he said, 'It wasn't me. It was the other people on the record'." *Never Let Me Down*, meant as a rebirth, would be state's evidence of his shocking decline as a composer and a performer.

It was his ugliest-sounding record since *Diamond Dogs*. Both albums are the work of a Bowie with something to prove, down to playing the guitar solos; each inspired an over-the-top tour; each held clues for his next direction. The parallel goes only so far. He'd built *Diamond Dogs* from failures, filled it with blood and anger. He'd seen glam collapsing and had fought his way out. In *Never Let Me Down*, nothing was at stake except royalties. Becalmed, detached, Bowie was left with spectacle, which had served him well enough in the past.

Five-Piece Band Music

Bowie bought a Fostex sixteen-track and AHB mixing console to make intricate home demos (even getting lyrics done early for once) and brought them into Mountain Studios for a small crew to replicate. As on *Blah-Blah-Blah*, Erdal Kızılçay played keyboards and synthesizers, was the rhythm section, and provided any sound Bowie wanted. Frampton and Carlos Alomar were flown in for guitar overdubs. The tracks would be garnished with horns and singers in New York and mixed to be hits by Bob Clearmountain. "Very, very structured, this one," Bowie said. "I played the demos and said, 'I want it to sound exactly like this, but better'." Alomar wondered what the point was of having to copy demo guitar lines that Bowie had played in imitation of him.

It had been two years since he'd made an album for EMI — and he hadn't toured to support *Tonight*. He'd spent months writing and producing Iggy Pop's relative hit record for a rival label. EMI memos circulated about "the declining prospects of a viable product" from Bowie. With *Absolute Beginners* and *Labyrinth* flops, his reputation was in freefall. EMI wanted a chart-aimed record in the can by Christmas and a global tour to promote it in 1987.

Never Let Me Down was warped by contrary motives. Bowie wrote hard rock "protest" songs for a tour to be built around a giant spider prop. He crowned twisted verses with booming refrains. He wrote ambitious top melodies, some of which he struggled to sing and for which "rough" guide vocals were often used on the album. He gave them lyrics that, at best, attempted some surrealist urban reportage. He needed songs lengthy and repetitive enough for a dance troupe to use, but he also wanted a "stripped down" sound for a "five-piece band." Slavishly recreating his demos, he then went to the Power Station to crowd up the tracks. The Borneo Horns returned; a master funk percussionist, Crusher Bennett, was hired to play on supremely unfunky songs; Mickey Rourke did a guest rap. The album's cover photograph was apt. Circus performer Bowie is mid-leap in the ring, surrounded by clutter with vague connections to his lyrics. It was a Kit Williams puzzle with no prize rewarded.

Born in a Handbag

Frenetically monotonous, "Day-In Day-Out" was the album's lead-off track and single. It bursts open, rolling out its biggest hook like "Let's Dance" did, with a similar descending bassline. But instead of red shoes and serious moonlight we get a prostitute who was "born in a handbag" (an ill-timed Oscar Wilde joke) and who's in "in the pocket of a homeboy" (sung as "hoome-*boy*"). It devolves into a barked "gonna get a shawt-gun... POW!", with some of Bowie's phrasing reminiscent of David Byrne's on Talking Heads' "Stay Up Late."

   "A lot of the subject matter deals with the street," Bowie said of *Never Let Me Down*. This was his preferred adjective of the period — the "Day-In Day-Out" video was "street," his dancers for the Glass Spider tour were "street." The same abstract Street as in "Under Pressure," with visuals taken from movies like *Streets of Fire* and BBC reports about Los Angeles gang wars. "I'm like everyone else, I know what's going on in the world basically through television and the newspaper — one for the pictures, the other for the truth." He split the album between songs of "personal romance" and "some kind of statement or indictment of an uncaring society," then tried to bridge this gap within the same song, making for gruesome constructions. There was a theme of women being dominated by powerful men, and a vague commitment to "narrative" ("I used to write in a fragmented way but these days I write in a more linear fashion").

He said he wrote "Day-In Day-Out" to show society's indifference to its caste of undesirables. Los Angeles "is not that far from the situation in London or even Delhi… when you think you've got to the bottom of the pit, it gets even worse." Stuck at the bottom of the pit, the song shifts between two battling major chords, G and F. Verse and refrain are indistinguishable, the latter worsened with grade-school rhymes for its call-and-response hook. Bowie's in good voice, if hoarse-sounding in places (see the bridge's last set of *ooh! ooh!*s). Alomar and Frampton's guitars scrap nicely, Kızılçay's drumming is as solid as granite; the house-style piano (likely Philippe Saisse) that zips in for the second verse is a welcome novelty; Sid McGinnis' guitar solo wakes up the latter half. At some point a "Borneo Horns" brass arrangement was replaced by staccato synthesizer "horn" lines (the restoration of original brass tracks for the 2018 remix/remake of "Day-In Day-Out" show that the synths played their lines nearly note-for-note. The restoration also reveals there was a baritone sax line in the bridge — its synth equivalent is barely audible on the original track). Still, for his opening salvo and statement of intent, "Day-In Day-Out" was muddied sound, mild fury.

Its video, shot by Julien Temple in Los Angeles, had a cast that Bowie proudly noted included actual homeless people. It's a 1987 take on a Victorian slum tour, with Bowie as roller-skating narrator. In one scene, a prostitute is assaulted as Bowie rolls by on his skates; he looks into the car window, lip-syncing during an attempted rape. Temple then has the actress run down a street in her underwear, being groped by a gauntlet of men; she's arrested, with a last leering close-up. It was exploitative horseshit masquerading as social commentary. Recalling the video in 1999, Neil Tennant said:

> I always liked pop that has a sense of wonder about it. I mean, would you rather see David Bowie on roller skates — like he was in his "Day In, Day Out" video — or would you rather see David Bowie dressed as a clown, walking along the beach at Hastings with a bunch of New Romantics? I know what I would.

Too Dizzy

(Bowie, Kızılçay.) **Recorded**: *(backing tracks, poss. vocals) ca. September-November 1986, Mountain; (overdubs) ca. November 1986, Power Station. Bowie: lead and backing vocal, keyboards; Frampton: lead guitar; Alomar: rhythm guitar; Saisse: piano; Kızılçay: bass, drums, keyboards, Yamaha DX7, E-mu Emax, Akai S900; Bennett: percussion; Gardner: trumpet; Harrison: alto saxophone; Elson: baritone saxophone; Pickett: tenor saxophone; Clark, Groves, Gray, Grodie: backing vocals. Produced: Bowie, Richards; engineered: Richards, Pollack.*

First release: *20 April 1987,* **Never Let Me Down** *(EMI AMLS 3117/PJ-17267, UK #6, US #34).*

Notorious for being so bad that it was recalled (Bowie deleted it from *Never Let Me Down* reissues), "Too Dizzy" hails from the start of the short-lived collaboration of Bowie and Erdal Kızılçay. "A sort of tryout to see how we sparred as writers," Bowie called it. "That was just sort of a mess. We sat down at the piano and worked it out together in one session." Bowie wondered if "Too Dizzy" could work for Ronnie Spector, as "Girls" had for Tina Turner. He also said it was better suited for Huey Lewis, an insult to Lewis. Like many *Never Let Me Down* songs, it's a jarring mingle — a first-person abuser lyric set to some of the tackiest music he ever recorded. Bowie tries to keep a straight face ("who's this guy I'm gonna blow away?") but by the time he's singing "you can't have no LOV-AH" like a constipated Barry Gibb, the song's become a farce. Its arrangement distracts the ear from some unusual changes driven by Kızılçay's bass continually ascending the scale (F-sharp major verses and refrains, via an A major pre-chorus). The backing singers are malicious; the guitar and saxophone solos sound as if they were done to test microphone levels.

New York's in Love

Recorded: *(backing tracks, poss. vocal) ca. September-November 1986, Mountain; (overdubs) ca. November 1986, Power Station. Bowie: lead and backing vocal, lead guitar, keyboards; Frampton: guitar; Alomar: rhythm guitar; Saisse: piano; Kızılçay: bass, drums, organ, keyboards, Yamaha DX7, E-mu Emax, Akai S900;*

Bennett: percussion; Clark, Groves, Gray, Grodie: backing vocals. Produced: Bowie, Richards; engineered: Richards, Pollack.

First release: *20 April 1987,* **Never Let Me Down**. *Live: 1987.*

"New York's in Love" takes a wobbly metaphor — New York's a sexy lady! Watch her strut! ("that real vain aspect of big cities," as per Bowie) — and has fun knocking it down. While at the time he was calling out the Fall's Mark E. Smith for writing "fourth-form poetry," Bowie opens with "the city grew wings in the back of night/the clouds are stuck like candy floss." That's the high point of the lyric, along with a quote from "Sorrow" in the refrain. The verse melody, full of octave dips and swoops, was a challenge to record, as Bowie's audibly straining on "fam-i-ly" demonstrates — live recordings document some ragged singing. Built on a similar major-chord standoff as "Day-In Day-Out," it was crafted as a tour number — hence its refrain, paced leisurely enough for dancers to take their next positions between lines. Its weak life hangs on its bassline; the meat-handed guitar solos are Bowie's own. Hard truth lyric: "No one knows they've had their day."

Shining Star (Makin' My Love)

Recorded: (backing tracks, poss. vocal) ca. September-November 1986, Mountain; (overdubs) ca. November 1986, Power Station. Bowie: lead and backing vocal, keyboards; Mickey Rourke: rap; Frampton: lead guitar; Alomar: rhythm guitar; Kızılçay: bass, drums, drum programming keyboards, Yamaha DX7, E-mu Emax, Akai S900; Bennett: congas, percussion. Produced: Bowie, Richards; engineered: Richards, Pollack.

First release: *20 April 1987,* **Never Let Me Down**.

"Shining Star (Makin' My Love)" is a Frankenstein patchwork of a song, down to its title. Parts include a small set of augmented chords; simpering verses; an emotive pre-chorus whose lines include "life is like a broken arrow" and which sounds like Prince cosplay; a refrain meant to homage Smokey Robinson; an eight-bar rap by Mickey Rourke. Why Rourke? He

257

and Bowie were briefly a regular pair in the clubs, as if he was auditioning for Bowie's "wild man" companion after Iggy Pop sent in his notice. As ludicrous as it is, Rourke's rap is far from the worst offender. He's having a go at being Joe Strummer, as does Bowie, who sings "vermin... cowardice... lice" as if he'd heard "Straight to Hell" on the drive to the studio. (Replacing Rourke with Laurie Anderson for the remix — the remit here apparently being to turn "Shining Star" into a bad song from 1993 — was intriguing in theory. But she adds little, particularly as her voice is mixed too low and she's stuck saying the same words.)

The disjointed lyric — Jim Carroll doper casualties and Strummer mercenaries in verses; soul love in refrains — represented "how people are trying to get together in the face of so many disasters and catastrophes... never knowing if they're going to survive it themselves," Bowie said. "The one thing they have got to cling on to is each other." It's *Never Let Me Down* — "back-to-street situations" love songs for interpretive dancers — in a cracked nutshell. As Mario McNulty noted when remixing the track, "the programming is a mess" and it has one of Bowie's more excruciating vocals, peaking with the showboating high Gs on "I could make you happy ev'ry god-damn-sing-le-day of your liiiiiiiiiiife!" (Points for pronouncing "Chernobyl" the Russian way ("cherr-no-beel")). Its gaudy spirit would return decades later in "Girl Loves Me."

JULIE

Recorded: (*backing tracks, poss. vocal*) *ca. September-November 1986, Mountain;* (*overdubs*) *ca. November 1986, Power Station. Bowie: lead and backing vocal, keyboards, acoustic guitar?; Frampton: acoustic guitar?, guitar; Alomar: rhythm guitar; Kızılçay: bass, drum programming, keyboards, Yamaha DX7, E-mu Emax, Akai S900; Clark, Groves, Gray, Grodie: backing vocals. Produced: Bowie, Richards; engineered: Richards, Pollack.*

First release: *23 March 1987, EA 320.*

Recorded in the *Never Let Me Down* sessions, "Julie" was issued as a B-side, perhaps cut from the album because of similarities to "Bang Bang." There's also a connection to Bowie's 1969 song "Janine," with its game of deceptive, ill-matched love. Janine's an affected ingénue; Bowie's her equal as a fraud. There was a smile in his singing, in his blustering attempts to win a round against her.

In "Julie," Bowie retrieves a scenario from his singles of the mid-Sixties — the girl he loves barely knows he exists and he's willing to settle for her occasional attention. Single-tracked and keeping to a narrow range for the opening verse, his vocal builds with his ambition: double-tracked at the octave for the second, soaring to his higher register for the refrains (he harmonizes with a singer doing a Tina Turner imitation — was "Julie" intended as another Bowie/Turner duet?). In line with other *Never Let Me Down* songs, there's an undercurrent of domination and violence — the singer may have killed the man Julie loves and he's serenading her while she's in mourning. The mix gets out of the song's way, with acoustic and rhythm guitar lines over a keyboard bed, with synthesizer triplets as seasoning. One of the few songs to escape the period without much damage, its inclusion on *Never Let Me Down* reissues was a minor injustice corrected.

BEAT OF YOUR DRUM

Recorded: (backing tracks, poss. vocal) ca. September-November 1986, Mountain; (overdubs) ca. November 1986, Power Station. Bowie: lead and backing vocal, keyboards; Frampton: lead guitar; Alomar: rhythm guitar; Saisse: piano; Kızılçay: bass, drums, keyboards, Yamaha DX7, E-mu Emax, Akai S900; Bennett: percussion; Gardner: trumpet; Harrison: alto saxophone; Elson: baritone saxophone; Pickett: tenor saxophone; Clark, Groves, Gray, Grodie: backing vocals. Produced: Bowie, Richards; engineered: Richards, Pollack.

First release: 20 April 1987, **Never Let Me Down**. *Live*: 1987.

"Beat of Your Drum" uses the *Never Let Me Down* template of ominous verse and giddy refrain with an awkward pre-chorus as adhesive, but it works better here. The incongruous elements — sepulchral verses and a big dumb sex refrain nicked from Bruce Springsteen — complement each other, with sordid mumblings in the verse emptying into a pool of lust in the refrain.

Bowie casts himself as a photographer ogling a new model/conquest. His sole, and repellent, description of the song was that "it's a Lolita Number!

Reflection on young girls... Christ, she's only fourteen years old, but jail's worth it!" (In 2015, Lori Mattix claimed to a reporter that during the Spiders from Mars era, she'd slept with Bowie when she was fifteen.) "Beat of Your Drum" is a corroded *Labyrinth* song, with its intro's portentous synthesizer lines close to those of Trevor Jones' film soundtrack. It's Jareth scoping out another girl across a dance floor ("prison can't hold all this greedy intention"). Sounding inspired, Bowie manages to keep a coherent lyrical theme, with references to film — negatives, colors fading, "bright light destroys me" (whether developing photo or vampire).

Subtlety wasn't in the cards for a track that opens with a Morse Code ostinato synth pattern and sprawls all over the place (the LP edit, which trims three refrains, is its ideal cut). Bowie, in his death-croon register, sings a fragmented melody of three- or four-note phrases, aping both Scott Walker and Peter Murphy, fusing influence and influenced in one gargoyle vocal. Bowie liked the combination so much he'd use it again on "You Belong in Rock n' Roll." Midwifed by a harmonically-woozy bridge that ends with Bowie barely holding a high A ("taaaaame!"), the refrain pops in like a commercial. The lyric is ridiculous, the melody's mostly one priapic note. There's a horn/guitar riff on loan from Springsteen's "Glory Days," handclaps on all fours, fairground saxophone, barrages of keyboards, and it's capped off by a cheeseball Peter Frampton solo. If only the whole album had been as tacky as this.

Bang Bang

(Pop, Kral.) **Recorded**: (backing tracks, poss. vocal) ca. September-November 1986, Mountain; (overdubs) ca. November 1986, Power Station. Bowie: lead and backing vocal, keyboards; McGinnis: lead guitar; Alomar: rhythm guitar; Frampton: electric sitar; Saisse: piano; Kızılçay: violins, bass, drums, keyboards, Yamaha DX7, E-mu Emax, Akai S900, Bennett: percussion; Gardner: trumpet; Harrison: alto saxophone; Elson: baritone saxophone; Pickett: tenor saxophone; Clark, Groves, Gray, Grodie: backing vocals. Produced: Bowie, Richards; engineered: Richards, Pollack.

First release: 20 April 1987, **Never Let Me Down**. **Live**: 1987.

Iggy Pop and Patti Smith Group alum Ivan Kral wrote "Bang Bang" in 1980 for Pop's album *Party*. It began as "a song about the emancipation of women" until Pop rewrote the lyric with some usual themes — young heartbreakers and isolation. (He'd been inspired by Tom Wolfe's *The Right Stuff*: "one thing you don't want to do in rock is get hung up on girls. They'll fuck your band. They'll fuck up your music... Another part of having the right stuff is knowing that unless you've got the right girl, you ain't gonna get nowhere.") Arista brought in Tommy Boyce (who had co-written "Last Train to Clarksville") as a fixer. Though allegedly spending his time scoring drugs with Pop (the pair once locked Kral in a closet when he tried to hinder them), Boyce turned "Bang Bang" into a passable New Wave single, filling it with hooks: the title phrase coming down like rain; ominous descending organ/bassline; pizzicato strings; a sullenly-struck tambourine. It sounded as if Pop had joined some Satanic incarnation of the Cars.

Bowie's cover of "Bang Bang" closed *Never Let Me Down*. It's an understandable sequencing — given the pileup of disasters on the album's second side, "Bang Bang" at least had a pulse. But it was the third album in a row he'd padded with a Pop cover, and journalists were calling him out on it. "A lot of bands cover Chuck Berry or the Stones or whatever — I cover Iggy Pop," he retorted. He thought Pop's "Bang Bang" should've been a hit; so he was just cleaning it up. He kept the three-chord G major chord sequence (Em-D-C) for both verse and refrains, instead tinkering with the arrangement: during guitar solos, a chorus all but sings the harmonies of the Eagles' "Already Gone." Erdal Kızılçay overworks the pizzicato string line; Peter Frampton plays electric sitar.

With an eye on how the song could work on stage (as an interpretative dance where Bowie pulled a "random" girl from the audience to dance with, then groped her), Bowie turned Pop's grumbling intro into holiday-camp instructor banter: "This ain't the right thing to do! So... so let's... so let's *go*!" He gives a twang to lines like "you all oughtta be in pic-shuhs" and turns Pop's "I want no intimacy" into "I wander lonely to the sea," kicking off a brief period where he worsened lyrics of his covers via possible mishearings (see "Don't Let Me Down and Down").

'87 AND CRY

Recorded: (backing tracks, poss. vocal) ca. September-November 1986, Mountain; (overdubs) ca. November 1986, Power Station. Bowie: lead and backing vocal, lead guitar, keyboards?; Frampton: lead guitar; Alomar: rhythm guitar, backing vocal; Saisse: piano; Kızılçay: bass, drum programming, keyboards, Yamaha DX7, E-mu Emax, Akai S900; Bennett: rattles, chains, chimes, percussion; Elson: baritone saxophone; Pickett: tenor saxophone; Clark, Groves, Gray, Grodie: backing vocals. Produced: Bowie, Richards; engineered: Richards, Pollack.

First release: 20 April 1987, **Never Let Me Down**. *Live*: 1987.

In March 1974, Bowie left Britain for a tour, never to return except to visit. His home and work would be elsewhere — Los Angeles, Berlin, New York, Switzerland, Mustique — and his records were products of global capitalism. See "Let's Dance," made in New York by a British singer, a white Texan guitarist, and New York-based black and Latino musicians, and whose video featured Australian aboriginals.

"Many music celebrities simply chose to leave Britain, and it wasn't all about tax; America was the main global market for music," Pete Townshend wrote in his autobiography. He'd considered moving as well but realized "everything I am and have done for myself, all my artistic work, was rooted in the British way of life, the two world wars and the hidden damage they had done to four generations."

Bowie proved easier to uproot. Once among the most British of British pop singers, taking cues from Anthony Newley and Peter Cook, his records up to *Diamond Dogs* are set in a diseased England where the United States is a rumor, a pirate radio broadcast, a treasured test pressing. When he left, he became stateless, a traveler, the world's houseguest (though while filming in Australia or Polynesia, he came across as a genteel Englishman in the South Pacific).

He returned to Britain in "'87 and Cry" — the start of a renewed interest in his home country he'd develop on songs with Reeves Gabrels and for *The Buddha of Suburbia*. Things had changed in his absence. The Britain of 1974, despite the costumed rockers on *Top of the Pops*, wasn't radically different from that of his childhood. The Britain of 1987, eight years into Margaret Thatcher's reign, was sharper, flashier, more atomized. "An impression of

Thatcherite England" is how Bowie described "'87 and Cry" at the time, though as usual he refracted it through *Nineteen Eighty-Four* (see the "it couldn't be done without [diamond] dogs!" refrain line, which Bowie said referred to proles doing the dirty work).

"It took on all these surreal qualities of a pushy person eating the energies of others to get to where they wanted and leaving the others behind," he said of the song. "It was a Thatcherite statement made through the eyes of a potential socialist, because I always remained a potential socialist — not an active one" (potential socialists don't have to pay much tax, so it worked out for him). It was also a forty-year-old expatriate griping about how things had gone rotten back home, though at least not with the reactionary bile of the Rolling Stones' "Hang Fire." The second verse is threadbare Blitz nostalgia: the old days when men wore blue ties and women "dressed down for the enemy." He associated Britain with gossip and shame-mongering, with long-deferred obligations. He'd been attacked by the tabloids for not attending his half-brother's funeral, and in the following year the *Sunday Times* serialized *Alias David Bowie*, the first biography to excavate his life in Bromley and Beckenham, fat with quotes from relatives and friends whom he'd left behind.

"'87 and Cry" works best as competing lines of percussion: Carlos Alomar's guitar fills and Crusher Bennett working his shakers and chains (he'd drag the latter across a wooden table in the studio). As a composition, it's some clunking progressions in G major and F major linked by a bridge that manages the trifecta of being lyrically inane, gruesomely sung, and bafflingly arranged. Bowie's two-chord multi-tracked screech of a guitar solo ("mine is a lot of effects and ambiance, just trying to get an atmosphere rather than play. I don't know about 'playing'") sketches where he'd soon go with Tin Machine.

TIME WILL CRAWL

Recorded: (album) (backing tracks, poss. vocal) ca. September-November 1986, Mountain; (overdubs) ca. November 1986, Power Station. Bowie: lead and backing vocal, keyboards; McGinnis: lead guitar; Frampton: guitar; Alomar: rhythm guitar; Saisse: keyboards; Kızılçay: bass, drum programming, keyboards, Yamaha DX7, E-mu Emax, Akai S900, trumpet?; Bennett: percussion; Laurie Frink: trumpet?;

Harrison: alto saxophone; Elson: baritone saxophone; Pickett: tenor saxophone; Clark, Groves, Gray, Grodie: backing vocals. Produced: Bowie, Richards; engineered: Richards, Pollack; **("MM Remix")** *(overdubs) ca. early 2008, Looking Glass, 632 Broadway, New York. Sterling Campbell: drums; Krista Bennion Feeney, Robert Chausow: violin, Martha Mooke: viola; Matthew Goeke: cello (arr. Gregor Kitzis). Produced: Mario McNulty; engineered: McNulty.*

First release: *20 April 1987,* **Never Let Me Down***; (MM Remix) 29 June 2008,* **iSelect** *(UPDB001).* **Broadcast***: 17 June 1987, Top of the Pops.* **Live***: 1987.*

On 26 April 1986, while Bowie was recording at Mountain Studios, a reactor exploded in the Chernobyl nuclear plant in the then-Soviet Union. "It was a beautiful day and we were outside on a small piece of lawn facing the Alps and the lake," he wrote two decades later,

> Our engineer, who had been listening to the radio, shot out of the studio and shouted: "There's a whole lot of shit going on in Russia." The Swiss news had picked up a Norwegian radio station that was screaming — to anyone who would listen — that huge billowing clouds were moving over from the Motherland and they weren't rain clouds.

The memory of standing in the sunlight, fearing that radiation was sailing his way from the east — shades of the last Australians in Nevil Shute's *On the Beach* — inspired "Time Will Crawl," the track Bowie felt was most worth salvaging from *Never Let Me Down*. He remade it in 2008, and it's the only *NLMD* song to appear on the 2014 career compilation *Nothing Has Changed*, where it stands bewildered and alone, like a survivor of an airplane crash.

He'd written rapturous apocalypse songs before — "Five Years" rang out the death of the world like a pub chant — but Chernobyl showed how the world would more likely end: a holocaust of ineptitude, with a government cover-up getting underway during the chaos. Like the doomed characters in "When the Wind Blows," the singer of "Time Will Crawl" accepts what he's told and tries to ignore the obvious: "We only smelt the gas/as we lay down to sleep." (As per the title, even time's been beaten down.) The second verse is after-effects: rotting fish, anti-radiation pills, bloated corpses. In the refrain, man is another poor lost animal, as in "Glass Spider."

Bowie tersely documents horrors, keeping to a three-note span, dispensing with rhyme in favor of a nagging rhythm, as though being prodded to offer more details in a deposition. It's his best querulous Neil Young impression. Short phrases ("I felt a") hook into longer ones ("warm warm breeze"). "There is a rudeness about it musically. It doesn't do very much. It just sort of plows through," Bowie said at the time. Verses and refrains have the same chord structure — strides away from tonic chord B minor, out to G major or A major, then straight home again. The refrain (whose rhythms and phrasing have a touch of the verses of "Stay") is harsh, thanks to the title line with its sour "aw" phoneme.

In 2008, he released a remixed/partially re-recorded version of "Time Will Crawl," which he said corrected the sins of its original production. "Oh, to redo the rest of the album," he wrote then, a wish granted after his death (the remixes were allegedly done according to his detailed notes.) The problem was that "Time Will Crawl" was the least of the offenders on *Never Let Me Down*, its arrangement spartan by comparison to fellow tracks. Acoustic guitar rhythms sharpen the bite of Bowie's phrasings; Phillippe Caisse's keyboards are a nervy hook; Sid McGinnis roars in the second refrain, saying on guitar what Bowie won't; the trumpet is a pennon in the mix, its lamenting tone distorted and muted. The 2008 "MM" mix aimed for dramatic sweep, holding the drums in reserve until the first refrain, cranking up the guitars and Bowie's vocal, to the point of overpowering the newly-done string arrangement. The trumpet is a Geiger counter loop while Sterling Campbell vies to outplay the original's synthetic drums but comes up a draw. You can see why Bowie remade the song, but he didn't improve it.

GLASS SPIDER

Recorded: (backing tracks) ca. September-November 1986, Mountain; (overdubs) ca. November 1986, Power Station. Bowie: lead and backing vocal, keyboards, Mellotron, Moog; Frampton: lead guitar; Alomar: rhythm guitar, backing vocal; Kızılçay: bass, drum programming, bass sequencer, keyboards, Yamaha DX7, E-mu Emax; Bennett: sticks, percussion; Clark, Groves, Gray, Grodie: backing vocals. Produced: Bowie, Richards; engineered: Richards, Pollack.

First release: 20 April 1987, **Never Let Me Down**. *Live*: 1987.

An all-time low: a spoken/sung science-fiction track with "spooky" music and some of the silliest lines Bowie ever wrote. It's *Diamond Dogs'* "Future Legend," of course.

"Glass Spider" is the return of the Bowie of "Future Legend." The weird, dorky, juvenile Bowie. The embarrassing Bowie. The Bowie who Lester Bangs called "that chickenhearted straw man of suck rock you love to hate." Bowie as Jareth the Goblin King, not the cool, aspirational figure of the *Serious Moonlight* tour. "Bowie's most embarrassing moment in years," as Steve Pond of *Rolling Stone* described "Glass Spider." "It's probably not any dumber than... *Diamond Dogs*, but coming thirteen years later from an artist who's supposed to be sophisticated and intelligent, it sounds a hell of a lot dumber."

Elvis Costello once said his label kept hounding him for another *This Year's Model*, but when he finally made it — the bitter divorcé album *Blood and Chocolate* — they didn't know what to do with it. It's the same with "Glass Spider." Isn't this what everyone wanted? Back to space-age apocalypse, costumes, and dark theater? Back to scary monsters? Why was it all so silly now? Why could Bowie dress like a space pirate in 1974 and be the height of cool, but when he intoned his parable about glass spiders in 1987, it was laughable and pathetic?

The Smiths' "Rubber Ring" gets at the heart of this. Morrissey breaks the fourth wall in the song, telling his listeners of their upcoming betrayal. *These songs mean everything to you now, but soon enough you'll leave them behind and joke about your mopey Smiths phase.* "When you're dancing and laughing, and finally living/hear my voice in your head and think of me kindly," he sings. Because he's staying at the barricades. "Glass Spider" holds to the same line. *This is what I do, this is what I've always done, as ridiculous as it may seem now.* Its lyric is about being abandoned by your parents, of learning to live on your own. "You always think your mother's there, but of course she never really is," as Bowie said. It's sung by a man who will always be back in your childhood, wearing tights and a wraparound headset, standing atop a giant spider.

He had practical needs for the song: it would be his opening number for the tour and provide the central image for the stage set. Having seen a TV documentary about black widow spiders that littered their webs with pieces of their prey, Bowie lit upon the idea of a multi-tiered, corpse-strewn spider web as a housing project (another link back to *Diamond Dogs*) "with a kind of altar at the top." Like the black widows, he kept piling things on — his spider was a universal mother (albeit one from the "Zi Duang province of an eastern country") who leaves her children to the cold world. The third verse, with abandoned spiders looking for shelter, is Bowie's Fall of Man.

Its organizing structure suggests Michael Jackson's "Thriller" — Bowie does his take on the latter's Vincent Price section, then a bass sequencer kicks in, as on Jackson's record. Bowie speaks his parable over washes of Mellotron and Moog and the clack of Crusher Bennett's sticks. Sounding like Spinal Tap's Nigel Tufnel, he's a bit fuzzy on the details: "with almost apparent care," "one could almost call it an altar." It's ridiculously long — fifty-six bars, nearly two minutes. The latter half of the song is a horror-movie theme, with a few sharp lines ("life is over you") and a decent momentum, the "mummy come back" tag knifing its way into the last verses. It's the triumph of the 2018 *Never Let Me Down* remix because Mario McNulty took it completely seriously, having Bowie recite and sing over swirling and receding waves of keyboards and guitar and pummeling drums towards the close.

"Glass Spider" uses an old Bowie compositional trick of backing into establishing the key: while the spoken section lurks in E minor, the song hammers down into A minor, its progression similar to "Be My Wife" (Am-F-G, with the latter chords keeping A as the root note), while a chromatically descending bassline worries the "mummy come back" refrain. There's plenty that's ridiculous, from the diva moments in the verses to the whinnying Frampton interjections to the nasally "jah jah jahs." As silly as "Glass Spider" is, it's the sound of an artist reclaiming himself, or at least trying to.

ZEROES

Recorded: (backing tracks, vocals) ca. September-November 1986, Mountain; (overdubs) ca. November 1986, Power Station. Bowie: lead and backing vocal, keyboards; Frampton: lead guitar, electric sitar; Alomar: rhythm guitar; Saisse: piano; Kızılçay: bass, drums, keyboards, Yamaha DX7, E-mu Emax, Akai S900; Bennett: percussion; Gardner: trumpet; Harrison: alto saxophone; Elson: baritone saxophone; Pickett: tenor saxophone; Clark, Groves, Gray, Grodie, "The Coquettes" (Coco Schwab, Duncan Jones, et al.): backing vocals. Produced: Bowie, Richards; engineered: Richards, Pollack.

First release: 20 April 1987, ***Never Let Me Down***. *Live*: 1987.

Having made a "rock 'n' roll" album, Bowie wondered what the term even meant in 1986 — it was teenage music that teenagers had abandoned. "Rock and roll is for *us* — it's not for kids," he said. The Baby Boomer generation had inherited rock, they'd kept it up, they weren't going to pass it on. "We wrote it, we play it. We listen to rock. Kids listen to something else." You could have heard this from any Sixties rocker in the mid-Eighties, doing their part on MTV, looking for the hip drum sound, making guest appearances on younger people's songs. No one had imagined it could have gone on for this long. Rod Stewart, always up for a laugh and ready to hit the pub after half a day's recording, could keep the show running, but Bowie (telling journalists at the time "I've always been a fan of rock 'n' roll," as if it was a product line he was endorsing) felt a strain.

"Zeroes" is the result — the wild ambition, creative anxiety, and bungled execution of *Never Let Me Down* in microcosm. He meant to strip "away all the meanness of rock and com[e] back to the spirit with which one entered the thing. It's the ultimate happy-go-lucky rock tune, based in the nonsensical period of psychedelia... a naïveté song about rock, using a lot of clichés." But there's little "happy-go-lucky" about the song, which opens with demonic, synthetic audience screams.

Honored on *Time* or *Rolling Stone* covers, recycled in fashions, appropriated, trademarked, "The Sixties" was now a reactive force — a new conservative voting bloc. Sixties politics were a tableland of lost potential, full of martyrs; Sixties music was the perfected strain of rock 'n' roll, to which no music afterward could compare. All younger musicians could do was pay homage and hope for Sixties survivors to reunite (which most had by 1989). "We're trying to bring it back if we can. We've decided to believe, just for the sake of it," Malcolm McLaren said at the end of the Eighties. The Sixties had been shown up as a lie, as a scam, but it didn't matter — it was a lie you could live in, and that was enough. "People are trying desperately to be naïve," McLaren added. "The long dresses, the pasty faces, the whole nocturnal ideal of a ghostly image... people are trying to taste again a little of the Sixties."

In "Zeroes" the first verse is the lay of the battlefield: the young heroes are dead, their memory a weight on the survivors. The refrain is sung by someone whose muse has deserted him but whose label hasn't yet. There are lists of demands: another tour, another mediocre record review ("don't you know we're back on *trial* again today?" he sings, drawing out the sharpness of the vowels). He's still on stage, still singing that it's all for you, tonight I'm yours, God gave rock 'n' roll to you, everybody is a star. His band is called the Zeroes: a cipher of no value.

Each section of "Zeroes" — verse, refrain, coda — is in a different key, isolated from each other, sharing few common chords. The transitions are abrupt and wrenching until the D-flat major coda, a collapse into submission — Bowie exits by sinking into a trance of *doesn't matter*s. It's a memory-festival: Peter Frampton's Coral electric sitar is a curtain-raiser between verses and refrains; Crusher Bennett does a tabla impersonation during the "psychedelic" outro. Bowie built the track up like one of his scale models of Hunger City for *Diamond Dogs* — the denseness of its mix, its clutter of sounds, its sprawling cast (including a vocal chorus whose ranks included his son Duncan and his assistant Coco Schwab), being suffocated in a blanket of songs (Beatles chord changes and melodies ("Eight Days a Week," "The Fool on the Hill," "Sgt. Pepper"), Dylan phrasings, Prince's little red corvette). The remix, which set Bowie's high-octane vocals to a backing so plodding that it sounds mastered at the wrong speed, spoiled the fizzy charms of the original. Where "Heroes" was a future that would never come to pass, "Zeroes" is a false past, a stage-world fit for vampires, and there is no way out of it.

NEVER LET ME DOWN

(Bowie, Alomar.) **Recorded**: *ca. September-November 1986, Mountain; ca. November 1986, Studio A, Power Station. Bowie: lead and backing vocal, harmonica, synthesizers, keyboards; Alomar: lead and rhythm guitar; Kızılçay: bass?, drum programming; Bennett: woodblock, sticks, congas, other percussion. Produced: Bowie, Richards; engineered: Richards, Pollack.*

First release: *20 April 1987,* **Never Let Me Down**. **Broadcast**: *16 September 1987, Top of the Pops (USA).* **Live**: *1987.*

Written and recorded in the mixing sessions of *Never Let Me Down*, the album's title song was done in little more than a day. It honored Coco Schwab, who'd worked for Bowie for over ten years as best friend, bodyguard, enforcer, quasi-parent, and manager. Reticent about his relationship with Schwab, Bowie opened up in late-Eighties interviews, saying she had saved his life, that she was the only one who could reach him during the depths of his addiction. "On her strength, I got out of America," he said. "Coco and I have shared ten lifetimes together in happiness and depressions... We know so much about each other that we communicate almost in code."

"It's a reciprocal song: a song of loyalty," he said of "Never Let Me Down," having the dance performance for the Glass Spider tour symbolize this. He sang on his knees, wearing a straightjacket, while his soon-to-be girlfriend Melissa Hurley moved around him, "as if she's accompanying her pet in a park," leaning in to press an oxygen mask to his face. Though he called it a platonic song, he built it on a sexual one, taking top melodies and rhythms from Sylvia Robinson's early disco hit "Pillow Talk."

He'd been mulling over a new song during mixing at the Power Station (not surprising, given what he was mixing), so while Bob Clearmountain worked on "Zeroes," Bowie and David Richards found that Studio A was open and began recording over a discarded drum track from the Montreux sessions. Bowie wrote a three-verse lyric that begins in recollection (referring to "her name" and "she danced") and closes in intimacy (singing to "you"). It's sung and phrased well: in the pre-chorus his bobbing run of notes buoy "dance a little dance," which starts a long fall down an octave. By the evening Crusher Bennett came in to play sticks and woodblock, while Carlos Alomar added percussive guitar fills in the refrains. Bowie asked Alomar to spice up what he called a "funereal" chord progression, with Alomar using chords from a song of his called "I'm Tired," earning him a co-credit. The F major ninths, sevenths, and sixths in the intro and pre-chorus (which culminate in a pounded-home G7) sounds like a guitarist's doing.

Bowie said he meant it as a tribute to John Lennon, his vocal, harmonica, and whistling coda as Lennon shorthand. But which Lennon, though? Julian Lennon's "Too Late for Goodbyes" has a vocal line that darts up to falsetto, a bouncing rhythm sparked with bass flourishes, and a harmonica solo in place of a verse. Julian had appeared in late 1984 with a debut album on Atlantic: recorded at Muscle Shoals with top session players, its videos directed by Sam Peckinpah in his dotage. The full press worked. *Valotte* went platinum and had two Top 10 hits. Julian, who sounded and looked like a newly-hatched version of his father, was a commemorative edition John Lennon — young and single again, no political stunts, no screaming about his mother, no feminist broadsides. As Ben Greenman wrote, he was a "psychic replacement" for his father. If Bowie was referencing Julian, it was a mercenary's sense of where the action was. Julian was getting hits, and Bowie wanted "Never Let Me Down" to follow suit. It won a small place on American radio, the last Bowie single to crack the *Billboard* Top 40, and to chart higher in the US than in Britain, until "Lazarus" in 2015.

I WANNA BE YOUR DOG

(Alexander, R. Asheton, S. Asheton, Pop.) **Recorded**: *6, 7 or 9 November 1987, Sydney Entertainment Centre, 35 Harbour St., Darling Harbour, Sydney, Australia. Bowie: lead vocal, rhythm guitar; Charlie Sexton: lead guitar; Frampton: lead guitar; Alomar: rhythm guitar; Kızılçay, Richard Cottle: keyboards; Carmine Rojas: bass; Alan Childs: drums. Produced: Anthony Eaton.*

First release: *6 June 1988,* **Glass Spider** *(VC 4043/MP 1526).* **Live**: *(Pop and Bowie) 1977, (Bowie) 1987.*

The Glass Spider tour, 1987: eighty-six shows, six months, three continents. The spider, designed by Mark Ravitz, was sixty feet high and sixty-four feet wide. Spun out of fiberglass and metal, with vacuum tubes for legs, it weighed 360 tons. Bowie opened each concert by descending in a chair from its maw. During the encore opener, "Time," he sang atop the spider's head, standing on a three-foot-square steel plate. He likened the spider to a ship. When the winds were up (it was a summer spoiled by winds and rain), it was precarious for him to be up there.

In Europe, many Glass Spider shows were outdoors, and as it stayed light until 10 or 11pm, the spider wouldn't be fully illuminated until the show was nearly over, while the video-projected backdrops were hard to discern. So concertgoers saw an enormous, immobile, occasionally-glowing spider and, beneath it, performers running around in circles. Bowie wore bright red and gold suits so at least those in the nosebleed seats would know which speck he was.

A sub-par sound system, worsened by Bowie and his dancers wearing headset microphones, made a babble of between-song "dialogue" (not a loss, as lines included "it's rock 'n' roll, it's like kissing a blowtorch"). He took to miming a pre-recorded vocal track on the opening "Glass Spider," as he was often inaudible in his chair. Carlos Alomar and Peter Frampton got pushed upstage by the dancers, who occasionally stepped on their effects pedals.

The mood backstage was raw at times. Alomar, tired of being the agreeable sidekick, gave interviews in which he emphasized his importance to Bowie's records (never good for your standing in the Bowie organization), and asked to start gigs with a solo to show he was Frampton's equal. "On that tour, I was tired of being the sideman. I wanted my place. Give me a bone, Jesus!" he told David Buckley years later.

Bowie was manager and ringmaster, dancer and director, mapping out choreographed dance and lighting sequences during soundchecks. He sang while performing like a triathlete: climbing up to a catwalk on "Scary Monsters," being thrown around like a sack of grain on "Fashion." To no surprise, he grew exhausted and irritable, especially once pans came in: (*Melody Maker*: "the paucity of ideas is quite incredible," *Sounds*: "frenzied schlock"). The tour fared little better in the US press. The *Detroit Free Press* reported an "alarming number of people leaving the Silverdome by mid-show, many cursing about the show." "Often the band seemed to be losing the beat... Bowie is probably the worst dancer of all rock front men" (*Louisville Courier Journal*). He'd never put on a show on this level before, with $20 million needed to build two alternating sets, and a $1 million payroll for each week on the road. In 1974, he'd pulled the escape hatch, ditching the *Diamond Dogs* stage concept three months in, scrapping sets and revamping the show into a less formal "soul" revue. But in 1987, Pepsi was footing the bill, and everyone expected the spectacle: the giant spider, the routine where Bowie pulled his girlfriend out of the crowd on "Bang Bang," the abseiling and kickboxing dancers.

As with *Never Let Me Down*, Glass Spider was an arena-based hot-ticket event (shows generally sold out) that he'd envisioned as some kind of traveling performance-art circus, with dances inspired by Pina Bausch. The show was meant to be a "rock 'n' roll revue" that would "bring together symbolist theater and modern dance," marry "real American street dancing" with "European performance art," and explore "mixed media." Ravitz recalled that the whole show was never rehearsed "top to bottom, so it never had a total cohesiveness about it."

You can see what Bowie intended a year later, when he worked with the dancer Louise Lecavalier (see "Look Back in Anger"). Lecavalier was a percussive, whirling force, twirling around Bowie, vaulting across the stage — she fed off the music. In the Glass Spider shows, any erotic power or intimacy was lost because of how unwieldy the stage concept was, while some dance routines were witless and irritating — the five-person troupe came off as a gang of theater kids sabotaging a rock show. "After a while, trying to work out why there was a heap of bodies sprawled in a corner of the stage...became confusing" (*Sounds*). It didn't help that Bowie envisioned their characters as being, in his words, "a big girl," "a soft, ethereal girl," "an androgynous Jim Morrison kind of guy," "a large, aggressive black guy" and "a British punk."

The setlist was fresh: he played almost all of *Never Let Me Down* and revived relative obscurities ("Sons of the Silent Age," "All the Madmen," "Big Brother"). But the arrangements were as overworked as the choreography, with Frampton cluttering songs with whining lead lines. Bowie had never had such a tedious guitarist before. At its worst, the show was a revue of ersatz versions of Bowie classics — Frampton flailing at Mick Ronson's whinnying guitar parts on "Time"; anemic synth horns on "Let's Dance"; a would-be Neil Peart drum solo on "Chant of the Ever-Circling Skeletal Family."

As the tour wound down in Europe, Bowie started swapping in older rockers ("Jean Genie," "White Light/White Heat"), in part because he didn't have to dance during these numbers: he could strap on a guitar. By the American leg of the tour, he was doing the Stooges' "I Wanna Be Your Dog" in encores. Compared to his caustic performances of the song with Iggy Pop a decade earlier, Glass Spider takes on "I Wanna Be Your Dog" were guitar showrooms. A performance filmed in Sydney for the *Glass Spider* video finds Charlie Sexton and Frampton vying to out-cliché each other. But "I Wanna Be Your Dog" served its purpose: for the length of the song, Bowie was free from his tackiest show.

The tour ended in Auckland, New Zealand, on 28 November 1987. He'd never attempt anything of its like again. It had been a hard purging of illusions. He'd been ridiculed; it had worn him to the nub. Right after the tour ended, he started telling people he'd had the spider burned in a field in New Zealand — the sacrificial bonfire of his ambitions. The reality was more prosaic, if fitting: the stage props were broken down, most pieces wound up in landfills or were sold for scrap, and a few bits remain in a West Auckland warehouse today.

CHAPTER SEVEN:

THE BATTLE OF THE WILDERNESS

(1988-1992)

The wise do not get angry when they are driven into a corner, kings do.
— The Milinda Pañha (a corrupt English translation, favored by political scientists)

He does it to be king of his bankrupt domain.
— Steven Berkoff, *West*

I began to realize that the guitar had a very wide overtone, so maybe one guitar might sound like ten violins...I decided, well, I'm going to see if I can orchestrate this music that I'm playing and see if it can have a larger sound—and it surely did.
— Ornette Coleman

To be on the move, however, is better than nothing... The air creeps into one's clothes.
— Claudio Magris, *Danube*

A Konrad can go forward...or backward. He can play slow...or fast. And turn around. Isn't that wonderful?
Bowie, promotional sketch for his first band, ca. 1963

Be yourself. Whoever that is.
— Hunt Sales, 1989

THE KING OF STAMFORD HILL

(Bowie, Gabrels.) **Recorded**: *(vocal) ca. May-August 1988, Mountain Studios, Montreux; (overdubs) ca. 1994-early 1995, Sound City Studios, Van Nuys, CA; the Massachusetts Institute of Technology, Boston. David Bowie: lead and backing vocal; Gary Oldman:"running commentary"; Reeves Gabrels: lead guitar, rhythm guitar, "Guitar Orchestra, Greek Chorus and Self Destruct Guitars"; Matt Gruenberg: bass; Milt Sutton: drums. Produced: Gabrels, Tom Dube; engineered: Dube, David Richards.*

First release: *5 September 1995,* **The Sacred Squall of Now** *(Upstart 020).*

"If you do what I do — play out of tune, stretch time signatures, make noise — people assume you're an idiot. Because nobody would want to play out of tune, right?" Reeves Gabrels said in 2000. "So I needed the firepower to say, 'OK, this is what I could do if I wanted to wear a Lacoste shirt and chinos like you.' If I wanted to play on baked bean commercials, that's what I'd do. I'm already past that. I'm working on my vision, dammit. It might not be a good one, but it's mine."

Gabrels worked with David Bowie for eleven years. "Sideman" doesn't accurately describe his role: no other Bowie guitarist co-wrote entire albums with him. He embodied Bowie's Nineties, whether dressed in Prada suits or sporting kilts and boas. An agitator, he shrouded Bowie albums in noise. For solos, he ran vibrators across his guitar strings; he'd screech notes through his jack plugs. He saved Bowie from middle-aged mediocrity; he made Bowie look ridiculous. Most of all, he was an unknown and a latecomer. *Tin Machine*, issued right before he turned thirty-three, was his first major-label release. In early rehearsals, his bandmates the Sales brothers wondered who the hell the guitarist was. He'd come in through a side door: he was Bowie's friend first, then his collaborator. But after years of scrabbling with dead-end bands, playing hundreds of weddings and bar mitzvahs and teaching guitar lessons, he'd been around long enough to know what he didn't want to do.

The Captain's Son

Gabrels was born on Staten Island in 1956. His father was a tugboat captain, often away from home for weeks but "somewhere within a couple miles of our house, on a boat circling the island." He bought Reeves a guitar, hoping to make his son more social. Instead Gabrels spent even more time in his room, practicing. He went to the Parsons School of Design and the School of Visual Arts. Studying painting made him want to play music, as did living in the East Village at the peak of the CBGB scene. He switched to Berklee College of Music. At Parsons, an instructor told Gabrels he should play music because he was no good at art; at Berklee, a teacher said he should go back to art school.

Seeing Adrian Belew play with Talking Heads in 1980 felt like being struck by lightning (it helped that Gabrels dropped acid during the gig). "His solos didn't just move on the X/Y axis of harmony and melody," Gabrels recalled of Belew. "It was like there was a Z axis, a third dimension. ... Adrian could hold his guitar up and by changing the angle get different feedback notes." Going to Berklee no longer made sense. "That was the thing about Belew and Hendrix — that you could impact upon civilians." So he dropped out to play in a string of Boston bands. The city had a thriving scene at the time: the Neighborhoods (later to open for Tin Machine), La Peste, the Lyres, the Nervous Eaters, Mission of Burma, the Dark, Rubber Rodeo (Gabrels was in late editions of the latter two).

Forever monkeying with his guitar tones ("I'm not experimental. It's just that everybody else is hyper-conservative"), he took advantage of accidents. While he was rehearsing in a kitchen, electromagnetic interference from a refrigerator motor channeled through his pickups and chorus pedal. It sounded like a choir of angels, he said. At a gig where he didn't have his usual gear, he made do by "grabbing different notes and harmonics off the strings," doing little pull-offs "five frets above the notes of my solos." When his bass player complimented him for his new effects and harmonizer programs, he thought "why am I carrying all this stuff around if I can fool my own bass player without it?"

From his drawing technique came his picking style, making tiny circles to hit strings at an angle, at rapid speed, with his picks sharpened to a needle point. He favored newer-make guitars as he thought anyone who plays a Fender Stratocaster loses a battle against nostalgia. "Playing instruments that don't have clichés defined on them keeps me from playing licks from 1952," he said. In the late Eighties, his main guitar was a prototype "headless" Steinberger with a TransTrem vibrato mechanism; in the Nineties, he favored the lightweight Parker Fly.

He met Bowie on the American leg of the Glass Spider tour. Gabrels' journalist wife, Sara Terry, after writing articles on child exploitation (see "Shopping for Girls"), needed a break and became Bowie's press agent for a few months. Gabrels regularly visited her, and Bowie came to enjoy his company. As Gabrels said, he and Bowie had the least to do before a show. Though he'd played Bowie covers in high school bands, Gabrels didn't say he played music. "I figured I'm never going to play with the guy, so why ruin it?" Instead they talked about painters or watched *Fantasy Island* with the sound off, making their own dialogue.

Before Bowie left for the tour's Australian leg, Terry handed him a cassette that had some of Gabrels' recordings. Bowie was surprised: he'd thought Gabrels was a painter. Back home in Switzerland, he found the tape and figured it was worth a listen. He soon began recommending Gabrels, who had moved to London in the meantime, for session work. One afternoon in spring 1988, Gabrels came home after pasting flyers advertising his guitar lessons and got a phone call from Bowie. He thought it was a gag until Bowie mentioned *Fantasy Island*.

Cathedrals of Sound

Bowie was taking part in a La La La Human Steps dance routine for an Institute of Contemporary Arts benefit at the Dominion Theatre, planning to remake "Look Back in Anger" for the music. He'd booked his regular studio team at the time — Kevin Armstrong and Erdal Kızılçay — but wanted something fresh. The remake should sound as though it was carved out of a wall of guitars, he said. He invited Gabrels to Switzerland to audition as his architect.

There, Bowie gave Gabrels an inventory of his current interests. These included hard rock (Hendrix and Led Zeppelin bootlegs, electric bluesman Buddy Guy, downtown avant-gardists Sonic Youth and Glenn Branca, and Bowie's new love, the Pixies); a surrealist cookbook by Salvador and Gala Dali; books on art (including Robert Hughes' *The Shock of the New*) and medieval and Deconstructivist architecture. Bowie rattled on about flying buttresses and their descendants, the exposed structures of the likes of Centre Pompidou, tying this to the "cathedrals of sound" of Branca and Sonic Youth. He heard something similar in Gabrels' playing — ornamental guitar, not fitting "properly" into a song's harmonic structure but essential to its support.

"Look Back in Anger" was the test run. "It had only been a three-minute song, but he wanted another two-and-a-half minutes on each end of instrumentals while he was dancing," Gabrels said. "He said that he wanted it to be like the sonic equivalent of Gothic architecture and spires." His art school years paid off. Bowie liked to give musicians cues from painting or architectural styles (telling a horn section to "play Impressionist," for example). Gabrels was one of few who knew what he was talking about. He gave Bowie his spires and walls: "simple repetitive two-string things stacked up to create dense harmony, and close voiced."

After the ICA performance, Gabrels made a number of trips to Switzerland over the summer of 1988. He and Bowie would drive to Mountain Studios, work on demos, go home for dinner and *Fawlty Towers*. (Many years later, Gabrels marveled how Bowie "treated a fairly expensive recording studio the same way you'd treat a Tascam Porta One.") Gabrels had no ties to Bowie's past, hadn't seemed interested in music when Bowie met him. Over dinner one night, Bowie confided in him. He was lost. He felt obligated to write hits but no longer had the knack for it. Gabrels' response was: why be in the game at all? You're David Bowie. "The only barrier between you doing what you want and you doing what you think you should do, is you."

Smells Like Daisies

Steven Berkoff's play *West* premiered in London in 1983. It's set in Hackney, in a medieval Sixties (characters speak in Elizabethan Cockney). Mike, the local gang leader, agrees to take on a rival thug-lord from Hoxton in hand-to-hand combat. He walks to the fight alone — his gang has begged off, his girl is sick of him, his parents are ashamed of him. Berkoff said *West* was about the "courage to live according to your spirit and not the guidelines laid down for you by others... to be true to yourself, which may involve alienating others." Mike returns victorious and bloody, and his mother claims him as her own. "From me he saw that not to fight was to give in/ he saw that I never fought back/so he had to."

Bowie thought of adapting *West* as a musical or making a concept album about it, but believed the play was too obscure. EMI made it clear there wouldn't be a *Baal* on their dime. Who cares if only a few people like it? Gabrels responded. They wrote the Berkoff-inspired "The King of Stamford Hill," with Bowie doing a vocal over a Gabrels instrumental piece. It's from the perspective of Mike walking to the fight, taking in the sewage: "smells like *day*-sies." The cock-crow of the last honest man left in the city. "Ain't it fucking *cur-ee-ous* some other cunts are trying to *ditch* the *king*." While Gabrels re-recorded most of the instrumental tracks for his 1995 solo album, he kept Bowie's fantastic vocals from the Montreux demo sessions, making them the center of a pounding, screaming refrain: "gonna build an *army* march 'em to the *marshes*... someone's gonna *lose* 'is poxy *face*!" Bowie had a scheme at last. Now he had to build an army.

HEAVEN'S IN HERE

Recorded: 20 August-7 September, October 1988, Mountain Studios; (overdubs) 6-27 February 1989, Compass Point Studios, West Bay Road, Gambier Village, Nassau, Bahamas; (last overdubs, mixing) March-3 April 1989, Right Track Recording, 168 West 48th St., New York. Bowie: lead vocal, rhythm guitar; Gabrels: lead guitar; Kevin Armstrong: rhythm guitar; Tony Sales: bass, backing vocal; Hunt Sales: drums, backing vocal. Produced: Tim Palmer, Tin Machine; engineered: Justin Shirley-Smith.

First release: 22 May 1989, **Tin Machine** (EMI USA MTLS 1044/E1-91990, UK #3, US #28). *Broadcast*: 31 May 1989, International Rock Awards; 13 August 1991, Mark Goodier's Evening Session (BBC); 13 December 1991, The Arsenio Hall Show. *Live*: 1989, 1991-1992.

In Los Angeles in spring 1988, Bowie tried out a band assembled by Bon Jovi's producer, Bruce Fairbairn. It was some of Bryan Adams' group, guitarist Keith Scott and drummer Mickey Curry; the jazz bassist Rene Worst; Red Rider keyboardist John Webster. They cut demos, including a cover of "Like a Rolling Stone" later pawned off on Mick Ronson. The sessions, meant to sketch out his next album, were only months after the Glass Spider tour. Here he was again: another round of recording, another search for a single.

He went home to Switzerland, called up Reeves Gabrels. They started writing and demoing songs for an unspecified project (the first batch included "Bus Stop," "Baby Universal," "Pretty Pink Rose," and what became "Under the God"). Something had to change: he felt he couldn't do another *Never Let Me Down*. First to go would be Carlos Alomar. Gabrels recalled that Bowie and Alomar weren't getting along, and that Bowie said if he'd known Gabrels was a guitarist during Glass Spider, "I would have fired Carlos and hired you." Alomar was frustrated, too. "I knew David wanted to do a different kind of music, but he just didn't know how," he told David Buckley. "I always thought if I gave the music back to David, it would end up going back to the Spiders from Mars. That's exactly what happened."

One of Bowie's favorite bands at the time were the Screaming Blue Messiahs, who "have an exciting guitar player — a New Wave guitar player," he said in 1987. There was something more calculated at work. Gabrels later learned Bowie had spoken to a corporate image consultant, who allegedly told him "he needed to do something which was such a departure it would destroy everything that went before." Bowie was casting his demolition team. First, Gabrels. Then a new producer, Tim Palmer, who had recorded acts like the Mighty Lemon Drops and the Mission. For a rhythm section, some potential choices had art-rock pedigrees: drummer Terry Bozzio, a Mothers of Invention veteran, and bassist Percy Jones, who'd played on Eno's *Another Green World*. Bowie balked again. Sure, he could do *Scary Monsters 2*, which Gabrels and Palmer thought could be the plan. But wasn't that another version of the same trap?

For their "Look Back in Anger" remake, Bowie and Gabrels used drum machines to get a "thunderous nihilistic sound." Bowie said he wanted musicians who could play like that. As with Gabrels, Glass Spider did the introductions. In Los Angeles for a tour video launch party, Bowie saw Tony Sales, whom he hadn't talked to in years. He soon got Tony and his brother Hunt into a rehearsal room in LA, where they jammed as a trio. And there it was. For a rhythm section, the Saleses: the Katzenjammer Kids of rock. They weren't "checkbook musicians," as Bowie sniffed about the pros he'd auditioned, but road-scuffed R&B freaks who treated Bowie like he was their former keyboard player.

He was surrounding himself with people who all thought his Eighties records and tours were beneath him. He wanted a band as an obstacle, and he got one.

Hall of the Mountain King

In August 1988, Gabrels and Bowie had been working for about a week at Mountain Studios (writing "Baby Can Dance," "Pretty Thing," "Shopping for Girls," and other unreleased songs (see appendix)) when the Saleses arrived. Hunt walked into the studio wearing a "Fuck You, I'm From Texas" T-shirt, with a knife tucked into his belt. Tony was the other end of the spectrum. Having nearly died in a car accident a decade before, he'd become teetotal.

The Saleses made it clear they wouldn't be sidemen. They would sing, write songs, be loud about what they didn't like, and they didn't like a lot — they were the band's reactionary wing ("we were sick of turning on the radio and hearing disco and dance music and drum machines, which I think in the business they call 'crap'," Tony told *Spin* in 1989). They hazed Gabrels non-stop until he learned to ignore them. Hunt built his massive drum kit upon a riser (he had to use a ladder to reach it) and dominated the room, drumming so loudly the guitarists could barely hear themselves play. The recording philosophy was "an audio verité thing," as Gabrels later said. The band would cut tracks live in the studio, with as few takes as possible. No overdubs unless needed for a guitar solo, no synths, no lyric rewrites (that said, there apparently were a number of the latter). They would return from lunch to find Bowie had written a full lyric for whatever song they were working on. That was as far as he could go: he was held to his first instincts. "It's interesting to have to shut up," he said.

At first, Gabrels and Palmer thought the Saleses were a mistake. Palmer wanted to make "the greatest-sounding Bowie album ever," but soon realized he'd be happy getting a take where the band ended at the same time. "All these dreams went right out the window." Gabrels had spent a decade in groups and hated them. "I didn't want to be in a band anymore. Bands are a nightmare," he said.

But Bowie had picked the Saleses as a veto mechanism. He'd gotten too good at telling his musicians what he wanted. "That becomes a system. And once you've got a system you're really fucked up...That's the time that you have to break it," he said in 1991. Upon their arrival, he told the Saleses "let's ruin rock 'n' roll." The band they formed, Tin Machine, would be Bowie and Gabrels as brain and throat, the Saleses as guts and testicles. "Reeves went to school and I didn't," Hunt Sales said. "I got my education playing at jazz clubs with older musicians and in the street." At the same time, the brothers had an "amusing sense of rock star entitlement," Gabrels recalled.

"I think David was deliberately trying to go for a fucked-up sound," Palmer told Paul Trynka. "If it was too safe or polite, he'd dump it." Tin Machine favored songs "that didn't have too much orchestration," Bowie said. "If it started to get too chordy or arranged, it wouldn't be anything like what we wanted to do. The structure had to be as loose as possible so that everybody could improvise." Rather than reworking a song, they'd cut another one: *Tin Machine* easily could have been a double album. The standard was blues rock, the average song having less than five chords. *Tin Machine* — fourteen tracks in full — was a heavy listen. Few records are as exciting in miniature and as draining as a whole, encapsulated in the lead-off track "Heaven's in Here."

"Heaven's in Here" was the first track Tin Machine recorded as a full band, the first song they played live, and the last they would ever perform together. Tracked in a single day at Mountain, it's an E major vamp that starts with a whiff of feedback. A snarling rhythm guitar is overshadowed four bars in by the Saleses' entrance, while Gabrels plays a singing lead. Bowie's verse phrasing is a sly, mid-register insinuation, escorted by slide guitar; the refrain finds him channeling Jim Morrison (see "rocket *to* Mars," while the band all but rewrites "Love Me Two Times" in places). It's a tribute to sexual healing — for *Tin Machine*, Bowie alternated town-square rants with bedroom praises — but as it goes on, it sounds like a stripper bar band's begun to quarrel among themselves at the expense of supporting the main attraction.

It was "deconstructionist R&B," Bowie said. What set the band apart was its "struggling element." Tin Machine was allied against easy pleasures, always wanting to tear up and drag out songs instead of letting them groove. In "Heaven's in Here," the solos were confrontations between Gabrels and Hunt Sales, with Tony getting in an occasional outburst in support of whoever last got his attention. Gabrels goes off in his squall-world while Hunt's turnaround fills nearly knock the band off the tracks. Singing it live, Bowie threw in scraps of everything from "Cheek to Cheek" to "Fever" to Kraftwerk's

"Radioactivity" during its middle sections. Caught between his screaming guitarist and madman drummer, he was kept under siege, and he liked it.

IF THERE IS SOMETHING

(Ferry.) **Recorded***: 20 August-7 September, October 1988, Mountain Studios; Bowie: lead vocal, rhythm guitar; Gabrels: lead guitar; Armstrong: rhythm guitar; T. Sales: bass, backing vocal; H. Sales: drums, backing vocal; Produced: Palmer, Tin Machine; engineered: Shirley-Smith.*

First release*: 2 September 1991,* **Tin Machine II** *(Victory/London 828 272-1, UK #23, US #126).* **Broadcast***: 13 August 1991, Mark Goodier's Evening Session; 23 November 1991, Saturday Night Live.* **Live***: 1991-1992.*

Less than a year after forming, Roxy Music opened for Bowie in London, in summer 1972. They had become serious competition. "Virginia Plain" was in the charts, and their outlandish stage act lived up to songs such as "Re-Make/Re-Model," where a babbling synthesizer traded fours with a saxophone quoting "Ride of the Valkyries." Roxy Music was what Bowie never had: a band of autonomous, brilliant musicians working around and against a central figure. While Bryan Ferry wrote most of the songs and controlled the visuals, he turned over performances to his bandmates — Phil Manzanera, Andy Mackay, the fantastic drummer Paul Thompson — who kept him honest, or at least funny. There was a limit — Brian Eno, who challenged Ferry's authority, was soon gone — but at its best, Roxy Music in the early Seventies was an ironist collective that could swing harder than any other glam band.

Roxy Music's "If There Is Something" was the second track that Tin Machine recorded at Mountain Studios, after finishing "Heaven's in Here." "We were so exhausted that we didn't have it in us to write another song, so we used an old song to show how we as a band would approach someone else's material," Bowie said. While the track was left on the shelf along with many other *Tin Machine* outtakes, during the mixing of *Tin Machine II*, in spring 1991, Bowie "pulled it out to see how it sounded. We really got off on it."

The original "If There Is Something" begins as a country parody, with

Ferry drawling and Manzanera making asides on slide guitar. The first solo has Ferry and Manzanera still wearing their cowboy hats, but after a new, worrying motif, the song morphs into a torch ballad. "I would do anything for you, I would climb *mountains*," Ferry wails, applying ludicrous vibrato ("oceans bluuuuuuuuuuuuuuuuuuuuuue") to match the gigantism of his lyric. He'll swim oceans, climb Everest, plant potatoes *by the score*. Eno's synthesizer takes up the motif, Graham Simpson's bass rambles, a forty-bar progressive rock break ensues. When Ferry returns, he's mourning a lost romance, threatening to leap into an unexpected pitch at any moment. His gigantism is nostalgic: the grass was greener, the mountains higher, when he was young. It ends with mocking squiggles on Eno's synth.

Tin Machine could have a denseness, despite its singer and guitarist having deep senses of irony (Bowie said he loved Reeves Gabrels' playing because of this, whereas Stevie Ray Vaughan had meant every note he played: "It was *all heart*."). Covering "If There Is Something" was an invitation to go anywhere — turn the song into sonic spectacles; rope in more outlandish genres; do it as a straight-faced country and western piece. Instead, the Machine settled for volume: cranking up the amps, speeding up the pace, cutting corners, pounding through it, leaving it for dead. Bowie's most notable alteration was to sing "I would come all day" instead of climbing mountains. Tin Machine's "If There Is Something" was competent hard rock, with Gabrels introducing a hooky guitar riff in the latter section. But while they kept its structure intact, it was like a team assembling an Alexander Calder mobile from a set of Ikea instructions.

BUS STOP
COUNTRY BUS STOP

(Bowie, Gabrels.) **Recorded**: *20 August-7 September, October 1988, Mountain Studios; (overdubs) 6-27 February 1989, Compass Point Studios; (last overdubs, mixing) March-3 April 1989, Right Track. Bowie: lead vocal, rhythm guitar; Gabrels: lead guitar; Armstrong: rhythm guitar; T. Sales: bass, backing vocal; H. Sales: drums, backing vocal. Produced: Palmer, Tin Machine; engineered: Shirley-Smith.*

First release: *22 May 1989,* **Tin Machine**. *Live: 1989, 1991-1992.*

Hailing from Bowie and Reeves Gabrels' earliest songwriting efforts, "Bus Stop" wound up being an oasis of wit on *Tin Machine* ("I love you despite your convictions/that God never laughs at my jokes"). A London man tries to reconcile his religious skepticism with his lover's fervency; he's praying on his knees with her at the bus stop, grunts out a "hallelujah." It's a spiritual song centered on the body, from aching feet to grumbling stomach. "So English, it's almost vaudeville," Bowie said of "Bus Stop" in 1989.

Hard rooted in D major, "Bus Stop" is three chords, two verses and two refrains, with a brief outro; it runs on a similar tension-release guitar riff as the Damned's "New Rose." Hunt Sales bludgeons his snare four to the bar, his brother cues changes by speeding up or widening his span of notes. It spins to an end with a guitarists' scrap: Kevin Armstrong holding his ground, Gabrels trying to flank him. "It's about everyone's faith: where it comes from, when it comes out," Gabrels said. "When you really want something, I guess everybody prays in some way." On the road, "Bus Stop" was Americanized, possibly to lampoon televangelists in the news like Jimmy Swaggart. Over a reduced tempo, Bowie sang in a drawl close to his "Kentucky" accent in *Twin Peaks: Fire Walk with Me* (see "Boys Keep Swinging"). "Country Bus Stop" oversold a good joke; it was a relief when Gabrels ripped into the riff to spur Tin Machine to replay "Bus Stop" in its rocking-and-writhing version.

AMAZING

(Bowie, Gabrels.) **Recorded**: *20 August-7 September, October 1988, Mountain Studios; (overdubs) 6-27 February 1989, Compass Point Studios; (last overdubs, mixing) March-3 April 1989, Right Track. Bowie: lead vocal, rhythm guitar; Gabrels: lead guitar; Armstrong: rhythm guitar; T. Sales: bass, backing vocals; H. Sales: drums, backing vocal. Produced: Palmer, Tin Machine; engineered: Shirley-Smith.*

First release: *22 May 1989,* **Tin Machine**. **Live**: *1989, 1991-1992.*

Waiting to go to the movies and playing classical guitar figures, Reeves Gabrels wrote much of the music for "Amazing" in about ten minutes. After backing tracks were cut, the track was tabled until "David came back

THE BATTLE OF THE WILDERNESS

a month later and sang over it." It was one of several *Tin Machine* songs dedicated to Bowie's soon-to-be fiancée, the dancer Melissa Hurley. "The love songs are for my girlfriend, so I don't know what [the band] thinks of that," he said. Despite its title, "Amazing" isn't an unalloyed declaration of love — he fears she'll realize there's no future ("I'm scared you'll meet someone in whom you'll confide") and he's having nightmares about her leaving. He and Hurley would break up in 1990.

A power ballad in E major, shading to its parallel minor in refrains, "Amazing" is a crank's take on contemporary Aerosmith. Bowie took his verse melody from Gabrels' ascending scale playing — rises of a fourth ("you-*cray*-*zee*") answered by near-octave drops ("girl"). The rhythm is driven by multiple-tracked guitars, including some fine acoustic work, letting the Saleses rival Gabrels as lead players at times. As Bowie shelved many quieter pieces from the *Tin Machine* sessions to create a bristling mood for the album, by dint of surviving the cull, "Amazing" — leading off the album's second side — feels more substantial than it is. It doesn't end as much as it nods out, its composers doing vocal improvs and guitar doodles.

BABY CAN DANCE

Recorded: *20 August-7 September, October 1988, Mountain Studios; (overdubs) 6-27 February 1989, Compass Point; (last overdubs, mixing) March-3 April 1989, Right Track. Bowie: lead vocal, rhythm guitar; Gabrels: lead guitar; Armstrong: rhythm guitar; T. Sales: bass, backing vocal; H. Sales: drums, backing vocal. Produced: Palmer, Tin Machine; engineered: Shirley-Smith.*

First release: *22 May 1989*, **Tin Machine**. *Live*: *1989, 1991-1992*.

"The songs are almost secondary, to find a vehicle to work on, to improvise on," Bowie said of *Tin Machine*'s compositions. See album closer "Baby Can Dance," which starts as a group stomp, extending the curtain-of-feedback concept of the revised "Look Back in Anger" ("Now," a song Tin Machine played live in 1989, was another go at this). Solos drone over progressions with an E pedal point: Reeves Gabrels showers feedback-laden notes while the Saleses thunder around him; in refrains, he plays descending lines to harry Bowie's vocal melody. Tony Sales' walking bassline is a secondary hook to the tatty Bo Diddley riff that shakes through the song. Hunt, happily loose with tempo shifts, is gargantuan in sound — his snare hits sound like he's striking a bridge support.

Bowie's lyric is so dull that referencing his unreleased "Shadow Man" is a highlight. Struggling to get a foothold in the song, to the point where it seems like he's free-associating at the mike, his shakily-phrased verse lines jump-cut to an upward push on "bay-bee can float... bay-bee can dance." On stage, the band built out the song — a longer "it's over now" section, a "Flight of the Bumblebee" Gabrels solo. The coda, with Gabrels needling his way into a communal thud, summed up early Tin Machine as well as anything did.

PRETTY THING

> *Recorded: 20 August-7 September, October 1988, Mountain; (overdubs) 6-27 February 1989, Compass Point; (last overdubs, mixing) March-3 April 1989, Right Track. Bowie: lead vocal, rhythm guitar; Gabrels: lead guitar; Armstrong: rhythm guitar, Hammond B-3; T. Sales: bass, backing vocals; H. Sales: drums, backing vocal. Produced: Palmer, Tin Machine; engineered: Shirley-Smith.*

> *First release: 22 May 1989, **Tin Machine**. Live: 1989, 1991.*

"Pretty Thing" is a crass Bowie composition elevated by his lunatic band. A set of jokes, from its heavy metal progression (in F# minor, with feints to A major) to "laddish" lyrics ("something getting hard when you *rock it up*"), it's sung by Bowie in a nasal, clammy tone, as if summoning the forces of the counter-erotic. "A silly song," he called it. "Zippy the Pinhead... yuppie glam rock." A skydiving Reeves Gabrels introduces a Mod soul interlude, with Kevin Armstrong on Hammond B-3 organ, that's soon closed out by Hunt Sales' best Gene Krupa imitation. Returning for an endless round of refrains, "Pretty Thing" finally expires with a taunting on drums.

TIN MACHINE

*(Bowie, Gabrels, H. Sales, T. Sales.) **Recorded**: 20 August-7 September, October*

1988, Mountain; (overdubs) 6-27 February 1989, Compass Point; (last overdubs, mixing) March-3 April 1989, Right Track. Bowie: lead vocal, rhythm guitar; Gabrels: lead guitar; Armstrong: rhythm guitar; T. Sales: bass, backing vocals; H. Sales: drums, backing vocal. Produced: Palmer, Tin Machine; engineered: Shirley-Smith.

First release: *22 May 1989,* **Tin Machine**. **Live**: *1989.*

Tin Machine was "the first band I've been in — as opposed to led or directed — since the Konrads," Bowie said at the time. And he meant it, at the time. On or about 6 September 1988, Bowie decided that he, the Saleses, and Reeves Gabrels should form a true band, named after one of the songs they were working on in Montreux. Their debut album was credited solely to Tin Machine (though EMI stickered the cover to remind buyers who the bearded member was), who signed a legal agreement in which each member was an equal partner, paying for a fourth of every band expense (and owning a fourth of the publishing of all songs on *Tin Machine II*.) "*Tin Machine* is not a David Bowie record. Tin Machine is a band," Hunt Sales said in 1989. Tony Sales often introduced the band on stage. In TV interviews, Bowie tried to not talk over his bandmates; in a 1989 *Spin* profile, all but Bowie spoke. This collective front pleased few at his label and his organization: Gabrels later said Bowie's assistant Coco Schwab "felt Tin Machine was bringing down the value of the currency of the David Bowie name."

Visually, Tin Machine was Bowie's Power Station, the mid-Eighties supergroup in which Robert Palmer hooked up with Duran Duran and Chic. Like Palmer, Tin Machine wore designer suits (Bowie gave each of them $1,000 to suit up in Prada for their debut gig); like Power Station, they liked loud R&B workouts and T. Rex riffs. Unlike Power Station, they looked like a support group for ex-husbands. Tin Machine was a Power Station gone mad, a band who liked to implode on stage. In interviews, the band spent much of its time arguing that it was a band, with Bowie supporting the idea and also sending it up. "In other tours, people were working *for* you, while we're together," Hunt Sales told him in a group radio interview. "Togetherness in hostility," he replied. "There's unity and purpose in this band," Hunt lobbed back. "Unity Mitford," Bowie cracked, referring to one of Britain's more glamourous Nazi sympathizers.

Their name was arbitrarily chosen. "We couldn't think of a good name, so we picked [one] from a song on the album," Bowie said in 1989. Gabrels had wanted to call the band White Noise but Bowie said it sounded racist (in an alternate life, Bowie fronted Crack City). Tin Machine, a play on Led Zeppelin and Iron Butterfly, signaled Bowie's hopes for the band: a vehicle to get him on the road going somewhere else.

The Saleses liked having a theme song, like the Monkees. It livened up a deadpan group — there's often something unavoidably goofy when a band uses its name for a song: see the Clash, who kept at it with diminishing returns. "Tin Machine" is the closest the band came to hardcore, but it's hardcore as a jotted-down concept — simple, short, angry, fast — delivered by a band with too many chops and which goes too slow. There's no buildup or breakdown: "Tin Machine" packs off in a sulk. The arrangement aims for [Glenn] "Branca-sonic," with multi-tracked guitars including "facsimile bagpipes" — Gabrels playing a six-string in his lap like a slide guitar, while stomping on a Wah-Wah pedal. Hunt Sales spares his crash cymbals and adds a fuel-injection fill in the second verse.

In a flat, clipped vocal, Bowie does the sort of "fractured word" spleen-vent that plagues much of *Tin Machine*: "mindless maggot glare," "night that spews out watchmen," "humping Tories." There's wordplay of sorts ("blue-suede tuneless") and callbacks to his recently-revived "All the Madmen" ("I'm not exactly well"). He tears through the bridges, howling lines that expire in a choked-out "hell" — it's a mannered rage.

RUN

(Bowie, Armstrong.) **Recorded**: *20 August-7 September, October 1988, Mountain; (overdubs) 6-27 February 1989, Compass Point; (last overdubs, mixing) March-3 April 1989, Right Track. Bowie: lead vocal, rhythm guitar; Gabrels: lead guitar; Armstrong: rhythm guitar; T. Sales: bass, backing vocals; H. Sales: drums, backing vocal. Produced: Palmer, Tin Machine; engineered: Shirley-Smith.*

First release: *22 May 1989,* **Tin Machine** *(EMI USA CDP 7-919990-2).* **Live**: *1989.*

For Tin Machine, Bowie had a convert's devotion to tradition. A band meant the Beatles mold of two guitars-bass-drums and four distinct visual personalities. As this meant he had one musician too many, Bowie demoted rhythm guitarist Kevin Armstrong, who didn't appear on the album cover, only given a passport photo on the back. He was recast as the genial session guy brought in for support ("Kevin does what I pretend to do," Bowie said).

When the band reconvened at Compass Point Studios in the Bahamas, early in 1989, Bowie broke the news to Armstrong. Though disappointed, Armstrong bore no ill will and later said he'd had "mixed feelings" about Tin Machine anyhow (Bowie "allow[ed] Reeves and Hunt and Tony to steer the whole thing"). He left after Tin Machine's short 1989 tour and was missed: he was the one supporting player in a pack of lead actors ("I think of myself as the easiest one to get along with, of course, but I was a controlling fuck," Gabrels said), his guitar sometimes all that held performances together.

Armstrong co-wrote the music for "Run" with Bowie. As they'd worked on *Blah-Blah-Blah* together, and as Armstrong played on Iggy Pop's subsequent tour, "Run" sounds like it's written for Pop — the refrains in particular for Pop's baritone. Bowie's vocal melody has similarities to "Loving the Alien," while his lyric is a scrap pile — a Velvet Underground reference in the title, another sailor adrift (see "Shake It"), a "goldman (Sachs?) in a soaring tower." Using the same four-chord A minor progression for verses and refrains, "Run" has a solid guitar hook, an arpeggiated near-octave-spanning figure, but it's filler on an overstuffed record.

VIDEO CRIME

(Bowie, H. Sales, T. Sales.) **Recorded**: *20 August-7 September, October 1988, Mountain; (overdubs) 6-27 February 1989, Compass Point; (last overdubs, mixing) March-3 April 1989, Right Track. Bowie: lead vocal, rhythm guitar; Gabrels: lead guitar; Armstrong: rhythm guitar; T. Sales: bass, backing vocals; H. Sales: drums, backing vocal. Produced: Palmer, Tin Machine; engineered: Shirley-Smith.*

First release: *22 May 1989*, **Tin Machine**.

The near-tuneless "Video Crime" is the least of the "social commentary" songs on *Tin Machine*, a hodgepodge of serial killers ("trash time Bundy," "late night cannibal"), urban decay ("wonder where the Third World went") and "video nasties." The latter, a scare courtesy of the usual suspects (Mary

Whitehouse, the *Sun*), concerned the popularity of direct-to-VHS horror/ sex films (in a *Young Ones* episode, the gang rents *Sex With the Headless Corpse and the Virgin Astronaut*). Bowie's narrator, his imagination steeped in slasher movies, wants to make one of his own or become a killer himself ("chop it up!" is an editor's and killer's move). There was something to make of the cultural vogue for serial killers, but it wasn't found here. With a nattering, four-note vocal (its ancestor was the equally grating mass-killer "Running Gun Blues"), "Video Crime" was the only song on *Tin Machine* never played live. A slog, it runs on two chords, briefly escaping to a third in the solos, and has an imposition instead of a groove. The usual tricks keep things moving — Hunt Sales' snare fills; Gabrels' high-pitched leads. Credit to Kevin Armstrong, who's in-the-pocket rhythm guitar suggests a better song is somewhere in the morass.

UNDER THE GOD

Recorded: 20 August-7 September, October 1988, Mountain; (overdubs) 6-27 February 1989, Compass Point; (last overdubs, mixing) March-3 April 1989, Right Track. Bowie: lead vocal, rhythm guitar; Gabrels: lead guitar; Armstrong: rhythm guitar; T. Sales: bass, backing vocals; H. Sales: drums, backing vocal. Produced: Palmer, Tin Machine; engineered: Shirley-Smith.

*First release: 22 May 1989, **Tin Machine**. Live: 1989, 1991-1992.*

Rewriting a demo called "Night Train" as "Under the God," a song about neo-Nazism, Bowie said he wanted to avoid metaphor and high-flown language in favor of "something that had the same simplistic, naïve, radical, laying it down about the emergence of a new Nazi so that people could not mistake what the song was about." This attitude was in keeping with his *Tin Machine* persona. Reeves Gabrels and the Sales brothers were sonic extremists, so Bowie had to be as radical and overbearing in his vocals and lyrics. He'd never sounded angrier, but it was a thin anger, diffused through woeful lyrics and phrasings warped to fit the songs' bent shapes.

He'd first seen neo-Nazi skinheads towards the end of his Berlin years. "They were very vocal, very visible... you just crossed the street when you saw them coming," he said in 1993. "I thought — this is not a place to for Joe [his son, now known as Duncan] to be growing up. This could get worse." By the time of *Tin Machine II*, Germany had over fifty nationally-known "fascho-bands," including Zyklon B and Endstufe. "We'd like to dedicate [this] for all those unfortunate enough to be immigrants in this decaying Western world," as Bowie introduced the song on stage in Munich in 1991. It wasn't only Germany: there was Skrewdriver, a British punk band aligned with the National Front and white power groups, and "you can see it in Orange County," Bowie told an American interviewer in 1989. "It can happen here."

In the late Eighties, skinhead Nazis were still marginal, "threatening and pathetic, full of bravado yet highly pessimistic," as Timothy S. Brown wrote. Bowie believed it was just the first stage, and that this pessimism would give way to an increasing sense of power once the right realized what forces it could corral. A democracy carries the bacillus of its own destruction: the freedom of identity it gives its citizens is easily corruptible. "It's painful being a democracy because one of the fucking things you have to do is allow people to say what they want to," he said in 1991. Freedom of speech could be weaponized. Should a David Duke be allowed to run for office, to broadcast his racism? Bowie wondered. Hunt Sales pointed out that Duke had failed at the ballot box. Bowie replied that Duke "created a power base for himself. He should not be taken lightly, we have not seen the last of him by any means at all."

Like "Crack City," the song had a self-loathing, confessional aspect. Bowie had dabbled in Nazi affectations in the Seventies, to the point where he earned praise from the Young National Front's *Bulldog* and the neo-Nazi magazine *Spearhead*. "Under the God" is a loud demystification — no more sacred Himmler realms and thin white dukes, but a stupid, drunk skinhead retching into a toilet bowl. Its subtlest argument was to use a guitar riff from the Yardbirds' cover of Billy Boy Arnold's "I Wish You Would" (which Bowie had covered on *Pin Ups*), showing rock to be fundamentally an African-American music.

As the punk scene had been self-policing for years (see the Dead Kennedys' "Nazi Punks Fuck Off," from 1981), "Under the God" was late to the game, clumsily opportunistic and even cheesy, from the Saleses' "white trash!" backing vocals to Bowie's phrasing of lines like "ten steps into the *crazeee crazee*." Reeves Gabrels plays a solo that sounds like the "Meow Mix" theme, with tea-kettle-whistle feedback at the close. With one of the muddiest mixes on *Tin Machine*, "Under the God" had more power live, with a 1991 performance on the *Oy Vey Baby* video its most pulverizing version.

SACRIFICE YOURSELF

(Bowie, H. Sales, T. Sales.) **Recorded***: 20 August-7 September, October 1988, Mountain; (overdubs) 6-27 February 1989, Compass Point; (last overdubs, mixing) March-3 April 1989, Right Track. Bowie: lead vocal, guitar; Gabrels: lead guitar: Armstrong: rhythm guitar; T. Sales: bass, vocals; H. Sales: drums, vocals. Produced: Palmer, Tin Machine; engineered: Shirley-Smith.*

First release*: 22 May 1989,* **Tin Machine**. **Live***: 1989, 1991-1992.*

Though written by Bowie and the Saleses, "Sacrifice Yourself" is Reeves Gabrels' show. Given a blurry harmonic structure and a punishing tempo, Gabrels defaces riffs, picks at Bowie's two-note refrain melody, chews scenery. The rhythm guitar sounds like a detuned piano; Hunt Sales fills whatever he finds open. Buried on *Tin Machine*'s second half (and not included on the LP), "Sacrifice Yourself" became a live favorite, often the high-voltage set opener. Howled into the din is a lyric with affinities to "I Can't Read": a spent-out artist figure gone respectable, taking digs at his ex-wife and stardom ("thirty-five years pass him like an evening at the circus"). The last verse references snorting coke, Iggy Pop's "Bang Bang," "Suffragette City," and the Book of Ecclesiastes. The refrain's another way of saying "keep yourself alive": rationed hope for a withered time. On stage, Bowie sang "Sacrifice Yourself" at a breakneck pace, slowing only to soak "yourself" in contempt.

PRISONER OF LOVE

(Bowie, H. Sales, T. Sales, Gabrels.) **Recorded***: 20 August-7 September, October 1988, Mountain; (overdubs) 6-27 February 1989, Compass Point; (last overdubs, mixing) March-3 April 1989, Right Track. Bowie: lead vocal, rhythm guitar;*

Gabrels: lead guitar; Armstrong: rhythm guitar; T. Sales: bass, backing vocals; H. Sales: drums, backing vocal. Produced: Palmer, Tin Machine; engineered: Shirley-Smith.

First release: *22 May 1989,* **Tin Machine**. **Live**: *1989.*

One of the better tracks on *Tin Machine*, "Prisoner of Love" is a communal songwriting effort — where Bowie typically wrote all lyrics, Tony Sales contributed some lines here (hopefully not "like a sermon on blues guitar/ love walked into town," one of the grimmer similes in the Bowie oeuvre). Bowie's phrasing is graceful: see the rich internal rhymes and consonance in the first verse ("what*e*ver it takes... *I've believed I b*elonged to you for a long t*i*me"), or his gently arcing line in the bridge where, after hitting a high G ("don't be"), he sinks an octave. Like "Amazing," it was a pledge to Melissa Hurley, who was two decades younger than him, religious, and less worldly ("just stay square"). "The fact she is young, very naïve and kind of straight is something I'd like her to retain as long as she can," he said in 1989. Or see the lyric, sung in the voice of "Too Dizzy": "I'll break any thug that maps out your passage to ruin." This being Bowie, "Prisoner of Love" also references Jean Genet's last work on Palestinian guerrillas, and a James Brown single.

It's a valentine for electric guitar: Kevin Armstrong's rhythm lines bolster the vocal melody, while Reeves Gabrels is an orchestra: a Hank Marvin-style twanging opening riff; a "string section" for bridge and refrains; chiming harmonics from picking between the trapeze tailpiece and bridge of an old Gretsch; the outro's weeping lines.

WORKING CLASS HERO

(Lennon.) **Recorded**: *20 August-7 September, October 1988, Mountain; (overdubs) 6-27 February 1989, Compass Point; (last overdubs, mixing) March-3 April 1989, Right Track. Bowie: lead vocal, rhythm guitar; Gabrels: lead guitar; Armstrong: rhythm guitar; T. Sales: bass, backing vocal; H. Sales: drums, backing vocal. Produced: Palmer, Tin Machine; engineered: Shirley-Smith.*

First release: 22 May 1989, **Tin Machine**. *Live*: 1989.

Sean Lennon was friends with Bowie's son, and was around for some of the Nassau sessions, where Tin Machine played his father's "Working Class Hero" in tribute. The song appeared on *Tin Machine*, with Bowie saying he'd wanted to bring a neglected John Lennon masterpiece into wider circulation. "Working Class Hero" dissects working-class life: the few paths open to the masses, their gulling by the ruling class. "A working-class hero is *something to be*," Lennon sang, biting on the latter words. Its five verses are one life: birth, school, work, the narcotic comforts of adulthood, and the sanctioned way out of the hole: the escape clauses for a handful, whether via lottery tickets or pop music.

Lennon plays a game of bluffs as to his sympathies, with righteousness, scorn, or pity in any given phrasing. "[John] was not the big 'Working-Class Hero' he liked to make out to be. He was the least working class of the Beatles actually. He was the poshest because his family almost owned Woolton at one time," as Paul McCartney said. For a time, Lennon embodied the "classless" Britain of Swinging London: a Scouse-accented creator of psychedelic pop and Joycean books. When he recorded "Working Class Hero" in 1970, a time he was involved in radical politics, he demoted his rank. "I'm working class and I use few words," he said to Dick Cavett. "I'm not an intellectual, I'm not articulate."

Like Lennon, Bowie had been raised middle-class, but he'd never pretended otherwise, apart from his occasional claims he'd grown up on the hard streets of Brixton. His perspectives were surreal suburban and alien tourist. A Bowie take on Lennon's already-conflicted class anthem was ripe for further ironies. He didn't have the band for it, though. As on "If There Is Something," the hope was that "by playing someone else's song, you can hear what the band sounds like," Reeves Gabrels said at the time. "Our writing doesn't get in the way of our playing." Tin Machine made "Working Class Hero" into a rocker with a lumpen swagger. Where Lennon's song is in the Dorian mode, sounding as if he'd revived an ancient ballad (it's the same scale as "What Shall We Do with a Drunken Sailor"), Tin Machine clamps it into standard A minor. Where Lennon is cyclical — shuttling between chords; playing the same acoustic guitar figure, paced by bass notes he sounds on an open string — they settle in for a bluesy sag. Gabrels takes a solo after the third verse; the track's book-ended with the usual drubbing.

Bowie hustles through the song, hoarsely inflating words like balloons. Lennon precisely sounds each consonant of "pick a career," savoring its bureaucratic coldness and playing on the double meaning of "career" as something spinning out of control. Bowie sounds like he's in a checkout lane: "*pick*-uh *c'reer*." He flatly sings or mumbles the lyric's curses, which Lennon had deployed as land mines, while his screaming at the close is an admission of interpretive defeat.

CRACK CITY

Recorded: 20 February 1989, Compass Point; (last overdubs, mixing) March-3 April 1989, Right Track. Bowie: lead vocal, rhythm guitar; Gabrels: lead guitar; Armstrong: rhythm guitar; T. Sales: bass, backing vocal; H. Sales: drums, backing vocal. Produced: Palmer, Tin Machine; engineered: Shirley-Smith.

First release: 22 May 1989, **Tin Machine**. *Live*: 1989, 1991-1992.

In 1977, the Clash's Joe Strummer and Mick Jones went on holiday to Kingston, Jamaica. They walked to the docks, looking for Lee Perry's studio and to score drugs. On the streets, they were called "white pigs" and threatened ("the only reason they didn't kill us was that they thought we were merchant seamen off the ships," Strummer recalled). They spent the rest of their stay in the Pegasus Hotel, smoking grass and writing songs, one of which, "Safe European Home," was a self-mocking memoir of their trip.

A decade later, Bowie, while recording in the Bahamas, walked around Nassau a few times and was shocked at how pervasive the drug use was. "The crack situation down there was just trouble on legs, it was hateful... usually the foggy underbelly of a city is fun. This isn't fun," he said. ("They were selling crack in the hotel!" Tony Sales added.) But while the scenario was similar — white musicians in a post-colonial Caribbean city — the resulting song wasn't. "Safe European Home" had wit, deprecation and hooks. "Crack City" rips off "Wild Thing" for its riff and I-IV verse progression, while lines include "they're just a bunch of assholes/with buttholes for their brains." (Bowie explained that "I think there are a bunch of assholes out there who are really screwing up young people.") The lyric's artlessness was due to its making: Bowie improvised it on the spot, the band cutting the track on the same night in Nassau as they did "I Can't Read."

The time was ripe for a cynical look at the crack plague, which had become a new way for the police to harass African Americans and which had spawned racist urban legends. (See the idea of a generation of "crack babies," which had no medical foundation — even Neil Young's "Rockin' in the Free World" has a crack mother leaving her baby in a garbage can.) But "Crack City" uses crack as a stalking horse for other concerns: Bowie's past drug use and the glamour that he felt rock 'n' roll gave to addiction.

During the Tin Machine era, Bowie stopped drinking. He'd weaned himself off cocaine with alcohol, which was apparently a greater burden for him than he let on — a few stories got out about his antics (most notably in 1989, when a reportedly drunk Bowie hit on Axl Rose's girlfriend, Erin Everly, causing Rose to chase him down an LA street screaming "I'm gonna kill you, Tin Man!"). At the turn of the decade, he did a twelve-step Alcoholics Anonymous program and during sessions for *Tin Machine II*, he invited the album's cover artist Edward Bell to a Narcotics Anonymous meeting. Some of Bowie's precepts for Tin Machine were similar to AA quotes. "449 says you are in the place you're supposed to be," he told an interviewer, referring to page 449 of AA's basic text: "I can find no serenity until I accept that person, place or thing as being exactly the way it's supposed to be at this moment. Nothing in God's world happens by mistake." "We were talking about drug and sex addiction — all kinds of addiction," Tony Sales recalled. "Deep, injured stuff."

Bowie would describe himself as "a former drug addict" in interviews, and once snarled about the Happy Mondays that "you look at them with their pro-drug stance and you look at [Rene] Magritte, who never touched anything other than a pipe in his life, and you wonder who came off better." "Crack City" alternates between cursing dealers and rock 'n' rollers, "the icon monsters" who play "drug dirges," including the Velvet Underground and, in live performances of the song, Jimi Hendrix (Bowie would sing "'scuse me while I kiss the sky"). He included himself among the guilty: "'Jean Genie' was the romantic side of it, whilst 'Crack City' is the reality."

Tin Machine makes it catchy: the "hit-crack-citaaay!!!" vocal hook, Reeves Gabrels' bloody-minded playing in the verses and sustain-riddled solo. Live, the band improved on the studio arrangement, backing off to let the verses breathe more. Because most anti-drug songs were "all intellectual... written for other writers," Bowie said he wrote bluntly so that the street could hear him. What it heard was would-be heavy metal Bob Dylan, a "Masters of War" for the crack years.

I CAN'T READ

(Bowie, Gabrels.) **Recorded***: 20 February 1989, Compass Point; (last overdubs, mixing) March-3 April 1989, Right Track. Bowie: lead vocal; Gabrels: lead guitar; Armstrong: rhythm guitar; T. Sales: bass, backing vocals; H. Sales: drums, backing vocal;* **(remake)** *ca. August-September 1996, Looking Glass Studios, New York. Bowie: lead and backing vocal; Gabrels: lead guitar, rhythm guitar; Mark Plati: keyboards, rhythm guitar; Gail Ann Dorsey: bass; Mike Garson: piano; Zachary Alford: drums. Produced: Palmer, Tin Machine;* **(remake)** *Bowie; co-produced: Gabrels, Plati. Engineered: Shirley-Smith; (remake) Plati.*

First release*: 22 May 1989,* **Tin Machine***; (remake) 21 October 1997,* **The Ice Storm** *(Velvel Records VEL 79713).* **Broadcast***: 8 April 1997, 99X Breakfast Show (WNNX), WBCN; 5 September 1997, CKZZ; 8 September 1997, Breakfast Show (KNDD); 9 September 1997, Johnny Steele Breakfast Show (KITS); 10 September 1997, Tammy Bruce Show (KROQ); 16 September 1997, KFOG; 26 September 1997, CFNY; 16 October 1997, WXRT; 7 November 1997, Rock & Pop; 29 January 1998, WHFS; 23 August 1999, VH1 Storytellers.* **Live***: 1989, 1991-1992, 1996-1997, 1999.*

Bowie called "I Can't Read" *Tin Machine*'s best song and revised it in 1996, keeping it in live sets for the rest of the decade. A Beckettian epilogue to his earlier songs-of-songwriting, "I Can't Read" answers "Quicksand," written at the vertiginous height of his compositional powers, "Sound and Vision," and "Ashes to Ashes." It's a man bled clean of inspiration, left a husk in a dry season.

"I Can't Read" (mostly written by Bowie and Gabrels on the former's yacht in Mustique in January 1989) stings of wounds from the *Never Let Me Down*/Glass Spider debacles. In the past, whatever his frame of mind, Bowie had tacked down and delivered. Now he faced the prospect that he could no longer write well. He always said he wanted to be a painter and a director, and that music was the vehicle to get him there. It was what he could do well, his backstop. Now that foundation was gone. "The structure seems to be decaying. What is the purpose of daily life?" he told a TV interviewer in 1989, in what he said were his son's thoughts. "It doesn't seem to have any values that really mean anything." To another interviewer four years later, he said, "what happens is you wake up one morning and you feel absolutely dead. You can't even drag your soul back into your body."

Tin Machine was his group therapy — "I've cried in front of the band," he said in 1991. "Pain I'm going through now... All that pretending you're okay that doesn't work anymore... Problems are too big. And life is quite fucking short." He recalled needing to "ice up" his emotions by the age of five, "you find a façade that will keep everybody happy," and that he "battled very arduously to block his emotions on all levels until... I didn't even know what I felt." The band was his most dedicated effort to dismantle "David Bowie" since *Low*; one possible title for the first Tin Machine album was *The Emperor's New Clothes*.

In "I Can't Read," illiteracy stands for creative barrenness — the loss of a faculty which once had come easily. "Things like "I Can't Read" come from my own desperations, not from watching or observing other people," Bowie said. He tries to capture a melody but can't play it. The constituent parts of music — the notes, chords, guitar tones, phrasings — are illegible. The track is washed in howling feedback, as though noise is all he can muster. He watches TV, flicks from *Countdown* to cop show; he sees himself on a magazine cover: a man trapped in his famous face. Andy Warhol appears as a ghost. Bowie had once danced Warhol through his tribute song for him in 1971, using Warhol's maxims about art and fakery. Now he's reduced to celebrity arbitration: *Andy, where's my fifteen minutes?*

Its creation, however, was a compositional resurgence. Gabrels recalled Bowie sitting with a book open on a music stand and improvising a lyric on the mike, spying a word or phrase on the page, using it to fill in a line or two, and quickly weaving the song into a whole. Recorded in an hour one night in Nassau, "I Can't Read" moves at a crawl, sounding on the verge of collapse after every verse. "It is so dangerously overbalanced. You expect it to topple off," Bowie said in 1989. "It seems to sort of stagger to starts and stops, and you never think it will actually pick itself off the floor again." It takes nearly a minute to get started: snare hits, an occasional bassline, feedback. Bowie begins to sing, keeping on a single note (just above the chord's root note) until sinking to the root note to close a phrase ("I-can't-read-and-I-can't-write *down*"). A blankly observational tone, like a man who's been in a car crash recounting what he can remember. Phrases trail off, leaving empty bars for guitars to fill — a grinding riff, like an engine stuck between gears.

The refrain is summoned by Hunt Sales' table-rapping. Bowie soars up a fifth, sounds light-headed. "I — can't *read shit* anymore... can't get it right," delivering the latter lines in a mocking sing-song, as though he's taunting the listener. *You want a melody? Here: blah blah blah.* (The chords are meat-and-potatoes rock 'n' roll, I-IV-V.) Feeling pain in his bones, he closes in exasperation: I can't read *shit*, I can't *read* shit. The players regroup, run through the intro sequence again. Anyone could stop and the song would die.

Tin Machine's lack of a common language works here: each player is a mass of contrary emotions. The hiss of Hunt's ride cymbals, his fills, rollick Bowie's admissions of defeat. Tony Sales' refrain hook suggests the bassline that drove "Suffragette City"; other times he makes leaps down his bass neck. Kevin Armstrong's rhythm guitar fits the barren mood of the vocal melody; Gabrels' exuberance is the Janus face to it.

In their short 1989 tour, Tin Machine slowed the tempo (the studio take goes at a fairly fast clip), making the song even more purgatorial, with Bowie throwing in lines from Dylan's "Maggie's Farm," which they were covering at the time. By the following tour, they were flaying "I Can't Read" open, with the bass singing through the intro. No matter how shambling a particular gig was, the band always locked in on this song. Gabrels played a siren wail over the "watch the police car" line, Bowie mimed being crucified while singing "when you see a famous smile"; they trashed the refrains, killing off momentum as it crested, then revving it up again.

For a studio remake, recorded in the *Earthling* sessions in mid-1996, the song gained a studied melancholy, verses now set to acoustic guitar strums, with Gabrels taking an elegant acoustic solo. It was mostly Gabrels' doing, building the track out of rehearsal tapes for the Neil Young Bridge Benefit. The remake would be used in Ang Lee's *The Ice Storm*, and Lee wanted the refrain in a minor key (there was also a revised lyric, with the second verse now the last, while for a new second verse, Bowie sang more earnest lines like "can I see the family smile? Can I reach tomorrow?") Gabrels rerecorded some instruments under the refrain vocal to move the key center and harmony from C major to A minor without changing the melody, so that Bowie's vocal still worked.

"I Can't Read" was restored to its original shape for its last go-round for his 1999 tour, where the refrain had a cold majesty and Bowie sang the Warhol line as if cursing over his grave. But none of the later versions surpassed Tin Machine's takes on the song: it was their nightly exorcism. "Music on the edge of improvisation becoming fixed composition, like writing words in concrete," as Gabrels said. Bowie's long bid to reclaim his title in the Nineties is inconceivable without "I Can't Read" — a reckoning and confession; a song in which failure was a muse.

MAGGIE'S FARM

(Dylan.) **Recorded**: *25 June 1989, La Cigale, 120 Boulevard de Rochechouart, 18th Arrt., Paris. Bowie: lead vocal, rhythm guitar; Gabrels: lead guitar; Armstrong: rhythm guitar; T. Sales: bass, backing vocal; H. Sales: drums, backing vocal. Engineered: Westwood One.*

First release: *ca. 28 August 1989 (EMI USA MT 73, UK #48).* **Live**: *1989.*

Tin Machine's promotional tour in June-July 1989 was a dozen gigs in medium-sized venues in the US, Britain, and Europe (including New York's The World, Amsterdam's Paradiso, and London's Town & Country Club.) The lighting was as severe — stark whites and shadows, like the Isolar tour — as the setlist. They played no Bowie solo songs but nearly all of *Tin Machine* and got respectful reviews, if often regarded as "Prince and the Pauper wish fulfillment" for Bowie. "This is not gonna be a circus," Tony Sales said at the time. "We are first and foremost playing for *us*," Bowie added.

The band played two Sixties rock standards in the tour, debuting a cover of Bob Dylan's "Maggie's Farm" in Hamburg, Germany, on 22 June 1989 (a recording from La Cigale in Paris was issued as a single in September). "Maggie's Farm" resounded in summer 1989 in Britain, where growing resistance to the Poll Tax would help bring down Margaret Thatcher the following year. Bowie sang verses as sets of irritations, bellowing the last lines, while the band imposed Dylan's melody upon the chassis of T. Rex's "Jeepster." They downplayed how comical Dylan's song is, an absurdist parody of the standard "Down on Penny's Farm," and discarded the song's wry fatalism (say what he likes, the singer's never getting off the farm) for macho defiance.

SHAKIN' ALL OVER

(Kidd.) **Recorded**: *1 July 1989, Newport Leisure Centre, 1 Kingsway, Newport, Wales. Bowie: lead vocal, rhythm guitar; Gabrels: lead guitar; Armstrong: rhythm guitar; T. Sales: bass, backing vocal; H. Sales: drums, backing vocal. Mixed: Gabrels, Dube.*

First release: *19 August 1991 (LONX 305/Victory 869 403-1).* **Live**: *1989, 1991-1992.*

Another live cover on the 1989 tour was a brass-knuckled take on Johnny Kidd's "Shakin' All Over." Released in 1960 into a somnolent British pop market, "Shakin' All Over," with its lust-stung vocal, creeping bassline, and cranked-up guitars, hit like a cannonball: the first great UK #1 of the decade. Stunned by a girl ("I get the shakes all over me!"), Kidd's left a victim of erotic circumstance. Joe Moretti's guitar solo helped invent British rock; Mick Ronson paid homage by playing Moretti lines on Bowie's cover of "I Can't Explain." Taking the Who's *Live at Leeds* version for its cue, Tin Machine made "Shakin' All Over" into a catch-all rock 'n' roll homage, with scorching Reeves Gabrels solos and sometimes references to other quivering hits — "Whole Lotta Shakin' Goin' On" and "Shake" — as if doing a medley on a Bizarro World episode of *Cher*.

BABY UNIVERSAL

(Bowie, Gabrels.) **Recorded**: *(backing tracks) 20 August-7 September, October 1988, Mountain; (overdubs) ca. early September-early November 1989, Studios 301, 301 Castlereagh St., Sydney, Australia; (further overdubs) ca. late 1990, Cherokee Studios, 751 North Fairfax Ave., Los Angeles; (mixing) ca. early spring 1991, Eel Pie Studios, the Boathouse, Twickenham. Bowie: lead vocal, rhythm guitar; Gabrels: lead guitar; T. Sales: bass, backing vocal; H. Sales: drums, backing vocal;* **(studio remake, unreleased)** *ca late August-11 November 1996, Looking*

Glass. Bowie: lead and backing vocal; Gabrels: lead guitar; Plati: keyboards, rhythm guitar; Dorsey: bass; Garson: piano; Alford: drums. Produced: Palmer, Tin Machine; (remake) Plati, Bowie; engineered: Shirley-Smith, Guy Gray, Simon Vinestock, et al.

First release: *2 September 1991,* **Tin Machine II**. **Broadcast**: *3 August 1991, Paramount City; 13 August 1991, Mark Goodier's Evening Session; 29 August 1991, Top of the Pops; 23 November 1991, Saturday Night Live.* **Live**: *1991-1992, 1996.*

In September 1991, Tin Machine put out a second album. "Hot tramp! We loved you so. Now sit down, man, you're a fucking disgrace." So ended *Melody Maker*'s review, which was far from the only hatchet job. *Spin*: "a follow-up as eagerly awaited as *Mannequin 2: On the Move,*" with Bowie "made ridiculous by adhering to rules he himself wrote for his most rickety and least publicly subscribed persona." *Entertainment Weekly*: "anonymous, grinding rockers... songs with passable chorus hooks and nothing in the verses to support them. Meaningless lyric after meaningless lyric."

EMI had refused to release the album, and Bowie soon left the label. "It didn't seem that his output, quality-wise, had lived up to his legend or his ability, and actual sales seemed to bear out our assessment," EMI's senior VP for marketing Jim Cawley said in 1991. *Never Let Me Down* had been relatively disappointing, sales-wise; Bowie's only major tour of the period was to promote reissues on another label (see "Pretty Pink Rose"), and *Tin Machine*, though it moved a million copies worldwide, "came out at a time when unless you were selling at least six million copies, your album was a failure," Reeves Gabrels recalled. "We took Michael Jackson money for a Pixies album, which is only going to piss people off."

No Bowie album to this point had such a long genesis; no Bowie album would be as publicly despised. The great majority of *Tin Machine II* was tracked months after the band's mini-tour in 1989. In good spirits ("I'm so up on this I want to go and start recording the next album tomorrow," Bowie said) and working at a clip, the band cut enough tracks for an album to come out in fall 1990, right after Bowie's solo tour. "We finished the next album and we're going out immediately once this tour's over," he said at a January 1990 press conference. But EMI's rejection, and Bowie becoming consumed by a tour that got extended by months, meant that *Tin Machine II* lingered in a state of half-completion for well over a year, with further, sporadic recording sessions in Miami, London, and Los Angeles. Finally completed in spring 1991, the album came out that September to indifference or hostility.

The band was spoiling for a fight. It wasn't just the "we're four dicks" cover illustration of Greek kouroi, which caused a flap when some US distributors refused to carry the album until the statues' genitalia were obscured. The group persona of Tin Machine could seem surly at times, with Bowie in particular never so unpleasant a public figure, once condescendingly telling an interviewer "you seem like a smart girl — why are you asking me this?" when she brought up the cover art.

Tin Machine II is the only Bowie album that, as of the time this book went to press, is entirely out of print — not streaming; not on CD or vinyl; not downloadable. It deserves better. It's Bowie trying to forge a style for a new decade, and halfway succeeding; it's a band moving beyond its founding principles to become a working unit. "The songs on the first record were excuses to make noise," Gabrels said in 1991. *Tin Machine II* had a wider palette, with softer hues. "It's sensitively aggressive, the next album... presented in a more melodic context," Bowie said in 1990.

It was Gabrels' album in many ways. "He really was eager for us to solidify the band and I think I got caught up in his enthusiasm," Bowie said. While Bowie toured throughout 1990, Gabrels kept after him, booking studio time on Bowie's off days, cutting overdubs on his own and with the Saleses, recording dozens of solos, mortaring walls of guitars. On "You Belong in Rock n' Roll," his guitar dubs took up the majority of the fifty-six tracks. "I'm still convinced the guitar has got a world of sounds in it," he said in 1991. His lead playing was a series of "events... [that] get people from the verse to the chorus, or through the second verse after they've heard the melody once... the current listener's horizon time is shorter in terms of how often you have to give them things to keep them interested." He was experimenting with "modal chromaticism," which entailed using modes with a common tonic chord — he could play any note in a number of scales "as long as you end on a right note." This led to excesses but also created passages of uncanny melody, or counterpoints to elevate a chord progression. Bowie was amused by it: "Reeves will present himself with his own obstacles."

The album was the work of a tighter band, with Bowie contributing more rhythm guitar (to a point: as chord voicings were more complex on new songs, Gabrels once tuned Bowie's guitar "in all roots and fifths and said, 'you just play with one finger and it will be okay.' But he was only going to play guitar when he felt like it.") and saxophone. When the band assembled in Sydney in early September 1989, they were in high spirits. Enjoying the Australian springtime and away from distractions, they flourished. Tracks like "You Belong in Rock n' Roll" and "Shopping for Girls" "have a bigger horizon to them, sonically," Gabrels said. "I think Australia had something to do with that. It's a place that moves slower and it's so wide open, almost like Texas."

The *Tin Machine* sessions had been so fecund that the band could have made another album from its leftovers. Instead, they wrote a batch of new songs (Bowie said they cut twenty-five in Sydney), in tacit agreement to reduce the guitar-drums barrages to emphasize melody and structure. "Do some slowed-down shit that's *melodic*," as Hunt Sales told Gabrels. There was surf music, pop metal, dressing-room blues. Yes, the drummer got to sing two songs and Tin Machine hadn't lost its habit of beating promising material to death. But the greater half of *Tin Machine II* had some of Bowie's strongest tracks in years.

Baby Baby Baby

Bowie and Gabrels wrote and demoed "Baby Universal" in their first songwriting collaboration in 1988. Bowie set it aside during *Tin Machine* — from producer Tim Palmer's perspective, Bowie considered the song too catchy. Holding it back until 1991 suited it, with "Baby Universal" becoming as much of a decade-opening statement as "Oh! You Pretty Things" had been for his Seventies — "Hallo Spaceboy" and "Looking for Satellites," among others, begin here. It's the sound of *Earthling*, for which he and Gabrels remade the song (while it wasn't released, you can hear what it sounded like in 1996 live recordings — a drum 'n' bass-inspired rhythm track with the same harmonic structure as the Tin Machine version).

A strong album opener, with Tony Sales playing Kim Deal to Gabrels' Joey Santiago, it had a lively mix (tambourine in the pre-chorus, Hunt Sales' lightning fills to trigger chord changes in the verse) and Bowie's lyric had more craft than usual for a Tin Machine song (see the internal rhyme of "humans" and "assume"). It's another space messiah, viewed skeptically in the A major verses, given a grand annunciation in the G major refrains. The new Ziggy Stardust is the spoiled product of indifferent cosmic parents. Ziggy, the Pretty Things and the Starman had promised liberation, but the Baby's self-contained, jaded ("it doesn't matter — I've seen everything anyway"), with humanity an afterthought. The chanted "baby" opening, with barely-audible interjections (including "thinking/walk" and "lost/found"), suggests the messiah is a stream of binary code. The verse, with its guitar/organ accompaniment, builds to its thrashing refrain, with Bowie howling the title line, letting it expire with a last slurred "*yoo*-ni-vers-*ull*." A parallel is "Scary Monsters (and Super Creeps)," with which "Baby Universal" shares a mood, arrangement and percussive sounds, particularly in its 1996 live versions.

SORRY

(*H. Sales.*) **Recorded**: *ca. early September-early October 1989, Studios 301; (further overdubs) ca. late 1990, Cherokee; (mixing) ca. early spring 1991, Eel Pie; (saxophone overdub) spring 1991, Larrabee Studios, West Los Angeles. H. Sales: lead vocal, drums; Gabrels: lead guitar; Tony Sales: bass, backing vocal; Bowie: backing vocal, saxophone. Produced: Tin Machine, Palmer; engineered: Guy Gray, Vinestock, et al.*

First appearance: *2 September 1991,* **Tin Machine II**. **Live**: *1989, 1991-1992.*

When Tin Machine first met the press, Hunt Sales' brooding looks and shoulder-length hair made him a striking visual, and he dominated interviews with his Catskill comedian personality. By 1991, he looked more vampiric, sporting new tattoos, cropped bleached hair and sunglasses affixed to his face. His self-penned "Sorry" has some pathos, especially in its closing verse: "I guess I've thrown it away." He said he'd written the song about the past — "It's honest, just very very honest... I was in sad shape, so let's talk about it, you know?" It was a fuck-up's half-apology (B minor verses lead to combative C major "I'm sorrry!" refrains). Bowie said he related to it "because I had my own addictions, and that song was instant recall. It has more to say about addiction without mentioning addiction... than any other I know of."

It's hard to extricate "Sorry" from various stories in Bowie biographies that issues with drugs during the 1991-1992 tour was one factor in the collapse of Tin Machine (David Buckley quoted Carlos Alomar saying Bowie was "depressed because of his inability to deal with that drug problem... It's a terrible blow when you find that one of the band members is lying to you and, most importantly, lying to himself"; Paul Trynka quoted Eric Schermerhorn, rhythm guitarist on the tour: "[Bowie] watched Hunt self-destruct and I think it angered him, in that he was trying to help him."). Bowie's newfound sobriety may have been part of this: he was less tolerant about band members using than in the past. In 1999, he said that "personal problems within the band became the reason for its demise... it became physically impossible for us to carry on" and, in 2000, that this "really destroyed the band, more than anything else. It got to a situation where it was just intolerable. You didn't know if the guy was going to be dead in the morning. We just couldn't cope." A rocker in the 1989 tour, the revision of "Sorry" as a ballad for *Tin Machine II* made it a study in abasing neediness. Bowie's backing vocals and saxophone and Reeves Gabrels' harmonics color a sad footnote.

Betty Wrong

(Bowie, Gabrels.) **Recorded**: ca. early September-early November 1989, Studios 301; (further overdubs) ca. late 1990, Cherokee; (mixing) ca. early spring 1991, Eel Pie. Bowie: lead vocal, rhythm guitar, saxophone; Gabrels: lead guitar; T. Sales: bass, backing vocal; H. Sales: drums, percussion, backing vocal. Produced: Tin Machine, Palmer; engineered: Gray (remix: Michael Arminger, Michael Stavrou).

First appearance: (earlier mix) ca. October 1990, **The Crossing** (Regular Records TVD 93336/Chrysalis CDP 3218262); 2 September 1991, **Tin Machine II**. **Live**: 1991-1992.

The first track released from the *Tin Machine II* sessions, "Betty Wrong" played on the end credits of the 1990 Australian film *The Crossing*, starring a young Russell Crowe. With different overdubs than the album mix, mostly saxophone and woodblocks in the verses, the track (its title a play on the singer Betty Wright) was mooted as a possible single — its hooky refrain fit the sub-*Rebel Without a Cause* scenario of *The Crossing*.

With its intro a sickly echo to that of Midnight Oil's "Beds Are Burning," "Betty Wrong" is lyrically in the vein of "Amazing": a fallen man transported by love and pledging his faith in a broken time, though the decent lines ("nurtured on grime, good will and screams") are outweighed by the likes of "the kiss of the comb/tears my face." Gabrels' closing solo was an experiment to see what it would sound like if the blues guitarist Otis Rush played over an unusual chord sequence: C#min7-A major-G7-G# minor. "The difference is to move one note in the right direction," Gabrels said. "The strongest statement that you can make is often the shortest distance: just a half-step away from the note that's ringing. That's hardest to hear."

"Betty Wrong" was substantively reworked on Tin Machine's 1991-92 tour. A typical performance (e.g., the *Oy Vey Baby* video) began with Gabrels showboating, followed by a breathy Bowie saxophone solo, narrow in tone, in which he moved from playing lengthy, circling lines to a stagger-step up the scale to announce the full band's entrance. After the song proper, another sunset-to-daybreak saxophone solo (complete with police sirens) led to a final band instrumental reprise. Night after night, these were among the most confident saxophone performances of Bowie's life, and foreshadowed his jazz ambitions on *Black Tie White Noise*.

NEEDLES ON THE BEACH

(Bowie, Gabrels, H. Sales, T. Sales.) **Recorded**: *ca. September 1989, 301 Studios. Gabrels: lead and rhythm guitar; Bowie: rhythm guitar; T. Sales: bass; H. Sales: drums. Produced: Palmer, Tin Machine; engineered: Gray, Dube.*

First release: *25 October 1994, **Beyond the Beach** (UPSTART CD 012).*

Drawing on Bowie and Reeves Gabrels' Pacific travels and Tin Machine's stay in Sydney, a recurring theme of *Tin Machine II* was of paradise gone rotten. While some songs — "Shopping for Girls" and "Amlapura" — made it onto the album, the instrumental "Needles on the Beach" wound up on a 1994 "surfbilly" compilation issued on a Boston indie label, making it one of the more obscure official releases in the Bowie catalog. Its title referred to Sydney's then-filthy Bondi Beach, which was covered in used syringes, courtesy of local and visiting junkies. There's a Gabrels musical joke as well, as the chord changes are taken from Jimi Hendrix's psychedelic surf track "Third Stone from the Sun" — specifically the progression when Hendrix murmurs "you'll never hear surf music again." "Needles on the Beach" varies between Gabrels' guitar riff, similar to the opening of Hendrix's song, playing over a shuffle, and a slightly-altered riff over straight-on drums, with a three-chord descending line for turnarounds. The released track was faded before its full close, with a pick slide à la Dick Dale, while a dreamy rhythm guitar track became a rumor in the mix.

Exodus

(Gabrels?) **Recorded**: *(unreleased) ca. September 1989, 301 Studios. Gabrels: lead guitar, acoustic guitar?, handclaps?; Bowie: acoustic guitar?; T. Sales: bass; H. Sales: drums. Produced: Palmer, Tin Machine; engineered: Gray.*

Another surf instrumental from early in the Sydney sessions, "Exodus" (bootlegged in 2008) has Reeves Gabrels channeling Robert Fripp on Eno's "St. Elmo's Fire," an exuberant bassline underpinning the acoustic guitar, and handclaps as percussion.

"You Better Stop"

(H. Sales?, Gabrels? T. Sales? Bowie?) **Recorded**: *(unreleased) ca. late October-early December 1989, Studios 301 or ca. late 1990, Cherokee. H. Sales: lead vocal, drums; Gabrels: lead guitar, rhythm guitar; Bowie: guitar?; T. Sales: bass. Produced: Tin Machine, Palmer; engineered: Gray.*

An outtake from either the Sydney sessions or the Sales-Gabrels overdub sessions in LA a year later, "You Better Stop" (its bootleg title — it's often lumped into a longer set of blues improvisations) is a Hunt Sales-sung blues, with franchise blues club guitar licks. Sharing a title with Sonny Rhodes' soul classic, its lyric is half-written: Hunt cues the band with "bridge!" Not bad, nor tragic that it wasn't developed beyond this.

SHOPPING FOR GIRLS

(Bowie, Gabrels.) **Recorded**: *(demo, backing tracks) 20 August-7 September, October 1988, Mountain; (overdubs) ca. early September-early November 1989, Studios 301; (further overdubs) ca. late 1990, Cherokee; (mixing) ca. early spring 1991, Eel Pie. Bowie: lead vocal, guitar; Gabrels: acoustic guitar, lead and rhythm guitar; Armstrong: piano; T. Sales: bass; H. Sales: drums. Produced: Tin Machine, Palmer; engineered: Gray, Shirley-Smith, Vinestock, et al.*

First release: *2 September 1991,* **Tin Machine II**. **Broadcast**: *ca. 6 January 1997, ChangesNowBowie.* **Live**: *1991-1992.*

In 1987 Sara Terry, a reporter for the *Christian Science Monitor*, wrote a series of articles about exploited children, under the umbrella name "Children of Darkness." Among her most harrowing profiles was thirteen-year-old Kham Suk, "a small child with a delicate face," whose mother walked her across the border from Myanmar into Thailand and sold her to a brothel, where the rate was $4 a client. Terry's husband, Reeves Gabrels, accompanied her on research trips and helped her by pretending to hire child prostitutes so that Terry could interview them away from their brothels. Bowie had been to Thailand during his 1983 tour and seen similar horrors. He and Gabrels pooled their experiences into a song about the child sex trade. "It's collectively autobiographical," Bowie said.

It took him months to write a lyric. The problem, he later said, was that the subject was so horrific that it was impossible to write a rock song about it. He scrapped draft after draft for being too sensationalist, too didactic. "The moment I got fingerwagging about it, or moralistic, the whole thing just went to pieces and became embarrassing," he said in 1991. Using the prophet-of-rage voice of "Crack City" and "Under the God" would've been disastrous. Inspiration came from Lou Reed's *New York*, on which Reed was an amoral narrator, letting details do the work for him. "Shopping for Girls" has a cold, clipped third-person perspective (reminiscent of "Repetition") that shifts to second person for a last, abbreviated verse. It's the detached perspective of a sociopath who sees his actions as if on a television screen, paralleled by the song's shifting tonality, with verses shading between E minor and its parallel major.

Bowie sings in a rapid patter that barely rises above the conversational —

an unnerving recitative. (He'd develop it further on *1. Outside.*) He sounds as if he's wormed into the song. The first verse has him dashing through lines, dispensing with rhyme or meter, with a consonant-heavy string of phrases ending with "these are children riding naked on their tourist pals." He sings the first "shopping for girls" coldly, later he registers more disgust. A Michael Jackson song plays (Bowie spitting out Jackson's name); a john talks about how back home it's winter; the room smells of the tropical flower frangipani, favored by Victorian decadents. Songs of love and bliss play on the radio in some Phuket child brothel. They could be Bowie songs — "Let's Dance" or "Golden Years" for some $4 transaction. The title references the Coasters' "Shoppin' for Clothes," a distorted riff following the second refrain uses the hook of "Raspberry Beret" (the joy of sex in Prince's song curdled into evil here).

"You can't distance yourself from that," Bowie said in 1991. "You can see a magazine article and say, 'ooh that'd be a good idea for a song,' but it's not the same as walking down Patpong [in Bangkok] and having an eight-year-old say, 'do you want blowjob, mister?' That's fairly fucking heavy." The *Christian Science Monitor* series on child exploitation disturbed readers, embarrassed governments, and won prizes; the child sex trade continues thirty years later. ("No one over here reads the papers, pal.") What could a song on a Tin Machine album have done? "Shopping for Girls" has no rallying points. It's not "Biko," it's not "Free Nelson Mandela." All Bowie and Gabrels could do was indict the song's narrator, writers, performers, its listeners, compilers, and critics.

AMLAPURA

(Bowie, Gabrels.) **Recorded***: ca. early September-early November 1989, Studios 301; (further overdubs) ca. late 1990, Cherokee; (mixing) ca. early spring 1991, Eel Pie. Bowie: lead vocal, acoustic guitar?; Gabrels: acoustic guitar, lead guitar; T. Sales: bass; H. Sales: drums. Produced: Tin Machine, Palmer; engineered: Gray, Vinestock, et al.*

First release*: (Indonesian vocal) 19 August 1991 (LON 305); 2 September 1991,* **Tin Machine II***. Live: 1991.*

Amlapura is the largest town in east Bali, the island east of Java. Indonesian guidebooks don't consider it worth a visit until you've done the top-tier attractions. Its palaces, filled with Dutch paintings, are a reminder that the kings of Amlapura bowed to the Dutch in the late nineteenth century and so kept the trappings of their rule while other Balinese states were conquered. After a volcanic eruption in 1963, which nearly destroyed the town but spared its temple, the town's name was changed from Karangasem to Amlapura. A sign of rebirth, or a hope that the volcano would pass it by next time.

Bowie visited it in July 1989 during a vacation in Indonesia, and something about the place stuck with him. "There's one town in Bali I particularly love," he told a Japanese interviewer. The song that he and Reeves Gabrels wrote about it mixes colonial-era imagery (tall ships, flying Dutchmen, "boogies"– i.e., bugis, traders and pirates) with the more recent past — dead children under lava, flowers blooming around a statue's mouth. Bowie's Amlapura is a dreamspace invaded by the killers and traders of the West, as well as the site of an oblique romance which he described as being about falling in love with a stone statue of a priestess who lived two-hundred years ago.

In his earlier Indonesian song, "Tumble and Twirl," the mood had been absurdist. "Amlapura" is mistier, with Bowie singing a semitone flat to convey sadness and loss. Tin Machine, working out the song, quieted down — Hunt Sales' drums, prominent in early takes, were reduced to kick beats for intro and first verse. Verses are carried by three acoustic guitars spread across the stereo spectrum — the left-and-right guitars play chord clusters; the center-mixed guitar, arpeggios. Amlapura may well be Bowie's last resting place — after his cremation, his ashes were said to be scattered in Bali, perhaps near the town he'd honored in an evanescent song.

STATESIDE

(Bowie, H. Sales.) **Recorded**: *ca. early September-October 1989, Studios 301; (further overdubs) ca. late 1990, Cherokee; (mixing) ca. early spring 1991, Eel Pie. H. Sales: lead vocal, drums; Bowie: vocal, rhythm guitar, saxophone; Gabrels: lead guitar; T. Sales: bass, backing vocal. Produced: Tin Machine, Palmer; engineered: Gray, Vinestock, Ferry, et al.*

*First release: 2 September 1991, **Tin Machine II**. Broadcast: 13 August 1991, Mark Goodier's Evening Session. **Live**: 1991-1992.*

Tin Machine II's travel songs end — how else? — with a horny drummer in Sydney, wanting to go home. The sins of "Stateside" are venial — crassness, dullness, overstaying its welcome — and mortal: the way Hunt Sales whine-sings "she wanted my lovin'... *my lovin'.*" Reeves Gabrels' lengthy solos are in quotation marks: cliché-filled lines in the spirit of Blues Hammer. Bowie adds a saxophone solo, his tone so dwarfish that he sounds like he's tootling on a plastic toy, while the bridge is a Trash Americana landscape, similar to Bowie's spoken riffs during performances of "Young Americans" in his 1990 tour — e.g., from Niagara Falls ("American dream... let's get some rock 'n' roll and blue jeans. Walk down the street and hope you won't get killed"). Here it's inflatable Marilyn Monroe dolls, Kennedy convertibles (still blood-stained?), and lines from "Summertime," "Home on the Range," and, naturally, the band America. Performed at every Tin Machine gig in 1991-1992, inflated to colossal length, complete with wedding band asides ("this is Chicago, home of the bloooz — I'm Hunt, you don't have to hunt"), "Stateside" became hateful, a tax levied by its composer on audiences across the globe. Bowie checked out, taking cigarette breaks during the solos. A happy consequence of Tin Machine's breakup was that he never had to play the song again.

You Can't Talk

*(Bowie, Gabrels, H. Sales, T. Sales.) **Recorded**: ca. early September-early November 1989, Studios 301; (further overdubs) ca. late 1990, Cherokee; (mixing) ca. early spring 1991, Eel Pie. Bowie: lead and backing vocal, rhythm guitar; Gabrels: lead and rhythm guitar; T. Sales: bass, backing vocal; H. Sales: drums, backing vocal. Produced: Palmer, Tin Machine; engineered: Gray, Vinestock, Simkins, et al.*

*First release: 2 September 1991, **Tin Machine II**. Live: 1991-1992.*

The guitar squiggles during the intro of "You Can't Talk" are fair warning. Half-rapped verses, with a "Beauty and the Beast" reference to remind you of better days, lead to refrains whose hooks sound as if the band had leased them. In earlier takes, Bowie sang "I know you don't blow me… away," while he cut the last word in the final mix, hobbling his dumb joke. Hunt Sales hustles it along, Tony makes it halfway danceable, Gabrels is Gabrels. Solid rhythm guitar, reminiscent of early Talking Heads. But there's a hole in the center of this music.

A BIG HURT

Recorded: early September-early November 1989, Studios 301; (further overdubs) ca. late 1990, Cherokee; (mixing) ca. early spring 1991, Eel Pie. Bowie: lead vocal, rhythm guitar; Gabrels: lead and rhythm guitar; T. Sales: bass, backing vocal; H. Sales: drums, backing vocal. Produced: Palmer, Tin Machine; engineered: Gray, Vinestock, Simkins, et al.

First release: 2 September 1991, **Tin Machine II**. **Broadcast**: 13 August 1991, Mark Goodier's Evening Session; 13 December 1991, The Arsenio Hall Show. **Live**: 1991-1992.

The only solo Bowie composition on *Tin Machine II* was "A Big Hurt," his harried attempt to write a Pixies song — see its stub of a guitar riff, stop-start dynamics, and screamed-mumbled vocal. Tin Machine worked like a cruiserweight: guitar/kick drum exchanges in refrains; speed-metal banshee Reeves Gabrels solos. "If you heard this in the context of the older material, it would sound at home," Gabrels said of this track. "If you give them a burst of ugly guitar noise in the right place, where it's going to make somebody go, 'ooh, what's that?'… you serve two masters." Bowie's lyric ("I'm a believer/you're a sex receiver") has the phrasing it deserves — he all but belches out "big *hurt*." At its best, "A Big Hurt" is a spoof of toxic masculinity, with the band attacking on multiple fronts; it's rarely at its best.

HAMMERHEAD

(Bowie, H. Sales.) **Recorded**: ca. early September-early November 1989, Studios 301; (further overdubs) ca. late 1990, Cherokee; (mixing) ca. early spring 1991,

Eel Pie. Bowie: lead vocal, rhythm guitar, saxophone; Gabrels: lead guitar; T. Sales: bass; H. Sales: drums. Produced: Palmer, Tin Machine; engineered: Gray, Vinestock, et al.

First release: *(vocal) 19 August 1991, "You Belong in Rock n' Roll," LONCD 305; (instrumental) 2 September 1991,* **Tin Machine II**.

There are two versions of "Hammerhead," a Bowie/Hunt Sales composition: a minute-long instrumental that appeared uncredited at the end of *Tin Machine II* and a rant-thrash piece issued as a B-side. It was the same track, as the instrumental was the B-side's lopped-off coda. Singing a slurred tribute to a femme fatale, Bowie likens her to a shark, boxers (including turn-of-the-century champion George Dixon), Cher, and Bruce Lee (a mumbled "enter the dragon"). He's out of her league in any case, particularly as his jaw seems wired shut.

It's Tough

Recorded: *(unreleased) ca. September-early November 1989, Studios 301. Bowie: lead vocal, rhythm guitar, saxophone; Gabrels: lead and rhythm guitar; T. Sales: bass, backing vocal; H. Sales: drums, backing vocal. Produced: Palmer, Tin Machine; engineered: Gray.*

Considered for *Tin Machine II* (its place possibly taken by the revived "If There Is Something"), "It's Tough" vanished until a few takes of it leaked in 2008. According to one source, Bowie played a rough mix of the album to an Australian friend who called "It's Tough" the weakest track. But Tin Machine had worked "It's Tough" into shape, hardening its "Lust for Life" bassline, doing a multi-guitar intro (while the underlying figure sounds like a sequencer, it's most likely a rapidly-picked guitar, like the opening of Talking Heads' "Burning Down the House") and revising its structure: earlier takes overused the "it's tough! but! it's okay!" refrain, while the most complete-sounding one has greatly overhauled verses and two saxophone solos.

Bowie scrapped some luridly violent lines ("someone driving a 4×4 threw acid on her face/she told the cops that she hacked him up/with the sharpened edge of his license plate") for a more obscurantist lyric that quotes Dean Martin. While his earlier vocal was more malicious-sounding, there was still a spit in his delivery: "All the rats are winning... Squeezing out a generation/waiting for the next... So I *lie! lie! lie!*" Any circulating version of "It's Tough" has more kick than the lesser half of *Tin Machine II*; its omission was a mistake.

You Belong in Rock n' Roll

(Bowie, Gabrels.) **Recorded**: *ca. early September-early November 1989, Studios 301; (further overdubs) ca. late 1990, Cherokee; (mixing) ca. early spring 1991, Eel Pie. Bowie: lead vocal, rhythm guitar, tenor and baritone saxophone; Gabrels: lead and rhythm guitar, vibrators; T. Sales: bass, backing vocal; H. Sales: drums, backing vocal. Produced: Palmer, Tin Machine; engineered: Gray, Vinestock, Simkins, et al.*

First release: *19 August 1991 (LONCD 305, UK #33).* **Broadcast**: *3 August 1991, Paramount City; 14 August 1991, Wogan; 29 August 1991, Top of the Pops; 18 October 1991, Eleva2ren; ca. 27 October 1991, Double Jeu.* **Live**: *1991-1992.*

At Tin Machine's last North American show, in Vancouver, Bowie was introduced in the encore as "Mr. Rock 'n' Roll" and appeared wearing a silver Lurex suit, Ziggy Stardust boots, a platinum blonde Jareth-style wig, and pink lipstick. It was the spirit of *Tin Machine II*'s lead-off single "You Belong in Rock n' Roll," a seeming parody of U2's "With or Without You," with which it shared a bass-driven, crooned verse, a dynamic shift for refrains (triggered by the title phrase) and half of a chord progression. Compared to U2's Christian erotica, however, "You Belong in Rock n' Roll" has Reeves Gabrels playing guitar solos with a vibrator.

After the bridge-burning of *Tin Machine*, "You Belong in Rock n' Roll" was a realignment, a band trying to fit back into contemporary rock. There's some Buddy Holly in how Bowie toys with phrases, hollowing vowels, stretching a word to fill the space of three: luh-uh-huh-hove, say-uh-hay-hay. He builds to become the archangel-voiced Bowie of pop memory: on FIRE! on FIRE! on FIIIYAH!

Asked at the time if there were any new ideas in rock 'n' roll, Bowie said no, and that innovation lay in what you fed the old beast. Tin Machine was a self-consciously veteran band, in all senses of the word. "Talking about the feelings that you have between your mid-thirties and mid-forties... there are endless experiences there," he said,

> The whole weight of having gone through the apocalyptic vision of the Seventies, the greed and vanity of the Eighties: these are things that none of the younger bands knew about or experienced. So they're just a result of it. With a band like Guns 'n' Roses, lyrically there's a kind of abandon there. But abandon from what?

He'd never been reverent about rock music, calling it an aging tart back in his Ziggy Stardust days. Twenty years later, he was in a hard rock band but still played the tart. In the video, Bowie preened into a mirror, wriggling out of his lime-green jacket; on stage, he mimed slapping on foundation. The guiding spirit was Marc Bolan in his prime: *I love the velvet hat — you know the one that caused a revolution*. Bowie's come-ons in "You Belong in Rock n' Roll" are shopworn by comparison: the girl's walk reminds him of cheap streets, she says cheap things, she brings bad luck. Bolan knew he was the prize — the come-ons were for show, as he'd already closed the deal. Bowie has to work the sale. The title refrain hook, triggered by the song's one chord change, ends with "well, so do I," but his deflated phrasing of the last words suggests he knows it's a dubious claim.

While most of its rhythm tracks — a rumbling Tony Sales bassline, acoustic guitar flourishes, Hunt Sales' piledriving kick drum — were nailed down in the Sydney sessions, Gabrels spent a year on guitar dubs. He'd loved Nine Inch Nails' *Pretty Hate Machine*, and as "You Belong in Rock n' Roll" was "basically a bass song, I wanted to lay in some industrial stuff against it," he said. After experimenting with an electric razor, he realized he needed something with variable speeds so he could better tune it. A trip to Sydney sex shops bagged a generous selection of vibrators — "you can use [a vibrator] as a sound source and also as a string driver by laying it against the bridge," he said. Bowie said he expected to go into a music store and find vibrators with effects pedals and slides: an inspired vision of commerce that sadly never came to pass.

Gabrels' main solo, an eight-bar bridge between refrain and verse, is a series of steadily-rising chords, while his vibrator dubs work as mood colors. The track had plenty of hooks — the jumble of Gabrels' tones, the Saleses' backing vocals as an elaboration of Bowie's murmurings, Bowie's saxophone as secondary bassline — but in autumn 1991, few wanted to hear it.

GOODBYE MR. ED

(Bowie, H. Sales, T. Sales.) **Recorded**: *early September-early November, Studios 301; (vocal overdubs) ca. October-November 1990, Criteria Studios, Miami; (further overdubs) ca. late 1990, Cherokee; (mixing) ca. early spring 1991, Eel Pie. Bowie: lead vocal, guitar; Gabrels: lead guitar; T. Sales: bass; H. Sales: drums. Produced: Palmer, Tin Machine; engineered: Eric Schilling, Gray, Vinestock, et al.*

First release: *2 September 1991*, **Tin Machine II**. *Live: 1991-1992.*

"America became like a myth land to me," Bowie recalled of his youth to the documentarian Alan Yentob in 1974, while sitting in a limousine going through the California desert. Some fifteen years later, the dreamland was gone. "I was fantasizing about America when I was a lad and writing things like 'Aladdin Sane'," Bowie said in 1991. "I didn't actually know America at all, but I wrote about what I thought America would be like. Now I have the knowledge."

He'd seen an episode of the PBS show *Tony Brown's Journal* about the Lenape, the former inhabitants of Manhattan island, who according to legend were the biggest suckers in real estate history. American history is the story of conmen and their marks, and the Lenape were king marks, royal dupes: they sold Manhattan to the Dutch for sixty guilders' worth of trade goods. In "Goodbye Mr. Ed," the ghosts of "the Manhattoes" stand atop Philip Johnson's AT&T Building at 550 Madison Avenue, another capitalist shrine erected upon some lost farm or burial ground. The Manhattoes take in the view, then jump off, screaming. But the name was wrong. "Manhattoes" was a name coined by white colonists, used centuries after the tribe's removal by writers like Washington Irving and Herman Melville. Suicidal ghosts denied their true name, they jump from a landmark skyscraper, predicting the New York catastrophe of a decade later.

With this as a founding image, Bowie wrote "Goodbye Mr. Ed" by "juxtaposing lines which shouldn't really fit, free-association around the idea of 'bye-bye, Fifties America,'" he said. The title references the talking horse of the TV sitcom, an American sage. "Someone" — an indifferent angel, the blank eye of a television, a quizzical talking horse — sees it all, watching the wrack of a civilization pile up: Andy Warhol's skull in a Queens shopping mall; Brueghel's *Landscape with the Fall of Icarus*; a soured nursery rhyme; the Sex Pistols and their inheritors, seeding demon eggs. The Pistols as the end-stage cancer of rock music, Britain's revenge on its lost colonies.

Bowie's vocal keeps to a narrow range, with a melody nicked from Acker Bilk's "Stranger on the Shore" (cf., the descending "shrieking as they fall"). In the verses, Bowie's lines are a loose iambic trimeter, with a strong-beat/weak-beat rhythm (*"And*y's *skull* en*shrined"*), while he sings the title line with the same cold intonation on each syllable. The miraculous and the uncanny are now bric-a-brac. "My brain hurt like a warehouse," he'd once sung. Now he was absently going through the archives, wondering why he'd bothered to fill them up in the first place.

"Goodbye Mr. Ed" began as what Tony Sales recalled as a "tuning-up thing" from the Sydney sessions and "was just a rhythm track until we got to Miami," Gabrels said. The Sales brothers wrote the music with Bowie: Tony plays restless basslines, making a wistful ascent before the first bridge, with querying notes in the solo; Hunt varies his buildups to start each verse, with snare fills throughout and thundering kick drum hits in the bridges. Gabrels is a more modest presence after the intro, where he tracked multiple electric guitar dubs over rapidly-picked acoustic guitar. He plays an ostinato, then some singing phrases before the first bridge. After Bowie's final goodbye, the players fade out and creep back in: the last thing heard is a repeating busy signal via feedback.

Despite having been pieced together over continents, "Goodbye Mr. Ed" was one of the best group performances of Tin Machine — within its span, they were the band they said they were. It's the song of another of Bowie's dry men, the spent figure of "I Can't Read" unraveling a myth he'd once needed to live. A peak of the Tin Machine era and its worthy epitaph.

PRETTY PINK ROSE

Recorded: (backing tracks) 11 November 1989, Royal Recorders, 7036 Grand Geneva Way, Lake Geneva, Wisconsin; (vocals) 15 January 1990, Right Track Recording, New York. Bowie: lead vocal; Adrian Belew: lead vocal, guitars, synthesizers, keyboards, bass, drum programming. Produced: Belew; engineered: Rich Denhart.

First release: *8 May 1990,* **Young Lions** *(Atlantic 7567-82099-2/82099-1, US #118).* **Live**: *1990.*

By the end of 1989, *Tin Machine II* became a sideshow for Bowie, whose priorities now were to promote an elaborate CD reissue campaign for his back catalog, with a world tour planned for his past's last chapter.

Though compact discs outsold LPs for the first time in 1988, Bowie's pre-EMI catalog was out of print on CD. Initial runs of RCA discs ("their rights were expiring and [RCA] wanted to milk the catalog for all it was worth," as Rykodisc's Jeff Rougvie wrote on his blog) were now only found in the secondary market. (In September 1988, *Billboard* ran a list of "most wanted" albums on CD as per retailer requests, with *Ziggy Stardust* and *Changesonebowie* topping it.) Entertaining licensing offers, Bowie was unhappy with labels' conservative sales estimates (as per Rougvie, one estimated a *Changesonebowie* reissue would sell 25,000 copies in its first year; it wound up moving 500,000 in that time). He was intrigued by Rykodisc, an independent label from Salem, Massachusetts. They proposed kicking off a campaign with a 3-CD retrospective set, then reissuing albums for which they could charge full price by having outtakes as bonus tracks. (Precedents were Bob Dylan's *Biograph*, on which Bowie's *Sound + Vision* set was based, and Frank Zappa's recent CD reissue campaign with Rykodisc.) Charging a premium instead of the typically-reduced catalog price was a fundamental change in record retailing — an artist could sell an album that their fans already owned (say, *Ziggy Stardust*) as a new release. Thus began rock 'n' roll's archivist, collector's edition phase, which shows no sign of ending.

After Bowie signed an agreement in March 1989, Ryko shipped his tapes from a dumpy, prison-like facility in New Jersey to a state-of-the-art site near Salem. "We picked the vault clean," Rougvie said, noting that Bowie cleverly let Ryko assume the costs of storing, cataloging, and digitizing his tapes. *Sound + Vision* would be tripartite: release a box set in September 1989; stagger-release CD reissues (the last batch didn't appear until spring 1992) that would have about two dozen bonus tracks all told; and promote it with a tour. The latter was a happy coincidence: the idea of doing a "greatest hits" revue had been in the works since 1988, and now Bowie had an impressive reissue campaign to promote.

For the tour, he needed a lead guitarist familiar with his catalog, and presumed he'd use Reeves Gabrels. But Gabrels declined. He thought the tour would've meant bad blood with the Sales brothers, who weren't invited, and that he wasn't the right fit. The audience for this type of tour wouldn't tolerate assaults on Bowie classics. So Bowie went with one of Gabrels' inspirations: Adrian Belew.

The Return of the Native

On 4 August 1989, Belew was sitting by a swimming pool in San Diego with members of the band America when he got Bowie's call. It was a tempting offer. He'd be the tour's musical director and could use his own band. But Belew owed an album to Atlantic by early 1990. "I had about ten weeks to write, develop, and record *Young Lions*," he said. "Recording in the day, writing at night." Bowie pitched in, offering a song for Belew to use on his album and which also could be a duet piece for the tour.

The problem was the song, "Pretty Pink Rose." Bowie sent Belew a cassette that dated from his first writing sessions with Gabrels in 1988. Years later, Belew was unsparing about it. "Oh gawd, it was awful!...Here I was on the verge of touring for a year with David Bowie and thinking we might produce a duet of perhaps a 'hit' song of David's, only to be confronted with something which sounded lifeless, limp, and plodding. I didn't know quite what to do."

Working at a studio near Lake Geneva in Wisconsin, Belew salvaged the song. He began with the backing tracks. Recalling a Beatles trick in which Paul McCartney played straight 4/4 while Ringo Starr played a shuffle (or vice versa) to create a "pulling" sensation "that seems almost like half-time but isn't," Belew took a "growling" bass sample and worked against it on a 1955 Ludwig drum set. Then he wrote a tongue-in-cheek grandiose intro, a quasi-classical synthesizer musing on the refrain melody that's upended by wailing guitar. He replaced a keyboard ostinato that ran under the refrain vocal on Bowie's demo with a double-tracked guitar line. For verses, Belew found how Bowie's vocal melody "sat" inspired responses on guitar, forging a dialogue between guitarist and singer.

As for his guitar tracks, Belew used "Stratocasters equipped with Kahler tremolos at the time… I discovered you could adjust the tip of the Kahler tremolo arm downward facing the strings and then play the strings using the tip itself. Like 'tapping,' only using the tip of the tremolo arm instead of your right hand fingers." The finished track danced between sixteen-bar uptempo verses and refrains that felt more like bridges, tailor-made for the Bowie croon. Belew made a potential hit single out of a song that hadn't made the cut for Tin Machine.

Bowie and Belew cut their vocals in New York on 15 January 1990, taking a break from tour rehearsals. Though they scrapped a spoken intro, "she had tits like melons… it was love in the rain," (a throwback to a ditty that Bowie once sang at Glastonbury in 1971), a goofiness remained in the song, a kiss-off to the Cold War. "She's just been to Russia and they're dying their faces," Bowie sings. It's capitalism triumphant, the funfair rumbling East across the falling borders. Its video had Bowie and Belew as rock 'n' roll emissaries being brought to heel by Julie T. Wallace playing a dominatrix in traditional Russian garb.

The woman at the center of "Pretty Pink Rose" is righteous chaos: "the poor man's gold, she's the anarchist crucible!" Upturning civilizations, tearing up Paris looking for Tom Paine, who's slipped loose from jail. In 1990, it seemed for a moment that history's tragedies could be rewritten as comedies, but the second verse had a dead-on premonition of thirty years down the road: "the left wing's broken, the right's insane."

GUNMAN

(Bowie, Belew.) **Recorded**: *(backing tracks) 3 November 1989, Royal Recorders; (vocals) 15 January 1990, Right Track. Bowie: lead and backing vocal; Belew: lead and rhythm guitar, Roland GR-50 synthesizer, keyboards, bass sample, drum programming. Produced: Belew; engineered: Denhart.*

First release: *8 May 1990, **Young Lions**.*

After cutting his vocals for "Pretty Pink Rose," Bowie listened to backing tracks Adrian Belew was considering developing for *Young Lions*. One, an uptempo piece with a guitar hook and a tom-centered beat, caught his ear. Sitting down with a beer and a legal pad, Bowie wrote a lyric in under a half-hour, then recorded his vocal in a few takes.

Belew had built the piece on a drum track with an up-tuned tom, on which he played steady eighth notes and then added delay "in time with the tempo." The bassline was the same "growling" sample on other *Young Lions* tracks, while for rhythm guitar he used the Roland GR-50, a guitar synthesizer that generated different tones for each string. He "added a harmony note to each string but a different note from string to string. In this way I could make up very unusual chords and patterns for the rhythm guitars."

Bowie, who titled the song "Gunman" before he wrote his lyric, opened the song in a guttural voice that worked against the beat. Taking his vocal hook from Belew's two-chord guitar phrases ("gun-man"), Bowie sang six- or eight-line verses and four-line "refrains" over contrasting sections with arpeggiated guitars. Asked by Belew to do some spoken lines (he considered whether to go with an American or English voice — Belew voted for the latter), Bowie sang the latter half of the track in an exaggerated accent — "my sohrt of stahh... a rock of coh-*cay*ne... like a gr*ay*ve stone" — rubbishing the title gunman in a run of snotty asides, like a gangster from Stepney jibing at some run-of-the-mill American psychopath.

YOU AND I AND GEORGE

(Kelly.) **Live***: 21 May 1990, Tacoma Dome, 2727 East D Street, Tacoma, Washington. Bowie: vocal, acoustic guitar.*

The Sound + Vision tour opened in Québec City in early March 1990 and closed on a September night in Buenos Aires. Touring without a new album to promote, Bowie instead sold a box set and CD reissues, with the hook being that this tour was *it*: the last time he'd play the hits. (It wasn't, for the most part.) Seemingly the opposite of Tin Machine, the tour had the same intention: to be a firebreak between Bowie and his past. "I've purposefully painted myself into a corner and given myself no option other than to develop new material." It was also coffer replenishment, with higher ticket prices than average, letting Bowie reap arena-sized profits for playing theaters.

He wanted a minimalist response to the bloat of Glass Spider: no horn sections, backing singers, or dancers, just a Tin Machine-style quartet — Adrian Belew, Belew's keyboardist and drummer, and Erdal Kızılçay on bass. Yet as they had to play everything from "Let's Dance" to "Life on Mars?," "the instrumentation needed to portray such a varied catalog was far beyond the abilities of a four-piece band," Belew said. He and keyboardist Rick Fox put orchestrations into sequencers, distilling songs to "signature components," which meant more and more Roland samplers.

In theory, Bowie could sample a hook, whether David Sanborn's saxophone on "Young Americans" or Mary Hopkin's vocal on "Sound and Vision." He'd unveil his old treasures while computer-sequenced film and video clips were projected on a forty-foot diaphanous opera screen. Audiences ate it up (the opening "Space Oddity," with Bowie alone on acoustic guitar, was phenomenal — you could feel the auditorium shake when he walked on stage) but the tour was Bowie starring in a musical revue of his life.

The roughly thirty-five-song setlist was determined by fan votes, with selections catering to Britain, the US, and Europe (Americans wanted recent hits; the *NME*, "Laughing Gnome"; Europeans, "Heroes"). It showed that democracy is fundamentally bland. There was nothing from the Sixties besides "Space Oddity." Nothing from *The Man Who Sold the World*; most albums were represented by their singles; only three songs came from the "Berlin" trilogy. Bowie said he didn't mind revisiting most songs though he thought a few, such as "Rebel Rebel" ("written for a particular generation") were no longer relevant, and even "Heroes" was "a series of situations which are no more," given the recent fall of the Berlin Wall. "I find I'm throwing them away a bit. I hope it won't show." His motivation, he joked, was that with each show "I get that much closer to never singing 'ground control to Major Tom' again." He said he loathed "Young Americans" and had little use for "John, I'm Only Dancing," which he once introduced on stage as "same shit, same period," and cut after the first month.

On stage, there was a visible hierarchy — Belew and Bowie were the leads; the band, clumped stage left and often kept behind the projection screen, backup. "[Bowie] wasn't very happy on that tour. Something wasn't working. It was a weird atmosphere," Kızılçay said. Fox, who mostly kept the sequencers in sync with performances and triggered film clips via his keyboard, sometimes ate his dinner on stage, and Belew said Fox occasionally would turn off his live keyboard and play lines from other songs while the samplers blared out, say, "Space Oddity." The tour was draining, trundling across the US and Europe, increasingly to second- and third-tier markets (St. Johns, Newfoundland; Schüttorf, Germany). Bowie lost his upper register ("Ashes to Ashes" became a struggle) and sometimes his voice — at a show in Modena in September, he threw down his guitar, groaning "fucking nightmare!" Because of the sequencing to keep film clips in sync, shows were so tightly choreographed that roadies needed to time their offstage appearances to light cigarettes for Bowie. "Stay," funk centerpiece of the 1976 and 1978 tours, was flaccid; "Ziggy Stardust" was heralded by synthesizer fanfare.

Only a few times per gig could Bowie shake loose — mostly on "Young Americans" and the usual encore "Jean Genie," which he and the band extended to ten minutes, Tin Machine style, with Bowie throwing in bits of everything from "A Hard Rain's a-Gonna Fall" to "Maria" from *West Side Story*, Funkadelic's "(Not Just) Knee Deep" and Johnny Cash's "I Walk the Line." But on 21 May 1990, playing the Tacoma Dome near Seattle, Bowie broke the format and sang Red Kelly's "You and I and George" alone on guitar.

He was honoring a local hero. Kelly was a jazz bassist who played with Stan Kenton, Woody Herman, and Charlie Parker and had retired to Tacoma, where he ran for mayor on a platform of reviving cable cars and riverboat gambling. Kelly sang "You and I and George" during his time with Kenton, who immortalized it on 1961's *Kenton at the Tropicana*. Shuffling to the mike, a doleful Kelly announced that the next song was written by someone who preferred to remain anonymous. It's one verse: George, Kelly, and a woman walk along a brook; George falls in and drowns; the woman winds up with Kelly, possibly her second choice. Bowie honored Kelly's self-mocking tradition. "You boo it when you're fed up with it!" he told the crowd in Tacoma, then gave a performance with phrasings similar to "The Drowned Girl." (He'd sing "You and I and George" once more, at a Bridge Benefit Concert in 1996.)

After the tour, Bowie and Belew parted ways. Bowie promised to give Belew a call for further collaborations, and never did. Sound + Vision walled off an era like a television retrospective. He'd given the people want they wanted; now, he said, it was his turn for a while.

One Shot

(Bowie, Gabrels, H. Sales, T. Sales.) **Recorded**: *(first version, unreleased) early September-early November 1989, Studios 301; (vocal overdubs) ca. late 1990, Criteria;* (**Tin Machine II** *version) ca. March-April 1991, A&M Studios, 1416 N. LaBrea Avenue, Los Angeles. Bowie: lead vocal; Gabrels: lead and rhythm guitar; T. Sales: bass, backing vocal; H. Sales: drums, backing vocal. Produced, engineered* (**Tin Machine II**): *Hugh Padgham.*

First release: *2 September 1991,* **Tin Machine II**. **Live**: *1991-1992.*

Though he'd griped about his labels, Bowie had been built by RCA and EMI, their worldwide sales channels, their sacks of promotional dollars. If unhappy with a *Low* or *Tin Machine*, the labels still bought trade ads and in-store promo material, still pushed them on the radio, if indifferently. It was a level of patronage inconceivable for someone of Bowie's bent today. Even he would never have its like again. He'd spend the Nineties a free agent, jumping labels, always on the hustle: a preview of the musician's life in the 2010s.

After EMI, he needed a new record deal, with little more than a rapidly-eroding commercial reputation and the rough mixes of *Tin Machine II* for enticement. His back catalog, now licensed to Rykodisc, couldn't be used as bait. Amidst filming *The Linguini Incident* and an episode of *Dream On*, Bowie shopped for labels and found a taker in early 1991. Victory Music was the first-ever US-based label launched by a Japanese company, the electronics giant JVC. Run by former Atlantic Records exec Phil Carson, Victory had a cut-rate strategy of signing "classic rock" icons past their prime. Their roster included Tin Machine, Yes, and Emerson, Lake and Palmer.

As *Tin Machine II* would be Victory's first big release, the label wanted the band to remake "One Shot," a track cut at the 1989 Sydney sessions, for a single, using a popular producer. So this session, at A&M Studios in Los Angeles, was run by the albatross of Bowie producers, Hugh Padgham, last seen on *Tonight*. Earlier (apparently 1989) circulating rehearsal takes are at a slower tempo and in a different key, with Gabrels trying out guitar tones and solo ideas. The album version has some structural variations to lessen monotony — a vocal-and-drums-only third verse; a lyric change in the third bridge repeat. As it turned out, the new, flashy "One Shot" was basically a note-by-note remake of the final 1989 take of "One Shot," just recorded to a click track with a different hi-hat pattern in the refrain and with what Gabrels considered to be a better guitar solo.

Bowie's vocal, all empty-shell bravado, was in the service of a cliché-strewn lyric ("ten dollars tore us apart... one shot put her away": there's livelier writing in James Patterson book jacket copy). Ian MacDonald wrote that when Lennon and McCartney were slumming it as lyricists, they sang about buying their girlfriends jewels. In some of Bowie's writing in the late Eighties, when inspiration falters, a woman gets abused. Whether attempting some spavined critique of domestic violence, or just being a shock-value ploy, the cumulative effect of these songs was of a coarseness never found before in Bowie's music.

Dragged out across two verses and three bridges, the lyric contrasts a hard-knock couple in some firetrap and the man looking back on the few good times they had — minor-key bridges, with its softly ascending phrases, as respites to harsh verses. Bowie uses empty lines for emotional hits (the woman was a "spitfire" who gave him "hot love"), so when the guy shoots her (or, as Bowie sings it, "put her ah-way-uh-hey-hey!"), there's no remorse or disgust. It's a paper doll killing another paper doll. Gabrels' guitar solo, which Tony Sales called "smooth, almost sax-like," has a strong melodic arc to it (weighed against this are his fifty-six bars of shredding in the outro, trimmed by a minute in the single edit.) The vocal harmonies in the intro and refrains demonstrate how undeveloped that aspect of the Machine was.

After all the talk about Tin Machine, how hard they pushed audiences, how they sold scones instead of Big Macs, Bowie was back with Padgham, grinding out a track that came off as an Eddie Money gangster record. It was a label concession, of course. But at the time, Neil Young was making feedback concertos to rival Sonic Youth; Bob Dylan was holed up in his garage taping murder ballads. Even the Rolling Stones put out a half-decent Gulf War protest single. Where was Bowie? Sounding aesthetically bankrupt.

Debaser

(Thompson.) **Live**: *1991-1992. T. Sales: lead vocal, bass; Bowie: backing vocal; Gabrels: lead guitar; Eric Schermerhorn: rhythm guitar; H. Sales: drums.*

Bowie had talked up the Pixies since he'd heard them, praising their "pure dynamics," their pulp of trash TV and art museums, Black Francis' stage presence ("his mass of screaming flesh"). His favorite Pixies song was "Debaser," which led off 1989's *Doolittle*. It was all-American, full of sex and shame. "That's the whole formula of the Pixies, that one song," Joey Santiago once said of it. "All the sound qualities are there. That's what it represents." A boy stumbles across *Un Chien Andalou* and gets turned on by the idea of being a worm in society. As Francis screams "De-*base*-er!," Kim Deal quietly repeats it after him, as though she's trying to calm a disturbed child.

Tin Machine played "Debaser" throughout their 1991-1992 tour. It was tribute and evangelism, as Bowie considered the Pixies shamefully neglected. Tony Sales sang lead while Bowie was a hype man, jabbing and weaving (in a Tokyo performance, Bowie intoned the "ha ha ha ho" lines). The performances were more admirable in concept than execution. Sales couldn't match Francis' yawp (his "Andalucia" was more "Andaloser") and Tin Machine discarded the Pixies' clockwork arrangement — how "Debaser" crests from Deal's bassline to Santiago's guitar riffs to David Lovering's drum fills — in favor of an equalized thrashing.

Go Now

(Banks, Bennett.) **Recorded**: *24 October 1991, Docks, Spielbudenpl. 19, Hamburg, Germany. T. Sales: lead vocal, bass; Bowie: rhythm guitar; Gabrels: lead guitar; Schermerhorn: rhythm guitar; H. Sales: drums.*

First release: *6 July 1992,* **Oy Vey Baby** *(Victory 085 320-3/London 085 320-3).* **Live**: *1991-1992.*

After months of rehearsals, warm-up gigs, television appearances and poorly-received record retailer promotional shows, Tin Machine began its first and last full tour in October 1991. They moved westward, starting in Europe (during which Bowie proposed to the model Iman Abdulmajid in Paris – they had started dating the year before), going to Britain in early November, North America later that month, Japan early the following year.

They generally played clubs, a response to Bowie's large-scale 1990 tour and an acceptance that there was a cap on Tin Machine audience sizes. "There's a fair amount of improvisation in terms of how we approach some songs. And that wouldn't hold well in a large place — particularly at this stage," Bowie said at the time. "The people don't know the material at all. I don't know how many people would be interested in coming to see a Tin Machine show in an arena. I'd imagine a lot might come along hoping I'd be doing old songs or something. We don't want that feeling at all."

Though sometimes they could be interminable (see "Stateside"), the band honored its claims of being foremost a live act. They played well off each other, made weak studio cuts stronger ("A Big Hurt" could sound like "Son of 'Blackout'"), and Bowie worked himself on stage, stripping off his garish sportscoats to be shirtless by the end of sets, playing guitar and saxophone, all while smoking like a factory.

On 20 December 1991, the band closed its US leg in Seattle, playing the Paramount Theatre. By then, "Smells Like Teen Spirit" was on MTV and the city was in a gold rush of record labels and promoters. As grunge blew up, Tin Machine was getting middling to scathing reviews (Greg Kot, on the Chicago show: "there was nothing noble about a group of graying rock 'n' rollers collectively working through a midlife crisis on stage and then having people pay to watch it"), and Bowie signaled his experiment was ending. "A small room packed with people is a cool thing, but it's not economical," he recalled to Kot in 2002. "I was paying for that band to work, and I was gradually going through all my bread, and it became time to stop. I had to build my audience back up again." (Gabrels responded on his website at the time that Bowie's depiction of Tin Machine's finances here was "simply misinformation.")

Bowie had said Tin Machine would be a three-album project ("it will take three albums, possibly, for people to start to understand where we're coming from," Tony Sales said), and Gabrels hoped they could become for Bowie what Crazy Horse was to Neil Young: a wild bunch he used for tours and to back the occasional solo album. "I think our intention is to stay together as long as all of us have the same enthusiasm that we have now," Bowie said during the tour. "I think once it starts to feel like a job, I think that's the last thing we want to feel." When the tour was over, so was the band. The last song of Tin Machine's life, at the Budokan on 17 February 1992, was the first song they'd recorded, "Heaven's in Here," which Bowie sprinkled with bits of Roxy Music's "In Every Dream Home a Heartache" and Perry Como's "Dream On Little Dreamer."

There's poignancy in Tony Sales' performances of "Go Now," sung throughout the tour (a version from Hamburg is on the *Oy Vey Baby* video). Often lost amidst Hunt's antics, Gabrels' demolitions, and the charismatic lead singer, he was a fine bassist and R&B singer for whom Tin Machine was the payoff in a professional life of near-misses. "Go Now," a song written for Bessie Banks that the Moody Blues hit with in 1965, was originally a waltz built on descending piano thirds. Its title proved an easy target, as some in the audience yelled the line back at Tony. It was the long, heartfelt, frustrating end to Tin Machine, and to Bowie's time in the ranks. Oy vey, baby, and amen.

CHAPTER EIGHT:

FAMILY ALBUMS

(1992-1993)

I suppose the best way to find out where you've come from is to find out where you're going and work backwards.
— The Doctor (Tom Baker), "City of Death"

It's the process, not the result, that matters to me.
— Hanif Kureishi, *The Buddha of Suburbia*

Periodically I drop back and say, where do I come from? What am I doing? Like standing back from a canvas you've painted.
— David Bowie, 1983

But I am the same one who lived here, and here I came back... Or are we all the I who have been here or have been?
— Fernando Pessoa, "Lisbon Revisited (1926)"

REAL COOL WORLD

Recorded: ca. spring 1992, 38 Fresh Recording Studios, 1119 N Las Palmas Ave., Los Angeles; Mountain Studios?; The Hit Factory, New York. David Bowie: lead and harmony vocal, saxophone, programming; Nile Rodgers: guitar; Dale Schalow?: programming; uncredited musicians: keyboards, bass. Produced: Rodgers; engineered: Hugo Dwyer.

First release: 14 July 1992, **Songs from the Cool World** (Warner 9-45009-2, US #89).

Mere months after the end of Tin Machine, Bowie was recording with Nile Rodgers. "We used to laugh about Nile Rodgers and then it's funny he goes back and works with him," Hunt Sales told Marc Spitz. "[Bowie's] idea to work with him was to recapture what they had, but that's bullshit. You can never go home again." The point of Tin Machine was to build a wall between Bowie and *Let's Dance*, and here he was making the latter's sequel.

But "there was always a lot of pressure to make money," Reeves Gabrels recalled. Bowie didn't have a solo record contract, he'd funded a fourth of the Tin Machine tour, and he was newly-married, establishing domestic life in properties like a palatial getaway in Mustique. Then upstart label Savage Records threw a bundle at him for what Savage hoped would be *Let's Dance II* (reportedly a $3.4 million minimum advance, plus $100,000 for Bowie's own promo efforts).

Black Tie White Noise, though it briefly hit #1 in Britain, was a relative dud, especially in America. Bowie sabotaged his compromise: consigning a potential single to a CD bonus track, filling half the record with instrumentals and covers. Rather than the album that everyone (including Rodgers) expected — a New Jack Swing era *Let's Dance* — he made an abstractly personal one, full of guilts and ghosts, with its covers as autobiography, and commemorating his wedding in textures. "I wanted to experiment on *Black Tie*. I love doing a hybrid of Eurocentric soul, but there were also pieces like "Pallas Athena" and "You've Been Around," which played more with ambience and funk," he said in 1995.

First to appear from a long series of recording sessions (Rodgers said where *Let's Dance* had taken three weeks to make, *Black Tie* "took a year") was "Real Cool World," done for the film *Cool World*, the animator Ralph

Bakshi's response to *Who Framed Roger Rabbit?*, complete with a cartoon temptress. The intro alone, with its mesh of percussion (hi-hat pattern mixed left; heavy snares), syncopated sequencer lines, a synthesizer holding high root notes, and a staggered introduction of bass and Bowie's saxophone, was the sharpest Bowie arrangement since Rodgers had last produced him.

For his vocal, Bowie gave an icy performance, his phrases often double- and triple-tracked, with a bass synthesizer effect on lower harmonies. He's the unreadable center of the track, the still point of a synthetic circulatory system, only rousing in the bridges, which lift out of B minor to shine in C major (even then Bowie barely ventures above a middle C). His phrasing suits the tentativeness of the lyric, in which he finds himself in love but is too paranoid to accept it. "Color me doubtful," he murmurs, listening for footsteps: a sentiment that belied the album he'd soon release.

You've Been Around

(Bowie, Gabrels.) **Recorded**: *(some backing tracks for Gabrels' version) 20 August-October 1988, Mountain; (Bowie version) ca. April-November 1992, 38 Fresh, Mountain Studios, Hit Factory. Bowie: lead vocal, saxophone, programming; Reeves Gabrels: lead guitar, rhythm guitar; Rodgers: rhythm guitar; Lester Bowie: trumpet; Richard Hilton, David Richards, Phillipe Saisse, Richard Tee: keyboards; Schalow?: programming; Barry Campbell or John Regan: bass; Poogie Bell or Sterling Campbell: drums; Gerardo Velez, percussion; Fonzi Thornton, Tawatha Agee, Curtis King Jr., Dennis Collins, Brenda White-King, Maryel Epps: backing vocals;* **(Gabrels version)** *Bowie: lead and harmony vocal; Gary Oldman: lead and harmony vocal; Gabrels: lead and rhythm guitars, vocal; Tom Dube: harmony vocal; Matt Gruenberg: bass; Hunt Sales: drums, percussion. Produced: (**Black Tie**) Bowie, Rodgers; engineered: Jon Goldberger, Gary Tole, Andrew Grassi; (**Sacred Squall**) produced: Gabrels; engineered: Dube.*

First release: *5 April 1993,* **Black Tie White Noise** *(Arista 74321 13697 1/ Savage 74785-50212-2, UK #1, US #39); (Gabrels) 5 September 1995,* **The Sacred Squall of Now**. **Live**: *1989.*

Sequenced as the first vocal track on *Black Tie White Noise* and marking Bowie's return to the solo stage, "You've Been Around" was a holdover from Tin Machine: the band recorded it for their debut album and had played it live in 1989. Bowie later said it hadn't worked with Tin Machine, blaming his obstinacy — he didn't like what the band wanted to do, so he shelved the song.

The remake of "You've Been Around" was a subtle (only hardcore fans knew its provenance) acknowledgement that the Tin Machine era was over. While the *Black Tie* version didn't alter Bowie's lyric, it effectively erased co-composer Reeves Gabrels. In the original "You've Been Around," Gabrels' grungy ostinato held together an oddly-structured piece whose rambling verses trailed into refrain tags, with Bowie's irregular phrasings responding to a shaky drumline. Bowie and Nile Rodgers centered "You've Been Around" on a synthesizer "bed," a pulsating bassline, a punch of live drums and programming. Bowie had Gabrels cut fresh guitar tracks, which are barely audible at times; the main solo went to Lester Bowie on trumpet while "I had the chance to mix Reeves way into the background. I thought that would doubtlessly really irritate him, which indeed it did," Bowie said with a smile, introducing the song's promotional video.

For *Black Tie*, Bowie had altered his compositional habits again. He was working from the ground up, creating some beats and sequencer patterns at a Los Angeles studio, 38 Fresh, then shipping tracks to the Hit Factory in New York for Nile Rodgers to build them into songs (Gabrels recalled that most of the album was done at the Hit Factory). "You've Been Around" begins as raw materials. "What I like about the first half of the song is that there's no harmonic reference," Bowie said. "It's just drums, and the vocal comes out of nowhere — you're not sure if it's a melody line or a drone. It's an ominous feeling." (That said, the harmonic references are established early on — G major chords alternating with B minor ones, with a move to E minor in refrains.)

Fragments — ringing percussion, shards of guitar, laconic bass — coalesce to support the first verse, in which Bowie's voice, doubled with distorted echoes, sings disjunct phrases, some sinking by a fifth on the last note ("violent *night*," "many *years*"), building to a "viii-oh-lin" that he drags through two bars and sinks nearly an octave. Like several of Bowie's vocals on *Black Tie*, he's deep in the well of Scott Walker (see "Nite Flights"): dark crooning, near-recitative top melodies. The undulating low synthesizer is another Walker touch. As for Gabrels, he cut "You've Been Around" for his 1995 solo album — in a tit-for-tat, he replaced Bowie's vocals in the second verse with those of Gary Oldman, who sounded like Bono doing a Bowie impression.

THE WEDDING
THE WEDDING SONG

Recorded: ca. April-November 1992, 38 Fresh, Mountain?, Hit Factory. Bowie: lead vocal ("Wedding Song"), harmony vocal, tenor saxophone; Rodgers: rhythm guitar; Michael Riesman: harp, tubular bells; Hilton, Richards, Saisse, Tee: keyboards; Schalow?: E-Mu SP1200, Akai S2000; B. Campbell or Regan: bass; Bell or S. Campbell: drums; Thornton, Agee, King Jr., Collins, White-King, Epps: backing vocals ("Wedding Song"); uncredited musicians: strings (arr. Riesman). Produced: Bowie, Rodgers; engineered: Goldberger, Tole, Grassi.

*First release: 5 April 1993, **Black Tie White Noise**.*

On 6 June 1992, David Bowie married Iman Abdulmajid for the second time. They had been wed by a magistrate in Lausanne two months earlier. In Florence, they staged their union in part for the tabloid *Hello!*, which ran a twenty-three-page spread on the event. It was a wedding as a Jeff Koons installation: two glowing celebrities (the groom as tanned as a tennis pro) posing for the cameras while fans massed outside the St. James Episcopal Church.

Brian Eno attended, as did Yoko Ono and Bono (someone had fun with the seating arrangements). Later that summer Eno gave a lecture on it. "It was a lovely wedding. And I was totally confused." He had trouble accepting how something could be so promotional and private at the same time. To his lecture audience, he said, "are we troubled by our inability to locate this event comfortably either in the category *real life* or the category *theatre?*... is it possible to manipulate a situation at the same time as being moved by it?" For Bowie, the answer was an obvious yes. In Iman, he'd made an ideal match. Another single parent, she was worldly, had a sharp business sense, and had long mastered how to have a private life within a public one. Their *Hello!* wedding in Florence was a performative union. "We didn't really feel married," he said. "I know the forms were signed but at the back of our minds our real marriage, sanctified by God, had to happen in a church in Florence."

Responsible for the music (he and Iman agreed Wagner's "Bridal Chorus" was appalling), he wrote a composition to symbolize the marriage of a man from Bromley and a woman from Mogadishu. "It was important for me to find something that had no representation of institutionalized and organized religion." "The Wedding," which would lead off *Black Tie White Noise*, was built on three-chord progressions in A major, with a foray into B-flat major in its bridge. It's a set of pairs: two tracks of tubular bells for the intro, two main keyboard lines, a fifths-and-roots bassline — the hook of Melle Mel's "White Lines," tonally jarring for a wedding song (well, maybe not Bowie's). And there are two saxophone lines: a thick-toned "R&B" one and an "Arabic" saxophone — a tenor saxophone distorted and varisped — that's more discordant and exuberant.

Months after the wedding, he wrote a lyric for the piece, closing *Black Tie* with a sung reprise of its instrumental opener. "The Wedding Song" was a saccharine ode to his wife, a regal version of Paul McCartney's "The Lovely Linda." "I'm so happy that people want to strangle me most of the time," as Bowie told Arsenio Hall in 1993. Though he called "The Wedding Song" confectionary, "all icing with a couple on top," there's fatalism in it. A wedding is a public defiance of time: a couple makes an impossible stand against their inevitable demise ("The Wedding Song" ends with the tubular bells of the instrumental's intro). If Iman's his personal angel, "she's not mine for eternity" but a temporary embassy from heaven. "I'll never fly so high," Bowie sings, in a processional sweep up a fourth. But "I'm smiling."

PALLAS ATHENA

Recorded: ca. April-November 1992, 38 Fresh, Mountain?, Hit Factory. Bowie: lead vocal, tenor saxophone; Rodgers: rhythm guitar; Lester Bowie: trumpet; Hilton, Richards, Saisse, Tee: keyboards; Schalow?: E-Mu SP-1200, Akai S2000?; B. Campbell or Regan: bass. Produced: Bowie, Rodgers; engineered: Goldberger, Tole, Grassi.

First release: ca. March 1993, Arista MEAT 1. **Broadcast**: 6 May 1993, Arsenio Hall. **Live**: 1997.

For *Black Tie White Noise*'s worldwide distribution, Bowie signed with BMG/ Arista, in part thanks to Martyn Watson, an Arista A&R consultant and Bowie fan with clubland ties (also Arista, fat on earnings from Whitney Houston's "I Will Always Love You," was throwing away money at the time). The label purposed Bowie as a club figure, commissioning remixes of *Black Tie* tracks by Meat Beat Manifesto, Brothers In Rhythm, and Leftfield (Watson lobbied for Underworld, to no avail; Andrew Weatherall turned Arista down). In 1993, when Bowie was considered a joke by Watson's friends, Watson felt that "I had to try to make him cool. I loved him more than my mum." He hand-delivered to a select group of DJs a promo 12" stamped only with the track's title, "Pallas Athena." It got some play in London and New York clubs, with word spreading that David Bowie was groaning *"God... is on top of it all"* over a techno beat. Showing that you just can't win, *Billboard* criticized Bowie's anonymity: "it would be mutually beneficial for his name to appear somewhere... it's not enough to glean a bit of hipness without giving something back."

"Pallas Athena" holds to four notes, its central melody of B-flat-G-A-G in constant repetition, carried by whole notes on synthesized cello, soon squired by quarter notes on synthetic violins — the higher the notes, the faster they're played. Along with the occasional bassline shift, the free agent is Bowie's saxophone, which tears off on excursions, often starting with a rising triplet figure. Lester Bowie's trumpet adds community. Over this are chanted refrains — a mountainous *"God* is on top of it all" in a Bowie vocal so distorted and slowed that it sounds like a sample of an African-American preacher, along with the more recognizably Bowie refrains of "that's all" and "we are, we are."

"God is on top of it all" sounds definitive: God's in control, relax. As the track develops, the vocal lines blur: "that's all that's all we are" or "we are we are God"; "we are we are" sounds like "Yahweh." Talking about his wedding, he affirmed that God was "the cornerstone of my existence" ("I have an unshakeable belief in God. I put my life in his hands every single day. I pray every morning.") But he was still a Gnostic, saying that "I believe man develops a relationship with his own God," and that man can judge God as well (after all, "I tend to judge a man or a woman by their actions"). The title carried other suggestions. The temple of Athena Nike is on the Acropolis: God is an empty ruin standing above a city that no longer worships her; the goddess Pallas Athena was hatched from the

head of a god. "I don't know what the fuck it's about," Bowie said of the track to the *NME*.

LUCY CAN'T DANCE

Recorded: ca. April-November 1992, 38 Fresh, Hit Factory. Bowie: lead and harmony vocal; Rodgers: rhythm guitar; Hilton, Richards, Saisse, Tee: keyboards; B. Campbell or Regan: bass; Velez: percussion; Thornton, Agee, King Jr., Collins, White-King, Epps: backing vocals; uncredited musicians: trumpets. Produced: Bowie, Rodgers; engineered: Goldberger, Tole, Grassi.

First release: 5 April 1993, **Black Tie White Noise**.

While Nile Rodgers has made his peace with *Black Tie White Noise*, at times he vented his frustration with its making. To David Buckley, Rodgers said his hands were tied, that Bowie hadn't wanted to make the radio-ready smash the world expected from a Rodgers/Bowie reunion (*"Star Wars 2"*). Bowie wanted to make a personal album on a platinum budget and kept rejecting guitar licks Rodgers played him ("maybe the licks I thought of stank — who knows? But all I knew was that they couldn't all suck!").

Bowie couldn't have made *Star Wars 2* if he'd wanted to. Approximating what he thought a mass audience would find palatable had only gotten him *Tonight*, and his Tin Machine years had left him hungry to experiment — during the Sound + Vision tour, he told Erdal Kızılçay he wanted his next album to be a jazz record, and he talked of collaborating with Glenn Branca. Instead, Bowie made an experimental record in the guise of a commercial one —undermining his pop comeback. Hence the fate of "Lucy Can't Dance" ("a guaranteed number 1 record," Rodgers said. "I was already accepting my Grammy"), a potential single that Bowie demoted to a CD bonus track.

That said, it's a stretch to think the trebly "Lucy Can't Dance" would've been a guaranteed #1 in 1993. Like "You've Been Around," it was an older composition, dating to the Tin Machine years. Rather shapeless, its lengthy verse/refrains, alternating between A major and G major, have to brave a harmonically-turbulent bridge before reaching the hooky refrains. As on "Let's Dance," Rodgers worked the song over, making it pop with clacking percussion (the opening burst sounds like pencils rattled in a metal can), underwater-sounding guitar fills, trumpet blasts, a synth bass.

Lyrically it was a take-down of another musician who'd been "David Bowie" better than the original had been in the Eighties: Madonna. As with Gary Numan, Bowie lacked his typical generosity towards younger musicians when talking about her. He could be crass (winking about her getting tied up by her ex-husband on "Pretty Thing") and dismissive ("I would get behind [her career] a lot more if I really felt anything for her music. It's conventional in the extreme. I guess I've seen too much, because I don't really find her provocative, either"). She made him sound like a cranky old Yorkshireman. In reference to her "La Isla Bonita" video, he said in 1987 "well, I don't understand how she can run her fingers over her pussy and in the next shot be clutching a crucifix... I find that has something a lot more perverse about it than anything in my video ["Day-In Day-Out"].

"Lucy Can't Dance" came at a time when Madonna was inescapable, the era of *Erotica* and her *Sex* book. Hence "Lucy, I know what you're going to do" (he's already done it); "you're looking for God in exciting new ways" (predicting her Kabbalist period); "who died and made you material girl?" (she only takes form when someone else (cough) leaves the stage.) The refrain indicts a soulless "soul" musician, and like many indictments, it applies to the accuser as well: see the bridge lines knocking Bowie's own word-salad lyricism. Madonna inducting an absent Bowie into the Rock and Roll Hall of Fame was the appropriate end to it all. ("She's a top-drawer plate-spinner," he admitted in 1998.)

DON'T LET ME DOWN AND DOWN

(Tahra, Valmont). **Recorded:** *ca. September-November 1992, Hit Factory. Bowie: lead and harmony vocal; Rodgers: rhythm guitar; L. Bowie: trumpet; Hilton, Richards, Saisse, Tee: keyboards; B. Campbell or Regan: bass; Bell or S. Campbell: drums; Velez: percussion; Thornton, Agee, King Jr., Collins, White-King, Epps: backing vocals. Produced: Bowie, Rodgers; engineered: Goldberger, Tole, Grassi.*

First release: *5 April 1993,* **Black Tie White Noise**.

The most obscure cover of Bowie's life was a wedding gift. Going through Iman's record collection early in their courtship, he came across a CD that he thought was Arabic at first and was intrigued by a song he heard on it. "Don't Let Me Down and Down" was "one of those tracks that sort of in a diary-like way records the beginnings of a relationship," he recalled.

The musician, Tahra Mint Hembara, was born in Néma, in southeast Mauritania. She was a hereditary griot, one of a caste of poets and musicians who keep strict gender roles: female griots play a harp variant, the ardin. Living in France by the late Seventies, she studied at the Sorbonne until casting her lot with professional music, getting a record deal with Pathé Marconi. Her 1988 album *Yamen Yamen* had compositions rooted in Mauritania's modal system (in which a musician plays in five modes and three "ways," the latter roughly equivalent to scales and often called "black," "white," and "mixed"). One song, "T Beyby," built on fretless bass, keyboards, and drum programming, was a vehicle for her harsh, unearthly voice — its refrain, a hypnotic "den eden dani den edani," was a two-note ardin line in words. Her producer Martine Valmont wrote an English lyric, renaming the song "Don't Let Me Down and Down." Where "T Beyby" is the voice of a man whose lover has left her husband ("he rejoices and thanks God"), Valmont made the song obsessive: a woman trapped in a cycle of love and despair.

"It was so extraordinary and just out of kilter with what should be Western music — this extraordinarily plaintive little voice expressing this pidgin English lyric," Bowie said. He apparently didn't bother with the lyric sheet, as he thought one of Valmont's best lines, "judge and jury in my memory," was "you jog-jog in my memory." Lifted out of 3/4 into standard time, its arrangement rivalled *Tonight* at its immaculate nadir, with a glittering wall of keyboards and backing singers doing elaborate phonetic harmonies. Worse, in the spirit of cultural fusion he'd tried in "The Wedding," Bowie sang in some ghastly attempt at a Jamaican (?) or French (?) accent ("steel I keep my lurve for youuu") in a croaking timbre. As though shamed by Lester Bowie's fluttering beauty of a trumpet solo, he corrected course, lunging to his high register for the last refrains. It was too late: "Don't Let Me Down and Down" was another tonally adrift Bowie cover.

LOOKING FOR LESTER

(Bowie, Rodgers.) **Recorded**: *ca. September-November 1992, Hit Factory. Bowie: tenor saxophone; L. Bowie: trumpet; Mike Garson: piano; Rodgers: lead and rhythm guitar; Hilton, Richards, Saisse, Tee: keyboards; B. Campbell or Regan: bass; uncredited musicians: trumpets, trombones (arr. Chico O'Farrill). Produced: Bowie, Rodgers; engineered: Goldberger, Tole, Grassi.*

First release: *5 April 1993,* **Black Tie White Noise**.

With his goatee and lab coat, Lester Bowie was jazz's mad scientist, part of the jazz faction that favored commotion, play, and activism instead of being custodians of "America's Classical Music." Bowie said he'd known Lester's brother, trombonist Joseph Bowie, in Sixties London and had always wanted to use Lester on an album. On *Black Tie White Noise* he got the works. Lester (asked only to play on "Don't Let Me Down and Down") hung around for days at the Hit Factory, winding up on four other tracks. He preferred not to hear tracks before he played on them: "you roll the tape and he jumps in. Sometimes he's madly out of tune," Bowie said. Nile Rodgers rigged up a rhythm track for the two Bowies to solo over: a "basket of sounds" whose breezy main theme was carried by players arranged by bandleader Chico O'Farrill.

"Looking for Lester" (the title was Bowie's, a play on "Chasin' the Trane") has a hammering drum loop, intertwined synthesized and electric basslines, and a blend of piano and synthesizer colors. Lester opens with descending triplets that land on a long-held F# that he coaxes down a tone. His first solo varies on the main theme, finding little pockets of melody, closing with a sweet, soaring phrase. After a theme reprise, with Lester doodling in the margins, he's freer in the second chorus, casting off allegiance to the melody, building to short, punchy phrases choked off by a massed trumpet retort. In the studio, "you have to follow him around with a microphone because he won't stand still," Bowie said.

As it was Bowie's album, he got the longest solo. He starts with two moaning phrases (the second one grows especially wheezy); soon enough he finds a sweet spot and burrows into it, closing with a blast of genteel skronk. And for the last solo chorus, Mike Garson returns, back in the Bowie fold after almost twenty years and sounding as if it had only been a week.

He makes spiky runs across his piano, rumbling on the bass keys, musing on the treble ones. "Looking for Lester" is the equivalent of a weekend getaway where well-off dads spend $10,000 to jam with Peter Frampton — an eternal amateur saxophone player gets to duel with a brilliant trumpeter and have his producer box it up. An indulgence, not an embarrassment.

BLACK TIE WHITE NOISE

Recorded: ca. July-November 1992, Hit Factory. Bowie: lead vocal, saxophone; Al B. Sure!: lead vocal; Rodgers: rhythm guitar; L. Bowie: trumpet; Dan Wilensky: saxophone?; Hilton, Richards, Saisse, Tee: keyboards; B. Campbell or Regan: bass; S. Campbell: drums; Thornton, Agee, King Jr., Collins, White-King, Epps: backing vocals. Produced: Bowie, Rodgers; engineered: Goldberger, Tole, Grassi.

First release: 5 April 1993, Black Tie White Noise. Broadcast: 6 May 1993, Arsenio Hall; 10 May 1993, Tonight Show.

Having flown to Los Angeles for apartment shopping at the end of April 1992, Bowie and Iman were in the city when riots started on the afternoon the Rodney King verdict was announced. "It really felt like a prison riot, more than anything else, or the beginnings of a revolution," Bowie said the following year. He claimed he'd seen buildings afire, either from his windows or rooftop, and that he'd kept his jeans, car keys and money near his bed in case he and Iman had to flee when their apartment building got torched. Whether embellished or not (let's say embellished), this Ballardian image of a rich man in his suite, watching a riot unfold in the city below and feeling vaguely euphoric about it, inspired the title track of Bowie's new album.

It began as a critique of interracial-brotherhood songs: that the likes of "Ebony and Ivory," "We Are the World" and "We Shall Overcome" ("I Got You Babe" weirdly added to their ranks here) become slogans to make white liberals feel better without doing anything — these songs strove to find "white sameness within everybody," Bowie said. "We're far too keen, as white liberals, to suggest to black people how they should improve their lot... They've got their own ideas of how they can improve their lot, and they couldn't give a fuck what we think. They don't want our advice." The best that any white person could do is start being honest about institutional racism. "There's the denial in America that slavery ever took place," he said in 1995. "I think there should be a confrontation and... a museum of Black America." His "black tie" image was to acknowledge his own great debts to black American culture. He had a deep collection of black literature, urging band members to read novels like Ann Petry's *The Street*; he called out MTV in 1983 for not playing black artists, refusing to let VJ Mark Goodman get away with explanatory platitudes.

In 1993, Arsenio Hall asked Bowie if he and Iman, as an interracial couple, had gotten hostility. Bowie was blunt: never, because they were celebrities before they'd married ("you get the occasional snide remark, but nothing of any weight"). To consider their marriage a typical interracial union would be, as his opening line went, getting your facts from a Benetton ad. (Bowie used his marriage as a motif throughout *Black Tie*. The night he and Iman first met, he'd worn white denim and she black leather, and the title was their public personae — sartorial elegance, abrasive music.) Considering the future of his (then hypothetical) bi-racial child, Bowie was optimistic, in an apocalyptic way. Where Tom Petty had issued "Peace in L.A." (for whom?) in response to the riots, Bowie's song said peace wasn't the answer. "Change is no easy thing, and it's not going to happen without a certain amount of violence... I think there is no revolution without violence. It's not a soft solution, but there is a positive outcome." Or as he had Al B. Sure! sing: "there'll be some blood, no doubt about it."

Unfortunately, then there's the song. The nuances of Bowie's conversation get lost in a contorted composition whose verses stew in E-flat major until giving way to lengthy bridges in A-flat. It had a traffic jam of an arrangement: jawboning wah-wah guitar, ebullient trumpet and saxophone, over-mixed drums, and every vocal track given great doses of reverb, including backing singers whose staccato "black! tie! white! noise!" is the closest there is to a hook.

To duet, Bowie chose Sure!, an R&B journeyman whose recording career ended soon afterward, although Lenny Kravitz had lobbied for the part. Sure! was more amenable to coaching: "I had a particular thing that I wanted to do with this song, and he spent a long time working through it... it was often quite punishing for both of us," Bowie said. Too punishing: Sure! got shoehorned into a performance that was anonymous when not overly mannered. It didn't help that he had to sing lines like "I've got a face, not just my race." In the bridges, Bowie and Sure! face off as if it's the last reel of *Reservoir Dogs* ("you won't kill me! you won't kill me *no!*"), while throughout Bowie veers from singsong ("I won-der *why*, I wond-er *why*") to a horrific "no-oy-oy-oy-se" to a nasally cod-reggae "*crank*-ing *out*." A recording that leaves one seasick, it verifies the Oscar Wilde quip that "all bad poetry springs from genuine feeling."

MIRACLE GOODNIGHT

Recorded: ca. July-November 1992, Hit Factory. Bowie: lead and harmony vocal; Rodgers: lead guitar, rhythm guitar; Hilton, Richards, Saisse, Tee: keyboards; B. Campbell or Regan: bass. Produced: Bowie, Rodgers; engineered: Goldberger, Tole, Grassi.

First release: 5 April 1993, **Black Tie White Noise**.

Opening with a relentless synthesizer riff that's been compared to a Balinese frog chorus and the first notes of the *Sanford and Son* theme, "Miracle Goodnight" soon augments this with further keyboard lines (the long-held notes singing overhead in the second verse) and a mix of live and synthetic bass. With a near-conversational, and at times *just* conversational, vocal in a three-note range until the refrains, it breaks up its bridegroom reveries with flashes of despair ("burning up our lives," "I wished I had a future," "ragged, lame and hungry"). The second spoken break is a blunt compromise: let's agree we don't talk about who we used to sleep with. The title line's a man bidding goodnight to the woman he can't believe he married, knowing the good times will have to end someday: "don't want to say goodnight," he sings towards the fade.

A harmonically spare song moving between G major and A major, like two generals dancing with each other, "Miracle Goodnight" still has a lightness of touch — the easy transitions between verses and refrains; the keyboard solo of florid rising sixteenth notes in homage to Handel's "Arrival of the Queen of Sheba." For the guitar solo, Bowie asked Nile Rodgers to play as though the Fifties had never happened; that is, as if white pop music hadn't been invigorated by black guitarists ("I don't want to hear a single blue note.") Rodgers responded with twangy, spiraling lines suggesting Les Paul and an alternate font of musical influence, the guitar styles of West African highlife. In an album on which he was a frustrated presence at times, Rodgers is free to roam for four bars.

COSMIC DANCER
I KNOW IT'S GONNA HAPPEN SOMEDAY

(Bolan ["Cosmic Dancer"], Morrissey, Nevin ["Someday"].) **Recorded**: *["Someday"] ca. July-October 1992, Hit Factory. Bowie: lead and backing vocal; Wild T. Springer: lead guitar; Hilton, Saisse or Tee: piano; B. Campbell or Regan: bass; Bell or S. Campbell: drums; Thornton, Agee, King, Collins, White-King, Epps, Frank Simms, George Simms, David Spinner, Lamya Al-Mughiery, Connie Petruk, Bowie, Rodgers: choir; uncredited musicians: horns. Produced: Bowie, Rodgers; engineered: Goldberger, Tole, Grassi.*

First release: *5 April 1993,* **Black Tie White Noise**. **Live**: *["Cosmic Dancer"] 1991.*

For teenage Steven Morrissey, David Bowie was a god. "Manchester, then, was full of bootboys and skinheads and macho-macho thugs, but I saw Bowie's appearance as the ultimate bravery," Morrissey recalled in 2008. "To me, it took guts to be David Bowie, not to be a shit-kicking skinhead in a pack." When he bought the "Starman" single in summer 1972, "that was a truly extraordinary time for me. I was falling in love with the potency of the pop moment. That's why I am here...because the pop moment in my life was the only thing that ever spoke to me."

The two met at a Bowie show in Manchester in August 1990. By then, Morrissey had co-founded and disbanded the Smiths, who were for disaffected Eighties teenagers what Bowie had been for Morrissey. One night the following June, when Morrissey was playing the Great Western Forum in Los Angeles, Bowie came on stage to sing T. Rex's "Cosmic Dancer" with him. The crowd went mad: on tapes, you can barely hear the singers above the din. It was Bowie anointing Morrissey as heir presumptive of glam, with a Marc Bolan song as coronation hymn.

The mutual admiration society continued when Bowie covered a Morrissey song on *Black Tie White Noise*. There was a dig in his choice, though, as "I Know It's Gonna Happen Someday" was Morrissey's attempt to do a "Rock

347

'n' Roll Suicide," whose coda saxophone arrangement he might as well have sampled. "It occurred to me that he was possibly spoofing one of my earlier songs, and I thought, I'm not going to let him get away with that," Bowie said. Mick Ronson, who produced Morrissey, returned from cancer treatment to hear playback of "I Know It's Gonna Happen Someday" and, as per the song's co-writer Mark Nevin, had an "are you kidding me?" expression on his face.

Bowie had contrary ideas for his cover — he wanted it to be "weepy and silly," singing in the histrionic vein of Johnny Ray, but also wanted it to sound as if being performed during the *Diamond Dogs* tour: decadent and fervent. Set to 4/4 instead of the whirling 12/8 of the Morrissey original, its centerpiece was a guitar solo by Wild T. Springer, a "lilting" take on Hendrix's "Little Wing." Its mix was accorded great glops of "choir" vocals and horns. Bowie strained to carry the song — see his vocal fills before the closing "wait, don't lose faith." By spoofing what he considered a Morrissey spoof (in the video, Bowie holds aloft a cigarette lighter and solemnly sways his arms during the guitar solo), Bowie made a cynical misreading. Morrissey's track opens with static, shimmering into range as though broadcast from behind enemy lines. Its tone is sincere, its message one of constancy, a typical Morrissey pledge to adolescents that they can get through it. At the end of his "Everyday Is Like Sunday" video, a girl with mousy hair finds Morrissey through her spyglass and sees that her face is on his T-shirt: she's his idol as much as he's hers.

In autumn 1995, Bowie asked Morrissey to open for him on some British and European dates. Soon there was friction about everything from publicity materials (which touted Morrissey as a "very special guest" but only featured Bowie's photograph) to soundcheck times. Morrissey reportedly opened one set with "good evening, we are your support group" to a half-empty Wembley Arena. His fans were "a crowd, that is, of precisely eleven rows deep and twenty seats across," *Melody Maker*'s Jennifer Nine noted. "Not that Bowie and Morrissey lack points of comparison: both of 'em once meant the world; both now make mediocrity on a regular basis. Both are doomed to play gigs that ticket-buyers will shrug mildly over." Morrissey said the breaking point was Bowie's request, as with Nine Inch Nails earlier in the tour (see "Reptile"), to interchange opening and lead bands while Morrissey and Bowie duetted to open Bowie's set. Morrissey considered it a diva move to deprive his fans of a proper closer.

After nine shows, he abandoned the tour before an Aberdeen gig, and for years afterward lambasted Bowie as a has-been and a charlatan. "You have to worship at the temple of David when you become involved [with him]...He's not the person he was. He is no longer David Bowie at all. Now he gives people what he thinks will make them happy, and they're yawning their heads off. And by doing that, he is not relevant. He was only relevant by accident." Bowie only said that Morrissey had gone to soundcheck, got into a car, "and that's the last we heard of him."

JUMP THEY SAY

Recorded: ca. April-November 1992, 38 Fresh, Hit Factory. Bowie: lead and backing vocal, saxophone; Rodgers: rhythm guitar; L. Bowie: trumpet; Hilton, Richards, Saisse, Tee: keyboards; Schalow: programming; B. Campbell or Regan: bass; Bell or S. Campbell: drums; Thornton, Agee, King Jr., Collins, White-King, Epps: backing vocals. Produced: Bowie, Rodgers; engineered: Goldberger, Tole, Grassi.

First release: 15 March 1993 (Arista 74321 139424, UK #9). **Broadcast**: 6 May 1993, Arsenio Hall. **Live**: 1995-1996.

On the snowy morning of 16 January 1985, a patient left the grounds of Cane Hill Hospital, crossed to Coulsdon South station, and walked to the end of the platform. When the express train appeared in the distance, he jumped onto the track, lay his head upon the rail and turned his face away from the train, which killed him. He was Terry Burns, David Bowie's half-brother.

A family tragedy became the sport of tabloids. The *Sun* attacked Bowie for alleged neglect of Burns and for not attending his funeral (he thought he would have made it a press circus, had he gone). The papers gave a platform to an aggrieved aunt. The following year brought Peter and Leni Gillman's biography, *Alias David Bowie*, with said aunt as a key source, which depicted the Bowie family as being riddled with insanity and argued that Bowie's relationship with his mentally ill half-brother, and his own fears of going mad, was central to his songwriting.

Barring a note with the flowers he sent to Burns' funeral, Bowie kept silent about his half-brother. Two years earlier, while promoting *Merry*

Christmas, Mr. Lawrence, he said he'd found in his character, a soldier haunted by having once abandoned his brother, "all too many areas of guilt and shortcomings that are a part of me. I feel tremendous guilt because I grew so apart from my family... I have a step (sic) brother I don't see anymore. It was my fault we grew apart and it is painful — but somehow there is no going back."

Bowie's elder by ten years, Burns had helped turn David Jones into "David Bowie," introducing his half-brother to everything from Tibetan Buddhism to jazz. Their last period of regular contact, the 1970-1971 Beckenham era, when Bowie would introduce himself to guests as "Terry's brother," coincided with Bowie's quantum leap in songwriting: "All the Madmen," "Five Years," "The Man Who Sold the World," "Bewlay Brothers." Bowie made Burns a vessel into which he could channel his fears. Looking back in 1993, Bowie said he hadn't really known his half-brother, who would disappear for years and then turn up in Bromley without warning. "I think I unconsciously exaggerated his importance. I invented this hero-worship to discharge my guilt and failure, and to set myself free from my own hang-ups."

Writing a song "semi-based on my impression" of Burns produced "Jump They Say," a desolate midtempo track that became a British hit: Bowie's last solo appearance in the UK Top 10 in the twentieth century. It's similar in tone and structure to "What in the World," with which "Jump They Say" shares an alternating two-chord progression and a similar rhythmic base: the little girl with grey eyes has grown up to be a shaking man "with a nation in his eyes." "What in the World" is on the manic end of *Low*'s emotional spectrum, while "Jump They Say" is reserved, withdrawn, a piece of harmonic and rhythmic stasis — the bassline scarcely varies, nor do the percussion loops (left-mixed synthesized hi-hat and right-mixed tambourine sixteenths). Bowie's vocal, which stays within the range of a fifth except in the bridge, chills a lyric in which a suicidal figure is observed in the distance, as if by a scientist: "look at him climb!"

Breaking through the permafrost are distorted trumpets in the intro, a reversed horn figure from a Stan Kenton recording, Lester Bowie's solo (in the *Outside* tour, this section was fought over by Reeves Gabrels and Mike Garson) and Bowie's agonized saxophone responses to the crowd calling for the man to jump: a piercing melody that he gave words to in the last refrain: "you've got to *believe somebody*." Its video had further scenarios — Bowie as a deranged-seeming corporate raider; scenes from lost futures (*La Jetée* and

2001); and recreating Evelyn McHale's "beautiful suicide" of 1947. McHale leapt from the Empire State Building and was immortalized in death by a passing photographer, her body crumpled into a Cadillac roof. "Tell my father, I have too many of my mother's tendencies," her farewell note read.

I FEEL FREE

(Bruce, Brown.) **Recorded**: *ca. summer-autumn 1992, Hit Factory. Bowie: lead vocal, saxophone; Mick Ronson: lead guitar; Gabrels: rhythm guitar; Hilton, Richards, Saisse, Tee: keyboards; B. Campbell or Regan: bass; Bell or S. Campbell: drums; Thornton, Agee, King Jr., Collins, White-King, Epps: backing vocals. Produced: Bowie, Rodgers; engineered: Goldberger, Tole, Grassi.*

First release: *5 April 1993,* **Black Tie White Noise**. **Live**: *1972.*

Cream's "I Feel Free" had personal resonance for Bowie, as his half-brother once had suffered a schizophrenic episode outside a hall where Cream was playing. Bowie sang it live in 1972, considered recording it for *Pin Ups* and *Scary Monsters* (see "Is There Life After Marriage"), and finally did so on *Black Tie White Noise*. Though Reeves Gabrels cut a solo, he was erased in favor of the ailing Mick Ronson, whose performance here was among his last recordings.

NITE FLIGHTS

(Engel.) **Recorded**: *ca. July-November 1992, Hit Factory. Bowie: lead and harmony vocal, saxophone; Gabrels: rhythm guitar; Hilton, Richards, Saisse, Tee: keyboards; B. Campbell or Regan: bass; Bell or S. Campbell: drums. Produced: Bowie, Rodgers; engineered: Goldberger, Tole, Grassi.*

First release: *5 April 1993,* **Black Tie White Noise**. **Broadcast**: *10 May 1993, The Tonight Show.* **Live**: *1995-1996.*

Noel Scott Engel, born in Ohio in 1943, went to Britain for fame and stayed there. David Robert Jones, born in Brixton the day before Engel's fourth birthday, struck for fame in Britain and died in America. Jones became David Bowie, Engel became Scott Walker. Each was precocious, ambitious, handsome. But in the mid-Sixties, only Walker was a pop star, the heartthrob of the Walker Brothers; at the time, Bowie was just polite aspiration.

The Walker Brothers made maudlin, shabby pop. Their hit singles, sung in Scott's glum baritone, were dirges. Britain especially took them to heart. Beneath the shine of Carnaby Street, there was a nation that hadn't gotten over the war, and for whom "Make It Easy on Yourself" and the doom-struck "The Sun Ain't Gonna Shine Anymore" rang truer than "All You Need Is Love," whose promise extended only to the young and beautiful. Though they looked like surfer gods, the Walkers lived in darkened rooms, enduring desertions and morning-after regrets. And years before Bowie created a plastic rock star, there were the Walkers (not brothers; none really named Walker), who didn't play on their records or tours. As their biographer Anthony Reynolds wrote, the Walker Brothers were only Scott and John Walker's recorded voices. "The Walker Brothers *felt* real, but did not actually exist in any recognizable reality."

Scott Walker hid in movie theaters, sat alone in nightclubs. He took Valium to bring himself down, uppers and vodka to get through sessions and shows. Writing B-sides for publishing royalties, he found escape. In "Archangel," built on a Bach-inspired pipe organ figure recorded at the Odeon Cinema in Leicester Square (a moviegoer's whim indulged), and the kitchen-sink drama of "Mrs. Murphy" was the breadth of his imagined London: the gossipy life in a two-up two-down, where angels appear at the windows.

Going solo, Walker took the Belgian singer Jacques Brel for a liberator, using Brel's songs for cover, exotica, notoriety. The *Scott* records of the late Sixties had fervid Brel songs, country/folk forays, and Walker-penned songs, the latter peopled with squandered dreamers on fire escapes and terraces. They were the sort of albums the couple in Paul Simon's "The Dangling Conversation" would have on their hi-fi. The music of the aspiring middlebrow of the Sixties, a lost world of Cabernet, mime, arts labs, Buddhism, poetry readings, underground theater. The world of Bowie and his girlfriend, the dancer Hermione Farthingale, in 1968.

Around this time, Bowie discovered Walker. At first Walker was a portal to Brel, with Bowie soon incorporating takes on Walker's covers of "Amsterdam" and "My Death" into his own sets. But the original *Scott* songs are in the sediment of Bowie's late Sixties, too: the bedroom of "hessian and wood" in "An Occasional Dream," the paper-strewn room of "Conversation Piece," in Major Tom's desire to slip free from the world and float off like a balloon.

As Bowie became a star, Walker faded. No longer singing his own compositions, Walker released albums that seemed to be commissioned by charity shops. He grubbed them out, cutting his vocals in a day, going through a bottle of vodka in the booth. He sang anything he was given, often beautifully, often as if demoing for other singers. As Andy Zax said of these records, "their emptiness is startling." "I hated myself so much for all the years of bad faith," Walker said in 2006. "I still do. I'm very wary of it. It bothers me that I wasted all that time, you know? I was making records to pay off bills."

By late 1973, with the Spiders from Mars in ashes, Bowie was listening to Walker again. On *Diamond Dogs*, a parody of Walker's recent "Any Day Now" surfaces in "Future Legend," while the ghoulish *basso profondo* that opens "Sweet Thing" sounds like a zombie Walker going through Hunger City, looking for rough trade. It's a Walker purged of his middlebrow crooner affectations, clarified to dark camp, and it's one possible ending: Walker as a Bowie character, another influence absorbed.

The Electrician and the Lodger

The Walker Brothers reunited in 1975, to fleeting success. With enough label money left to fund a last record in 1978, they cut their own songs. Scott brought *"Heroes"* to the studio, where it became "the reference album when we were making *Nite Flights*," the engineer Steve Parker told Reynolds. "If we'd had an Eno character in there, it would have been even more stunning, I think." *Nite Flights'* peak was Scott's "The Electrician," where he pushed beyond Bowie and Eno. In its refrain, he corrodes his voice, hanging between being sharp and on the note. It suited the lyric, a love song about American complicity in Central American torture regimes. There was nothing of its like in 1978. Released as a single, "The Electrician" was a future no one wanted (see "The Motel").

In September 1978, Eno brought *Nite Flights* to Montreux, where he and Bowie were recording *Lodger*. Bowie was stunned. One can't blame him. Imagine if a great stone face you've been making offerings to for years

353

rumbles up a response. Over a decade later, Bowie returned the volley by covering *Nite Flights'* title track.

Bowie said he chose "Nite Flights" to symbolize the unease and danger he and Iman had felt upon embarking on a new marriage relatively late in life. As with "I Know It's Gonna Happen Someday," there was also vanity in his choice — "Nite Flights" is the closest Walker ever came to sounding like Bowie, from its "Heroes" callbacks ("we will be gods") to its arrangement. Bowie and Nile Rodgers smoothed Walker's insistent disco by slowing the tempo and letting the song groove, freed from the piano, snare, and hi-hat pulse of the Walker track. They wove a thick curtain of sound. Where Walker makes the chord change to B-flat major on "blood-lite" portend something awful, Bowie breezes through it. He sings Walker's bizarre, violent lines ("the dark *dug up by dogs!*... the raw meat *fist you choke!*) with cool poise, taking the first octave leap — "it's so *cold!*" — without blinking.

"Nite Flights," Bowie covering Walker's most Bowie-colored song, was an exception for two artists who usually stood at an influential imbalance. Bowie was a Scott Walker fan (hearing a recording of Walker wishing him a happy fiftieth birthday nearly made Bowie weep, saying "I see God in the window"). Walker, whenever he mentioned Bowie (rarely), did so with gracious reserve, the quiet complimentary manner of an artist to a distant patron. They were two planets in the same system: one more favored by the sun, a rich world with a host of satellites wheeling around it; the other smaller, less hospitable, given to long, elliptical orbits. Sometimes the two have been in sync, or have eclipsed the other. But their dance is over. The larger world has stopped moving; it hangs suspended now, a preservation of its best days. The lesser orb still goes on its way.

LIKE A ROLLING STONE
COLOUR ME

(Dylan ["Rolling Stone"]; Ronson, Morris ["Colour Me"].) **Recorded**: *("Rolling Stone" vocal, backing tracks) Los Angeles, spring 1988; (lead guitar, vocal overdubs, backing tracks ["Colour Me"]) ca. autumn 1992, Hit Factory? Bowie: lead vocal ["Rolling Stone"], vocal ["Colour Me"]; Mick Ronson: lead and rhythm guitar, bass, vocal; Joe Elliott: vocal ["Colour Me"]; Keith Scott: guitar; John Webster: keyboards; Sham Morris: keyboards ["Colour Me"]; Rene Wurst: bass; Mick Curry:*

drums; Martin Barker: drums ["Colour Me"]. Produced: Bruce Fairbairn, Ronson; engineered: Erwin Musper.

First release: 10 May 1994, **Heaven and Hull** (Epic 474742/53796.)

In late 1991, Mick Ronson learned that he had inoperable liver cancer; he died less than two years later, at age forty-six. Bowie heard the news while promoting Black Tie White Noise in America, and eulogized Ronson on the Arsenio Hall Show. Since splitting with Bowie in 1973, Ronson had settled into a sideman's life, working with everyone from Bob Dylan to John Mellencamp (he's greatly responsible for the arrangement of "Jack and Diane") to Morrissey. Learning that Ronson was making a solo record, Heaven and Hull, Bowie sent him "a box of tapes" which unfortunately hailed from the uninspired 1988 Bruce Fairbairn sessions in Los Angeles. There was little Ronson could do with Bowie's clumping version of Bob Dylan's "Like a Rolling Stone" except overdub as much guitar as the tape could take (Bowie did additional vocals, possibly during the Hit Factory Black Tie sessions when Ronson cut his solo on "I Feel Free"). Bowie also sang vocals with Joe Elliott for a middling Ronson composition, "Colour Me." It was a weak finale to a great partnership: play "Moonage Daydream" instead.

THE BUDDHA OF SUBURBIA

Recorded: ca. August 1993, Mountain Studios. Bowie: lead and backing vocal, alto saxophone, twelve-string acoustic guitar?, synthesizer; Erdal Kızılçay: synthesizers, keyboards, lead guitar, acoustic guitar?, bass, drums; Lenny Kravitz: lead guitar ("rock" version). Produced: Bowie, Kızılçay; engineered: David Richards.

First release: 8 November 1993, **The Buddha of Suburbia** (Arista/BMG 74321 170042, UK #87).

Black Tie White Noise failed to reestablish Bowie as a major commercial presence. This was just as well, as he'd been ambivalent about being reestablished. He avoided touring the album, confining promotions to two television appearances and a few magazine interviews. One of the latter was the springboard into his next project.

The writer Hanif Kureishi spoke to Bowie in early 1993 for *Interview*, a conversation that touched often on Bromley, where both had been raised. Bowie was already in a nostalgic mood, having helped compile an issue of *Arena* that cataloged his past and giving a *Rolling Stone* interviewer a guided tour of London and its suburbs. At the time, Kureishi was adapting his semi-autobiographical novel *The Buddha of Suburbia* into a miniseries for the BBC, and he asked to use songs like "Fill Your Heart" and "Time." Bowie agreed. Working up the nerve, Kureishi asked if he also felt like contributing original material. A few months later, Kureishi and director Roger Michell were in Switzerland, listening to Bowie's score for the series.

His incidental music was motifs — combinations of guitar, synthesizer, trumpet, percussion, sitar. Kureishi found it surreal to watch footage of his film on a TV monitor while the idol of his adolescence worked the mixing desk; he also found it daunting to tell his idol that the music wasn't quite right. After revising the soundtrack, Bowie thought he could rework it into a new album, a quasi-soundtrack. "He said he wanted to write some songs for it because he wanted to make some money out of it," Kureishi recalled to Dylan Jones. (Bowie was always surprised to discover how poorly the BBC paid.)

During his nostalgic turns in early 1993, Bowie also had been wondering if he could make a fourth "Berlin" album out of scattered pieces of the trilogy, a fake "Lost Tapes" album that "never existed." Ryko bonus tracks like "I Pray Olé" and "Abdulmajid" had been trial runs, with Bowie using bits from his late-Seventies sessions and fashioning new tracks out of them. And on *Buddha of Suburbia*, he remixed his soundtrack, making new shapes by distorting and slowing down tracks.

Relying on his usual jack-of-all-trades Erdal Kızılçay, Bowie worked at Mountain Studios in summer 1993 to extend his *Buddha* motifs into six- or eight-minute loops, isolating their "dangerous or attractive elements," then recording vocals and instrumental lines over these elements. After a week's recording and a fortnight of mixing, he had a fifty-minute album. It appeared in November 1993, listed as the soundtrack it wasn't, distributed only in the UK and Europe, and eclipsed, sales-wise, by the near-simultaneous release of Bowie's *Singles Collection*. *The Buddha of Suburbia* was a ghost record, and his finest in a decade.

Stockpile of Residue

Seven years Bowie's junior, Kureishi had attended the same school, Bromley Tech, and had a similar trajectory: escaping to London for a professional life in the arts. (Similar to Kureishi, *The Buddha of Suburbia*'s protagonist, Karim Amir, is the son of an Indian father (Kureishi's was Pakistani) and an English mother.) Bowie found in Kureishi's work an observation that rang true: the curse of being a suburban artist is a self-conflicted ambition, a need to feel you're bettering yourself while fearing being found out as a fraud. "It's a miracle," Bowie once told Tin Machine guitarist Eric Schermerhorn as their tour bus went through Brixton. "I probably should have been an accountant. I don't know how this all happened."

Once asked why Orwell's *Nineteen Eighty-Four* had been such an influence on his work, Bowie said "for those of us born in South London, you always felt like you were in [the book]. That's the kind of gloom and immovable society that a lot of us felt we grew up in." The *Buddha* characters who thrive are those who transform themselves, like Karim; those who wither, like Karim's fundamentalist uncle Anwar, are those who can't shake free of the past. Yet in *Buddha* this self-transformation, this multi-ethnic suburban counterculture, is ultimately twinned with Thatcherism — novel and series end on the night of the general election in 1979. The ferment generated by suburban hippies and punks paralleled the economic "liberation" of Thatcher. The revolution, when it came, would be a suburban one.

Working on *Buddha* triggered something in Bowie. The film had lovingly recreated early-Seventies Bromley for him. Writing his new songs, he drew from what he called a "personal memory stock" that ranged from his teenage years in Bromley through the late Seventies in Berlin. Bowie's *Buddha* would be an impressionist autobiography. As he wrote in his liner notes, "a major chief obstacle to the evolution of music has been the almost redundant narrative form. To rely upon this old war-horse can only continue the spiral into the British constraint of insularity. Maybe we could finally relegate the straightforward narrative to the past."

That said, he had to write a straightforward narrative for the series' theme song, played over the end credits of most episodes. "The Buddha of Suburbia" was a homage to Bowie's turn-of-the-Seventies "Beckenham" songs: the guitar break from "Space Oddity" (and the suspended, diminished and augmented chords); the "zane zane zane" coda refrain of "All the

Madmen"; the flavor of its verses — Bowie's octave-tracked voice in a framework of acoustic guitar, bass, and synthesizer — suggested "Bewlay Brothers" and "After All."

His lyric holds to the path of Kureishi's book, which is divided into "In the Suburbs" and "In the City" sections. The opening verse is suburban misfit angst, the singer pushing for experience ("full of blood, loving life and all it's got to give"). The second verse finds the kid in the city, changing himself, or at least his clothes. The melancholy custodian of his folk years in verses (arpeggiated guitars; yearning top melodies), Bowie becomes an Anthony Newley figure for the refrains ("down on my *knees* in suh-*bur*-bee-yah"). Bowie the jazz saxophonist takes the first solo; the power-chording glam rocker gets the second. (Lenny Kravitz played lead on the song's "rock" mix: it was his usual simulacrum work.)

SOUTH HORIZON

Recorded: ca. August 1993, Mountain Studios; (piano overdub) ca. September 1993, O'Henry Sound Studios, 4200 W Magnolia Blvd., Burbank, California. Bowie: alto saxophone, synthesizer?; Kızılçay: synthesizers, trumpet, bass, drums; Garson: piano; Richards: drum programming. Produced: Bowie, Kızılçay; engineered: Richards, Mike Ruggieri.

First release: 8 November 1993, **The Buddha of Suburbia**.

In his *Buddha of Suburbia* liner notes, Bowie listed Ronnie Scott's club in Soho, where as a teenager he'd seen jazz players. From a soundtrack motif he conjured a jazz piece, "South Horizon." Starting with a trumpet/synthesizer loop, he isolated melodic peaks of the trumpet melody, layered in percussion, then "all elements, from lead instrumentation to texture, were played both forwards and backwards. The resulting extracts were then intercut arbitrarily." It was his favorite track on the album.

Rather than being "intercut arbitrarily," however, the track is in obvious halves (the join is at 2:24): a "traditional jazz" section with live drums playing ride beats and an "acid jazz" section with drum machine — the lesser half, as the beats sound like someone playing on a tissue and comb. In the opening half, perspective shifts from bass to drums (a dialogue of ride cymbal, hi-hat, and kick) to piano, while the latter section, kicked off by a groaning "three blind mice" synthesizer hook, has a fresh trumpet line (sprightlier and sweeter, happy to escape the loop that claimed its predecessor) and Bowie's saxophone, playing variations on the synthesizer melody.

Bowie called Mike Garson, asking if he could do piano overdubs on an afternoon when Bowie was in Los Angeles, with Garson given only three hours to cut his performances on "South Horizon" and "Bleed Like a Craze, Dad." On the former, Garson begins playfully, winking through scales, rumbling away on the bass end of his piano. When the drum machine kicks in, Garson darts through a melody, pounds chords, plays a sweet contrast to a trumpet motif. Devoting as much care to the spaces between notes as to the notes he plays, he closes with a fractured lullaby on his highest keys. On his "Aladdin Sane" solo, Garson sounded like he'd soaked up every speck of music he'd ever heard and could reproduce it at will, like God's player piano. His work here is more concise, conciliatory. Knowing he could play anything, he often keeps silent, or hints at some greater pattern.

THE MYSTERIES

Recorded: ca. August 1993, Mountain. Bowie: keyboards, synthesizers; Kızılçay: guitar, trumpet, piano, keyboards, synthesizers. Produced: Bowie, Kızılçay; engineered: Richards.

First release: 8 November 1993, **The Buddha of Suburbia**.

"Sometimes I felt the whole world was converging on this little room," Hanif Kureishi's narrator says of his Bromley bedroom in *The Buddha of Suburbia*. And Bowie once called his teenage bedroom "my entire world. I had books up there, my music up there, my record player. Going from my world upstairs out onto the street, I had to pass through this no-man's-land of the living room and out the front hall." Calling the suburbs a conformist, soulless place ignores their nourishing side: the freedom they give the imagination. Stuck in a small house with the rumble of their parents' television coming through the wall, a teenager maps escape routes, living in, as Amanda Petrusich wrote, "the heavy emotional sanctity of the suburban bedroom." It's no coincidence so many pop musicians are suburban kids. The suburban misfit welcomes the future; they are nocked like an arrow towards it.

"The Mysteries" is a mind at roam over a bed of synthesizer loops (double-tracked washes of sound, with high whistles and "foghorns" appearing later — a lower-mixed loop sounds like a choir) as the drone of everyday life. As with "South Horizon," Bowie took a tape (possibly a synthesizer track from "Strangers When We Meet," whose verse melody appears in lengthy, broken intervals) and slowed it to "open up the thick texture dramatically," thus allowing Erdal Kızılçay to "play the thematic information against it." The latter included phased and reverse-tracked piano and, after two minutes, acoustic guitar: fraying strings of sound, not expanding on first observations but repeating patterns or starting new ones tentatively. A descending three-note motif becomes, with each repetition, more resonant — its last appearance, late in the track (5:52), rings in triumph.

DEAD AGAINST IT

Recorded: ca. August 1993, Mountain. Bowie: lead and backing vocal, guitar, synthesizer; Kızılçay: guitars, keyboards, synthesizers, bass, drum programming; Richards: drum programming. Produced: Bowie, Kızılçay; engineered: Richards.

*First release: 8 November 1993, **The Buddha of Suburbia**.*

Getting out of the suburbs is only the half of it. Karim's first encounters with London are a series of insecurities — the city "seemed like a house with five thousand rooms, all different." Bowie in the Sixties knew London as a Mod commuter and had to set up in Beckenham to mature as a songwriter. Ziggy Stardust was an exile in suburbia, a city-born hipster who was carrying the news to kids in Sussex.

"Dead Against It," with its whirligig instrumentation (a battery of synthesizers, sequencers, wafer-thin drum machines and, after the first refrain, dueling guitars), its trebly mix and caffeinated tempo is that of the Mod Sixties. It's also a homage to the madcap organists of the New Wave: Steve Nieve, Barry Andrews, Jimmy Destri (one keyboard hook has a taste of Blondie's "Dreaming"). Mod and punk were urban movements; the latter, like disco and hip-hop, a response to Seventies rock and its songs about life on the farm or the highway. Britpop, emerging around the time Bowie cut this track, was another re-engagement with the city: Pulp's Sheffield, Blur's Camden Town, Saint Etienne's "Mario's Cafe," whose patrons buzz on the prospects of London life, where your friends live around the corner and your family's nowhere in sight.

Of the *Buddha of Suburbia* tracks, "Dead Against It" most sounds like its making: Bowie and Erdal Kızılçay camped out in the studio, eating hamburgers and listening to Prince, making odd little tracks. (Bowie would consider remaking it throughout the Nineties, proposing a group improvisation over "Dead Against It" in the early *1. Outside* sessions and slating it as an *Earthling* remake, though the latter wasn't recorded.) Three lengthy instrumental stretches bookend and break up verses and refrains — an arpeggiated synthesizer line is answered by one on guitar. Bowie's larking vocal is full of ascending phrases, sinking only when reality sets in ("begins to sigh," "my words are worn"). His lyric is clotted with internal rhymes and consonance: "I couldn't *cope*/or'*d* h*ope* el*oped*/a *dope* she r*oped*." There's a barb in this spun sugar — he stares at her while she sleeps; she reads to avoid talking to him but talks to strangers on the phone — but it's lost in the blissful waves of guitars that close out the track.

SEX AND THE CHURCH

Recorded: ca. August 1993, Mountain. Bowie: lead and backing vocal, synthesizer, saxophone; Kızılçay: trumpet, organ, keyboards, synthesizers, bass, drum programming; Richards: drum programming. Produced: Bowie, Kızılçay; engineered: Richards.

*First release: 8 November 1993, **The Buddha of Suburbia**.*

An open marriage of Prince's *The Black Album* and Laurie Anderson's early Eighties records, "Sex and the Church" is an overlong experiment with a varisped, vocoder-distorted Bowie vocal. The backing tracks showcase Mountain Studios' 1993 inventory of drum machines and sequencers; Bowie takes a saxophone solo, Erdal Kızılçay plays organ, trumpet, and bass. There's an interplay between Bowie's near-spoken phrases, musing on reconciling the demands of flesh and spirit, and the surging instrumental motifs, like a pulsing organ line, which come down on the side of the flesh. (Bowie once

361

said the underlying thread of *Black Tie White Noise* was to unify passion "and the spiritual font from which it flowed; the wedding thing.") It ends with a rave-up ending a la "Jean Genie" and some moans, like a virtual reality sex program punched up by a Philip K. Dick character.

BLEED LIKE A CRAZE, DAD

Recorded: *ca. August 1993, Mountain; (piano overdub) ca. September 1993, O'Henry. Bowie: lead and backing vocal; Kızılçay: synthesizer, organ; Garson: piano; Rob Clydesdale: guitar; Paul Davidson: bass; Isaac Prevost: drums. Produced: Bowie, Kızılçay; engineered: Richards, Ruggieri.*

First release: *8 November 1993,* **The Buddha of Suburbia**.

The why-not ethos of the *Buddha of Suburbia* sessions led Bowie to use a rock trio cutting an EP at Mountain Studios at the time — 3D Echo, with whom he shared an engineer. The result was "Bleed Like a Craze, Dad," whose lead guitar sounds as if had been commissioned for a carpet emporium ad. The lyric is full of near-homonyms (astral/kestrel, footnote/footstone, parlous/parlors, Shirley/Charley); the title phrase puns on Mod London's favorite gangsters, the Kray Twins (and "friends of the Krays I had known," Bowie wrote). If there's a Kray narrative here, it's them as Bewlay Brothers on the town ("how they drank from the jazz," "seek for a leather journey," "living on a movie"). Mike Garson on piano manages to land anchor in an inhospitable track — opening with what sounds like a Debussy prelude, he dabs his way through the bludgeoning guitars, playing secretive scales.

UNTITLED NO. 1

Recorded: *ca. August 1993, Mountain. Bowie: lead and backing vocal, keyboards, saxophone, guitar; Kızılçay: guitar, keyboards, synthesizers, bass, drum programming; Richards: drum programming. Produced: Bowie, Kızılçay; engineered: Richards.*

First release: *8 November 1993,* **The Buddha of Suburbia**.

Bowie called *The Buddha of Suburbia* one of his favorite albums. He had nothing at stake when he made it. With Erdal Kızılçay as his hands, he recorded whatever came into his head. Some of it was lovely, some of it odd, all of it held together, humbly coherent — his tidiest concept album.

He closed it with a thematic pair. Where "Ian Fish, U.K. Heir" is an ebbing — what's left when the tub's drained — "Untitled No. 1" is the waters rushing in. With a simple chord progression, the latter song is open to anything poured into it. The little melodies that Bowie and Kızılçay keep adding, like spinning plates upon a table; a rising scale figure answered by groaning bass, like sunlight rousing a sleeper; the stately entrance of the synthesizers; the swirling synth figures in the breaks; Bowie's warm, adhesive oooooohs; the guitarist playing a line so entrancing that he won't let go, sounding the last notes again and again; the jangling countermelody to the opening scale motif that becomes a barrelhouse piano line. The saxophone motif at the end of the first verse, soon bestowed on piano and keyboards. The breakdown into a quasi-Indian dance track until a guitar strums things to a close.

It's two verses and a refrain of blur-words, cut to fit the generous spread of music: "Now we're swimming rock [farther/harder] with [the doll/the gull] by our sides." An indecipherable chorus hook: Sleepy Capo? Cynical Fool? Shammi Kapoor? (the first word in particular mutates throughout). A prayer is buried in the second verse. A bleating vocal suggests that Bowie's lovingly parodying his lost friend, Marc Bolan. But it's a tribute that more honors the living, the gracious hours that we have left to us. The most distinctly-phrased words are "it's clear that some things never take" and "never never." "Untitled No. 1" burgeons. There are a few times where Bowie could have stood up and never recorded again: eddies of finality in which everything reconciled for a moment. This is one of them.

IAN FISH, U.K. HEIR

Recorded: *ca. August 1993, Mountain. Bowie, Kızılçay: guitar, keyboards, synthesizers, percussion, loops. Produced: Bowie, Kızılçay; engineered: Richards.*

First release: *8 November 1993, **The Buddha of Suburbia**.*

Bowie's most devoted attempt at creating ambient music was "Ian Fish, U.K. Heir" (anagram of "Hanif Kureishi," one of his successors in Bromley and in Britain). Something ingrained in his compositional habits made him struggle at this. Brian Eno once said of his ambient works that he needed to balance between making and listening to them. "As a maker, you tend to do too much, because you're there with all the tools and you keep putting things in. As a listener, you're happy with quite a lot less." A congenital "maker," Bowie couldn't help but provide scads of sonic information in recognizable patterns, developing textures and melodies in (generally) traditional forms, even in his most would-be radical tracks.

For its canvas, "Ian Fish" takes the "zane, zane, zane" section of "The Buddha of Suburbia," slows it to a crawl and greatly distorts it. There's a slow fade-in of sounds, including the voice of someone who seems to be singing in another apartment. In the right channel, a string loop repeats a croaking phrase. There's static, some white noise: crackles and buzzes that wrap other ghost sounds in a loose blanket. Later, a trickle of piano, quickly stopped up. Deep in the mix, a ceaseless two-note pattern, like the sound of a phone left off the hook.

Yet underlying this random information is a compositional order. The white noise makes a ceiling, the low drone a floor. The layers of reversed vocals are in harmony, as are the synthetic drones in different octaves. There's a "verse" section where an acoustic guitar plays the "Buddha of Suburbia" top melody, slowly and in pieces: a few notes sounded on the high E string, some consonant twangs of lower strings, a lonely arpeggio or two. A finger's slight impositions on strings, the hollow body of the guitar responding. There's even something of a refrain (starting at 2:41), with a fresh, droning keyboard progression and the return of a plucked "harp" motif heard earlier. As the track fades, its background gathers dimension. The voice grows more distinct, hanging on the cusp of being audible. You realize there's been a 4/4 rhythm kept throughout, and just how many instruments have helped to build the track. Some bow before going off stage, like members of a troupe.

STRANGERS WHEN WE MEET

Recorded: *ca. August 1993, Mountain. Bowie: lead and backing vocal, guitar, synthesizer; Kızılçay: guitar, synthesizers, bass, drums; (**1. Outside remake**) ca. summer-autumn 1994, Mountain; West Side Studios; January 1995, The Hit Factory. Bowie: lead and backing vocal; Carlos Alomar: guitar; Gabrels: guitar; Tom Frish: guitar; Garson: piano; Kızılçay or Yossi Fine: bass; Campbell or Joey Baron: drums; Eno: treatments. Produced: (original) Bowie, Kızılçay; (**1. Outside**) Bowie, Eno; engineered: Richards.*

First release: *8 November 1993, **The Buddha of Suburbia**; (remake) 25 September 1995, **1. Outside**. Broadcast: 27 October 1995, The Tonight Show; 9 November 1995, Top of the Pops; 2 December 1995, Later with Jools Holland; 26 January 1996, Taratata. **Live**: 1995-1997.*

One of Bowie's most transient songs, "Strangers When We Meet" appears on two albums, neither of which it suited. On *Buddha of Suburbia*, a fairly minimal incarnation was still ornate enough to make its fellow tracks sound like demos; on *1. Outside*, sequenced as a closer, "Strangers When We Meet" sounded like a bonus track appended to the album after having first appeared in a film. For Bowie's label, at least, "Strangers When We Meet" was the antidote to the darkness of *1. Outside* — it was issued as the album's second single. After performing a vicious "Hearts Filthy Lesson" on Letterman, Bowie's next TV appearance in 1995 was doing "Strangers When We Meet" on Leno, a performance that could have been subtitled "Back to Normal" — Bowie wore business-casual and was cordial.

"Strangers When We Meet" was the thread that tied *Black Tie White Noise* to *Buddha* to *1. Outside*. It was first attempted (and recorded) during the *Black Tie* sessions in New York by Bowie, Reeves Gabrels and the latter's then-current band, Modern Farmer. It's a *Buddha* track in its magpie construction — a bassline lifted from the Spencer Davis Group's "Gimme Some Lovin," for example — and in its aggressive use of cut-up for its lyric: "No trendy rechauffe... humming Rheingold... we trade by vendu... heel head over."

Its emotional charge comes from how it questions and undermines the elated mood of *Black Tie* — it's what had to be buried before the wedding. In 1989, Bowie had come close to marrying the dancer Melissa Hurley, but they split during the Sound + Vision tour. "It didn't work out," Bowie recalled a year later. "It wasn't [a relationship] built on honesty, at least not from my side." On *Tin Machine*, he'd written songs praising her youth and "squareness," but these qualities apparently proved irreconcilable with life as "David Bowie." "I liked the idea of her not being in the music business, but in the end we realized we were worlds apart."

As a title, "Strangers When We Meet" had an adulterous backstory — a Kirk Douglas film about secret lovers who need to part to preserve their marriages. They meet for a last time in the empty house that Douglas, an architect, has built and get mistaken as husband and wife by a stranger. Bowie draws on this, and also on the broken couple of "Heroes" — a pair so consumed by passive-aggressive emotional violence that they no longer recognize each other. In "Heroes," the act of being together is courageous. Here's the other side of it — a relationship that survives out of habit, the cowardice of someone knowing the match won't work but refusing to admit it; it's a union never to be blessed by a wedding. The TV's a blank screen, as is the window ("splendid sunrise, but it's a dying world"). The man weeps in bed, cringes when she tries to embrace him. By the final refrain, he welcomes this state: if they're strangers again, they could fall in love again.

A standard progression in A major, its verses banked to sweep in the dominant chord, E major ("secrets") after a tense stop on a B 11th ("thin and frail"); the refrains reverse course, going from E major back home to the tonic chord. The *Buddha* version is tense, more compact, nervier; the *1. Outside* take is full of new characters: a ruminative Mike Garson; Reeves Gabrels, who discards the hook in the original's verses for subtler lines (he also adds an Adrian Belew "elephant roar" in the intro). (Gabrels once said he thought its best performances were on the *Earthling* tour: "for some reason that song and its lyrics (blank screen tv...) had a lot of resonance on the road.") On *Buddha*, Bowie had kept pace with the song, worked as its motivator. On *1. Outside*, he resists the flow of his melody. His emphases land on unexpected beats, he lets the last word of the title phrase trail off — fixating on "when." In the closing refrain, accompanied by a ghostly harmony vocal, he makes his last lines hard-fought delusions, but doesn't absolve himself of his role in the mess.

CHAPTER NINE:

IN THE REALMS OF THE UNREAL

(1994-1995)

Effect before everything.
— Philip Johnson

It's all just paint, right?
— Nile Rodgers, on making recordings

There is a constant appeal to sense, but it remains unfulfilled, because the pieces keep moving and shifting and when "sense" appears it is transitory. Therefore, what is important is not to discover the truth at the end of the investigation, but the process itself.
— Alain Robbe-Grillet

Even his fakes were on a Titanic scale.
— Micheál Mac Liammóir, on Orson Welles

LEON
NOTHING TO BE DESIRED
LEON TAKES US OUTSIDE
SEGUE: NATHAN ADLER
SEGUE: RAMONA A. STONE/I AM WITH NAME
SEGUE: BABY GRACE (A HORRID CASSETTE)
SEGUE: ALGERIA TOUCHSHRIEK

(Bowie, Eno, Gabrels, Garson, Kızılçay, Campbell.) **Recorded**: *ca. 1 March-summer 1994, Mountain Studios, Montreux; West Side Studios, London; (Eno "Segue" overdubs, treatments) late 1994, 4-6 January 1995, Brondesbury Villas, Kilburn; (last overdubs) January 1995, The Hit Factory, New York. David Bowie: lead and backing vocals, Korg, Ensoniq; Brian Eno: Yamaha DX7, Eventide H3000, Lexicon JamMan, E-Mu Procussion, Korg A3, transistor radio; Reeves Gabrels: guitar; Carlos Alomar: guitar (overdubs); Mike Garson: piano, keyboards; Erdal Kızılçay: bass; Yossi Fine: bass (overdubs); Sterling Campbell: drums, percussion; Joey Baron: drums (overdubs), Bryony, Josey, Ruby and Lola Edwards: backing vocals (overdubs). Produced: Bowie, Eno; engineered: David Richards.*

First release: ("Nothing to Be Desired") 11 September 1995, "The Hearts Filthy Lesson" (Virgin 7243 8 38518 2 9); ("Segue: Ramona," "Segue: Adler," "Segue: Baby Grace," "Segue: Touchshriek," "Leon Takes Us Outside") 25 September 1995, **1. Outside** *(BMG/Arista 74321303392 /Virgin 7243 8 40711 2 7, UK #8, US #21.)*

David Bowie's wedding in Florence was the first time he'd seen Brian Eno in years. At the reception, they talked about work. Bowie commandeered the DJ's system to play some current demos, pieces with "distressed instruments." Eno was intrigued. Bowie seemed awoken from a long slumber. They agreed, tentatively, to collaborate. "We were suddenly on the same course again," Bowie later said.

Eno had spent the Eighties making ambient instrumental albums, brewing perfumes, mulling ideas like "quiet clubs" and "research gardening," doing a Tropical Rainforest Sound Installation for the World Financial Center, and being half of the production team that delivered U2's *The Unforgettable Fire* and *The Joshua Tree*. In September 1989, he told an interviewer "I'm sure I could, if someone held a gun to my head, crank out a record of songs, but at this point in time I know it wouldn't be any good, because there's no conviction to carry it forward." Nine months later, he was quarrelsomely working on a record of pop songs with John Cale, *Wrong Way Up*. Other "song" albums would follow.

And Bowie, in jigs and jags, had tried to experiment: with Tin Machine, on *Black Tie White Noise* and, particularly, *The Buddha of Suburbia*, which Eno considered strong work. Talking to Dylan Jones in 1994, Bowie said he wanted to "stop mucking about" and write for himself instead of an audience. (Axl Rose recalled Bowie saying "one side of me is experimental and the other side of me wants to make something that people can get into and I don't know fucking why! Why am I like this?") Pairing with Eno would strengthen his resolve. "I think my big contribution was in encouraging [Bowie] not to retreat from his extreme positions," as Eno said of the *Low* period.

In the year after Bowie's wedding, Eno was his usual beehive, releasing, producing and co-producing over a half-dozen albums, along with lectures, exhibits, and a daughter. He and Bowie would talk on the phone and mail or fax each other "mini-manifestos... so that at least when we went in [to the studio] we'd have a set of concepts that would enable us to avoid all the things we find boring and bland in popular music," Bowie said. In late 1993, Reeves Gabrels became their translator. On tour with Paul Rodgers, Gabrels would return to his hotel after playing "Feel Like Makin' Love" on stage to find faxes from Bowie and Eno asking, for example, how songs in 11/8 and 4/4 playing simultaneously could align on the same note.

They knew what they didn't want to do: the fourth "Berlin" album. "We don't want to make another record of a bunch of songs," Eno said. "There's got to be a bigger landscape in play than that." They had a scatter of ideas — a musical; pieces for the La La La Human Steps dance troupe; a "heavy" CD-ROM. "Brian and I are developing something from which the user will genuinely feel he has had a full participation creatively," Bowie said of the latter.

Each released a CD-ROM in 1994 — Bowie had *Jump*, where one could isolate tracks from *Black Tie White Noise* and watch blurry videos; Eno had *Headcandy*, advertised as a "mind-altering experience without the drugs," in which users donned "prismatic glasses" to see 3-D images shifting to an Eno soundtrack. Eno soon wrote off CD-ROMs as "a typically disastrous new media adventure," but he liked the idea of an overstuffed, incomplete album for which listeners controlled the narrative, "releasing something which says 'here's a whole lot of things. You sort it out'." CDs had already killed LP listening habits — now you jumped around a disc or programmed it to play only your favorite songs. On his *Nerve Net*, Eno had two mixes of the same track, figuring listeners would skip the one they liked less.

"Make the medium fail. Do something that sounds like it's bigger than something that can be fitted onto a CD," Eno said. He expected musicians to release unfinished tracks, "something evolving on the cusp between 'music,' 'game' and 'demonstration,'"; the musical equivalent to *SimEarth*. The artist would provide backdrops; the listener would be the player. Hence all the raw scenario ground up into Bowie and Eno's *1. Outside*, an album that seems like an interactive text videogame gone awry, leaving players stranded in its matrix. "I like things that tend to be endless puzzles," Bowie said while promoting it in 1995.

Fodder

For their first recording session, "we would come in armed with fodder," Bowie said. His inputs came from a recent immersion in the art establishment. He'd become an avid collector (favoring British painters like David Bomberg) and was on the board of *Modern Painters*, where he scored a coup by interviewing his Swiss neighbor Balthus. He was taking his own painting more seriously. Soon he'd collaborate with Damien Hirst and would have his first solo exhibition at The Gallery on Cork Street, London ("New Afro/ Pagan and Work, 1975-1995"). "I don't think it's enough anymore to make a record," he said while making *1. Outside*. "It's a visual society now." He'd taken to heart what Malcolm McLaren said in 1989: "Only the visual artists know what's going on. Musicians always have to be catching up."

From the art world, Bowie took a few shiny bits, "components that were bitten off from the periphery of the mainstream." The work of Viennese Actionist Rudolf Schwarzkogler, wrongly believed to have castrated himself in performance (he did fall out of a window to his death), and to whose *Aktions* Bowie paid homage by being photographed similarly: swathed in bandages, with dead fish taped to his torso. Hermann Nitsch, who performed blood rituals using animal carcasses; Chris Burden, whose gallery works included being shot (see "Joe the Lion"); Ron Athey, for whose "scarifications" he and his collaborators had their skin penetrated, with the tissues that sopped up the blood hung like tiny flags. Bowie thought Athey's work was becoming domesticated, given the popularity of piercing and tattooing, which suggested to him a growing paganism and tribalism among the young.

This flowed into a broader channel: Bowie's idea that the West would binge and purge before the millennium. The peaceful, prosperous late-twentieth-century West liked blood and fear in its entertainments: serial killer movies and TV shows; paranoia soaked into everything from *JFK* to *The X-Files*; Hirst's shark and sheep cadavers; the influence of the late fashion photographer Guy Bourdin, a developer of the heroin-chic waif look, who had posed his models like corpses. "Art murder," one narrative concept of *1. Outside,* was the natural next step, after "conceptual muggings" ("Murder may be art. If you get away with it," Bowie said in 1995. "Like, perhaps, O.J. Simpson.") A favorite novel of his at the time, Peter Ackroyd's *Hawksmoor*, has an architect consecrating his churches with killings.

Eno regarded Bowie's obsessions with blood and ritual with bemused tolerance. He was more interested in game strategies, creating scenarios to keep artists fresh ("role playing is essential in Brian's life, it seems," Bowie said. "I don't know how much he takes it into his private life.") For Bowie's recording session, Eno scripted characters for musicians and engineers to play, with his usual caveat for no one to reveal their instructions. These were in the vein of science-fiction pieces he'd recently written for the *Whole Earth Review*. Bowie was a griot, a town crier figure ("it was my job to pass on all the events of the day... in a society where the informational networks have broken down"); Gabrels was in the house band on the third moon of Jupiter (his recollection) or in an underground club "in the Afro-Chinese ghetto in Osaka" (Eno's); drummer Sterling Campbell was, variously, a disgruntled member of a South African rock band or playing on a moon satellite; Mike Garson was a morale booster for a "small ragtag terrorist operation" (or "just be Mike Garson"); bassist Erdal Kızılçay had to play Arabic funk to win over the father of a woman he wanted to marry ("I don't need a letter to play Oriental stuff," Kızılçay later sniped to Paul Trynka).

Kızılçay more played the role of Carlos Alomar on *Lodger* — a longtime Bowie collaborator frustrated by the art school hijinks of Eno, of whom Kızılçay once said "cannot even play four bars...cannot play two harmonies together." It was the last time Kızılçay played with Bowie. He later wondered why Bowie, after a decade, turned cold and stopped using him. Bowie said he'd hand-picked musicians he thought "wouldn't find themselves in an inhibiting or embarrassing position when asked to do things which musicians maybe aren't generally comfortable with... I needed adventurers, seamen, fellow pirates." Gabrels, Garson, and Campbell were game; Kızılçay apparently not so much, though his dismissal was more part of an overall Bowie purge of his Switzerland period — he would also never again work with David Richards, nor record again at Mountain Studios.

Annunciation

Recording began at the start of March 1994 at Mountain. Gabrels came a week earlier to reconnect with Bowie, whom he hadn't seen since the *Black Tie* sessions. While they did some composing and tracking ("Thru' These Architects Eyes" and "The Voyeur of Utter Destruction (As Beauty)" were begun at this time), Bowie more wanted to talk. He'd wade into his album. On the first day, an overall-clad Bowie greeted everyone with tools — paintbrushes, wallpaper hangers, canvases. Before playing, they would redecorate the studio. Each musician got a corner of their own. Bowie made an atelier, painting and sketching for days before he sang a note.

It was a variation on what Eno had done the previous summer with the Mancunian band James. During the day, they made a "structured" pop album, *Laid*. At night, in a second studio with dim lighting, they made what Eno called a "shadow album," *Wah Wah*, going through lengthy improvisations. At Mountain, Eno and Bowie would create another shadow album, one without a counterpart. While Kızılçay recalled hearing demos ("really terrible... the demos just didn't work because they weren't any good"), the impetus was on unstructured jamming, the musicians punching in around 10am, breaking for lunch, jamming through the afternoon; five days a week, for weeks. As with *Wah Wah*, hour-long tape reels captured everything. Eno used "strategies designed to stop the thing from becoming over-coherent" or, worse, becoming blues jams. His "fodder" included an "archive of strange sounds," Bowie recalled. Eno employed it whenever he heard a conventional jam, piping into everyone's headphones loops of clock chimes, French radio broadcasts, samples from Motown tapes. So Sterling Campbell could lock into a French weather report loop, alter his drum pattern and shift the direction of the improvisation. Eno's directions were often George Lucas-esque: "continue, continue."

In a 3 March 1994 journal entry, Bowie wrote how happy he was that the music the band was playing had no connection to his past works, though he planned to introduce "Dead Against It" the following day to see if it could be "transformed." The peak moment came a week later, on 12 March 1994 (or, as Bowie recalled in another interview, 20 March 1994). Standing before a table covered with pages he'd ripped from books and magazines, and sheets of computer-generated "cut-up" lines, Bowie started riffing. During this "blindingly orgiastic" session, he made a setting — Oxford Town, New Jersey, a suburban take on his Hunger City via *Twin Peaks*. "Placing the eerie environment of the *Diamond Dogs* city now in the Nineties gives it an entirely different spin," he said. Then he sketched people who lived there: "a guy called [Nathan] Adler and this other guy called Leon and this very scary woman named Ramona [A. Stone] and there was some kind of murder thing that happened, and it had to do with the art world."

Gestation/Abduction

Anywhere from twenty-five to thirty-five hours of material came from the sessions: what remained after Bowie and Eno sliced up the daily reel-to-reels and kept what they liked. What followed was a nearly year-long revision. Gabrels went to Switzerland several times in 1994, working on new songs, developing pieces pulled from the improvisations. Eno was doing the same at his studio in Kilburn, and in late spring-early summer 1994 there were further sessions and initial mixing at West Side Studios in London (drummer Neil Conti was called in, but apparently not for any released take).

The rough edits were of an "improvised opera" provisionally called *Leon*. What we can hear of this piece today are three bootlegged "suites," each between twenty-two and twenty-seven minutes long, that were pared from a three-hour work. Gabrels said this bootleg comes from someone nabbing initial mixes from West Side in summer 1994 and later chopping them up into "suites." So the *Leon* bootlegs are not unreleased edits by anyone involved in the recording, but the work of a bootlegger imposing their aesthetic ideas upon those of Bowie and Eno. This bootlegging also lessened Bowie's interest in developing *Leon* further.

So now we have another, unknown author imposing themselves

into an already-confusing story. It's a bit fitting, given the nature of the project. Let's start with the section of *Leon* that the bootlegger titled "I Am with Name." What exists of it on *1. Outside* is its intro, some of which was reworked as "Segue: Ramona A. Stone/I Am with Name" (with a new mix — the drums are jacked up on *1. Outside*), and the first "Segue: Nathan Adler," the latter having a different vocal and backing tracks possibly recorded as late as the sessions in New York in January 1995. The soundscape of *Leon* often has Kızılçay and Campbell as support poles (sounding looped at times) while Gabrels and Garson swirl around them — Gabrels ripping chords, Garson with fills and reaction shots. Bursts of applause and crowd noises are heard throughout — loops triggered in the studio when someone liked where a jam was going.

Keeping to instructions of being a reciting storyteller, Bowie cycles through words, shuffling them: *laugh hotel, fishy, good-time drone, slug-male (slug-mail), an OK riot, I wanna be chrome, small friends, Oxford Town, heart-skin, anxiety descending*. He has a taste for jargon from computer magazines. "She was a router and a swapper," Adler says of Ramona A. Stone. "A fuckin' update demon" (Demon was one of Britain's first internet service providers). Algeria Touchshriek is "a domain name server." Later come "packet sniffers" (a term for tools to diagnose network bottlenecks).

More voices appear than on *1. Outside*. There's a character who, four minutes into the suite, sounds as if rats are climbing over his body: *I won't eat me it will hide me he should take them I won't tell it she can't take them it won't do this he said tell it he said strongest he should do this he should be there!!* After Adler and Ramona A. Stone's sections (see below), a more melodic piece marks the suite's halfway point: "We'll Creep Together," sung languidly over Garson's piano and gunshot noises. Later, a parody of the Doors' "The End" ("this is the Chrome, my friends") and the march of the "Leek Soldiers," with Bowie flogging a new dance: "twist *fly boy*! Back front heaven erect! *Twist hardware*, fleece the ziplock *twist hardware*!" Things disintegrate: more chanting; Bowie does a ventriloquist act; Garson sounds like he's following a possessed metronome.

Editorial Apparatus

What the bootlegger packaged as *Leon*'s "The Enemy Is Fragile" suite has for its centerpiece a tremendous title section — a stretch of art funk with a slamming bassline and drum pattern, whirring percussion, and a corral of Bowie voices. The suite opens with a character who didn't make the cut for *1. Outside* — a "dramatic" narrator enunciating each word as if going for an elocution prize. Backdrops include murmuring goblin voices, train noises, accordion, spasms on Garson's piano, and Gabrels' "Spanish" guitar soloing. After appearances by Nathan Adler, reminiscing about "a dame called Ivy, who drove around in a hearse," and Ramona A. Stone ("I think we're stuck in a web... a sort of nerve-net... we might be here for a long time"), the narrator returns to tout a CD-ROM, floridly rolling his "r"s. For this compilation of Wolof music, "the editors have done an excellent job... the editorial apparatus of this CD-ROM leaves nothing to be desired."

A bassline has been snaking beneath him. Now he gives over to it, his last four words becoming a mantra. ***Nothing** to be **desired***. He's joined by a chorus whose ranks include "Laughing Gnome" voices, and they shift to another chant — *mind changing change your **mind** changing **mind** changing*. Ad copy as religious invocation. The chants build, driven by pounded piano chords, Bowie bracing himself ("stand by! stand by!") until the tension breaks with a drum fill.

This segment (6:35-7:35 of the "Enemy Is Fragile" suite) was the only officially-released music from *Leon,* apart from the intro and character segues on *1. Outside.* Titled "Nothing to Be Desired," it was a bonus track on the "Hearts Filthy Lesson" CD single. For its release, the *Leon* extract was prefaced by a minute of heavily-mixed drums, a new bassline and guitar dubs that persisted through the vocal section. Barely remembered in the twenty-five years since, "Nothing to Be Desired" is a strange orphan, dressed up and cast out into the world with no letters of introduction.

The Art Murderer: Leon

The final bootlegged *Leon* suite was named "Leon Takes Us Outside." All that's been released from it are its intro, which became *1. Outside*'s opening track, and a tantalizing glimpse of Bowie and Eno recording "We'll Creep

Together," a middle section, in the album's electronic press kit. The full piece is a series of jumps through questionable links, broken dialogues, perhaps all the dream of Leon Blank: artist, outsider, suspect, possible killer or martyr.

Bowie described Leon, the mysterious central character of the "opera" improvisation, as a twenty-two-year old of mixed race, with a rap sheet ("plagiarism without a license"). A Nathan Adler segue has Leon jumping on stage at midnight and cutting "zeroes" in objects with a machete, ripping a hole in "the fabric of time itself." Visually (Bowie used the image of a young black man (with his own features) to represent Leon in the *1. Outside* CD booklet: it was obviously based on a photo of the musician Tricky), Leon was his homage to two contemporary artists — Tricky, and the late painter Jean-Michel Basquiat. Some Tricky effects appear on *Leon* — ambient noise, particularly the sound of rain, and in the intro Bowie even attempted Tricky's murmuring flow. In 1995, *Q* magazine asked Bowie to interview Tricky, hoping for a "Paul Weller Meets Noel Gallagher" type feature. Bowie instead turned in a batshit fictional piece in which he cast Tricky as Leon Blank and himself as Adler. They climb a building, chatting about "the War" and the "haunting Nineties," until Tricky, out of malice or mercy, kicks him and Bowie falls to his death.

The "Leon Takes Us Outside" suite begins as *1. Outside* does — Bowie murmurs dates and holidays over surf guitar and twinkling piano. A melody develops on synthesizer; guitar and piano form ranks, jabbing against it. It's a stream of data, both American and British (Michaelmas and Martin Luther King Day; July 6th and "5th March"), as though reciting a sequence of information that will wake up a program. (Its similarity to the buzz-and-murmur opening of U2's (Eno co-produced) *Zooropa* is likely no coincidence.) The suite moves outward: a section where Bowie chirps "choir! choir!" over loops of congas; a cut to Bowie singing, in plaintive voice, "the first time... that I saw the boil... put it on the neck"; a babbling Nathan Adler monologue ("as sure as you can see the nose on my face or the greys on my arm... or the foot on my ankle or the car in my garage"); an arrival in Oxford Town ("moving on the sidewalk, faces on the ground").

A lengthy central sequence has Bowie in his Adler voice. Over an "on the four" drum pattern, Gabrels plays arpeggios, Garson adds a few asides. After some ranting, Adler settles into his story. "It was the night of an *OK riot*," he recalls. Ramona Stone was there, "with her wavy hair, and her research grants." It builds in intensity, Adler consumed with Ramona, howling her down. *"I'd rather be chrome*! Beauty is A. Stone!"

Scene change. Bowie now in patrician English voice, close to a Margaret Thatcher impression. A man on a balcony, watching the Leek Soldiers marching before him; a British Quisling or Pétain. He's a remnant of some fallen order (like Adler's, it's another dead twentieth-century voice, a decayed hauteur associated with Merchant-Ivory films and Noël Coward records). *"Friends* of the *trust!"* (applause loop) "You've been a *breath-filled* crowd tonight... you've been positively... *fly boys."* (applause) "As far as I'm concerned, you are all *number one packet sniffers*!" He begins a lullaby. *"We'll creep together...* you and I. Under a *bloodless* chrome sky." From there, it's a slow retreat until the fade. Adler bows out, saying "it would end in chrome... but wait, I'm getting ahead of myself." Gabrels plays a three-note figure that he alternates with descending scales; a synthesizer melody sounds like bottled Vivaldi. The suite closes with feedback and a judicial drum fill.

The Diary

Leon began its reinvention as *1. Outside* towards the end of 1994, when *Q* asked Bowie to contribute to their one-hundredth issue by keeping a diary for ten days. Recording at Mountain at the time, he figured a true day-to-day account would be "incredibly boring." He wondered what his private detective character would write instead. This became the "Diary of Nathan Addler, Or the Art-Ritual Murder of Baby Grace Belew" which, with slight revisions (such as Adler and Baby Grace's last names), would be the CD booklet of *1. Outside*.

After the *Leon* improvisations, "David...after becoming aware of what the lyric content implied, looked into it further and revised and rewrote," Gabrels said in 2000. "The order and plot were imposed/invented by David after the fact." *Q*'s deadline got things into a semblance of order. On *Leon*, characters are voices, moving in and out of focus. Now, like a game of *Clue* (or *Cluedo*, depending on your country), five were given distinct looks and possible motives. "They're all based on me," Bowie said. The Nathan Adler Diary "was a great skeleton to put the texture on... the story is the skeleton and flesh and blood on the feeling of what it's like to be around in 1995."

Pay the Private Eye: Nathan Adler

Speaking in an Englishman's attempt at a hard-boiled gumshoe's voice, Nathan Adler is the alleged protagonist of *1. Outside*. His direct ancestors were Phillip Jeffries, the FBI agent Bowie played in *Twin Peaks: Fire Walk with Me*, and Jack Grimaldi, played by Gary Oldman in the 1993 film *Romeo is Bleeding* — a corrupt cop in a sexually obsessive relationship with a psychotic Russian mob assassin.

A private eye is the walking means to advance a detective story. He doesn't know anything, so he asks questions, pokes around, stumbles upon bodies and secrets; he shades in the plot. Nothing like this happens with Adler. The more he talks, the more confusion there is. (His name was originally "Addler," after all.) He's not even trying to solve a murder, only determine if it qualifies as art, perhaps for tax purposes. He's also a commercial artist — based out of Mark Rothko's old apartment, with some previous investigation reports displayed at the Tate. A citizen of narrative in a postmodern world, Adler "looks back rather nostalgically to a time when there was a seeming order in things," Bowie said. "He's really rather despondent that things are broken into this fragmented chaotic kind of state."

On *Leon*, Adler is more of a presence — he's heard in all three suites, a rambling, opaque narrator whose voice is often mixed under guitar and piano tracks. The "official" Adler, as heard in his *1. Outside* suites and as read in the Diary, is more terse. He even swings a bit: for his first *1. Outside* segue, he talks over a minute-long funk piece that's hooked to what sounds like Carlos Alomar's rhythm guitar.

Wavy Hair and Research Grants: Ramona A. Stone

Ramona A. Stone is the apparent villain of the piece. She first appears in Adler's diary in "Kreutzburg (sic), Berlin," June 1977, running a Caucasian Suicide Temple, "vomiting out her doctrine of death-as-eternal-party into the empty vessels of Berlin youth." She's a punk rock "no-future priestess" (the Sex Pistols were in West Berlin a few months earlier in 1977) who helps a score of Berliners kill themselves. At century's end she's in London, Canada, running a "string of body-parts jewelry stores." She's a cyborg, a "good time drone" who says, "in the future, everything was up to itself."

She's also every accusation levied against Bowie in one cyborg body —
vampire artist, control freak (see Angela Bowie's typically barbed comment
to Peter R-Koenig: "David wants to be a dictator, not God. His fixation is
with himself and he strives to ignore his own self-loathing"), futurist fascist,
a vain high priestess ("I was an *artiste*! in a *tunnel*"), someone so disgusted
by aging ("a MIDI-life crisis") that she dreams of becoming a machine. To
play Ramona for the CD booklet, Bowie put his face upon a She-Hulk figure
sporting a Mohawk; for her voice, he multiply-tracked himself, altering each
vocal with harmonizing synthesizers, including Eno's Eventide H3000. It
was a premonition of Andy Serkis' "Gollum" voice. On *1. Outside*, the only
things left untreated on "I Am with Name" are Garson's gusts of piano — a
last bit of old humanity left in the mix.

The Victim, Fourteen Years of Age: Baby Grace Blue

Every mystery needs a corpse. On *1. Outside,* it's Baby Grace Blue (renamed
from "Belew" in Bowie's original Adler diary for *Q*), whose eviscerated and
dismembered body is found at the Museum of Modern Parts, in Oxford
Town, New Jersey. It's described in loving detail in the first section of the
Nathan Adler diary, while the first character "segue" on *1. Outside* is Grace's:
her last words, discovered on a "horrid cassette."

On the bootlegged *Leon* edit "The Enemy Is Fragile," Grace's testimony
runs from 8:11 to 11:00 ("the first monologue...was 15 minutes long and
was very *Twin Peaks*," Bowie said) — the *1. Outside* version is shorter, cutting
some SF jargon ("I've got this soul-brain patch... I got the shakers on it
with this neurotransmitter") and having a rerecorded vocal. On *Leon*, Bowie
tries to imitate a teenage girl's voice in an altered tone — it's close to his
phrasing on "When I'm Five"; on the *1. Outside* segue, he's sped up to near-
Chipmunk pitch. What remains is Grace's gauzy recollection of being given
"interest drugs" and being allowed to listen to "popular musics," but now
"they just want me to be quiet... I think something is going to be horrid."

"It's Baby Grace's voice that touches me most. Perhaps because I based her
story on a girl I know very well and who's been through a whole bunch of
bad relationships in which she was abused," Bowie said in 1995. "It seemed
like she really picked that kind of man each time." There was a tangle of
other references: Laura Palmer, the dead girl at the heart of *Twin Peaks*,

and as Nicholas Pegg noted, the Moors killers, who taped the ten-year-old Lesley Ann Downey pleading for her life. The "horrid cassette" was also now a horror trope. With tape recorders and video cameras widely available, horror films used videotaped killings (see *Henry: Portrait of a Serial Killer*) and "found" video/audio footage to heighten realism, culminating in *The Blair Witch Project*, which bored Bowie after fifteen minutes.

Promoting *1. Outside*, Bowie retconned Grace's death — now she symbolized the twentieth century, her ritual murder needed for the next century to begin. It was the century turned backwards, killed in its helpless old youth.

Harmless, Lonely: Algeria Touchshriek

The last character segue on *1. Outside* is for Algeria Touchshriek, a refugee from Bowie's Sixties songs: the confirmed bachelors and elderly shoplifters, Uncle Arthur and the Little Bombardier, the Austrian shopkeeper and the sad scholar of "Conversation Piece." Bowie also spun Touchshriek from Charrington, a junk shop owner in Orwell's *Nineteen Eighty-Four*, a man who leads a "ghostlike existence," who rents a room to Winston Smith, and who turns out to be in the Thought Police, baiting the trap that lands Smith in Room 101.

Touchshriek is a seventy-eight-year-old shopkeeper who "deals in art drugs and DNA prints [and a] fence for all apparitions of any medium." He's described as "harmless, lonely." Lonely, yes. Harmless? In a *Leon* sequence, he mentions walking near the Museum of Modern Parts, where Grace's body was displayed. He might rent the room above his shop to a fugitive, Wolof Bomberg (a mix of Bowie's "griot" character and a favorite painter, David Bomberg). Perhaps Grace was once kept there. He says that he "knew Leon once." His segue, an edited/revised version of the segue in the "Enemy Is Fragile" suite (its last substantive section), opens with Edward Lear and James Joyce-style wordplay. Bowie builds Touchshriek's empty cupboard of a world in a handful of lines. In the *Leon* "Enemy Is Fragile" suite, Touchshriek speaks over piano glissandi and guitar arpeggios; on his *1. Outside* segue, guitar and piano whisper underneath, as if debating whether to believe him.

Twentieth Century Dies

Given its incomplete state, it's impossible to predict how *Leon* would have been received if some form of it had appeared in 1995, a three-CD set to rival Prince's *Crystal Ball*. It likely would have gained a cult following and, given how most Bowie albums were received by critics in the Nineties, it likely would have been ridiculed. But in 1994, for the third time in as many years, he was without a record deal, and as with *Tin Machine II*, he had tapes that few labels would salivate over. "Nobody would take *Outside* when we first recorded it," he recalled a few years later. "It was held back for a year until we could find somebody to distribute it in America." By early 1995, he was making more conventional songs for a more conventional album. Gabrels and Eno had pushed for some version of *Leon* to come out: a two- or three-CD set, issued without name or hype. "It would have been a very serious musical statement (and maybe pissed off more people than Tin Machine)," Gabrels wrote on his website years later.

The slow tempos and strange asides in *Leon*, their murky flow and formlessness, convey in music what the internet in 1994 felt like. You click through obscure, barely-readable sites (recall the plague of green script on black backgrounds), stalling out, landing in places you didn't expect. It's a stream of continuous juxtaposition. All the distorted and cartooned versions of Bowie's voice were akin to his love of Photoshop. Creating a character once needed makeup artists, costumers, hairdressers and photographers. Now he could do it in ten minutes, sitting at his desktop.

Leon is Bowie doing comic and horrific voices over a backdrop of semi-improvised art rock. It's one of the most "Seventies" things he ever did, suggesting he (or maybe Garson) drew on prog-rock instrumental albums like Roger Powell's *Cosmic Furnace* for a backdrop. Yet it's fascinating — truly odd, and truly different from anything he'd recorded before. Had *Leon* been released as a CD-ROM, listeners could have remixed the suites, bringing up the guitars and machine-gun noises, fading down Ramona Stone.

Once *Leon* was reincarnated as *1. Outside*, it was meant to sound like 1995, Bowie said — a year pressed onto disc, like flower petals crushed in a book. He and Eno would release a new album each year until the millennium, and so chronicle the dying century in a "contextual diary" and continue the un-storyline of *1. Outside*. Bowie said he'd use his computer to find out who killed Baby Grace, wrapping up the "plot" early on so he could move on to more interesting things. "One foresees at the end you may well have twenty to twenty-five different characters flying around," he said. "It'll be the *Nicholas Nickelby* of rock by the time it's finished." It would culminate in a performance in 1999 or 2000, held at the Salzburg Festival, directed by Robert Wilson, and starring Bowie as Adler. It would be "like Grand Guignol" and would be possibly eight hours long. "Pack a sandwich!"

A SMALL PLOT OF LAND

(Bowie, Eno, Gabrels, Kızılçay, Garson, Campbell.) **Recorded***: (backing tracks) ca. 1 March-April 1994, Mountain; (overdubs) May-December 1994, Mountain, West Side, Brondesbury Villas. Bowie: lead and backing vocal; Eno: Yamaha DX7, Eventide H3000, JamMan, E-Mu Procussion, Korg A3; Garson: piano; Gabrels: guitar; Kızılçay: bass; Campbell: drums. Produced: Bowie, Eno; engineered: Richards.*

First release*: 25 September 1995,* **1. Outside***.* **Live***: 1995-1996.*

Along with character segues, a few songs on *1. Outside* were quarried from the *Leon* improvisations. "A Small Plot of Land" opens with Mike Garson on piano, parrying against a drum pattern — steady fours on the kick; rockslide fills on snare; hi-hat insistence. Reeves Gabrels nags at a pair of notes. The bass is a specter, turning up in corners of the song, as if not caring for the atmosphere.

About seventy percent of Bowie's lyric (his estimate) came from his computer-generated cut-up program, the "Verbasizer," likely the mother of lines like "he pushed at the pigmen." The title was either from the French philosophers Deleuze and Guattari's *A Thousand Plateaus* ("try out continuums of intensities segment by segment, have a small plot of new land at all times") or the pop standard "Thou Swell" ("give me just a plot of, not a lot of land"), or both.

The backdrop slowly expands as if lights are being turned on, one by one, in a house — synthesizers emerge as a faction; eventually, there's a murmuring sea of backing vocals. Bowie plays against it, singing at times in a different key from the arrangement, building and falling, running variations (with some "Nite Flights" in it: "swings through the tunnels").

He sets a funereal pace with two-note phrases (*"poor* soul," *"prayer* can't," *"brains* talk"), holding the first while letting the second quickly expire (this culminates in the three-bar endurance of *"poooooor,"* followed by a soft "dunce"). But he never holds to this pattern for long, as he'll extend lines or raise closing notes in pitch ("inn-o-cent *eyes"*). Gabrels' solo has him digging in, while Garson rumbles along the bass end of his piano. Bowie picks his way through the debris in the closing minutes.

In autumn 1994, Eno made a mix of "A Small Plot of Land," setting Bowie's voice over "long, drifting overlays" of synthesizers, like battalions of machines humming. Another stripped-down mix appeared on the *Basquiat* soundtrack: the build to the final *"poor* soul" was now a humbly-sung, double-tracked closing phrase — the churchyard instead of the cathedral. Julian Schnabel, *Basquiat's* director, thought it superior to the *1. Outside* version. At a performance in New York in September 1995, accompanied only by Garson, Bowie followed this course, lessening his severity — a gorgeously-sung *"poor* dunce" swept into a Garson solo that churned up "Rhapsody in Blue."

During the *Outside* tour, Bowie often put "A Small Plot of Land" dead-middle in sets, prefaced by a Beckettian monologue about the poor dunce: "he wasted all his life, he was dumb, he deserved to die and now he's dead!" He'd sing with his back to the audience or pace in a circle. During Gabrels' solo, Bowie walked across the stage pulling on cords, tugging down banners. Some reviewers thought this symbolized his alienation from the audience, but it was more something for him to do during the solo, and to set the stage for the following number. "Functional theatricality," as Gabrels called it.

THE HEARTS FILTHY LESSON

(Bowie, Eno, Gabrels, Garson, Kızılçay, Campbell.) **Recorded**: *(backing tracks) ca. 1 March-April 1994, Mountain; (overdubs) May-December 1994, Mountain, Brondesbury Villas, West Side. Bowie: lead and backing vocal, Korg, Ensoniq; Eno: Yamaha DX7, Eventide H3000, JamMan, E-Mu Procussion, Korg A3; Gabrels: lead guitar; Garson: piano, keyboards; Kızılçay: bass; Campbell: drums, percussion; Bryony, Josey, Ruby, Lola Edwards: backing vocals. Produced: Bowie, Eno; engineered: Richards.*

First release: 11 September 1995 (RCA/BMG 74321 30703 2, UK #35, US #92). *Broadcast*: 25 September 1995, Late Show with David Letterman. *Live*: 1995-1997.

Another outgrowth from the *Leon* sessions in March 1994, "The Hearts Filthy Lesson" was released as *1. Outside*'s lead-off single. Its Samuel Bayer-directed video had minotaurs, Pinhead piercings and a goth-punk Last Supper, but its essential performance was on the *Late Show with David Letterman*, the day before *1. Outside*'s release in the US. Clad in black leather and wearing eyeliner and black nail polish, Bowie had a hostile, jittery vibe. He acted as if the audience wasn't there, that he was singing to a mirror, then acknowledged the camera with leers and cryptic smiles. Mike Garson played a solo like a Teppanyaki chef; Gail Ann Dorsey was cool charisma.

Officially the perspective of Nathan Adler, its lyric was "made up of juxtapositions and fragments of information. [It] doesn't have a straightforward coherent message to it. None of the album has any message; it's really a compression of information, it's just information: make of it what you will," Bowie said. While "Ramona" hails from the character segues, other names without backstories, Paddy and Miranda, have as much dramatic import in the song. ("Paddy" could be a nickname for God, a fellow Art Crime detective.) Bowie once said the heart's filthy lesson was the certainty of one's death: "that realization, when it comes, usually later in life, can either be a really daunting prospect or it makes things a lot clearer." The heart is a blood-sponge, a dirty waterworks, an ever-flexing muscle we've turned into a warm red icon to represent love. The body's a prison and we flatter our warden.

What became "The Hearts Filthy Lesson" was taped in the March 1994 group improvisations and then left alone until Reeves Gabrels, Bowie, and engineer David Richards tailored it to a more conventional form that summer. Its foundation was a G-flat bass pedal, droning throughout, that becomes a gravity well — other sections yearn to escape (a Db minor verse, a move to Gb minor on "something in our skies," the Fb major refrain sections), but "Hearts Filthy Lesson" ultimately sinks back into Gb major, collapsing into itself.

"We moved some of the instrumental hooks around a bit to make them more 'hooklike'," Gabrels said. These included a Bo Diddley bassline; piano fills in homage to "Raw Power"; a guitar riff that trills along the low E string, punctuating with quick descending runs on the D string. A dog-whistle sound on alternating refrain downbeats; waves of static; what sounds like shaken chains; a guitar so distorted it could be synthesized strings (around 3:15). Stitching includes an eight-bar Garson piano solo and a sudden sigh to trigger the second bridge ("Paddy will you carry me"). A last touch is the sibilant backing vocals of the Edwards family, four siblings who were in West Side Studio for a workshop for underprivileged children run by the heiress Sabrina Guinness.

Revising the song, Bowie cut a new vocal with a lyric that Gabrels recalled being about "English landscape painting" (one of Bowie's "inputs" for the *Leon* lyric improvisations). Gabrels gently told Bowie that this would ruin the song. After restoring his original lyric, Bowie had a fantastic vocal — the snarling presence in his opening verse phrasings, the aspirant lines flooded with reverb, his bridge sequence of "Oh Ra-*moan*-a... if there was *on*-ly" that he upends with "be-*tween* us" while keeping the stress rhythm.

Studied alienation, gasps and mutters, a Nine Inch Nails-style video: for some critics, it was Bowie chasing a moving train while trying to catch his breath. But there was a YouTube comment on its video a few years ago, by someone who'd been fifteen at the time. "Hearts Filthy Lesson" was the first Bowie song they had ever heard, and it had freaked them out. On *Letterman*, there was an unease in the studio after Bowie's performance; guest Doc Severinsen likely cracked during the commercial break "what was that all about?" *Tell the others*, Bowie murmured towards the end. *Tell the others*. There's a generation gap in Bowie fandom between those who grew up in the Seventies and those who first knew him with *1. Outside*. For the latter, this cadaverous aging creep, muttering about Ramona and blood and filthy things, was their Ziggy Stardust.

SEGUE: NATHAN ADLER (2)

(Bowie, Eno.) **Recorded**: *ca. May-December 1994, Mountain, West Side, Brondesbury Villas. Bowie: lead and backing vocal; Eno: Yamaha DX7, Eventide H3000 SEK, JamMan, E-Mu Procussion, Korg A3. Produced: Bowie, Eno; engineered: Richards.*

First release: *25 September 1995, **1. Outside**.*

Unlike other character segues, which hailed from the *Leon* sessions of March 1994, the second "Nathan Adler" segue was a later addition composed by Bowie and Eno. Bowie reworked lines from Adler monologues on *Leon* while speaking over similar-sounding "jungle" beats as those heard on "I'm Deranged." Barely thirty seconds long, it's sequenced on *1. Outside* as an epilogue that, properly, resolves nothing.

THRU' THESE ARCHITECTS EYES

(Bowie, Gabrels.) **Recorded**: *ca. March-summer 1994, Mountain, West Side. Bowie: lead and backing vocal; Gabrels: lead guitar; Kevin Armstrong: rhythm guitar; Eno: Yamaha DX7, Eventide H3000, JamMan, E-Mu Procussion, Korg A3, Garson: piano; Kızılçay: bass; Campbell: drums. Produced: Bowie, Eno; engineered: Richards.*

First release: *25 September 1995*, **1. Outside**. *Live: 1995.*

Thwarted in his plans to make "The Hearts Filthy Lesson" about English landscape painters, Bowie got his art history piece onto *1. Outside* via "Thru' These Architects Eyes." It opens with Philip Johnson, American Modernist and brutal aesthete (the "Manhattoes" in "Goodbye Mr. Ed" jump off Johnson's AT&T Building), and British architect Richard Rogers, in whose Centre Pompidou or Lloyd's Building the structure's "guts" — pipes, elevators, gas lines, cables — are exposed, turned into barriers against the street. By the mid-Nineties, Johnson and Rogers' buildings were inescapable in Western cities.

The singer walks in the shadow of steel and glass towers built by great architects for great multi-nationals. Capitalism's won, history's over, so get to work. "This goddamned starving life": digging for your gold, or the life of an artist, always having to feed on the world. The song hums with resentment, a man cursing in the shadow of Johnson's Lipstick Building, which housed Bernie Madoff's office at the time, or seeing Rogers' Millennium Dome blight Greenwich. (What city is he in? Not New York, which at the time had no Rogers buildings, nor London, where there are no Johnsons. For literalists, say it's Madrid, where you can look from Johnson's Puerta de Europa towers and see Rogers' terminal at the Barajas Airport.)

Which architects, though? A Christian Gnostic heresy is that the world wasn't created by God, but by a lesser being; that man is a fallen god himself, and gnosis ("knowledge") reveals this condition. St. Thomas Aquinas wrote that "God, Who is the first principle of all things, may be compared to things created as the architect is to things designed." For the Gnostics, a poor architect, a bungler who left tectonic plates to crack against each other, who condemned swathes of the globe to ice and desert. Gnostic thought has darker implications: freeing the God within oneself can lead to a "liberation" from society, a ruthless capitalist or fascist life. A young Philip Johnson went to Nazi rallies in Potsdam and Nuremberg and got turned on ("all those blond boys in black leather"), penning pro-Hitler articles. "Hitler's 'racism' is a perfectly simple though far-reaching idea," Johnson wrote. "It is the myth of 'we, the best,' which we find, more or less fully developed, in all vigorous cultures."

"Thru' These Architects Eyes," an ode to vigorous culture, has little reason to be on *1. Outside*, though I assume there are theories linking it to the builder of Oxford Town, etc. But its interpretive density suits the album and it was a strong performance, particularly Bowie's aggrieved vocal. He's an irritant in his own song, pushing against its harmonic movements, bright A major (verses) yielding to ashen B minor (the bridges), the keys clashing in the refrains. Its weave of guitar tracks is a Tin Machine reunion — Kevin Armstrong and Reeves Gabrels, playing together one last time. Mike Garson closes with a piano figure that, if not for the fade, sounds as if it would keep slowing to a crawl for eternity.

THE VOYEUR OF UTTER DESTRUCTION (AS BEAUTY)

(Bowie, Eno, Gabrels.) **Recorded**: *ca. March-summer 1994, Mountain, West Side. Bowie: lead and backing vocal, Korg, Ensoniq; Eno: Yamaha DX7, Eventide H3000, JamMan, E-Mu Procussion, Korg A3; Gabrels: lead guitar; Garson: piano; Kızılçay: bass; Campbell: drums, percussion. Produced: Bowie, Eno; engineered: Richards.*

First release: *25 September 1995, **1. Outside**. **Broadcast**: 14 December 1995, The White Room; 26 January 1996, Taratata; 29 January 1996, Karel. **Live**: 1995-1997.*

With one of the most ungainly titles in the Bowie catalog, "The Voyeur of Utter Destruction (As Beauty)" is aligned in spirit with the *Leon* improvisations but like "Thru These Architects' Eyes," it was a composition Reeves Gabrels began before the sessions, presumably here given enough Eno input to justify a co-write. Its opening guitar lines are Gabrels' tribute to Adrian Belew (see King Crimson's "Thela Hun Ginjeet"); its clatter of rhythm tracks, tom fills against buzzing insurgencies of electronic percussion, points towards *Earthling*.

Another lyric from the alleged perspective of an Artist/Minotaur figure (see "Wishful Beginnings"), it's Bowie riffing on his interests of the time: body modification, scarification, erotic torture (*"the screw… is a tightening atrocity"*). There's some Scott Walker phrasing on lines like "sober Philistine." In a very Bowie moment, his refrain hook, "turn and turn again," honors both T.S. Eliot (see the opening lines of "Ash Wednesday") and Christmas pantomime routines ("turn again, Dick Whittington!": the errant servant who becomes Lord Mayor of London, summoned by the Bow Bells).

Its arrangement is devoted to propulsion: "O Superman" metronomic vocal loops, Mike Garson sketching with his piano's treble keys. After a key change so jarring it's as if another song has invaded, the track swirls into the maelstrom for its closing minute. (The bridge and outro sound so overcooked that it could possibly be an engineering error.) Performances of "Voyeur" in the 1995 tour often bettered its studio take, with Gail Ann Dorsey's vocals as undercurrent, Gabrels and Carlos Alomar swapping guitar lines, and Garson and Bowie going further upriver.

Get Real

(Bowie, Eno.). **Recorded***: ca. March 1994-January 1995, Mountain, Brondesbury Villas, West Side, Hit Factory. Bowie: lead and harmony vocal, Korg, Ensoniq; Eno: Yamaha DX7, Eventide H3000, JamMan, E-Mu Procussion, Korg A3; Gabrels, Alomar: guitar; Kızılçay or Fine: bass; Baron: drums. Produced: Bowie, Eno; engineered: Richards.*

First release*: 22 September 1995,* **1. Outside** *(Japanese ed., Arista BVCA-677).*

Bonus track and B-side "Get Real" is an odd leftover from the *Leon/1. Outside* sessions. Its guitar tracks suggest Bowie's unlamented mid-Eighties while its melancholy bridges, the bass tolling through the chord changes, reflect his late Sixties and predict *'hours...'* and *Toy*. With a lyric that started life through his Verbasizer (a sheet dated 6 March 1994, included in the *David Bowie Is* exhibit, has Bowie's handwriting over paragraphs of computer-generated text), it's a modest mid-life crisis ("you can't stop meaningful teenage cries/from deep behind fifty-year-old eyes"), with Bowie asking the kids what's happened while he's been holed up in Switzerland.

WISHFUL BEGINNINGS

(Bowie, Eno.) **Recorded:** *ca. summer-December 1994, Mountain, West Side, Brondesbury Villas. Bowie: lead vocal, Korg, Ensoniq; Eno: Yamaha DX7, Eventide H3000, JamMan, E-Mu Procussion, Korg A3. Produced: Bowie, Eno; engineered: Richards.*

First release: 25 September 1995, **1. Outside**.

One of the few *1. Outside* songs never performed live, "Wishful Beginnings" was even cut from some reissues (where deleting "Too Dizzy" was an act of criticism, axing the 5:09 "Wishful Beginnings" was done for a more practical reason — room was needed on a lengthy CD for the "Hallo Spaceboy" remix, a minor hit). Its lyric was the perspective of an "Artist/Minotaur" figure that Bowie made the occasional gesture at explaining. He once said it was one of his Diamond Dogs reincarnated, and he made postcard drawings of a minotaur for a 1994 exhibit in London ("Minotaur Myths and Legends"), one showing a muscular beast-man grasping his enormous cock. That same year he made "We Saw a Minotaur" (by "Joni Ve Sadd"), an art piece about an unfortunate play performed only once at the Globe Theatre in 2002 due to the "hideous construction playing the part of the Minotaur" and, in a foreshadowing, "the density and complexity of the script, written in part by a Macintosh Quadra 650 computer."

The world of *1. Outside* is a bloody one. Fourteen-year-old girls are gutted for art; Mark Rothko slashes each arm below the elbow and is found lying in a pool of his blood. The young pierce and ink themselves. There are severed limbs, diamond-studded umbilical cords, intestine webs, bloodstained tissues strung on wires. The galleries have casts of heads filled with blood, and the bisected corpses of cows. Bowie called it modern paganism, going "back to the Romans and their drinking the blood and eating the meat of the bull to enable us to go forward into the new era... a kind of appeasement to the gods to allow us to go into the next millennium." Some lines in "Wishful Beginnings" suggest the Minotaur's performing a sacrificial ritual on himself ("I'm no longer your golden boy... flames burn my body").

There was a shallowness to *1. Outside*, with Bowie taking concepts from art pieces, yanking them out of context, reducing them to gore. He deconsecrated works: for instance, turning Ron Athey's scarifications, with their sacramental reflections on AIDS and its ravages of the body, into little more than tongue-piercing or a knock-off *Silence of the Lambs* scenario. He'd always worked this way, true, but it used to be more fun. His need for an artistic pedigree, to give his stolen goods some weight, bogged down his lesser songs. Imagine an exploitative comic book with pages of footnotes.

"Wishful Beginnings" has a wintry soundscape. Bowie sings over a few loops, including a "chime," a thudding kick sample on every other downbeat, a three-note "death rattle" and a thwacked tambourine. At first, the only harmonic structure is a synthesizer chord synced to the kick sample. His mostly single-tracked voice flutters around the mix. Patterns alter, gather dimension — more melodic fragments; the tambourine loop lengthens and shortens. By the midpoint, where Bowie's at his gentlest ("we *flew* on the wings"), a few tiny melodies escape via keyboard, but the track ends as it began.

It was a dark revision of Lou Reed's "Make Up" (compare Reed's "you're a slick little girl" with Bowie's "you're a sorry little girl"): where Reed had warmly detailed a makeup ritual, Bowie describes someone as meat readied for the blade or, in its best-case scenario, the submissive in a BDSM relationship. His greatest debt on "Wishful Beginnings" was to himself: his 1967 song "Please Mr. Gravedigger," another horror piece with a spoken-sung melody and scant harmonic grounding. "Are you going to re-record 'Please Mr. Gravedigger?'" a fan asked in a 1998 web-chat. "I did already," Bowie said. "It was called *1. Outside*."

THE MOTEL

Recorded: ca. March-summer 1994, Mountain, West Side. Bowie: lead vocal; Gabrels: lead guitar; Garson: piano; Eno: Yamaha DX7, Eventide H3000, JamMan, E-Mu Procussion; Kızılçay: bass; Campbell: drums. Produced: Bowie, Eno; engineered: Richards.

First release: 25 September 1995, *1. Outside*. *Live*: 1995-1997, 2003-2004.

As recording sessions for *1. Outside* kept on, so did Bowie's role-playing. A fresh idea: he'd create the album that Scott Walker never would. Walker had vanished after 1984's *Climate of Hunter*; his reputation had preceded him. He was a critical nullity in the Eighties, particularly in his birth country, where he was mostly out of print: none of his records are listed in the 1983 *Rolling Stone Record Guide* and various editions of the *Trouser Press* guides; he merits a single line in a brief Walker Brothers entry in the *Rolling Stone Encyclopedia of Rock 'n' Roll*. In Britain, the *Sunday People* offered a reward for Walker sightings, as if he was a Yeti.

Walker's "The Electrician" still fascinated Bowie and Eno, fifteen years on (see "Nite Flights"). Eno called it a lost future of music; he said he was frustrated to hear new bands content to rip off Roxy Music instead of moving beyond what Walker had done in 1978. "The Electrician" opens with massed atonal strings, a tolling bass, Walker's groaning baritone; it shifts to a section where Scott and John Walker harmonize; it cuts to a flight of strings and Spanish guitar. These shifts have no dramatic impetus; the song resets itself each time it moves. It's tropical extremes of mood, from violation (the torturer drills through the spiritus sanctus) to resistance (whose dream is the strings-and-guitar idyll? the torturer? the person on the rack?). Walker's opening lines are set in the torture chamber, and the Ink Spots could have sung them: *Baby, it's slow/when lights go low*.

Whenever asked for a list of favorite songs, Bowie cited "The Electrician," but he never tried to claim it on stage as he did another favorite/obsession, "Waiting for the Man." On *1. Outside* he channeled "The Electrician" into a new song, a centerpiece for a centerless album.

"The Motel" opens in the lobby. Murmurs of conversation; in one corner, an effusive pianist, a secretive bassist. A guest wanders over. "For we're living in the safety zone..." Everything's provisional, fluid. A motel is a nowhere, a purgatory, a vestibule between reincarnations. Chords blur from F major to F-sharp, Bowie often moves between singing A or B-flat notes. A brief interlude: dancing piano, fretless bass figures. Drums kick in. Bowie sharpens his tone, singing "there is no hell," a line he took from "there's no help" in "The Electrician" and what he'd seen on a Gugging Clinic wall: THIS IS HELL (see "Outside"). The pianist becomes grandiose. Bowie closes the refrain with his highest notes yet: "it's *lights up, boys.*" A body twists in an electric chair; inmates are rousted from their beds.

Another verse, but upon the "there is no hell" hook, Bowie keeps on, elaborating his melody, hitting a high E-flat as the song hardens into E-flat major. He gave "The Motel" a grand finale, a Judy Garland spotlight moment, with vocal pyrotechnics for the benefit of a clunky last verse: "re-exploding you... like everybody doooo." The motel lobby becomes a Vegas stage; Bowie ended "The Motel" as he had "Rock 'n' Roll Suicide."

While Bowie was making his Scott Walker sequel, so was Walker. Learning that Walker would release a new album, *Tilt*, in 1995, Eno wrote in his diary that he feared *Tilt* "could occupy much of the territory of Bowie's" and, if so, "Bowie won't release those things and, as time passes, more will get chipped away or submerged under later additions." Bowie got an advance copy of *Tilt*. He phoned Eno, relieved: it sounded nothing like their album. When first played in the *NME* offices, *Tilt*'s opener, "Farmer in the City," reportedly caused staffers to beg for someone to yank the CD. On "The Cockfighter," Walker sings over what sounds like a rat gnawing through paper; later, a horn sounds like a horse being slaughtered. Bowie's favorite album of the year, *Tilt* was the record *1. Outside* could never be. Nearing its twenty-fifth anniversary, *Tilt* still stands apart from its time; the future hasn't risen to meet it yet.

"He's true to himself, whereas other artists are traitors to themselves," Bowie said of Walker in 1995. For the rest of his days, Bowie used Walker as a symbol of the uncompromised artistic life, as a boundary rider off in the wilderness, from whose sporadic reports he'd chart his own future movements (see "Heat").

Now
Outside

(Bowie, Armstrong.) **Recorded**: *ca. summer 1994, Mountain, West Side; January*

1995, Hit Factory. Bowie: lead and harmony vocal, Korg, Ensoniq; Eno: Yamaha DX7, Eventide H3000, JamMan, E-Mu Procussion, Korg A3; Gabrels: lead guitar; Alomar: rhythm guitar; Garson: keyboards, piano; Kızılçay or Fine: bass; Campbell or Baron: drums. Produced: Bowie, Eno; engineered: Richards.

First release: *25 September 1995,* **1. Outside**. **Live**: *1989 ("Now"), 1995-1997 ("Outside").*

Many Bowie albums come from multiple revisions: *1. Outside* was an extreme case. Things kept being troweled on. One was an interest in "outsider art." There wasn't much of this on *Leon*, which was more a pulp of the internet, CD-ROMs, millennial terrors, and body artists. But in September 1994, Bowie and Eno visited the Maria Gugging Psychiatric Clinic, which housed patients with artistic inclinations in a wing where they could paint walls, couches, even trees. Bowie sketched the artists and their work; Eno recorded conversations.

Outsider art, a term coined by Roger Cardinal for a 1972 survey, was the focus of an exhibit, "Parallel Visions: Modern Artists and Outsider Art," that had run at museums near Bowie's homes: the Los Angeles County Museum of Art in late 1992, and Kunsthalle Basel in summer 1993. Exhibited artists included Karl Brendel, who modeled figures he made from chewed bread; Carlo Zinelli, who graffitied hospital walls with bricks and nails; J.B. Murray, who drew "spirit script" on bank calendars and receipts; Martin Ramirez, who made collages on paper scraps that he glued together with mashed potatoes.

What united them, the institutionalized and the obscure, was being "compulsive visionaries," argued exhibit curator Maurice Tuchman. An outsider artist had extreme focus, fixating on repetitions of patterns or structures, as if compelled to flush an image from their mind and trap it on paper. Alfred Kubin, an early advocate, admired their work's "secret regularity... these wonders of the artists' minds that come from the depth outside all thoughtful thinking and make you happy just looking at them." During their time at Gugging, Bowie and Eno met artists including August Walla, who had painted a room floor-to-ceiling with mythical beings and unknown alphabets. "We felt an exhilaration watching them work," Bowie said. "None of them knew they were artists. It's compelling and sometimes quite frightening to see this honesty. There's no awareness of embarrassment."

He'd always been taken with obscure, prickly, even possibly deranged musicians — Wild Man Fischer, Biff Rose, The Legendary Space Cowboy, Vince Taylor — and bohemians like Brion Gysin (see "Hallo Spaceboy") and William S. Burroughs. "These 'outside' people were really the people I wanted to be like," Bowie said. "I derived so much satisfaction from the way [Burroughs] would scramble life and it no longer felt scrambled reading him." He thought they had greater access to the "realms of the unreal," as titled the outsider artist Henry Darger's fifteen-thousand-page opus. Bowie's creative process was one of trying to outfox his mind, setting snares to push him outside his parameters. He rarely needed such tricks for composition — his chord progressions, those of a self-taught experimentalist, could be strikingly odd, harmonically "erratic" yet following a sound internal logic. It was elsewhere, in his lyrics and structuring concepts, where he struggled with overcoming self-awareness.

1. Outside, in its final form, is a would-be "outsider" work — the dense amounts of cryptic detail, the indecipherable symbology of the liner notes, the sense of some overarching structure that the audience can't quite discern. It was a move away from the liminal, flowing *Leon* suites towards a more clotted-up, hermetic work. Eno, hearing the final album, noted this: "strong, muddy, prolix, gritty, Garsonic, modern (self-consciously, ironically so)... Some acceptable complexity merging into not-so-acceptable muddle... The only thing missing: space — the nerve to be very simple. But an indisputably 'outside' record. I wish it was shorter."

Its title track, however, didn't come from a group improvisation, wasn't generated via Eno's role-playing scenarios. It was a rewritten Tin Machine song from 1989, originally called "Now."

Bowie kept potentially strong songs on retainer, holding off on finishing pieces until the mood was right (see "Bring Me the Disco King"). Written by Bowie and Tin Machine rhythm guitarist Kevin Armstrong, "Now" was played twice during the band's 1989 tour (they may have cut a studio version as well). It had developed from Bowie's reworking of "Look Back in Anger" with Armstrong and Gabrels, being bookended with similar guitar barrages. Its downtempo verses and bridges, presumably in part Armstrong's work, hung on an ascending four-note bass hook. Bowie's lyric was so threadbare — "I need your love! Talk about love!" — that he apologized for it before the song's live debut (all he kept for "Outside" was the "now... tomorrow...

yesterday" hook, which may derive from a line in Steven Berkoff's *West* ("it's not tomorrow any more/ it's now/ the readiness is all").)

The 1995 "Outside" is colder, more reserved. It holds back and never quite climaxes — Bowie doesn't move to his higher registers until the second bridge, doesn't double-track his voice until the third verse. (On stage, he sang the first verses and bridges seated, rising to his feet for the climactic section; by 1997, he'd turned the song over to Gail Ann Dorsey.) Its harmonic base is two stereo-panned guitar volume swells that parallel the ascending bassline. In the last bridges Gabrels shadows the bassline, then solos off it. The drums are tremendous: the little fill to bring in the bass hook; the subtle shifts in patterns to trigger the bridges; the widescreen tom fills at 2:38. The percussion roster includes tambourine in the first verse, chimes and congas in the second, Eno squiggles throughout.

The album's grandmaster of ceremonies, "Outside" would be a statement of purpose for Bowie's embattled mid-Nineties tours. It was his hard. commitment to the present; he wasn't singing "Space Oddity" tonight. *"Now... **not** tomorrow,"* he'd sing. "It happens *today*."

WE PRICK YOU

(Bowie, Eno.) **Recorded**: 13-16 January 1995, Hit Factory. Bowie: lead and backing vocal; Eno: Yamaha DX7, Eventide H3000, JamMan, E-Mu Procussion; Alomar: rhythm guitar; Fine: bass; Baron: drums. Produced: Bowie, Eno; engineered: Richards.

First release: 25 September 1995, **1. Outside**. Live: 1995-1996.

In mid-January 1995, Eno flew to New York for more work on an album he felt might never be done. Sessions booked at the Hit Factory were meant for overdubs, but Bowie showed little sign of wanting to refine his songs. In his journal, Eno wrote that upon arriving in New York, Bowie called him "full of tangential ideas, the kind of ideas people usually have when their lyrics aren't ready... no mention of actually finishing the album, for which I'm ostensibly here."

Eno wanted "to leave here with some kind of result, not just more promising bits and pieces, all half-finished." On the first day of recording, devoted to a track called "Dummy" (see "I'm Afraid of Americans"), he went over what he and Bowie had recorded in 1994. It sounded "underdisciplined... rambling, murky, over- and over-dubbed — things just left where they happened to fall." He blamed forty-eight-track consoles, which had too many options. If Bowie was the director who kept shooting new footage, Eno was the film editor who had to get a work print out of it.

On the afternoon of 13 January 1995, Eno started a new track based on the drum programming he'd done for "Dummy." By the following day, "Robot Punk," whose refrain went "we fuck you — we fuck you" ("[it] leaves something to be desired," Eno wrote), was coming together quickly. Eno created new drum loops and added synthesizer colors like "marimba" fills and a four-note riff slightly distorting towards the close. By 16 January, the track was "pretty well finished" — Bowie had cut his vocals and Carlos Alomar, for refrains, played a hustling guitar line worthy of the Miracles' "Love Machine." Eno was amazed: "he plays like a kind of liquid, always making lovely melodies within his rhythm lines."

"We Prick You" (its final title) moves from modest beginnings (a bassline over two drum loops, mixed far left and right; soon joined by drum machine and two main keyboard tracks) to become baked in hooks: loops of "ooohs" high in the mix in later verses; low counter-melodies ("shoes, shoes, little white shoes"); a righteously-sung *tell* the *truth*!" and the title line, repeated thrice like an anathema, pummeled by snare fills. Bowie wanted Camille Paglia for the "you show respect, even if you disagree" vocal loop, but had to do it himself, his voice sped up to sound like an officious house elf (he called Paglia's office, but she thought it was a joke and never responded). On stage Bowie responded to the voice as if being annoyed by God; he'd talk back and shake his head.

His lyric shares the density of the arrangement: his refrain lines alone are a dirty joke; a *Merchant of Venice* nod ("if you prick us, do we not bleed?"); a prosecutor in the trial of Leon Blank ("tell the truth!"); a reference to the alchemical symbol of Christ being pierced with a spear, and to body scarification, inspired by Ron Athey's *Four Scenes in a Harsh Life*, where Athey carved patterns into the flesh of another performer. A compression of scattered ideas into a tight ball of sound, "We Prick You" is a minor masterpiece.

I'M DERANGED

(Bowie, Eno.) **Recorded**: *ca. late 1994, Mountain; January 1995, Hit Factory. Bowie: lead and harmony vocal, keyboards; Eno: Yamaha DX7, Eventide H3000, JamMan, E-Mu Procussion; Gabrels: lead guitar; Alomar: rhythm guitar; Garson: piano; Fine: bass; Baron: drums. Produced: Bowie, Eno; engineered: Richards.*

First release: *25 September 1995,* **1. Outside**. **Live**: *1995, 1997.*

Another song inspired by Bowie and Eno's trip to Gugging Clinic, "I'm Deranged" references an artist inmate who called himself the Angel Man, who told Bowie "I was exactly who I was up until the 5th of February 1948, and then I became an angel... it was just after lunch." Bowie said the inmate "believed that his old person disappeared, and his angel took over him. He was totally reborn at that moment."

Bowie puréed a lyric via his Verbasizer software, then improvised more, possibly on the mike ("be real" becomes "before we reel"; "blonde" summons "beyond"). Its perspective is of someone with high hopes of growing mad ("I'd start to believe... if I were to bleed," he sings, gently extending his long eees), while some lines suggest Bowie was reading John Rechy's *City of Night* again ("cruise me baby," "the fist of love"). Though assigned to his Artist/Minotaur figure (see "Wishful Beginnings"), any attempt to fit "I'm Deranged" into the *1. Outside* storyline would devote more effort than its composer did.

Making the track was a grueling process. Reeves Gabrels worked for two days on "serious orchestrated guitar stuff" that got scrapped; Carlos Alomar recalled a three-part harmony track later removed. Eno didn't think much of "I'm Deranged" when he turned to it on 17 January 1995 at the Hit Factory. "A poorly organized song with no meaningful structure. It goes something like ABBBBBBBBBCBBBBBBBB but the hook is A. I've had relationships like that, where the bit you liked never happens again." It embodied the "lack of rigour" of some *1. Outside* material and by lunch he gave up, not referencing the song again in his diary. Bowie apparently carried it to the finish line in later sessions that month.

With an F minor progression that's a long, winding path before landing on the home chord, "I'm Deranged" was indebted to Eno for its would-be drum 'n' bass rhythms, though it also owes something to Bowie and Nile

Rodgers' "Real Cool World" (there's even "Billie Jean" in its opening four-note synthesizer hook). The arrangement is both propulsive and tinny — the drum machines sound like video game effects at times; piano interludes seem generated from a sampler track labeled "Off-Kilter Mike Garson Solo."

Bowie considered it a strong song, "with a really intelligent use of jungle... that sort of quasi-Arabic melody line and the really rather disturbed words." Its strongest element is his vocal. There's a cool precision in his opening lines — by the second verse, he's weighing each word, miring himself in syllables, building to his long, lovingly strangled "deraaaanged"s. It suited the title sequence David Lynch had it score on *Lost Highway* — a driver's-eye shot of a cranked-up stream of highway center lines, a loop of auto-motion.

Hallo Spaceboy

(Bowie, Eno.) **Recorded**: *(backing tracks, loops) summer 1994, Mountain; 17-20 January 1995, Hit Factory. Bowie: lead and backing vocal; Gabrels: lead guitar, loops, textures; Alomar: rhythm guitar; Eno: Yamaha DX7, Eventide H3000, JamMan, E-Mu Procussion; Garson: keyboards; Fine: bass; Baron: drums. Produced: Bowie, Eno; engineered: Richards.*

First release: *25 September 1995,* **1. Outside**. **Broadcast**: *2 December 1995, Later with Jools Holland; 14 December 1995, The White Room; 20 January 1996, Det Kommer Mera; 26 January 1996, Taratata; 29 January 1996; Karel; 19 February 1996, Brit Awards; 29 February 1996, Top of the Pops; 27 June 2000, Bowie at the BBC Radio Theatre.* **Live**: *1995-1997, 2000, 2002-2004.*

Brion Gysin was a poet, historian, mystic, painter, filmmaker, musician, inventor (of "the Dreamachine," a trance-inducing light-box). Born in Britain during World War I, Gysin lived in New York, where he was a ship welder and Broadway set designer; Tangier, where he ran a restaurant whose house band was the Master Musicians of Joujouka; and Paris, where he died in 1986.

His greatest legacy was his cut-up method, in which he applied techniques from painting and film (collage and montage) to the assembly of words. After slicing through a stack of newspapers, he'd make poems from the filleted strips of paper. For Bowie, it became his standard method for writing lyrics.

Gysin's was an unrefined creativity, compared to the austere order of a Scott Walker. For Gysin, being a dilettante was a noble calling. Life's a game, not a career, he often said. Bowie's "Hallo Spaceboy" is, among many things, a eulogy to Gysin, an architect of *1. Outside*: a tribute to a force of motion stilled by death. "Your silhouette is so stationary... Don't you want to be free?" "Moondust will cover you" references a line in Gysin's *The Process*: "I look for my guide to find him, too, buried in moondust."

"Hallo Spaceboy" opens with a tornado on the horizon — a swirl of synthesizers, a chopping loop mixed right, a distorted guitar line. Sixteen bars in: a cannonade of electronic beats and crushing drums, undergirded by a low-mixed bassline and bursts of guitar. If the "Moonage Daydream" guitar hook was glam in miniature — *dream this: go!* — the hook of "Hallo Spaceboy" finds you out, hunts you down. In refrains, the guitars spit and tear from B major to G major chords (the main harmonic sequence, along with a brief A major progression in the bridges). Before the second refrain, Bowie holds off the onslaught for a few bars, whispering "moondust" before the door's kicked in. The rest is counter-rhythms: ping-ponged electric guitars; a mousechase across piano. Bowie's muttered syllables work as crash cymbals.

One starting point was Eno's "Third Uncle" (esp. as covered via Bauhaus); another was the Swiss industrial band the Young Gods, particularly on *T.V. Sky* (1992): see "Skinflowers," with its buzz-swaths of guitar (a hollered "outside!," too) or the juxtaposition of guitar loops and percussion on "Dame Chance." Another source was closer to home. During the second *1. Outside* recording session in Montreux in summer 1994, Reeves Gabrels wrote and recorded an ambient instrumental piece. Bowie then recited some lines over it, including "moon dust," which Gabrels said came from a "book of poems" Bowie was reading in the studio (possibly this was his slight misremembering of Gysin's *The Process*). After that "I did a bunch of long sustain guitars thru a vocal formant patch from an Eventide 4000 signal processor (which makes it sound like a human voice) and I used a slight variation on the ava rava (sic) middle eastern scale," Gabrels wrote on his website in 2003. On a subsequent visit to Switzerland, Gabrels asked about the track, provisionally called "Moondust," but Bowie said "he didn't feel there was anything special going on with that piece and that he'd pretty much forgotten about it."

However, he had apparently recalled "Moondust" by the New York sessions in January 1995. On 17 January, he and Eno broke the song down "to almost nothing," as Eno wrote in his diary. "I wrote some lightning chords and spaces...and suddenly, miraculously, we had something." Bowie came up with the "hallo spaceboy" vocal hook, Eno added "a bass sax thing" and a bass part that he described as "very African, with wide, bouncing intervals — pygmy anarchism with Lagos Mack-truck weight."

Upon hearing "Hallo Spaceboy," Gabrels noted its similarity in harmonic structure to "Moondust," but Bowie had no interest in sharing credit with anyone but Eno. Gabrels, who knew when to pick his battles, let it drop. But in 2003, he noted that "Hallo Spaceboy" "follows the chord changes of my original 'ambient' track which was dismissed as just being 'ambient' and not really a song or contributing to the existence of 'Spaceboy'." For Bowie, "Hallo Spaceboy" was a song that he'd alchemized from an unpromising ambient piece that he'd then conveniently forgotten about.

God can be an ironist: "Hallo Spaceboy" was itself nicked from Bowie. When the Pet Shop Boys asked to remix "Hallo Spaceboy," Bowie agreed, as he let the world and his wife remix his songs. But upon learning Neil Tennant would sing new, "Space Oddity"-connected lyrics, Bowie had doubts. *1. Outside* was meant to be his pre-millennial tension record and here was bloody Major Tom/Starman again. ("I only used [the word] 'space' — there's nothing about it that's even remotely like 'Space Oddity,' frankly," Bowie said in a press conference in 1995.) In an inspired move, Tennant cut up the lines of "Space Oddity" Gysin-style, with words put into new alliances: "Ground to major bye-bye Tom/dead the circuit countdown's wrong/Planet Earth is control on?" The remix shifted the song's axis: "this chaos is killing me!" became the voice of an astronaut strung out in heaven.

Issued as *1. Outside*'s third single, the remix nearly broke into the UK Top 10. On British TV performances, Tennant calmly sang while Bowie thrashed around, as if in a zoo exhibit. Bowie would spend the last decade of his performing life trying to get "Hallo Spaceboy" back under his thumb, sometimes succeeding (three drummers pounded the song into submission at his fiftieth birthday concert), sometimes acting as if he was covering it.

I HAVE NOT BEEN TO OXFORD TOWN

(Bowie, Eno.) **Recorded**: *17-20 January 1995, Hit Factory. Bowie: lead and*

backing vocal; Gabrels: lead guitar; Alomar: rhythm guitar; Eno: Yamaha DX7, Eventide H3000, JamMan, E-Mu Procussion; Fine: bass; Baron: drums. Produced: Bowie, Eno; engineered: Richards.

First release: *25 September 1995,* **1. Outside**. *Live: 1995-1996.*

Abandoning "I'm Deranged," Eno started making a track from scratch. He'd clear the air instead of overdubbing another half-finished song. As Bowie wasn't in the studio, Eno worked up a rhythm piece with Carlos Alomar and Joey Baron, appropriately titled "Trio." A basic G major progression, its verses kept on G, a refrain shifted between G and C major, a bridge brought in the dominant chord, D major. The following evening, Eno embellished "Trio" so that by the next morning, 19 January 1995, he had a new track for Bowie to consider.

Though frustrated by Bowie, Eno was awed by how quickly his collaborator could move. "He's the hunter to my pastoralist — he hangs around for a long time and then springs for the kill." In a half-hour that morning, Bowie wrote and cut his vocal for "Trio," renamed "Toll the Bell" and finally "I Have Not Been to Oxford Town." He began writing during the first playback, then asked for a replay and for five tracks to be cleared for vocals. As Eno wrote in his diary, "he went into the vocal booth and sang the most obscure thing imaginable — long spaces, little incomplete lines." His second vocal track complemented the first, the third posed a "'question' to which tracks one and two had been the answers," and he devoted the last two to his top melody. "He unfolded the whole thing in reverse, keeping us in suspense for the main song."

Using an F major to A minor turnaround as the hinge of his two-note backing vocal hook ("all's... well"), Bowie made his words work as rhythms first and foremost ("my attorney seems sincere": the internal rhyme of "nee" and "seem," the conga line of esses). Subconsciously or not, he channeled David Byrne's vocal on Talking Heads' "Once in a Lifetime" — his verses have a similar chant-like phrasing, which Byrne had picked up from evangelical radio, "where the text was almost turned into music." Long repetitions, mainly keeping on one note, that pay off with soaring, rhyming phrases ("behind the wheel of a large automobile!"). On "Oxford Town," Bowie favors short vowels, gives curt appraisals of each syllable, letting some pass, haranguing others ("Baby Grace is the victimmm"). It's balanced by the jovial lightness of his refrains: one long, dancing melodic line.

It swings thanks to Alomar. "I do my stuff knowing a lead guitarist will come in. So I stay away from certain frequencies, concentrate on making a sturdy frame," he said. In the second pre-chorus, Alomar counters the verse melody, then connives against the beat in the refrains. He plays arpeggios in the bridge and riffs through the verse returns. By the last forty seconds, his guitar makes filigrees around Bowie's vocal lines. The track ends with Alomar alone, a sideman holding the spotlight, hooking into a riff.

Bowie's lyric, whether it was fully improvised or a working-through of ideas he was already considering, shows how he'd internalized the scenarios he'd done in the past year. He was an actor who'd gone off book, able to dash out a fresh lyric about Leon Blank and Ramona Stone without blinking. And he wrote as close to a finale as *1. Outside* would ever have.

Leon Blank, accused killer, is seen through the eyes of others until "Oxford Town" finally gives him a voice. It's his last words from a jail cell, a favorite scenario from Bowie's youth (see, in *Rebel Rebel*, "Bars of the County Jail" and "Wild Eyed Boy from Freecloud"). The food's bad, the bedding's good, his attorney means well, the priest's willing to listen. In the bridge, Leon talks to his author: "This is your shadow on my wall... this is what I could have been." *I have not been to Oxford Town* isn't an alibi, it's a criticism. Leon kicks against the cheap story he was conscripted into and walks out of it. On stage in Paris a year later, Bowie gave another possible ending. Someone threw a white scarf on stage. He took it up, played with it, twined it around his neck, made a sling with it for his arm. Then he strung it into a noose and, while singing the end refrains, aped hanging himself.

No Control

*(Bowie, Eno.) **Recorded**: 19-20 January 1995, Hit Factory. Bowie: lead and backing vocal; Gabrels, Alomar: guitar; Eno: Yamaha DX7, Eventide H3000, JamMan, E-Mu Procussion; Fine: bass; Baron: drums. Produced: Bowie, Eno; engineered: Richards.*

***First release**: 25 September 1995, **1. Outside**.*

Bowie and Eno's late lucky strike in New York produced in four days as many new tracks, finally solidifying *1. Outside*. Having amassed enough "commercial" material to balance the remnants of *Leon* and more esoteric tracks like "Wishful Beginnings," Bowie soon had a deal with Virgin Records to release the album.

On 20 January 1995, Eno's last day in the studio, he and Bowie completed another track they had pulled out of the air: "No Control." Eno started it the night before with engineer David Richards. The following morning, he added "a lovely descending bell line" so when Bowie arrived at the Hit Factory, he "heard the body of a great song," as Eno wrote in his diary. Along with Eno's purling banks of synthesizers and sequencers, Carlos Alomar was the pivotal rhythmic force, his guitar lines spinning webs beneath Bowie's mood-swing phrasings.

Soon Bowie was in the vocal booth and had his tracks done within the hour. For a melody, he cribbed from his childhood favorite "Inchworm" and, as Momus noted, "Well Did You Evah" from the Fifties musical *High Society*: another melody that "slides ascending phrases down a chordal slope." In an octave-doubled vocal for the verses, Bowie warns a collective "you," his nearly one-note melody hooked to the song's harmonic progression (A major moving to its flattened VII chord, G major, on "deranged"). He has a wider-ranging, ascending melody in the bridge, a loftiness in his single-tracked intonation over the same progression in G major.

Then in the second bridge, Bowie moves to a stagy phrasing that suggests a character from *Oklahoma!* has turned up in Oxford Town. "Watching him tune it to just the right pitch of sincerity and parody was one of the most fascinating things I've ever seen in a studio," Eno wrote. "You've gotta have a scheme! You've gotta have a plan!" Bowie sings in a booming, open-throated optimistic voice, with "one arm extended to the future," as Eno described it. It's the voice of a fanatic ad man, of a propagandist who believes his lies, selling the delusions he's warned against in the verses.

As with some other late *1. Outside* tracks, Bowie mostly discarded his art-murder storyline, with a few lines here ("stay away from the future," "don't tell God your plans") having the aphoristic bite of his best Seventies songs. "No Control" was a strong closer that got lost in the over-heaped platter of *1. Outside*, especially as Bowie never played it live. Bizarrely enough, its stage debut came in 2016 with *SpongeBob SquarePants: The Broadway Musical*, fitted with new lyrics by Jonathan Coulton.

A Contaminated Epilogue

In 1999, the satirical newspaper the *Onion* ran a series of letter-writing campaigns to celebrities. One begged Bowie to finally complete his *1. Outside* storyline:

> Your musical tale of the art-murder of Baby Grace was all fans could talk about for months; during that time, you could step into any small-town bar and the topic of conversation would always be the same: Who killed Baby Grace? Some suspected tyrannical futurist Ramona Stone.

By then, the idea that Bowie would ever finish his art-murder mystery was as shaky as the storyline itself. In the immediate years after *1. Outside*, Bowie kept promising that sequel albums would appear, along with a theatrical production. In January 1995, Eno wrote how Bowie was "excited about his idea for a staging of 'Leon': a conflation of the original Leon things and what we're doing now. He's tempted both by the prospect itself and by the vaguely offered financial backing." But the proposed five-album "hypercycle" was soon diminished to a trilogy. While *2. Contamination*, slated for spring 1997, would have "some bearing on the first one… it's completely different," Bowie said. "It goes backwards and forwards between Indonesian pirates of the seventeenth and eighteenth centuries and today… it's really becoming a peculiar piece of work."

In 1997 Eno relocated to Saint Petersburg, Russia, while Bowie spent much of the year touring *Earthling*. The sequel albums were still always about to begin. Along with the sequels, Bowie and Eno would release an outtakes album called *Inside Outside* ("that stuff is pretty far-out, and I'm not sure if it has much of an audience at all… it'll be available — although I wouldn't recommend that you put it on at a party"). In March 1997, Bowie said he and Eno had "formulated the storyline and decided to do it ourselves with no other musicians and to not meet while recording it… we'll send the tracks back and forth between St. Petersburg and wherever I am." The Vienna production directed by Robert Wilson was still underway, but *Contamination*'s internet component was going to do a lot of the work ("what we'd like to do is bump up all kinds of stuff on the internet, so you get lots of photographic references… it's kind of a Ripley's Believe It or Not premise").

While pirates were still in the mix, the focus now centered on infectious diseases ("Ebola, AIDS, that new tuberculosis"), hence the title. Trent Reznor and Goldie were supposedly recruited. More time passed. The director of the

Salzburg Festival went public, saying that he'd stopped hearing from Bowie and that the millennium stage production wouldn't happen (Bowie later said he was thinking of having the artist Tony Oursler stage a performance). In a late 1999 web-chat, Bowie said he still hadn't found time to sift through the "over 24 hours of material." In February 2000, he told BowieNet users *this* would be the year he "pieced together" *Contamination*. Instead he played Glastonbury and re-recorded his Sixties songs (see "Hole in the Ground").

There would be nothing else. No CD-ROMs, websites, operas, movies, new Adler diaries. No grand concert with Eno to mark the millennium in Vienna. (No more work, ever, with Eno.) Bowie ended the twentieth century doing everything but continuing the *Outside* sequence. It may have been a blessing: *2. Contamination* and its follow-up (per fan rumor, *3. Afrikaans*, though Bowie never said this) could've been his *Matrix* sequels.

The jig was up by 1999, when Bowie said in a few interviews that he lacked the time or interest to go through the tapes, and Eno showed no signs of wanting to revive a project that had been such a slog in its first go-round. *1. Outside* and its sequels were more a conceptual art project that Bowie (and to a lesser extent, Eno) conducted in the press. From the beginning, Bowie was thinking of this as the endgame, writing in his 1994 journal about "falsifying a concert at a mythical venue" and at a 1995 press conference saying he and Eno "wanted to create some kind of situation that never really happened, but film it as though it had happened, document an event which never took place." The longer that the sequels and concerts didn't exist, the grander they became. When fans circulated hoax sequences of *2. Contamination* ("Ebola Jazz," "Segue: The Mad Ramblings of Long Beard"), it was as inspired an ending as any.

His last thoughts on the project were in 2003. "We did record an awful lot of stuff, and there really is every intention of going through it and putting out Part II and Part III... it would have been nice to have somehow done it as a theatrical trilogy. I just don't have the patience. I think Brian would have the patience." Toward the end of his life, Bowie reportedly wanted to pick up the threads, get back together with Eno to finally complete *1. Outside*. Who's to say it wouldn't have happened — he did finally write his musical, after all. But the end products were beside the point. The process is what mattered. The vast pile of stuff, the reels of tape, the role-playing games, the asylum visits, the Minotaur paintings and obscurantist diaries — Bowie had needed all of it, a sprawling apparatus, a great jerry-rigged dirigible, to get off the ground. Still, now he was in the air.

CHAPTER TEN:

THE BOTTLE IMP

(1995-1997)

Every time you reach the edge, the edge move ahead of you.
— Marlon James, *A Brief History of Seven Killings*

People my age, they don't do the things I do.
— Neil Young, "I'm the Ocean"

Remember, with all original numbers the audiences are hearing numbers they've never heard before — so this makes for a varied stage act. It's risky, because the kids aren't familiar with the tunes, but I'm sure it makes their musical life more interesting.
— David Bowie, 1966

REPTILE
HURT

(Reznor.) **Live**: *14 September-31 October 1995. David Bowie: lead vocal; Trent Reznor: lead vocal, guitar; Reeves Gabrels, Carlos Alomar, Robin Finck: guitar; Mike Garson, Peter Schwartz, Charlie Clouser: keyboards; Danny Lohner, Gail Ann Dorsey: bass; Chris Vrenna, Zachary Alford: drums; George Simms: backing vocal.*

Each of David Bowie's recent tours had been unhappy in its own way. "When I go on the road again, it will have to be something that I have the utmost belief in," he said in 1990. Five years later, to promote *1. Outside*, he sifted together a band of regulars (Reeves Gabrels, Carlos Alomar, Mike Garson, the singer George Simms) and newcomers Zachary Alford and Gail Ann Dorsey. The tour grew to six weeks in America and four months in Britain and Europe. Honoring his vow to retire the hits, he kept older songs mostly to those with allegiances to *1. Outside*: "Scary Monsters," artist profiles "Andy Warhol" and "Joe the Lion," Scott Walker homages "My Death" and "Nite Flights." And half the setlist was from an album that, in the tour's first weeks, hadn't been released. "I really want, for the rest of my working career, to put myself in a place where I'm doing something that's keeping my creative juices going, and you can't do that if you're just trotting out cabaret-style big hits," he said. "Before, I tended to pander to the audience."

His biggest gambit was asking Nine Inch Nails to open the US leg. They were a generation younger, a road-hardened artillery unit outselling him in America. *The Downward Spiral* and *Pretty Hate Machine* had gone platinum, "Closer" was a constant on MTV. Decades later, Reznor recalled Bowie saying "right off the bat, 'you guys are going to blow us off the stage because I'm not [playing] what people want to hear… we've made a difficult new record with Eno and we're going to focus on that… Nobody really wants to hear that, and I know that, but this is what I need to do right now'." At the time, Reznor was a remake of 1975 Bowie: coked and cracking up, with occult pretenses. Bowie became a grounding point for Reznor, offering the prospect of a future. Having diminished his vices to smoking, he was settled but not self-satisfied, and hustling for a new audience.

But the NIN and Bowie crowds stayed separate tribes. Some Bowie fans came late or tailgated until NIN was done, while once Bowie was on, many NIN fans left. Only half the audience remained by the end of one Meadowlands show, while in St. Louis "most of the young crowds... streamed steadily out of the gates." Those who remained sometimes booed or pelted Bowie on stage. In Philadelphia, there were shouts for Tin Machine. In Seattle, a reviewer wrote "most of Bowie's newer stuff left the crowd arm-crossingly bored." Bowie said he knew much of his audience were "there decidedly to see Nails. I think most of them haven't a clue what I do." They moshed and body-surfed while he emoted through "My Death" and "Teenage Wildlife."

Trying to convert NIN fans, he was alienating his own. "We had to adjust emotionally to the fact that we were going to be challenged every night," Bowie said. "It did help me understand a certain aesthetic that was needed to do live performances in front of younger crowds." A prickly middle-aged gumption kept him going. He didn't *have* to do this — he could sing "Changes" at Wembley. But no, he'd sing "The Voyeur of Utter Destruction (As Beauty)" to teenagers. "I just wanted to move away from the preconception of what an artist of my so-called stature should be doing," he said. Not knowing how the audience would react after each song excited him. As he said towards the end of the NIN leg, "I much prefer creating a phenomenal disaster than an exercise in predictable mediocrity."

Bowie and Reznor designed a sequence to bridge their sets. Bowie, then his band, would join NIN, then the latter would leave the stage, with Reznor remaining. The interim set started with "Subterraneans," "Scary Monsters," and NIN's "Reptile." For "Reptile," a song in which sex is corrosion, ejaculation is contamination, and a lover is a succubus, Bowie and Reznor traded verse lines (still in character from "Scary Monsters," Bowie sang his lines in Mockney — "she leaves a trayl of hunn-eh") and harmonized in refrains. When he wasn't singing, Bowie swayed upstage, as if buffeted by winds.

After "Hallo Spaceboy," the NIN/Bowie sequence ended with "Hurt," the closing track of *Downward Spiral*. The song was a "valentine to the sufferer," Reznor said. Performing "Hurt," Reznor burrowed into the song while Bowie kept at a remove, making its drama stagier, intoning the opening verse in the Dracula-is-risen voice of "Cat People." In his refrain duets with Reznor, Bowie took the higher harmony, Reznor sounding like a kid sullenly following his lead.

Critics often knocked or condescended to the tour, and while Bowie sold out some arenas, others were three-quarters full. His new songs were "oddly made, as if designed to envelop the listener rather than to leave catchy memories," as per the *New York Times*. The UK leg was less confrontational — no NIN; "Moonage Daydream" and "Diamond Dogs" as regular encores — but many in the audience were still indifferent-to-apoplectic about the new material. What remains are the live recordings (with hope, there'll be an official release soon). Freed from the expectations and resentments of their time, they document Bowie in fighting trim, backed by one of his finest bands, blasting through some of his most adventurous sets. His mid-Nineties renaissance was as much a stage creation as a studio one.

I'M AFRAID OF AMERICANS

(Bowie, Eno.) **Recorded: (Showgirls version)** *ca. late 1994, Mountain Studios, 11-13 January 1995, Hit Factory;* **(Earthling remake)** *ca. 26 August-11 November 1996, Looking Glass Studios, New York. Bowie: lead and backing vocal, keyboards, loops; Eno: keyboards, synthesizers, loops (orig.); Alomar: guitar (orig.); Gabrels: guitar; Garson: electric piano (remake); Mark Plati: keyboards, synthesizer, loops (remake); Dorsey: bass (remake); Alford: drums (remake); Produced: Bowie, Eno (orig.); Bowie, Gabrels, Plati; engineered: David Richards (orig.); Plati.*

First release: *26 September 1995,* **Showgirls** *OST (Interscope 92652-2); (remake) 3 February 1997,* **Earthling** *(RCA 74321 449442/CK 92098, UK #6, US #39).* **Broadcast**: *10 April 1997, Late Night with Conan O'Brien; 29 January 1998, Howard Stern Birthday Party; 22 November 1999, MusiquePlus; 29 November 1999, Later with Jools Holland; 27 June 2000, Bowie at the BBC Radio Theatre; 15 June 2002, A&E Live by Request; 23 September 2003, Sessions @ AOL.* **Live**: *1997-2000, 2002-2004.*

"I'm Afraid of Americans" is a *Showgirls* soundtrack song, an *Earthling* album track, and a six-remix single. A "stateless" song like "John, I'm Only Dancing," it has no definitive version, though Trent Reznor's "V1" remix is its most recognizable face: the last time Bowie troubled the *Billboard* Hot 100 until 2015. Like "Young Americans," it was a critique of a country he'd been fascinated by since childhood. "I loved all the things that America rejects," Bowie said. "It was black music, it was the beatnik poets. It was all the stuff that I thought was the true rebellious subversive side... what makes America great is its pioneer, independent spirit, not its corporate togetherness." And the corporate side was winning. "I was traveling in Java when [its] first McDonald's went up: it was like, 'for fuck's sake'."

Originally called "Dummy" (a Portishead nod?), its first version was recorded around late 1994 or in the first weeks of 1995: a sour concoction of drum patterns, synthesizer and distorted vocal loops, a few of which — a "laughing" hook and a synth hook pinging around an E-flat octave — survived in subsequent remakes. By the time Brian Eno arrived in New York in January 1995, "Dummy" was slated for the soundtrack of *Johnny Mnemonic*, a Keanu Reeves movie adapted from a William Gibson short story. The original refrain has Bowie howling "I'm afraid of the *animals*!," which became "Americans" towards the fade. Before tracking his vocal, "David would have an identity in mind. He'd know who the person singing it was and their attitude," Eno said in 2016. "I remember him recording 'I'm Afraid of Americans' and saying, after one of the early takes, 'No, he's got to be more self-doubting than that.'" Later in 1995, the retitled "I'm Afraid of Americans" was shifted from *Johnny Mnemonic* to *Showgirls*, where lines like "dummy wants to suck on a Coke" read like script cues for poor Elizabeth Berkley's character.

Bowie remade it for *Earthling*, starting with the *Showgirls* version's forty-eight-track masters. "We pulled things off several different reels to make this new composite. It was quite a clean-up job, not the most enjoyable," its co-producer Mark Plati recalled. Bowie renamed its subject "Johnny" (a callback to *Mnemonic*, or his own "Repetition") and transposed verses — the *Showgirls* opening verse became the *Earthling* version's third. It remained in F major, mainly keeping to the home chord, with Bowie's verses penned to a two-note range while spanning fifths in refrains ("afraid of the *world*"). New additions were live bass and drum tracks, Mike Garson's electric piano, and every fuzzbox Reeves Gabrels owned, including a Univox Super Fuzz and a Roger Mayer Octavia. "I plugged them direct into the board. I tracked as many guitars as I could until I ran out of fuzz boxes," Gabrels said. The *Earthling* mix grew as cluttered as a closet: gurgles, feedback whistles, static bursts, twinging loops.

For his remix, Reznor scrubbed this jiggery-pokery, giving his arrangement a tighter scope — a grinding bass figure mixed right is boosted to dominate the first refrain, while each verse gets a different rhythmic base. A looped

"God is an American" is the last word, where the *Earthling* version rode its refrain hard to the close. The video was a European tourist's nightmare of walking in an American city. Some thuggish Yank singles you out for your weird clothes and accent and chases you down; everyone's armed; the cabbies are lunatics; the place is full of Christian fanatics. Reznor, wearing a civilian take on Travis Bickle's army jacket, played a convincing heavy. (Another remix has Ice Cube pursuing Bowie as Reznor does in the video, harassing him with advertisements: "shut up and be happy!" "Superbowl Sunday!")

[KODAK] COMMERCIAL

Recorded: ca. 1995? Bowie?: vocals, guitar, synthesizer, drums?

A brief, mostly-instrumental piece Bowie reportedly licensed for a Kodak Advantix ad which aired in early 1996, its origins are murky, said to hail from everywhere from *Lodger* to the *1. Outside* sessions. A thirty-second fragment heard on a commercial that's found on YouTube as of this writing (look for "1996 Kodak Advantix Film"), if it's Bowie's work at all, is more aligned with the sound of *'hours…'* than anything else.

TELLING LIES

Recorded: (backing tracks) ca. February-March 1996, Mountain Studios; (overdubs) ca. mid-May 1996, Looking Glass. Bowie: lead and backing vocal, loops, keyboards; Gabrels: lead guitar, Roland VG-8, GR-09, loops; Plati: loops, synthesizer; Garson: keyboards; Dorsey: bass; Alford: drums. Produced: Bowie, Gabrels, Plati; engineered: Plati.

First release: 11 September 1996 ("Paradox Mix," download); 3 February 1997, *Earthling*. *Broadcast*: 17 February 1997, Nulle part ailleurs. *Live*: 1996-1997.

A few months after the *Outside* tour, Bowie played a string of Asian shows and European festivals. He'd fallen in love with his touring band, which he winnowed to a quartet: Gail Ann Dorsey, Zachary Alford, Reeves Gabrels, and Mike Garson ("the band that it probably should have been when we started," he said). Though needing to compensate for losing Carlos Alomar's rhythm guitar, Gabrels also downsized, in part to get off festival stages faster. Once carting around twenty-space and sixteen-space racks of gear, he converted to the Roland VG-8 ("virtual guitar") system, which replaced most of his amps, preamps, effects, and speaker cabinets, while adding a Roland GR-09 guitar synthesizer.

It was the start of Bowie's drum 'n' bass period. He'd discovered the genre, which he called "jungle" interchangeably, a few years before — a London friend who was a huge "clubber" had made the introductions. "What's great about [Bowie] is that he's constantly looking for new input... he just wades right in, like an old lady at a basement sale," Gabrels said. He would do reconnaissance, going to raves and taking ecstasy while Bowie played Goldie singles at home. Always sniffing around for contemporary R&B and dance rhythms, Bowie found drum 'n' bass an appealing fit. It was (in good part) British and had less "street" connotations than hip-hop. He liked to say the producer Photek was a white guy who "lives in Ipswich, I think, and does it all in his bedroom — he's never been to a club in his life!"

To some, the move was Bowie in flagrant denial of approaching fifty. He was talking up jungle, wearing a Doctor Strange costume on stage, dying his hair copper (so audiences could see him better at daylight festival gigs, he said), growing a goatee. Co-opting a once-underground genre like drum 'n' bass was something you *expected* Bowie to do in 1996. "If Bowie was associated with something, it was instantly OK," Martyn Ware said at the time, recalling the Seventies. "If only that was the case now." Bowie's statements had the overheated taste of a press release. Jungle was "the great cry of the twentieth century." Or "jungle is a new vocabulary... these hectic snare volleys reflect how information is pounding on us today... a metaphor for our whole way of thinking."

He said he had no intention of being a "legitimate" drum 'n' bass musician (he was David Bowie, for God's sake), and that drum 'n' bass itself was a scavenger's music, made from sped-up samples and drum loops — he was just an amateur scrapper. It started with Brian Eno making percussive loops for two late *1. Outside* songs — "I'm Deranged" and "We Prick You." By early 1996, working for the last time in Montreux (he'd soon put his Lausanne home on the market), Bowie was experimenting on his own, laying the groundwork for at least one track, "Telling Lies."

Before hitting the road, Bowie brought the tapes of "Telling Lies" to New York for his band to complete; they'd play it on stage that summer. The song was his "first formal approach to juxtaposition between jungle and aggressive rock and using a melodic line as a kind of easing the situation," he said. "It became an exercise piece, it kind of mutated throughout the tour." Mark Plati recalled it being "a quickie, done in a couple of days, most of the time devoted to the live drums." Plati remixed "Telling Lies" later that year ("the Feelgood Mix"), as did A Guy Called Gerald ("the Paradox Mix") and Adam F. These were released as downloads, week by week, on Bowie's website that September.

Recording *Earthling* at the time, Bowie wanted another go at "Telling Lies." He polished the lyric, Gabrels added some Roland lines, Dorsey a melodic bassline, Garson played keyboards, Plati dropped in sounds from his remix. "The major change was in the structure, where after the second chorus we cleared the track out, leaving Mike's synth pad and a piano part from the remix," Plati said. "Then the song built itself up again." It was one of the album's weakest tracks, a shamble between A minor and E major, its verses affixed to overlong refrains. Bowie's top melody was a stitchwork, some verse phrasings in hock to Leonard Cohen's "The Future" and the Beach Boys' "I Just Wasn't Made For These Times." He mandated the revised "Telling Lies" make the cut for *Earthling*, calling it "the most successful of the juxtapositions." It worked better on stage, where he sang lines like "gasping for my resurrection" and "come straggling in your tattered remnants" with a tart vigor.

"DEAD MEN DON'T TALK"

Recorded: ca. 20-24 May 1996, Looking Glass. Bowie: lead vocal; Gabrels: guitar, loops; Garson: keyboards; Dorsey: bass; Alford: drums.

First shown: 6 September 1997, **Inspirations**.

In spring 1996, Bowie was filmed for *Inspirations*, a documentary by Michael Apted about the development of artists' styles. Much of his sequence has Bowie in the studio. After reading a front-page article from the 17 May 1996 *New York Times* about a disgraced admiral who shot himself, he types the headline and some sentences into his word-scrambling Verbasizer program, which generates a clump of text that includes "the top kills himself" and "dead men don't talk." "The choices that I now make from this form I can then reimbue with an emotive quality, if I want to, or take it as it writes itself," he tells an off-camera Apted. He makes "dead men don't talk" a refrain hook and sings some other lines over a guitar feedback loop. Apparently not developed further, the piece previews *Earthling*, cut with a similar spontaneity and dispatch in three months' time.

LAW (EARTHLINGS ON FIRE)

(Bowie, Gabrels.) ***Recorded****: ca. 26 August-11 November 1996, Looking Glass. Bowie: lead vocal; Gabrels: guitar, Roland VG-8, GR-09, loops; Plati: keyboards, loops, synthesizer, bass. Produced: Bowie, Gabrels, Plati; engineered: Plati.*

First release*: 3 February 1997, **Earthling**.*

Bowie booked the Looking Glass Studios in New York for a month, starting in the last week of August. He wanted to cut an album at a trot, even getting in a few East Coast club shows while recording. "It was just the feeling that we're bloody good and we really want to get it down on record," he said in 1997. "Reeves and I virtually wrote an album to show off the band's abilities, and where we were at. I think that you feel a lot of the aggression and momentum of the band on the album."

The songs were written (Bowie: "eight days," "nine days," "nine-and-a-half days") and recorded ("three weeks," "eleven days," "twelve days," "two-and-a-half weeks") in a burst: a response to the year he'd spent on *1. Outside*. "We don't want to spoil the energy," he said while mixing the album in late 1996. "I might even go with some rough mixes with no effects." Where *1. Outside* was "a forum for a lot of artsy, intellectual analysis on the part of Eno and myself," the new record was a Polaroid of his band. "An interruption... [it] wasn't an expected album. It really came out of the touring situation," he said. "I rushed into it and then thought gosh, this is going to mess everyone up because they're expecting the next Nathan Adler diary." As usual, there was misdirection at work. *Earthling*, allegedly "written as almost a vanity showcase for the band," was more a studio experiment like *The Buddha of Suburbia* than any attempt to document his live sound.

At Looking Glass, a studio on Broadway that had begun as the workspace of its namesake, Philip Glass, the main engineer was Mark Plati. Having worked with Arthur Baker and Junior Vasquez and run the desk on Deee-Lite's *Infinity Within,* Plati had over the years collected samples from discarded takes, microphone tests, and monitor mixes, stockpiling these for use as compositional material. During a studio visit in May 1996, Gabrels found a simpatico soul in Plati, with whom he crafted some loops for the summer tour.

A month after the tour ended, the *Earthling* sessions kicked off as a three-man workshop. Bowie and Gabrels had made demos on the road, songs written on Fernandes ZO-3 "travel" guitars "in a very conventional manner against the [chord] sequence. Then we'd lose the guitar once the song was done," Gabrels said. Plati's prep work was to make a "load of playback tracks," loops to jump-start compositions. As Gabrels said, "you felt like there was already a song at work. You eliminated the dead air of a few people sitting there and going 'okay, how do we start this?'" Soon enough, "we were cranking these out one per day," Plati said. "Reeves would be coming up with guitar parts and sounds, I'd be at the computer recording him or working on the arrangement, and David would be on the couch, writing the lyric. At day's end he'd do a vocal." Songs were flattened to "rhythmic landscapes" — chords, drum loops, Roland lines. They would move up sets of faders at random to "see what the combinations sounded like together," Bowie said. "There was no suggestion of melody. Once we developed a kind of mattress, then I would go into the studio and just free associate against that."

The latter half of the *Earthling* sessions brought in the rest of the band, mostly for overdubs. Unlike his improvisatory role in the *1. Outside* sessions, Mike Garson had to work with mostly-set song structures (he also didn't find drum 'n' bass interesting, melodically). The band were sampled, turned into a synthetic, distorted version of their stage presence. Garson's piano was piped through a guitar amp; some Gail Ann Dorsey basslines were loops of her jiggering with her pedal board without knowing she was being taped (particularly on "Little Wonder"); Zachary Alford was heard more in sped-up drum loops than live tracks (see "Battle for Britain").

Tired of "straight" (even his conception of "straight") electric guitar, Gabrels went to town on his Roland VG-8 processor. Cutting a single guitar track on his Parker Nitefly, he had hundreds of possibilities — he could change amp sounds, bend a note, retune a single string for more "jagged" intervals, drop all the strings down a whole step. He'd play three lines "as identically as possible but using sounds that emphasize the bottom, the top, or the midrange — like a bottomy Les Paul thing, something with razor-edged, hex-fuzz-type distortion and a Rat pedal-type sound up the middle." It made the guitar as suspect as the rest of the pieces that *Earthling* was built upon. "We transferred a lot of what we did on the guitar to the synth and then played them as recurring pieces," Bowie said. "Exactly the same notes, played in exactly the same manner, keep recurring throughout a piece."

Earthling was also the first digitally-recorded Bowie album, which let him easily reset the bones of a song. "David would say 'let's hear a verse, a chorus, a verse, a double chorus, a break' and I would be able to do all that in about thirty seconds," Plati said. As there was no need to conserve tape, Plati kept everything from rehearsals to scratch takes, and Bowie soon had more tracks than first envisioned. *Earthling* was originally an EP's worth of new songs to be sequenced with remakes of "Telling Lies," "I'm Afraid of Americans" and slightly older compositions — "Baby Universal," "Dead Against It," "I Can't Read," and "Bring Me the Disco King" were all planned (and mostly cut) for the album. By the end of the sessions, there was enough new material to render most of the "covers" superfluous.

Against Certainty

The first track Bowie, Gabrels, and Plati worked on was "Law (Earthlings on Fire)," a piece "based on one of Reeves' hotel-room ideas called 'Bits,'" Plati said, "It changed direction a few times, until it assumed more the shape of a sound collage. It's also the only track with a real guitar amp — the rest of the record is VG-8 and pedals."

It was a trial run like "Telling Lies," more a frenzied atmosphere than a song. A sequel to "Pallas Athena," it is eight- or sixteen-bar sections pasted together, including "verses" with spoken lines like "a wallet drops and money flies into the midday sun" and a two-note bassline; and refrain/hook sections with a chanted "with this sound mark the ground" and the parenthetical title line, which Bowie sings as if announcing a superhero. The rhythms have little to do with jungle — the track's far more in line with late-Eighties industrial trash pop like My Life with the Thrill Kill Kult. "Law" has sustained abuse of the Eventide Harmonizer, a looped Bowie chanting, synthetic vibraphone, guitar-synth yawps, regular guitar yawps (Gabrels on a Seventies Gibson Firebird reissue) and old standbys like motorcycle revs, shattering glass, and door-slams.

Bowie scratched together a brief lyric, taking his hook "I don't want knowledge! I want certainty!" (sung into an empty water cooler bottle) from a paraphrased 1964 Bertrand Russell interview. Russell hadn't made this demand: rather, he called it a fundamental human error, as "our nature is as much a fact of the existing world as anything, and there can be no certainty that it will remain constant." Russell "was right, mean old bastard that he was. As you get older, you become more desperate for certainty," Bowie said. The alternative was to "relax your hold on the idea of ever acquiring it and enjoy the process of gaining information. I'm quite happy with the latter. What-is-my-purpose? doesn't hang so heavy in my sky."

In his youth, he'd been hungry for belief — it drove songs like "Quicksand" and "Cygnet Committee." Now he was more sanguine about never learning the answers. "I'm not looking for a faith. I don't want to believe anything. I'm looking for knowledge," he said in 1995. Going through boxes in the attic was all one could do. Don't waste time wondering who put them there. "To me, it's the avenue to insanity, to presume if you keep studying you'll find the answers," he said. "As I got older, I was more able to accept the idea that you don't have certainty on this earth; rather than make you more perplexed and worried, it actually lightens the load when you realize there are no certainties." Another line in "Law" has a man falling dead, his last words "what a morning." These were reportedly Samuel Beckett's father's last words, though Beckett's father also said something else before he died: *fight fight fight*.

Looking for Satellites

(Bowie, Gabrels, Plati.) **Recorded**: *ca. 26 August-11 November 1996, Looking Glass. Bowie: lead and backing vocal; Gabrels: lead and rhythm guitar, Roland VG-8, GR-09, loops; Garson: keyboards; Plati: keyboards, loops; Dorsey: bass; Alford: drums, drum loops. Produced: Bowie, Gabrels, Plati; engineered: Plati.*

First release: 3 February 1997, **Earthling**. *Live:* 1997.

The second track started in the *Earthling* sessions, "Looking for Satellites" began as Mark Plati's attempt at an electronic track in waltz time, using "samples from lots of records I'd done before. [I] reshaped them, twisted them, made them into new sounds through manipulation and combination with other sounds." Keeping some of this foundation — rhythm, chord information, a few melodic lines — Bowie and Reeves Gabrels reset the song in 6/4 and wrote a new verse progression around a diminished chord, though keeping Plati's D major key for a mantra/refrain, as many of his samples were tuned to D. "It was a case of David and Reeves jamming against the track to come up with chord sequences," Plati said. Bowie wrote a refrain and first verse in "a whirlwind of cigarettes and Post-It notes," cutting guide vocals that wound up used on the album. During overdubs, which included a soaring bassline, Bowie added another verse. And the track closed with a guitar solo against its player's wishes.

"David insisted, so what you're hearing is me being pissed off," Gabrels said of his solo. Bowie didn't only demand a solo, he added an Eno-style constriction: Gabrels had to stay on his low E string until the chord changed. Then he could move to the next-highest string but had to stay there until the next change and so on, all while playing constant sixteenth notes. The result, pieced together from multiple takes, had an "orgasmic form," as Gabrels said. "A nice starting point, a plateau stage, a peak, a climax and its resolution. In a way it's a statement of dick control." When confined to his low E string, he plays distorted bass figures (Dorsey's overdubbed bassline glides beneath his notes). He sounds like he's flailing underwater, with each move up a string a fresh, desperate breath. Reaching his A string sends him kiting, wringing lines full of yo-yoing theremin sounds. "At the very end of it, you can hear me trying to kick out the walls of the box," he said. As revenge, Gabrels kept going beyond his allotted bars, plowing his way into the last refrain. It was one of his finest solos on a Bowie record, an inspired frustration.

Bowie's lyric was another knowledge-versus-certainty match like "Law." This time he set God against television, putting odds on TV. "The initial lines are just a shopping list of words that I associated with consumer culture," he said. "That was to prop up the idea of a spiritual search between an orthodox religion and a technological age... Sort of, 'Who is God — shall we kill Him so that we can reinvent him for our own purposes?'" Derived from Verbasized cut-up, the mantra is eight iambs sung by a double-tracked Bowie (with a third voice on "TV"). It's a "seed phrase," in a term from cryptology — a meaningless string of words that can be translated, by those with the key, into a passcode. The words move in dragging procession, their rhythms pegged to a thumb hitting a remote, clicking through war, shampoo ad, Boyzone video (Bowie sang "Boy's Own," allegedly unaware it was a boyband homonym). From the start, there's interference — a guitar whistle, a counter-melody on synthesizer.

It wound up religious, the satellites of its title as observing angels. "Satellite's gone/up to the skies," Lou Reed sang in 1972, with Bowie in the control booth. Each year more satellites hang above the planet, watching hurricanes form in the Caribbean, spying on us, beaming *Baywatch* to Chennai or directions to a driver in Fresno. They tend to the knotting and binding of the world. Satellite television, honored in a stupefied chant of images, cleared the ground for the internet: the small flood before the great flood. An age of miracles that's left us as lonely as a moon, and like the moon, we live on stolen light, half in darkness. "It's as near to a spiritual song as I've ever written," Bowie said.

SEVEN YEARS IN TIBET

> (Bowie, Gabrels.) **Recorded**: ca. 26 August-11 November 1996, Looking Glass. Bowie: lead vocal, alto saxophone; Gabrels: lead and rhythm guitar, Roland VG-8, GR-09, loops; Garson: Kurzweil organ; Plati: keyboards, loops; Dorsey: bass, vocal; Alford: drums, drum loops. Produced: Bowie, Gabrels, Plati; engineered: Plati.

> **First release**: 3 February 1997, **Earthling**. **Broadcast**: 3 March 1997, The Rosie O'Donnell Show; 8 April 1997, 99X Breakfast Show (WNNX), WBCN. **Live**: 1996-1997.

"When I was about nineteen, I became an overnight Buddhist," Bowie said in 1996. He'd found Buddhism through books like Heinrich Harrer's memoir *Seven Years in Tibet*. Harrer wrote himself as an existentialist hero, unburdened by family or nationality (convenient if you were a once a Nazi), who discovers an isolated Buddhist kingdom in its last days of independence.

"So much of what first appealed to me about Buddhism has stayed with me," Bowie said. "The idea of transience, and that there is nothing to hold onto pragmatically, that we do at some point or another have to let go of that which we consider most dear to us, because it's a very short life." ("I managed to cope with most things when I worked with David — except the Buddha," quipped Kenneth Pitt, his manager in the Sixties.)

Maoist China's crackdown on Tibet sent the Dalai Lama and other lamas into exile. Some of the latter found refuge in London's Buddhist Society, where they encountered a teenager from Bromley with endless questions. Bowie learned of monks being tortured and murdered, monasteries and holy places sacked. His 1968 mime *Jetsun and the Eagle* was a fable of a boy under the foot of Chinese Communists, and his "Wild Eyed Boy from Freecloud" revised the scenario — a monk being sentenced to death brings down the wrath of nature upon a village of occupiers.

Thirty years on, it had only grown dimmer in Tibet. Upon listening to some Dalai Lama lectures, Bowie said he felt guilty "that I've known about this situation quite well and quite intimately for many, many years — [but] I hadn't actually come out and made my stance on what I feel about it." So he wrote "Seven Years in Tibet," about "a young Tibetan monk who's just been shot. His last experiences in the snow as the Chinese helicopters fly over." A monk watches the sky fade, gets off a last prayer. Bowie processed his voice through a ring modulator, giving it a crackling, papery sound. It was the voice of "young Tibetans who have had their families killed and themselves have been reduced to mere ciphers in their own country." That said, Bowie found his opening lines from a fabricated article circulating the internet in 1996: an exploding biscuit container hits a woman on the head. She thinks she's been shot and frantically tries to hold in her brains, which are in truth the oozing biscuit dough. The track's working title was "Biscuit Lady."

The song began as a Reeves Gabrels instrumental called "Brussels," which Bowie first considered "incredibly hack, with a very predictable self-serious quality. I said, 'dump this one, Reeves.'" Gabrels eventually won him over. Its salvaging, Mark Plati said, was "a case of taking a preconceived idea and finding new chords": D minor verses and F major refrains, each built around an absent home chord. It was the usual *Earthling* songwriting routine — Bowie chose samples he liked from Gabrels and Plati's collections, worked out chords on guitar with Gabrels, then quickly wrote a lyric.

The dreamy lead guitar called back to Fleetwood Mac's "Albatross," a Sixties signifier along with Mike Garson's Farfisa organ tone (a setting on his Kurzweil) and Bowie's alto saxophone, meant to give "a Stax influence... the sort of sound you might imagine behind Al Green or Ann Peebles." (Gabrels evoked "Albatross" mostly to "oppose it to the ton-of-bricks chorus," a distortion-fattened wall of guitars and keyboards.) The track ran to the death-beat of "Nightclubbing" as routed through Nine Inch Nails' "Closer," garnished by loops that sound like kettle drums and tympani strikes. Gail Ann Dorsey makes quick, descending fills in the turnarounds. The coda has velociraptor shrieks, mosquito buzzes and baby cries; Garson's "Farfisa" gets the last word with a droning E major chord.

A few months before "Seven Years in Tibet" was cut, the first Tibetan Freedom Concert was held in San Francisco. Tibet became a hip political cause right when the Clinton administration normalized trade relations with China, and today the idea that China will recognize Tibetan independence has the same odds as the US giving Florida to the Seminoles. Bowie played Tibet House benefits, spoke out in the press, hung a Tibetan flag in the studio, and sang a version of "Seven Years in Tibet" in Mandarin Chinese that would be the last #1 single in British-controlled Hong Kong. "Seven Years in Tibet" had its composer's blend of Gnosticism and Buddhism: something within us will outlast conquerors and life. It's heard in Dorsey's voice in the final refrain, when she sings "nothing!" as a grand departure.

DEAD MAN WALKING

(Bowie, Gabrels.) *Recorded*: ca. 26 August-11 November 1996, Looking Glass. Bowie: lead vocal; Gabrels: guitar, Roland VG-8, keyboards, loops; Garson: piano; Plati: Moog, keyboards, synthesizer, loops; Dorsey: bass, backing vocals; Alford: drums. Produced: Bowie, Gabrels, Plati; engineered: Plati.

First release: 3 February 1997, **Earthling**. *Broadcast*: 3 March 1997, The Rosie O'Donnell Show; 4 April 1997, Late Show with David Letterman; 8 April 1997, 99X Breakfast Show (WNNX), WBCN; 10 April 1997, Late Night with Conan O'Brien; 17 April 1997, Top of the Pops; 18 April 1997, Jack Docherty Show; 5 September 1997, CKZZ; 8 September 1997, Mountain Morning Show (KMTT); 9 September 1997, Johnny Steele Breakfast Show (KITS); 10 September 1997, Tammy

Bruce Show (KROQ); 16 September 1997, KFOG: 25 September 1997, Live from Studio One; 2 October 1997, World Café (WXPN). **Live:** *1997.*

Watching Neil Young and Crazy Horse play in 1996, Bowie found "a sense of grace and dignity about what they were doing... an incredible verve and energy. It was very moving, watching them work under the moon," he said. Young had become a shaman figure for audiences half his age. "This grand old man of American rock, a pioneer loaded with integrity," as Bowie effusively called him, did the same feedback-bloodied, two-guitars-bass-drums stomp he'd done in 1969. He'd stood still, and the world had spun back to him. That night Young and Crazy Horse were "turning around, like in a tribal circle, very slowly," Bowie said. "And it seemed to me that they were doing that to catch back their dreams, to find youth again, to not allow the energy to escape."

"Dead Man Walking," Bowie's homage "to rock and roll that is still young while we are all growing old," was the first track in the *Earthling* sessions written in the studio without drawing on earlier demos. Bowie originally wanted a techno-influenced track in the Underworld vein (he also thought he'd write about his old flame Susan Sarandon, who'd recently won an Oscar for the same-titled film). After Mark Plati and Reeves Gabrels came up with rhythm tracks, Bowie played a guitar riff he'd used in "The Supermen." Jimmy Page had showed it to him when cutting Bowie's "I Pity the Fool" single in 1965 — an alternating movement of F# barre chord to open E string, G chord to open E string. "It was just opening up that E string. That's made me so aware of keeping the E's open and taking chords through it," Bowie said. "[Page] probably started me off on 'Space Oddity' without realizing it." On "Dead Man Walking," the riff collides with a Roland guitar-synth line, which buzzes along beside it joined by keyboard arpeggios, feedback spurts, percussive loops. Yet when the riff closes out a refrain, it's a gavel pounding to make other voices fall in line.

Plati wrote a Moog part for the intro, Gabrels did guitar lines for the verses, Bowie wrote a lyric and cut a vocal (much of it was wiped when Plati backed up the hard drive, so Bowie had to sing it again). Yet "Dead Man Walking" stalled out and was nearly cut from the album. The rest of the band weren't fitting in. "Instead of focusing the track like the other songs, they made it even more blurry. Too many elements on tape! It was a bit hard to listen to for a while," Plati said. He spent five days on a mix that had a dramatic arc — the track "begins completely programmed, and by the time it's finished, it's completely live," with Zachary Alford's snare fills and cymbals, Gail Ann Dorsey's bass as a sinuous foundation for the outro, and Mike Garson playing what he considered "straight jazz" and closing with a fresh Latin-style melody, as if saying: let's go *here* now.

Lyrically it was a blur. An older man watches a clip of his youth on a screen. He gets up, packs up his thoughts as he walks down the aisle (airplane? marriage?). As the pre-chorus begins, with its downshift to E-flat minor, he feels clean of the past, as if he's finally outlived it. In the counterpoint refrain, with Bowie singing two alternating notes, he's in mid-air, falling up through time. As the riff kicks in, he dives away. In the morning, he'll wake up wearing dried mascara and feel the hangover deep in his bones (that's the acoustic revision of "Dead Man Walking" that Bowie and Gabrels played in 1997). Until then he's gone, toe-tapping on angels' heads.

LITTLE WONDER

(Bowie, Gabrels, Plati.) **Recorded**: *ca. 26 August-11 November 1996, Looking Glass. Bowie: lead vocal; Gabrels: lead and rhythm guitar, Roland VG-8, loops; Plati: keyboards, loops; Garson: harpsichord pad; Dorsey: bass; Alford: drums, drum loops. Produced: Bowie, Gabrels, Plati; engineered: Plati.*

First release: *27 January 1997 (Arista 74321 452072, UK #14).* **Broadcast**: *24 October 1996, VH1 Fashion Awards; 8 February 1997, Saturday Night Live; 11 February 1997, The Tonight Show; 17 February 1997, Nulle part ailleurs; 22 February 1997, Wetten... dass?; 27 June 2000, Bowie at the BBC Radio Theatre.* **Live**: *1996, 1997, 2000.*

To commemorate Bowie's fiftieth birthday in the *Times,* Caitlin Moran asked readers to imagine that "this orange-faced bandwagon jumper" was a primary school teacher who'd recorded *Earthling* in his shed at home. "Do we really believe that record companies would eagerly sign up a fifty-year-old man with no new ideas, wonky eyes, manky hair, LA teeth and a tartan suit, who talks like an animatronic statue in Picadilly's Rock Circus?...What is the *point* of David Bowie now?"

Earthling-era Bowie was a wonky, manky older man scampering on stage in his professionally-torn jacket. "I don't like it, 'cause it's sort of like your dad embarrassing you, isn't it?" as Blur's Graham Coxon said at the time. The video for leadoff single "Little Wonder" had Bowie as a rave cathedral gargoyle. "I seem to be going into a kind of demented persona now on stage. I guess it's 'cause I can't sell youth. 'Cause I'm not a youth," he said. "So I'm selling whatever it is I *am* as a persona, which tends to be this kind of ironically enthusiastic older guy who's still into this like crazed sound." The album was "very hard-nosed... had no compromises on it whatsoever."

This wouldn't do. Any rocker entering their fifties needs dignity and perspective. *This next one is called "Oh, You Pretty Things" (applause) and it's about the homo superior. Remember the homo superior? (Audience chuckles) Ah you **do**, you **do**. Well, it's hard to believe you're one of 'em if you can't get out of bed without groaning! (Sympathetic laughs).* Instead with "Little Wonder," Bowie tried to become an MTV regular again and make the cover of *Spin*, not succeeding on either front; he played summer festivals where kids took ecstasy and got drunk instead of those where people brought their kids.

"Little Wonder" came from the Prodigy, with whom he'd toured in summer 1996 — a mash of arena rock and what the American press had started calling "electronica," with some of Bowie's stage moves and costuming suggesting an arch take on Prodigy singer/dancer Keith Flint. By late 1996, the Prodigy had been signed by Madonna's Maverick label and "Firestarter" was on MTV's Buzz Bin, as was the Chemical Brothers' "Setting Sun," complete with Noel Gallagher guest spot. The elements looked aligned for a garish hard rock/electronica single from a British rock legend.

But Bowie couldn't just grab for the ring: he had to go about it sideways. He prefaced his thumping refrain, slam-full of guitars and "Helter Skelter" harmony vocals, with verses where he keeps below a middle B and closes phrases down an octave ("grum-*py gnomes*"). It's not a festival voice, but a cabaret one: the voice of a decaying British institution who never translated well overseas, renting some jungle loops and singing over them in his Mockney accent: "Sit on my karma! Dayme meditation! Tayke me away!"

"Little Wonder" started with a tape of noises Reeves Gabrels had made via his Roland VG-8. The opening guitar riff alone was three different samples. The first note is the sound of a popped low E string sent through an envelope filter and distorted, the second the same tone up two octaves and whammied, the third an exospheric E that Gabrels played on the 24th fret of his Parker and kicked an octave higher via a Fernandes Sustainer. "It gets squeaky up there: it sounds like two pieces of metal rubbing together," he said at the time. "My playing on this record is like making head cheese: you put the parts in, boil it and scrape off the distilled thing that comes to the top." Before performing "Little Wonder" live, he had to figure out how to play his riff on stage.

Given a rhythm track by Gabrels and Mark Plati, Bowie took a miniature Fernandez guitar and strummed together a chord sequence he described as "street corner singing" — a doo-wop progression he rattled by raising its last chord a half-step. The track took time to build, with the refrains set in place before the verses. Finding a Disney catalog in the studio, Bowie used the names of the Seven Dwarfs for his lyric, adding "Stinky" and "Shaky" ("the dwarf in rehab," Mark Plati said later) to their ranks. At one point "Little Wonder" grew to be a "nine-minute jungle-electronic epic — much longer than on the album, but essentially the same idea," Plati said. The middle break was a montage of stolen sounds, distorted instruments, bass queries, studio verité footage, even a snippet of a drunken roadie introducing Steely Dan in 1974. "All sorts of shit," Gabrels said. Edited to roughly two minutes for the album mix, the break was shortened further for the single, with pieces from it distributed throughout (e.g., the train noise after the second verse). It added up to a minor UK hit, a dud on the American charts, and a song that already sounded, when Bowie sang it for the last time in 2000, like a dated piece from a lost world.

BATTLE FOR BRITAIN (THE LETTER)

(Bowie, Gabrels, Plati.) **Recorded**: *ca. 26 August-11 November 1996, Looking Glass. Bowie: lead vocal; Gabrels: guitar, Roland VG-8, GR-09, loops; Plati: keyboards, loops; Garson: piano; Dorsey: bass; Alford: drums, drum loops. Produced: Bowie, Gabrels, Plati; engineered: Plati.*

First release: *3 February 1997,* **Earthling**. **Live**: *1997, 2003-2004.*

The cover of *Earthling* is Bowie standing in the ultra-verdant fields of England, taking in the view like a general or an extraterrestrial surveyor. He's wearing an Alexander McQueen distressed frock coat, a remake of

Pete Townshend's Union jacket from the Sixties. "The ultimate anti-icon," Bowie said of McQueen's coat. "A retelling of the British flag joke, again torn and stained... the tatty remains of a metaphysical empire." The photo's a fake: Bowie's surveying a green screen, Photoshopped into a postcard.

It suited his symbolic return to his home country. When he recorded *Earthling*, he hadn't lived in Britain for over two decades. He was considering repatriating, particularly upon the birth of his daughter in 2000 (see "Dollar Days"). "At some point in my life I would like to go back to Britain," he said. "I miss the gossip... I quite miss a particular way of looking at the world." But he stayed in New York. He blamed the tabloid culture in London, saying the red-tops would never leave his family in peace, whereas in New York it's considered a point of pride to ignore celebrities. And maybe he'd been gone too long. The Britain that had formed him was a ghost of a memory. "It probably comes from a sense of 'am I or am I not British?', an inner war that wages in most expatriates," he said of his "Battle for Britain (The Letter)." "What Britain is very good at is keeping people re-evaluating their own standards in a hostile and quite cruel fashion."

Earthling arrived at the peak of second-edition Swinging London: Britpop battles sponsored by the national press, an election in which Tony Blair played a slimmed-down (in multiple senses) Harold Wilson, name-dropping the Stone Roses and being praised by Noel Gallagher, and with galleries full of the work of hip young artists like Tracey Emin and Damien Hirst (both Bowie pals). "There's so much energy there. It's as if we've finally understood that we don't have the rest of the Commonwealth, or the world, to support and comfort us, that we have to do things on our own now to prove who we are," said Bowie at the time, sounding like a freelance promoter for the country. Britain had

the greatest architects in the world... In the fashion world, we're taking over; in the art scene, there's nobody to touch us and the best music is coming out of Britain now. In every aspect of world culture we are leaders. Quite rightly! The whole thing will all fall down in a year or two when we realize that, once again, we have no idea how to market it, and all our original ideas will run off to Italy and America, and we'll get all whiney about it.

There were the requisite "Cool Britannia" articles in *Vanity Fair* and

Newsweek but claims that Britain was enjoying another Sixties looked shaky in any head-to-head match, whether the Beatles versus Oasis, Michael Caine versus Hugh Grant, or the World Cup versus Euro 1996. Burning out quickly and feeling like it was its own twentieth-anniversary retrospective while it was still happening, the Britpop era was a fairly inhospitable place for Bowie, who was regarded more as an old irritant than a national treasure.

"Battle for Britain" starts as a letter from an exile, as though dropped, addressed to BRITAIN, in an airport mailbox. "My my, the time do fly," he begins, "when it's in another pair of hands" (he later puns on "fly" and "pair of pants"; Gail Ann Dorsey responds with a descending bassline as if elegantly backing away from him). He's scuffling around the old neighborhood, popping pills for his ailments. He doesn't regret leaving. Yet when he's about to teeter into spite, the last bars of the pre-chorus shift to A major, pivoting to a refrain where he tries to make amends. "Don't you let my letter get you down." No one cares he's back; no one remembers he was gone. By the second verse, he's grown bored with himself, cutting off a line with a weary *la-di-dah*.

Like "Looking for Satellites," it began as a Mark Plati experiment — here trying to make "a jazz-tinged jungle track." Bowie and Gabrels scrapped the original chord sequence, creating a new constellation of B major (verses), G major (pre-chorus) and C major (refrain) progressions. Plati thought "The Letter" (its original title) got the album in focus — a sign that Bowie wanted strong melodic and harmonic structures so that *Earthling* would be "actual songs over intense atmospheres."

Plati turned to solving one of the album's puzzles: its drum tracks. Bowie wanted samples kept "in house," so Zachary Alford made four- or eight-bar loops, with different timings and patterns, at roughly 120 beats per minute. After speeding the loops up to 160 BPM, Alford improvised on his kit against them. It was a bespoke version of the frenetic double-time feel of jungle, and similar to how Dennis Davis had sparred against his Harmonized beats (see "Breaking Glass"). The challenge was to keep Alford in sync with his 160 BPM alter ego. "He had to play exactly in time or it would sound like a train wreck," Plati said. The solution: Alford's half-time drum tracks were loaded into the computer "and manipulated on each and every beat to match the programming. It took days," Plati said. On "Battle for Britain," Alford pushes his way in, starting with ride cymbals and tom fills, then settling into a jumpy heartbeat snare pattern. Future Bowie collaborators

Mark Guiliana and Jason Lindner would cite *Earthling* as a key album of their youth, with Alford's drum work in the bedrock of *Blackstar*.

For a finishing touch, Plati added a "Being for the Benefit of Mr. Kite"-inspired carousel of sound he culled from his scraps collection, capped off with a skipping Bowie vocal (at 3:33) intended to make a listener wonder if the CD's scratched. Lindner praised Gabrels' "garbled, sampled guitar noise — that Eighties pop/heavy-rock guitar sound." Mike Garson got the most challenging brief: Bowie asked for a piano solo in the style of Igor Stravinsky's wind octet (unfamiliar with the piece, Garson had to buy the CD at the E. 4th Street and Broadway Tower Records). Garson interpreted Bowie's request as a series of thin-sounding atonal chords with a brassy feel and treble key runs that leave spidery traces of melody. Alford challenges Garson halfway through, slipping snare hits between piano notes, unsettling Garson's runs with a rolling tom fill, and whacking the solo to a close.

THE LAST THING YOU SHOULD DO

(Bowie, Gabrels, Plati.) **Recorded**: *ca. late October-11 November 1996, Looking Glass. Bowie: lead vocal, synthesizer; Gabrels: guitar, keyboards, loops; Plati: guitar, bass, keyboards, drum loops; Alford: drum samples. Produced: Bowie, Gabrels, Plati; engineered: Plati.*

First release: *3 February 1997,* **Earthling**. **Live**: *1997.*

"The Last Thing You Should Do" was such an afterthought it wasn't even noted on *Earthling*'s production chart. A prospective B-side, it instead got a late-in-the-day promotion to the album, bumping an "I Can't Read" remake, heard on the soundtrack of *The Ice Storm*, and a "Baby Universal" revision, still unreleased. Reeves Gabrels and Mark Plati built a track on "obtanium" ("discarded overdub bits"), adding guitar, bass, and keyboard lines. Bowie "popped in the studio for a bit and liked what he heard, made up three verses on the spot and then split," though not before playing a "Laughing Gnome"-inspired synthesizer line in the break. Gabrels added a rhythm guitar solo and more overdubs, then Plati mixed it.

Gabrels lobbied for its inclusion on *Earthling* at the expense of the two Tin Machine remakes. "Because I co-wrote both of those T.M. songs, that meant

431

I could stand on the higher moral ground, as I was fighting against my own offspring." Adding "The Last Thing You Should Do" turned *Earthling* "from a ten-song album pastiche… to a nine-song cohesive statement," he said. The track was *Earthling* in miniature: sonic trash loops, melancholic verses with a word-slosh lyric, occasional shrieks and groans, its sections in a fraying non-aggression pact. In the three verses, built on a foxing progression that zips between F minor, F# minor and A-flat major, a synthesizer drone hangs like a storm cloud. In breaks, Gabrels makes a slashing progress through three power chords, encouraged by spliced-in Bowie "yeahs!"

"I think it's very much of its time as a song: one has to be very selfish and protective about oneself if you're going to survive these days," Bowie said of it. He repeats a line three times, then closes with the title phrase, whose last syllables he sours. Clubtime is over; a man who should've been in bed hours ago waits for a cab, wondering how much his life has cost him. Though sequenced midway through *Earthling*, it was the album's spent-out coda.

I'M A HOG FOR YOU

(Leiber, Stoller.) **Live**: *19 October 1996, Shoreline Amphitheatre, 1 Amphitheatre Parkway, Mountain View, California. Bowie: vocal, acoustic guitar; Gabrels: lead guitar; Dorsey: bass.*

In October 1996, Bowie played at Neil Young's annual benefit concert for the Bridge School. On acoustic guitar, supported only by Reeves Gabrels and Gail Ann Dorsey (both plugged in), Bowie opened his first set with "Aladdin Sane," then played "Jean Genie" for the first time in six years. Dorsey tapped out the bassline like a code-breaker. After reminding Gabrels how to play the riff, Bowie sang a refrain and bridge from "I'm a Hog for You," a wonderfully dirty 1959 Coasters song by Jerry Leiber and Mike Stoller. It's a teenage boy as a root hog, lying in torture in his bed at night, his frustrations and emissions conveyed via grunting saxophone and a single-note guitar solo. Bowie got into the spirit, altering Leiber's lyric to spell things flat-out, to the delight of the audience.

DIRTY BLVD.

(Reed.) **Live**: *9 January 1997, Madison Square Garden, New York. Lou Reed: lead vocal, rhythm guitar; Bowie: lead vocal, twelve-string acoustic guitar; Gabrels: lead guitar; Garson: keyboards; Dorsey: bass; Alford: drums.*

First broadcast: *8 March 1997, David Bowie & Friends: A Very Special Birthday Celebration.*

"An aging rock star doesn't have to opt out of life. When I'm fifty, I'll prove it," Bowie said in 1979. Upon turning fifty in January 1997, he threw a party at Madison Square Garden, broadcast on pay-per-view television. There would be no partial Spiders from Mars reunion, no Luther Vandross singing "Young Americans." It was a promotional launch for *Earthling*, released a month later, with all but two songs from the album performed. Guests were younger musicians who got more radio play than he did — Billy Corgan, Frank Black, Dave Grohl, Robert Smith. Some fans and former colleagues thought it came off as desperate. "That whole thing was a political thing for him, to get together with the people who he thought would project him into the future," as Carlos Alomar (not invited to play) told David Buckley. But Bowie doing a *Last Waltz*-style retrospective was never going to happen.

The only person on stage that night who had influenced Bowie, not the other way around, showed up towards the end. Introduced by Bowie as "the king of New York," Lou Reed sang and played guitar on "Queen Bitch" (Gabrels had to teach him the chords) and duetted with Bowie on "Waiting for the Man." Bowie sang it reverently; Reed changed phrasings on a whim. In keeping with the unsentimental mood, their last duet, rather than something from *Transformer*, was "Dirty Blvd." from Reed's 1989 *New York*. It had a thick guitar riff and a lyric whose last verse feels workshopped (in another life, Reed taught creative writing at the University of Iowa). Bowie closed the show alone, performing "Space Oddity" on twelve-string acoustic guitar. "I don't know where I'm going from here," he told the crowd. "But I promise it won't bore you." He'd opted in for a while longer.

BLUE MOON

(Rodgers, Hart.) **Broadcast**: *18 February 1997, Paris. Bowie: vocal, forbearance.*

French radio DJs call Bowie's Parisian hotel; he sings the refrain of "Blue Moon" over shower noises they supply. It's a wonder that he stopped doing interviews in the 2000s.

PLANET OF DREAMS

(Bowie, Dorsey.) **Recorded**: *ca. 14-15 March 1997, Metalworks Studios, Toronto. Bowie: lead vocal; Dorsey: lead vocal, bass; Gabrels: guitar; Plati: keyboards; Garson: piano; Alford: drums, percussion. Produced: Bowie; engineered: Plati.*

First release: *23 June 1997,* **Long Live Tibet** *(EMI 7243 8 33140 2 7).*

As this book chronicles, the story of David Bowie's musical life is that of a boy's club. Of the handful of female musicians with whom he toured and recorded, only one lasted the distance: Gail Ann Dorsey. Even then, she didn't play on many Bowie albums of her era. Some of her absence was due to timing, as she was in demand for sessions and tours; some of it was that producers Mark Plati and Tony Visconti were also bassists, so "it's hard for me to get a look in," as she said in a 2003 webchat.

Around the time of the 1996 tour, Bowie wanted to produce a Dorsey solo album — he told a BBC interviewer it would come out in 1998. The tracklist would include songs she sang on stage at the time — "Under Pressure," "O Superman," "Outside" — along with "The Motel" and some newly-written material. The idea faded, but from it came a single Bowie—Dorsey collaboration, "Planet of Dreams," issued on a 1997 compilation to benefit the Tibet House Trust. It was cut over roughly two days at Metalworks Studios in Toronto in March 1997, while Bowie and his band were there to film the "Dead Man Walking" video.

A gentle contrast to *Earthling*, "Planet of Dreams," with its glacial tempo and wide-panned stereo mix, has the sort of soundscape found in Daniel Lanois productions and documentaries set in the Himalayan region. A single verse, with Bowie singing each line over the same melody, has intimations of reincarnation, Clark Gable's eyes and "Eisenhower blam[ing] the poor," and closes with a move to the chanted title phrase. It's the Mahayana Buddhist concept of māyā — we perceive the world like a crowd at a magic show, taking the stage illusions as real. Dorsey's harmonies, arriving midway through the verse, shroud Bowie's single-tracked, wavering vocal like a tunic. What saves "Planet of Dreams" from loftiness is its scrapper's utility: see the "Walk on the Wild Side" tribute or the piano hook from George Michael's "Freedom."

TRUTH

(Goldie.) **Recorded**: *ca. May 1997, Manic One Studio, 17 St. Anne's Court, London, and/or Trident Studio, London. Bowie: lead vocal; Goldie: synthesizers, programming, loops; Mark Sayfritz: programming. Produced: Goldie; engineered: Will O'Donovan.*

First release: *27 January 1998,* **Saturnz Return** *(FFRR 828 990 2, UK #15).*

Bowie and the drum 'n' bass artist Goldie collaborated in a film (*Everybody Loves Sunshine*, gruesomely retitled *B.U.S.T.E.D.*) and on a track. Born in Walsall in 1965, Clifford Price, whose nickname came from his grills, built his music from his "case of sonics": samples that he'd collected, distorted, and mutated. His muse was length. "Timeless" (1994) was over twenty minutes; *Saturnz Return* opened with an hour-long track.

In spring 1997, while Bowie was rehearsing in London for a tour, Goldie recruited him to sing on "Truth," a relatively brief track on *Saturnz Return*. Bowie had expected a jungle banger but got a ballad whose lyric was owed to "acid and coke," as Goldie later recalled. Bowie's vocal is a highwire act over panned and flanged synthesizer washes and piano loops. On quieter downtempo stretches, he sings more melodic phrases; over jump-cut synth patterns, he's freer in phrasing and range, at times sinking to his lowest register. Goldie applied liberal echo to the vocal, at some points smudge-smearing Bowie's lines. Bowie stood at the mike, chain-smoked and took direction. "I was telling him what I could see in my head," Goldie said in 1998. "He was great, totally tuned in… I was laughing my bollocks off, man. I mean, David Bowie being told what to do by me!" (as per sources who knew Bowie at the time, Bowie was a bit rankled at this, though naturally he never let it show). He'd been talking up doing more work with Goldie, but it ended here.

Is It Any Wonder
Fun (Funhouse)

Recorded: ("Is It Any Wonder") ca. late 1996, Looking Glass; ("Fun") January 1998, Looking Glass. Bowie: synthesizer, alto and baritone saxophone; Gabrels: loops, guitar; Plati: loops, programming; Garson: keyboards; Dorsey: vocal, bass; Alford: drum loops.

First release: ca. September 1998, CD-ROM for BowieNet subscribers. *Live*: 1997.

By 1997, Bowie had become a road dog, spending five months that year touring from Ireland to Argentina. On a more intimate scale and with a lesser price tag, the *Earthling* tour ran the gamut from small clubs to festivals. There was more overt use of digital audio tapes on stage for supplementary beats, vocals, and synthesizer lines, which freed up the players — Gail Ann Dorsey could move to keyboard at times. Aggressive, flashy, even shocking (clips of hardcore porn were shown during "Fashion"), it was the last great costume tour: Bowie in his cowls and frock coats, Reeves Gabrels in his boas, Dorsey sporting horns or a crucifix mask.

In his dress rehearsal concerts (four gigs in Dublin and London), he unveiled his planned structure for the tour — shows would have "rock" and "drum 'n' bass" sets, the latter typically including "I'm Deranged," "Pallas Athena," "V-2 Schneider," "The Last Thing You Should Do" and "Telling Lies." The Hanover Grand shows in London in early June 1997 were a coming-out party for Bowie's drum 'n' bass stylings — Goldie and DJ Rap were in the crowd ("some nice music bits, but for me it lacked rhythm and soul," DJ Rap said. "Maybe he needs to work with some people in the scene and study the form a bit more."). As the audience at the first Hanover gig ebbed after the rock set (not so much a critical judgment as that they had to catch the last train), Bowie opened with his dance set the following night. Some journalists regarded it as one would someone igniting farts on stage. See the *Observer*'s Barbara Ellen: "We all have to stand around for an aeon to what sounds like the cast of *Star Wars* falling down a fire escape... for God's sake man, you're a living legend. In future, play the old stuff and stop trying so hard."

But Bowie's bid for a younger audience was paying off, as seen in battles between fans wanting to dance to the *Earthling* numbers and those standing still, arms crossed, sometimes pushing back at the kids ("I was verbally abused: some guy even grabbed my neck and squeezed until I stopped [dancing]," wrote John Sellars, a contributor to the *Teenage Wildlife* fansite, about one of the Hanover gigs. "In the end I gave up and went to the bar to get pissed."). "Yeah, that's the stuff — fuck yer dance shite!" as someone in the Barrowlands, Glasgow audience yelled when Bowie sang an oldie. After a few weeks, Bowie scrapped his split-set plan in favor of interweaving drum 'n' bass pieces with rock songs, though he revived the idea one last time at the Phoenix Festival in July, playing in the radio/dance tent under the name Tao Jones Index.

In the dance sets, and throughout later months of the tour, the band played an instrumental piece, "Is It Any Wonder," that had been built from various backing effects created to accompany performances of "Fame," with a vocoded Dorsey vocal hook for the "is it any wonder" line. Bowie was often barely audible over the barrage, if managing to make his baritone saxophone groan like a wounded elephant.

When Gabrels and Plati were mixing a live album from the *Earthling* tour in January 1998 (see "Tryin' to Get to Heaven"), Bowie thought to make a new track out the elements of "Is It Any Wonder." Gabrels changed and added some verse chords and Bowie wrote some end-of-the-season lyrics ("my summer turns to fall... and I'll miss you"). This new track, called "Fun" but also known as "Funhouse," was issued to BowieNet subscribers on a CD-ROM later in 1998 and, remixed by Dillinja, appeared on the 2000 *liveandwell.com*, its only official release to date.

PERFECT DAY

(Reed.) ***Recorded****: ca. summer 1997, various studios in London & New York. Vocals: Lou Reed, Bowie, Bono, Boyzone, Tom Jones, Brett Anderson, Laurie Anderson, Burning Spear, Emmylou Harris, Dr. John, Elton John, Robert Cray, Tammy Wynette, Evan Dando, Shane MacGowan, Heather Small, Skye Edwards, Lesley*

Garrett, Gabrielle, Ian Broudie, Joan Armatrading, Suzanne Vega, Thomas Allen,
Huey Morgan, Visual Ministry Choir, et al; Sheona White: tenor horn; Courtney
Pine: soprano saxophone; Brodsky Quartet, BBC Symphony Orchestra: strings,
horns, winds, percussion. Produced: Simon Hanhart.

First release: *17 November 1997 (Chrysalis CDNEED01, UK #1).*

Lou Reed's "Perfect Day," arranged and produced in 1972 by Mick Ronson
and Bowie, was revived a quarter-century later thanks to Danny Boyle using
it for an overdose scene in *Trainspotting*. In "Perfect Day," a sociopath spends
a day doing "normal" things — goes to a zoo, sees a film, has a picnic —
which seem surreal. He's so bent out of shape, his world so corroded, that
banal existence is strange and beautiful. The perfect day for him is one that
the good and prosperous people of the world would soon forget.

A few months after the first Labour parliamentary victory in two decades,
the BBC celebrated itself with a promotional film of a constellation of stars
singing lines from "Perfect Day." Released as a single, with proceeds going to
Children in Need, it would be Bowie's last (if collaborative) UK #1. He sang
in montage with the likes of Brett Anderson, Emmylou Harris, Boyzone, Dr.
John, Shane MacGowan, and Tom Jones, the latter belting "you're gonna
REEEAAAAP" as if auditioning for the part of an operatic Galactus.

O SUPERMAN

(Anderson.) **Live**: *17 May-31 October 1997. Dorsey: lead vocal, bass; Bowie:*
harmony vocal, baritone saxophone; Gabrels: guitar, loops; Garson: keyboards;
Alford: drums.

On the 1997 tour, Laurie Anderson's "O Superman (For Massenet)" was
Gail Ann Dorsey's spotlight moment, often sequenced late in sets. She sang
it as if she'd summoned it, though often not quite nailing Anderson's first
"O *juuuuu*dge." With Bowie on lower harmony and baritone saxophone,
the tour arrangement replaced Anderson's minimalism — her voice looped
on an Eventide sampler (as the writer Isaac Butler described it: "a pulmonic
egressive 'ha' repeats, calling out from 1981, exhaling middle C") — with
thudding drum loops and laces of guitar feedback.

A woman sits at home. The phone rings, she lets the machine get it. The first call is from her as-usual worried mother. The second one is a voice that unnerves her so much that she picks up the phone, asks who it is. *This is the hand,* the voice says. *The hand that takes.* It sings a lullaby, and she falls into it. A beautiful power, corroding the words of the Post Office and the Tao Te Ching. When justice is gone, it sings, there's always force. The voice reassures you: you have no choice in the matter. This is how it always ends: with mom.

The answering machine put a screen against the world: you weren't a slave to a ringing phone anymore. But before, a wrong number didn't happen when you weren't at home; a threat could only be heard once. Now the machine kept the voices. The other actors of "O Superman" were the American planes ("made in America"), up in the skies of the voice's reverie.

In the context of Anderson's 1983 *United States* show, "O Superman" was a variation on a plane crash theme she'd used throughout — she was the calm voice of the pilot telling you to brace yourself. After 9/11, "O Superman" became prophecy. *American planes... Smoking... or non-smoking?* There was no going back to before that morning. Singing "O Superman" a week after the attacks, Anderson had a mournful reserve: the song had been taken away from her. Four years before, Dorsey and Bowie had stood on stage and sang this future to their audiences. *All of this is coming, and it's coming soon.*

CHAPTER ELEVEN: TOMORROW ISN'T PROMISED

(1998-2000)

He looked around him wildly, as if the past were lurking here in the shadow of his house.
— F. Scott Fitzgerald, *The Great Gatsby*

Nostalgia's no' the way it used to be.
— The Big Elastic Band, "When Big Roy Sang on Annie McGregor's Juke Box"

*Even though I think more about **this** world, I actually belong emotionally to another one. To one that still exists but is fading out, I suppose. I'm still made very uncomfortable by being forced to live in different times, in what I call the present.*
— Brian Eno, 1992

Memory, some say, is fate's shorthand. I do recall at some time in the Seventies the revolutionary Yippie Abbie Hoffman saying to me over a drink: "Tomorrow isn't promised."
— Bowie, introducing "Seven," 1999

He understood that he was granted eternal life, but not eternal youth.
— Agata Pyzik, "Thomas Jerome Newton, A Biographical Note and Possible Obituary"

TRYIN' TO GET TO HEAVEN

(Dylan.) **Recorded**: *ca. January-28 February 1998, Looking Glass Studios. David Bowie: lead and backing vocal, acoustic guitar, baritone saxophone; Reeves Gabrels: lead and rhythm guitar, keyboards; Mark Plati: bass, guitar, keyboards, drums. Produced, engineered: Plati.*

First broadcast: *8 November 1999, "Radio Dos 84," 105.8 FM (Girona, Catalonia).*

David Bowie, Reeves Gabrels, and Mark Plati spent the first weeks of 1998 mixing a tour album provisionally called *Earthling Live*, which eventually became *Liveandwell.com*: a swift descent in title from the obvious to the ridiculous. They also cut potential bonus tracks (see "Fun"), one of which was Bowie's impromptu decision to sing Bob Dylan's "Tryin' to Get to Heaven," from the recently-released *Time Out of Mind*. "Like 'Planet of Dreams,' it just sort of popped up from out of nowhere. Which was fine by me!," Plati said. "I was psyched about it because it was a completely live track, and after all the programming we'd been doing, it was a nice break in the cycle." (Bowie said upon first hearing *Time Out of Mind*, "I thought I should just give up.")

As a young man, Dylan had squatted in old songs; on *Time Out of Mind* he broke them up, used them for kindling. In "Tryin' to Get to Heaven," which he rewrote several times in the album sessions, he took from Woody Guthrie ("This Train Is Bound for Glory," "Poor Boy"), Furry Lewis ("I Will Turn Your Money Green") and a songbook's worth of traditionals ("Miss Mary Jane," "Lonesome Valley," "Rising Sun Blues"). For a refrain, he used a nineteenth-century hymn, "The Old Ark's a-Movering" ("she tryin' to get to heaven 'fo they close the do'"). He wanders from New Orleans to Baltimore, across valleys and train platforms; he comes to rest in the parlor, hoping for sleep, wondering if death will come in its place.

In Dylan's late style was some of Bowie's: history cycling through lesser variations; disappearing into your old fakes. Bowie cut the second verse and merged the last two, making room for a refrain in the spaces he cleared. Where Dylan's phrasings had a circularity, Bowie went for dramatics. Tim Curry once said that when playing villains, he'd give different wattages for different takes: under the top, over the top, top over the top. Bowie goes top over the top here: a rattled "cha-huh-*hain*," a triumphant "clo*hh*ose the door!," a feverish "I've been! to Sugar Town! I've shook! the suh-gur! down!" Dylan sang the latter line as if recalling a repossessed life, Bowie as if passingly familiar with the English language. The track was never released: a Catalan radio broadcast (reportedly of a promo CD-R) in 1999 is the source of subsequent bootlegs.

The Battle Hymn of the Republic

(Howe, Steffe.) **Recorded**: *ca. 3-15 June 1998, Garfagnana, Tuscany. Bowie: vocal, acoustic guitar.*

First release: *14 December 1998,* **Il Mio West***.*

Paying a tithe to indie cinema, Bowie acted in three cheap movies, back to back, in the spring and summer of 1998. He flew to Tuscany in June for one of them: *Il Mio West*, a would-be Spaghetti Western with Harvey Keitel. Bowie played the shades-wearing "psychopath" Jack Sikora, using a squirrel soup of an accent for lines like "this place stinks worse'n a mule's ass... and somebody's already shittin' their pants!" Accompanied by a photographer and a crew of albino, Rastafarian, and fashion plate gunfighters, Sikora has a taste for headlines ("I'm gonna suck the fame outta you!" he hisses at Keitel). In homage to *The Night of the Hunter*, Bowie and gang surround Keitel's house at night to threateningly serenade him. Bowie caps a raspy performance of "The Battle Hymn of the Republic" by breaking his guitar on the head of the village idiot.

A Foggy Day (Suite for a Foggy Day)

(Ira & George Gershwin, Badalamenti.) **Recorded**: *ca. July 1998, National Recording Studios, Edison Recording Studio and/or Excalibur Sound Productions, New York. Bowie: lead vocal; Al Regni: alto saxophone; Steve Badalamenti: trumpet; John Campo: bassoon; Angelo Badalamenti: keyboards; Andre Badalamenti: clarinet, bass clarinet; Sherry Sylar: oboe; Todd Coolman: bass; Grady Tate: drums; The String Orchestra at SoHo: orchestra (arranged & conducted, Badalamenti). Engineered: Artie Freeman, Art Pohelmis.*

First release: 6 October 1998, **Red Hot + Rhapsody** *(Antilles 557 815-2/314 557 788-2).*

The only studio recording Bowie released in 1998 was a collaboration with Angelo Badalamenti for a *Red Hot* compilation: a version of George and Ira Gershwin's "A Foggy Day." It was brooding and strange, with Badalamenti weaving two of his compositions, "Overcast" and "The Rainbow," into George Gershwin's music, making a new intro with a four-note rising theme, massing strings for Bowie's entrance. "I picked ["Foggy Day"] because I knew I could take that song with its verse and darken it up and make it very slow and make it very Angelo Badalamenti," Badalamenti said in 2014.

One of George Gershwin's last pieces, "A Foggy Day" was covered in his fingerprints: the melody's repeated notes; rich chords for jazz musicians to feast on; melancholy dispelled by jumps of fourths and fifths (the elated leap on "for suddenly"), paralleling the sun breaking through the fog in the lyric; the unusual structure, with the refrain escaping its thirty-two-bar confines with two more bars full of harmonic tumult and winking at the tune "Country Gardens." In the Bowie/Badalamenti recording, the stormy verse is lighter in feel, with an oboe playing the sun, struggling to shine. In the transition to the refrain, night and fog descend in low strings and winds (bass clarinet and bassoon) and a drooping bassline. Bowie sings as if he's walking into a headwind. Then he sees her, the fog lifts, the song breaks open. But he sings the last line, "through foggy London town, the sun was shining," with sadness, recalling a lost happiness. He's still a stranger in the city. One of his finest covers.

(SAFE IN THIS) SKY LIFE
SAFE

(Bowie, Gabrels.) **Recorded:** *("(Safe In This) Sky Life," unreleased) ca. early August 1998, Sear Sound, New York; ("Safe") 8 August-ca. 15 September 2001, Allaire Studios, NY; ("Safe" overdubs) ca. 1 October 2001-31 January 2002, Looking Glass. Bowie: lead and backing vocal, twelve-string acoustic guitar, Stylophone; Gabrels: guitar ("Sky Life"); David Torn, Gerry Leonard?: guitar ("Safe"); Jordan Rudess: keyboards; John Conte ("Sky Life"), Visconti: bass; Clem Burke ("Sky Life"), Matt Chamberlain ("Safe"): drums; Richard Barone: backing vocals ("Sky Life"); uncredited musicians: strings. Produced: Bowie, Visconti.*

First release: ("Safe") ca. June 2002 (BowieNet download).

In 1999, Bowie had a new look: flannel shirts, a rat-brown fringe, tinted granny glasses (when sporting the latter, he looked like a premonition of Diane Keaton's Sister Mary in *The Young Pope*). It was the wardrobe of a decommissioned rock star, now the caretaker of his past lives. This shift began, as one might expect, with the cartoon *Rugrats*.

Karyn Rachtman, musical supervisor of *The Rugrats Movie*, asked Bowie for a song, and a "David Bowie song" at that: Ziggy Stardust guitars, sweeping strings, Thin White Duke croon, the build of "Heroes" and "Absolute Beginners." Bowie reworked a piece he'd written with Reeves Gabrels earlier in the year. As "(Safe In This) Sky Life" was neither released nor bootlegged, there are only descriptions of its elaborate making, including a twenty-four-piece string section, harmony vocals by Richard Barone (the Bongos), bass by John Conte, and drums by Clem Burke (Blondie). (It helped that the *Rugrats* producers were paying for all the session time.) And to produce it, Tony Visconti.

He and Bowie hadn't seen each other in fifteen years. There had been sore feelings on both sides: Visconti for being elbowed out of *Let's Dance*, Bowie for Visconti's oversharing in the press. "I'd become annoyed at how much he would feel it was necessary for him to be the essayist on my relationship with my son," Bowie said in 1993. "I just got tired of the incessant gossip: he was turning into a real old woman." The reconciliation was simple enough. Bowie called Visconti, they began talking occasionally, and met again in New York at the string sessions for "Sky Life." "We spent three hours reminiscing," Visconti said.

"Sky Life" was cut from *Rugrats* during editing, once the sequence for which it was intended was deleted. "He delivered a song far beyond my wildest dreams, and now I can't even use it," Rachtman mourned. Saying it "doesn't fit in with what I'm doing at the moment," Bowie shelved it until the *Heathen* sessions of 2001, when he and Visconti rebuilt it from the ground up as "Safe," retaining only the strings from the 1998 session (it would be a B-side).

Like "Tryin' to Get to Heaven," "Safe" feels pulped from a catalog — in this case, Bowie's. The verse top melody suggests "The Supermen" (*cf.* "when all the world was very young" to "frozen to the glass again") and a "period" synthesizer effect sounds like a Stylophone. Visconti's strings, anticipating and challenging the vocal, have the lushness of his work on "Win" or "In the Heat of the Morning." It was sensory triggers for fans — the rising progression in the verses, the guitar-smeared shifts to the refrains, the extended "skyyy-liiiiiife."

Ziggy Played Guitar (Slight Return)

By the time he recorded "Sky Life," Bowie was planning a *Ziggy Stardust* sequel on a major scale, filling the conceptual gap left by his never-made *1. Outside* sequels and concerts. To commemorate the album's thirtieth anniversary, there would be a film ("an objective piece about how [Ziggy] is viewed and perceived by his audience," Bowie said), a theater piece ("more internal, more reflective of the immediate repercussions of Ziggy and his effect on the people around him... his close intimates, how he thinks and what his perception of the world really is," and so suggesting an early draft of *Lazarus*), and a Web segment meant as "pure fun, with hypertext links so you can find out who [Ziggy's] mum was, and things like that — a huge exploration of his background... startlingly info-packed maps and photographs." (This was something he'd considered doing in 1972 —having one part of *Ziggy Stardust* be from Ziggy's parents' perspective.)

Of course there'd be tie-ins: a Mick Rock photo book, a concert DVD, and a double-CD with re-recorded *Ziggy Stardust* outtakes. To Radio One in 1998, Bowie said

> I've found bits and pieces of songs that I obviously had written for [*Ziggy Stardust*] but never finished off. It's as if I'll be complementing what's already there with other pieces that were started but not actually finished at the time, so they have an authenticity of the period about them... It's just a question of finishing off what might be a ninety-second or a two-minute piece, taking it obviously the way it wanted to go and finishing it off and keeping the sound of the material in the period.

He'd done that with *Low* and *"Heroes"* outtakes on Ryko reissues (see "Abdulmajid") but pulling such tricks on *Ziggy Stardust* outtakes would be a new level of audacity. Reeves Gabrels later said the only way it might have worked would have been complete period devotion, using sixteen-track decks, vintage amps and microphones. Otherwise Bowie risked something like the surviving Beatles' ghost-duets with John Lennon for *Anthology*: a dodgy appendix to his old music, relying on fans suspending disbelief.

The *Ziggy* project was in part Bowie looking for a franchise to rival what Pete Townshend had pulled off with the *Tommy* musical in the early 1990s. But it also was a counter-offensive against Todd Haynes' *Velvet Goldmine*, a 1998 film that Bowie disparaged, having denied Haynes the rights to use his songs. He said Haynes had missed the tone of the glam era, that it was more fun, cheap, and silly than his morose film implied. But *Velvet Goldmine* is also an angry film, of betrayal and defeat, of the diminishing of a free cultural moment and of a glamorous bisexual who is Bowie in all but name: Brian Slade, played by Jonathan Rhys Meyers. In *Velvet Goldmine*'s "present day" 1984, Slade has become a Billy Idol-esque stadium rocker called Tommy Stone (parallels to *Let's Dance* Bowie are unavoidable). Stone is never shown performing, nor do viewers ever hear his music. He's just an inescapable presence — seen on posters or in press conferences. Everyone loves him in a hollowed-out way. Asked in 2012 about a scene with a young fan who gets a press pass to a Stone gig, Haynes said she's

> so ecstatic about Tommy Stone because that's all that generation has. That's what they got — it's not their fault that the same desire, the same need for something special is expressed, but it's just not radical, or progressive, or culture-changing. But it's what they got and I didn't want to blame them because they are part of a culture that had to clamp down around categories again, resume control of those categories that were seeping into each other so surprisingly for a brief time.

It was Haynes' misreading of, and unwanted pity for, the generation that grew up with *Let's Dance* and *Labyrinth*. But the aesthetic conservatism he mentioned was certainly to be found in a fifty-five-year-old Bowie making some *Ziggy Stardust* prequel. Happily, the projects fell prey to Bowie's usual distractions. Hanif Kureishi, recruited to help Bowie write a script, said Bowie soon discarded the idea of doing a crowd-pleasing *Tommy*-style musical, wanting something more avant-garde, possibly with La La La Human Steps, and "he didn't really quite know how to do that," he told Dylan Jones. "He got really nervous and said this was going to be a disaster" (see "Lazarus").

So the *Ziggy* anniversary was commemorated only by an uninspired CD reissue in 2002, when Bowie looked back in horror at his idea. "I'm running like fuck from that one. Can you imagine anything uglier than a nearly sixty-year-old Ziggy Stardust?" he said. A *Ziggy* movie or play could have "close[d] all the doors that maybe a lot of people had opened for themselves and hopefully I helped open up and gave their own imaginations a run for their money. I wouldn't want to stymie all that by presenting some nerd in a red wig, having run through a really slack-arsed movie script." As with deciding to rerecord his old Mod songs on *Toy* (see "Hole in the Ground"), Bowie's ambitions at the end of the twentieth century were mostly-unrealized excavations of his past. "Safe," a "Bowie-sings-'Bowie'" track cut from a cartoon movie and released as its own cover, sums up the period well. There's a borrowed majesty in "Safe," and one line from it foreshadowed Bowie's early post-millennial years: "The things will move more slowly."

MOTHER

(Lennon.) **Recorded**: *(unreleased) ca. June-July 1998, uncredited studio, Nassau, Bahamas; (overdubs) ca. early August 1998, Sear Sound, New York. Bowie: lead vocal; Gabrels: acoustic guitar, lead guitar, Roland VG-8; Rudess: piano; uncredited musician: organ; Visconti: bass, harmony vocal; Andy Newmark: drums; Barone: harmony vocal. Produced: Visconti.*

"Mother" led off John Lennon's solo debut, *Plastic Ono Band*. When his mother Julia was struck by a car and killed in 1958, teenage Lennon became caustic, cruel, utterly consumed with rock 'n' roll. On *Plastic Ono Band*, which came from his and Yoko Ono's "primal scream" sessions with Arthur Janov ("at the center of all that fame and wealth and adulation was just a lonely little kid," Janov said), "Mother" was a last curse at Julia, who forever abandons Lennon, his larynx-scraping "mama dooon't GOOOO" met by the hammer blows of "*dad*dy-come-*home*."

Plastic Ono Band was a touchstone for Bowie. A journalist saw him playing the album during the *Pin Ups* sessions, nodding off as if in a trance, then lifting the needle back to "Mother." Many years later, he covered "Mother" for a tribute album for Lennon's would-have-been sixtieth birthday in October 2000 (the album remains unreleased). He tracked the song in Bermuda in summer 1998 with Reeves Gabrels and the drummer Andy Newmark (the latter's first appearance on a Bowie record since *Young Americans*). Newmark, living in Bermuda at the time and booking bands for a local club, got a bassist and a keyboard player (both of whose names no one recalls) from a local church. Bowie decided to have the track mixed at the Tony Visconti-produced "(Safe in This) Sky Life" session that August in New York ("we were looking for a stepping stone to do something together again, and this totally autonomous piece seemed to me to be convenient," Bowie said). They kept the original vocal, despite bleed-through from Newmark's drums (as Bowie needed to do some punch-ins, Visconti had to find the same type of microphone he'd used in Bermuda), and added Jordan Rudess' piano, Visconti's bass, and his and Richard Barone's harmony vocals. "It is not the most polished production of our careers," Visconti said. "The recording was made on that now defunct digital system ADAT and it was one of my first attempts at manipulating music in a computer."

Bowie couldn't summon the raw neediness of Lennon's recording, the sound of a man breaking himself into a crying child — even Lennon couldn't have done it again. He sang the verses in his lower registers, as if doing counterpart harmonies to Lennon's record, and gravely extended notes in the closing refrains. The production's messiness worked in its favor — Bowie's voice sounds blown out at times — but he gives nothing to the song, only takes.

20ᵀᴴ CENTURY BOY

(Bolan.) **Broadcast**: *16 February 1999, London Docklands Arena. Brian Molko: lead vocal, guitar; Bowie: lead vocal; Stefan Olsdal: bass; Steve Hewitt: drums. Recorded: Visconti.*

Upon hearing their demo, Bowie hyped the band Placebo, who would regularly open for him on his mid-Nineties tours. Mascara-sporting Goth scamps with a taste for unusual tunings, Placebo began as Brian Molko, small and nasally, and Stefan Olsdal, who stood like a ship's mast. A collaboration with Bowie was inevitable. At the February 1999 Brit Awards, they performed T. Rex's "20th Century Boy," which Placebo had covered for *Velvet Goldmine* (Molko and Bowie agreed to avoid the subject). "20th

Century Boy" was the T. Rex formula in its basic elements: a guitar hook so overwhelming the song barely needs a refrain; a lyric of boasts and come-ons. "We weren't too bad, we were in key at least," Molko told *Melody Maker*. "But we could never really get the lyrics right. We had a fucking laugh." He was being diplomatic: he was letter-perfect, where Bowie stumbled through his verses, playing his Tin Machine-era "headless" Steinberger and looking like Placebo's trying-too-hard-to-be-hip guest.

WITHOUT YOU I'M NOTHING

(Placebo.) **Recorded**: *(Bowie vocal) 28 March 1999, Looking Glass Studios. Molko: lead vocal, guitar; Bowie: harmony vocal; Olsdal: bass; Hewitt: drums. Produced: (orig.) Steve Osbourne, (remix) Visconti; engineered: Adrian Bushby, Visconti.*

First release: *16 August 1999 ("Without You I'm Nothing," FLOORCD 10).* **Live**: *1999.*

Along with playing with them live, Bowie wanted to work with Placebo in the studio. But the band had recently released an album and there was no time to write a fresh track. With Tony Visconti mixing the performance of "20th Century Boy" for a possible single, Bowie proposed doing harmony vocals for a remix of "Without You I'm Nothing," the title track of Placebo's 1998 record. An obsessional piece whose title came from a Sandra Bernhard film, the song was meant "as a message to each other. And it's a message to our fans — which is that old Judy Garland thing," Brian Molko said. Bowie tries to break into the song, starting as a lower harmony to Molko's lead, holding back his strength until the refrains. But there he finds Molko already so cranked up that all he can do is add supplementary howls.

NEW ANGELS OF PROMISE

(Bowie, Gabrels.) **Recorded**: *(demos) ca. February-autumn 1998, various home/ hotel studios, New York, London; (first version) ca. autumn 1998, Mute Records Studio, Harrow Road, London; (overdubs, retakes) ca. February-May 1999, Looking Glass; (last overdubs, mixing) ca. May-June 1999, Chung King Studios, 36 West*

37ᵗʰ St., New York. Bowie: lead and backing vocal, keyboards; Gabrels: lead and rhythm guitar, keyboards, synthesizer, drum programming; Plati: bass, keyboards; Sterling Campbell: drums. Produced: Bowie, Gabrels; engineered: Kevin Paul.

First release: *21 September 1999, 'hours...' (Virgin CDV 2900/7243 8 48158 2 0, UK #5, US #47).*

There was once a pane of tinted glass between Bowie and his audience. A star like Bowie shouldn't be seen *eating*. He'd chafe under his reputation sometimes, say he was an ordinary guy, make a big deal of walking to the corner store to buy bread. At the turn of the century, he made himself more ordinary than ever before, as if following a weight-loss regimen for the mystique. When Mark Zuckerberg was still in high school, Bowie was bracing for the twenty-first century, for having to turn oneself into a business card, distributed upon request. He also saw opportunity. On 1 September 1998, he launched BowieNet, whose early motto was "everyone has a voice."

It wasn't the typical rock musician's webpage of the time, with a few heavily-pixelated concert photos and text all but plagiarized from fan sites. BowieNet had legitimate exclusives: downloads; live recordings; scans of Bowie's paintings; his book and film picks. Contests where fans could write lyrics (see "What's Really Happening?"), polls where they choose single mixes and album covers. Intimate-seeming journal entries, with Bowie writing how much he loved Iman, or musing how, in another life, he'd be walking his grandchildren around Bromley. He was a chatroom regular, with some Q&A sessions exploring fresh horizons of banality: *Do you shop at Wal-Mart? Is it possible for you to market some of your better paintings in poster versions for like much cheeper* (sic)*? Bowie when you were filming Exhuming Mr. Rice in Vancouver, did you ever stop by Subeez Cafe??*

Throughout the Nineties he was both an internet evangelist and skeptic. He found in his chat rooms many artists and graphic designers, or at least people who claimed they were, and regarded it as a virtual version of his neighborhood Arts Lab from thirty years before ("there's something added [in] not actually knowing who the other person is in reality, but only having a sense of that person: it's almost metaphysical.") The potential "of what the internet is going to do to society — both good and bad — is unimaginable," he said in December 1999. "We're actually on the cusp of something exhilarating and terrifying." He predicted the recording industry would be shattered, that making a living by selling albums would be an impossible dream for younger generations of musicians, that rock music would mean less to people. "Once everyone can sample what they want at home on a cheap computer, the medium suddenly becomes the message," he said in 2000. "And the message seems to be 'this is lifestyle music, not attitude music.'... It's no longer the replacement to church."

He was caught up in the goldrush, too. By the time BowieNet launched, the dot-com boom was at its peak, with companies with no remote path to profitability having millions thrown at them. In 1994, Bowie said, "I don't like being considered a multi-media person — it sounds a bit Bond Street to me." Six years later, the *Financial Times* noted he'd branched into realms "unrelated to [what you] might call his core competencies." There was the David Bowie Radio Network for *Rolling Stone*'s website. He'd co-formed UltraStar, an internet service provider that ran the website of the New York Yankees, among others. There were the Bowie Bonds, music royalty securitizations that let him pay off Tony Defries and get sole ownership of his songs — a Bowie business partner, Robert Goodale, said in 2000 that "we wouldn't rule out 'Bowie's Trading Desk,' if someone came to us with a good proposal." Then there was BowieBanc: an internet-only venture whose account holders got an ATM card that had a photo of Bowie's austere face. ("What he is doing is taking his fan base, which twenty years ago had an affinity for wearing a T-shirt of his, and maybe ten years ago graduated to wearing a golf shirt of his, and in the last three or four years has developed to being part of his online service, and trying to create that same affinity with what he is doing with online banking," Bowie's financial adviser Bill Zysblat said.) This collapsed in little over a year, a strange footnote. But what was he doing with his face on bank cards? It was like Greta Garbo on a box of breakfast cereal. BowieBanc was the mad culmination of this need to be everywhere, to leverage his legend.

Another project in the late Nineties was *Omikron: The Nomad Soul*, a PC game developed by Quantic Dream and released by Eidos Interactive. It mingled *Tron* (gamers are trapped in a videogame world) and the *Final Fantasy* franchise (gamers could go "off narrative," walk around and hang out in bars, which was Bowie's preference). One premise of *Omikron* was that your "nomad soul" could move from body to body: reincarnation as a gaming strategy.

Bowie appeared in the game as "Boz," leader of the subversive band

"The Dreamers" and aligned with a resistance movement called "The Awakened" (like *The Matrix*, another 1999 release, *Omikron* dabbled in a futurist Gnosticism). "I saw Boz as being a kind of digital patchwork quilt," he said. "Made up of all sorts of shifting patterns, fleeting thoughts, and fractured memories — someone who would slip in and out of focus, one moment drifting and world-weary, the next absolutely concise and direct." While on Earth Bowie was in conference calls with bankers, in *Omikron* he was young, playing dives, running a musical resistance. He and Reeves Gabrels wrote much of the game's music, drawing from a pile of new songs (see "Survive"). There were in-game "Boz" performances of "Survive," "Something in the Air," and "The Pretty Things Are Going to Hell." "I approached it as though I was doing a movie," Bowie said. "There's ambient music, fight scene music and all that, and being a French-designed game there are plenty of strip clubs."

Neu Engel

"New Angels of Promise" scored *Omikron*'s opening credits (in the album version's refrains, Bowie replaces a lustily-sung "*Oh*-mi-kron!" with "suspicious minds"). As with other *'hours...'*/*Omikron* tracks, he was presuming a familiar audience. Gone was the itch to convert new listeners or aggravate old ones. Like "Safe," "New Angels of Promise" was Bowie making a "Bowie song," a piece so weighted with his past it's barely coherent as itself.

"Sons of the Silent Age" in particular was tapped for melodic blood transfusions: "I am a blind man, she is my eyes" is close to how he sang "Sam Therapy and King Dice." Both tracks have a snaky instrumental opening, an eight-line verse with Bowie's near-conversational voice alternating with guitar and keyboards, and a modulation to a harmonized refrain. "New Angels of Promise" sits within the traces of "Sons of the Silent Age," as if it inhabits the same radio frequency at a different point in time.

The "angel of promise" is a vague concept in Christian theology — an angel who heralds a covenant with God. As the centuries went on, particularly once the United States got going, the angel of promise became more of a guardian angel, a harbinger of prosperity. But angels of promise don't necessarily bring good news. In a nineteenth-century sermon by

George Davis Herron, "the angels of promise are always on the wing... God is always speaking, but man does not hear." Bowie's new angels of promise are passersby: one's blind. They're a pair of "tabular lovers": immovable objects, like pillars (or the stone-and-wax Bewlay Brothers) or lines of data. It's possible he meant to suggest the players of *Omikron*, working at some tenuous line of resistance, looking for meaning in a scripted world.

There's a lethargy in it— an entire verse is repeated, Bowie's vocal tics might as well be samples, a rhythm guitar line sounds like a hangover from an earlier mix (the *Omikron* mix is a bit livelier.) The verse is built on a standoff between tonic and flattened VII chord; the refrain's shift to F# minor is a dogged advance. Does its intro keyboard figure suggest Peter Gabriel's "San Jacinto"? The whole piece is a suggestion, its parts greater than its sum.

Logging Off

Around 2004, BowieNet began to stagnate. Once Bowie semi-retired, there were far fewer updates; the exclusives dried up. It slumbered through the rise of YouTube, Facebook, Twitter. In 2006, Bowie's ISP business was acquired by the concert promoter Live Nation. Finally, in March 2012, his Facebook page confirmed what had been obvious for years: "the old BowieNet, as we have known it, is kaput!"

On his birthday the following year, he put a new video up on YouTube, sold the song on iTunes. He worked the internet hype cycle like a pro, but he was no longer the glad-handing figure of the dot-com years. He wasn't chatting, wasn't doing Q&As. His revived website was functional, well-designed, and had little pretense of being a two-way link between him and his fans. For the rest of his life, he would make videos and songs and release them without notice and with little explanation. You would hardly ever hear his speaking voice. He was back behind the glass, and there he stayed.

QUALISAR
JAHANGIR (JANGIR)
THRUST
1917

(Bowie, Gabrels.) **Recorded***: ca. February-autumn 1998, various home/hotel studios, New York, London; ca. autumn 1998, Mute Records Studio. Bowie: lead vocal, Roland TR-707; Gabrels: lead and rhythm guitar, keyboards, synthesizers, drum programming. Produced: Bowie, Gabrels; engineered: Paul.*

First release*: ("1917") 20 September 1999, "Thursday's Child" (Virgin 7243 8 96268 2 7 VSCDF 1753); ("Thrust," "Qualisar," "Jangir") 31 October 1999,* **Omikron: The Nomad Soul***.*

Of the brief instrumentals that Bowie and Reeves Gabrels wrote for *Omikron*, two — "Jahangir" and "Qualisar" (both names of game sectors) — weren't apparently developed further. But the *'hours…'* B-side "1917" (the Russian Revolution? Marcel Duchamp's *Fountain*? The true beginning of the twentieth century? The hotel suite where Bowie wrote the song?) was an elaboration of "Thrust," an *Omikron* piece used to score a demon fight scene. Mumbling over a blocky synthesizer/guitar figure that's close to the hook of Led Zeppelin's "Kashmir," Bowie is distorted and indecipherable, singing what sounds like "I'm a man" most of the time. A holdover from the *Earthling* era, "1917" is fun and deservedly obscure, with a false ending halfway through a cruel surprise for those who lack a taste for presets and guitar squeals.

AWAKEN 2
NO ONE CALLS

(Bowie, Gabrels.) **Recorded***: ca. February-autumn 1998, various home/hotel studios, New York, London; ca. autumn 1998, Mute Records Studio. Bowie: lead and backing vocal, Roland TR-707, keyboards; Gabrels: guitar, keyboards, synthesizer, drum programming. Produced: Bowie, Gabrels; engineered: Paul.*

First release*: ("No One Calls") 20 September 1999, "Thursday's Child" (Virgin*

*7243 8 96268 2 0 VSCDT 1753); ("Awaken 2") 31 October 1999, **Omikron: The Nomad Soul**.*

"No One Calls" (though Bowie sings "nobody calls" throughout) was one of a few *'hours...'* bonus tracks that hint at the more unsettling album it could have been. As Nicholas Pegg noted, the track may have come from Bowie appropriating Trevor Jones' "Thirteen O'Clock," from the *Labyrinth* soundtrack — the melody of "no-body-calls" is close to the first synthesizer melody in Jones' piece — and an earlier version of the piece appeared as the "Awaken 2" instrumental in *Omikron*. Built on the Roland TR-707, "No One Calls" has a twinned, eerie keyboard melody that seems to have crept in from a Dario Argento horror film, and a processed guitar, sounding like an Indian esraj, to parallel the vocal. The fragmented lyric, sung in a loose phrasing, double-tracked down an octave, or given a demonic counterpart, is an isolate's monologue, someone left behind in a post-apocalyptic world: "counting the windows" (left unshattered); "nobody phones anyone at all" (because no one else is left). It ends with some doleful "not at alls," trailing off into synthetic rainfall.

SURVIVE

*(Bowie, Gabrels.) **Recorded**: (demos) ca. February-autumn 1998, various home/hotel studios, New York, London; (first version) ca. autumn 1998, Mute Records Studio; (overdubs, retakes) ca. February-May 1999, Looking Glass; (last overdubs, mixing) ca. May-June 1999, Chung King. Bowie: lead and backing vocal, twelve-string acoustic guitar, keyboards, Roland TR-707; Gabrels: lead and rhythm guitar, acoustic guitar, synthesizer, drum programming; Brendan Gallagher: guitar (Marius De Vries mix); Plati: bass, Mellotron; Levesque: drums. Produced: Bowie, Gabrels; engineered: Paul.*

***First release**: 21 September 1999, '**hours...'**. **Broadcast**: 23 August 1999, VH1 Storytellers; 8 October 1999, TFI Friday; 19 October 1999, Cosas que importan; 20 October 1999, Nulle part ailleurs; 25 October 1999, Mark Radcliffe Show/Saturday Music Show/Breakfast Team; 22 November 1999, MusiquePlus; 29 November 1999, Later with Jools Holland; 5 December 1999, Quelli Che... Il Calcio; 8 December 1999, Inte Bara Blix; 27 June 2000, Bowie at the BBC Radio Theatre; 18 September*

2002, Live and Exclusive. **Live***: 1999-2000, 2002.*

By 1998, Bowie had put his Swiss home on the market and relocated to Bermuda, where he lived in Sea View, a 4,500-sq-foot mansion on the tip of the "hook" of the Bermudan island. Its front living room was his new writing and recording space. He hadn't done any substantial composing in nearly two years — his time had gone to his tour, his movie projects, his Ziggy Stardust revival (see "Safe"), his art world plans, his internet ventures, and being a happily-married man of property and wealth. Now he had to come up with the goods again. So he and Reeves Gabrels composed throughout the year at each other's homes and in hotel suites, often using their jointly-owned Pro Tools rig that Gabrels set up in his New York apartment. They worked "up a small storm and we are fairly pleased with the songs," Bowie wrote in a 27 November 1998 journal entry. "We've got around thirty good pieces and they're still coming." By mid-December, Bowie wrote that he was going "bonkers" with songwriting and worried he was neglecting his painting.

Some songs were pegged as *Omikron* pieces, others for a Gabrels solo album (including what became "The Pretty Things Are Going to Hell," "Seven," and "Survive"). The original plan was to approach songwriting more "organically" as compared to the group improvisation-spawned *1. Outside* songs and the scrapper-sampler aesthetic of *Earthling*. He'd enjoyed doing acoustic versions of songs like "Dead Man Walking" live. So the concept would be akin to Bowie's folk music duo with John Hutchinson in the late Sixties: two singers, two guitars (one Pro Tools rig). But Bowie and Gabrels came to be at loggerheads as to what they wanted. Gabrels felt that there should have been a quick follow-up to *Earthling*, the *Aladdin Sane* to its *Ziggy Stardust*. "The music had evolved, the band was playing great, the window of opportunity (time-wise) was there," he told David Buckley. But Bowie was heading towards the opposite pole, wanting to make an "anti-*Earthling*," as Mark Plati described it: "a stripped-down affair, just songs, no electronics, no big production. I know [Gabrels and Bowie] were at odds over that — Reeves definitely wanted to go in the direction of *Earthling 2*, so to speak... there was also talk of it not even being an album, but simply music for... *Omikron*."

By the end of 1998, Bowie told a reporter the songs were so disparate in tone — some electronic, some acoustic, some rockers — that it made sense to "record all [of them] to see what will come out of it." He talked of reuniting the *Earthling* band, of having Tony Visconti produce with Gabrels and himself. And he again felt pressured to deliver a commercial product. "If I'd had my druthers, I'd rather not have put out an album right now," he said in 1999.

> Virgin wanted me to put this album out now, because everyone has gone for the end of the millennium thing. I don't mind. But I would rather have had it come out earlier this year or waited until the beginning of next year. But at least it will come out and I can move onto the next one — which is how I tend to think.

In the autumn of 1998, Bowie and Gabrels cut a full album in London, working at Mute Records' studio on Harrow Road. Jason Cooper of the Cure drummed and Bowie and Gabrels played everything else (various 1998 sessions provided the "demo" versions of *'hours...'* tracks that appeared on reissues, as well as versions on the *Omikron* soundtrack). After it was mixed in early 1999, the two were again at odds. Gabrels liked the mix because "I thought it had a certain *Diamond Dogs* quality." But "David said it was too raw... he wanted it to be more slick and polished and have fretless bass" (a reoccurring Bowie craving — he'd push for fretless bass on *The Next Day*, too).

So at Looking Glass Studios in New York in spring 1999, Bowie and Gabrels overhauled the tracks, using Mark Plati on bass and Mike Levesque on drums (Sterling Campbell also appeared). Plati recalled to Paul Trynka "looking for where the songs would land, as opposed to on *Earthling* where we pretty much just ran with our first impulse... Some songs went through multiple treatments, different drummers, structure shifts."

Mixed and mastered by the end of June 1999, it wound up as *'hours...'* — Bowie's last twentieth-century record — an unsettled, moody, lovely, sketchy, washed-out collection of unreconciled songs that's the most neglected of Bowie's late albums: a lesser work that knows it's lesser, and takes modest pride in it. A finer album lies within it, just out of reach.

Never Get Old

Carnival was over and Bowie was in a Lenten mood. The album's cover photo played on Michelangelo's Pietà, with Bowie's new somber majordomo persona cradling the dying "rave uncle" of *Earthling*. Its videos put Bowie in surreal domestic situations. The one album on which Gabrels received full co-composition credit is the one on which he's the most muted. And Bowie wanted to sing "just like a bloke. To give them a feeling of: anybody could sing these songs. They're not difficult."

"His circle of friends was more in his age group and they were listening to Luther Vandross and things like that... and I wasn't," Gabrels recalled to Brian Ives in 2017,

> He actually made a comment to me at one point, "I want to make music for my generation." And I said, "You always just made music that you wanted to make, and if you want to make music for your generation, you're ten years older than me. So where does that leave me in this equation? I don't know how to produce that. I don't know how to help you if that is the new criteria." The whole thing started to feel claustrophobic to me.

Being unaligned with his generation was a core Bowie quality, at least for Gabrels. "He evolves as an artist," he said of Bowie in a 1993 radio documentary. "Otherwise you age with your fans — when your fans are forty you're forty, and you're playing music for that group of people as opposed to being driven by a creative need or desire." Bowie had avoided this trap, "he's always done so and continues to do, and that's why he's not *old*," Gabrels emphasized.

Yet he was starting to be perceived as old. "Wrinkled, shaggy-haired David Bowie looked slightly lost, a visual reminder of how time passes quickly in MTV's world of pop music," as per an Associated Press report of a 1999 awards appearance. After a decade of trying to be "outside," it was time to come in. The album's title played on unforgiving time and a generational bond: *hours/ours*. Bowie said he'd hit "every cliché in the book" in the Eighties, wondering "should I be with younger people or should I let go of the youthful feelings? Am I now supposed to settle back into something?... I just treat the rest of whatever life I've got as the adventure it used to be, so I'm not just kind of by myself, just left on the sands of this awful, nostalgic, rather poignant, sad old life."

He worked up a narrative voice, called it a distillation of alleged "friends" who, hitting fifty, regretted their lives. Musing on middle age in 1991, Bowie said "people get mellow. They relax, they get wrapped up in finances and careers. They lose the fire, or perhaps they never had it. They never find themselves. They aren't true to their lives." At the end of the decade he was equally harsh. "I've watched [my friends] flounder a little over the last ten years, when they're reaching that stage where it's very, very hard to start a new life," he said. "Some of them are affected with resignation and some of them, a certain bitterness maybe... they found themselves in relationships that aren't what they had expected to be in when they were younger."

The *'hours...'* perspective was of fumbling desperation, sung in the voice of someone convinced, as Zygmunt Bauman wrote in *Liquid Love*: "that one is living a lie or a mistake; that something crucially important has been overlooked, missed, neglected, left untried and unexplored; that a vital obligation to one's own authentic self has not been met." It feels like an early draft at times, with keyboard presets rather than string arrangements and instrumentation as if worked out through an arbitration hearing. As with his "average joe" vocals (which sound pretty much like Bowie vocals), something has fallen through in the performances — it's a record that charts sadness and mediocrity like surveying an ocean shelf. The question, left to the listener, is whether this mood is intentional, if the diminished figure in these songs is another mask, or if it's the only voice Bowie could muster in an uninspired time.

One of These Things First

The first track released from the *'hours...'* sessions, "Survive" allegedly came from Bowie meeting later in life someone whom he'd once desperately loved. "And boy was the flame dead!" It's close to the scenario of "Strangers When We Meet," but it's tempting to think he was hinting at his ex-girlfriend Hermione Farthingale, whom he'd once used to symbolize everything he'd lost in the Sixties. Biographical criticism only goes so far. The woman in "Survive" is more abstract, a place-filler used by a sad man to stand for his loss of potential.

There are Sixties shadows: Mark Plati's Mellotron, "Time Is on My Side," "You Keep Me Hangin' On." And "Survive" answers, obliquely, Nick Drake's

1970 "One of These Things First." In Drake's song, a young man thumbs through possible lives. He could have been steady, he sides with inconstancy. He could have been a real lover, not a half-one, and "a whole long lifetime/ could have been the end." Committing would end his freedom, close off the other avenues that lie before him. He wants to remain in a conditional tense.

"Survive" turns him up decades later, still lost in the could-have been. The verses run out of breath, while the refrains are scant hopes, feinting at A major but still trapped in the verses' D major. A descending bassline holds him to the Earth. Gabrels is a bright color, playing a dancing phrase after "I miss you," a counter-melody for the second refrain, an eight-bar solo that's a puff of hope, descending arpeggios to shadow the ambivalence in Bowie's vocal. (Marius De Vries' remix, used for the UK single mix and later included on *Nothing Has Changed*, ditched much of Gabrels' work for a "spacier" contemporary sound, with new guitar lines by Karma County's Brendan Gallagher.)

He sees her across the floor. They could've been something once. "I should've kept you," he says. "I should've tried." She's the mistake he never made, he says, but she sees through him as someone who never deserved the better life that he waited for in vain. The song is a circle, opening and closing on the same augmented D major chord, its two refrains bracketed by its two verses, and it ends in a sad defiance, Bowie's voice waning more each time he sings the title line, until he lets the song expire in his place.

SOMETHING IN THE AIR

(Bowie, Gabrels.) **Recorded**: *(demos) ca. February-autumn 1998, various home/ hotel studios, New York, London; ca. autumn 1998, Mute Records Studio; (overdubs, retakes) ca. February-May 1999, Looking Glass; (last overdubs, mixing) ca. May- June 1999, Chung King. Bowie: lead and backing vocal, keyboards, Roland TR- 707; Gabrels: lead and rhythm guitar, Roland VG-8, keyboards, synthesizer; Plati: bass; Levesque: drums. Produced: Bowie, Gabrels; engineered: Paul.*

First release: *21 September 1999,* **'hours...'** **Broadcast**: *20 October 1999, Nulle part ailleurs; 25 October 1999, Mark Radcliffe Show; 22 November 1999, MusiquePlus; 29 November 1999, Later with Jools Holland.* **Live**: *1999.*

Bowie said of "Something in the Air" that "there's a terrible conflict... it's probably the most tragic song on the album." It autopsies a relationship: a man who once worshiped life with his partner has become an unbeliever. "'I can't believe I'm asking you to go, you, my entire life. I imbued you with so many future inspirations.' It's terrible," Bowie said, outlining his character's plight. A couple is paced through their last days ("we smile too fast/then can't think of a thing to say") by a bassline that follows the lead of a no-nonsense programmed drumline.

At the end of the century, Bowie said he thought the world had a "present sensibility," that "history has receded into the distance, and so has the future." It was a rebuke to his idea of a there being a cultural purge for the new millennium. Maybe no one had wanted the house to burn down after all but were content to stay inside as it collapsed. The couple in "Something in the Air" exist in this present sensibility, over arguing/altering pairs of chords: C minors broadening to C minor ninths; D minors versus F majors; F-sharps blunted to F majors, then sharpened again.

It's Bowie as a "faux novelist," in his words. But there's all of this other information packed into the song. Its title references a lost revolution anthem, Thunderclap Newman's 1969 "Something in the Air," which had called for the streets and houses to get blocked up, for arms and ammo to be passed around. The song would soundtrack an ad in the 2000s, the revolution now a faster mobile service. The death of a relationship is the cover story: there's a greater betrayal beyond Bowie's markers — an aesthetic and cultural exhaustion, a rumination on old emotional violence. He sings the opening line, "your coat and hat are gone," like "you're cold and had a gun," while under the verses is the jabbing riff of "Straight to Hell" ("we can't avoid the Clash"), another wartime song from would-be pop revolutionaries. And his coda (which brings in live drums) homages Annette Peacock's "I'm the One," a song he'd loved for decades. After making brilliant, uncompromising records and supporting radical movements, Peacock had burned out by the end of the Eighties. "I used to be extremely optimistic," she said. "Now I'm more realistic about man's ability to transcend his basic nature, or his basic conditioning. Unless people start becoming active, in terms of doing what they can actually do in their own sphere of activity... yeah, there is no hope."

A failed marriage, a failed revolution, a failed world: they hang together like old coats in a closet. There's grandeur in Reeves Gabrels' lead lines, in Bowie's voice in the coda. What did he have to mourn? The counterculture's collapse had been the best thing for him: his public image in the Seventies was of a man who showed up after everything went south. Having invested in the idea of the future, having been the future's champion, he had tired of it. The future hadn't been worth it, after all. Let me go back into history, let someone else offer alternatives. Goodbye to all the oppressive tomorrows. "Danced with you too long," he sings. It's a scraping performance, with his voice twisted and torn through a ring modulator. "Something in the Air" is spun from old dreamers' songs but has no dreams left in it.

THE DREAMERS

(Bowie, Gabrels.) **Recorded**: (demos) ca. February-autumn 1998, various home/hotel studios, New York, London; ca. autumn 1998, Mute Records Studio; (overdubs, retakes) ca. February-May 1999, Looking Glass; (last overdubs, mixing) ca. May-June 1999, Chung King. Bowie: lead and backing vocal, keyboards, Roland TR-707; Gabrels: lead and rhythm guitar, synthesizer, keyboards, drum programming; Plati: bass; Campbell: drums, chimes. Produced: Bowie, Gabrels; engineered: Paul.

First release: 21 September 1999, 'hours...'

"The Dreamers" is a Bowie album finale as if scripted for the David Bowie Is exhibit. Imperiously sung in its opening minutes, with Bowie obscurities ("Shadow Man") amidst the lyric's apocalyptica (black-eyed ravens, a sky "flame-filled" and "vermillion"), it twines the main strands of 'hours...' — gamer drama ("the Dreamers" are Bowie's fellow musical insurrectionists in Omikron) and middle-aged lamentations. A few lifts here and there, like the riff of T. Rex's "Jeepster" in the bridges or a keyboard/guitar line from Genesis' "Follow You Follow Me."

It's devoted to Bowie's past yet unwilling, or unable, to get even halfway there ("so it goes," as Bowie sings, a homage to Kurt Vonnegut's Slaughterhouse Five, where the phrase accompanies each death in the novel). With its acerbic chord structure, shifting rhythms, lengthy coda, and Gotterdammerung lyric, it needed something like the "Wagnerian orchestra" that Tony Visconti had arranged for "Wild Eyed Boy from Freecloud" in 1969. Instead, beds of synthesizers and stabbing guitars bear the weight (Sterling Campbell's drums in the 'hours...' version give it more of a kick than the drum-programmed

463

Omikron mix). "The Dreamers" comes off as an overcooked demo that got promoted to an album closer.

BRILLIANT ADVENTURE

(Bowie, Gabrels.) **Recorded:** *ca. summer-autumn 1998, New York, London, Bermuda; ca. autumn 1998, Mute Records Studio. Bowie: koto, keyboards, percussion?; Gabrels: keyboards, synthesizer, percussion? Produced: Bowie, Gabrels; engineered: Paul.*

First release: *21 September 1999,* **'hours...'**

"A luverly instrumental, again with koto, that Reeves and I did in the front room in Bermuda," as Bowie recalled of the slight "Brilliant Adventure." Considered for incidental music in *Omikron*, it would be sequenced as an ampersand on *'hours... ,'* linking Sturm ("New Angels of Promise") and Drang ("The Dreamers"). It possibly started with Bowie listening to, and playing along with, a Balinese orchestra recording ("something very odd came from all this and I must get it to Reevz (sic) and see what he makes of it," he wrote in an August 1998 journal entry).

Bowie's other koto instrumental, "Moss Garden" on *"Heroes,"* was the work of an inspired amateur, plucking the strings of an instrument he could scarcely play. "Brilliant Adventure" is a tiny ship corked in a tiny bottle. It begins with an eight-bar sequence: over a bed of chimes and a (soon-diminishing) repeated bass note, its melody is carried on a falling koto and synthesizer "flute" line that, with a chord change, is reduced to koto, which rallies to close with a rising figure, winding up back on its starting note. At forty-two seconds, "Brilliant Adventure" ends; it's reborn a moment later. The sequence repeats, with slight variations. Another ending, another resurrection. This rebirth proves too much: midway through the first eight-bar sequence, it shuffles off. Life isn't quite worth the effort after a few rounds.

THURSDAY'S CHILD

(Bowie, Gabrels.) **Recorded**: *ca. February-autumn 1998, various home/hotel studios, New York, London; ca. autumn 1998, Mute Records Studio; (overdubs, retakes) ca. February-May 1999, Looking Glass; (last overdubs, mixing) ca. May-June 1999, Chung King. Bowie: lead and backing vocal, keyboards; Gabrels: lead and rhythm guitar, synthesizer, drum programming; Plati: bass; Levesque: drums; Holly Palmer: backing vocal. Produced: Bowie, Gabrels; engineered: Paul.*

First release: *20 September 1999 (Virgin 7243 8 96265 2 0, UK #16).* **Broadcast**: *21 August 1999, Top of the Pops; 23 August 1999, VH1 Storytellers; 2 October 1999, Saturday Night Live; 15 October 1999, Les Années Tubes; 16 October 1999, Wetten... dass?; 19 October 1999, Cosas que importan; 20 October 1999, Nulle part ailleurs; 21 October 1999, Francamente me ne infischio; 28 October 1999, WB Radio Music Awards; 16 November 1999, Late Night with Conan O'Brien; 17 November 1999, The Rosie O'Donnell Show; 22 November 1999, MusiquePlus; 5 December 1999, Quelli che... il Calcio; 8 December 1999, Inte Bara Blix; 11 December 1999, BingoLotto.* **Live**: *1999-2000.*

On *'hours... ,'* Bowie was a sad clown again. The figure of "When I Live My Dream" and "Letter to Hermione," the cabaret and mime Bowie: regional thespian, bedsit saddo, Mod worshipper of Judy Garland. "Thursday's Child" is another loser at love. Take the Mr. Pitiful tone of the opening verse, where yearning emphases ("doing my *best*," "whisper of *hope*") are cued to B minor chords. While the refrains are an escape, hoping a new love can break the cycle, its vacillation between major and minor chords makes it a tenuous one, despite the desperately sung "everything's *falling* into *place*!"

Its verse melody, a dance of mild leaps and falls, suits its lyric: it's Bowie's "September Song." His title came from Eartha Kitt's autobiography, an erotic memory of his youth (that and D.H. Lawrence, he said) that fit the *'hours...'* theme of middle-aged reckoning, of flipping through mold-speckled records from his youth, like Ray Charles' "That Lucky Old Sun," a man in the middle of life who envies death. But the title's also a medieval prediction rhyme: "Thursday's child has far to go." Thursday was a day of great fortune, under the sway of Jupiter. (David Robert Jones was born on a Wednesday, "full of woe.") So the singer being a Thursday's child jars with his nothing-ever-goes-right backstory ("a teethgrinding, I'll-get-this-job-done guy," Bowie said of his character). A Thursday's child could be lucky, ambitious: a Kitt or a Bowie. "Doing my best with what I had" becomes a modest boast, "shuffling days and lonesome nights," those of a stage life.

Composed in Bermuda in late 1998, "Thursday's Child" never lost its homebound quality — the opening melody and chordal support throughout are the work of cheap-sounding keyboards, rather than a string section (the "Rock Mix," where many keyboard lines are shifted to guitar, demonstrates how it could have been worse) and the cymbal-fixated drums plod. From early on, Bowie saw a prominent role for a female singer. After considering Mark Plati's six-year-old daughter for the "Inchworm"-inspired "Monday, Tuesday..." line ("she said she'd rather sing with her friends than with grown-ups," Plati told David Buckley), Bowie was ready to ask the R&B trio TLC. It was a savvy move, as in the late Nineties a Baby Boomer legend could get hits by pairing with someone half his age (see Santana, Carlos). But it didn't sit well with Gabrels, who considered it his brief to keep Bowie weird, to stop him from embarrassing himself. His veto of TLC would be his last strategic win. The singer was instead his Boston friend, Holly Palmer, whose voice is a brushwork in the mix, mostly harmonizing beneath Bowie's lead and with close-miked vocalese for color; it's an ecstatic coffeehouse ambiance. Palmer soon joined Bowie's touring band.

The last piece was Walter Stern's video. "Bowie" and his partner ready for sleep in their tasteful Williams Sonoma-style bedroom. They brush their teeth, she takes out her contacts (verrry slooowly), the faucet plashes water into the sink, he coughs, mumbles, half-sings along to "Thursday's Child" playing on the radio. He looks in the mirror, surveying his face. A twist of the glass and reflecting back are his younger self and a young woman who's possibly, likely, not his partner. The mirror pair, stunning vampires, regard the older couple with the cold pity of what Bowie once called "the coming race." Transfixed, Bowie plays the Marx Brothers' *Duck Soup* mirror game with his double, whose face is composed greatly of cheekbones. Bowie's attention turns to the mirror girl — the one he should have gone with back then, who's still there for him in the past. He kisses her in the mirror. Then his partner switches off the faucet and radio, stranding him in his life.

WE ALL GO THROUGH

*(Bowie, Gabrels.) **Recorded:** (demos) ca. February-autumn 1998, various home/ hotel studios, New York, London; ca. autumn 1998, Mute Records Studio; (overdubs, retakes) ca. February-May 1999, Looking Glass; (last overdubs, mixing) ca. May-June 1999, Chung King. Bowie: lead and backing vocal, twelve-string acoustic guitar, keyboards, synthesizer; Gabrels: lead and rhythm guitar, synthesizer, keyboards; Plati: bass; Levesque or Campbell: drums. Produced: Bowie, Gabrels; engineered: Paul.*

First release: *20 September 1999, "Thursday's Child."*

"We All Go Through," with its sturdy E major structure and dreamy verse melody, is one of the sunnier tracks of the *'hours...'* sessions, with even Reeves Gabrels in gentle spirits. The "lunarscape" of the verses warms to refrains with swooning falls into the arms of the home chord. It was the end credits piece for *Omikron*, a victory lap for gamers. Stripped from the game narrative, the lyric was obscure, full of homonyms (morning/mourning, lunarscape/loon escape, nobody's eyes/nobody sighs) and line scrambles — instead of the expected "we'll be all right," it's "we'll *all* be right," while "Dog [a backwards God] is in every word."

With a production aesthetic out of 1989 (Tears for Fears' "Sowing the Seeds of Love" an apparent guidebook), synthetic strings provide a "faux-psychedelic chantin' drone," as per Bowie. His harmony vocals blight vowels ("hooouur by hoouuur"). A bassline snakes through the outro, working against stage-clearing acoustic guitar strums and a non-standard-tuned Gabrels lead. "A writer giving us a series of transitions without scenes on either side of them," as Momus said of the song. Like many other *'hours...'* tracks, "We All Go Through" is jellied in an interim state, if happily enough here.

SEVEN

*(Bowie, Gabrels.) **Recorded**: (demos) ca. February-autumn 1998, various home/ hotel studios, New York, London; (first version) ca. autumn 1998, Mute Records Studio; (overdubs, retakes) ca. February-May 1999, Looking Glass; (last overdubs, mixing) ca. May-June 1999, Chung King. Bowie: lead and backing vocal, twelve-string acoustic guitar, keyboards; Gabrels: lead and rhythm guitar, synthesizer,*

drum programming; Plati: bass; Campbell: drums; Everett Bradley: percussion. Produced: Bowie, Gabrels; engineered: Paul.

First release: *21 September 1999, **'hours...'** Broadcast: 23 August 1999, VH1 Storytellers; 19 October 1999, Cosas que importan; 20 October 1999, Nulle part ailleurs; 22 November 1999 MusiquePlus; 27 June 2000, Bowie at the BBC Radio Theatre.* **Live**: *1999-2000.*

Written on acoustic guitar, "Seven" was, or so Bowie claimed in its debut performance, "a song of nowness." "Seven days to live, seven ways to die," he said. "I'd actually reduce that further to twenty-four hours to live. I'm very happy to deal and only deal with the existing twenty-four hours I'm going through. I'm not inclined to even think too heavily about the end of the week or the week I've just come through. The present is really the place to be." Using "seven" as an organizing symbol worked against this, though, as it's barnacled with the past — seven deadly sins, holy virtues, seals and veils and hells and penitential psalms. He called "Seven" a "hippy dippy" thing, too, but a city "full of flowers" has a bridge full of "viole(n)t people" — the hippies have let down the side as well.

It got lost between incarnations, as its "demo" version (included on a reissue) is richer than the *'hours...'* mix, with a more fore-grounded slide and acoustic guitar and organ. Its *Omikron* mix has a more prominent bassline; a Marius De Vries mix, pushed up in key, was used for the single release.

Talking to Charlie Rose in 1998, Bowie foreshadowed "Seven" by saying he'd escaped his Eighties doldrums by wanting "for each day to be really good... I've got maybe this finite amount of time left... it's something I want to keep on the front burner, every day. I want it to be just like that until death strikes." "Seven" is a song of deliberate forgetting — of the gods, and whatever his mother and father told him. "Not necessarily my mother, father and brother; it was the nuclear unit thing," he told David Quantick in 1999,

Obviously I am totally aware of how people read things into stuff like this. I'm quite sure that some silly cow will come along and say (adopts silly cow voice) "Oh, that's about Terry, his brother, and he was very disappointed about this girl back in 1969, whenever he got over her..." I am only the person the greatest number of people believe that I am.

A family of blank faces; the song of a willing orphan. Losing your parents is the last act of becoming an adult: you look up to find there's no roof on your house. If there's just seven days left (we once got five years in a happier doomsday), Bowie plays in churches (the gods' tombs), wanders empty cities; his movements in the verses' C major progression, one as overused as any in pop music, are a strike outward, a wistful moment alone, a move to avoid going home, then home anyway. The ash-emptied "Seven" says goodbye to the forgotten, ringing with a guitar that holds notes long enough that it seems they'll break, then bends them anew.

THE PRETTY THINGS ARE GOING TO HELL

(Bowie, Gabrels.) **Recorded**: *(demo) ca. September 1998, "Sea View Studio" (Bowie's home), Bermuda; (first version) ca. autumn 1998, Mute Records Studio; (overdubs, retakes) ca. February-May 1999, Looking Glass; (last overdubs, mixing) ca. May-June 1999, Chung King. Bowie: lead and backing vocal, keyboards; Gabrels: lead and rhythm guitar, synthesizer; Plati: bass; Levesque: drums, tambourine, percussion. Produced: Bowie, Gabrels; engineered: Paul, Plati.*

First release: *21 September 1999,* **'hours...'** **Broadcast**: *23 August 1999, VH1 Storytellers; 23 September 1999, MuchMusic Video Awards; 4 October 1999, Late Show with David Letterman; 19 October 1999, Cosas que importan; 20 October 1999, Nulle part ailleurs; 22 November 1999, MusiquePlus.* **Live**: *1999-2000.*

"The Pretty Things Are Going to Hell" started life as a riff Reeves Gabrels wrote, tagging it for his solo album. Bowie, cutting a vocal some months later, claimed the song, considering it a potential single (it was nearly the lead-off) and a good fit for an *Omikron* sequence where "they want[ed] something more rambunctious." He kept providing interpretations, calling it a take-off (or "put-down") of the glam era, and that he'd been inspired by the "bright young things" of Evelyn Waugh's 1930 novel *Vile Bodies*, which had also fueled "Aladdin Sane." "I think their day is numbered," Bowie said of Waugh's lovelies. "So I thought, well, let's close them off. They wore it well but they did wear themselves out... there's not much room for that now. It's a very serious little world." It was also a comedy song, he said. Its "rawk" stylings send up glam, or inept takes on glam, like a parodic critique of the music of *Velvet Goldmine*. Looking back on his performing life, "I wasn't sure if I was doing songs or stand-up," Bowie said. He complained reviewers missed his favorite pun, writing that he sang "life's a bitch" when it was "life's a bit and sometimes you die." "It's stand-up! I wrote a song about stand-up!"

With grudging exchanges of C major and F major chords as its primary harmonic movement, "Pretty Things Are Going to Hell" has Gabrels' "bonehead" main riff — mostly a bend and release of one string, tarted up with artificial harmonics — and power chords moving like a shiver of sharks. Mark Plati described his equally "bonehead" bassline as "low and ugly and simple — and perfect," while Mike Levesque played under the influence of a Keith Moon biography he'd read, with wild fills and kick and snare hits spiced with tambourine and cowbell. It wound up being exhausting (the single edit mercifully crops a bridge repeat), the sort of joke told by a man who keeps saying "do you get it?" after he tells it.

WE SHALL GO TO TOWN

(Bowie, Gabrels.) **Recorded**: *ca. February-autumn 1998, various home/hotel studios, New York, London; ca. autumn 1998, Mute Records Studio; (overdubs, retakes) ca. February-May 1999, Looking Glass; (last overdubs, mixing) ca. May-June 1999, Chung King. Bowie: lead and backing vocal, twelve-string acoustic guitar, keyboards; Gabrels: lead and rhythm guitar, synthesizer, drum programming; Plati: bass, synthesizer; Campbell: drums. Produced: Bowie, Gabrels; engineered: Paul.*

First release: *20 September 1999, "Thursday's Child" (Virgin 7243 8 96268 2 7 VSCDF 1753).*

One last straw for Reeves Gabrels was when "We Shall Go to Town" got demoted to a B-side ("I thought it was a key track," he said decades later). He said the song was about a pair of horribly disfigured people so grotesque "that people would stone them on the street, and they grew tired of having to live in the shadows. And they think 'tonight's the night we go to town. This might be our last night on earth because people will probably kill us.' That was a little less jolly than 'Thursday's Child.'"

Over wary movements between B-flat major and E-flat minor chords, it runs along competing rhythm lines: Mark Plati's fretless bass, singing a rising phrase throughout; Sterling Campbell's warning shuffle patterns on snare and low toms; a rhythm guitar figure in the latter halves of verses and refrains (panned right to left). There's a sour flavor in Bowie's vocal, sung in a diseased-sounding, distortion-riddled low register, his lines full of alliteration and consonant rhymes (br*ing* your th*ing*s), with syllables dragged violently across bars ("deliiiight," "forgehhhht," "the foooooool").

"That song was done in a heartbeat, and it was always one of my favorites," Plati told me. "Probably because it *was* done in a heartbeat, and that kept the mood pure — sometimes, that dynamic yields the tastiest fruit. Reeves' solo is a thing of broken beauty... and, given that he didn't get many of that sort on that record, I suppose he went to town as it were." It's a solo of fits and rages that break off after a few shrieks of strings, as if now being channeled elsewhere, out of range, only to slash back in again.

IF I'M DREAMING MY LIFE

(Bowie, Gabrels.) **Recorded**: *(tracking) ca. February-May 1999, Looking Glass; (last overdubs, mixing) ca. May-June 1999, Chung King. Bowie: lead and backing vocal, twelve-string acoustic guitar, keyboards; Gabrels: lead guitar, synthesizer, keyboards, drum programming; Chris Haskett: rhythm guitar; Plati: bass; Levesque: drums. Produced: Bowie, Gabrels; engineered: Paul.*

First release: *21 September 1999, '**hours...**' Broadcast: 23 August 1999, VH1 Storytellers.* **Live**: *1999.*

"If I'm Dreaming My Life" is one of Bowie's longest studio recordings, in the same set as "Station to Station," "Width of a Circle," "Blackstar," "Cygnet Committee," "Bring Me the Disco King." It was one of the last songs made for *'hours...,'* cut in the Looking Glass sessions of spring 1999, with former Rollins Band member Chris Haskett on rhythm guitar (he was provisionally slated to join Bowie's touring band in 1999).

Its sprawling structure (four verses interspersed with guitar solos — the second and last verses with tagged-on refrains — and a three-minute bloodletting of a coda) and quirky, motivic chord progressions give "If I'm Dreaming My Life" an uneasy presence on *'hours...'*: it's a blank quadrant of

471

the map, with some notes penciled in. Bowie drifts into emotive "ooohhhs"; the second guitar solo sounds like it began with Gabrels noodling lines from "Under the Bridge." In the lyric, nothing pans out, everyone misses cues, the timing's off. Even the air she breathes comes at the wrong time.

Bowie's performance in the coda is a theatrical exhaustion: he tries to complete a phrase but often only gets out a "dreaming myyyy" before having to start over again. He's carried by keyboards dressed as a horn/wind quartet (a role assumed by Mike Garson's organ in the song's few live performances) but gathers supporters when he manages to finish his line: chiming guitar; a choir of secondary Bowies; a melodically generous bass.

What's Really Happening?

(Bowie, Gabrels, Grant.) **Recorded**: *(tracking) ca. autumn 1998, Mute Records Studio; (overdubs) ca. February-May 1999, Looking Glass; (lead and backing vocals, guitar and bass overdubs) 24 May 1999, Looking Glass; (last overdubs, mixing) ca. May-June 1999, Chung King. Bowie: lead and backing vocal; Gabrels: lead and rhythm guitar; Plati: bass; Levesque: drums; Alex Grant, Larry Tressler: backing vocals. Produced: Bowie, Gabrels; engineered: Paul, Plati.*

First release: *21 September 1999, 'hours...'*

Being a fan is transactional. You buy the records (well, you once did), join the fan club. Get an autographed picture in the mail, or a Christmas record. First dibs on concert seats. Win a contest to go backstage, or have lunch with the star, or at least the drummer. The more time and money you give, the further you go into the circle, but only so far. Fandom could be a one-sided, abusive relationship: fan clubs milked for cash; fans sexually harassed by roadies, bodyguards, and hangers-on for backstage access.

BowieNet would level things, be less exploitative. For a relatively cheap subscription, you could talk to Bowie online and, in late 1998, co-write a song, "What's Really Happening?" As a guideline, he gave would-be lyricists a hummed top melody track: three sets of four lines, mainly seven syllables each. He claimed he read most of the 25,000 submissions (one rewrote "Laughing Gnome," another wag sent in "Wind Beneath My Wings" unaltered), many of which were in the vein of the as-yet-released *'hours...,'* "very soul searching and angst-ridden" stuff. He chose a twenty-year-old Ohioan, Alex Grant, whose lyric "was impertinent, it scanned well, and it was easy to sing." Grant was an early adopter of being publicly exhausted by the internet, one of the twenty-first century's major literary genres. His opening verse contrasts "virtual" life to the natural mechanics of our bodies' "outdated clocks." This concept eroded by the last verse, where glass clouds sink "like the shattered past," though to be fair these were pretty Bowie-esque lines.

A G Dorian piece whose melody is two cups "You Keep Me Hangin' On," one cup "Pictures of Matchstick Men," its refrain, with its glum accumulation of major chords, found Bowie recycling a line from "One Shot." Its clutter of a mix helps distract the listener from realizing the song should end by the two-minute mark (there's a hard edit at 2:36, suggesting the intro section was looped back in). Touted as the first "Cyber Song," the Looking Glass session for Bowie's lead vocal, Grant and his friend Larry Tressler's backing vocals, Reeves Gabrels' lead lines, and Mark Plati's bass overdubs was simulcast to BowieNet via a Lucent 360 "BowieCam." BowieNetters gave color commentary: "Is David drinking a Zima?" "What a boring song," "Reeves is a Teletubbie," "You haven't missed anything except David wailing the same line incessantly." Imagine the live thread had fans been able to watch Bowie and Eno cut "Warszawa" in the studio: "Is this in Portuguese?" "I MISS RONNO."

Originally planned as a BowieNet-exclusive track, "What's Really Happening?" wound up on 'hours...' possibly as a publicity hook. It was a curio of noble intentions, as never again would Bowie have such a degree of fan participation in his work.

JEWEL

(Bowie, Black, Plati, Gabrels.) **Recorded**: *12 February 1997, Westlake Recording Studios, 8447 Beverly Blvd., Los Angeles. Frank Black: lead vocal, rhythm guitar; Gabrels: lead vocal, lead and rhythm guitar; Bowie: lead vocal; Plati: bass; Dave Grohl: drums, backing vocal. Produced, engineered: Plati.*

First release: *4 November 1999,* **Ulysses (Della Notte)** *(EMA-61050-2).*

Many Bowie collaborators got a "your services are no longer required" notice. Reeves Gabrels quit. His last performance with Bowie was a *VH1 Storytellers* concert shot in New York on 23 August 1999. One can look for signs of the break in their interactions, in a tense exchange about Tin Machine. But Bowie was reportedly blindsided, having to scramble to find a lead guitarist for his promotional tour (it would be Helmet's Page Hamilton).

Gabrels was tired of Bowie's management and advisors, of having to scrap for songwriting credit. And he sensed the mood was turning. Tony Visconti was back, the *Ziggy Stardust* anniversary boondoggle was still underway (see "Safe"), there were more hits in the setlists. "A big part of [Bowie's] legacy is the pursuit of the new. When I became more aware of the desire to do more old songs and eliminate the sequential information and loops from our new music, I realized that what David wanted from the music was quickly diverging from what I needed," Gabrels told David Buckley. As *'hours...'* was already "becoming a little too VH1," the future would only hold more struggle — his clash with Bowie about using TLC in "Thursday's Child" was another warning sign. "I realized that I was constantly imposing my will, in terms of what I wanted from music and being younger than David," he said. "Why should I look at him as being the singer in my band?" He feared becoming a hack, dutifully playing Mick Ronson lines on stage and being "everything I disliked in musicians I had known... or I was gonna die because I would be so miserable I would just drug myself to death," as he told Paul Trynka. He called his solo album *Ulysses*: a lost man trying to make his way home.

One of the fullest creative partners Bowie ever had ("his workload got heavier and heavier and I think that wore him down a bit," Zachary Alford recalled), Gabrels was Bowie's extended middle finger, and someone who could always crack him up. He didn't honor the myth: interview after interview finds Gabrels busting Bowie's chops, to Bowie's delight. He had the audacity to believe his work, his insights, could be as vital. This could make for hard stretches — some solos feel intended to kill the songs they're housed in – and his departure was welcomed by some quarters of fandom, for whom Gabrels embodied everything they disliked in Bowie's Nineties. Now it was safe to go to a Bowie show again.

On Gabrels' 1999 album *Ulysses (Della Notte)*, Bowie appeared on one track, "Jewel," along with Frank Black, Dave Grohl, and Mark Plati. In the after-party for Bowie's fiftieth anniversary concert, Grohl said that he,

Gabrels, Charlie Sexton, and Black should form the alt-rock Blind Faith. The closest they came was "Jewel," on which Grohl drummed, Black sang a verse, and Gabrels the refrains, sounding like a more morose J. Mascis (if intended to be Neil Young). In Los Angeles to play the *Tonight Show* with Bowie in February 1997, Gabrels called Black and Grohl, who happened to be there as well. Soon they and Plati were in Gabrels' hotel room writing a song, cutting it at Westlake Studios on the evening of the same day that Bowie's star was unveiled on Hollywood Boulevard. The honoree wrote his verse via his analog cut-up method, scissoring lines from Jerzy Kosinski's *Cockpit*, Matthew Barney's Hugo Boss prize exhibit at the Guggenheim, and some issues of *Spy*, spreading sheets of paper across the studio floor, then singing his lines in a flush of voices.

SECTOR Z
MAN WITHOUT A MOUTH

(Albee, Gutter, McNaboe, Noyes, Roods, Ward, Zoidis.) **Recorded***: ca. May 1999, Avatar Studios; July 1999, Looking Glass. Dave Gutter: lead vocal, guitar; Bowie: lead and harmony vocals; Spencer Albee: keyboards, vocals; Dave Noyes: trombone; Jason Ward: baritone saxophone; Ryan Zoidis: saxophone; Jon Roods: bass; Tony McNaboe: drums. Produced: Visconti, Dave Leonard, Rustic Overtones.*

First release*: 5 June 2001,* **Viva Nueva** *(Tommy Boy TBCD 1471).*

"The overriding feature of much of the Nineties was working with bands that few people had heard of," Tony Visconti wrote in his autobiography. One was Portland, Maine's Rustic Overtones, a band Arista's Clive Davis envisioned, with their saxophone/trombone section and funk/ska sound, as his response to RCA's Dave Matthews Band. Recording with Visconti in spring 1999 at Avatar Studios, the band felt like "the Beverly Hillbillies," lead singer Dave Gutter told me. Their one indulgence was having a ping-pong table brought in. Visconti kept saying Bowie would love them, to the point where it became a running joke. Then one day, Bowie walked in. "We freaked out," Gutter said.

With Bowie chain-smoking everywhere despite the "no smoking" signs (Gutter mailed his mother some Bowie cigarette butts), they developed a track called "Sector Z," Bowie playing an alien broadcaster, alternating spoken asides with phrases "in his Ziggy voice," as Visconti recalled, and swathing them in harmonies. It's a world away from *'hours...'*. And when the band was overdubbing at Looking Glass in July 1999, Bowie said he thought he could do something for another song. For "Man Without a Mouth," he sang harmonies with his usual economy: triple-tracking lines in twenty minutes. "Oh, that was shit," he'd say upon hearing one of his (usually perfect) vocals in playback.

The Rustic Overtones were caught in the music industry's post-Napster collapse ("when the wall fell down," Gutter said). Their album, *Viva Nueva*, had an early 2000 release date until Davis' departure left them without advocates — Arista soon pulled it. After a year in limbo, they escaped with their album masters. The strain took its toll: while the album came out in summer 2001, the band broke up a year later (they've since reformed). They had one regret about working with Bowie: they had wanted to ask him to play ping-pong but chickened out — he was a serious artiste, after all. Later, the band heard that he was an avid player who once had an epic match with Lou Reed.

HOLE IN THE GROUND

Recorded: (unreleased) ca. 5-20 July 2000, Sear Sound, Studio C, 353 W. 48th St, New York; ca. late October-early November 2000, Looking Glass. Bowie: lead and backing vocal; Earl Slick: lead guitar, acoustic guitar; Mike Garson: piano, keyboards; Plati: guitar, keyboards; Gail Ann Dorsey: bass; Campbell: drums; Lisa Germano: recorder. Produced: Plati; engineered: Pete Keppler.

For many years, David Bowie started with "Space Oddity" in 1969. What came before was juvenilia. "Aaargh, that Anthony Newley stuff, how cringey. No, I haven't much to say about that in its favor," he said in 1990. Into the memory hole went his Decca, Parlophone, and Pye singles, his 1967 Deram album, "The Laughing Gnome," the King Bees and Manish Boys and the Riot Squad: five years of candled ambition. His oldest tracks fell in and out of print, scattered through decades of cheap compilations.

In the Nineties, his pre-1969 work was at last thoroughly compiled by Rhino and Deram and by the end of the decade Bowie was mulling the idea of revisiting it. Upon remaking "Let's Dance" as an acoustic piece, he said "there can be a point where you can start getting back into those things with a new invigorated sense of purpose." In an October 1998 journal entry, he wrote of "the possibility of re-recording some extremely early songs with contemporary arrangements and techniques." A year later, he played his 1966 single "Can't Help Thinking About Me" at *VH1 Storytellers*, introducing it by rubbishing his lyric. But the song cooked on stage, thanks to Sterling Campbell's drumming — it felt fresher than some *'hours...'* songs. He also revived "I Dig Everything" in his 1999 promotional tour and played "Karma Man" and "Conversation Piece" in rehearsals.

Bowie said his plans for the year 2000 were to assemble *2. Contamination* (no), make the long-rumored Tony Visconti album (not quite), and to remake songs he'd released between 1964-1969, "not so much a *Pin Ups II* as an *Up Date I*." The latter idea soon ballooned in scope. The sessions would be simulcast via webcam. He wouldn't just remake his old singles but also ghost songs, outtakes that fans knew only as titles.

Iman was pregnant and due in August, so he planned a burst of activity for early summer: some live shows and cutting "the Sixties album." "I hate to waste the energy of a show-honed band," he said. "I've pulled together a selection of songs from a somewhat unusual reservoir and booked time in a studio. I cannot wait to sit in a claustrophobic space with seven other energetic people and sing till my tits drop off." During rehearsals, Bowie and his band (the 1999 touring unit plus Earl Slick as new lead guitarist) revived all but two of his 1964-1966 singles and some choice Deram pieces like "Let Me Sleep Beside You." He wanted them to crack into the songs. "We weren't out to duplicate the original tracks at all," said Mark Plati, who Bowie chose to produce the album.

On stage that summer, Bowie broke his *Sound + Vision* tour pact and flung open the catalog. His first gig at the Roseland in New York, a three-hour set on 16 June 2000, began with "Wild Is the Wind" and went on through "Life on Mars?" "Golden Years," "Absolute Beginners," "Rebel Rebel," and "Changes," some of which he'd hadn't played in a decade. In Britain he sang "Starman" on television for the first time since the Heath ministry (you expected him to appear in Ziggy Stardust makeup by this point). Two days later, he headlined Glastonbury.

He'd last played it in 1971, its debut year, when it was Glastonbury Fayre, one of the free festivals then cropping up around Britain (its pyramid-shaped stage was built on a ley line). In 2000, Glastonbury was now £87 tickets and 100,000-strong crowds. Wearing a glam bishop's vestments, his hair at *Hunky Dory* length, Bowie made the rest of the bill look second-rate. For an encore he did "Ziggy Stardust," "Heroes," "Let's Dance," and a stonking "I'm Afraid of Americans." The UK press genuflected: "a masterclass of superstardom" (the *Mirror*), "an object lesson in How to Be a Rock Star" (the *Times*), "a level beyond and above anyone else at this festival" (*NME*). All was forgiven. In the prophecy year 2000, he rode in on the past.

Down in the Hole

Soon upon their return to New York, Bowie and his band cut thirteen tracks for the "Sixties album," eventually titled *Toy* (a word in lyrics of two songs remade for the album, "Baby Loves That Way" and "London Boys"), in about nine days in July 2000 at Sear Sound. Engineer Pete Keppler recalled Bowie "belting his brains out and the band just roaring away behind him," cutting a first-take lead vocal, overdubbing himself in the second take, adding harmonies for every further take.

At least two "lost" song remakes were tracked: "Shadow Man" (see *Rebel Rebel*) and "Hole in the Ground." Bowie had written the latter for his friend George Underwood in late 1969 — its demo was cut by mostly the same crew as on the *Space Oddity* album, its lyrics were typical Bowie apocalyptic portents of the era (stay home until he gets there — he's been outside and he's seen the hole in the ground). As the demo wasn't bootlegged (even Underwood said he'd forgotten what it sounded like), it's impossible to say how the *Toy* version altered the song. Mike Garson recalled it developing from a studio jam, though its phrasings and acoustic guitar strum patterns are reminiscent of 1969's "Janine," which also had a slacking-off in lieu of an ending. "Hole in the Ground" has a welcoming groove — keyboards and recorder as shifting backdrops, Gail Ann Dorsey paying homage to "Walk on the Wild Side" with some sloping fills. But its revival mostly showed that Bowie had been right in deep-sixing it. Time hadn't improved the song, only made it novel.

Your Turn to Drive (Toy)

Recorded: ca. 5-20 July 2000, Sear Sound?; ca. late October-early November 2000, *Looking Glass. Bowie: lead and backing vocal, Stylophone; Slick: lead guitar; Garson: piano; Germano: violin; Cuong Vu: trumpet; Plati: guitar, keyboards, bass?; Dorsey: bass?; Campbell: drums; Holly Palmer, Emm Gryner: backing vocals. Produced: Plati, Bowie; engineered: Plati, Visconti, McNulty.*

First release: 15 September 2003 (download, HMV orders of **Reality**).

On *Toy*, Bowie revived his failures and obscurities, making few alterations in lyrics, chords, or melody, mostly slowing tempos and singing in an ashen tenor or baritone. At best, he cast an agreeable pall: "Conversation Piece" burnishes its loneliness, "Liza Jane" is a dirty carnival barker's song, "Baby Loves That Way" a lament of a humiliated old fool, "Silly Boy Blue" was unruinable. But the lesser remakes were an amateur's songs made more professional, with the rough edges of teenage ambition sanded down.

In late summer 2000, Mark Plati was listening to the *Toy* mixes and felt something was missing. Catching the Eels at their 10 August show at the Bowery Ballroom, Plati was taken with their guest violinist Lisa Germano ("her vibe would be just perfect for us"). In late September, he scheduled two days with Germano and Bowie at his apartment in the East Village. She turned up with a "small arsenal of eccentric instruments," including a recorder-flute, a 1920s Gibson mandolin, "and an old tiny tortoise-shell blue-green Hohner accordion with a strap so old and tired we had to beg it to stay together (assisted by duct tape)," Plati recalled. Bowie arrived, happy to work (it was his first time making music since his daughter's birth). He sat on Plati's couch, played guitar and tried his hand at violin "playing some cool drones, like a John Cale vibe." There was a good chemistry and Germano was recruited for overdubs.

An effusive Bowie wrote in his journal that "the songs are so alive and full of color... It's really hard to believe they were written so long ago." Yet by now he was reconsidering *Toy*. With an eye on its commercial prospects, he didn't want to have an entire album of re-recorded songs. He'd "written a couple of new songs... in a style I may have written them in the Sixties."

One of these was "Your Turn to Drive," later issued as a download-

479

only bonus for *Reality*. Originally called "Toy," it possibly started in the Sear Sound sessions but seems more the product of overdub sessions at Looking Glass that October. A tell is Bowie's Stylophone, heard on other newly-written tracks like "Uncle Floyd," and trumpeter Cuong Vu, who also cut a solo at Looking Glass for "Liza Jane." Even less cohesive than "Hole in the Ground," it's a dreamy refrain of alternating ascending phrases, bookended by piano and a two-minute coda that's hazy with Vu's trumpet lines. Bowie is a softer presence than the piano or trumpet, with his vocal a loose alliance of sounds: he could be singing "die tonight" or "lie tonight." An intriguing trifle.

PICTURES OF LILY

(Townshend.) **Recorded**: *ca. 10-13 October 2000, Looking Glass. Bowie: lead and backing vocal, Stylophone; Plati: lead and rhythm guitar, bass, backing vocal; Campbell: drums, backing vocal; Germano: violin. Produced: Bowie, Plati; engineered: Plati.*

First release: *4 June 2001,* **Substitute: The Songs of the Who** *(Edel 0126242ERE/ ED183022).*

A first order of business once Bowie reconvened his band in early October 2000 was a Who cover. Pete Townshend had asked him to take part in a Who tribute album and Bowie chose "Pictures of Lily," one of an astonishing run of Who singles between 1965 and 1967 — a kid falls in love with a dead pin-up, Townshend's guitar playing is a curse at time. Done within hours, Bowie's take was a trio performance with him, Mark Plati on guitar and bass, and Sterling Campbell on drums (Lisa Germano's violin was overdubbed later). It "came out sounding like a glam version of Crazy Horse... complete with Stylophone solo, Ronson homage outro and football hooligan chanting," Plati wrote. At a molasses tempo and over shoegaze guitars, Bowie sounds like he wants to grow up to *be* Lily, not fantasize about her.

Afraid

*Recorded: (**Toy** version, unreleased) ca. October-early November 2000, Looking Glass; (overdubs for **Heathen**) ca. autumn 2001, Looking Glass. Bowie: lead vocal, acoustic guitar; Plati: acoustic guitar, electric guitar, bass, backing vocal; Gerry Leonard: guitar; Germano: violin (**Toy**); Campbell: drums; uncredited musicians: strings (**Heathen**). Produced: Plati (**Toy**), Bowie, Visconti (**Heathen**); engineered: Plati (**Toy**), Visconti.*

*First release: 10 June 2002, **Heathen** (ISO/Columbia COL 508222 9/CK 86630, UK #5, US #14). **Broadcast**: 18 October 2002, Late Night with Conan O'Brien; 25 October 2002, The Early Show. **Live**: 2002-2004.*

Another impetus for Bowie doing a self-covers album was that with Reeves Gabrels gone, he no longer had a co-composer. He feared he'd gotten out of shape for songwriting. So "Afraid," a song he whisked together in the *Toy* mixing sessions, was a breakthrough — showing he could still produce when put under pressure, if in this case as a joke. He was recalling an anecdote from Rolling Stones manager Andrew Loog Oldham's memoir *Stoned*, where Oldham had locked Mick Jagger and Keith Richards in a flat until they wrote a song. Mark Plati, following Oldham's lead, sent Bowie to the Looking Glass lounge, telling him "not to come back until he had the goods!" And so he did. Bowie returned with "Afraid," working out the song on Plati's mini Stratocaster.

It had affinities to *Toy*'s "new songs in the vein of old songs" concept, with traces of "Heroes," "Conversation Piece," and "I Can't Read" (especially its Nineties revision, whose lyric Bowie all but quotes in the last refrain). He'd gone back again to John Lennon's *Plastic Ono Band*. On that album's "God," after knocking down a set of false idols, Lennon ends his purge with the Beatles. Here Bowie sings that he believes in Beatles, as well as aliens and/or God ("we're not alone"). Another old song shifts beneath it. "Cygnet Committee," from 1969, is Bowie as a young man willing himself into becoming an artist, screaming "I want to believe!" "Afraid" questions the idea of belief, whether it's worth even having dreams. It's a numbed perspective, a man recalling past heights ("I used to walk on clouds"), now living a flattened life. In 2002, Bowie took pains to distance himself from his character: "I don't see it as being representative of me." His narrator does what society expects, striking a bargain of spiritual conformity for security. "An interesting deceit, but it's not mine," he clucked.

Plati and Bowie honed "Afraid" during late October, debuting it on a livestream on BowieNet on 2 November. By the time of this performance (Bowie on acoustic guitar, Plati on electric), most of the song was in place: the intro guitar riff, the G minor verse progression, and the lyrics. It was recorded around the same time, becoming a major new piece for *Toy*, which was scheduled to come out in early 2001 but would not be released in Bowie's lifetime (see "Uncle Floyd").

A year later, working with Tony Visconti on *Heathen* (see Chapter Twelve), Bowie had lost hope for *Toy* and began salvaging from it. "Afraid" was an obvious choice, as it thematically fit his new album. He and Visconti kept the original backing tracks, with Plati called in for guitar overdubs and Visconti writing a string arrangement. Most revisions came in the mixing. The first verse on *Toy* was carried on acoustic guitar, while the *Heathen* mix has prominent electric guitar, the left-mixed acoustic making interjections until getting shuffled to the center and submerged. Visconti's strings emboss the refrains, where Bowie's quavering lead vocal stands exposed. "I think it could be a great live song," Bowie said of "Afraid," and it became a regular of his last shows. "Of course, it's kind of sardonic in its assertion that if we play the game everything will be alright." He'd believed in a great many lies in his life, but never that one.

UNCLE FLOYD
SLIP AWAY

Recorded: ("Uncle Floyd," unreleased) October-November 2000, Looking Glass; ("Slip Away," backing tracks, vocals) 8 August-ca.15 September 2001, Allaire Studios; (overdubs) ca. October 2001-January 2002, Looking Glass. Bowie: lead vocal, Stylophone, piano; Plati: acoustic guitar, keyboards, bass, backing vocal ("Uncle Floyd"); Leonard: lead guitar; David Torn: guitar ("Slip Away"); Germano: violin ("Uncle Floyd"); Jordan Rudess: keyboards ("Slip Away"); Tony Levin: bass ("Slip Away"); Campbell: drums, backing vocal ("Uncle Floyd"); Matt Chamberlain: drums ("Slip Away"); Coco Schwab, Holly Palmer, Jo Lloyd, James Wright, Dave Magee, et al: chorus vocals ("Uncle Floyd"). Produced: ("Uncle Floyd") Plati; ("Slip Away") Bowie, Visconti. Engineered: ("Uncle Floyd") Plati; ("Slip Away") Visconti.

First release: ("Slip Away") 10 June 2002, **Heathen**. **Broadcast**: 15 June 2002, A&E Live by Request; 27 June 2002, Friday Night with Ross & Bowie; 14 September 2002, BingoLotto; 25 October 2002, The Early Show. **Live**: 2002-2004.

The Catholic Church no longer believes in limbo, but they're wrong: it exists, and it's in New Jersey.

Floyd Vivino was a showbiz kid. His brothers were in Conan O'Brien's house band, his niece was in the original *Les Miserables*. He tap-danced at the 1964 New York World's Fair, worked burlesque shows, nightclubs, amusement parks, and circuses: singing, playing piano, doing impressions. Like other vaudevillians, he found refuge in television.

At twenty-three, he pitched a kid's show to WBTB, Channel 68 in West Orange, New Jersey. WBTB had to devote airtime to children's programming, so they took on *The Uncle Floyd Show* (also, Vivino said he'd sell ads). As Uncle Floyd, Vivino wore a plaid coat, bowtie and porkpie hat. He played upright piano and cracked off-camera to his crew, who laughed at random moments (in part because they were seeing skits for the first time). The show's production values consisted of lighting and microphones. Vivino often used food as a prop because he could buy it cheap at Pathmark. He had Oogie, a clown puppet he'd found in a Times Square magic store, and Bones Boy, a skeleton whose catchphrase was "snap it, pal!"

Bowie got hooked on *Uncle Floyd* during the months he starred in *The Elephant Man*. A John Lennon and Iggy Pop favorite, *Uncle Floyd* was a weird kids' show where the Ramones would show up to play. "We used to love falling around watching this guy," Bowie said in 2002. "The show looked like it was done out of his living room in New Jersey." (Close enough — it was a house built on the site of a burned-down circus.) Wearing an Uncle Floyd button, Bowie went to a live taping at the Bottom Line in 1981 and told Vivino how much he loved his show. Vivino didn't know who he was at first and wanted him kicked out of backstage.

In 1982, a syndication aired *Uncle Floyd* nationally; around the same time, Mercury Records released an *Uncle Floyd* cast album. The show had moved to Newark — the studio had an air conditioner and a former *Sesame Street* director was brought in, soon appalled by the lack of rehearsals. Sketches were filmed thirty times. Episodes got cut to bits. Some NBC affiliates revolted, one calling the show "garbage." The syndication deal was over after a single season. *Uncle Floyd* ended up back in New Jersey, shown on the New Jersey Network, then the Cable Television Network, who wound it down in 1992. There was a last brief millennial revival on Cablevision. Around that time, Floyd got a phone call from Bowie. "He said he was thinking of doing a song about me, and wanted to know what I felt about it."

Let's Dance, Bones and Oogie

Down in space it's always 1982. Uncle Floyd's pivot year was Bowie's. Like Uncle Floyd, he went on a larger stage than he'd ever played before; unlike Uncle Floyd, he made the big time.

Toy is Bowie remaking the songs of someone who never charted, whose shows never sold out, whose name was rarely in the press. *Uncle Floyd*'s lost chance at fame haunts the album. Imagine a world where Bones and Oogie are film stars (promoting *Uncle Floyd's Big Adventure*, Amy Adams gushes about how as a kid she loved Bones Boy. "I can't believe we're working together!"). A New York where Oogie is inflated to the size of a city block as a Thanksgiving Day float. "Once a time they nearly *might have been*," Bowie sings, with a delicate weight on the last syllables. "Bones and Oogie... on a *million screens*."

In October 2000 at Looking Glass, Bowie and Mark Plati started working on a new song. "It began its life with a semi-out-of-tune piano and some grainy synth strings which sounded like they were pulled off of an old 78rpm record," Plati wrote. "Both sounds gave the effect of someone playing in a basement of some small, sad, lonely house." The Irish guitarist Gerry Leonard, who would become Bowie's final bandleader and one of his last co-composers, came in for overdubs; Lisa Germano added violin. While Plati worked on a rough mix of the backing tracks, Bowie wrote a full lyric. For his refrain, he used Corinne Schwab, Sterling Campbell, Holly Palmer, some Looking Glass staff and Stretch Princess, a British alt-rock band recording in the adjacent studio.

For an intro, there was an opening routine with Oogie that reminded Germano of "a Mark Ryden painting... sweet and strangely disturbing." Oogie crooks his round head. His empty eyes watch us through the camera as he wonders about the death of his world. *Didja ever stop and think if there wasn't an Uncle Floyd show what everyone on the show would be doing?* A Stylophone fades in, singing in its nasal range. Bowie takes the first verse over it, singing along to a music box, as he would on a Madison Square

Garden stage a year later.

Piano settles the song down, builds a floor. The verses are journeys off the ground (F major, "Once a time… ") up to a G major diminished chord ("Bones and Oogie"), then slowly falling to Earth. Leonard and Germano are satellites. The last verse seems about to drift off until Campbell stops time with a fill, rolling across his toms. *Don't* **forget** *to keep your* **head warm**… *twinkle* **twinkle***, Uncle Floyd*. In his cavernous refrain, sung with friends and strangers, Bowie makes Uncle Floyd a legend of a world where there are stars named after Bones and Oogie. You can see them from the beach on Coney Island, hanging above the World Trade Center towers.

Plati and Bowie completed *Toy* during the 2000 election, taking breaks to see which candidate appeared to be president at the moment. On New Year's Day 2001, BowieNet announced *Toy* was scheduled for March, though the release date was soon pushed to May. In June, in a web-chat, Bowie said "I'm finding EMI/Virgin seems to have a lot of scheduling conflicts this year which has put an awful lot on the back burner. *Toy* is finished and ready to go and I will make an announcement as soon as I get a very real date." A month later he mentioned "unbelievably complicated scheduling negotiations." EMI had posted an £8.1 million operating loss for the first half of the year, thanks in part to the onset of digital song swapping, a recession, and many ill-considered and costly strategic moves. Needing a *Let's Dance*, they got the most self-indulgent album of Bowie's career. In October, Bowie said the label was going with an album of "new material over the *Toy* album. Fine by me. I'm extremely happy with the new stuff." But "I won't let *Toy* slide away. I'm working on a way that you'll be able to get the songs next year as well as the newie."

So *Toy* became "a reservoir of B-sides and bonus tracks." "Afraid" and a remade "Uncle Floyd" were on *Heathen*. "Shadow Man," "You've Got a Habit of Leaving" and "Baby Loves That Way" were *Heathen* B-sides, "Conversation Piece" was on a *Heathen* bonus disc, "Let Me Sleep Beside You" finally appeared in 2014. The rest of *Toy*, including the brilliant original "Uncle Floyd," still remains unissued, though it leaked as a full bootleg in 2011, and can be found on YouTube. Visconti told the writer Dan LeRoy, who included *Toy* in his book of lost rock albums, that Bowie would never talk about it, that he'd taken the rejection hard. Yet by 2003, the need to save *Toy* had lost its urgency. Bowie was frank. "You know what? New writing just takes precedence. It always does."

Slip Away

It was as if Bowie shot a second pilot, remaking "Uncle Floyd" as "Slip Away" a year later with Tony Visconti. No puppets. No Stylophone, at first. Now it opens with artificial harmonics on electric guitar. A piano is front and center in the first verse, Tony Levin's bass and Matt Chamberlain's drums take over in the second. The biggest change was to move up the refrain (it now came after the second verse) and dispense with the guitar solo. It made sense — why hold back your biggest hook until four minutes in? — but it also spoiled the slow arc of "Uncle Floyd." Pete Keppler told LeRoy he thought "Uncle Floyd" "was way cooler than the one that came out on *Heathen*. The mix that Mark did on that song was so much more haunting." In Bowie's last live performances, he restored some of the original framework, including the Oogie intro. At Jones Beach in 2004, he brought on the Polyphonic Spree to sing the last refrains.

Bowie included "Slip Away" on *Heathen* because "I wanted something on the album that pointed to a nicer time, a better time, a more fun time, even if it wasn't necessarily true," he said in 2002,

> For me it was a fun time, the late Seventies, it really was… Saying "Uncle Floyd where are you now?" is really like Ray Davies saying, "Where Have All The Good Times Gone?"… That's my yearning song, as far as looking backwards. But most of it is about looking rather anxiously into the future.

The New York City of *The Uncle Floyd Show* is gone. The Bottom Line, CBGB, Brownies, Kim's Video, Coliseum Books are long closed, some with afterlives as abused trademarks. WBTB, its original call letters long retired, was bought by Univision. All of the original Ramones, Lou Reed, and David Bowie are gone. All that remains from your childhood are photos, toys (Stylophones, skeleton puppets), and television signals. "Just waves in space," as Thomas Jerome Newton once said (he would have liked *Uncle Floyd*). Signals that, if converted, will recreate *The Uncle Floyd Show* and make 1982 appear again, are sailing across the solar system. Everything goes, everything ends, and even Oogie will crack apart one day, but some things survive. At least television will. *Uncle Floyd* is dead, long live Uncle Floyd.

Isn't It Evening (The Revolutionary)

(Bowie, Slick.) **Recorded**: *ca. 12 March 2001, Alice's Restaurant, New York. Bowie: lead and backing vocal; Slick: lead and rhythm guitar; Plati: bass, keyboards, drum programming. Produced, engineered: Plati.*

First release: *9 December 2003,* **Zig Zag** *(Sanctuary 06076-84671).*

A mainstay of Bowie's last tours and albums, Earl Slick was also the last link to Bowie's past. Of *The Next Day* players, only he and Tony Visconti had worked with Bowie in the Seventies. Bowie considered Slick a fearless "blue-collar" guitarist, the guy you called for your rock 'n' roll deliveries. John Lennon had hired Slick for *Double Fantasy* because "he wanted one street guy in there" among the studio aces, a player with attitude in his string bends and pick attacks.

Slick had grown up in Brooklyn and Staten Island. After kicking around local bands, he got recommended for Bowie's *Diamond Dogs* tour, and he'd later play on the 1983 tour. By the Nineties he'd cleaned up and burned out, living near Lake Tahoe with his dogs. Around New Year's 2000, after an email invitation was sent to his webmaster, Slick became Bowie's lead guitarist again. It was a good fit: Bowie was reviving older songs and his newer material suited Slick's style — he wasn't being asked to do drum 'n' bass numbers.

In early 2001, Slick planned his first solo album in a decade. He thought of an instrumental record, with Mark Plati producing, "almost like making a demo to get [film] scoring jobs," Slick said. Bowie "overheard a conversation I was having... and said, 'I guess you're not interested in me maybe doing a little something on the record'." This became "Isn't It Evening," recorded in a day at Plati's home studio ("Alice's Restaurant") in New York. Slick sent Bowie "seven really rough pieces" and he picked one, writing a top melody and a lyric with a few striking lines ("one dies on the lawn/his face turned away from it all"). "We recorded it shortly thereafter, if not at that moment, which is what we would usually do if he was writing lyrics," Plati said. "Isn't It Evening" (its odd parenthetical added after mixing), as Plati told me,

sat around for a long time, with the rest of Slick's solo album, as we kept looking for collaborations and waited for a label to get onboard. I remember

487

in the intervening years between recording and mixing that I would play "Isn't It Evening" for people on the sly, trying to generate some interest for the project... and they seemed to really dig it... One guy at Geffen Records said it was the best DB song he'd heard in a decade. Which was not bad, considering the track's humble origins (Slick, DB, and myself at my place). We didn't bother to add anything else to the original demo, it just had a thing.

NATURE BOY

(Ahbez.) **Recorded**: *(Bowie vocal) ca. 2 March 2001, Looking Glass; ("orchestra take" backing tracks) ca. late 2000-February 2001, uncredited studio; (Massive Attack tracks) ca. early 2001, Massive Attack, Christchurch Studios, Bristol, UK. Bowie: lead vocal; Craig Armstrong: conductor/arranger ("orchestra take"); strings, winds, horns, percussion: uncredited musicians (poss. the London Orchestra); Robert Del Naja, Neil Davidge: keyboards, samplers, programming (Massive Attack version). Produced: Visconti (Bowie vocal); Armstrong, Baz Luhrmann, Anton Monsted, Josh Abrahams (orchestral); Del Naja, Davidge (Massive); engineered: Geoff Foster (orchestral), Lee Shepherd (Massive).*

First release: *14 May 2001,* **Moulin Rouge** *(Interscope 06949 3035 2).*

While Bowie was making *Toy*, the Australian director Baz Luhrmann was shooting *Moulin Rouge*, where Belle Epoque French bohemians sing contemporary pop songs. Along with letting Luhrmann use "Heroes" and "Diamond Dogs," Bowie agreed to sing the standard "Nature Boy," which was *Moulin Rouge*'s theme, its last line a motif, its verses sung by various characters. Bowie wasn't integral to the film: his "orchestral" version of "Nature Boy" is heard in a few scenes, while an alternate version produced by Massive Attack, originally slotted for end credits, was pulled as "Bowie and Massive ended up being, in a sense, so dark that we needed to resurrect the audience during the credits," Luhrmann said.

"Nature Boy" was debuted by Nat King Cole in 1948 and written by eden ahbez (an early hippie, one too bohemian for capitalization), who first presented his score to Cole on soiled parchment, as though he'd written it on a mountainside as the First Epistle to the Californians. ahbez got his melody from Dvořák's Piano Quintet No 2. and probably "Shvayg Mayn Harts," a Yiddish pop song. (The latter's composer, Herman Yablokoff, sued ahbez, who claimed the melody had come to him "as if angels were singing it," to which Yablokoff replied they "must have bought a copy of my song." They settled out of court.) "Nature Boy" has no refrain, only sixteen-bar verses with slight harmonic and melodic differences. What Cole and later interpreter John Coltrane found in the song was a freedom of movement: you could alter rhythms, twist and belabor the melody, play ahbez's notes over an assault on his chord structures (Coltrane did all of that at once).

Bowie cut his vocal in New York in March 2001, with Tony Visconti producing, likely during the early planning for *Heathen*. Luhrmann attended the session and was startled when Bowie asked him how he should end, a traditional way or a more "operatic" closing. Luhrmann said he should do both. So Bowie cut two "vocally pristine" takes, as Luhrmann recalled. In the "orchestral" version of "Nature Boy," Bowie tinkers his phrasings, sidesteps the expected rise on "very far," stresses fools rather than kings, gravely responds to the scarlet moods of Craig Armstrong's orchestration. Yet as the song readies to wind down, Bowie does a pole-vault for his last note: "RETUUUUURRRRN!"

The Bowie/Massive Attack "Nature Boy" starts as if another song is being eaten. A repeating two-note bassline becomes a pulsebeat. Other loops ebb and flow: a three-note phrase on plucked strings, a wavering synthesizer figure. Bowie's voice sounds sped up, thinned out, his phrasings are minor effects. His rise on "many things" is washed out by guitar. Instead of a grand dame finale, it closes with a slow collapse. Seconds before the end, Nicole Kidman whispers of love and the hope of being loved back.

CHAPTER TWELVE: FORWARD INTO REMOVE

(2001-2002)

Our culture, our civilization, all this beautiful stuff, as exalted or as funky as it gets, it's just nail polish on the claws, and the nail polish has begun to crack and flake and the claws are showing through.
— Leonard Cohen, 1993

He'd spent too long being disappointed by the world.
— Lev Grossman, *The Magicians*

I have more memories for the past than for the future. I wouldn't think about the future. I would only have expectations, and they'd all be very good.
— Bob Dylan, 1968

The End is what we want, so I'm afraid the End is what we're damn well going to get. There. Set that to music.
— David Mitchell, *Cloud Atlas*

I'VE BEEN WAITING FOR YOU

(Young.) **Recorded***: 8 August-ca. 15 September 2001, Allaire Studios, 486 Pitcairn Rd., Shokan, New York; (overdubs) ca. 1 October 2001-31 January 2002, The Looking Glass Studios, New York City. David Bowie: lead and backing vocal, rhythm guitar, Chamberlin, Korg Trinity, EMS Synthi AKS, theremin; Dave Grohl: lead guitar; Tony Visconti: bass; Matt Chamberlain: drums, percussion loops. Produced: Visconti, Bowie; engineered: Visconti.*

First release*: 10 June 2002,* **Heathen***.* **Broadcast***: 15 June 2002, A&E Live by Request; 18 October 2002, Late Night with Conan O'Brien.* **Live***: 1991-1992, 2002-2004.*

In June 2001, David Bowie drove up from New York City to West Nyack, where Tony Visconti had a studio in a loft apartment. They were making, at last, the album they'd been talking about making for three years.

Bowie had spent the spring writing "serious songs," as he later put it — devoting a more-than-usual amount of time to composition, to recording demos. "They were pretty much cut and tailored before I went in," he said of the songs. He and Visconti had met in March in New York, ostensibly to listen to albums like Beck's *Midnite Vultures* "for little creative tags to incorporate for the new album," as Visconti wrote in his autobiography, but before long Bowie was playing Neu! and Little Richard records again. Noting how Bowie had domesticated his addictions, brewing pot after pot of coffee on the hour (he was even trying to shake cigarettes), Visconti wrote that "I couldn't help thinking how great it was that we'd survived the indulgences of rock 'n' roll. We were alive and sober."

Alive and Sober could have titled the album. Knowing a Bowie and Visconti reunion meant great expectations from fans and the press, the pair figured some grandiosity was inevitable, especially when they had a "crock of songs [that] come out of a general feeling of anxiety I've had in America for a number of years," Bowie said. Drawing on what he heard in Bowie's demos, Visconti proposed a "magnum opus" concept: autumnal pieces fattened with "layers of layers of overdubs." It suited Bowie's introspective mood, but he didn't want the album to traffic in memory. It inevitably would be compared to *Scary Monsters* but it shouldn't *sound* like *Scary Monsters*.

Visconti found a new deliberateness in Bowie's songwriting. "His knowledge of harmonic and chordal structure had vastly improved... there was more depth to his melodic and harmonic writing." Bowie's songs were united harmonically as well as lyrically, with a particular taste for A minor and F major pairings. In West Nyack, they cut four demos. A convert to Pro Tools and Logic Pro software, Visconti "cut up beats and sections of a song, made beat loops and pasted them in other places." The album would be a testament to Pro Tools, its tracks full of loops: percussion, vocals, synthesizers, guitars ("sometimes we're trebling up on loops," Bowie said).

The next day, they drove north to the Catskills, where there was a recording studio called Allaire. It was southwest of Woodstock, on Mount Tonche, atop whose crest the Pittsburgh Plate Glass heir Raymond Pitcairn had built a summer manse, Glen Tonche. An 18,000-square-foot "hideaway" with a commanding view of the Ashokan Reservoir, its nautical-themed rooms had what Bowie called "very American but aristocratic pieces of work," as if a tide of wealth had ebbed through the house. Pitcairn's heirs had sold Glen Tonche to the musician Randall Wallace, who converted rooms, including a dining hall blessed with forty-foot-high ceilings, into recording studios. Tipped off about Wallace's studio by guitarist David Torn, Bowie and Visconti were on a reconnaissance trip.

Allaire's isolation was sublime. "This is not cute, on top of this mountain: it's stark and it has a Spartan quality about it," Bowie said. "Remote, silent and inspirational." He'd found the right setting for his songs — a luxurious colony nestled in a wood-world of black bears, wild pigs, and deer. "Walking through the door, everything that my album should be about was galvanized for me into one focal point... I knew what the lyrics were already. They were all suddenly accumulated in my mind." In 2003, Bowie bought 64 acres of a mountain in the area and would spend some of the year in Woodstock, where he was a regular at coffee shops and school festivals. He reportedly died in his home there.

For the Allaire sessions, which began in the first full week of August 2001, it was primarily Bowie, Visconti, and drummer Matt Chamberlain, who they'd met during their scouting visit. Bowie rose around dawn to work in the studio, while Visconti and Chamberlain woke at a more civilized hour and showed up around 10:30am, upon which Bowie would present them with the song of the day. They worked until dinner. Bowie kept writing at night while Visconti and Chamberlain watched DVDs or sacked out early. "This certainly wasn't a rock 'n' roll life, by any stretch of the imagination,"

Visconti wrote. A productive life, though. In roughly two weeks they got down nineteen tracks, dispatching the "epic" pieces first. "I wanted to make sure that the bookends were firmly in place before I got on with the rest of the album," Bowie said.

Losing Once or Twice

One track, a cover of Neil Young's "I've Been Waiting for You," was paying an old debt. Young had infused Bowie's *Hunky Dory*-era songs, particularly "Kooks," "Bombers," and "Bewlay Brothers." He also saw in Young how to thrive in an industry where age is considered a personal failing. "Neil Young and Bob Dylan... have both made a few disastrous albums, but they always end up coming back to the point of what they started in the first place," Bowie said in one of his last interviews, in 2004. "You've got to go back to what you were doing when you were rooting around with experimentation, ideas that are going to work for me, not my audience."

"I've Been Waiting for You" was on Young's 1968 self-titled debut, which has a piece for string quartet, dolorous folkie ballads, a Western movie theme, and a few songs devoted to unattainable, mystifying women. Among the last was the Hendrix-inspired "I've Been Waiting for You," with "Foxy Lady"-style heavy breathing and a guitar solo for which Young sent his guitar through an organ's Leslie speaker, then straight into the soundboard.

Set in A minor, the song's reappearing D9 chord ("for a *woman*") is a liberation declined. Rather than use the D9 to brighten into A major or D major, Young keeps sliding back into A minor. Some life-redeeming woman is about to arrive but never does, perhaps with good reason. A concise obsession, "I've Been Waiting for You" is a single verse, a refrain with a descending chromatic bassline ("waiting for *you*... coming to *me*") and anguish via guitars.

It was one of Kim Deal's favorite Neil Young songs. During their *Bossanova* sessions, the Pixies knocked off a version where Deal sounded cheery, even when she sang "losing *once or twice*." This version would be Bowie's template, as he used the Pixies' edits: recycling part of the verse after the solo and halving the solo's length. Tin Machine played "I've Been Waiting for You" on stage, with Reeves Gabrels on lead vocal. On the *Heathen* take, Bowie used a synthetic "choir," likely a Chamberlin, to recreate the wailing harmonies that he and the Sales brothers had sung to buttress Gabrels. For lead guitar, Bowie recruited Dave Grohl, who literally mailed in his solo, a run of blocky chords that lacked the build and release of Young's solo. It was overshadowed by Chamberlain's drums.

In the verse, Bowie sounded more callow than Young had in 1968; in refrains, he shaded his longing with menace. This purgatorial "waiting" appears throughout Bowie's work, from "Look Back in Anger" through "Cat People" to the borrowed line here. Waning powers, with endurance replacing action. In his closing refrain, Bowie sang "long time now" as if he could taste each hour of each wasted year. The track gave up the ghost with an unmoored bassline, a guitar clanging like a ship's bell, and a choir snuffed out in a breath.

SUNDAY

Recorded: 8 August-ca. 15 September 2001, Allaire; (overdubs) ca. 1 October 2001-31 January 2002, Looking Glass. Bowie: lead and backing vocal, guitar, Chamberlin, Mellotron, EMS Synthi AKS, Roland TR-707, alto and/or baritone saxophone; David Torn: guitar, Electrix Repeater; Visconti: bass, backing vocal; Chamberlain: drums, percussion loops. Produced: Visconti, Bowie; engineered: Visconti.

First release: 10 June 2002, **Heathen**. **Broadcast**: 18 September 2002, Live and Exclusive. **Live**: 2002-2004.

Heathen was Bowie's take on the composer Richard Strauss' Four Last Songs, or so he claimed. "There's a certain sense of universality in those songs that Strauss wrote at the end of his life... they're the most terribly romantic, sad, poignant pieces that I think have ever been written," he said in 2002. "I kind of used them as a template."

His Four Last Songs would be his album's opener and closer, "Sunday" and "Heathen (The Rays)," and (though less thematically linked) two mid-sequenced ones, "5:15 The Angels Have Gone" and "I Would Be Your Slave." These were end-of-life musings, November still lives, parceled regrets — in retrospect, a first draft of *Blackstar*. And like *Blackstar*, it was an album conceived of as being a side-stage event, a chamber piece curtained off from the rest of the festival. "Especially in one's mid-fifties, you're very aware that that's the moment you have to leave off the idea of being young. You've got to let it go," Bowie said, adding he was no longer becoming but simply being. For someone who'd built his life on continually becoming, wasn't this death? He dressed his songs as if it were, setting them in departure lounges, empty train stations, cold beaches.

He'd had some mortality to process of late — his mother had died in spring 2001. But the death-haunted man of *Heathen* was as fictive a personality as Ziggy Stardust. Bowie was fifty-four, thirty years younger than the Strauss of the Last Songs. He was playing with how pop stars age like dogs. If the world thought him an old man, he'd play one in drag: a sexless, morose figure, so time-withered he can barely move, wanly gesturing towards the sunset.

It aimed for the mood of an album of five years before — Bob Dylan's *Time Out of Mind* (see "Tryin' to Get to Heaven"). As with *Heathen* and 9/11, *Time* was colored by events after its recording — in Dylan's case, an alleged-near death hospitalization. Having almost met Elvis, as Dylan joked, deepened the morbidity of the album, with its somnolent tempos, its lyrical wanderings and dislocations. Bowie also noted the rapturous critical reception Dylan got for his "return to form" — he won three Grammys, even. If an aging singer is expected to harp about death and lost time, why not serve up a double? Maybe sell some records, too. It was the next step after *'hours...'* The aging melancholic falls to the gravedigger.

What set *Heathen* apart was its "non-professional approach... [there's a] kind of British amateur-ness about it," Bowie said, comparing the album to the work of "a man who, only on Sundays, will build a cathedral out of matchsticks, beautiful but only to please himself and his family and friends." Bowie liked synthesizer pre-sets and made a patchwork of digital loops, using antique synthesizers like the EMS Synthi AKS, Chamberlin and Mellotron instead of choirs or strings. *Heathen* was a quirky homebrewed apocalypse, like "Kafka meets Ed Wood," as Pete Townshend said upon hearing its rough mixes.

"Sunday" (*Heathen* starts like a calendar week) begins on a remote E-flat minor chord. A guitar birdsong figure; the occasional bass note, like someone dropping stones in a well; a bed of keyboard-summoned voices to cushion the lead vocal and establish chords, rising and ebbing (Bowie likely started the song by playing three near-consecutive black keys (Ebm), then moving left and right on the keyboard to find answering chords). David Torn's opening loop introduces the "glitched-out" guitar sound of Bowie's late albums, where tones and loops are used as melodic and percussive colors.

He sings advice for foragers. Watch out for drifters and cars. Shafts of light on the road mean death. Keep under the bracken for safety. Run when the rain lessens. Follow the sun west, where the heat goes. It's a rabbit's life. "When you've got no past, you've got no future," Bowie said at the time. "You're just in this crashing now place… trapped in this terrible little rowboat on this sea of chaos and anxiety and terror." As "Sunday" wanders through its verse, it gathers shape, firming up in A-flat major. The guitar is freed from a loop; a bass drum pattern begins. A mantra chorus offers consolation: "in your fear, seek only peace," a line Bowie found in Kahlil Gibran's *The Prophet* ("but if in your fear you would seek only love's peace and love's pleasure/then it is better for you that you cover your nakedness and pass out of love's threshing-floor") and sung mostly by Tony Visconti, who had learned Tuvan "throat" singing, which let him sound two notes at once. Mixed left is Bowie in his Scott Walker register, burning in the pyre, rising in the air. Associations with the smoldering World Trade Center were unintentional, he said, swearing he'd written his lines before the attacks (see "America").

Much depends upon suggestion: guitar loops; eight bars of gravid ooohs; a solo section with faint saxophone; an abbreviated second verse that acknowledges the Sixties folk standard "All My Trials" (instead of his trials being over, his will be remembered — he'll bear a grudge after death). One last defiant "chaaaanged" and Matt Chamberlain crashes in, hammering his snare. On stage, Bowie let Earl Slick play out "Sunday" for minutes, wailing low on his guitar neck, but on *Heathen*, the closing struggle is percussive, soon fading away. Sunday might be the day of resurrection, but night falls on it without fail.

I WOULD BE YOUR SLAVE

Recorded: 8 August-ca.15 September 2001, Allaire; (overdubs) ca. 1 October 2001-31 January 2002, Looking Glass. Bowie: lead vocal; Torn and/or Leonard: guitar; Visconti: bass; Chamberlain: drums, percussion loops; Gregor Kitzis: 1st violin; Meg Okura: 2nd violin; Martha Mooke: viola; Mary Wooten: cello. Produced: Visconti, Bowie; engineered: Visconti.

First release: 10 June 2002, **Heathen**. *Live:* 2002.

The first original *Heathen* composition performed live (at a Tibet House Benefit Concert in February 2002), "I Would Be Your Slave" was a vehicle for voice, arpeggiated guitar, percussion loops, bass, and string quartet. The latter were the Scorchio Quartet, a freshly-formed group that Bowie named — they became a regular of Tibet House's benefit concerts.

"I Would Be Your Slave" is aimed as much at God as another human being — a typical Bowie love song. Like "Word on a Wing," it's prayer as labor negotiation. The overarching theme of *Heathen*, or so Bowie said, was of a world that had dispensed of its gods. He plays one last believer, convinced that God's laughing at him in the quietude where He's retreated. "An entreaty to the highest being to show himself in a way that could be understood," as Bowie described the song.

His concession to God is that he "would be your slave" — he's not committing. It's love as offering oneself as the slave drive to a master processor, but also recall Jareth's last temptation of Sarah in *Labyrinth*: "I ask for so little. Just fear me, love me, do as I say and I will be your slave." Rather less Goth is the line "no footprints in the sand," referencing a kitschy poem in which a man walks beside God on the beach, then turns to see one set of footprints — God has carried him in times of trouble. Bowie's beach has no trace of God or the lonely human.

There are loops of wheezes and ticks, like someone in an iron lung, and a circularity in the chord structure, a semi-tonal rise and fall from an F-sharp major chord (aided by the bass, which descends to mark each return to F#). A feint to B-flat minor ("show me who you are!") leads back to F# major again. The A minor bridge breaks the spell, igniting fresh changes in latter verses. With its Deram instrumentation and stagy lyric ("a chance to strike me down!"), "I Would Be Your Slave" sounds like a late Sixties Bowie song, in particular "When I Live My Dream," that's stranded in a new century.

The Scorchio Quartet gave a sting to the chords (in part because each player was miked through a guitar amp). Their arrangement was mostly Bowie's, composed on his Korg Trinity keyboard, hence the chordal scoring, with few solo passages apart from a droning cello line in the third verse. The strings cling together for comfort, gloss the bass fills, span peaks in latter halves of verses. Scorchio recorded their parts days after September 11, making it up to Shokan from New York City despite irregular trains and closed roads. "As they pointed out, it was the necessary break that was so needed by all of them," Bowie said. The greatest mourners on *Heathen* were the strings.

5:15 THE ANGELS HAVE GONE

Recorded: 8 August-ca.15 September 2001, Allaire; (overdubs) October 2001-January 2002, Looking Glass. Bowie: lead and backing vocal, guitar, Korg Trinity, Roland, Chamberlin; Torn: guitar; Jordan Rudess: piano; Visconti: bass; Chamberlain: drums, percussion loops. Produced: Visconti, Bowie; engineered: Visconti.

*First release: 10 June 2002, **Heathen**. Broadcast: 15 June 2002, A&E Live by Request; 18 September 2002, Live and Exclusive; 20 September 2002, Later with Jools Holland. **Live**: 2002-2004.*

A tattered end to Bowie's angelic trilogy ("Look Back in Anger," "New Angels of Promise"), "5:15 The Angels Have Gone" is another world abandoned by God, or at least one whose inhabitants are sick of Him. "A man who could once see his angels — hopes and aspirations, maybe? — can't see them anymore," as Bowie described the song. "And he blames the crushing dumbness of life for it."

"Look Back in Anger" had an angelic bureaucrat; the new angels of promise were avatars in a game that most computers can't play today. In "5:15," even these intermediaries are gone — in some of the album booklet's defaced reproductions of Renaissance paintings, angelic observers are cropped out of the frame. Like "I Would Be Your Slave," "5:15" is a love song of an estranged man and estranged god. "*Weeee* never **talk** an-nay-more!" Bowie pleads in refrains, as if singing Cliff Richard's disco hit of the similar title. He's numbed, dulled, fogged, stuck in a foreign station, being rained on: a purgatorial life. "We create so many circles on this straight line we're told we're traveling," Bowie said. "We are arriving and departing all at the same time."

Muted colors include a Chamberlin choir, piano scampering through refrains, grudging nods on bass. The guitar riff is a shrug of a melody on three low strings — one line starts and ends on an open G string; the other soon cuts off, as if thwarted. Matt Chamberlain's drum loop sounds like he's hitting an anvil: it keeps on through the A minor verses through the F# minor refrains — numbed grief met by spasms of anger.

The title invokes the Who's "5:15," the train that Jimmy the Mod took to Brighton. Bowie's departed angels are Mods: thin on the ground, all legs and wings, strange sandy eyes. The Mod could "pass." In his sharp suit and neatly-cut hair, he could sit and not disturb anyone with the impropriety of being young, even though he was off his head on amphetamines and dreaming about setting fire to the train. The last angels in our midst, at least in this song.

HEATHEN (THE RAYS)

Recorded: 8 August-ca. 15 September 2001, Allaire; (overdubs) ca. 1 October 2001-31 January 2002, Looking Glass. Bowie: lead and backing vocal, guitar, piano, Chamberlin, baritone saxophone, Stylophone; Torn: lead guitar; Visconti: bass, backing vocal; Chamberlain: drums, percussion loops. Produced: Visconti, Bowie; engineered: Visconti.

First release: 10 June 2002, **Heathen**. *Broadcast*: 18 September 2002, Live and Exclusive; 20 September 2002, Later with Jools Holland. **Live**: 2002-2004.

There was salvation, of a sort, in Bowie "quest" songs like "Quicksand" and "Station to Station." Answers, or at least hints that there were answers. He'd rummaged through accounts of Nazi occultists, burrowed through religions. "I was young, fancy free, and Tibetan Buddhism appealed to me at that time. I thought, 'There's salvation.' It didn't really work," he said in 2004. "Then I went through Nietzsche, Satanism, Christianity, pottery, and ended up singing. It's been a long road..." His was a credulous mind, starving to believe. "He is what he reads," as Carlos Alomar recalled. "And at that time in his life, he was reading so much bullshit."

Bowie had inherited his father's skepticism of organized religion, especially of "Henry's church" (of England), and his religious fancies were a set of lab tests, like an alchemist putting stones to a flame. Yet in his crooked way, he was a religious songwriter. In 1973, at the peak of Ziggy Stardust, he said he'd always felt like a vehicle for something else, but then I've never sorted out what that was. I think everybody, at one time or another, gets that kind of feeling: that they aren't just here for themselves... there's a feeling that we are here for another purpose. And in me it's very strong.

Five years later, he talked of his "belief or let's call it the usual force. Or God? Yes, sure. It's a lukewarm relationship at the best of times, but I think it's definitely there."

His work said there *was* something else, grand and inexplicable, besides mundane reality. Even on *1. Outside*, he thought there would be new rites for a new century; that body scarification could be the new communion wafer. But the voice of "Heathen (The Rays)," the closing track of *Heathen*, the far shore across from "Sunday," is that of an unbeliever, its sodium-lit mood that of Philip Larkin's last poems, especially "Aubade" ("the sure extinction that we travel to/And shall be lost in always.") Its temperament is, as Bowie put it to *Der Spiegel* in 2002, "Why now, when I [finally] understand myself and others, should I die? What a shitty game. Is there no one you could revise the rules with?"

He'd gotten the new century wrong. He'd expected too much in the Nineties, had hoped all of the millennial frenzies and purgings would clear the way for a spiritually-revived world. Instead it was, as Stanley Hauerwas wrote in 1995, "people who believe they should have no story except the story they choose when they have no story." A refined barbaric world, one suited for fanatics of all stripes, but freelancers now: no longer the need for a Hitler or Mao to employ them. Hence the album's title ("*Philistine* was too on-the-money," Bowie said). "Heathenism is a state of mind... I'm referring to one who does not see his world. He has no mental light. He destroys almost unwittingly. He cannot feel any God's presence in his life," Bowie said. "Someone who's not even bothered searching for a spiritual life anymore but who's completely existing on a materialistic plain."

"Heathen" is a mistranslation from a fourth-century Gothic bishop's version of the Book of Mark, which used the Gothic *haiþnô* ("woman of the heath") for someone referred to in Mark 7:26 as a Greek woman, *hellēnis*. The foreign unbelievers were no longer the pantheistic Greeks but the "wasteland dwellers" of the heaths. But in either translation, the heathen was a potential convert. Bowie's heathens are instead immaculate barbarians. In the album's photographs, he played one, shredding dictionaries, striking out words, defacing religious paintings — blinding the Virgin with blots of white paint, bisecting St. Sebastian's face, gouging out Mary Magdalene's eyes.

The one photograph of non-desecrated art was of a shelf of replacement bibles. Friedrich Nietzsche's *Gay Science*, in which God is dead, so stop worshiping His ghost. Einstein's *General Theory of Relativity*, in which time and space aren't absolutes (Ortega y Gasset thought Einstein had turned reality into cinema — time could be cranked to Keystone Kops speed or move in slow-motion). And Freud's *Interpretation of Dreams*, in which dreams are the "royal road" to the cellar of our unconscious (where Bowie's going in one album photo). In dreams, man is a superman: Freud's dreams "are the blessed fulfillers of wishes." If we can fulfill our own wishes, what need is there for God?

"All these things culminated in the idea that everything we knew before was wrong," Bowie said. "We start out the twentieth century with a clean slate. We are now the gods. And the greatest thing we could do as God in that century was... to create the bomb. That's what we were good at doing." Maybe there was no purpose, and there never had been. "Are we mature enough to accept that there's no plan, there's no going somewhere, there's no gift of immortality at the end of this?" He mocked the likes of a Peter Thiel, tech "visionaries" who say "'if we evolve far enough, we may never have to die.'... Maybe we can't live like that. Maybe we have to exist and live, [know] that we have one day at a time. Can we do that?"

Paperweight World

Looking out a window at Allaire one morning, drinking his first cup of coffee, Bowie saw deer grazing on the mountainside, and beyond them, a car passing along the Ashokan Reservoir. "There was something so still and primal about what I was looking at outside," he recalled. He wept, began to write.

What was it? A glimpse of a depeopled world, one left to the deer and crows. But the car was part of it. Mankind in harmony with plants and animals, or in its usual role of oblivious despoiler? How we depart from life one morning and the animals take no notice, the sun keeps on its pace. The absurdity of a rock star sitting in a recording studio in a plutocrat's mansion weeping over these thoughts. "How beautiful and wonderful life is, and how I regret that I will have to relinquish my hold upon it," he said later. There was another reference in his opening lines, "steel on the skyline/sky made of glass." In *Nineteen Eighty-Four*, Orwell describes a paperweight that Winston Smith keeps in the room he rents for his assignations with Julia. "It was as though the surface of the glass had been the arch of the sky, enclosing a tiny world with its atmosphere complete." For Smith, it's a tiny piece of history that Big Brother has forgotten to alter, a message from another world. But when it's smashed on the floor by the Thought Police, he sees "how small it always was."

"Heathen" coalesces as it begins, with loops of David Torn's guitar entwining, unraveling, entwining again, moving around the tones of an E-flat 7 chord. Two grand chords, sounded on synthesizer with baritone saxophone mixed in: D-flat and Eb7. Only upon shifts to A-flat ("made for a") and F minor ("real world"), swept in with drums, does the song find its footing in A-flat major. The same key as "Sunday," on the far side of the album. Its three verses are more like three bridges in a song whose refrain has gone missing. Chords swap in and out of the main progression, as if in a three-card monte game: never escaping the A-flat key but undermining it, coloring it, much as how Bowie's high notes extend the underlying chords into sixths or sevenths.

Though it's Bowie as consumptive diva ("I can *feel* it *die!*"), the musicians undermine the pathos, from the brisk tempo (nearly 120bpm, rather fast for a dirge) to a rockabilly guitar riff. The drums are a child at a funeral. A Stylophone tootles by. The guitars look to escape into a livelier song. As death approaches, it's cheered like a boxing champion entering the ring, with handclaps near the close. In "Modern Love," Bowie had ticked off everything that had failed him, from marriage to God and man. No confessions! No religion! "Heathen" is what's left behind after the house is emptied. Its live performances in 2002, especially in Berlin, were brilliant — Bowie pantomiming losing his sight, then being led offstage by Gail Ann Dorsey while the band kept playing, as though he knew he'd depart before the rest of them.

CACTUS

(Thompson.) **Recorded**: *8 August- ca. 15 September 2001, Allaire; (overdubs) ca. 1 October 2001-31 January 2002, Looking Glass. Bowie: lead and backing vocal, lead guitar, twelve-string acoustic guitar, piano, EMS Synthi AKS, Longwave theremin, Chamberlin?, Korg Trinity, baritone saxophone, drums; Visconti: bass. Produced: Visconti, Bowie; engineered: Visconti.*

First release: *10 June 2002,* **Heathen**. **Broadcast**: *2 June 2002, Top of the Pops; 14 June 2002, The Today Show; 15 June 2002, A&E Live by Request; 18 June 2002, Late Night with Conan O'Brien; 1 August 2002, Last Call with Carson Daly; 12 August 2002, The Tonight Show; 11 September 2002, Hypershow; 18 September 2002, Live and Exclusive; 6 October 2002, Quelli che... il Calcio; 15 October 2002, VH1/Vogue Fashion Awards; 25 October 2002, The Early Show.* **Live**: *2002-2004.*

At age twenty, Charles "Black Francis" Thompson went to Puerto Rico for a semester abroad. He hung out at a sailor's brothel, "this massive barroom, full of these sailors and these slithering whores. They'd circle the room like vultures, seeing who was ready to fuck in the back room... It was like it had been that way for a hundred years and nothing had changed." Sex was everywhere except in his bedroom. A girl he liked took up with a local and he was too broke and scared to try the portside brothel. He wrote a postcard to Joey Santiago, a friend back at UMASS, saying they should start a band. They did. The Pixies' "Cactus" came from Thompson's trip: a song of sexual deprivation and revulsion. A man is locked up somewhere — a prison cell, an asylum — and writes to a woman. He's got a letter, sure, but he wants more, wants her to cut her hand on a cactus, wipe the blood on her dress, and mail it to him. Thompson sang as if his lungs were infected with lust.

Bowie called the Pixies the great American band that America didn't appreciate (see "Debaser"). "They broke up virtually penniless. They were so important but they never meant a thing outside New York and Los Angeles," he said in 2002. It was especially galling at the turn of the century, when the hushed-verse/loud-refrain Pixies formula, refined through Nirvana, was the sound of "modern rock" radio.

In "Cactus," Bowie knew a glam song when he heard one, despite Steve Albini's austere mix. The Stooges were in its progression (tonic chord (E5) to flat III chord (G5), a Ron Asheton move) and Thompson's vocal, which was Iggy Pop's stage games projected inward. It also took from T. Rex's "The Groover" for a chanted "P! I! X! I! E! S!", which Bowie naturally amended to "D! A! V! I! D!" He kicked the song into A major and cut octave-doubled vocals (playing both Kim Deal and Black Francis), using synths for his backing singers. Where Thompson sounded like he wanted to wear someone else's skin, Bowie delights in his depravity — it's the nastiest old man he ever played. *Send it to meeee!* "My little humoresque," he called his cover. Apart from Tony Visconti on bass, it was all Bowie: acoustic and electric guitars, synths, "I Wanna Be Your Dog" piano, and even drums, playing "over my own loop" with shaky hi-hat and thudding kick. It was a carnal relief from the Grand Old Man-isms of *Heathen*. A triumph: one of his best covers.

I Took a Trip on a Gemini Spaceship

(Cowboy). **Recorded**: *8 August-ca. 15 September 2001, Allaire; (overdubs) ca. 1 October 2001-31 January 2002, Looking Glass. Bowie: lead and backing vocals, rhythm guitar, Longwave theremin, Chamberlin, baritone saxophone; Torn: guitar; Visconti: bass; Chamberlain: drums, percussion loops; Kitzis, 1st violin; Okura, 2nd violin; Mooke: viola; Wooten: cello. Produced: Visconti, Bowie; engineered: Visconti.*

First release: *10 June 2002,* **Heathen**. **Broadcast**: *2 June 2002, Top of the Pops 2.* **Live**: *2002.*

As a teenager, Bowie loved Frank Edwards' *Strange People,* a chronicle of real or fictional people with ESP or third eyes or who'd been struck by lightning and could talk to ghosts. He found their equivalent in performers like the Legendary Stardust Cowboy. "I think David thought that he was more practical and that they were loonier artists in the real sense of artists as madmen," the manager Danny Fields told Marc Spitz. "Because David was never a madman. I think he felt guilty [about that], because how could you really be a good artist without being a madman?"

On a ramble through the internet, Bowie found the website of the Legendary Stardust Cowboy, aka Norman C. Odam. It had a JPEG of Odam's birth certificate and a scan of a handwritten letter in which "The Ledge" wrote of financial troubles. "It sure would be nice if David Bowie would pay me something for using part of my name in 'Ziggie Stardust,' as appeared in the August 20 1984 issue of *People* magazine with Richard Burton on the cover." Long ago, Bowie had used the Cowboy's name for his plastic rock 'n' roll star. Now the Cowboy was so broke he didn't have a computer to see his own website. "I got guilty and wanted to make amends immediately," Bowie said. "So I covered one of his best songs, 'I Took a Trip on a Gemini Spaceship,' although he sings 'Spacecraft' on the record."

Talking up the Cowboy also fit Bowie's "outsider music" designs. As guest editor of the July 2002 *Mojo*, he commissioned some pieces about oddballs (reserving The Ledge's tribute for himself). He curated Meltdown Festival that summer, favoring "outsider" performers like Daniel Johnston and the Cowboy (that said, Coldplay and Pete Yorn also made the cut). For his article, Bowie listened to the Cowboy's singles again, which "got me into a quiet reverie or two... the Ledge was instrumental in creating, unwittingly, the now current Outsider Music genre." As Cowboy guitarist Frank Novicki once said, "Norman can't carry a tune, and he doesn't really sing in time, but you don't have to know any of that stuff to be good at music. Boy, is he proof of that."

Odam grew up in Lubbock, Texas, in the years after Buddy Holly left. He'd stand on the steps of his school to be pelted by classmates with pennies and dirt clods while singing songs like "My Underwear Froze to the Clothesline." After watching the Cowboy perform in the 2000s, the musician Joe Ely, a former classmate, said the repertoire hadn't changed much.

Upon seeing Tiny Tim on the *Tonight Show* in 1968, the Cowboy knew television was ready for him. He set off for New York but got stuck in Fort Worth. There, some vacuum cleaner salesmen, stunned by his performance at a nightclub, hustled him into a recording studio. On duty was the twenty-year-old T. Bone Burnett, who'd been up all night and close to hallucinating. The salesmen waved some money around, so Burnett rigged up microphones, put a fresh reel on the deck and got behind the drums. The Cowboy told him "beat the heck out of the drums, which he did." The result was "Paralyzed," a song intended to be "wilder than anything Elvis had ever done. His music was too slow for me!" the Cowboy boasted. He war-whooped and played bugle, as if he was both sides of the Battle of the Little Bighorn.

A hit on Fort Worth's KXOL, "Paralyzed" attracted a local impresario, "Major Bill" Smith, who became the Ledge's manager. Mercury released "Paralyzed" nationally. It cracked the *Billboard* Top 200 and got the Cowboy on *Laugh-In*. Yet like the *Uncle Floyd Show*, the Cowboy struck out in the major leagues. A musicians' union strike prevented TV variety shows from booking live musicians — he had offers from the *Ed Sullivan Show*, the *Tonight Show* and *American Bandstand* and couldn't accept any of them. By the time the strike ended, "Paralyzed" was off the charts. His follow-up singles (including "Gemini Spaceship") flopped, and Mercury dropped him. The rest of the century was a strange epilogue. The Cowboy was jailed for vagrancy. He unspooled a master tape down Henderson Street in Fort Worth to spite Major Bill. By 2001, he was working as a security guard and living with eight roommates in San Jose, "two stop signs and nine traffic lights from the freeway," he told a reporter. Then Bowie covered his song.

"I Took a Trip on a Gemini Spaceship" was Odam's life in west Texas, where he'd painted the moon's Sea of Tranquility on his car's roof and spent nights looking at a sky he wanted to hide in. "That song is about somebody isolated in space," Bowie said. It was also an undeclared rewrite of Jimmy Van Heusen and Johnny Mercer's "I Thought About You," as sung by Frank Sinatra. The Cowboy stripped it of tonality and turned Mercer's cars and trains into spaceships. ("There's such a redneck cowboy approach to the thing," Bowie said. "You jump in your Gemini, I'll jump into mine! And this guy is writing seriously.") The Cowboy strangled words ("Gem-uh-nee," "jew-pit-err"), jostled phrases along like boxcars. The drummer kept to a clunking pattern until, as if taunted, he started clubbing fills in every bar. The organist sobered up at times to play lines of haunting beauty.

Bowie's "Gemini Spaceship" dresses the Stardust Cowboy for the festival circuit. In a nightclub seducer's croon, he goosed innuendos ("I shot my *space gun*"), with sighs, drawls and plummeting notes (the "weeelllllll" at 3:14 is one of his lowest-sung notes on record). "There's no melody," Bowie said. "It's virtually a poem against abstract, loud, impossibly incohesive music." He played glum-Gus baritone saxophone, a "woeful-sounding" theremin, strings with some Bollywood in them, washes of David Torn guitar atmospheres, a bassline that hops along on root notes, and Matt Chamberlain trying to keep things together. Singing "Gemini Spaceship" on stage in 2002, Bowie bopped along like a sugared-up kid.

Unlike many stories, this one has a happy ending. The Cowboy got some royalty checks and Bowie flew him out for Meltdown. Two months later, when Bowie's tour hit San Francisco, the two met at last. "David Bowie was much more intimidated by the Ledge than vice versa," the filmmaker

Tony Philputt told Richard Skanse a year later:

> When he came walking into to the room, he yelled out "Ledge!" and ran to him to try and hug him. And Norman was having none of that — he stepped back slightly and David ended up giving him the two hands on the arms squeeze as opposed to a full hug... and Bowie had this grin on his face like somebody had just handed him a syringe of the sweetest smack in the world.

The tale of Bowie and the Ledge shows how damned *normal* Bowie was, relatively speaking.

WOOD JACKSON

Recorded: 8 August- ca. 15 September 2001, Allaire; (overdubs) ca. 1 October 2001-31 January 2002, Looking Glass. Bowie: lead vocal, rhythm guitar, keyboards, synthesizer; Torn: lead guitar; Rudess: Hammond organ; Visconti: bass, recorder, backing vocals; Chamberlain: drums, percussion loops. Produced: Visconti, Bowie; engineered: Visconti.

First release: 3 June 2002, "Slow Burn" (ISO/Columbia COL 672744 2).

In "Wood Jackson," Bowie honored another "outsider" musician, Daniel Johnston, "a lad who had a lot of problems with thinking." Born in 1961, Johnston lived in Austin, Texas, working at McDonald's and making "funny little cassettes of all his songs, on an out-of-tune piano or guitar: beautiful, poignant, sad little pieces," Bowie said. Johnston's reputation was built on his tapes, particularly *Hi, How Are You*, whose cover Kurt Cobain often sported as a t-shirt.

Johnston is bipolar and has had schizophrenic episodes. Convinced he was Casper the Friendly Ghost, he nearly killed himself and his father by yanking the keys from the ignition of a two-seater plane and throwing them out a window while in flight. Once, in a psychotic episode, he made an elderly woman leap from a second-story window. Such stories gilded his legend. "When a child hits a piano, he makes untainted music, and that's there in Daniel," Spiritualized's Jason Pierce rhapsodized. Everything about

Johnston — his wavering voice; his calmly surreal lyrics ("hearts upon his sleeve and his blade," as Bowie sings) — was a rebuke to the professional musician. He was an artist's anti-artist. "It seems as though he's stumbled upon a truth of some kind, and I think it's irresistible to believe the idea," Bowie said of Johnston. "It's a very pagan thing, to want to believe that the fool has a straight through-line to the truth." Yet to wax how "untainted" Johnston's music is, to rack up his breakdowns and institutionalizations as if they were batting statistics, is to diminish him. You become a slum-tourist, marveling at the ruin of his life.

Recorded in the *Heathen* sessions and issued as a B-side, "Wood Jackson" is as spacious as a three-story house. It opens with Jordan Rudess on Hammond organ, a grand version of the toy organ that Johnston would use. A drum loop, bassline, and spectral lead guitar are a jostling set, along with shaker and congas and a late-arriving acoustic guitar. Bowie's Wood Jackson is both Christlike (taking beatings, threatened by mobs) and satanic, exchanging cassettes for souls. There's some "Bewlay Brothers" ("to tayke away") and "All the Madmen" (with Tony Visconti back on the recorder), Bowie's old pledges of allegiance to the raving men. "Wood Jackson" would be his last homage to those who'd burned brighter than he had. He'd used them for his own ends; now he said goodbye and wished them well.

When the Boys Come Marching Home

Recorded: 8 August-ca. 15 September 2001, Allaire; (overdubs) ca. 1 October 2001-31 January 2002, Looking Glass. Bowie: lead and backing vocal, Chamberlin, Korg Trinity, Mellotron, theremin?; Torn: lead guitar; Carlos Alomar: rhythm guitar; Rudess: piano; Visconti: fretless bass, keyboards, backing vocal; Chamberlain: drums, percussion loops; Kitzis: 1st violin; Okura: 2nd violin; Mooke: viola; Wooten: cello. Produced: Visconti, Bowie; engineered: Visconti.

First release: 3 June 2002, "Slow Burn."

Though written before the 9/11 attacks (or so Bowie said), the B-side "When the Boys Come Marching Home" invokes the autumn of 2001 in the US, with a nation afraid to open its mail thanks to the anthrax scare, the start of the forever war in Afghanistan, color-coded government freak-outs, the establishment of the Department of Homeland Security, and the Iraq war in its blueprint stage. There's a martial feel throughout, from the snare pattern to the title (referencing the US Civil War song "When Johnny Comes Marching Home Again" or its British counterpart, "Johnny I Hardly Knew Ye"). "There's nothing to learn from history, as we've repeatedly shown," Bowie said in 2002. "We're not willing to learn. We've slipped straight back into what we usually do — we've fallen for a religious war."

Its G# major progression is close to that of "I Would Be Your Slave," and its lyric is a pile of images Bowie earthed up, a cut-up version of *Heathen*'s themes: "outsider" artists in a battle-numbed Europe; cities and countries as prostitutes; a fisherman moon, his tides hauling in nets of souls; a moth-eaten old man. A descending synthesizer line heard in early verses soon departs; marginal commentaries of violins and viola spark the refrains; Jordan Rudess plays a nimble piano line near the close that itches to break into stride. A strong, if gnomic track, its exile from *Heathen* suggests there were just too many downtempo songs for one album. Its drum loop would live again in "Bring Me the Disco King."

A BETTER FUTURE

Recorded: 8 August-ca. 15 September 2001, Allaire; (overdubs) ca. 1 October 2001-31 January 2002, Looking Glass. Bowie: lead and backing vocal, acoustic guitar, keyboards, Korg Trinity; Torn, Leonard?: guitar; Visconti: bass; Chamberlain: drums, percussion loops. Produced: Visconti, Bowie; engineered: Visconti.

First release: 10 June 2002, **Heathen**. *Live*: 2002.

There's a photograph taken by Brian Aris in September 2000, with Bowie lying on his back, holding his infant daughter to his chest. Behind them, a large window shows an unscathed Manhattan skyline. A smiling Bowie stares up at the ceiling. Within the year, he would write "A Better Future," another conversation with God, whom he treats like a lover who's let him down, enough to consider breaking up unless things change.

"I had rosy expectations for the twenty-first century, I really did," he said in 2002. "The whole idea was lifting my spirits quite a lot during 1998 and 1999. But it has become something other than what I expected it to be.

And it's obviously a pretty typical parental concern to wonder what type of a world you have brought your child into."

"A Better Future" was a plea "to whoever that higher spirit is… because I want a place where my daughter can grow up safely, walking open-eyed into her ambitions — not having to dodge bullets." He has little to bargain with. The lofty bridge ("nothing is moooooooviiiiiing") is a cameo by an indifferent God and the verse's perspective could be His as well, singing a landlord's blues to His tenants. Likely composed on acoustic guitar (it sounds like Bowie's playing), the song is a sunny three-chord progression in A-flat (Ab-Bbm-Eb) built on slides up and down the neck. There are guitar gales and a synthesizer hook that's close to the vocal tag of "Do You Know the Way to San Jose," a song about giving up on your dreams and heading out of town.

EVERYONE SAYS "HI"

Recorded: (vocals, guitar) ca. 1 October 2001-31 January 2002, Looking Glass; (overdubs, backing tracks) ca. December 2001- January 2002, SubUrban Studios, South London. Bowie: lead and backing vocal, keyboards; Carlos Alomar: rhythm guitar; Brian Rawling: programming; Gary Miller: guitar, programming; Dave Clayton: keyboards; Philip Sheppard: cello; John Read: bass; Sola Akingbola: percussion; Visconti: backing vocal. Produced: Rawling, Miller, Visconti.

*First release: 10 June 2002, **Heathen**. Broadcast: 2 June 2002, Top of the Pops; 27 June 2002, Friday Night with Ross & Bowie; 11 July 2002, Die Harald Schmidt Show; 1 August 2002, Last Call with Carson Daly; 12 August 2002, The Tonight Show; 11 September 2002, Hypershow; 14 September 2002, BingoLotto; 18 September 2002, Live and Exclusive; 19 September 2002, Parkinson; 3 October 2002, Wetten… dass?; 6 October 2002, Quelli Che… Il Calcio; 10 October 2002, Live with Regis and Kelly. **Live**: 2002.*

"Everyone Says 'Hi'" was outsourced to the London-based production team of Brian Rawling and Gary Miller (Rawling had co-produced Cher's "Believe"). Though it marked Carlos Alomar's return to the fold, much of the track is played by London musos: bassist John Read, percussionist Sola Akingbola (Jamiroquai), cellist Philip Sheppard (Scott Walker, Jarvis Cocker), and keyboardist Dave Clayton (ABC, Simply Red). "I just worked from the vocals. It started off like a remix, but ended up as a fully fledged production," Miller said. He and Rawling made a bauble, its hook Sheppard's electric cello line, its undercarriage a chugging acoustic guitar (and some Alomar rhythm fills), and its mix garnished with whooshing loops, Akingbola's chimes and rattles, and synthesizers playing charades (now an accordion, now a whistle, now a bassoon).

Issued as a British single, "Everyone Says 'Hi'" barely cracked the Top 20. It was sappy, sentimental, and as much a rumination on death as the "Last Songs" of *Heathen*. In an interview at the time, Bowie said its impetus came from a memory of his father's death in 1969. "I kind of thought that he'd just put his raincoat and his cap on and that he'd be back in a few weeks or something. And I felt like that for years." (The single was released the same day on which, twenty-five years earlier, his friend Marc Bolan had died.)

We tend to face death by "making do," with platitudes, busy-work, weak jokes: the need to get "back to normal" paramount. If "Everyone Says 'Hi'" is a shallow response to death, so are many of ours. Take how Bowie sings, "didn't know the right thing... to say." He gets tongue-tied, makes a joke. A trot through the C major key is matched by a chutes and ladders vocal ("a *big* trip" jolts up a seventh, slides down a third). The key line is "buy a little frame: something cheap." The frame is the track itself: its sweet melody, its shiny mix.

"We all feel very alone, don't we: often," Bowie said in a TV interview in 2002. "Too often: that's why we make such a thing about being with people... It's very scary to know that in those last moments we'll be absolutely alone." When Claudia Brücken covered "Everyone Says 'Hi'" a decade later, complete with a Major Tom video, it was a song for the then-vanished David Bowie. Brücken wishes he'd send a letter, let us know how he's doing. ("Someone told me that David wrote that [song] for me. That made me cry," Reeves Gabrels said in 2017.) And on the morning when news broke of Bowie's death, "Everyone Says 'Hi'" was reborn as a song for a world that would have to make do without him.

AMERICA

(Simon.) **Broadcast**: *20 October 2001, Madison Square Garden, New York. Bowie: vocal, Omnichord.*

First release: *(edited) 27 November 2001,* **The Concert For New York City** *(Columbia C2K 86270).* **Live**: *2001-2002.*

I don't live in America. I live in New York. It's another country.
— Bowie, July 2002.

When the first tower was hit, there was a rumbling. Take an oil drum, turn it on its side and play on it with mallets, amplify, give it heavy bass: something like that. It lasted for over five seconds.

At 195 Broadway, a block east from the World Trade Center, I went to the window to see if a truck had overturned on the Brooklyn Bridge, but there was nothing but traffic. Kevin came in. He was the sort of overgrown boy who made for a good reporter on Wall Street. "Plane hit the Trade Center," he said, and soon went back down to the street. I figured it was a Cessna, someone out of Teterboro who'd gone off course in a bad way. I crossed to the other side of the office, where a small window had a view of Church Street and the base of 2 World Trade. Smoke and bits of paper were in the air. A man on the intercom said there was no need to leave. Kevin returned. People were starting to jump, he said. "It's worse than you think." I sat at my desk, sipping coffee, refreshing a news website that said nothing. I kept going to that small window, watching papers whirl and scutter in the air: photocopies, envelopes, manila folders.

When the second plane hit, there was a loop of flame high in the air. Our building shook; screams came from the street. The man on the intercom calmly said we should go.

I'd worked in 2 World Trade five years before, on the eighteenth floor. The guards wore maroon jackets. There was so little light. In our office, the light was rationed to editors, each of whom had an office with a window-strip, leaving us reporters clustered in semi-darkness. It was like working in a mineshaft. On the ground floor, corridors and lobbies linked the two towers with the lesser buildings of the Trade Center complex. At Christmas, they set up a giant electric train set. There were statues of Bugs Bunny and

Daffy Duck as stockbrokers, feet up on their desks, in one shop window. A Duane Reade whose aisles in winter were full of lunchtime coughers. Tourists just went up to the observation decks. Only we who worked there knew the neighborhood, walked the scaffold-filled streets whose storefronts were mostly small-time importers, rug dealers, shops that repaired toasters and radios.

There was broken glass on Broadway that morning — the windows of Au Bon Pain were shattered, as were those of a Mrs. Fields cookie shop (its manager now busy pulling down gratings). A crowd had filled the street, were looking up at the towers. There was a sudden fluttering down the length of 1 World Trade: someone had fallen. I couldn't watch any more.

I walked up Church Street, trying to process what had happened — had there *been* a second plane? Had a gas main burst? A van disgorged FBI agents. I determined this because they wore windbreakers with "FBI" in great yellow letters. One looked excited. She wore an FBI baseball cap as well. Maybe she had a boring desk job and now here she was, pulling an *X-Files*. In a parking lot on Canal Street, I stopped to watch the towers again. Fires were eating through them, making great black clouds that the breeze sailed over to Brooklyn. These were the only clouds. Otherwise the sky was so clear and fine that you could see the sleeping moon. I was in a small knot of people. "It's going to burn for a long, long time," an elderly man said, with shaky authority. Two college kids filmed with handheld video cameras. "Check it out, dude," one said, offering the other a view from his monitor as if sharing a flask.

On Greene Street, I fell into step with two men in suits. We heard something and turned to see 2 World Trade fall into a pile of smoke. There was a low, bustling sound, like a train crossing in the distance. Only one tower stood now, ruling over a mountain of dust. I looked at the shorter of the men, said something like "can you believe this" and he gave me a why-are-you-fucking-talking-to-me face. "We've got to get *out* of here, it's not *safe* here," he said. In Washington Square Park, some hundred people stood in rows near the arch, as if at an outdoor concert. Everywhere I walked, I saw people carrying children and dogs.

I went into the First Presbyterian Church on Fifth Avenue and sat in a back pew for a time. As I was leaving, the crowd in the street gasped as one. The remaining tower was crumbling, again into a grey cloud, again with a soft rumble. "Oh God, all of those *people*," a woman said, her last word a long, piercing note of sadness. The air went out of me and I sat on the street.

When I got to my girlfriend's office on Seventh Avenue, I drank water, took in the speculations (Camp David was bombed, Congress was bombed, the president was missing). I figured I'd have to walk home to Queens at some point, so why not start. There were lines everywhere in midtown: at pay phones, bars, pizza shops, bank machines. In front of a bodega was an easel with draft paper on which you could write the name of anyone you wanted a prayer said for. It had a few names already, including "Everyone." A man was jogging down Third Avenue, headphones on, shirtless, oblivious.

I reached the Queensboro Bridge around noon. "We're representin' *Queens*," a man yelled. "This is the *real* Million Man March!" It was a holiday atmosphere by now, everyone sent home early from work. There were no police on the bridge. Men jumped on bumpers of barely-moving trucks, drinking Budweiser, ogling women, calling for them to strip. We were in a retreating, deteriorating army. Midway across I felt that a plane would come and shear through the bridge, and I wondered how it would feel to hang in the air for a moment before falling into the East River. In Queens Plaza the crowd divided, the greater half flowing towards Queens Boulevard, the lesser taking Northern Boulevard to Astoria. I was in the latter stream, and soon forked east to Sunnyside. At home, I sat with my feet in a bucket of warm water. I had no idea how I would get through the rest of the day.

At the Center of It All

Bowie and Tony Visconti were upstate at Allaire that morning, winding down the *Heathen* sessions. Visconti's son was living down by the Towers; he got out in time. Bowie and Iman's place in Soho was close enough that she heard the second plane hit while on the phone to him. She fled with their baby twenty blocks north ("Iman is a very fit woman," Bowie said in admiration).

Bowie was away from New York during an attack that seemed like something he'd have written for Hunger City in his *Diamond Dogs* film script, a crisis whose street actions were out of "Five Years." The visceral horror of the attacks, their simultaneous broadcast and dissemination on television, the whole apocalyptic spectacle was that of an early Seventies Bowie song: there was a crack in the sky, a hole in the ground; the nightmares were here to stay. Bowie was adamant that he'd written his *Heathen* lyrics before the attacks, in part to avoid looking like he was capitalizing on the tragedy. "I hope that a writer does have the antennae that pick up on low-level anxiety and all those Don DeLillo resonances within our culture," he said in 2002. But he also was stunned at what he'd invoked. As the spiritualist Robert Lees said in Alan Moore's *From Hell*, "I made it all up, and it all came true anyway."

A month later, Bowie took part in the Concert for New York at Madison Square Garden. It's hard to watch this concert today, with its sense of exhausted mourning, the open anger, the boorish comedians. The night's Anglo-American unity theme, with the Union Jack and Old Glory comforting each other above the stage and Paul McCartney writing the official 9/11 recovery theme song, seems a premonition of a shared disaster.

Bowie and his band's performance of "Heroes" was everything the audience needed that night. Many had lost friends; some would contract cancer and emphysema because of their work in those weeks. It's churlish to begrudge him for doing the expected; doing the expected felt like a luxury. "I felt duty-bound to do something," he said a week after the concert.

But he'd opened the show alone. He sat at the edge of the stage, his legs tucked under him, looking as if he'd been recruited from the Beckenham Arts Lab to warm up the crowd. He played an Omnichord keyboard, on which he set up a waltz pattern. Another toy instrument, like the Stylophone. He missed his cue and spent the first verse off-kilter, the keyboard waltzing ahead of him, making his phrasings halting and unsettled.

He sang Simon and Garfunkel's "America." Like the World Trade Center, it was from a lost Sixties. The America of Paul Simon's song is an old country, a departed country, like that of the Hardy Boys novels with their jalopies and automats. Mrs. Wagner's Pies, men in gabardine suits and bowties, young people hitchhiking without fear. He'd written some of it in England, made his English girlfriend Kathy Chitty a supporting character. He missed home enough to make pilgrims of cars stuck on the New Jersey Turnpike.

Why "America"? Bowie said he "was looking for something which really evoked feelings of bewilderment and uncertainty, because for me that's how that particular period really felt… Simon's song in this new context really captured that." He likely first heard it from the Scottish band 1-2-3, who regularly played the Marquee Club in 1967 (they covered one of Bowie's songs back when no one did, as they played Simon's song before

Simon himself released it, basing it on a demo he'd made in London). They turned "America" into a nearly ten-minute span of time and key changes, with newly-written interludes (Yes used a similar arrangement for their early Seventies cover).

Fitting into the song by its second verse, Bowie takes his time, stressing "for" over the crowd-pleasing "America." A world fades as he sings. Michigan goes like a dream. Saginaw's in another country. A busload of sleepers rolls East and night inks in the fields and towns they pass. What was it like, he asks on behalf of the lost kids at the Marquee, to have lived in such a place? And what will be there when it's gone?

SLOW BURN

Recorded: ca. early October 2001-ca. 31 January 2002, Looking Glass; (lead guitar) ca. November-December 2001, Pete Townshend's home studio, London. Bowie: lead vocal, keyboards; Townshend: lead guitar, acoustic guitar; Kristeen Young: piano, vocal; Visconti: bass, backing vocal; Sterling Campbell: drums; Lenny Pickett: tenor saxophone; Steve Elson: baritone saxophone; Stan Harrison: alto saxophone. Produced: Visconti, Bowie; engineered: Visconti.

*First release: 3 June 2002 (ISO/Columbia COL 672744 2). **Broadcast**: 2 June 2002, Top of the Pops 2; 10 June 2002, Late Show with David Letterman; 14 June 2002, Today Show; 15 June 2002, A&E Live by Request; 18 June 2002, Late Night with Conan O'Brien. **Live**: 2002.*

One of the last songs completed for *Heathen*, "Slow Burn" was its lead-off single in Japan and Europe. Bowie sang it in American promo appearances but it soon was out of his setlists. Perhaps it had been difficult to replicate the vocal accompaniment on stage (though he had two fine singers in Gail Ann Dorsey and Catherine Russell), but its absence also showed that "Slow Burn" had stiffed and few in the audience would clamor for it (the single was never released in the UK).

It has a droning "Heroes" opening, a portentous vocal with hawk cries (the ninth-spanning "sloooow BURRRN!," which gets a hard edit on its last notes), harmonic circularity (shuttling between F major to A minor), a doomsday lyric. In the latter, biblical references ("the walls shall have

517

eyes/and the doors shall have ears." See Luke 12:3 — "that which ye have spoken in the ear in closets shall be proclaimed upon the housetops") meet Simon and Garfunkel ("echoes in tenement halls," where presumably the words of the prophets are written). More conventional in structure (verse/refrain/solo/verse etc.) and in rhythm than many of its sister *Heathen* tracks, "Slow Burn" ticks to an eighth-note bassline, the drums kicking in when one would expect.

It felt bled out, with Bowie carrying the whole thing on his back. Kristeen Young pounds chords on piano ("they needed someone to play their piano line and I just happened to be at the studio," she told me. "If it was up to me... I would have played something different as it's not my style of playing.") The Borneo Horns nudge their way into the second verse, offering counter-riffs, doing a staircase-fall descent in one turnaround. And Pete Townshend, playing the intro hook on his Stratocaster, answers sustained chords with bent notes. He hangs on through the second verse, hooked into a choppy chord as if itching to cut Bowie short. After hearing rough mixes in New York, Townshend added solos to a Pro Tools file in London. Bowie picked the first one, which he thought had "a contained anger in it. It's so representative of Pete."

Though Bowie took pains to say he'd written his lyrics before the attack, his words invoke Manhattan that September. *Here are we, at the center of it all* (a line he'd reuse in "Blackstar"), while its most prophetic lines were earlier in the song: *who are* **we/So small** *in times such as these...*

HOP FROG

(Reed.) **Recorded***: ca. October-early November 2001, Sear Sound and/or Looking Glass, New York. Lou Reed: lead vocal, guitar; David Bowie: lead and backing vocal; Mike Rathke: guitar; Friedrich Paravicini: keyboards; Fernando Saunders: bass; Tony Smith: drums. Produced: Reed, Hal Willner; engineered: Tim Latham.*

First release*: 28 January 2003,* **The Raven** *(Sire/Reprise 48372-2, UK #122).*

In 1966, Bowie heard the voice of Lou Reed for the first time: flat, unimpressed, with an eye for details. *Up to Lex-ing-ton: ONE-TWO-FIVE.* Five years later, he produced *Transformer* for Reed, focusing on the vocal arrangements: a Crystals-esque "spoke spoke" in "Wagon Wheel," acidic counterpoint in "New York Telephone Conversation." Despite the occasional public dust-up, Reed and Bowie became friends and in 2001 they lived within walking distance of each other in New York. Reed was working on an album based on Edgar Allan Poe stories and poems that would be a Viking funeral for his recording career: a two-CD, thirty-six-track opus guest-starring everyone from Ornette Coleman to Steve Buscemi. "This might be a nice way to say 'Goodbye', a good way to go out," Reed said at the time. "I don't think you'll get a chance to make records like this with people downloading their music."

Asked to sing on a track, Bowie chose "Hop Frog." In Poe's story, Hop-Frog, a limping dwarf who's the slave and jester of a cruel king, devises a scheme. After having the king and his ministers dress up as escaped orangutans for a masked ball, Hop-Frog chains them together and sets them ablaze. In Reed's "Hop Frog" the jester boasts as the bodies ignite in feedback. Bowie holds back in the first verse, creeping in to shadow Reed's voice, then sets about taking over the song through his harmonies. *You can see me in the **bed**room! You can see me in the **woods**! Hop! Hop Frog!* He closes with a wail; Reed plays a fanfare on guitar.

PEOPLE HAVE THE POWER
GET UP STAND UP

(Smith, Smith ["People"], Marley, Tosh ["Get Up"].) **Live**: *("People") 26 February 2001, 22 February 2002, ("Get Up") 28 February 2003, Carnegie Hall, New York. (All years) Bowie, Philip Glass, various monks, (2001) Moby, Dave Matthews, Natalie Merchant, Emmylou Harris, Rahat Nusrat Fateh Ali Khan, (2001-2002) Patti Smith, (2002) Dana Bryant, Adam Yauch, Bebel Gilberto, Marc Anthony Thompson, (2002-2003) Nawang Khechog, Ray Davies, (2003) Angelique Kidjo, Ziggy Marley, Lou Reed, Laurie Anderson, Rufus Wainwright, Tsering Wangmo: vocals.*

Among the best Bowie performances of the early 2000s were the annual Tibet House Benefits, held at the end of the long New York winter at Carnegie Hall. Bowie's trio of appearances (2001 through 2003) had the most striking arrangements of his final performing years: "Silly Boy Blue," sung with the Tibetan monk chorus he'd always wanted for the song, and a Scorchio Quartet-led "Heroes." He also took part in the group-singalongs at the finale of each concert — twice on Patti Smith's "People Have the Power" and, in 2003, on the great anthem "Get Up Stand Up."

SAVIOUR

(Young.) **Recorded**: *ca. late 2001/mid-2002; (Bowie vocal retake) February 2003, Looking Glass. Kristeen Young: lead and harmony vocal, keyboards; Bowie: lead and harmony vocal; Richard Fortus: guitar; Brian Ion: bass; Jeff White: drums. Produced, engineered: Visconti.*

First release: *13 June 2003,* **Breasticles** *(N Records ZM 00103).*

At the end of 2001, Bowie left Virgin to form his own record company. It was the culmination of decades of frustration with the music industry and, most recently, with Virgin, which had rejected *Toy* and hadn't wanted him to release a live album online. "Many times I've not been in agreement with how things are done and as a writer of some proliferation, frustrated at how slow and lumbering it all is," he said. His new label, ISO, soon got a distribution deal with Columbia, an agreement which remained until his death.

As an independent artist, he had a growing penchant for guest-starring on other indie artists' albums. Tony Visconti introduced him to a songwriter and pianist named Kristeen Young. A half-Apache, half-German child adopted by fundamentalist Christians, Young survived a turbulent adolescence (her adoptive mother would smash her Prince records), by finding refuge in punk and indie music, becoming pen pals with Jello Biafra. She sent Visconti a copy of her second album, *Enemy*, in 1999 (reportedly finding his name in a music industry directory). Taken by what he described as her "part rock, part Bartok" sound and four-octave "gutsy voice... with its high soprano register," Visconti agreed to produce her. They recorded in New York around the time that Bowie was making *Heathen*. As she sang and played piano on the latter, Bowie offered to sing on one of her tracks — "Saviour," where Bowie took the second verse, getting a kick out of the line "American landfill... *laaand*-fill," and traded lines and harmonized with Young for the rest of the song.

I Feel So Bad
One Night

(Willis ["Feel So Bad"]; Bartholomew, King, Steinman ["One Night"].) **Live**: *16 August 2002, The Gorge Amphitheatre, 754 Silica Road, George, WA. Bowie: lead vocal; Leonard: lead guitar; Earl Slick: lead guitar; Mark Plati: guitar; Mike Garson: piano; Gail Ann Dorsey: bass; Campbell: drums; Catherine Russell: backing vocal.*

Planned as a dash through the European summer festival circuit, Bowie's 2002 tour began as him at his most curatorial. He performed *Low* in (mostly) sequential order, wearing a version of his Thin White Duke suit, tailored for his more advanced age. Then after changing outfits, he performed *Heathen* in sequential order. The albums "feel like cousins to each other," he said. "They've got a certain sonic similarity."

Around 1998, it became common for bands to play their classic LPs in order live, particularly once performance became their primary way to make a living. ("You'd better be prepared for doing a lot of touring because that's really the only unique situation that's going to be left," Bowie told the *New York Times* in June 2002.) Choosing *Low* was a savvy move, as the album was considered his masterpiece in the *Pitchfork* era — there was some ad man's hustle in the pairing (*"Heathen* is the new *Low"*). In performance, the *Low* songs were played well, sung richly, and felt constricted. Once-experimental works had hardened into standards, with Bowie guiding his audiences through cathedrals of his making. Late summer brought an alternating-headline slot Moby's Area 2 Festival in North America, with Bowie now mingling *Low* and *Heathen* songs in his sets, seasoned with hits.

On the last night of the Area 2 tour, at the Gorge Amphitheatre east of Seattle, he changed his encore. As it was the twenty-fifth anniversary of Elvis Presley's death, and as he thought Presley's birthday had always eclipsed his own, Bowie sang two Elvis songs. One was "I Feel So Bad," which Presley had cut in 1961 — a Chuck Willis R&B number, as sung by a man about to vanish into bad movies for a decade ("sometimes I wanna stay here/then again, I wanna leave"). During Boots Randolph's saxophone solo, Presley had walked over to cheer, as if he'd bet on Randolph in a horse race. "One Night" was a filthy Smiley Lewis song, a man shaking from an orgy ("the things I did and I saw/would make the earth stand still"). Presley cleaned it up for his 1958 cover, a minor hit. As Bob Dylan said, "you can't fault

Elvis — it was the taste of the times and he'd already broken enough rules." Presley went back to "One Night" a decade later, for a TV special. There he's joking, mugging for the camera, not giving a shit, and in a breath he's *there*, howling BEEN **TOO LONELY** *TOO LONG!* He lurches up, forcing someone to rig a mike for him; he slashes away at his guitar as if he wants to snap off the strings.

Bowie's covers were respectful karaoke. He sang "I Feel So Bad" in his lowest register, sliding into the refrains, keeping his Elvis mask on. "One Night" was livelier: Bowie got caught up enough in the song to wonder where it was going. "Bye-bye, Presley," he said as the band closed it out.

In October, after a small tour of Britain and Europe, he did a last run of shows, a five-borough sprint whose trajectory followed the New York Marathon route. It was his tribute to his still-battered adopted city. The first date was Snug Harbor, west of the ferry terminal on Staten Island ("Earl Slick country," Bowie said). Then St. Ann's Warehouse in the rapidly-gentrifying DUMBO (one sign of gentrification: getting an acronym like "DUMBO") neighborhood of Brooklyn. Joe Strummer had played St. Ann's earlier that year: he'd been late, saying his cabbie hadn't known where to go. Then he ripped into "Bank Robber," singing it like Elvis. Bowie played Colden Center at Queens College, Jimmy's Bronx Café, and the Beacon Theatre on the Upper West Side, where he closed with "Ziggy Stardust." "It didn't seem like the end of a long and grueling year, but a new time with a horizon that went on forever," he wrote in 2003, when he was cutting another album and planning a global tour. How could it ever end?

CHAPTER THIRTEEN:
INAUTHENTIC REALITY
(2003-2007)

We feel ourselves tangled in a constant, lashing web of crisis.
— George Steiner, "Tomorrow"

I would like to talk about reality sometime, authentic reality, inauthentic reality, and what we have to accept of what we see.
— Hillary Rodham, Wellesley College commencement speech, 1969

For us, there is only the trying. The rest is not our business.
— T. S. Eliot, "East Coker"

My integration into civilian life was not easy. It was very gradual.
— Matthew Weiner, on the end of *Mad Men*

Make the best of every moment. We're not evolving. We're not going anywhere.
— Bowie, 2004

NEVER GET OLD

Recorded: (backing tracks) ca. 10 January-15 February 2003; (overdubs) March-May 2003, Looking Glass Studios. David Bowie: lead and backing vocal, rhythm guitar, Korg Trinity, keyboards; Earl Slick: lead guitar; David Torn: guitar; Mark Plati: bass; Sterling Campbell: drums; Gail Ann Dorsey, Catherine Russell: backing vocals. Produced: Tony Visconti, Bowie; engineered: Visconti, Mario McNulty.

*First release: 15 September 2003, **Reality** (ISO/Columbia COL 512555 2/ CK 90576, UK #3, US #29). **Broadcast**: 4 September 2003, Trafic.musique; 11 September 2003, Friday Night with Jonathan Ross; 17 September 2003, Last Call with Carson Daly; 18 September 2003, The Today Show; 17 October 2003, Die Harald Schmidt Show; 21 April 2004, The Tonight Show; 23 April 2004, The Ellen DeGeneres Show. **Live**: 2003-2004.*

A hook for his most ambitious tour in thirteen years, *Reality* became something far different in the late 2000s and early 2010s: David Bowie's Last Album. With each year, it appeared more likely that he had retired without notice, thus leaving *Reality* as his *Abbey Road*, his *Avalon* — a "thrusty" (his favored adjective for it) overlong rock album with a wide-eyed anime Bowie as a cover image. His return in 2013 loosed *Reality* from this trap, restored it to what it always had been: a minor album whose songs were built to be blasted on stage; the work of a man at an armistice with his past, frightened of the world, holding it together for his kid's sake.

Unlike *Heathen*, there was "no through line" in *Reality*, he said. It was a collection of loud major key rock songs and a few covers pulled from his one-hundred-plus-song *"Pin Ups 2"* list. In its inessentiality was freedom — as a newly-independent artist (see "Saviour"), Bowie was no longer stuck in the release cycles of major labels. "I can put out stuff whenever I want," he boasted (but as he said, "going back on my word is part and parcel of what I do for you. Part of my entertaining factor is lying to you"). There's more thematic coherence in *Reality* than he let on. Like *The Man Who Sold the World*, it's an album of extreme figures — Pablo Picasso as cock of the walk, a gluttonous rock star vampire, a Dick Cheney stand-in — and diminished ones: lonelyhearts, frustrated wives, sad husbands.

As he was planning a tour once his daughter was old enough to travel, his sets needed an overhaul: more oldies and new uptempo songs. The rapid pace of his "five borough" shows in 2002 invigorated him. By year's end, he was "percolating" new songs, recording demos via his home setup: a Korg Trinity, ARP Odyssey, a Korg Pandora effects processor, and a lifetime's accumulation of guitars. "I was back at home with the baby and wife and doing daily things and I started writing immediately."

At the time, Tony Visconti was renting Studio B in Looking Glass Studios on Broadway, close to Bowie's Lafayette Street home (from now on, Bowie used studios within walking distance). Bowie kept a domestic schedule — internet binging and walks in the early morning, breakfast with his daughter, off to the studio around 10am, back for dinner. He could try something on a keyboard at home, play it in the studio a few hours later, take the file home and edit it that night. It was homespun record-making, a far cry from staying up all night at Sigma Sound.

In mid-January 2003, Bowie and Visconti demoed about seven tracks (top melody sketches and scratch keyboard, bass and guitars over a click track), then did overdubs of guitar, vocals and keyboards. "Inevitably we'd hardly redo anything," Visconti said. "A lot of the demo parts ended up on the final version." After a break in which Bowie wrote more, he gathered a small group for rhythm tracks, cutting eight in as many days. It was Bowie on guitar and keyboards, drummer Sterling Campbell and bassist/guitarist Mark Plati all crammed into Studio B, with its 12x10 isolation booth. Bowie could have rented the more spacious Studio A, but he liked being boxed in for "a real tight New York sound," said Visconti, who said he could better judge bass tones in the smaller studio. "We found that this MCI board had a lovely transparent sound and that the room had nice acoustics, with a very honest low end," he said soon before cutting *Reality*. "It helped to have a lot of my old gear there — some nice vintage stuff like dbx compressors, a Saturator, a Shure Level-Loc, an old Audio & Design Scamp processing system, and all the synths and modules we could possibly need."

Plati had been positioned to become Bowie's regular producer in the late Nineties, but the return of Visconti and the collapse of *Toy* gave Visconti a stronger hand. For *Reality*, Visconti often wanted Plati to ink in his demo basslines (Visconti's original parts remain on "The Loneliest Guy," "Days" and "Fall Dog Bombs the Moon"), and he'd looked askance at Plati's use of the Line 6 Bass POD, a preamp that let you "dial up" the sound of whichever bass amp and cabinet you wanted; Visconti preferred to direct-inject his '67 Fender Precision into the console. For guitars, there was Earl Slick (cranking through a huge Marshall stack), David Torn (again providing "atmospheres," though he also got some lead riffs, such as on "New Killer Star"), and Gerry Leonard. Bowie was keen to play some Supro guitars he'd bought on eBay, including a retrofitted 1957 Dual Tone and a patched-up twelve-string. He also played scads of Korg Trinity, his old Selmer baritone saxophone, and tried his hand at harmonica again.

By May, he had an album. Bowie typically cut three lead vocals for each track — one right after the rhythm tracks were done, one midway through the sessions, and the last during mixing. Visconti synced them (he'd made sure Bowie used the same mike, a Manley Gold, for all takes) and stitched together master vocals, following a line Bowie had sung in February with one from May. And he was in strong voice — having given up cigarettes at last, he said he'd recovered five semitones.

Angry Old Men

Before *Reality*'s release, Bowie filmed an ad for Vittel water. He's a chic brownstone owner sharing house with his discarded personae: Ziggy Stardust in the bathroom, the Thin White Duke at the breakfast table, Thomas Jerome Newton on the stairs ("never gonna get *Low!*"). The "real" Bowie walks off into the morning, out for a coffee or a Bikram yoga session, leaving the freaks back home. He looks great. The soundtrack is "Never Get Old."

Unlike many of his peers, Bowie in his mid-fifties had stayed thin, kept his hair, and could pass for at least a decade younger. He'd recently cut a remake of "Changes" with Butterfly Boucher, where he sang "pretty soon you're gonna get older!" with a smile. "It's a rather silly song," he said of "Never Get Old," about "a petulant fifty-six-year-old... sitting in a half-darkened room saying, 'I'm not gonna get old.' I had to write it before someone else my age did." Playing an aging, egomaniacal creep was too juicy a role to decline. "Today we're a generation of angry old men," he said.

In "Never Get Old," the E major refrains are bloated, full of whining guitars. A grotesque man won't leave the table, wanting more: cash, food, drugs, women (live, Bowie sang "never gonna be enough bullets!," making a gun shape with his fingers). Beneath the refrains, a distorted bassline is a gurgling stomach. There are the usual borrows from old songs: a winding verse melody from "Karma Man," the last vocal tag sharing similar harmonies with the closing ones of "Sgt. Pepper's Lonely Hearts Club Band." The verse starts on G major, sharpens the chord, returns to G, then moves to F major ("care of me"). The second time around it ends on E minor, the pre-chorus on C major. These qualified, fleeting movements, driven by a rhythm guitar nagging on one string, underscores a lyric of regret and loneliness. A man locks himself in his room. He goes to the movies, like the mousy-haired girl of "Life on Mars?" The moon floats along, its airy progress the little piano break.

During the album's promotion, Bowie said he wanted to see his daughter grow up, that he was trying to brighten his despairing nature. *Reality* was a lightshow meant to keep your eyes from the exits. "I desperately want to live forever," he said,

> I just want to be there for Alexandria. She's so exciting and so lovely so I want to be around when she grows up. I think, "When am I gonna let go of her? When she's twenty?" Nah, I wanna see her get married. When she's thirty? Nah, I wanna see what she's like as a mother. I don't want to let her go.

The demands for more and more from a rock star glutton is the human predicament in cartoon form. Life is absurd, and there's never enough of it. In the early 2010s, a blog commenter disputed my choice of words, as I'd written "when Bowie dies." Surely I meant *if?*, they asked. A wonderful complaint, and a true one. Bowie would never die, he couldn't die: we wouldn't let him.

REALITY

Recorded: (backing tracks) ca. 10 January-15 February 2003; (overdubs) March-May 2003, Looking Glass. Bowie: lead vocal, Korg Trinity, synthesizers; Slick, Torn: guitar; Plati: bass; Campbell: drums. Produced: Visconti, Bowie; engineered: Visconti, McNulty.

First release: 15 September 2003, Reality. Live: 2003-2004.

George Steiner was born in 1929 into the sort of cultured Viennese Jewish family that would be slaughtered and dispossessed during the war. The

Steiners were lucky. Having moved to France, they fled "in the last American boats" to New York before the Nazis invaded. Thirty years later, Steiner, now a writer and professor, delivered the T.S. Eliot Memorial Lectures at the University of Kent in Canterbury. Collected in book form, his lectures were *In Bluebeard's Castle: Some Notes Towards the Redefinition of Culture*, in which he argued that after the world wars and the Holocaust, the chain of Western high culture was broken. We were in a "post-culture" now. This wasn't necessarily tragic. Western civilization had ravaged cultures, animal species, and environments in the name of "progress." It may well have been an evolutionary mistake. But "we cannot turn back. We cannot choose the dreams of unknowing," Steiner concluded.

In Bluebeard's Castle was one of Bowie's favorite books. In interviews for *Reality*, he repeatedly brought up Steiner to frame his intentions for his title track, one of the first songs he'd written for the album. "That book just confirmed for me that there was actually some kind of theory behind what I was doing with my work," he said. "I have an undiminished idea of variability. I don't think there's one truth, one absolute." What he'd found in Steiner was a vocabulary to explain his own catholicity of taste, his love for Anthony Newley, Little Richard and Steve Reich, *the Beano* and Nietzsche. The glam aesthetic. "There were several of us dealing in this newly-found pluralistic vocabulary," he recalled. "This whole George Steiner-ism of life, you know?"

But even Roxy Music, who had *Lolita* and *Guernica* doing the Strand, or Bowie, who fused Jacques Brel, Judy Garland and doo-wop in "Rock 'n' Roll Suicide" ("wow, you can do anything!" as he described writing that song), became predictable, he said. "I think that the world caught up really quickly and everybody is so totally aware of the kind of vocabulary that we were throwing around at the time, that one feels kind of superfluous now." In his 2003 interviews he played a man disappointed in the world he'd helped create. He'd been a vanguard of change but that had long since been co-opted by marketers. Even the internet, his last infatuation with the future, was only further atomizing people. He kept up his *Heathen* theme of a played-out barbaric future. "I don't think we want new things. I think we're kind of scrounging around among the things we know to see if we can salvage some kind of civilization which will help us endure and survive into the future. We don't need new. We are fucked. We've got enough new. Enough!"

Playing *Reality* to a journalist, Bowie introduced one track (not identified) as "based on this author who wrote rather bad science fiction stories." One candidate is the title track, his description being an inside joke. Who was David Bowie but an author of bad SF? He enjoyed being a fraud. "I hid among the junk of wretched highs," as he sings in "Reality." It was life in Steiner's post-culture: you'll to have live off the land more, so learn to compost. David Bowie "is the medium for a conglomerate of statements and illusions," he'd said in 1976. Like "Heroes," reality exists in quotations. *Reality* has a saucer-eyed anime Bowie that, once the CD cover was flipped open, is replaced by the "real" Bowie, who's merely the image that David Jones chose to represent himself in 2003. "There's a fakeness to the cover that undermines" its title, Bowie said. "It's the old chestnut: what is real and what isn't? It's actually about who's stolen this world."

"Reality" is built of clashes between major chords (D and E for verses, C and F# for refrains) and has a lyric where Bowie's an aging rake, lusting for youth in the mirror. The track soon starts shaking apart — the guitars are at war. The refrain is someone walking off a movie set, with a run of *ha-ha-ha-ha*s like slaps to the face. Bowie sings one of his self-epitaphs: "I still don't remember how this *happened*/I still don't get the wherefores and the whys." A life devoted to change had wound up not dissimilar to one where you had hunkered down: a David Jones who stayed in Beckenham, watching television with his grandchildren in 2003, regarding post-modern life with the same bewilderment as the pop singer promoting his twenty-third album and talking about George Steiner.

Bowie has a blast in "Reality," in its guitar-crazy recording and raucous live performances — throwing himself around in it. In a post-culture, "progress" is for suckers. "If you accept that we live in absolute chaos, it doesn't look like futility anymore," he said.

It only looks like futility if you believe in this bang up structure we've created called "God" and all. [But] all of these structures were self-created, just to survive, that's all... It wasn't handed down to us from anywhere... We're leaving those old structures behind, whether we like it or not; they are all crumbling.

Let's dance and watch them fall.

PABLO PICASSO

(Richman.) **Recorded**: *(backing tracks) ca. 10 January-15 February 2003; (overdubs) March-May 2003, Looking Glass. Bowie: lead and backing vocal, rhythm guitar, baritone saxophone, Korg Trinity, keyboards, Yamaha digital piano?; Gerry Leonard: "Spanish" guitar; Earl Slick: lead guitar; Garson: digital piano?; Plati: bass; Campbell: drums. Produced: Visconti, Bowie; engineered: Visconti, McNulty.*

First release: *15 September 2003,* **Reality**. **Live**: *2003-2004.*

Jonathan Richman of Natick, Massachusetts, like Lou Reed of Freeport, Long Island, was a suburban Jewish boy saved by rock 'n' roll. Richman's catalyst was Reed's Velvet Underground. By the time he was twenty, Richman had his own band, the Modern Lovers, and was making demos with John Cale. Richman sang of the straights of the Sixties, those who only knew the counterculture from television. His "Roadrunner" isn't on the open road but on Route 128, the traffic-thick belt encircling Boston. He found the sublime in Stop 'n' Shop supermarkets and AM radio; he honored old people, praised the functionaries of Boston's charmless Government Center. Hippies, when they showed up, were wastrels and creeps.

"Pablo Picasso," which he wrote around 1970, was the Picasso from a *Life* profile: a bald, short, intense man living with beautiful women in canvas-strewn ateliers. He was photographed shirtless, thrusting his chest out, king gorilla of the art world. Richman makes Picasso king greaser of the block, as seen through the eyes of an envious geek. The song vamps on an E minor chord, a lower-rent take on the VU's "Sister Ray." ("They were like the Velvet Underground, except with whimsy," Bowie said of the Modern Lovers.) On the Cale-produced demo of "Pablo Picasso," there's a piano/bass drone, the drums in a chugging pattern (Richman wanted to invoke a New York subway train), guitar solos as jitters along the Em scale. "The original is a little dirgelike," Bowie said. "It doesn't move much, which gives it a power, but it gives it the power of another era."

Wanting "a more contemporary feel," Bowie changed the lyric (as everyone from Iggy Pop to Richman had done) and fattened "Pablo Picasso" with new chords, in part because he'd jacked up the tempo and needed some embellishments, like an ascending sequence (Bb-C#-G#-Bb-G#-F#) for an intro/bridge section. Gerry Leonard played an out-of-phase, panned "Spanish" lead guitar, and later soloed against Bowie's baritone saxophone (Bowie's refurbished Supro is likely one of the scraping rhythm guitars). A digital piano makes incidental sounds for a desktop; Sterling Campbell's drums were among those Tony Visconti remixed at Allaire Studios for more reverb. Bowie called it *Reality*'s equivalent to his cover of "Cactus" on *Heathen*, but it was more a sequel to his other painter song, "Andy Warhol." It's a comic-strip autobiography — replace "Pablo Picasso" with "David Bowie" in the lyric and it works as well. Good luck coming up with a better rhyme than Richman's, though.

FALL DOG BOMBS THE MOON

Recorded: (backing tracks) ca. 10 January-15 February 2003; (overdubs) March-May 2003, Looking Glass. Bowie: lead and backing vocal, rhythm guitar, keyboards; Slick, Torn, Plati: guitar; Visconti: bass; McNulty: drums, percussion. Produced: Visconti, Bowie; engineered: Visconti, McNulty.

First release: 15 September 2003, **Reality**. **Broadcast**: 4 September 2003, Trafic. musique; 23 September 2003, Sessions @ AOL. **Live**: 2003-2004.

A wartime album, made during the United States' invasion of Iraq in spring 2003, *Reality* was written by a British expatriate living in a city whose attack was the war's justification. "The sword... is unsheathed. The blade... stands ready," as Oliver North intoned on Fox News, two days before the invasion began.

Bowie favored a news service called Truth-Out.org, "a fabulous storehouse of information of what's written in the alternative press, or the rest of the world's press, that never really sees the light of day here." There he discovered that Kellogg Brown & Root, five days after the invasion, had won a bid to repair and operate Iraq's oil fields. KBR had been accused of bribery, expense padding, and sexual abuse and intimidation of employees. Until July 2000, its parent company Halliburton was run by the soon-to-be vice-president, Dick Cheney.

Cheney lived to claim power and brooked no checks on it. He didn't care what you thought of him. Carrying on about Halliburton just meant that you weren't serious. His public persona was of a doctor telling you that the news isn't good and the bill's due. "What tends to happen is that a thing like an issue or a policy manifests itself as a guide," Bowie said. "It becomes a character of some kind." He began the song with a Cheney caricature. "There's this guy saying, 'I'm goddam rich... throw anything you like at me, baby, because I'm goddam rich. It doesn't bother me.' It's an ugly song sung by an ugly man."

"Fall Dog Bombs the Moon," similar in chords and tempo to "New Killer Star," came together quickly: Bowie said he wrote the lyric in a half-hour. Neil Young and Crazy Horse are heard in its plaintive vocal and artless drums, the latter by engineer Mario McNulty. Bowie kept Tony Visconti's demo bassline and layered in guitars: a pack of players vying to be the lead, with a harmonized solo for the outro. "It's pretty enjoyable to thump about at extremely loud volume," he said.

Some read its title as George W. Bush, a "fall dog" instead of a fall guy, with the "moon" the Islamist star and crescent. A soldier sees a girl in a marketplace with a bomb strapped to her. She runs towards him; he waits, as if ready to embrace her. Soon he's an exploding man, whether victim or bomber. Yet despite Bowie framing his song as a picture of a late capitalist, his phrasings undermined his own reading. He sounds wistful, lets lines trail off. His Fall Dog (sometimes sung as "full dog") is Iggy Pop's dog — a man who yearns to submit. The second verse is the United States' endless need for a fresh enemy, but also applies to someone sitting at home chuckling at the news on *The Daily Show*. Who was Bush but a convenient moron to take the heat? "This whole world is run by brutes for the common and the stupid," Bowie had said in 2002. *These blackest of years... No shape, no depth, no underground*. In the twenty-first century, even the villains lack stature.

LOVE MISSILE F1-11

(James, Degville, Whitmore.) **Recorded**: *(backing tracks) ca. 10 January-15 February 2003; (overdubs) March-May 2003, Looking Glass. Bowie: lead vocal, rhythm guitar, Korg Trinity, keyboards; Plati: bass; Campbell: drums. Produced: Visconti, Bowie; engineered: Visconti, McNulty.*

First release: 29 September 2003, "New Killer Star" (ISO-Columbia COL 674275 9/ISO-Columbia 38K 3445).

A cover of Sigue Sigue Sputnik's "Love Missile F1-11" cut during the *Reality* sessions was issued as a B-side of the European/Canadian "New Killer Star" single. Bowie didn't try to top the original in excess; if anything, his version is closer in spirit to "the anarchic dub sound of the [track's] Portastudio demos," as Sputnik leader Tony James described them.

According to legend, EMI signed Sigue Sigue Sputnik for £4 million (it was reportedly far less). For its investment, the label got a #3 single ("Love Missile") and a brief tour marked by performative violence. Sputnik used film dialogue in its songs and wanted companies to buy ad space between LP tracks (L'Oréal and *i-D Magazine* did): they were the KLF 1.0. "I want to be successful and yet never out of touch with things. I don't want to be someone who's made into a pop icon and then doesn't know how to save himself," Sputnik's Martin Degville said in 1986. "I don't want to become David Bowie or Mick Jagger... they've cheated an awful lot of people. They've manipulated an awful lot of people and they've become cliches of themselves." (That said, Sputnik's Neal Whitmore later told Nicholas Pegg he'd been thrilled that Bowie had covered him.)

"Love Missile F1-11" had a Cold War sex and drugs lyric (nuclear missiles as hard dicks and heroin needles), Bo Diddley beats and Eddie Cochran riffs, and a Giorgio Moroder mix with chunks of dialogue from *Scarface* and *A Clockwork Orange*. Bowie recognized the single for what it was — the *Ziggy Stardust* of 1986, and a flashier beast than old Ziggy had ever been. He sang it straight, digging into his lines ("there goes my love rocket red!"), cheerleading another American war underway.

NEW KILLER STAR

Recorded: (backing tracks) ca. 10 January-15 February 2003; (overdubs) March-May 2003, Looking Glass. Bowie: lead and backing vocal, rhythm guitar, Korg Trinity, keyboards; Slick, Torn: lead guitar; Visconti, Plati: bass; Campbell: drums; Dorsey, Russell: backing vocals. Produced: Visconti, Bowie; engineered: Visconti, McNulty.

First release: 15 September 2003, **Reality**. **Broadcast**: 4 September 2003, *Trafic. musique*; 11 September 2003, *Friday Night with Jonathan Ross*; 17 September 2003, *Last Call with Carson Daly*; 18 September 2003, *The Today Show*; 22 September 2003, *Late Show with David Letterman*; 23 September 2003, *Sessions @ AOL*; 17 October 2003, *Die Harald Schmidt Show*; 24 February 2004, *Rove Live*. **Live**: 2003-2004.

He keeps a lost city in his head but keeps losing pieces of it. Was there a cobbler stand on Dey Street? Were the non-fiction books in the World Trade Center Borders upstairs or downstairs? Were there trees in the lobbies? What kind? What color were the walls of the Cortlandt Street subway station? Who but we remember these? No, we'll forget them, too.

"I'm not a political commentator, but I think there are times when I'm stretched to at least implicate what's happening, politically," Bowie said in his promotional piece for *Reality*. "There was some nod, in a very abstract way, towards the wrongs that are being made at the moment." "New Killer Star" shares qualities of other "public" Bowie songs, its disconnected details like those recounted by the shell-shocked narrator of "Time Will Crawl." After visiting the empty bowl that once was the World Trade Center, the singer watches the skies and TV, cottons his memory in old movies, waits for the next blow to fall. "There is a feeling [in NYC] that it's not over yet," he said in 2003. "I think everyone's sort of expecting something else to happen. I think the idea of terrorist action in bars and restaurants and that kind of thing, being cited as targets, is somewhere in everyone's mind."

The song structure is another *Reality* comic strip: a four-panel grid (bubbles and actions, little details in color) with establishing shot, start joke, build joke, punchline. Here: "stuttering" guitar riff, A minor verse, pre-chorus, E-flat refrain (punchline: a Brit mocks how the President of the United States pronounces "nuclear"). Eight-bar break. Repeat. The guitar/bass riff becomes the pre-chorus vocal melody (duh-*dah dah*, "I'm *red-ee*"). Guitar atmospherics by David Torn are hurricane weather. "New Killer Star" was another Bowie magpie construction: its bass/guitar riff is the chorus hook of Little Peggy March's "I Will Follow Him," while as Nicholas Pegg noted, "'87 and Cry" was shaken down for melodies and hooks.

Without intending to, Bowie had become a New Yorker. "It's a bit like being on holiday in a place I've always wanted to go to, that doesn't come to an end," he said of living there. "I always feel like a stranger here. I am an outsider... But I've got friends here. I probably know this town better than I know the new London." "New Killer Star" was a native's response to his city being made the stage of a national tragedy. "Others are watching us [now]. I don't think we ever felt that before," he said in 2003. "There's a slight unease. We really felt freewheeling and that 'tomorrow belongs to us,' anything can happen. Now there's not quite that swaying surge of hopefulness." He'll do his part and be optimistic despite everything that he sees and hears. "The ghost of the tragedy that happened [in NYC] is reflected in the song, but I'm trying to make something more positive out of it."

Looking for Water

Recorded: (backing tracks) ca. 10 January-15 February 2003; (overdubs) March-May 2003, Looking Glass. Bowie: lead and backing vocals, rhythm guitar, Korg Trinity, keyboards, synthesizers; Torn, Slick, Leonard?: guitar; Plati: bass; Campbell: drums, tambourine. Produced: Visconti, Bowie; engineered: Visconti, McNulty.

*First release: 15 September 2003, **Reality**. Live: 2003-2004.*

"Looking for Water" shifts location from a burned Manhattan to a Middle Eastern country picked to answer for the crime. Bowie started with another comic-strip idea: the cliché of a man wandering lost in the desert, looking for palm trees. Instead he finds an American perversion of deliverance — a row of oil derricks. There was also *The Man Who Fell to Earth,* where Thomas Jerome Newton comes looking for water for his depleted planet, and "Glass Spider," with its "the water's all gone" hook. "Virtually looped" between D major and F# minor, "Looking for Water" has verses incited by guitar breaks ("a secondary consideration was the melodic content on top," Bowie said). Against a single left-mixed guitar that keeps to its high strings, there's a blunt retort: a descending riff doubled on bass and some ferocious counterpoint figures, starting around 1:40. This sound — bright, guitar-fattened, punched through with overdubs — would be the template for *The Next Day* tracks like "The Stars (Are out Tonight)."

QUEEN OF ALL THE TARTS (OVERTURE)

Recorded: (backing tracks) ca. 10 January-15 February 2003; (overdubs) March-May 2003, Looking Glass. Bowie: lead and backing vocal, guitar?, Korg Trinity, keyboards, tenor saxophone; Torn, Slick, Leonard: guitar; Plati: bass; Campbell: drums; Dorsey, Russell: backing vocals. Produced: Visconti, Bowie; engineered: Visconti, McNulty.

*First release: 15 September 2003, **Reality** (limited edition: Columbia/ISO COL 512555 9).*

Used as pre-show music for the *Reality* tour, "Queen of All the Tarts (Overture)" is a guitar impasto, with a militant line heard towards the outro. The two-tiered (likely two-fingered) synthesizer solo is courtesy of the composer; Mark Plati sounds as if he's downed a few espressos; Sterling Campbell tracks in some thudding tom fills (there are also low-mixed sleigh bells, possibly synthetic). Its refrain, a vocalized keyboard line that suggests the track was a late-in-the-day upgrade of an instrumental, has two-note harmonies from a multi-tracked Bowie, Gail Ann Dorsey, and Catherine Russell. It's a throwaway with some intriguing details — take the arpeggiated diminished C# passing chord (first heard at 0:20). Bowie's use of passing chords (chords often not in the song's underlying key but which "bridge" two that are) is, as Momus noted, a favorite composition trick, done to inject feelings of transience and unease into a song's progression (see "Ashes to Ashes" or "Absolute Beginners"). Here the passing chord derails a confident progression in B-flat major, as if the title Queen has stumbled into a darkened room.

SHE'LL DRIVE THE BIG CAR

Recorded: (backing tracks) ca. 10 January-15 February 2003; (overdubs) March-May 2003, Looking Glass. Bowie: lead and backing vocal, baritone saxophone, harmonica, rhythm guitar, synthesizers, marimba?, handclaps; Slick, Torn, Leonard?: guitars; Plati: bass; Campbell: drums; Dorsey, Russell: backing vocals. Produced: Visconti, Bowie; engineered: Visconti, McNulty.

First release: 15 September 2003, **Reality**. **Broadcast**: 4 September 2003, *Trafic. musique*. **Live**: 2003-2004.

On *Reality* Bowie revived his framework for '*hours...* ,' pairing a desperate husband (see "Fly") with a desperate wife. In "She'll Drive the Big Car," the latter speeds along Riverside Drive in Manhattan, wondering if she should cut the wheel and plunge into the Hudson. "My favorite suicide song," he called it. "All her plans have been disassembled by her thoughtless boyfriend." The cad was supposed to "take her back to the old bohemian life" but instead he stands her up, like the friend of the girl in "Life on Mars?" So she's "stuck with this middle-class family and is absolutely, desperately unhappy as she's peeling along Riverside Drive. In my mind she just swings it off to the left and takes the whole lot down."

With some wordplay (Riverside Drive is a sylvan place with "cormorants and leaves"), the lyric's central image is of a family always about to crash in the same car, with the driver's useless husband sitting behind her and her eyes on a daughter whose life she's thinking about ending along with her own. The verse's move from home chord (C major) to subdominant (F major) is paralleled in the lyric's shift from lost hopes ("back in millennium/ meant racing to the light") to potential death on Riverside. The refrains sink to F# minor, more an immersion than an escape. The refrain of the song-within-the-song — blasting on the radio "so that she doesn't have to think anymore" while she drives like a demon — is the Isley Brothers' "Shout" or, in a more self-referential world, Bowie's 1964 cover of "Louie Louie Go Home," which had borrowed the refrain.

A trudge of a song, it lived in its overdubs: Bowie's harmonica, heard for the first time since "Never Let Me Down,"; a twanging guitar figure mixed left in refrains (a feedback burst at 3:22 is like a rip in the mix); a synthesizer bed that sounds like a harmonium; marimba fills; a snare drum hiccup to cue the refrains; Bowie's baritone saxophone as a dark layer in the foundation. The harmonies are Bowie as frantic advocate and Gail Ann Dorsey and Catherine Russell, spanning octaves, as reassurance.

FLY

Recorded: (drums) ca. August-September 2001, Allaire Studios; (backing tracks) *ca. 10 January-15 February 2003; (overdubs) March-May 2003, Looking Glass. Bowie: lead and backing vocal, guitar; Carlos Alomar: lead guitar; Slick, Torn, Leonard?: guitars; Plati: bass; Matt Chamberlain: drums; Dorsey, Russell: backing vocals. Produced: Visconti, Bowie; engineered: Visconti, McNulty.*

First release: *15 September 2003, **Reality** (limited edition).*

The marooned suburbanite is a constant of Bowie's songs. Dana Gillespie, a girlfriend from his teenage years, once recalled how grim the Jones' house was in Bromley, that it had seemed like Bowie's parents kept silent when no one else was there. Bowie flew away: Los Angeles, Berlin, Bermuda, New York. His turn-of-the-century albums find him regarding those who didn't escape as creatures in a zoo. What's it like to have lived only in one's imagination? In the refrains of "Fly," a broken father takes refuge in his dreams, a jarring D# minor chord ("but I can fly") giving him unexpected turbulence.

A man sits in his car in his driveway, weeping, watching the TV play to an empty room in his house. His wife is bored, his son might be on drugs, the kids down the street are playing "on their decks" in a garage, working up a set for an "all-night rave" (Bowie hadn't been getting out much in the early 2000s). None of this seems particularly tragic, even a line about a kid overdosing. It's more in the line of the Police's "On Any Other Day," with middle-aged suburban ennui played for dark laughs. The world of "Fly" and "She'll Drive the Big Car" would return in Floria Sigismondi's video for "The Stars (Are out Tonight)" a decade later, with Bowie playing a haunted suburban husband.

"Fly" is an Eighties waxwork — its guitar riff is derived from Devo's "Whip It"; a holiday camp keyboard is a tinny voice in a mix overrun by stray instruments. There are even some party bits, like a "dying for the *weekend*" tag. It marks the end of the line for Bowie and Carlos Alomar. By the late Seventies, Bowie and Alomar had developed a sort of industrial songwriting: Bowie as foreman/engineer, Alomar as shop steward. "He comes up with the goods and makes sure of delivery all down the line," as Scott Walker once said of Bowie. But it was Alomar who ensured that the deliveries were made. He hung on through *Tonight* and *Never Let Me Down*, toured Glass Spider, was the odd man out on *1. Outside* and its subsequent tour. His riff on "Fly" is barbed with hooks, as his riffs always were — it's one last funky blessing from Bowie's finest collaborator.

THE LONELIEST GUY

Recorded: (backing tracks) ca. 10 January-15 February 2003; (overdubs) March-May 2003, Looking Glass. Bowie: lead and backing vocal, guitar?, synthesizers; Torn: lead guitar; Garson: Yamaha Disklavier; Visconti: bass; Campbell: drums. Produced: Visconti, Bowie; engineered: Visconti, McNulty.

*First release: 15 September 2003, **Reality**. Broadcast: 27 November 2003, Parkinson. Live: 2003-2004.*

"A very despairing piece of work," Bowie said of "The Loneliest Guy," whose subject is "a guy qualifying his entirely hermetic, isolated existence by saying 'actually I'm a lucky guy. I'm not really alone — I just have myself to look after.'" This type, someone cooped in his room and subsisting on art and memory, is another version of the coked-up magus trapped in his circle, overlooking the ocean; the shut-ins of *Low*; old Algeria Touchshriek. If one end of the Bowie spectrum is the charismatic performer, "The Loneliest Guy" is in his deep ultraviolet range.

Content in domesticity and a parent again, Bowie said he no longer had "that sense of loneliness that I had before, which... became a subtext for a lot of things I wrote." There's no subtext to be found in "The Loneliest Guy," whose sense of lugubriouness and despair is so overwhelming it borders on parody. Bowie's character is such a colossal sad sack that he calls to mind Steve Martin's *The Lonely Guy*, who eats at a table for one with a spotlight trained on him and queues on the Manhattan Bridge to jump into the East River.

Bowie said he'd been inspired by the idea of "a city taken over by weeds," the modernist city of Brasília, which had been built from scratch in the Sixties. The city of a future that never came, its neighborhoods were built in grids, its squares full of modernist stadiums and concert halls. For critics such as Robert Hughes, Brasília was "miles of jerry-built platonic nowhere infested with Volkswagens... the last experiment of its kind. The utopian buck stops here." Bowie called Brasília

the perfect standard for an empty, godless universe... The architect Oscar Niemeyer designed all these places thinking that they were going to be filled with millions of people and now there are about 200,000 people living there, so the weeds and the grass are growing back up through the stones of this brilliantly modernistic city. It's a set of ideas... being taken back over again by the jungle.

This wasn't true about Brasília, whose population is well over two million and is not returning to the wild any time soon. It suggests more Bowie's Hunger City, a modernist grid that's become a dystopian playground, or the capitalist wasteland of "Thru These Architects' Eyes." But the metaphor of a fallen Brasília, the modernist dream consumed by nature, fits the track. "The Loneliest Guy" rots from within, moving as if sleep-stung, rousing to life only to gutter out again, shivering with waves of David Torn's atmospherics (it's possible Bowie recalled the Pretty Things' "Loneliest Person," with its arpeggiated acoustic guitars). Its remote E-flat minor key allows embassies from E major — it yearns to pull into the major in the third verse ("all the pages that have turned...") until an Eb minor chord snuffs out the coup on a precisely-timed sad "oh."

WATERLOO SUNSET

(Davies.) **Recorded**: *(backing tracks) ca. 10 January-15 February 2003; (overdubs) March-May 2003, Looking Glass. Bowie: lead and backing vocals, acoustic guitar, Korg Trinity, keyboards, theremin; Torn, Slick: lead guitar; Garson: Yamaha Disklavier; Plati: bass; Campbell: drums. Produced: Visconti, Bowie; engineered: Visconti, McNulty.*

First release: *10 November 2003 (UK-only download).* **Live**: *2003.*

At a Tibet House concert in 2003 (see "People Have the Power"), Bowie duetted with Ray Davies on "Waterloo Sunset." In the days before the show, they walked around Soho together and Bowie also recorded the song in the studio, issuing it as a bonus track later that year. He and Davies had met in 1964, and for a time shared a producer. More essentially Davies, through his songs, had taught Bowie how to write. He's deep in Bowie's work, from the debut album to the not-so-hidden pieces in later compositions (see "Baby").

"Waterloo Sunset," from 1967, was a capstone for its time. "I started writing a song about Liverpool that implied that the era of Merseybeat was coming to an end, but I changed it to 'Waterloo Sunset' not only because that gave me a bigger canvas to work on but because it was about London, the place where I had actually grown up," Davies wrote in his semi-fictional memoir *X-Ray*. He began with a memory of Waterloo Bridge, watching the Thames nearly cresting its banks. As in many of his songs, an older, homelier England is washed away. If the Beatles promised the world could be new, Davies sang of what was being thrown out: steam trains, china shops, palais halls, dance bands, virginity. The singer of "Waterloo Sunset" keeps to his flat, watches the young on the streets, writes their stories. There's such restless life outside: the dirty river, flowing ever eastward to the sea; the millions in Waterloo Station, pooling from across London and streaming in veins to the suburbs.

Bowie chased away the song's melancholy, made a "Waterloo Sunrise." Embellishments included a nagging two-note synthesizer riff, handclap-fattened drums, shimmering theremin as scene-changer. Only in the coda did he attempt the original's plangent harmonies. In "Waterloo Sunset" the world of movement still has its hiding places — sunset lingers for a while in the summer. Bowie's version has no need of these: it's the sound of a winner's Sixties, a flattened Sixties.

DAYS

Recorded: (backing tracks) ca. 10 January-15 February 2003; (overdubs) March-May 2003, Looking Glass. Bowie: lead and backing vocals, twelve-string acoustic guitar, synthesizers, baritone saxophone; Torn?, Slick: lead guitar; Visconti: bass; Campbell: drums. Produced: Visconti, Bowie; engineered: Visconti, McNulty.

First release: 15 September 2003, **Reality**. **Broadcast**: 4 September 2003, Trafic. musique; 23 September 2003, Sessions @ AOL. **Live**: 2003 -2004.

Tucked midway through *Reality*, "Days" is a sunny self-evisceration. An obvious reference was the Kinks' "Days," that most generous-spirited of breakup songs, in which Ray Davies is heartbroken but grateful for the happiness he was allotted. His memories are all he has left: his gratitude is obsessive. In Bowie's "Days," a man has taken his lover/muse for granted: "all I've done, I've done for me/all you gave, you gave for free." He's racked up such emotional debt that he could never repay it; in the bridge, he finds the nerve to ask for more. Call it another thanks to longtime assistant Coco Schwab (see "Never Let Me Down"), or a prayer (see the Psalm 23:6 reference for the title line, "surely goodness and mercy shall follow me all the days of my life"), a man atoning to a God he doesn't believe in. "I sometimes feel I wrote this song for so many people," Bowie said on stage in Melbourne.

Feinting at G minor to steady itself in F major in refrains, "Days" opens with a modest arrangement — three acoustic guitars, a lead guitar peeking in every other bar until settling down to arpeggiate, a conga/kick drum rhythm. The second verse carts in drums and a piano line soon taken up by synthesizer, which in turn is chased by baritone saxophone. The bridge has a descending bassline, a rumpled bed of synthetic strings, and a small gallery of Bowie voices. Over in a wink, with Bowie sweetly atoning for past and future offenses, its sound would return on *The Next Day*, especially in "So She."

TRY SOME, BUY SOME

*(Harrison.) **Recorded**: (backing tracks) ca. 10 January-15 February 2003; (overdubs) March-May 2003, Looking Glass. Bowie: lead and backing vocal, guitar, Korg Trinity, keyboards; Visconti: bass. Produced: Visconti, Bowie; engineered: Visconti, McNulty.*

***First release**: 15 September 2003, **Reality**. Live: 2003-2004.*

George Harrison died in November 2001. Two years before, he was knifed by a psychotic housebreaker in an attack — close to fatal, with one stab wound nearly puncturing his superior vena cava — that left him weakened against the lung cancer that claimed his life. (In a way, half of the Beatles were murdered at their homes by so-called fans.) A bus driver's son from Liverpool, Harrison was a pop emperor by twenty-one. He tried to ground his wealth and fame in a Hare Krishna blend of stoicism. To use a Philip Roth line, he was the Beatles' unchaste monk, and by middle age, he cared more for gardening than making records. The Beatles songwriter voices were autobiographer (Lennon), novelist (McCartney) and, with Harrison, sermonizer. His sermons could be trying. He lived in a mansion while singing of the illusions of material life; he decried the false wisdom of drugs after having spent years tripping. Yet throughout his work he kept to the same truths. Life is brief, we spend it worrying over pointless things, we lie to ourselves and to each other too much, everything we love will die, and we ultimately know nothing about existence. Why not make peace with your god, or at least tend to your garden?

"For [Harrison], there is a belief in some kind of system," Bowie said in 2003,

> But I really find that hard. Not on a day-to-day basis, because there are habits of life that have convinced me there is something solid to believe in. But when I become philosophical, in those "long, lonely hours," it's the source of all my frustrations, hammering away at the same questions I've had since I was nineteen. Nothing has really changed for me. This daunting spiritual search.

Written in 1970, Harrison's "Try Some, Buy Some" was a song of māyā, the Hindu/Krishna concept that the perceived world is illusory. The material world is a funfair. You overeat, go on rides, buy trinkets, but one day you need to go home. The verses look back to the Sixties — drugs, sex, celebrity parties — while his refrains face the future, to a humbled reconciliation with God. It was a typical Harrison piece in construction. His songs moved like orreries, in weighty orbits "through an unending series of harmonic steps," as Simon Leng wrote. Composed on piano, which Harrison said led to all the "weird chords," its spine was a descending chromatic bassline that hits every semitone from E to B, and a progression that starts on A minor and corkscrews down to D major. As if wanting to make the song more ungainly, Harrison wrote a seesawing top melody and set the piece in 3/4 and in a G minor key that Ronnie Spector, for whom it was intended, found uncomfortable. She said she didn't understand a word of the lyric (nor did he, its composer reportedly replied) but she was a trouper, mastering the rhythms and hitting the high notes.

Issued as Spector's debut single, "Try Some, Buy Some" only hit #77 in the US and didn't chart in Britain. Among the few who bought it at the time was a Beckenham songwriter with a yen for obscurities. "I got [the single] because I was totally ga-ga over Ronnie Spector," Bowie recalled.

"I always thought she was absolutely fantastic." He'd wanted to cover "Try Some, Buy Some" as far back as 1979, when he raved about it during a BBC guest DJ gig. "For me it was a Ronnie Spector song," he said. "It never really occurred to me that I was actually covering a George Harrison song." He said he'd never heard Harrison's version.

"We were pretty true to the original arrangement but the overall atmosphere is somewhat different. It's a dense piece," Bowie said of his cover, which he shifted to D minor. He wanted to free the song from Phil Spector's over-arrangement and give it a more forgiving setting. Unfortunately, this meant a chintzy-sounding Korg Trinity bed. There are some fine touches — his baritone saxophone leading the march to the basement and a guitar hook to distract from the harmonic grinding underneath — and Bowie doesn't try to out-sing Spector but keeps to a comfortable range. Harrison, in his take on the song, had strained at the top of his range, giving it a desperate quality. There's little desperation in Bowie's version, but plenty of sadness. "My connection to the song is about leaving a way of life behind me and finding something new," he said, which suggests he wrote "She'll Drive the Big Car" inspired by it.

His favorite Beatle was his friend John Lennon, but as the years went on Bowie's work became more aligned with Harrison's, even if Bowie could never bring himself to become a believer, or even a gardener. "Try Some, Buy Some" sits near the end of *Reality*, taking up space, spoiling the mood. Harrison would have approved: the song was never meant to go down easily.

BRING ME THE DISCO KING

Recorded: ("first version," unreleased) ca. summer/fall 1992, Hit Factory. New York. Bowie: vocal; Nile Rodgers: guitar?; Garson: piano; Barry Campbell or John Regan: bass?; Sterling Campbell or Poogie Bell: drums?; ("second version," unreleased) ca. August-November 1996, Looking Glass. Bowie: lead vocal; Reeves Gabrels: guitar, loops; Plati: keyboards, loops; Garson: piano; Dorsey: bass; Zachary Alford: drums, loops; (Reality version) (drums) ca. August-September 2001, Allaire Studios; (vocal, piano) ca. spring 2003, Looking Glass. Bowie: lead vocal; Garson: Yamaha S90; Chamberlain: drums; ("Loner Mix") Bowie: lead vocal; Maynard James Keenan: lead vocal; John Frusciante: lead guitar; Lisa Germano: piano, vocal; Danny Lohner: synthesizers; Josh Freese: drums; uncredited musicians:

*strings (arranged: Ed Shearmur). Produced: Visconti, Bowie, Lohner (the "Loner");
engineered: McNulty, Visconti.*

First release: *2 September 2003 ("Loner Mix"),* **Underworld** *(Lakeshore LKS
33781); 15 September 2003,* **Reality**. **Live***: 2003-2004.*

Interview transcript, 5/9/2005, D. Osterman, Rhinebeck, NY:

*I missed the '76 tour but I was there at the Garden in August '77. You've heard the
show, right? Yeah, right? My kid got that boxed set a while back. I didn't want to
hear it. I heard it there, you know? All you need. All **I** need, at least. [inaudible]
Well, okay, the show took forever to get going. Like two hours of lights dimming
and going back up, to all these big moaning groans from the crowd, and this metal-
shredding noise kept playing on the PA, setting everyone on edge. The mood, you
can expect, was just… off. Everyone in my group, five of us, was seriously high —
we had some ludes and some pot that was laced with who knows what. Not just
us. The **whole** crowd was high on something, or were just tensed for something.
Finally the lights went down for good and Bowie came out. He was pin-thin and
wore all black — black suit coat, black rosette in his lapel, black shoes. Black hat?
Maybe. Black cane. Leaned on it a lot. His face and hands were just… I've never
seen skin shine like that. Like moon-skin. And he was still living in LA then,
right? I guess he never went outside [laughs].*

*He started, I remember, with "Five Years," and it was just the slowest,
most dragging version that you could imagine — it was like a year between
the drum hits. And he just stood there, just propped against the mike stand,
and after a long while he started singing, low, real ghostly. [sings] "Pushing
through the market square…" You know how it goes. Then he seemed to kind of
wake up and the band really kicked in. He had, maybe, three guitarists? A guy
on a huge keyboard too. Drummer had a gong.*

*There was a bunch of disco stuff, really savage-sounding stuff. Couldn't
really dance to it: too fast… like "Fame," "Stay," "Calling Sister Midnight,"
"Gimme Sweet Head." He would sing some, then let his band jam for like ten
minutes, then pick it up again. While they played he looked out at the crowd,
like he was looking for someone he knew. He did some new stuff, too, maybe
ones he never recorded, like this one song I just remember he was yelling "bring
me the disco king!" over and over again. That was most of it. His hands were up*

in the air, like someone had a gun on him. Then he did this lunge, this weird
pivot, at the mike and said something like, [deep voice] "here's a new one for
you New Yorkers, it's called 'Blackout!'"

*And remember the blackout had just **happened** just the month before*
*and everyone in that room was probably **there** during it and… I mean, parts*
of the city were probably still on fire then! And he sent what was like an electric
current through the place. Have you ever been on a boat during a storm? The
crowd was… listing? Listing, like, say, the right side of the Garden kind of
convulsed and then it sort of shivered across until the left side got all worked
up. Screams, really big screams, you know. This guy the row down from us
started shaking, having a fit. Making this awful noise, I still remember it, this
little hut-hut-hut-hut-hut sound. Bowie was really caught up in the song, just
wailing, but then he'd crouch, almost squat down on stage, like he was like
holding off punches. I couldn't breathe all of a sudden and my friend Cindy was
crying, so when the strobe lights started, I figured we just had to get out of there.
Nearly got in a fight just getting into the walkway.

We got out on Eighth Ave., probably by "Station to Station," when that
kid got stabbed, right? I was happy to be out. Though I loved Bowie, you know?
Really. I was such a fan. But that wasn't a good place. And what happened to
him in '78 — well, you can't be surprised, really, though, can you?

"It kind of crawled along through the years with me," Bowie said of "Bring
Me the Disco King." The song dated to the start of the Nineties, its first
version recorded in the *Black Tie White Noise* sessions, with Mike Garson
brought in to play a "rather eccentric" piano part for it. Thanks to a journalist
for the *Straits Times* who heard it on a demo tape in 1993, we know that
much of its final lyric was there at the start: "Bowie sings of a time of 'stiff
bad clubs,' 'streets with the good-time girls' and 'a river of perfumed limbs,'
as if bitterly contemptuous of that horrid chapter of his life."

He cut it from *Black Tie* because it clashed with the overall mood, he said
in 1993. "I think the song was written with a sense of irony. I have some
fond memories of the Seventies, especially near the end when I was living
in Berlin, but yes, the song was more about the negativity of the Seventies."
Ten years later, he said the song had been him

trying to summarize my feelings about certain events in my past. I was in
a very happy period when I wrote 'Disco King' in 1991. I was just the most

delighted guy, in a bright new groove. It was a glorious time in my life back then, and I can still feel that vibe now... But I couldn't get the actual feeling of the song right; it was too cynical when I was doing it before.

The track came off too parodic, "play[ing] to the title, alarmingly... I wanted it to sound cheesy and kitschy, and be a kind of real uptempo, disco-y kind of slam at late Seventies disco. And the trouble is, it *sounded* cheesy and kitschy, ha ha! It just didn't work. It didn't have any weight to it." He filed it away and moved on.

Excerpt from Musician and Performer, May 1990 ("The London Boys Are Back"):

Musician: So everyone in the group was in London with you? In the '60s?

Bowie: Yes, although we didn't all work together then, except for John [Hutchinson] and I. Andy [Mackay] wasn't quite there — he was still at university until 1969 or 1970, I believe. But he knew the scene, went to a lot of the shows, same as I did. Bill [Legend] of course was Marc Bolan's drummer, on all the great T. Rex singles. Oh and yes, Herbie [Flowers] was on one of my records and one of Lou's, and he even produced a single of mine that no one ever remembers, called "Holy Holy."

M: And the band's name is a tribute to one of your other old singles? That no one remembers?

B: [Laughs]. It was too obscure to be forgotten! But I always considered it my first proper recording, my first proper song, and it meant a great deal to me. Though to be fair we weren't quite proper London Boys! I was in Beckenham until 1971 or 1972. Hutch was in Canada.

*M: Have you gotten flak for going down this nostalgic route? You're going to be playing a lot of old songs, and you haven't made any new records since **Never Let Me Down**.*

B: Which has few friends, I've found. No, I wouldn't call us a nostalgia act at all. There's a Buzzcocks song that goes, "nostalgia for an age yet to come." Well this is a nostalgia for a past that never was. I think we bring something new to the table. Though of course we've all been on the scene for quite a while. But never quite in this combination.

M: *And this is the last time you're singing your old songs? Are you recording new ones?*

B: *That's the plan, yes. Once we're back from South America later this year, we're going to see what happens in the studio. One possible title is* **Bring Me the Disco King** *[laughs]. You can see the cover image, right? Henry V, ordering some flamboyant conquered foe to be brought to him in irons.*

Bowie had another go at "Bring Me the Disco King" in the *Earthling* sessions four years later ("we did it in a sort of muscular way, like the band was at that particular time"). The second version is documented in a *Rolling Stone* article on a late *Earthling* session in which Mike Garson — through-line of all the song's incarnations — is playing an overdub for it. "It's more Kurt Weill than Hollywood strip," Bowie tells Garson. "Keep it expressionistic and float between the chords... Think Gil Evans — think of the long, plaintive notes in the *Taxi Driver* score! Less virtuosity, more anguish!"

The *Earthling* version had a "pulsating, Kraftwerk-style synth groove," which Bowie described as having "the strange gloss of the Seventies attached to it." Again, there was too much of the past inscribed into the song — he said it still couldn't escape feeling like a heavy-handed parody. Though in the running for *Earthling* until late in the day, "Bring Me the Disco King" again was an outtake.

Excerpt from Simon King, The Royal Scam: A Misspent Youth in the Advertising World (Clearwater: 1999):

Bill said DJ wanted me in his office yesterday. First, a trip to the men's room (I still had some coke from the night before). I was bracing for the worst. So, it seemed, was Bill. "King, bring me the disk before you go upstairs," he said as I was putting on my jacket and pinching some life into my face.

I'd never ever spoken to DJ before, only seen him from across the floor. He worked in three offices — London, Tokyo, here in New York — but was more like some global embodiment of Jones & Bond, his official residence a first-class airplane seat. DJ was a figure of terror in our office. He'd show up on a Friday afternoon and within an hour three people would be sent packing and you'd be reassigned to a new account with a project due Monday morning at 8 AM.

His secretary, who looked like a Modigliani come to life, waved me through. DJ was at his desk, which had nothing resembling work on it. He asked me to sit. It's hard to describe how incredibly striking he was. He was around forty but looked at least a decade younger. No visible work done, just a sense that life hadn't managed to touch him yet. He was steeped in charisma. This was a guy who'd started in the business in '63, when he was barely out of high school or whatever the Brits have, and in two years he was all but running the show at Collett Dickenson Pearce. His own shop by '68. He could have been anything — an actor, a prime minister. (Rumor was that he cut a few Beatles-type singles back then, but no one at J&B ever turned up anything.)

I tried to meet his gaze but it was hard. He had an irregular right pupil, permanently dilated, so naturally you were drawn to it but you also kept trying **not** to stare at it. He, of course, was entirely aware of this situation and used it as a power play, making whoever sat across the desk look at something else. There was a small Japanese lute mounted on the wall, I noticed.

"Simon," he began. "You consider advertising to be beneath your talents. Is that a fair assessment?"

I must have flushed. "You spend your nights in the East Village and say that you're some sort of corrupted artist. I quite empathize, but you must realize yours is a rather tedious existence." He took a Gauloise from his jacket pocket and lit it with a bone-handle lighter that he produced out of thin air. "Substantive art is not born from such a cliché. I was in your shoes once, but I came to realize that advertising has a far greater purchase on the imagination than any painting. What's the promise of art, after all? Immortality? Fame? Sublimity? Power? No, if you want to colonize dreams, if you want to create a **true** desire, something that never existed until **you** thought of it — if you'd like to stage how people regard reality itself, my field, **our** field, offers great promise."

He retrieved another cigarette and pushed it across his desk. "A Tibetan lama once told me there are two forms of art — black magic to turn people's heads and "white" reality art. We've well enough of the latter. Simon, would you care to work on some black magic with me? It should prove interesting, at least."

"Bring Me the Disco King" first appeared in public in 2003, as a remix on the soundtrack of *Underworld* by Nine Inch Nails guitarist Danny Lohner. "We never got in the room with Bowie," Lohner said at the time. "He just sent me some vocals of some stuff he was working on for his new album. I just took the vocals and built a song around it. We used one mono mic on the drums, and they don't sound great... [But we] literally got an e-mail of a vocal and just did our thing. Then we sent it back and he said, 'sounds good.'"

The "Loner Mix" was an alternate version of a track that Bowie was still making, with Lisa Germano on piano and John Frusciante on lead guitar. Josh Freese drums, Maynard James Keenan sings much of it. With Frusciante's looped Fender lines and even a string arrangement, it makes the *Reality* version sound like a cold, polished demo. Given the song's broken history, it's easy to imagine this remix being the only version of "Bring Me the Disco King" ever released. That one of Bowie's great finales would only be known as a mood piece on a Kate Beckinsale vampire movie soundtrack.

"Expatriates In Berlin: Works, 1975-1995" (James Cohan Gallery, until May 23):

> ...*The exhibit includes six works by David Bowie, the former rock performer from the 1970s best known for his gender-fluid chameleon style. Bowie has worked as a painter and avant-garde filmmaker since his retirement. Yet on the canvas his technique shows little improvement over the course of two decades. His subject matter remains obscure and, in its way, provincial.*
>
> *Of the pictures (three in oil, one black pencil, two mixed-media), the most promising is "(Bring Me) The Disco King and His Wives," a 6' x 12' abstract with some furious brushwork and a good sense of scale. That said, it pales next to the work of the other Berlin-based artists featured, especially the Archine sisters. One has to wonder why Bowie has abandoned a field in which he was so capable to devote his time to one in which he'll always be so second rate.*

As there are no circulating demos or outtakes of the song's earlier incarnations, it's impossible to trace the evolution of "Bring Me the Disco King" but through speculation. As per articles at the time, the song apparently evolved from cheeky parody through aggression to end in solitude as the closing track of *Reality*.

On *Reality*, Bowie reduced "Disco King" to a trio of elements. A four-bar drum loop by Matt Chamberlain, taken from the *Heathen* session for "When the Boys Come Marching Home." It's a lesser tempo than the original speed of "Disco King" ("I had those drums on it, the works, you know, it's a 120-beats-a-minute," Bowie said of the *Black Tie* track). There was Bowie's vocal, which he recorded over the Chamberlain loop. And another Garson piano track.

Bowie played Garson the vocal/drum loop track and asked him to develop the song chordally on a Yamaha S90 — to be the middle ground between Chamberlain's loop and his own top melody. "A lot of the voicings and motifs in the chart were just improvised," Garson said in 2004. "I never play it the same way twice." It was meant as a demo performance — Garson returned home with the digital files and played them through his Disklavier MIDI grand player piano, capturing the results with top-quality mikes for a commanding sound. Then Bowie used the original Yamaha S90 track on the recording. Asked why by a baffled Garson, Bowie said he liked it, that's all.

"Short Picks," JazzWeb, 10 May 1998:

Label: King (Disco 1). ***"Bring Me the French Reserves."*** *Zurich free-jazz ensemble Malachi (reportedly including David Bowie among its ranks, though its LPs never have credits) offers two 30-minute free form jams, wildly-distorted alto saxophone, vibraphone, car horns and arco bass.* ★★★★

"Chordal solos can be very interesting. You don't always have to play lightning riffs: they wouldn't support this song's mood anyway," Garson said of his work on "Bring Me the Disco King."

It was a world away from his percussive wizardry on "Aladdin Sane," a piano solo that reportedly terrified Duncan Jones as a child. Garson went to his roots, playing rich jazz chords, his closing solo full of F# minor 11s, F minor 11s and 13s, Bb minor 11s. His opening riff sounds like a slow, truncated version of the intro to Steely Dan's "Kid Charlemagne." Favoring his bass keys, he uses briefly ascending and descending chord figures as hooks, laces Bowie's verse lines with discreet note runs, provides chordal support on Bowie's dramatic pauses, plays off Chamberlain's looped drum figure. In his closing solo, he often only plays two chords per bar, though moving through the occasional harmonic thicket (dense bars with falling triplet chord figures), his hands often working in parallel. In the last bars, he plays whole notes for a bassline and bristling chords with his right hand, keeping within the circle of F minor, E minor, and G minor (the closing chord). He works in gracious service to the song. It was his last performance on a Bowie record.

Excerpt from Hollywood's Greatest Disasters (Methuen: 1988):

*By May 1980, **The Cubists** was $10 million over budget, only four complete scenes had been shot and Tom Stoppard's script was still being revised. After having seen dailies, producer Dino De Laurentiis called a halt for a week and said that he would recast the Braque and Léger roles, much to the consternation of De Niro, who had developed a good rapport with Gérard Depardieu during the shooting of **1900** and was reportedly upset to learn Depardieu would no longer be Léger.*

The replacement leads, however, were warmly received, particularly David Bowie, who played well against De Niro. To the shock of all concerned, the first weeks of resumed filming went smoothly, with most Paris exteriors completed. The move to Cinecittà, however, proved disastrous. Walken fell ill with colitis, De Niro was acting increasingly erratic (at times speaking to the crew in his private dialect of Italian). A stage hand fell to his death, the atelier set was lost in a mysterious fire (some suspected the desperate producer's hand). There was, consecutively, a flood, a rat infestation, a bomb threat by the Red Brigades, a supporting actor suddenly becoming mute, and a second fire.

Throughout it all, Bowie was unflappable, even when summoned to the set by De Laurentiis calling "bring me the disco king." Bowie's long years in live television, co-hosting revues with Petula Clark and Cher, had inured him to chaotic situations on set, and he entertained fellow actors with impromptu songs he played on guitar during the many breaks in filming. De Niro recalled hearing one "about some kind of astronaut rock star" and wished Bowie would have made a "proper album, as he was never really given his due." Walken agreed. "Bowie was the only good thing about it," he said. "It should not have been his last movie."

Throughout "Bring Me the Disco King" Bowie plots the demise of a character he'd played for decades. A command to let him disappear. *Nothing left to release:* expiring in jail but free from the album cycle at least, as he'd earlier punned on "balance" as a life goal and bank statement. There are lines of half-remembered decadence: Los Angeles coke runs; nights in walled Berlin. *Killing time in the Seventies*: wasting one's life in nightclubs but also standing victorious over time (temporarily). *You promised me the ending would be clear*, he begins. Labored over for a decade, existing in a host of parallel lives, "Bring Me the Disco King" set the stage for a world in which David Bowie is a memory.

Song 2

(Albarn, Coxon, James, Rowntree.) **Live**: *7 October 2003- 25 June 2004. Bowie: lead vocal, rhythm guitar, twelve-string acoustic guitar, Stylophone; Slick, Leonard: guitar; Garson: piano, keyboards; Dorsey: bass, vocal; Campbell: drums; Russell: vocal, guitar, keyboards, percussion.*

Bowie's last tour — nine months, 22 countries, 112 shows — was hubristic in its energy and length. Every night he played for at least two hours and sometimes had thirty-plus song setlists. *Take it easy, man!* you want to yell when you see a concert clip. But fan reports, newspaper reviews, the tour diaries of Gail Ann Dorsey, and videos all document a man in apparent robust health, in fine voice, eager to play.

After his road-heavy mid-Nineties, where he'd held his own with Nine Inch Nails and the Prodigy, he'd gotten a taste for the stage. "It was not something I looked forward to very much," Bowie said of touring,

> I've always loved the putting together everything. I love the idea of making albums and writing albums and conceptualizing and all that side of the thing, you know? The actual going out on the road side of the thing — one, I never thought I was that good at it, and two, I just didn't enjoy the process too much. I don't know, maybe because I didn't feel competent as an artist.

Planned since 2001, the *Reality* tour's impetus was in great part financial (i.e., the impetus behind every tour). Bowie's later albums had sold modestly, and making a living by selling albums was becoming impossible, he said. "I don't see any hope for the industry at all. We're watching it collapse — it's definitely imploding — and it's become a source of irrelevance." It would be his widest-ranging tour in years: he hadn't been to Singapore and Hong Kong since 1983, Australia and New Zealand since 1987. Using the goliath Clear Channel Entertainment, Bowie's team drafted a flexible schedule — he'd play the arenas he knew could sell out but would book two-thousand-seat theaters in less predictable markets. He often underestimated demand. The tour wound up grossing $46 million, even with its premature end.

His band — Dorsey and Sterling Campbell, Mike Garson, guitarists Gerry Leonard (playing the "Fripp," "Belew" and "Gabrels" role) and Earl Slick (playing himself) and a recent addition: Catherine Russell, a utility player who sang, played keyboards, percussion and guitar — were an adept, no-nonsense crew who kept to established arrangements, aided by a sound mix in which "David's voice sits on top, but this is not a Vegas-style show. The band is every bit as present as they need to be," said front-of-the-house engineer Pete Keppler. Learning that Bob Dylan had seventy songs in his touring repertoire, Bowie pushed his band to learn sixty of his, altering the setlists regularly. This churn was hard on his players — after one show in Paris where Bowie swapped in a bunch of under-rehearsed songs, Dorsey wrote the band "all felt as if we had fumbled through a tough football match we knew we had lost from the beginning."

Bowie put hits ("singalong time," he called it) cheek-by-jowl with the likes of "The Motel" and "The Loneliest Guy" in a typical set. "I can't do a full evening's worth of those songs [like "Starman"] because I'll go barmy. You become a karaoke machine," he said ("look mum, I'm a jukebox!" he said after singing "Starman" one night). "Judging by the audience reaction, I think I've done the right thing," he said midway through the tour. "I think I've chosen quite accurately how far I can go with quite new and obscure things, and how much I should balance that with pieces everybody knows." The fair-weather portion of audiences grew impatient. "Give us some *hits*, Davey!" one man yelled in Toronto between songs.

Wearing a tattered jacket, jeans, t-shirt and scarf and leather boots or Chuck Taylors, Bowie had regular bits (a runway strut for "Fashion," Pierrot-isms for "Ashes to Ashes," drag queen moves for "China Girl"), joked and bantered with the crowd, had them sing "All the Young Dudes." "Constantly grinning," *Billboard* noted of his performance in New York. In Berkeley he "pranced theatrically, calling himself the Artful Dodger, imitated Americans and Americans imitating the British." It was shtick, he told journalists. "If there's a sense of seriousness, that comes in the songs themselves... Performing isn't a life-threatening situation in the scheme of things." He was back to being the fey, witty singer of his folk duo "Bowie and Hutch," who'd made his hippie audiences crack up between numbers. Or the would-be cabaret star from 1968, breaking into medleys during songs, he or Dorsey or Russell singing bits of Frank Zappa's "It Can't Happen Here" or Dionne Warwick's "Do You Know the Way to San Jose." A favorite bit was for the band to tear into Blur's "Song 2," revving up crowds, as if Blur had written the song for Bowie to use as incidental music.

Just for One Night

Early summer 2004 was dismal in northern Europe, with many Bowie festival appearances that June plagued by rains and wind. At the Norwegian Wood Festival in Oslo, on 18 June, he was struck in the eye by a lollipop, causing him to understandably lose his shit for a moment. The next festival, in Finland, passed uneventfully. Then came Prague.

He opened with "Life on Mars?" for the first time on the tour. Eight songs in, while singing "Reality," those in the front rows saw him struggling to finish the song. He left the stage, the band going into "A New Career in a New Town" and "Be My Wife" (sung by Catherine Russell). "That's not supposed to happen," Leonard recalled thinking. "He was really feeling terrible. It happened right there on the stage: that's showbiz." Returning to apologize, Bowie blamed a trapped nerve in his shoulder. He sang "China Girl" and left again after an aborted "Station to Station." The show still didn't end. The persona he'd developed, the music man who gave you a bang for your buck, wouldn't let him rest. He returned to finish "Station to Station" and sing "Modern Love" and "The Man Who Sold the World," sitting on a stool, clutching his arm. Maj Halova of Prague, who was at the show, told me that the crowd knew something was wrong: "There might have been a few boos because it got cut short, but I think mostly we were confused and a bit worried." Bowie apparently had a heart attack that night, and it may not have been the first. Reeves Gabrels later told Marc Spitz that he'd known for years that Bowie was dealing with chest pains.

There was one more show.

The annual Hurricane Festival is held on a motorcycle racetrack in Scheeßel, a German village southwest of Hamburg. It's an unassuming place to close a story that began on 16 June 1962, when the fifteen-year-old David Jones had his first-ever public gig, playing with the Kon-Rads at the Bromley Tech PTA Fete. At Hurricane, those in the crowd noticed nothing amiss during the set, with Bowie moving around and playing guitar (he seemed to have a twinge of pain during "Ashes to Ashes," clutching his arm again). As evening drew in, it got colder, the North Sea winds coming across the Lower Saxony plains. Bowie donned a grey hooded sweatshirt. He looked like a handsome, tired dad at a football game. Or as the writer Chris Barrus said, like a fishing boat captain weathering a storm.

The next day, at St. Georg Hospital in Hamburg, a surgeon performed an angioplasty to treat a blocked artery in Bowie's heart, inserting a stent to open a blood vessel narrowed by plaque. He was in hospital for over a week and cancelled his remaining festival appearances. He said he was unhappy that the tour had ended this way but that he was feeling better and hoped to "get back to work" within a month.

At Scheeßel, Bowie closes his main set with "Heroes." Leonard plays an ascending, choppy figure on guitar, moving against Campbell's snare and cymbals. Bowie holds back, knotting his fingers beneath his chin (he does a little dolphin dance). Slick comes in, cool and indifferent, chewing gum. At last, the wailing Fripp riff (via Leonard's EBow) and Bowie starts drawing power from somewhere in him, diving into the song, surfacing, pushing through it. *And the SHAME spread on the OTHER SIDE!*, gesturing towards Berlin to the east. *And NOTHING and NO ONE will HELP us!* Campbell plays hard enough to light a city. The moment has chosen itself. This is the wake for David Bowie.

(SHE CAN) DO THAT

(Bowie, Transeau). **Recorded**: *(vocals) ca. winter-spring 2005, Looking Glass. Bowie: lead and backing vocal; Kristeen Young: backing vocal; (music) ca. winter-spring 2005, Los Angeles. Brian Transeau: synthesizers, keyboards, programming. Produced: Transeau, Visconti.*

First release: *12 July 2005,* **Stealth** *(Epic EK 94475).*

For seven long years, the last new recording issued under Bowie's name was "(She Can) Do That," a dance track on the soundtrack of *Stealth*, a 2005 film that was a commercial and critical disaster. He wrote the lyrics and topline melody; the rest was by producer Brian Transeau (aka BT) and the Berklee professor Richard Boulanger. After he'd convalesced, after years of making brooding albums and "Last Songs," here was something new: *keep going — don't stop now — keep going — take cover — keep going — be cool.*

In early 2005, Bowie cut his vocal at Looking Glass, with Kristeen Young on harmonies. "I was just hanging around the studio. It was a time when (on a few songs) David had me double his vocal an octave higher," she wrote in 2016. Bowie "kept saying, 'I don't want to write this. Do YOU want to write this?' I was naïve and thought he was joking... but now, I don't think he was." Bowie sent the Pro Tools files to BT in Los Angeles, where BT filled the track with trademarks like "stutter" edits, vocal pitch shifting, and subtle time changes.

What was Bowie doing? A tip of the hat to the *Hamtaro* theme song? An update of "Right," another song where he'd bucked himself up in a dark time? Most likely he put as much thought into "(She Can) Do That" as he did his coffee order at Dean and DeLuca the morning he cut it. If the brief was to make a dance song for a Jamie Foxx version of *Top Gun*, updated for the War on Terror, there aren't many viable options.

It was a tentative step back into the studio after his recuperation. Visconti and Bowie were planning a new album, with Bowie telling jazz musician Courtney Pine, in a radio interview in September 2005, that he was currently writing songs ("it looks pretty weird, so I'm happy"). There was ambivalence in his tone. Asked what his fans were expecting, Bowie said "oh they don't expect anything these days, I think they just sort of wait and see what I put out... it's the luck of the draw and sometimes it works really well and sometimes it's godawful... but that's the way it goes and I like that." He wanted a break from the *Heathen/Reality* sound — cutting an instrumental album, doing something "experimental" or "techy," with David Torn in a central role. Did he listen to playback of "(She Can) Do That" and swear off making records for a decade? Happily, in 2013 this atrocity became trivia.

THE CYNIC

*(Eistrup). **Recorded**: March-April 2005, Sun Studio, Dortheavej 4, 2400 Copenhagen, Denmark; (Bowie vocal) ca. late April-May 2005, Looking Glass. Bowie: lead vocal; Kaspar Eistrup: lead vocal, guitar; Henrik Lindstrand: keyboards, guitar; Mads Tunebjerg: bass; Asger Techau: drums. Produced: Kashmir, Visconti, engineered: Visconti, McNulty, Andreas Hviid.*

***First release**: 10 October 2005, **No Balance Palace** (Columbia 82876 72767 2).*

Bowie spent the years after his operation in semi-retirement but not in seclusion. He sampled bands who played New York, wearing a cap and sporting, at times, a mustache and beard. He became a routine sighting for blogs like *Brooklyn Vegan*, to the point where if Bowie *didn't* show up at your gig, your band had some issues. How did he have so much time? Dave Itzkoff asked him in 2005. "Fortunately, I'm not working [laughs]. So I'm resting. I get out a lot... I love seeing new bands, art shows, everything. I get everywhere — very quietly and never above 14th Street. I'm very downtown."

"I remember turning around, at a Mission of Burma reunion show at the Bowery Ballroom, and seeing Bowie, alone, standing in the shadows, soaking the music in, slipping away before the last song," the writer Alex Abramovich recalled. "Friends in the city were always seeing him at shows — he might have been secretive, but Bowie was so distinctive, and so beautiful, he wasn't easy to miss — and not at all the ones you'd have expected him to attend." Bowie saw TV on the Radio and the Arctic Monkeys, Secret Machines and Scissor Sisters (he sent an email to the latter's Jake Shears, saying "it sounded very good from where I was sitting," causing Shears to frantically parse that line for days, wondering if it was an insult). He saw Franz Ferdinand at the Roseland Ballroom, Interpol at the Hammerstein Ballroom, Clap Your Hands Say Yeah! at the Knitting Factory, Arcade Fire at the Bowery Ballroom, the Killers at Irving Plaza.

Tony Visconti attended the latter (in October 2004), bringing as his plus-one the Danish singer and guitarist Kasper Eistrup of Kashmir, a band Visconti was planning to produce. They met Bowie in the VIP balcony.

True to form, Bowie knew Eistrup's band, praised their albums, then talked about culture, politics and whatever else was on his mind that evening. The three shared a ride afterward.

When working on Kashmir's album in Copenhagen in March 2005, Visconti thought one track, "The Cynic," ("it had the vibe of a Kurt Cobain song influenced by Bowie") could use a Bowie vocal, to the point where he did Bowie imitations for scratch vocals. In New York in late April 2005, when Visconti, Eistrup and Kashmir bassist Mads Tunebjerg were doing mixing and post-production at Looking Glass, Bowie appeared "fresh as a daisy and enthusiastically sang the be-Dickens out of 'The Cynic' as if he'd written it himself," Visconti said. Tunebjerg recalled that Bowie already had the track on his iPod, so he "had one or two runs and he was there." Bowie even played a role in the video, a Constructivist-inspired piece in which he, looking like the Patrick Troughton incarnation of The Doctor, played Death as a butler. "The Cynic" was adequate post-Radiohead rock, with Bowie easily handling Eistrup's melody, enjoying the long vowels of the refrains. Bowie could've fashioned a take on Interpol or Franz Ferdinand well enough, but he was happier in the audience now.

PROVINCE

(Malone, Sitek.) **Recorded**: *ca. June-August 2005, November 2005, Stay Gold Studio, Williamsburg, NYC. Tunde Adebimpe: lead vocal; Kyp Malone: lead vocal; Bowie: harmony vocal; Dave Sitek: guitar, bass, sampler, keyboards; Gerard Smith: piano; Jaleel Bunton: drums. Produced: Sitek; engineered: Sitek, Chris Coady.*

First release: *6 July 2006, **Return to Cookie Mountain** (Interscope B0007466-02/4AD CAD2607, UK #90, US #41).*

In 2003, Dave Sitek, an artist and musician from Brooklyn, gave a painting to Bowie's doorman, who promised he'd pass on the CD of Sitek's band, TV on the Radio. Two years later, Bowie sang on one of their tracks. (Advice to the ambitious young: cultivate good relations with doormen.) Sitek formed the band with fellow illustrator Tunde Adebimpe, soon adding Kyp Malone, Jaleel Bunton, and the late Gerard Smith. They were part of the turn-of-the-century Williamsburg scene that also spawned the Liars and the Yeah Yeah Yeahs (a short-lived era — Sitek had to close his studio in 2009 after his landlord tripled the rent).

Bowie mentored TV on the Radio, listening to early mixes of their first album. He was making up for lost time — for much of his life, he'd been so consumed with work that he'd had few opportunities to develop younger acts (like Devo, whose debut he'd wanted to produce but starred in *Just a Gigolo* instead). So when the band was recording in summer 2005, Bowie offered to help, even if it meant coming to Brooklyn. "I told him, 'If you want to come into the studio and be the boss of things, you totally can,'" Sitek said in 2008. "I gave him the demos of the songs, and 'Province' just really resonated with him... He just showed up at my studio and did it." The challenge was how to fit Bowie into an already-dense vocal arrangement with Adebimpe and Malone. He starts the first verse as the high end of the harmony (his typical guest-star role) but is soon overshadowed by Malone. He spends the rest of the track fighting to be heard, sometimes following Adebimpe's lead, capturing the occasional phrase, sliding in low for refrains. One of his more democratic moments since Tin Machine.

WAKE UP
REFLEKTOR

*(Butler, Butler, Chassagne, Kingsbury, Parry [+ Gara on "Reflektor"]) **Broadcast**: "Wake Up," 8 September 2005, Radio City Music Hall, New York. Win Butler: lead vocal, guitar, tambourine; Bowie: lead vocal, twelve-string acoustic guitar; Régine Chassagne: keyboards, vocals; William Butler: rhythm guitar, vocals; Richard Reed Parry: bass drum, tambourine, accordion, vocals; Sarah Neufeld: violin; Owen Pallett: violin; Tim Kingsbury: bass; Jeremy Gara: drums. **Recorded**: "Reflektor" (music) ca. 2011-2012, Sonovox Studios, Montréal; (Bowie backing vocal, ca. late March 2013, Electric Lady Studios, New York City). Produced: Arcade Fire, Markus Dravs, Mark Lawson, James Murphy.*

***First release**: ("Wake Up") 14 November 2005, **Live at Fashion Rocks**; ("Reflektor") 9 September 2013 (download, UK #44, US #99). **Live**: ("Wake Up") 2005.*

Some of it's the lighting and TV facepaint. For the first time in his life, Bowie looks frail and old. Something's been wrung out of him. The band Arcade Fire crowds around him on the stage and he's happy for the company, happy to be mistaken for one of them.

On 8 September 2005, he performed for the first time since his heart operation, for a ceremony in which the fashion industry donates to a catastrophe elsewhere (post-Katrina New Orleans that year) — "Fashion Rocks." Strumming a twelve-string acoustic guitar, Bowie takes the first verse of Arcade Fire's "Wake Up," his phrasing two-beat jabs. *Some-thing... filled up... my heart... with **nothing.*** His movements are guarded. On the communal refrains (even the string players join in), he holds back, stepping away from the mike then swaying back in, a shaky pitch in the harmonies.

It was a performance by "Bowie in Recovery." He'd shown up that night dressed as if he'd been in a fight, with a bandaged hand and one eye made up to look blackened, and he opened with "Life on Mars?" with only Mike Garson on piano. In diminished voice (the vault on "sai-lors" a modest lift), he took the song at a distance, appraising it. And he sang "Five Years," with Arcade Fire as his backing band. "Five years! God, that's all we got!" he shouted towards the end, his voice fraying.

Arcade Fire's Win Butler was an American, from Texas, no less, home of the president; his father had worked for Halliburton. He ran off to Canada, fell in love, formed a band in Montréal with his wife, brother, and friends. Arcade Fire trafficked in childhood: flip-books in their *Neon Bible* box, *Yellow Submarine* graphics in their videos, their neighborhood jamboree performances, the school music room garnishes — sleigh bells, accordions, harpsichords, xylophones. Bowie was fascinated. "Arcade Fire has a very strong theatrical flair, a boisterous, college kind of feel to what they're doing, and also there's a wave of enthusiasm to it," he said in 2005. "But their show is theatrical nonetheless, because it doesn't alter much from night to night." After the Fashion Rocks performance, Bowie joined the band the following week, singing "Queen Bitch" and "Wake Up" in their encore at SummerStage in New York.

Arcade Fire's records became more spacious, losing the edge of *Funeral*. The title track of their fourth album, 2013's *Reflektor*, was a secret reunion with Bowie (credited only in the "thank you" section of the liners). Soon after the release of *The Next Day*, he visited the band in New York while they were mixing. Richard Reed Parry said he liked "Reflektor" enough that "he basically threatened us... 'if you don't hurry up and mix this song, I might just steal it from you!' So we thought, well why don't we go one better, why don't you sing on our version?" A few days later, engineers set up a Neumann U47 mike and "when Bowie came in he sang quite a bit, giving us many options even though his was not necessarily a featured part," engineer Korey Richey said. In 2016, Arcade Fire would be among Bowie's more prominent mourners, organizing a second line parade for him in New Orleans.

ARNOLD LAYNE
COMFORTABLY NUMB

(Barrett ["Arnold Layne"]; Waters, Gilmour ["Comfortably Numb"].) **Live**: *29 May 2006, Royal Albert Hall, London. David Gilmour: lead vocal, lead guitar; Bowie: lead vocal; Phil Manzanera: guitar, vocals; Richard Wright: keyboards, vocals; Dick Parry, Jon Carin: keyboards, vocals; Guy Pratt: bass; Steve DiStanislao: drums, vocals. Produced: Gilmour.*

First release: *("Arnold Layne") 26 December 2006 (EM 717); ("Comfortably Numb") 17 September 2007,* **Remember That Night: David Gilmour, Live at the Royal Albert Hall** *(EMI 504 3119/Columbia Music Video 88697 13913 9).*

Pink Floyd's David Gilmour played the Royal Albert Hall for three nights in late May 2006. At the first show, with no fanfare, Bowie walked out to sing "Arnold Layne" and "Comfortably Numb." Along with his performances with Arcade Fire the previous autumn, it suggested he was testing the waters for a return to public life.

On Pink Floyd's misanthropic *The Wall*, "Comfortably Numb" has B minor verses with Roger Waters in his favorite role as a manipulative bureaucrat — here, a doctor reviving the catatonic rock star Pink so he can perform. Its Gilmour-sung D major refrains were the needle hitting the vein. On stage, Bowie struggled to find his footing in "Comfortably Numb," particularly the verses, which had a near-conversational melody that Waters had written for his cracked voice (it began as a Dylan parody), Bowie elevated his phrasings and worried through the song.

He was more comfortable singing "Arnold Layne," Pink Floyd's first single. The characters of Bowie's debut album — the little bombardier, cross-dressing barkeep and Uncle Arthur — were kin to the knicker-thief and jailbird Layne. Bowie savored the Mockney rhymes ("now 'ees *cort*/a nahsty *sort*") and jibed the refrains: "takes *two* to know! Two to *know*!"

flashing a V-for-victory sign. Gilmour and Waters keep on, with Waters still touring *The Wall*, which has been around longer than the Berlin one was. Bowie never performed in Britain again.

PUG NOSED FACE

(Bowie, Gervais, Merchant.) **Recorded**: *5-7 June 2006, Elberts, Pegs Lane, Hertford, Hertfordshire. Bowie: vocal; Clifford Slapper: piano.*

First broadcast: *21 September 2006, Extras (Series 2, Episode 2 "David Bowie").* **Live**: *2007.*

Bowie was a fan of *Extras*, Ricky Gervais and Stephen Merchant's follow-up to *The Office*. Where *The Office* was provincial failure, *Extras* diagnosed a broader malaise: millennial Britain's obsession with fame and status. Plots centered on the humiliations and grievances of Gervais' character, actor Andy Millman. Gervais asked Bowie to perform in an episode. The set-up has the barely-famous Millman at a high-end bar, hoping for a sympathetic ear from Bowie. After a few nods, Bowie turns to a piano for an impromptu song: "Little fat man, who sold his soul... chubby little loser... see his pug nosed face!" It's a fan's nightmare: you fail Bowie's hip test and get stilettoed in public.

Bowie asked for an English rock pianist, so producer Charlie Hanson contacted Clifford Slapper (who would later write Mike Garson's biography). Gervais and Merchant had written the lyric as part of their script, so both Bowie and Slapper were asked to write chords. When they met, they discovered their pieces were nearly the same: A major progressions with "classic" Bowie modulations, as Slapper told me. Bowie filmed his *Extras* scene in the first week of June 2006, with one day for rehearsal and another for filming. As "Pug Nosed Face" was cut live, Slapper played off-camera to voice the piano that Bowie played on set (the latter's action was disengaged). It was the last public image of Bowie for years: a nattily-dressed man leading yuppies in a round of joyous humiliation. In 2007, for his final performance in public, Bowie introduced Gervais at Madison Square Garden with an *a cappella* "Pug Nosed Face," the crowd joining on the refrain. He bowed out with a jeer.

FALLING DOWN
FANNIN STREET

(Waits ["Falling Down"], Waits, Brennan ["Fannin Street"].) **Recorded***: ca. late April-May 2007, Dockside Studio, 4755 Woodland Road, Maurice, Louisiana; (Bowie vocals) ca. late summer 2007, Avatar Studios. Scarlett Johansson: lead vocal; Bowie: harmony vocals; Bunton: acoustic guitar; Sitek: guitar, sampler; Nick Zinner: slide guitar; Sean Antanaitis: pump organ, "guitorgan," vibes, banjo, piano, bells, tambourine, synthesizer; Ryan Sawyer: drums, tambourine, vibraphone, tom tom. Produced: Sitek, engineered: Sitek, Chris Moore.*

First release*: 19 May 2008,* **Anywhere I Lay My Head** *(ATCO 8122 79925 8/ R1 454524, UK #64, US #126).*

Scarlett Ingrid Johansson is a New Yorker, born and raised. She's made over fifty films and is not yet thirty-five. Though she wanted to sing in musicals in her youth, she never got the Annie or Cosette roles thanks to having a deep voice even as a child. But in 2006, she sang "Summertime" for a compilation distributed by Rhino, who then asked her to record a full album. Knowing she'd get belittled for whatever she made, she decided to be truly indulgent and hit upon the idea of a Tom Waits cover album.

Early sessions with jazz musicians "sounded awful," so she sought out Dave Sitek from TV on the Radio. Sitek saw his chance to cut a Lee Hazlewood/Nancy Sinatra mood record, the dream of every indie dude in the 2000s. Cut in late spring 2007 in Louisiana, the album (*Anywhere I Lay My Head*) was mostly latter-day Waits compositions. Sitek went for what he called a "cough medicine tinker-bell vibe," making Johansson part of a gentle clatter: Tibetan bowls, music boxes, pump organs, bass harmonicas, kalimbas, cicada buzzes.

Johansson and Bowie had both acted in Christopher Nolan's *The Prestige*, though having no scenes together. Afterward they met at a dinner in New York, where Bowie said he'd heard she was working with Sitek. "I jokingly said, 'You know, let me know if you want to come! Anytime — I'll drive you!'," she said. "And then one day when I was in Spain shooting [*Vicky Cristina Barcelona*], I got this call from Dave, and he was like, 'You'll never guess who I have in the studio right now'." Bowie showed up at Avatar Studios during mixing, having gone to the trouble of getting sheet music.

Sitek had suggested he sing on "Falling Down" and "Fannin Street," which he did, and "I Don't Wanna Grow Up," for which he felt he couldn't add anything.

In "Fannin Street," Waits leaned on Leadbelly's song of the same title. He recalls a warning he'd never heed, with a refrain melody that seemed fished from a riverbed. For Leadbelly, "Fannin Street" was where the night never ends; for Waits, it's a damnation. In her version, Johansson slips into the murk on her lowest notes. She cedes the mourning to Bowie, whose four-part harmonies build, by the closing refrain, to gorgeous hysteria.

Given its line "come from St. Petersburg/Scarlett and me," her singing "Falling Down" was inevitable. Waits had exploited his smashed voice — a man, a hotel, a world is in freefall, shattering itself apart. Johansson moves through the wreckage, watching through glass like Iggy Pop's passenger. Bowie starts by muttering in the margins ("I've-come-five-hundred-miles" he whispers) and then rises to shadow her in the refrains. By the last verse he's her equal: sounding the loss that she refuses to accept.

CHAPTER FOURTEEN:

AGENT JEFFRIES REPORTS IN

(2011-2013)

Fortunately for me my right lung collapsed and put a stop to the whole charade. And I felt a great sense of relief, as if, once again, I'd been let off the hook.
— Brian Eno, 1977

It made him a prisoner of his own departure.
— Michel Foucault, *Madness and Civilization*

David did nothing by halves. When he dropped out, he vanished.
— Mick Ronson

The exile thing is within yourself.
— Scott Walker

I feel tempted to communicate some of my experiences to them, some fruits of my long solitude.
— Rainer Maria Rilke

You can't talk to the dead through a wireless. You have to do it another way.
— Howard Norman, *The Bird Artist*

One always thinks everything's got worse — and in most respects it has — but that's meaningless. What does one mean when one says that things are getting worse? It's becoming more like the future, that's all. It's just moving ahead.
— Paul Bowles

WHERE ARE WE NOW?

Recorded: (backing tracks) 13 September 2011, The Magic Shop, 49 Crosby Street, New York; (vocal) 22 October 2011, (last overdubs) ca. spring 2012, Human Worldwide, 27 West 20th St., Suite 801, New York. David Bowie: lead vocal, keyboards; Gerry Leonard: lead guitar; Henry Hey: piano; Tony Levin: bass; Zachary Alford: drums; Tony Visconti: strings. Produced: Bowie, Visconti; engineered: Mario McNulty, Visconti.

First release: 8 January 2013 (ISO MP3: 886443826403) (UK #6).

Wedding

An older man, wearing a grey topcoat and knit cap, walks through Berlin one winter morning. If you were to follow him, he'd appear to be rambling towards no apparent destination, going through neighborhoods, sometimes doubling back. But seen from the air, his progress follows stitch lines across the heart of the once-sundered city.

Pankow

On the morning of 8 January 2013, at 5am GMT, the video of David Bowie's new single "Where Are We Now?" appeared on YouTube, while his website noted that one could buy the track on iTunes and pre-order a new album. By the time the British workday began, Bowie's return was getting the sort of media attention reserved for royal births and separations (it helped that a handful of key journalists and media outlets had gotten a heads-up from Bowie's British PR firm the night before). Each longitude of the Western Hemisphere woke up to the news in turn. "It was his idea to just drop it at midnight on his birthday and just let things avalanche," Tony Visconti said. At midnight in New York, Visconti sat at his computer to watch "Where Are We Now?" pop into existence. He'd produced it but couldn't quite believe it was there.

Among the first "surprise" album releases of the 2010s, *The Next Day* was a catalog artist gaming a broken system. Eliminate the promo cycle and throw a new album into the world; get press by leveraging the reputation that your former labels built. Bowie pulled off his caper by using musicians whom he could trust (still, he had them sign non-disclosure agreements). He recorded in a discreet studio near his home and ran a tight ship: Coco Schwab and Bill Zysblat for logistics and finance, no office staff. At Sony, with whom he had a distribution relationship, he had no A&R supervision. Sony president Rob Stringer only learned of the new Bowie album about a month before its release.

Weißensee

Much of Bowie's "lost years" between autumn 2004 and the release of *The Next Day* is a blank, and may always be. Once a voluble emailer, Bowie cut off contact with many friends after his surgery, even for a time Visconti, who was startled when Bowie popped in during a Dean and Britta session in New York in late 2006. By the end of the decade, Bowie and Visconti had regular lunches, where Bowie said he had no interest in writing new music.

The paparazzi got a fresh photo on a semi-annual basis, usually a shot of Bowie, with ubiquitous laptop bag, walking downtown or hailing cabs. He did the occasional guest-vocal, issued a statement praising Barack Obama's victory; he spoke to the press as late as 2010, telling the *Observer* what was on his iPod (Champion Jack Dupree's "Junker's Blues" and John Adams' "El Niño," among others) and the *New York Times* that "I'm not thinking of touring. I'm comfortable." Fan websites were reduced to covering reissues, the deaths of Bowie's old friends and collaborators, and the doings of Bowie tribute bands. "I really don't know what he's up to at the moment," Gail Ann Dorsey said in early 2010. "I just hope, as much as anyone else, as a fan of music, that he returns."

He was rumored to be ailing. It was said he'd had a stroke, had suffered more heart attacks, had terminal cancer, to the point where Noel Gallagher said in 2011 that "I know [Bowie] hasn't been very well, but we need him," and Chuck Klosterman and Alex Pappademas began preparing a Bowie obituary in June 2012 after *Grantland*'s editor got a tip Bowie was on his deathbed. (The rumors were true, it turned out; it was just that the timing was off.)

Prenzlauer Berg

To the *Big Issue* in 1999, Bowie said his public persona "doesn't affect me as

Jonesy. Bowie was always a poster boy, his is the thing that goes out there in the entertainment world and Jonesy can stay at home." The poster boy was folded up. It was now only Jonesy: a late-middle-aged art collector, family man, voracious reader, comfortable tourist, and lover of police shows, whether American (*The Shield*), British (*Foyle's War*) or French (*Spiral*). He still led a public life, attending charity galas with Iman, but he was no longer public. His absence grew louder each year.

Then in early autumn 2010, while in London recording Kaiser Chiefs' *The Future Is Medieval,* Visconti heard from Bowie out of the blue. He said he wanted to record demos with Visconti, Gerry Leonard, and Sterling Campbell once Visconti was back in New York. "My relationship with David has always been like this," Campbell said. "I just get a call out of nowhere and it's great if it works out." As his fellow drummer Zachary Alford said, "from what I understand, [Bowie] didn't even wanna think about music for a number of years. Then all of a sudden, he's got twenty songs he wants to record."

In November 2010, the four of them worked for a week at 6/8 Studios in the East Village, a studio they described as "a matchbox," "a little dungeon," and "a small grimy room." Bowie brought in demos he'd made on digital recorders. To Visconti, these were "obviously things that had built up over the past ten years, sketches he'd had all along," complete with basslines and drum patterns (Leonard concurred: "It seemed evident that he had been writing a lot — [like] he was pulling ideas for songs from a hat"). Writing was never the issue. It was that his confidence was shaky, that he feared releasing an album only to see it be condescended to in the press: sounding a bit old, a bit tired, a bit boring. Another aging rocker's newest space-filler.

At 6/8, Bowie played a home demo, had Leonard transcribe a chord progression, asked the group for their interpretation. On their last day, they cut roughly a dozen full-band demos (Bowie played keyboards and sang guide vocals, mainly wordless melodies) on what Visconti called "a basic Pro Tools rig." Bowie packed up, said his goodbyes. No one heard from him for over four months.

Mitte

He resurfaced in early spring 2011, now wanting the same crew for a potential album. As Campbell was touring with the B-52's, Alford got the call. As did Dorsey — Visconti wanted to focus on producing and not bass parts. David Torn, the atmospheric element of *Heathen* and *Reality*, played live with fellow musicians for the first time on a Bowie album. Unfortunately, the studio was so cramped that Torn said he often took one for the team and played in the console room.

Recording began at the Magic Shop (close to Bowie's home on Lafayette Street) on 2 May 2011, for what would be the first block of the *Next Day* sessions. There was little groundbreaking about the new songs. Bowie knew his players' styles (though he urged Dorsey to play fretless bass for the first time), to the point where it sounded in places as if he was making the album he'd intended to do in 2004, when he told Leonard and Campbell he was considering hustling the band into the studio to cut a road-cooked album like *Earthling*.

He kept stressing that the sessions were an experiment, one he could well scrap. He came in each morning, played a home demo and its full-band demo (everyone was encouraged to ask questions, as if Bowie was a professor emeritus in a seminar with grad students). No more than five takes for each track; on average, two tracks a day. They played in the Magic Shop's "live" room, Studio A, with no separation between musicians barring some amp baffles. Bowie set up at a Baldwin piano, making a work station where he could play a Korg Trinity or his twelve-string acoustic, and use a digital mixer to reference demos. Engineer Mario McNulty said Bowie and Visconti wanted a treated sound at the point of recording, so that in-studio playback would "sound like a record on playback" (Bowie's long-preferred method — he'd been startled in early *Young Americans* sessions to hear his untreated voice on tape.) Using the studio's Neve 80 series wraparound fifty-six-input console, McNulty applied EQ in each stereo channel and put generous compression levels on most inputs.

Tiergarten

Of the first recording block, nine tracks made it onto *The Next Day*. That September, Bowie and Visconti organized another date at the Magic Shop. As Dorsey was touring with Lenny Kravitz, the bassist Tony Levin now played with Leonard, Torn, and Alford. It was the same premise as the spring session: hear demos, take notes, do takes, "I'll call you later."

Though Bowie started cutting vocals that fall, he was slowly writing lyrics and would spend over a year on his vocals. "In the beginning he was finding his voice," Visconti said. "He's not an opera singer, he doesn't practice every day." Dorsey and Leonard said they feared at times he'd abort the album. Brian Thorn, the Magic Shop's assistant engineer, said "I had no idea if the album would even be released. I was prepared to sit on it for as long as I needed to." Studio owner Steve Rosenthal summed up the mood: "This has been like an art project that he's created and is executing upon us all. I don't think any of us really believed it was going to come out until we saw the song online."

A turning point came when Bowie called Earl Slick to do what Slick had always done: "rock 'n' roll" guitar parts. "He never let me hear the demos," Slick told *Rock et Folk*. "I played where he needed me." Along with doing overdubs, Slick played on the last set of new tracks in July 2012, with Visconti on bass and a returned Campbell (see "(You Will) Set the World on Fire"). Thus after two years Bowie had about thirty tracks, with those needing more work tagged as potential B-sides or bonuses. After winnowing the tracklist to about twenty songs, Bowie worked on the sequencing for months.

Kreuzberg

> *Each Berlin is worlds distant from, and a stranger to, the other... indeed I have to admit that the Berlin of which I speak is actually not really Berlin anymore.*
> — Georg Hermann, *Kubinke*, 1910

One day in 2011, Bowie came in and said, "I wrote a song about Berlin," Visconti recalled.

He'd been kicking it around. Baz Luhrmann recalled Bowie wistfully telling him "let's go to Berlin!" sometime in the 2000s, while Dorsey said Bowie told her he "had this idea of writing about his time in Berlin. That it was a very intense time for him." "Bowie in Berlin" was one of his most enduring characters. Singing "Heroes" at Hansa by the Wall. Living with Iggy Pop on Hauptstraße, swapping clothes. Biking around the city. Making paintings of Pop and Yukio Mishima. Taking his breakfasts in the cafe down the street. Spending days at the Brücke-Museum, nights at the Dschungel and Chez Romy Haag.

His estranged wife Angela thought it was ridiculous: he and Pop dressing up like bohemian painters, reenacting *Jules et Jim* with Coco Schwab. But Berlin was *reality*, Bowie said, whereas America and Britain were fictions. John Lennon once said rock 'n' roll was real and everything else was unreal. Bowie found rock 'n' roll the most unreal thing of all, and Berlin was where he got free of it.

Visconti said of Bowie's retired years that he traveled the world "but you wouldn't know it, because he doesn't want you to." An obvious question: did Bowie go back to Berlin in the late 2000s? Walk through Schöneberg and on Nürnberger Straße, visit Hansa, catch a train at Potsdamer Platz? Drives through Brixton and Bromley had sparked *The Buddha of Suburbia*. Did a similar visit inspire "Where Are We Now?" Another speculation (offered by Momus): did Bowie consider making his comeback album at Hansa? It would have made a perfect circle, a lost man returning to the city he'd gotten lost in. Maybe too perfect. And keeping a secret was easier to do with a few New York engineers and his old touring band. It was growing harder to get lost in Berlin.

Friedrichshain

After the danger dissipated in Berlin, nothing was left.
— Klaus Schütz

The Berlin of *"Heroes"* is gone. The old city districts have been consolidated, streets have new names, once-battlefront neighborhoods are gentrified, rents are spiking. It's a capital again. In the Cold War, divided Berlin was a stage where West and East sported their colors. It lived on its nerves, a city "so restless at night that even the animals in the zoo pace around," as the British diplomat Harold Nicolson once said of it.

A creaky voice recounts a story, though it's not much of one. "Had to get the train from Potsdamer Platz," he begins, not quite nailing the accent. "You never knew… that I could *do that*," with faint amazement. He's singing to a ghost, to someone who didn't outlive the Wall. The Potsdamer Platz of divided Berlin was a blocked door — the train station was a ghost stop on the S-Bahn, a closed station that one only saw in passing. Today in Berlin you catch an eastbound train without giving it a second thought.

He tries other names, seeing if anything hits a strike. The lost Dschungel club on Nürnberger Straße. The department store KaDeWe. And thousands of East Germans crossing Bösebrücke one autumn day in 1989, fearing a trap, that guards will open fire. But into the West they go, puncturing a hole in the Wall, soon followed by other holes, soon followed by no Wall at all. It had been so easy. Maybe all you ever had to do was walk across the bridge, fingers crossed.

Treptow

Christopher Isherwood went back to Berlin after the war, in 1952, "to do one of those Berlin-revisited things for the *Observer*." The city was still on the stretcher, with many buildings still shell-pocked and piles of rubble pushed to the curbs. This was pulverized bits of Wilhelmine and Weimar Berlin, the cornices and windowpanes of the lost city of Isherwood, Brecht, Sally Bowles, and the Landauers; it was swept up in piles, carted off to make three great hills on the outskirts of West Berlin. In the Grunewald Forest, the highest pile became Teufelsberg, on which the Germans planted trees and shrubs and built a ski jump. The Americans built a radar station.

It's how Berlin has always lived: junk what you can't salvage, build over the rest. Most cities would have preserved the Wall, made it a memorial. The Germans chipped it down, hauled it off, sold some pieces, threw others in the garbage. *Walking the dead*, Bowie sings, but he might as well have sung *walking on the dead*, because Berlin has paved over thousands of bodies.

Neukölln

Even at the demo stage, Leonard was struck by a song known as "067," the file's name on Bowie's digital recorder. "There are beautiful changes to it," he said. "He had these chords on his keyboard. David is an amazing writer, but he's not a schooled guy, he just goes by his ear." When talking structures, Bowie would say "the middle bit" or "the other bit."

Leonard moved the keyboard progression to guitar. A verse like someone walking back and forth along a street — Fmaj7 ("had to get") to Dm/G ("Potsdamer"). A seesaw movement — Db/Eb ("never knew that"), Eb/Db ("I could") — hinting at a move to Ab major but instead returning to the home chord, F, now with a C bass note ("do that"). And closing with a move from G/C ("just walking the"), Ebm/C ("dead") to end on a C7, the dominant chord of the song's F major key, soon resolved by another return home. A refrain falls from F major to C major. Another verse is trimmed; another refrain blossoms into an outro that changes the refrain chords to F-Dm-C/E-C, repeating to the fade. There's a sense of not wanting to waste time: a slam back to the verse after the refrain, where the ear expects a solo or recapitulation of the intro; a move to the outro right after the second refrain.

The track is Leonard's guitar, Bowie's keyboards (and Henry Hey playing Bowie's piano lines, particularly in the outro), Levin's bass, and Alford's drums, with Visconti's strings in the background. At first it falls to Alford to keep the song moving: Leonard and Bowie mostly augment chords, Levin is a torpid foundation. The song takes flight as it ends — Alford plays a martial snare pattern and Leonard elaborates on the melody, arpeggiating, moving down his guitar neck, wringing higher and higher notes, weaving a line as mournful as Bowie's vocal.

Tempelhof

"Where Are We Now?" was an odd choice for an opening single, Visconti thought. He and other musicians took pains in pre-release interviews to say how anomalous the song was, that most of the album was uptempo, guitar-fat, and loud.

It being the first new Bowie song in a decade was a macabre joke, like him showing up at Fashion Rocks in 2005 dressed as if he'd been in a car crash. If the world thought he was dying, fine: here he was croaking a song about his lost youth, as if dictating a will. But even the fragility of his voice was a trick. "That's a vulnerable voice he has used time and time again," Visconti said. "It's part of his technique, to sing that way. He put that voice on like he's vulnerable, but he's not frail." The ploy worked: "elegiac" was inescapable in reviews.

Bowie may have taken the title from the opening shot of his son's film *Moon*: "Where Are We Now?" is a question that kicks off a corporate promo film selling the future. In his song, it's a question Bowie never answers. *As long as there's sun... as long as there's fire.* As long as these endure... well, what else? Me and you, he finally says. But the more he thinks about it, he's not sure what will stand. They took the Wall down with chisels and hammers.

Schöneberg

All that was left was to shoot a video. Bowie chose Tony Oursler, whom he'd worked with in the Nineties. In a cluttered loft (Oursler's New York studio), the faces of Bowie and Jacqueline Humphries are video-projected on two lumpen mannequins astride a pommel horse. Behind them play clips of contemporary Berlin — Hauptstraße, KaDeWe, Potsdamer Platz, the Reichstag. Bowie's face looks like a sad turtle's. Humphries (an artist and Oursler's wife) was chosen in part because she resembled Coco Schwab.

Bowie designed it all: conjoined dummies, piles of junk, what played on the screen. "It was a crystal vision of what it was going to look like," Oursler said. "I was completely flattered that he wanted to come to my cave and fulfill this." Towards the end of the video, we see the "real" Bowie at last, trim and impassive, wearing a "Song of Norway" t-shirt (a film that his old girlfriend Hermione Farthingale had acted in, and likely meant for her — they had met again in the late Nineties and kept in touch). He looks like a retired spy, like Bill Nighy's Johnny Worricker, an old agent who becomes a man of honor by standing still while the world rots around him. The video symbolizes the long making of *The Next Day*. Having gone through piles of discards (like the rubble of postwar Berlin), Bowie sets up a dummy and screens his face upon it while his "public" memories are shown behind it. *We were kind of a museum exhibit*, as a German artist said of West Berlin in the Sixties.

Hauptstraße 155

It's late in the evening of the 8th of January 1977. Bowie and Iggy Pop, Romy Haag, and Schwab are in a Parisian nightclub for Bowie's birthday. A few photographs, taken by Andrew Kent, are all that remain of that night. Bowie and Pop sport near-identical outfits; Haag is the most beautiful woman in the room. The look of the club, the waitresses' costumes, the lighting of the photographs all invoke decadent cabaret. But Bowie, Schwab, and Pop look like students on a semester abroad, seeing how far their dollars and pounds will take them.

A quarter-century later, a German interviewer asked Bowie where he'd lived in Berlin. The quick reply of "Hauptstraße 155 in Schöneberg" startled the journalist. "You still remember it after twenty-five years?" "I will never forget it," Bowie said. "They were very important years." Upon hearing "Where Are We Now?," Haag said Bowie sounded homesick. He didn't live in Berlin for very long, but it was the last place he was young.

THE NEXT DAY

Recorded: (backing tracks) 2 May 2011, Magic Shop; (vocals) 16 March 2012, Human Worldwide. Bowie: lead and backing vocal, guitar; Torn, Leonard: guitar; Gail Ann Dorsey: bass; Alford: drums, percussion; Antoine Silverman, Maxim Moston: violin; Hiroko Taguchi: viola; Anja Wood: cello (string arrangement: Bowie, Visconti). Produced: Bowie, Visconti; engineered: McNulty, Visconti.

*First release: 11 March 2013, **The Next Day** (ISO/Columbia 88765 46186 2, UK #1, US #2).*

Object one: Album cover art (CD: 5" x 5.5"; LP: 12.5" x 12.4").
Designer: Jonathan Barnbrook (photo: Masayoshi Sukita).
Designed: September-December 2012; issued: 8 March 2013.

"I thought some fan made a joke cover," as Tony Visconti recalled his thoughts upon first seeing Jonathan Barnbrook's *The Next Day* image. Barnbrook proposed that *The Next Day* should have the defaced cover of an older Bowie album. Experiments included covering Bowie and Twiggy's faces on *Pin Ups* with Mickey Mouse ears. *Aladdin Sane* was a more promising candidate but "subverting [*Aladdin*] didn't work because it's subversive already... if you subvert *Aladdin Sane*, then you're adding to it, not destroying it," Barnbrook said. But in Masayoshi Sukita's *"Heroes"* cover photograph "there's a distance," with Bowie looking like a god in a universe of one. Altering the god's face is an act of desecration, a cheeky iconoclasm.

Barnbrook scrawled over *"Heroes"* (giving the cover the scabrous recycled look of Pavement albums) but felt that didn't work. Then he struck upon having a white square obscure Bowie's face. "It had to be something that was in direct contrast to the image underneath but that wasn't too contrived," he said. "It would have been clearer to many people if we had scribbled all over the cover but that didn't have the detachment of intent necessary to express the melancholy of the songs on the album." While the album wasn't titled when Barnbrook started work (its code name was "Table"), *The Next Day* and the defaced *"Heroes"* image worked in tandem. "We can be heroes — just for one day," Bowie sang. Now his beautiful 1977 face is covered by a Post-It note. Because it's the day *after* being heroes, back to being mean and drinking all the time.

Object two: Music video (2:58).
Dir: Floria Sigismondi. Starring: David Bowie, Gary Oldman, Marion Cotillard, Megan Neal Bodul, Catherine Jolleys, Brigitte Hagerman, Folake Olowofoyeku, Joshua Blake Shiver. Cinematography: Jeff Cronenweth. Executive producer: Colleen Haynes (Black Dog Films.) Producers: Jennifer Chavarria, Oualid Mouaness. Released: 8 May 2013.

A dirty priest goes to a bar full of saints and icons. He dances with a woman there. The bar band is led by a prophet who looks like he's been out in the desert for a while. The woman develops stigmata, blood splatters everywhere. The prophet gets the blame and is beaten by priests and harlots until the *deus ex machina* ending, complete with heaven-sent white light, when he's raptured away.

The reaction to the "Next Day" video was to be expected. The Catholic League's Bill Donohue attacked Bowie, if more for aesthetic incoherence than blasphemy ("it's a sure bet [Bowie] can't stop thinking about the Cadillac of all religions, namely Roman Catholicism. There is hope for him yet."). A former Archbishop of Canterbury said Bowie didn't have the guts to play with Islamic imagery. YouTube briefly deleted the video (in error, not in response to complaints); tabloids ran spreads with blood and half-dressed women, which they always enjoy doing. While "troll the Catholics" is a tired provocation, Floria Sigismondi had a keen eye for a shot: Gary Oldman's priest, with his ducktail haircut, looking like an old greaser; Marion Cotillard's face swaying into the frame, her eyes lost in a private bliss.

"A song about a tyrant, let me leave it at that," as Visconti described "The Next Day," while to another journalist he classified said tyrant as a medieval Englishman [or "Catholic cardinal"] who "was very insignificant. I didn't even know who [Bowie] was talking about. But if you read the lyrics, it's quite a horrific story." It could be a reference to the future King Charles II, who hid in an oak tree after the Royalist defeat at the Battle of Worcester in 1651. But Bowie's character reads less as a royal and more as a grasping second-tier villain, a rabble-rouser whose rabble turns on him, hunting him through the streets. The video supports this idea, using medieval Catholicism for costumes (Joan of Arc's there, as is the eyeless St. Lucy, though the flagellant barback is more of a Dan Brown joke), its setting a dive bar where the holy go in their off hours.

Often on *The Next Day*, Bowie raided his library for his lyrics: candidates here include Albert Camus' *The Stranger*, Nietzsche's *Also Sprach Zarathustra*, and most openly Robert Palmer's *Deep Blues*, which has a passage on the griots of Senegambia, who "sing the praises of wealthy and powerful men... some of them are attached to royal courts, while others sing in the streets." Griots accrue wealth and power but are often despised "for they are thought to consort with evil spirits" and because their praise songs "when not properly rewarded, can become venomous songs of insult." When the griots die, they aren't buried with respectable members of society. "Their bodies were left to rot in hollow trees."

A rich, revered, aging singer, once known to consort with evil spirits, spies death on the horizon. He knows he won't be buried among the good and the prosperous, no matter how many awards they give him. They'll stick his body in a hollow tree like the rest of his ilk.

Object three: Musical composition/recording (3:27). Credits: see above.

The doctors tell me I shouldn't be here now. But I don't go to the doctors for chemotherapy or anything anymore. I just put one foot in front of the other, and the next day is the next day, and you do your best. I've still got so much to do.
— Mick Ronson, 1993

The first song Bowie tracked upon his return to the studio, "The Next Day" leads off its album and it *sounds* like a starter, something to get the band cranking — an easy construction, with long stays on home chord E7 (first and fourth verse, refrains, outro) and otherwise mostly moving between G7 ("bodies wash a-") and A7 ("-shore in the dark"). (Bowie avoids the dominant (B7), having IIIb and IV chords duke it out for the favor of his home chord.)

Zachary Alford has little time for fills, pacing the band with his kick and hi-hat. Gerry Leonard and David Torn have a corral of guitars: a crunchy off-beat figure throughout, a trebly line to needle against it, a spectral rising line to ladder to the refrains. Bowie's voice is front and center, to the point where the band sounds like it's been herded back in the mix to give him room, with the strings barely distinguishable from Torn's guitar lines (the former are most discernible in the track's last seconds).

It's Bowie alive, unwell, full of piss and vinegar, as if the whole thing's his fuck-you response to the Flaming Lips' "Is David Bowie Dying?" He held back on recording his vocals for "The Next Day" until well into the sessions, as though needing time to find the right degree of contempt. He starts by keeping on root notes, his voice an abrasive bass overdub, his phrasings full of consonant runs ("*p*ain of the**ir** *p*a**r**–tic-u-l**ar** di*s*-ea*s*-e*s*"), his rhymes all but grunts. As on "Breaking Glass," he severs a verse with *listen!* In refrains, when he's harping on the highest note in the underlying chord, he hollers down anyone who wrote a premature obituary for him. Who knows if a late Mick Ronson interview was on his mind, but his perspective has the same obstinate resistance. HERE I AM: NOT QUITE DYING. Persevering, despite the world's best intentions, with the bookkeeping of life, the small routines, the breaths, blinks, and stomach rumbles, the farts and bloody noses. On through tomorrow, and tomorrow, and tomorrow, as a doomed Scottish king once said, though at least they didn't stick him in a tree. And the *NEXT DAY* and the *NEXT* and *ANOTHER DAY*. Bowie roars the words as`if he's peeling them open. One foot in front of the other. Live, live, goddamn you: *live*.

ATOMICA

Recorded: *(backing tracks) 2 May 2011; (overdubs) July 2012, Magic Shop; (vocal) 26 August 2013, Human Worldwide. Bowie: lead and backing vocal, piano, keyboards; Earl Slick, Leonard, Torn: guitar; Dorsey: bass; Alford: drums; Alex Alexander: percussion; Erin Tonkon: backing vocal. Produced: Bowie, Visconti; engineered: McNulty, Visconti.*

First release: 4 November 2013, **The Next Day Extra** *(Col/ISO 8883787812, UK #89)*.

While its backing tracks were cut at the very start of *The Next Day* sessions, "Atomica" had a labored gestation. Sharing with the title track a guitar-heavy sound and harmonic stinginess (again, verse and refrain are the same chord), what became "Atomica" was assigned to the "this needs more work" pile. Overdubs were done in 2012 and Bowie didn't cut his vocals until August 2013 (it was finally released on *The Next Day Extra* that November).

Some of his lines read as if generated by bots; phrasings include jamming as many syllables as he can into a line ("when-you're-head-o-ver-heels-and-the-ma-gic-is-gone-it's-im-*poss*-i-ble," in little over a bar). He sings "police" like "puh-leeze," rhymes "covered-up pool" with "purple tulle"; his lines about being a rock star or pop star hacking away would get negated on his next album's title track; he gets in a "baybe" as a last word. A thirty-two-bar bridge threatens to swallow up the song, with Bowie fixatedly singing that he holds himself like a god, over slow-building gales of synthetic strings. The return of the opening guitar riff is the defibrillator to finally shock him out of it.

How Does the Grass Grow?

(Bowie, Lordan.) **Recorded**: *(backing tracks) 3 May 2011, Magic Shop; (vocal) 16 January 2012, Human Worldwide. Bowie: lead and backing vocal, keyboards; Leonard, Torn: guitar; Dorsey: bass, backing vocal; Alford: drums. Produced: Bowie, Visconti; engineered: McNulty, Visconti.*

First release: 11 March 2013, **The Next Day**.

"We're not very impressed with today's music," Tony Visconti said in his role as Voice of Bowie in 2013. "We weren't listening to anything current... It all sounds like it was made by the same person." That said, one contemporary album cast a shadow on *The Next Day*, if inadvertently. PJ Harvey's *Let England Shake*, released on Valentine's Day 2011, came about when she learned the Iraq and Afghanistan wars had official photographers and writers. She'd play the "official" composer of the Bush/Blair wars, though using World

War I for images: trenches, gas, strafed beaches, fields of poppies and blood. Like Bowie, she was long in making her album (though working in reverse, first writing the lyrics) and though she considered working in Berlin, she recorded the album down the street from her home, using her reliable crew of musicians.

Some *Next Day* songs are in the *Let England Shake* mold, ringing with old violence — most notably "How Does the Grass Grow?" Where *Let England Shake* was compact in sound, like a response to Cameronian austerity, "How Does the Grass Grow?" has a verse keyboard line that's a staccato support to the vocal, goblins singing and muttering in the margins, treated cymbal crashes, organ swells, a great groaning bass hook. The distortion applied in the verses makes Bowie sound like the bandpass-filtered voice of Foster the People's "Pumped Up Kicks." The guitar solos sample Bowie eras as if moving between aisles in a warehouse. Though Visconti said the track "was very different, new Bowie, new-style Bowie," its refrain is that of Jerry Lordan's 1960 instrumental "Apache," overt enough for Lordan's estate to get co-composition credit. Bowie kept Lordan's top melody while slightly altering the chords (Lordan's F-G-C becomes F#6-Ab-Bbm), then reversed the sequence for his verse progression.

It's set in an imagined Eastern Europe, another of Bowie's war-bled Warsaws, with wild boys on Latvian mopeds (the Riga-1, ca. 1965) and kids making a life out of nothing. (The "Apache" hook could be thematic, referencing a teenage gang by that name in early-twentieth-century New York.) Bowie found one line in a 1967 essay by Stalin's daughter, Svetlana Alliluyeva, describing the Russian village of Zhukovka ("television antennas stick up from the gray, tumbledown roofs and the girls wear nylon blouses and sandals from Hungary"). It's also a British wartime setting, as another source was Carol Ann Duffy's "Last Post," a 2009 poem on the Great War: "…watch bled bad blood/run upwards from the slime into its wounds." As in Duffy's poem, the singer wants to reverse time, have it run like a reel of film spooling backwards, so that "the girls would fill with blood" — the veins of murdered girls flow again, if also a menstrual image. "Balkan," "burial," and "reverse" were how Bowie described the song, in a list of forty-two words that he sent to novelist Rick Moody (this was his only comment on the songs of *The Next Day* — each three-word set corresponded with a song on the album, following the sequential order). Only the earth endures. Blow a hole in the ground, grass covers it; mow down trees, they feed mosses; mow down soldiers, their blood waters the grass. The refrain, an army marching chant, came from Bowie's reading on military training camps and likely *Full Metal Jacket*, where R. Lee Ermey leads troops in a variation of the chant.

With its thematic links to other *Next Day* songs, "How Does the Grass Grow?" is one of the album's connecting hubs: an interest in doomed teenagers of multiple generations; the bridge as an escape hatch from a claustrophobic song — here, a D major sequence where Bowie sounds as if he's shaken free of a bad dream. And a tongue-in-cheek recycling of a Bowie standard — in the outro, dancing to Gail Ann Dorsey's bassline, the band revives "Boys Keep Swinging." You can wear a uniform and have other boys check you out, until they take aim at you.

YOU FEEL SO LONELY YOU COULD DIE

Recorded: (backing tracks) 3 May 2011, Magic Shop; (vocal) 2 March 2012, Human Worldwide. Bowie: lead and backing vocal, twelve-string acoustic; Leonard, Torn, Visconti: guitar; Hey: piano; Dorsey: bass, backing vocal; Alford: drums; Silverman, Moston: violin; Taguchi: viola; Wood: cello; Janice Pendarvis: backing vocal. Produced: Bowie, Visconti; engineered: McNulty, Visconti.

First release: *11 March 2013, **The Next Day**.*

Like many Bowie songs of this century, "You Feel So Lonely You Could Die" is burdened with those of the previous one. A songbook was pressed into service here: verses with a touch of Leonard Cohen's beaten warhorse "Hallelujah," a title hook from "Heartbreak Hotel." Bowie's "Rock 'n' Roll Suicide" is in the guitar figure (the song's the first Bowie waltz in decades), "The Supermen" in the vocal arrangement. The outro is the drum pattern of "Five Years," which Woody Woodmansey once described as hopelessness in a drumbeat. Zachary Alford plays it faster, his snare hits are snappier: it fits a song of hope, if the hope for the death of a despised object.

Sequenced as the near-last word of *The Next Day*, "You Feel So Lonely" is a nest of spies, broken assignations, theft, outsourced torture, political killings ("the assassin's needle" invokes the murder of Bulgarian dissident Georgi Markov, killed by poisoned umbrella tip). It's a reckoning on a history ("Russian history," Tony Visconti specified) that's been crated and shipped out. All Bowie can hope is that the creep in his sights — a traitor, a sell-out, a lover who worked for the Stasi, or maybe it just felt like that — will one day pay for it (his "official" words were "traitor," "urban" and "comeuppance.") Yet his target doesn't know, or care, how much hate they've bred, how tight a grip they've had on his imagination. *No one ever saw you*, Bowie begins, recounting the creep leaving notes in a park. But *he* did. He can hope for justice all he wants. If it finally comes, he'll lose the light he's circling around.

Who's at the other end of the rifle scope? Speculations range from Morrissey (the song as a vicious parody of "I Know It's Gonna Happen Someday") to Bowie himself, an unrepentant thief fearing obscurity and death. There's a thick vein of black humor — Bowie's pissily-moaned "people don't *like* you," sung after he's called for the hangrope; the chord sequence of D!-E!-A!-D! under the final "die-ie-ie-ieee"s. Over knotty chord progressions in a George Harrison style, its arrangement is classic Bowie as seen in a smudged mirror. Bowie on his twelve-string acoustic (taking a last flourish before the outro), a string quartet that's part of a vocal chorus with Gail Ann Dorsey and Janice Pendarvis, singing a gorgeous malediction. It's a latter-day song of, as Lady Stardust sang so many years ago, darkness and disgrace.

IF YOU CAN SEE ME

Recorded: *(backing tracks) 4 May 2011, Magic Shop; (overdubs) September 2011? spring 2012; (vocals) 4 April 2012, Magic Shop, Human Worldwide. Bowie: lead and backing vocal, keyboards; Leonard, Torn: guitar; Dorsey: bass? backing vocal; Levin: bass?; Alford: drums, percussion. Produced: Bowie, Visconti; engineered: McNulty, Visconti.*

First release: *11 March 2013,* **The Next Day**.

"If You Can See Me" is at the center of *The Next Day*, set like a scarecrow to send the half-hearted listener packing, with its "very wide, beautiful, crunchy jazz chords" (Tony Visconti) and vexing meter, aptly described by Jason Lindner as "the drums are in 4 but it's hard to figure out what everything else is in." Its intro and refrains climb from a G-flat chord to B-flat minor until, after slipping to A-flat, finally struggle up to D-flat. Bowie sounds as if he's carrying a weight through three verses and a pre-chorus until he exultantly reaches the title refrain just as the song cements into D-flat. The verses are a shaky huddle around F minor, with Bowie singing over a stabbing keyboard figure and a syncopated bassline that works as the spine of the E major guitar riff but also undermines it by playing a flattened fifth note. As Clifford Slapper noted, the verses feel "jumpy, nervous, as if dancing on hot coals, before finding brief respite on F minor periodically" (e.g., on "meet me across the river").

The lyric has *1. Outside* touches — ritual sacrifice ("take this knife"), serial killing ("a love of violence, a dread of sighs"). There's voyeurism ("fear of Rear Windows") and more of *The Next Day*'s lyrical interest in youth, who swarm like bugs and wave their fists at God here. It's Bowie playing the tyrant, a favorite role in his earlier songs: the utopian genocidal Saviour Machine, the dictator of "We Are Hungry Men," the "Führerling" Alternative Candidate. He sings the last verse in the high register of a conqueror, sacking towns, burning fields and books, promising annihilation ("crusade, tyrant, domination," Bowie gave for a précis.) His taunts of "if you can *see me*, I can *see you*" are a child-god's, with a link back to his old "When I'm Five": "if I close one eye, the people on that side can't see me."

A hallway between the sound of *Earthling* and the soon-to-come "'Tis a Pity She Was a Whore" and "Killing a Little Time," its production is all over the place, with keyboard mixed to top the drums and a bassline as a quagmire (though backing tracks were cut in the Gail Ann Dorsey sessions and Dorsey recalled playing on the track, Tony Levin is credited on bass: either a later overdub or a liner notes error). She definitely sang the whirling vocal in the intro (shades of Clare Torry on Pink Floyd's "Great Gig in the Sky") and was the ceiling of Bowie's vocals. It's Bowie as the malevolent god of his album, its chaos centerpiece. "I was a fractured man," he recalled in 1997 of his Seventies life. "I wasn't aware of other people. I wasn't aware of a society. I really was the dictator of this empty world." He relishes lines like "American Anna fantasticalsation" and "shoots and ladders," having a blast playing Shiva, Destroyer of Worlds in his last refrains.

DANCING OUT IN SPACE

Recorded: (backing tracks) 4, 7 May 2011, Magic Shop; (vocal) 8 October 2012, Human Worldwide. Bowie: lead and backing vocal, keyboards, Korg Trinity; Leonard, Torn: guitar; Dorsey: bass; Alford: drums. Produced: Bowie, Visconti; engineered: McNulty, Visconti.

*First release: 11 March 2013, **The Next Day**.*

There are four versions of *The Next Day* as of this writing: the original fourteen-track CD/download; the deluxe edition with three bonus tracks, which is also the LP sequence; the Japanese deluxe release, with a fourth bonus track; and *The Next Day Extra*, which has a second disc with all of the aforesaid bonuses, plus four more bonus tracks and two remixes. In the analog age, he could have had a three-LP set; in the streaming era, *The Next Day* is a fluctuating set of tracks whose sequence and length depends on the listener's mood and patience.

In a tighter time, something like "Dancing out in Space" would have been a B-side at best, but now it's scattered on the floor with everything else. Bowie didn't record vocals until the tail end of the album sessions (October 2012), suggesting the track had been in a similar limbo as "Atomica." A well-made minor song, its verses shuttle between G major and E minor, its refrains pegged on parallel steps (on the "ooooohs"), first Db to Eb to C major, then to bridge the return to the verse's G major. The vocal arrangement has a doo-wop bass in refrains ("big *bay*-bee") and a little whoop mid-refrain. Gail Ann Dorsey and Zachary Alford, his drums coffined in reverb, rumble up a lower-stakes "Lust for Life" beat; the guitars are a collective February; synthetic harmonica fills give a taste of 1987; keyboards shiver through the track's last seconds.

The lyric is little more than crossword clues without answers, though a line about being as "silent as Georges Rodenbach" honors a novel that haunts Bowie's last albums — Rodenbach's 1892 *Bruges-la-Morte*, about a widower obsessed with his dead wife and subsequently with her double (it's the ur-text for *Vertigo*; for more, see "The Informer" and "Blackstar"). The line also invokes Rodenbach's tombstone in Père Lachaise: a patina bronze nude languorously rising from the grave, clutching a rose. Rodenbach would've been flattered by the reference, if raising an elegant eyebrow at

Bowie rhyming "ghost" with "ghost." Bowie used "funereal," "glide" and "trace" to describe his cemetery soft-shoe or, more accurately, sock hop, as his refrain borrows from Danny & the Juniors' "At the Hop."

LIKE A ROCKET MAN

Recorded: (backing tracks) 5 May 2011, Magic Shop; (vocal) 2 March 2012, Human Worldwide. Bowie: lead and backing vocal, keyboards; Leonard, Torn: guitar; Dorsey: bass, backing vocal; Alford: drums; Pendarvis: backing vocal. Produced: Bowie, Visconti; engineered: McNulty, Visconti.

*First release: 4 November 2013, **The Next Day Extra**.*

It's a shame that the joker in *The Next Day* pack was "Dancing out in Space" rather than the catchy, subversive "Like a Rocket Man," which was assigned to the *Extra* EP. Bowie was shameless in his steals here — a verse melody from the Beatles' "Help," hiccups from Buddy Holly, Elvis tics for backing vocal fills, with lines from *Taxi Driver* ("God's lonely man") and the Kinks' "Days." His title mocks an Elton John single that he'd always considered a "Space Oddity" rip-off.

Yet it's also as close as Bowie came to a first-person account of being a cocaine addict, of someone who had found, as per the novelist Edward St Aubyn, that cocaine "was an opportunity to experience the arctic landscape of pure terror." As on *Young Americans'* "Fascination," Bowie personifies coke ("Little Wendy Cocaine") as a "go-to" party girl who's bankrupting him spiritually and literally ("I'd found a soul-mate in that drug," he recalled in 2002.) He wrote a sunny melody for his dead-of-night terrors ("I'm crawling down the wall, I'm happy screaming, yes I am!"). It's easy to get lost in the house of mirrors here, as he's sending up his Kabbalist Coke Fiend tabloid image while having a ball with language — see the consonance of the title and "shaking hips and cuckoo ey-ay-ayes," or the triple-run rhyme scheme of "doxy/trolley/poxy" (suggesting he was reading Jacobean plays like '*Tis Pity She's a Whore* by this point). The brickwalled production aesthetic of *The Next Day* works in its service, its bright mix full of pairings: briskly-strummed acoustic guitar to match the snare/cymbal figure; low-mixed bass as the ground below David Torn's guitar figures; an arpeggiated opening riff answered by harmonized guitars in the coda. Bowie's lead vocal has a nasally timbre, with grazed notes ("tooo-mah-row" at 1:25) and a hard punch-in (1:27). Though it took nearly a year to complete, "Like a Rocket Man" sounds as if he'd whipped it up in an hour, not caring if it scorched while it cooked.

Born in a UFO

Recorded: *(first version, unreleased) 5, 10 May 2011, Magic Shop; (remade backing tracks) 23 July 2012, (vocal) 26 September 2012, Magic Shop, Human Worldwide. Bowie: lead and backing vocal, keyboards; Slick: lead, rhythm guitar; Hey: keyboards; Visconti: bass; Campbell: drums. Produced: Bowie, Visconti; engineered: McNulty, Visconti.*

First release: *4 November 2013,* **The Next Day Extra**.

A gonzo tribute to Bruce Springsteen (see the title, obviously, and the verse melody follows the rough contours of "Prove It All Night"), plus a Bob Dylan quote and Toni Basil's "Mickey" in its keyboard lines, "Born in a UFO" refashions the Fifties science fiction novelty song "Space Girl" (by the Earth Boys). A tale of finding the right person at last, someone so unexpectedly perfect that it feels like they've crashed out of the sky into your life.

Like "Atomica," it was long in the works. Bowie and Tony Visconti played a *Lodger* outtake during the first *Next Day* sessions in May 2011 (Visconti described it to Nicholas Pegg as being a "wild," if sub-standard track) for the band to take as a starting point — a contrast to the usual method of working off Bowie's home demos. As much of *The Next Day* is Bowie playing in his past styles, now he covers one of his "lost" songs. There are other *Lodger* affinities — its antic, parodic mood is that of "Red Sails" and it has harmonic similarities to "D.J.," using three rising chords as a hook. Unhappy with the first take, Bowie had Earl Slick, Visconti, and Sterling Campbell remake "Born in a UFO" from the ground up in July 2012, cutting vocals in his last set of overdubs. It was a lot of work for a song in which Bowie's mostly in love with his alien inamorata's fashion sense. With her A-line skirt, clutch bag, Perugia shoes, and lavender mesh ("she was all Courrèges!" he swoons), all she's missing is a bipperty-bopperty hat.

HEAT

*Recorded: (backing tracks) 6 May 2011; (vocal) 5 November 2011, Magic Shop.
Bowie: lead and backing vocal, twelve-string acoustic guitar; Leonard, Torn:
guitar; Dorsey: fretless bass; Alford: drums; Silverman, Moston: violin; Taguchi:
viola; Wood: cello (string arr.: Visconti). Produced: Bowie, Visconti; engineered:
McNulty, Visconti.*

*First release: 11 March 2013, **The Next Day.***

The photograph is of a room in a flat in West Berlin — 155 Hauptstraße,
Schöneberg, taken around 1978. David Bowie lies on his side on his bed.
His face is that of a sleeping child: Bowie-in-Berlin, in a stolen moment (or
was it? was the photograph staged for possible use?). The headboard is a
wooden sunrise. All that's on the yellow (not electric blue) wall is Bowie's
portrait of the Japanese writer Yukio Mishima. One of Bowie's favorite
paintings, and his best, it's a severe crop of Mishima's head, which seems
carved from stone. The almond eyes have a penetrating sadness.

Before he first toured Japan in 1973, Bowie immersed himself in the
country — he always did the research. He loved its art, photography, fashion,
food, film, temples, and likely a few of its citizens. Above all, the work
of Mishima, whose last novels were translated into English in the early
Seventies. Bowie was drawing sketches of Mishima as early as 1971, and
one tributary of "Heroes" is *The Sailor Who Fell from Grace with the Sea*, of
whose sailor Mishima wrote "he was perfectly aware he would leave [his
lover] in a day yet he was ready to die happily for her sake" (and recall
that "sailor" was Bowie's internet handle). The sailor washes up in *Lodger*,
an album with a Mishima counterpoint on dignity in "Fantastic Voyage," a
Mishima-esque decayed angel in "Look Back in Anger," and a name-check
in "Yassassin" ("just *Sun and Steel*"). "Because You're Young" and "Teenage
Wildlife" tick to the pulse of Mishima novels like *Thieves*, with their lovely
young suicides.

Entrance to the Stage

Like David Bowie, Yukio Mishima is a stage name. He was born Kimitake
Hiraoka in 1925, to a family of samurai heritage. Soon after his birth, his

formidable grandmother kidnapped him, having his cradle moved into her sickroom. He lived with her until he was twelve. Given dolls and origami for playthings, with his few friends vetted as if they were prospective servants, he was mostly left alone to dream and read. When his grandmother determined she was finally going to die, she bequeathed him to his parents.

During World War II, he waited to be called up for the last battles of the Pacific, "a genius destined for death," as he called his twenty-year-old self. A sympathetic recruiter rejected him (Mishima had played up a bout of tuberculosis), so he never fought. He became a writer who wished he'd died a soldier. His books, full of death, scandal, and glamour, were so popular that slang for an adulterous woman, *yoromeki fujin* ("lady misstep"), came from his novel *A Misstepping of Virtue*. "In whatever little compartment — as a clown (which he liked to be), as an actor, as a gangster, as an aristocrat — every little thing he tried to be, he also resisted," the writer Nobuko Albery said. He was a gay man who married a woman; a Europe-besotted aesthete who wanted to restore traditional Japanese culture and the sovereignty of the emperor. His work schedule was that of a banker while he dressed like a gigolo, wearing shades, sport shirts, black pegged trousers, and gold chains.

Frail in build but driven by his shame of failing the draft, Mishima started doing kendo and weight-training, crafting each muscle as he'd designed each room of his house. In his treatise on body fascism *Sun and Steel*, he wrote that he began life as a mind and had "to learn the language of the flesh, much as one might learn a foreign language." Once he learned it, he knew he would lose it — his body's inevitable decay appalled him. By the mid-Sixties, he decided to write his masterpiece and die by ritual suicide.

While writing *Spring Snow*, the first of his quartet *The Sea of Fertility*, he befriended a group of nationalist students, whom he'd incorporate into the following book, *Runaway Horses*. He joined the Self-Defense Force (Japan's equivalent to the US National Guard or UK Army Reserve). While he wrote *The Temple of Dawn*, he created a civilian counterpart to the SDF — a private army called the Shield Society (he wrote their theme song). He played a terrorist in a film, hoped that a leftist uprising would cause his Shield Society to be activated. "He was playing war, which had a special excitement for him because he hadn't been allowed to do so as a child," his brother said.

On 25 November 1970, Mishima and four disciples went to the SDF headquarters in Tokyo and took the commander hostage. Mishima stood on the balcony, called for the soldiers below to overthrow the government and restore the emperor; they jeered him. Returning to the commander's office, he knelt and drove a foot-long dagger into his left side, then drew it across his abdomen. His disciple fumbled the killing blow, failing twice to decapitate him as Mishima shook in pain, gushing blood and intestines. He had left on his desk at home the completed manuscript of the last book of his quartet, *The Decay of the Angel*, and a note: "Human life is limited, but I would like to live forever."

Sightseer's Misfortune

The first lines of "Heat," the last song on *The Next Day* (the last next day), refer to a scene early in Mishima's *Spring Snow*. Mishima's quartet is the life of Shigekuni Honda and his friend, Kiyoaki Matsugae, who dies each novel to be reincarnated in the following one. Honda — rational, slave to routine, "a kind of harbor and not a ship," faithful husband, reader, voyeur, survivor — is the control. The experiment is Kiyoaki, whose incarnations are marked by passion, beauty, depravity, improvisation, a will for death.

Spring Snow begins with Honda and Kiyoaki as teenagers on the latter's family estate in 1912, walking in a group to a waterfall on a hill overlooking the manor. A stream is diverted midway up the slope by the corpse of a black dog. It's hauled out and given a burial; an abbess leads the funeral blessing. The water-washed corpse harbingers Kiyoaki's death and subsequent deaths, the corruption of his reincarnations, his estate getting bombed during the war, Honda's withering. Bowie uses "we": his perspective that of Honda and Kiyoaki, Mishima's halves in one eye.

Starting a song by referencing a Mishima novel was how Bowie wrote much of *The Next Day*. His circle reduced to his family and friends, he retreated into books (he lived Mishima's childhood as an older man) and used them to build songs: Vladimir Nabokov and Evelyn Waugh, Jon Savage and Robert Palmer, Anatole Broyard and Mishima, Carol Ann Duffy and Svetlana Alliluyeva, a dozen others. He'd written his first album in a similar way, raiding Alan Sillitoe and Keith Waterhouse stories for lines. Now he wrote more obliquely: a traceable reference links to an untraceable one, making a lattice. He was working again in the mode of an old influence. Scott Walker's later songs, dense with references that only Walker has the key to, have little to hold them together but being sung by the same keening voice.

Mirror Portrait

A funny thing happened in the twenty-first century. Where David Bowie's life became a speculation, Scott Walker became a relatively public figure (see "Nite Flights" and "The Motel"). He cut a song for a Bond film, curated a Meltdown Festival, produced Pulp's final album, took part in a documentary about himself which he said he's never watched, letting cameras into the studio as he recorded *The Drift*.

Sporting skinny jeans and caps like a Williamsburg grandfather, he makes albums that have as much a brand identity as the *Scott* albums of the Sixties. Their covers, in muted colors, have photographs that could be lunar surfaces or microbe slides; tracks have titles like "Epizootics!" and "Psoriatic" and "Herod 2014." There are sudden shifts in dynamics, esoteric percussion as rhythm tracks, lead vocals that follow melodic lines unsupported by the music (or the noises). *The Drift* is his art rock slasher film masterpiece. *Bish Bosch*, from 2012, has a winning absurdity — Walker in his red giant phase. He'd map out chords on a keyboard at home, get most of a song set in his head, go to the studio and have his musicians give the rest to him. A workable aesthetic, one that Bowie used for *The Next Day* and *Blackstar*.

Hailstones from a Clear Sky

Mick Rock's 2016 book of the Ziggy Stardust period is the size of a small gravestone. It's a life in glam stills: photos of Bowie applying makeup, sitting in a train, singing on stage. A record of Bowie assembling a grand personality. The critic Donald Richie said of his friend Mishima: "He knew one of the great and best-kept secrets of being alive is that if you behave the way you **want** to be, you will become it." As Ziggy Stardust, Bowie rigged himself into being a star. For the rest of his life, he'd change costume and do it again.

Mishima practicing kendo, flying in supersonic aircraft, plotting revolutions, gutting himself, making sure the camera caught the right profile. For Bowie, he was *image*: heat and light, sun and steel. Scott Walker hiding in London studios, having his drummers thwack sides of meat. Existing as *voice*, as an artist without biography. "I'm trying to just be a person singing, without my personality or anything else particularly," he once told Jarvis Cocker.

The False Account and the True

With its F-sharp major key, "Heat" is *The Next Day*'s frontier checkpoint. After a long stay on the home chord, it moves to the IV chord (B major, "songs of dust") to lead to a D major refrain; it shifts between E and F# for the coda. But the F# home chord shades, sometimes every two bars, to an F# with a flattened fifth, as if a landscape is being shrouded in mist, then uncovered. Bowie sings only a few notes, rising by second or third intervals. A movement repeats like Morse code: a two-note rise ("Mi-*shima's dog*," "love is *theft*") that only reaches a third note to close a section, whether circularly ("blocking the *water*-fall") or ambiguously ("pea-*cock in the* **snow**"). The rhythm is keyed to Bowie's strums on acoustic guitar, the drums embellishing (cymbals hiss on chord changes), the fretless bass a softly persistent voice. The rest is smoke — a keyboard playing wavering chords, guitars making solitary gestures, wary strings that burst into flight in the coda.

It's a mix of Walker tropes, particularly his *Climate of Hunter*-era love of fretless bass (Gail Ann Dorsey, on an instrument she was unfamiliar with), blurred instrumentation and semitonal shifts in melody and chords. But it's also a frozen conception of Walker, one from decades before, not the man groaning on his late records. *The Next Day* is Bowie sampling his past, playing cut-up with it, and he does the same to Walker here.

"Tragic, nerve, mystification" are the last words Bowie gave Rick Moody, applying to "Heat." A tragic loss of nerve. An end by fading into the mystic. The endemic violence of *The Next Day* — dying men in trees, soldiers pinned down on beaches, high school shooters, traitors dangling from ropes — stops at last in "Heat," a world bled free of killing as anything else. It's the epilogue of a wartime album, the tale of how the twenty-first century fell into the medieval instead of becoming the floating tin-can world of Major Tom.

I am a seer, and I am a liar, Bowie sings. It's a pun: a see-er, a man who only knows what's right before him; a seer, who knows the future. And a liar, which he always claimed he was. *My father ran the prison, not me. I'm not guilty, but you can't believe a word I say, mind.* If much of *The Next Day* is a romp with his touring band, getting the gang back together for a last caper,

"Heat" leads towards the end of Bowie's recording life. A dock, from which he went off on a last trip. Or a pier, which, as James Joyce once wrote, is a disappointed bridge.

Grand Finale

In 2014, Walker recorded with Sunn O))), a band a generation younger than him. That same year, Bowie was at a New York club sizing up jazz musicians, some of whom hadn't been born when *Scary Monsters* was released. After Bowie hired him, Donny McCaslin started digging into his back catalog. "That's old stuff," Bowie told him. "I'm into different things now."

In 1970, months before his suicide, Mishima mounts an exhibition of himself in a department store. It has photographs of his stolen childhood and shots where he's posed as St. Sebastian, pierced by arrows.

In 2008, Walker helps create *Drifting and Tilting* at the Barbican, where his post-Eighties songs are performed live for the first time. He doesn't sing them, isn't seen on stage. Those inspired by him, like Jarvis Cocker, do his songs. Walker sits at the sound desk.

In the mid-2010s, *David Bowie Is*, a museum exhibition of David Bowie's life, moves from London to Paris to Melbourne to Tokyo to New York. Among the works on display is a painting of Mishima that once hung on a West Berlin apartment wall. In 2015, Bowie's last public appearance is the opening night of his musical, *Lazarus*, where he sits and watches actors sing his songs to him. Clear the waterfall, let the stream go where it will.

THE STARS (ARE OUT TONIGHT)

Recorded: (backing tracks) 9 May 2011, Magic Shop; (vocals) 26 October 2011, Human Worldwide. Bowie: lead and backing vocal, twelve-string acoustic; Leonard: lead guitar; Torn: guitar; Dorsey: bass, backing vocal; Alford: drums; Steve Elson: baritone saxophone, contrabass clarinet; Visconti: recorder; Silverman, Moston: violin; Taguchi: viola; Wood: cello; Pendarvis: backing vocal. Produced: Bowie, Visconti; engineered: McNulty, Visconti.

First release: 26 February 2013, ISO MP3: 886443861534 (UK #102).

Issued as a single soon before *The Next Day*'s release, "The Stars (Are out Tonight)" stalled out on the charts, peaking at 102 in Britain and a non-event in the US. Some of it was timing, as the excitement about Bowie's return that drove sales of "Where Are We Now?" had cooled. But "The Stars" was also just adequate, a late-career Bowie track with "star" in its title, the guitars not causing any trouble, and some requisite homages to the past, including a huh-huh-HUH-huh vocal tag from a British #1 of the Sixties, "Cinderella Rockafella."

The instrumentation does what it can to lighten up a harmonically torpid song whose refrains and verses both shuffle between F# minor and D major chords (suggesting an A major key that declines to establish itself). Given that "the chords stayed the same for a long time," Gerry Leonard said he developed guitar figures with "two or three different parts I could overlay over the same chords… to find a way to be part of the dynamic of the song, sculpt it a little bit." He worked against the underlying F# minor chords, playing high E notes (thus augmenting the chords to F#m7s) and sounding an open string for tonal contrasts. He played a "Spanish" style guitar break after the third verse; David Torn's squiggling lines knot up the ends of verses. The bridge, with a fresh chord change at last, has a four-note descending hook on Tony Visconti's recorder. Zachary Alford came up with the Motown-inspired rhythm, with the bassline deepened by Steve Elson's baritone saxophone and contrabass clarinet.

The lyric was banal, particularly the refrain (Bowie cut the most striking line of an earlier draft: "trembling in the quiet room"), but its concept had potential — a celebrity from a fading era assessing his successors. He'd wanted to be a star from the day he first heard Little Richard, and building a celebrity self was part and parcel of his early music. Being out of the game gave him perspective. The do-it-yourself stardom that he'd practiced (inspired by Andy Warhol's "superstars") had become increasingly desperate — the stars of the 2010s were in the late-capitalist cycle of working longer for fewer rewards. In tabloid shorthand — Brigitte and Brad, Jack and Kate ("Scarlet" was in the earlier draft) — Bowie's stars are parasites who watch us from behind their shades (a play on sunglasses, the blinds of their mansions, and their ghosts), always on the clock, left "sexless and unaroused" in their few downtimes, like porn actors off camera. They infest our dreams and envy our sleep.

In Floria Sigismondi's video, Bowie and Tilda Swinton are an older

597

suburban couple who are stalked and consumed by a young celebrity pair. There are mirrors within mirrors, like the use of Swinton, Bowie's unearthly twin for decades, and the Norwegian model Iselin Steiro, who'd dressed as Bowie for *Paris Vogue* (all that was missing was Kate Moss in a Ziggy Stardust outfit). There's an obvious homage to *The Hunger*, with the vampire couple as a spin on Bowie and Catherine Deneuve's nightclub-foragers, but the video also delights in the idea that David Bowie Looks Old, a cranky pensioner upset by his neighbor singing "Jean Genie" at all hours. "We have a nice life," he tells Swinton. Compared to the ever-hustling celebrities of today, he'd gotten off easily, and he knew it.

So She

Recorded: (backing tracks) 12 May 2011, Magic Shop; (vocal) 23 October 2012, Human Worldwide. Bowie: lead vocal, twelve-string acoustic guitar, keyboards; Leonard: guitar, keyboards; Torn: guitar; Visconti: guitar, bass; Alford: drums; Silverman, Moston: violin; Taguchi: viola; Wood: cello (arr.: Bowie, Visconti). Produced: Bowie, Visconti; engineered: McNulty, Visconti.

First release: 11 March 2013, **The Next Day** *(Deluxe edition) (ISO 88765 46192 2).*

A bonus track on *The Next Day*'s deluxe edition, "So She" is subtly intricate. After a rockabilly guitar intro, an initial melody (leaping and diving by sixths and sevenths) appears, soon to be recycled as a refrain hook and a motif in later verses. "So She" closes with the same melody, now played in a different key (B major), sounding as if it hasn't assimilated.

While backing tracks were cut in the first *Next Day* sessions, "So She" was reworked over the following eighteen months, with Tony Visconti doing a fresh bassline and overdubbing guitar, and Bowie completing his vocal only months before the album's release. With its foundation of acoustic guitar and restless bass (the latter courses under the rockabilly intro riff), "So She" lives for its embellishes — a sprinkle of piano notes (starting at 1:57); fluttering strings after Bowie sings the title line. A dark, obscure lyric brightens in the second verse, where he's found a love who makes him feel like he's never been born (maybe the title was originally "So She Said She Said"). It has depths it won't disclose. "So she" what? He'll never know, nor will we.

GOD BLESS THE GIRL

Recorded: *(backing tracks) 12 September 2011, Magic Shop; (vocal) 2 November 2011, Human Worldwide; (later overdubs) ca. spring-summer 2012, Human Worldwide. Bowie: lead and backing vocal, keyboards; Leonard: guitar; Morgan Visconti: acoustic guitar; Hey: piano; Levin: Chapman stick; Alford: drums; Alexander: woodblocks, tambourine; Dorsey, Pendarvis: backing vocal. Produced: Bowie, Visconti; engineered: McNulty, Visconti.*

*First release: 13 March 2013, **The Next Day** (Japanese edition).*

Bowie struggled with where to place "God Bless the Girl" (originally titled "Gospel") on *The Next Day*, finally slotting it in as a bonus for the album's Japanese deluxe release: a thank-you to a country where people still buy CDs. Though backing tracks were cut in the second round of album sessions in September 2011, there were many late overdubs, including Henry Hey's piano and Morgan Visconti (son of Tony, and owner of the Human Worldwide studio) playing a Bo Diddley riff on acoustic guitar. The verse rhythm section is an oddlot of Tony Levin on Chapman stick, Zachary Alford rumbling on toms, and percussionist Alex Alexander on woodblocks and tambourine. After a long intro — acoustic riff set in place, lead lines musing around a melody — the song sets up in standard C major verses and refrains, the last verse trimmed to get to the outro faster.

As Bowie's heroine could be a nun or a prostitute ("her work is love… God has given me a job"), so his narrator is both a penitent and a goon out of Iggy Pop's "Funtime," singing "I don't wanna *hurt* you, just wanna have some *fun*." A reoccurring line is *there is no other* — an assurance of God's supremacy or of a world without God. Bowie makes his Jackie a nursery rhyme figure sitting in a corner, then a Gnostic "slave without chains"; the refrains are entropic (wine becomes water, spring falls to winter, light ebbs to darkness).

Again using a past style as a template, "God Bless the Girl" is *The Next Day*'s edition of *Young Americans* and "Underground," with Bowie fashioning a "gospel" chorus of himself, Janice Pendarvis, and Gail Ann Dorsey. In the outro's vocal arrangement, Bowie's in a central choir with Dorsey and Pendarvis; the latter two also make up a right-mixed faction, while his lead voice is a solitary figure wending through them. As the song soars to a close, he sings, "the years pass so *swiftly*" in a despairing tone, all but lost in the swirl of voices.

I'LL TAKE YOU THERE

(Bowie, Leonard.) **Recorded**: *(backing tracks) 12 September 2011, Magic Shop; (vocals, overdubs) 2, 5, 14 March 2012, Human Worldwide. Bowie: lead vocal, twelve-string acoustic guitar, keyboards; Leonard, Torn, Visconti: guitar; Dorsey: bass, backing vocal; Alford: drums; Alexander: percussion; Pendarvis: backing vocal. Produced: Bowie, Visconti; engineered: McNulty, Visconti.*

First release: *11 March 2013,* **The Next Day** *(Deluxe edition).*

Though the May 2011 sessions gave him enough to build an album on, Bowie wanted to freshen the pot with new compositions. That summer he visited his guitarist Gerry Leonard in Woodstock, where Leonard had a house and Bowie most of a mountain. "He said, 'okay, I'll come over for coffee and maybe we'll do a little more writing,'" Leonard recalled. Borrowing a Roland TR-808, Leonard set up a studio in his back room. Two Bowie-Leonard compositions would make it onto *The Next Day*: "Boss of Me" on the original album, and "I'll Take You There" as a bonus track, both of which were recorded in September 2011.

Set in a B minor key that it's eager to escape, "I'll Take You There" is Bowie publicly reconciling with his Eighties — it sounds like he kicked off the tracking session by playing "Beat of Your Drum" for the band. It's excess in moderation: big stereo-panned drums; Leonard, David Torn and Tony Visconti punching in guitar lines (Bowie's credited on acoustic, which makes a cameo appearance in the bridge), with Leonard doing his best Earl Slick for a lead riff. There's a Reeves Gabrels-esque pneumatic drill intro/outro guitar line and loop-de-loop backing vocals. The bridge builds to a "look up... at... staaaaars!" climax that leaves Bowie stranded like a cat in a tree — the band has to ladder-walk him down for the next refrain.

His Leonard co-writes, along with "Love Is Lost," are Bowie working with themes of emigration and exile, as he'd do in the play he'd soon write (see "Lazarus"). "I'll Take You There" has border-crossing lovers named after, take your pick, Lev and Sophia Tolstoy or married authors Lev Grossman and Sophie Gee (Bowie liked Grossman's *The Magicians*). Its hook is "what will be my *name* in the *USA*?!," an immigrant writing the first chapter of a new life in what once was the country of the future.

LOVE IS LOST

Recorded: (backing tracks) 13 September 2011, Magic Shop; (vocal) 19 November 2011 (last overdubs) ca. March-July 2012, Magic Shop, Human Worldwide; (remix overdubs) ca. summer 2013, DFA Studios. Bowie: lead and backing vocal, organ, keyboards; Leonard: guitar; Dorsey: bass; Alford: drums; Hishan Bharoocha, James Murphy, Jordan Hebert, Matthew Thornley: clapping chorus (remix). Produced: Bowie, Visconti; Murphy (remix); engineered: McNulty, Visconti; (remix) Matthew Shaw.

*First release: 11 March 2013, **The Next Day**; (Hello Steve Reich Mix), 4 November 2013, **The Next Day Extra**.*

Struggle permeates *The Next Day*, in its overlong sequence and in its combative, narrow-span vocals. Tony Visconti, in late 2015, said the album had "started out trying to do something new but something old kept creeping in." Bowie did with his music what the Victoria and Albert Museum did with his archive (see "Blackstar"): put pieces of his life into juxtaposition, let each viewer or listener write a storyline to tie it together. As with the album cover, it was Bowie's past being recycled and defaced at once. While some of its references were obvious, in *The Next Day*'s strongest songs, like "Love Is Lost," there was a hard reckoning at hand.

In B-flat minor (the key of "Let's Dance"), "Love Is Lost" holds to its home chord in its verses, troubled with a descending eighth-note bassline and Bowie's organ lines, moving the same hand shape around the keyboard, mostly keeping to black keys. Quotes abound: Visconti "Harmonizes" Zachary Alford's snare to summon the loud ghosts of *Low*; Gerry Leonard wanted a sound like Peter Green on Sixties Fleetwood Mac records; the Beatles' "Sexy Sadie" is in a late verse — *oh **what** have you done?* — while the song's title is a cold sequel to John Lennon's "Love." (The bridge sounds pasted in from another song — its "chord progression came out of nowhere when David put it down on the Trinity," engineer Mario McNulty recalled.)

Using images of relocation and exile (see "Boss of Me" and "I'll Take You

There"), Bowie gave his most chilling variation on the theme ("hostage, transference, identity," as he described the song). "Your country's *new*, your friends are *new*," he sings. Being in love as living under witness protection, the confined life of a defector, rewarded for their treachery. New house, new maid, new tongue (Bowie razors "ack-scent" into two sharp syllables), new eyes, new teeth (one presumes). But the same old compromised soul — you feel so lonely, you could die. The last verses, where Leonard thrashes his guitar and Alford works his cymbals, cut in shots from an asylum or prison. Love as being kept in isolation, the lights always on, no sleep. Bowie's harmony vocals are a goon squad working you over to force a confession. *TELL THEM ALL YOU KNOW!... you KNOW... you **KNOW**! ... YOU **KNOW**! ... YOU KNOW!*

He'd never been one for love songs. There was "The Wedding" to crown a midlife summertime, but his youthful credo had been "Soul Love," where he likened love to a plague or infestation. In 1979, he told the interviewer Mavis Nicholson that while he'd used to fall in love easily, now "love can't get quite in my way. I shelter myself from it incredibly." "What are you sheltering yourself from?" she asked. "From losing the other eye!" The perspective of "Love Is Lost" is someone who's lost his sight while looking into the past: the darkest hour, age twenty-two (the year he wrote "Space Oddity") when your voice is new, when love can fork you off the path, send you into the woods. In his play *Lazarus*, Bowie gave "Love Is Lost" to Valentine, serial killer of lovers.

James Murphy's "Hello Steve Reich" remix ballooned "Love Is Lost" to over ten minutes. Murphy layered in more callbacks, notably to Reich's "Clapping Music" — hence the subtitle — and Roy Bittan's keyboard from "Ashes to Ashes," appearing like a surprise guest on a variety show. The verses are more aggressive, the bridge colder and grander. The video Bowie made for the remix was yet more attic-clearing: puppets intended for a "Pretty Things Are Going to Hell" video were pulled from their crates; Bowie makes a warlock face via Tony Oursler's video projectors (see "Where Are We Now?"); he's at the bathroom mirror again (see "Thursday's Child"). Turning his darkened office into a set, he shot the video for the cost of a new flash drive. He'd piled up so much of the past that he could use it for cheap.

BOSS OF ME

(Bowie, Leonard.) **Recorded***: (backing tracks) 14 September 2011; (overdubs) 26 November 2011, Magic Shop. Bowie: lead vocal, guitar; Leonard: lead guitar; Levin: Chapman stick; Elson: baritone saxophone; Visconti: recorder; Alford: drums; Dorsey, Pendarvis: backing vocals. Produced: Bowie, Visconti; engineered: McNulty, Visconti.*

First release: *11 March 2013,* **The Next Day***.*

"Boss of Me" may owe its title to one of co-composer Gerry Leonard's effects processors, the Boss ME-80. With his title cliché as a foundation stone, Bowie rhymes "cool... again" with "cool... again," has insights like "life has your mind and soul" and sings "the small town diiiiiies" like a Valkyrie. You could read the lyric as a tribute to his Somalian-born wife Iman (not really a small town girl, as she grew up in Mogadishu and Nairobi) and an insight into their relationship, but it's as likely Bowie drew from the same refugee/immigrant scenario as in "Love Is Lost" and "I'll Take You There." His words for the song were "displaced," "flight" and "resettlement."

There's a clever structural shift, as verse chords (Cm-Am-Bb-F) later become refrain chords, and it has one of *The Next Day*'s wider-ranging melodies, over an octave. There are nice touches with Tony Levin's Chapman stick, Tony Visconti's tippling recorder line in the bridge, Zachary Alford's cymbal work, and Steve Elson's baritone saxophone retorts, which sound like a bear grumbling awake. But there are nice touches even in the direst recording. Which this is — the nadir of its album, with Bowie making a bitter taffy of his title phrase. As he had a decade to create *The Next Day*, putting something so third-rate on it was an act of genial perversity.

THE INFORMER

Recorded: (backing tracks) 14 September 2011, Magic Shop; (vocal) 21 September 2011, Human Worldwide. Bowie: lead and backing vocal; Leonard, Torn: guitar; Hey: piano; Levin, Dorsey: bass; Alford: drums. Produced: Bowie, Visconti; engineered: McNulty, Visconti.

First release: 4 November 2013, **The Next Day Extra**.

Lyrically, *The Next Day* is like a song whose key is undisclosed, the listener having to guess its tonality from a few shadowy chords. Lines throughout the album seem displaced from a wider organizing concept, suggesting Bowie was writing with a musical play in mind (see "Lazarus"). There are repeated images of emigration and exile, of teenagerhood trying to survive in inhospitable climes; assassins and hitmen, revolutionaries and soldiers.

Then there's Bruges, Belgium, the album's undisclosed location (as in *Blackstar*). Clues are Bowie's name-drop of writer Georges Rodenbach (see "Dancing out in Space"), and the bonus track "The Informer," whose lyric is owed in part to Martin McDonagh's black comedy *In Bruges*, in which two Irish killers hide out in Bruges when a hit goes wrong. Their boss arrives to clean up the job and everything goes to hell. Bruges is an empty square, a nowhere place where memories and guilts rack up, a city as a beautiful morgue.

Though it had the first vocal that Bowie cut for the album, "The Informer" was held back until the *Extra* EP. Moving at lightning speed by *Next Day* standards, it was finished in about a week, with Bowie cutting his vocals right after the backing tracks. He recorded a dozen harmony tracks, the arrangement close to his work on Lou Reed's "Satellite of Love." The verse, built on strides between C major and a fluctuating G major (from a suspended fourth back to the G chord), could be the voice of Colin Farrell's character in McDonagh's film, a neophyte hitman whose debut assignment is to dispatch a priest, with a boy killed in the crossfire ("you were the prime assignment"). There's also John Ford's *The Informer*, where an IRA soldier betrays a comrade for money and goes on the run, like the rat hunted in "You Feel So Lonely You Could Die." And John Braine's *Room at the Top* (mentioned in the last verse), where a social climber gets everything he's dreamed of at the cost of the woman he loves, who dies in a car crash after he betrays her.

With its swooshing guitars, brusque rhythm section, and a mix like a battery of klieg lights, "The Informer" is the close of a long run; it's the sound of *Reality* pushed to the point of exhaustion. Bowie has to hector his way through it. The hitman's holed up in a bathroom, the windows shattered; he's down to his last clip. The end is closing in, so he arraigns his employers, tries to balance his accounts (in a "Changes" nod: "I still don't know/what we were looking for") Ford's informer died on a church floor; the tragedy for Bowie's traitor is if he manages to keep alive.

I'D RATHER BE HIGH

Recorded: (backing tracks) 15 September 2011, Magic Shop; (vocals) 9 May 2012; ("Venetian mix" overdubs) August 2013, Human Worldwide. Bowie: lead and backing vocal; Leonard: lead guitar; Levin: bass; Alford: drums; Hey: harpsichord ("Venetian mix"). Produced: Bowie, Visconti; engineered: McNulty, Visconti.

*First release: 11 March 2013, **The Next Day**; ("Venetian mix") 4 November 2013, **The Next Day Extra**.*

So thickly-settled that it has little room to move, "I'd Rather Be High" is the child of Bowie's bookworm retirement years, where Amazon packages were shipped by the score to his home each month. It opens by referencing Vladimir Nabokov's novel *The Gift*. One hot summer day, the Russian émigré Fyodor is sunbathing in Berlin's park district of Grunewald:

The sun licked me all over with its big, smooth tongue... My personal I... had somehow disintegrated and dissolved... assimilated to the shimmering of the summer forest with its satiny pine needles... and spermy odor of sun-warmed grass.

As Bowie sings more prosaically, "brilliant and naked/just the way that authors look."

He may not have read *The Gift* at all, though, as the Nabokov passage is quoted in a book that Bowie certainly *had* read, Otto Friedrich's *Before the Deluge: A Portrait of Berlin in the 1920s*, one of Bowie's maps to Berlin while he lived there. He harps on a single note (D) ("up-on-the-beach-at-Gru-ne-wald"), as if he can't stop pushing a doorbell, relenting at last by moving up a fourth to close each phrase ("au-thors *look*").

The setting cuts to a tea room in wartime London, a wartime out of time, as "Clare" is possibly Ivor Claire, a soldier facing desertion charges in Evelyn Waugh's World War II novel *Officers and Gentlemen*, while Lady Manners was the birthname of Lady Diana Cooper, muse and patron of a

World War I group of intellectuals who mostly died in the trenches. Waugh's Guy Crouchback (another *Officers and Gentlemen* character) turns up in Cairo to join his regiment. The refrains are the eternal present: a soldier on a battlefield (it could be Gallipoli or Fallujah), shooting at strangers, wishing he could blank himself out of reality as the sun had dissolved Nabokov's émigré.

Tony Visconti described "I'd Rather Be High" as "the lament of a demobbed World War II soldier who would rather succumb to base emotions than be a human being." (He also took pains to note that "Bowie does not want to be high. He is clean and has been an AA member for years.") "Indifference, miasma, pressgang," was all Bowie had to say. Put in constellation with "How Does the Grass Grow?," "The Stars (Are out Tonight)," "The Informer," and "Valentine's Day," "I'd Rather Be High" becomes part of a broader theme — civilization's recursive betrayal of its youth. His was a generation that, for once, hadn't been decimated in its prime by the wars of old men. Had he been born in 1895 or 1920, he could have been on a beach, bullets spraying around him, while dreaming of pleasures that postwar British teenagers took as their birthright.

In November 2013, Bowie appeared in a Louis Vuitton ad directed by Romain Gavras. The model Arizona Muse worked the Vuitton merchandise while Bowie and a would-be Louis XVI court provided the setting: it was in hock to the ballroom scene in *Labyrinth*, Adam Ant's "Prince Charming" video, and Sofia Coppola's *Marie Antoinette*. The ad was a hedge fund manager's idea of surrealism — the blemish on Bowie's otherwise perfectly-executed final act; one hopes he got a nice trip to Venice out of it. For Vuitton, Bowie did a new mix of "I'd Rather Be High," with Henry Hey on harpsichord to complement Gerry Leonard's guitar riff — it lessened the monotony of the album track, where the riff dulled itself through repetition, though the "Venetian" version also downmixed Zachary Alford's shuffle pattern. Bowie cut some fresh vocals for the outro, whose long-held "flyyyyying"s have the lysergic tone of the Beatles' "Rain" and "Tomorrow Never Knows."

DIRTY BOYS

Recorded: (backing tracks) 17 September 2011, Magic Shop; (vocal) 8 May 2012, (guitar and saxophone overdubs) ca. July 2012, Magic Shop, Human Worldwide.

Bowie: lead vocal; Leonard: lead guitar; Slick: guitar; Visconti: rhythm guitar; Elson: baritone saxophone; Levin: bass; Alford: drums. Produced: Bowie, Visconti; engineered: McNulty, Visconti.

First release: *11 March 2013*, **The Next Day**.

"A euphemism, and song, for all the glam rock stars that have ever been," Tony Visconti offered as his take on "Dirty Boys." His co-producer said "violence, chthonic, intimidation." Sequenced as a midtempo response to the title track opener, "Dirty Boys" is an E minor piece that runs to Steve Elson's fifth-spanning strut of a baritone saxophone figure, like a Carl Stalling theme for a Warner Bros. villain. Elson, who recorded and toured with Bowie in the Eighties, was among the last recruited for *The Next Day* — Bowie ran into him, had "a dad conversation," told Elson he'd "be in touch about something." "He's a little guy and he's got a huge baritone sax, and he plays this dirty solo that sounds like stripper music from the 1950s," Visconti said of Elson's work on "Dirty Boys."

Even when Elson cut his overdubs in mid-2012, *The Next Day* was still under construction, with most tracks having working titles and reference vocals. Bowie's directions included "don't even think about what key we're in" and "farther out." He told Elson he liked to leave in oddments "so you might find, in a record, things that only happened once that one time maybe — just to show we could do it... the gems hidden in the recording." See the saxophone squawks in the track's last seconds, which sound like someone yelping in the studio.

As with "Boss of Me," its arrangement sets Elson's saxophone against Tony Levin's bass, with guitars as foils for Bowie's verse lines (players included Earl Slick, who said of "Dirty Boys," "if you're going to have a title like that, I have to be on it"). The neatly-arranged verses are let down by the refrains, which never leave the ground. Elson swings "Dirty Boys" to a close, sinking low and then clambering up an octave: it's a big man stepping his way off a dance floor.

Ending some verse lines with sinking triplets ("lone-ly-*road*," "cric-ket-*bat*"), Bowie references "Tobacco Road" (whether the Erskine Caldwell novel, John Ford's film adaptation, or the unrelated Nashville Teens' 1964 hit) and his own songs ("we all go through"). His setting is Finchley Fair in North London, his scenario is Iggy and the Stooges starring in *Brighton Rock* (the song's use in *Lazarus*, sung by the killer Valentine, made a nebulous plot more nebulous). A street gang fanboy late in life, Bowie was so enamored with the period gangster TV show *Peaky Blinders* that its star Cillian Murphy gave him a Blinders flat cap for Christmas. A delighted Bowie sent back a photo of him wearing it — he was running with the dirty boys at last.

PLAN

Recorded: (drum track) 14 September 2011, Magic Shop; (overdubs) 19-20 January 2012, Human Worldwide. Bowie: guitar, keyboards, synthesizer, organ, percussion; Alford: drums. Produced: Bowie, Visconti; engineered: McNulty, Visconti.

*First release: 11 March 2013, **The Next Day** (Deluxe edition)*

In early 2012, when some players on *The Next Day* feared that Bowie would abandon the album, he was burrowing into the studio. He started the year with "Plan," an instrumental he built around a drum track cut by Zachary Alford for "The Informer," with Bowie playing the rest himself — guitars, synthesizers, organ, shaker. His first instrumental on record since "Brilliant Adventure," "Plan" (included on the album's LP/deluxe edition) fits the *Next Day* schema of doing fresh takes on past styles — here, the second sides of *Low* and *"Heroes."* A droning organ line builds in crescendo three times, flooding the mix, becoming an ebbing undertow. The last organ sequence goes out of phase, then sharply fades with a scene-change signaled on guitar (Marc Bolan's Fender Stratocaster, later heard on "Lazarus"). It worked as the intro of the "Stars (Are out Tonight)" video; on its own, it was a compelling fragment, if more a sketch than a plan.

(YOU WILL) SET THE WORLD ON FIRE

Recorded: (backing tracks) 25 July 2012, Magic Shop; (vocal) 27 September 2012 (last overdubs) ca. September 2012, Human Worldwide. Bowie: lead vocal; Slick: lead guitar; Leonard: guitar; Visconti: bass; Campbell: drums, tambourine; Dorsey, Pendarvis: backing vocals. Produced: Bowie, Visconti; engineered: McNulty, Visconti.

First release: 11 March 2013, **The Next Day**.

Still tinkering with *The Next Day* in summer 2012, Bowie got another crew — Earl Slick and Sterling Campbell, with Tony Visconti doubling on bass and console — for some last tracks. After a full remake of "Born in a UFO," they turned to two new compositions. Where "Valentine's Day" was an obvious pick for the album, the other piece made a puzzling addition to an already-crowded set — "(You Will) Set the World on Fire," a garish valentine to the Greenwich Village of the early Sixties, a tale of ambitious folkies set to the second coming of "Bang Bang."

Bowie was a fan of Anatole Broyard's *Kafka Was the Rage*, a memoir of Village life in the years after World War II, when "rents were cheap, restaurants were cheap, and it seemed to me that happiness itself might be cheaply had," Broyard wrote. Bowie's setting is the tail end of this period: the Kennedy years, with Village bohemianism becoming mass culture and folk albums going gold. "(You Will) Set the World on Fire" has Dave Van Ronk, Joan Baez, Phil Ochs, Pete Seeger, and Bob Dylan hanging out together at the Gaslight, like a folkie Justice League of America.

A candidate for the figure at the song's hub ("the black girl and guitar/ burn together hot in rage") is the folk singer Odetta, whose manager was Albert Grossman (Dylan and Peter, Paul and Mary were among his other clients) — the title line is a Grossman-type figure promising fame and immortality. But true to form, Bowie's title also references St. Catherine of Siena, a medieval nun who dictated visions while writhing in orgasmic ecstasy, developed stigmata (see "The Next Day"), had a mystical marriage to Christ (which she symbolized as wearing his foreskin as her wedding band), and helped reconcile the schismatic church. (Her epistle to Stefano di Corrado Maconi has a line translated as "if you are what you should be, you will set the whole world [well, all of Italy] on fire!")

But the singer who left MacDougal Street to sell magazines and leave his peers behind ("you're in the boat, babe/we're in the water") was most of all Dylan ("manipulate, origin, text," Bowie winked in his description of the song). In that light, "(You Will) Set the World on Fire" is Bowie's late-in-life bookend to "Song for Bob Dylan": one consummate thief and arch-manipulator honoring another. An overbearing track, its E major verses ram along to Earl Slick's chords while the E minor refrains are overworked rock musical ensembles, flooded with guitars and vocal harmonies; even the tambourine is aggressive. After some Slick fireworks, the song ends with its final cannon-blast refrains, where Bowie pushes to a high G, the top of his range on *The Next Day*, summoning a last strain of youth by force of will.

VALENTINE'S DAY

Recorded: *(backing tracks) 24 July 2012, Magic Shop; (vocals) 18 September 2012, Human Worldwide. Bowie: lead and backing vocal; Slick: lead guitar, acoustic guitar; Visconti: bass; Campbell: drums. Produced: Bowie, Visconti; engineered: McNulty, Visconti.*

First release: *11 March 2013*, **The Next Day**.

"Valentine's Day" bristles with purpose, gets its hooks in quickly. With just Earl Slick on guitar (from acoustic chording to lead lines to an arpeggiated hook in the refrains) and the rhythm section of Tony Visconti and Sterling Campbell, its structure has a similar economy of scale — D major progressions for verses and refrains, a B minor coda. Visconti said the song takes place "inside the mind of a high-school mass murderer named Johnny, inspired by the spate of shootings in US schools." As the shooter's aiming for "the football star," the 1999 Columbine killings were one possible inspiration, though any twenty-first-century school slaughter could have been: Red Lake, Virginia Tech, Nickel Mines, Northern Illinois U.

In Bowie's *Lazarus*, a main character is Valentine, whose casting description was:

The most ordinary of men — a person seemingly with little confidence — physically withdrawn to the point of invisibility; a loner who is in search of a friend — for some love — for a cause; but a man who is unable to edit his opinion and function as a "normal" person; psychotic.

Valentine, killer of lovers, performs "Valentine's Day" at a spotlight moment in the play. Splattered in blood, he sings with a smile while actors pop dozens of balloons covering the stage floor, making the popping sound of a rapid-firing gun, rather unnerving to hear in a small theater.

"Valentine" confides in the singer: it's the voice of a split personality, or that of an about-to-snap friend warning you to stay away from his target. "Isolation, revenge, osmosis," as Bowie described the song. The line central to the refrain — *he's got **something to say*** — perverts what Bowie offered his fans: the belief you can transform yourself, become a star in your own world, build a life on change. Now it's a demand — listen to *me*, look at *me* — at the point of a gun. The "terrorist position," as Leonard Cohen called it in the early Nineties. "So seductive that everybody has embraced it," he said. "Reduce everything to confrontation, to revenge."

It was the catchiest song on its album, with Bowie singing Beatles harmonies over Slick's arpeggios. Valentine's victims — "Teddy and Judy down" — echo Terry and Julie in the Kinks' "Waterloo Sunset." Lovers in Ray Davies' song, they're bodies in a classroom now, RIP hashtag names. Bowie's vocal is a sustained rage conveyed by walling in his melodies, moving from his opening fifth-spanning phrases to, in the coda, keeping to a single note until nudging away to break off a phrase ("it's-in-his-tiny *hand*").

One book in the background of *The Next Day* was Jon Savage's *Teenage*, the history of how adolescence seceded from childhood and how the adult world sought to rule it — by jailing adolescents, employing them, fearing them, molding them into a market, and, in the first half of the twentieth century, killing them in global wars. "Valentine's Day" is a horrific epilogue in which the job of breaking and culling adolescents has fallen to teenagers themselves.

Its video, directed by Indrani and Markus Klinko, was filmed at the Red Hook Grain Elevator. A casually-dressed Bowie plays a headless Hohner G2T guitar, which he grips like a rifle; a bullet sails across a thrummed guitar string. Demonically grinning as he mimes his refrains, it's the face of the Moloch god who sings "If You Can See Me," weighing judgment on his adopted home, where the regular slaughter of children is considered an act of nature. Hence the song's title — a day to commemorate lovers is some grubby killer's day of indiscriminate revenge. The Valentine's Day high school massacre in Parkland, Florida, in 2018 made Bowie's song prophetic, though in a country as gun-sickened as the United States, its prophesy was inevitable.

CHAPTER FIFTEEN:
NOEWHEMOE
(2014-2016)

For he is noewhemoe. Finiche! Only a fadograph of a yestern scene.
— James Joyce, *Finnegans Wake*

Our whole life is an Irish sea, wherein there is naught to be expected but tempestuous storms and troublesome waves... We bangle away our best days.
— Robert Burton, *The Anatomy of Melancholy*

Mr. Palomar decides that from now on he will act as if he were dead, to see how the world gets along without him.
— Italo Calvino, *Mr. Palomar*

He said: I know what it's like to be dead. He said... did he? Oh, that's very nice indeed.
— John Lennon, "She Said She Said" demo, 1966

The puzzle is not worth completing, and lies
In pieces, mostly.
— John Hollander, "9/17 (TO LYREBIRD)"

...there never was a world for her
Except the one she sang and, singing, made.
— Wallace Stevens, "The Idea of Order at Key West"

Be like the sun, never gone.
— Broadcast, "Long Was the Year"

SUE (OR IN A SEASON OF CRIME)

(Bowie, Schneider, Bateman, Bhamra.) **Recorded**: **(single)** *24 July 2014, Avatar Studios. David Bowie: lead vocal, Donny McCaslin: tenor and soprano saxophone (tenor soloist); Jesse Han: flute, alto flute, bass flute; David Pietro: alto flute, clarinet, soprano saxophone; Rich Perry: tenor saxophone; Scott Robinson: clarinet, bass clarinet, contrabass clarinet; Tony Kadleck, Greg Gisbert, Augie Haas, Mike Rodriguez: trumpet, flugelhorn; Keith O'Quinn, Ryan Keberle, Marshall Gilkes: trombone (Keberle: soloist); George Flynn: bass trombone, contrabass trombone; Ben Monder: guitar; Frank Kimbrough: piano; Jay Anderson: bass; Mark Guiliana: drums. Arranger, conductor: Maria Schneider;* **(remake)** *(backing tracks) 2 February 2015, Magic Shop; (vocals) 23, 30 April 2015, Human Worldwide. Bowie: lead vocal; McCaslin: tenor saxophone, clarinet, alto flute; Monder: guitar; Jason Lindner: Wurlitzer organ, Prophet '08, Prophet 12, Mopho X4; Tim Lefebvre: bass; Guiliana: drums; James Murphy: percussion. Produced: Bowie, Tony Visconti; engineered: Kevin Killen; (remake) Killen, Visconti.*

First release: *(single) 17 November 2014 (Parlophone 10RDB2014/88875028701, UK #81); (remake) 8 January 2016,* **Blackstar** *(ISO/Col 88875173862, UK #1, US #1).*

The last chapter opens on a Thursday night at the club Birdland, in midtown Manhattan. It's the eighth of May 2014, and David Bowie is there to see the Maria Schneider Orchestra. Someone sneaks a phone photo of Bowie sitting at his table, smiling broadly as Schneider stands before him, gesticulating— they look like old friends who've run across each other. The next day, they would start to write a song.

With his surprise return to making albums, Bowie avoided expectations by just being there again one morning, with no time to wonder what he'd sound like after ten years' absence. As it turned out, not greatly different from how he'd sounded in 2003. Where to go next? A side-step. He told his guitarist David Torn he expected to use the *Next Day* band for another album once he'd done with his experiment. He was going to make a proper jazz record.

He'd often talked about doing a jazz piece — *Black Tie White Noise* was one compromised effort. Jazz is a through-line of his work, from his 1965 Georgie Fame-inspired single "Take My Tip" through *Let's Dance*, which ticks to a big-band heart, to the cool fusion of "This Is Not America" to having Mike Garson solo in the voice of Cecil Taylor on "Aladdin Sane" to "Looking for Lester," a saxophone/trumpet duet with Bowie's namesake. But most of this was Bowie using primarily rock or R&B musicians. As he'd happily admit, he couldn't hold his own as a saxophonist in a jazz ensemble, while as a vocalist, he was so distinctive in tone that integrating him into a jazz band would be difficult — the closest he'd come was his and Angelo Badalamenti's "A Foggy Day."

Now Bowie was looking for someone similar to Badalamenti, a bandleader and arranger who composed in the style of the jazz idols of his youth, Stan Kenton and Gil Evans. During his last tour, he'd talk to Garson about this, with Garson telling him to look up Maria Schneider, who'd worked with Evans. A decade or so later, he did.

Hang Gliding

Schneider was born in 1960 in Windom, a farm town on the Des Moines River in southwest Minnesota. She's gone back there in her compositions, drawing on memories of flying in her father's propeller plane to North Dakota and Canada, over fields of flax and corn. When working with Gil Evans in the Eighties, she learned to make cocktails of instruments (so she may score a line for mute trombone and baritone saxophone to make them sound like an English horn). How to "dress a soloist," as she described how Evans arranged Miles Davis' *Sketches of Spain*: "there's all this fluttering — this movement... all these things going on — and when Miles enters, everything stops." How to create "struggling points" in compositions, such as scoring low instruments at the top of their range. She also studied with Bob Brookmeyer, who argued that structure shouldn't be rigid. Don't do a chord change because "it's time" for one. A solo shouldn't come after x many bars of a theme because that's when a solo always comes. A solo, he said, should only come when there are no other alternatives.

By the early Nineties, she had her jazz orchestra, playing the West Village club Visiones on Monday nights. She'd cab there with scores and music stands and pay each musician $25 a gig. "Every week it was logistical hell," she said. "You're different when you're younger. You just take it somehow." A breakthrough was *Allégresse* (2000), which had her first masterpiece —

"Hang Gliding," with its mixed meters and slowly overlapping lines, like a loose procession along a thoroughfare. The same album's "Dissolution" ranges from flute wanderlude to drum-and-guitar scrum. In "Bulería, Soleá y Rumba" (2004), saxophonist Donny McCaslin charges at the ensemble like a bull; "Cerulean Skies" (2007), its title sadly not a "Hearts Filthy Lesson" reference, opens with birdsong and moves like an upturned day.

Most of Schneider's orchestra (which ranges from seventeen to twenty musicians) play multiple instruments — trumpeters double on flugelhorn, saxophonists on flute, clarinet, or piccolo. She developed a core set of improvisers and tailored songs for them: McCaslin, the guitarist Ben Monder, the late trumpeter Laurie Frink, pianist Frank Kimbrough. Where often in ensemble jazz, a soloist plays over a harmonic structure the full band has introduced, Schneider said she writes "solo sections that continue the harmonic development of the piece. They're carrying the piece to some other place."

Liturgy

When he first visited Schneider's apartment, Bowie came to her with the first musical ideas for a song that he'd wanted to develop together into a piece. Over the course of a couple of months, it would become "Sue." "During that first May visit, we talked a lot and I listened to what he presented to me, and I thought 'you know, I think I can put something of my world into that,'" she told me. "I sat at the piano there in front of him and played around with harmony a bit, and I then said, 'maybe I can imagine doing something with this.' I experimented on my own for a couple weeks before we again met and started working collaboratively based on those ideas."

On 9 June 2014, Bowie and Schneider, along with McCaslin, Monder, trombonist Ryan Keberle, bassist Jay Anderson, and drummer Mark Guiliana, met to test out ideas and feel out the structure. Schneider wanted Bowie to hear first-hand the direction of the piece before they got into the studio with the whole band. "The first workshop version was very different," Schneider told me. She began by trying various metric modulations for the solo sections, with players improvising over an E major chord. At some point, it "felt like it was just way too much blowing. And while he loved it, I really felt it was over a line where it could feel too much like he was guesting with my band. When I explained that to him, he understood that could be the case."

So Schneider decided to make the E major chord a "B section" for him, in which he could sing something like an operatic recitative, or "when a priest sings the liturgy on one tone, making it feel almost liturgical." It was the right approach, as that style of singing gave Bowie freedom to keep changing lyrics and phrasings up until the point of recording, as the rhythms weren't locked in. Instead there were general tones for him to gravitate around: singing over eight bars of E, resting for four bars of G major (where Schneider referenced the first melodic phrase). But Bowie surprised her by switching it up at one point, skipping one E section to sing over the G section instead. It fit perfectly with what she'd written and "wiped out any predictability."

After another rehearsal about ten days later, Schneider did her final tweaks and then she, Bowie and her full orchestra recorded "Sue" at Avatar Studios on 24 July 2014. She had decided she didn't want jazz solos "as much as improvisational decoration and commentary around David," she told me. The soloing that Tony Visconti wound up using was mostly McCaslin's, with some of Ryan Keberle's work heard in the out-of-time section after "Suuuue...goodbye!" Both McCaslin and Keberle cut multiple solos in the session, sometimes going back and forth, with a delighted Bowie watching them. Schneider found that "the element of surprise was just natural to him — perfectly placed surprise — entirely unique... even some of the tones of the first melody — they are just so unexpected and wonderful."

She heard his lyric for the first time at the session. In 2015, she recalled that while she had known the general direction that the song was taking, "that changed — it became about Sue getting murdered for cheating. He wanted it to be really dark. I thought oh my gosh, am I going to get a lot of flak for contributing to a song about a man murdering a woman? But I didn't write the lyrics. And it does sound rather good."

When "Sue" first aired on BBC Radio 6 (on 12 October 2014), reaction was mixed. It was defiantly odd, hard to absorb. Bowie's vocal, with buffeting gales of vibrato, was true to the concept of him being a liturgical singer and solved the problem of how to integrate "David Bowie" into a jazz band — he becomes oversized, a persona the musicians have to work around. The jostling factions — instruments in loose confederations that soon break apart, moving at different tempos — give him freedom of movement. Some players work in Bowie's favor, others plot against him. Schneider constantly varies her instrumentation: take how many voices are heard over the seven-plus minutes, from Keberle's trombone grunts to Scott Robinson's contrabass clarinet, from Guiliana's cymbal work to the three-note closing plash of Kimbrough's piano. (There was enough of Plastic Soul's 1997 single "Brand New Heavy" in the bassline to merit the band sharing composer's credit with Bowie and Schneider.)

The fall of a marriage in eight verses (six in the single edit), "Sue" is a story full of blank pages. It opens in success — he got the job, they'll get the house. But something's amiss. Sue is ill, although the clinic's called, the X-ray's fine. The "theme" melody (a four-note phrase carried by brass and flutes, sung by Bowie in the first two verses) is Sue's motif. As his accusations mount, the motif returns in new shapes — the horns playing the notes at 5:57 sound they're in tatters.

Bowie keeps his character's motives hidden: is he a fool, a dramatist, a psychotic? Sue doesn't exist apart from the long stressed vowel of her name. If Bowie used Sarah Waters' 2002 novel *Fingersmith* (one of his "Top 100" recommended books) for the name, it's an inspired reference: the Sue of *Fingersmith* is a con artist who's a dupe in a greater game; she's the "I" of a story who doesn't know her identity is a fiction. In "Sue," a murder happens offstage. He dumps the body in the weeds, kisses the corpse, says goodbye. That's how the single edit ends. On the full "Sue," Bowie keeps talking, as if detectives have him in the box. He's found a note that tells the whole dirty story: "you went with *thaat clooowwwn*." Is the murder a revenge fantasy? Is he sitting in his empty house sketching the gravestone of his "virgin" wife? *Sue, I never dreamed*, as he starts the last verse. Or "Sue"/"I Never Dreamed": David Bowie's latest single backed by "I Never Dreamed," the first song he ever recorded, with his band the Kon-Rads in 1963. One of the latter's verses was *I never dreamed/Your caress could hurt so much*.

With Bowie so unreadable, the song's emotional weight falls on the man soon to become his collaborator. In Schneider's "Sue," Donny McCaslin improvises throughout. In the break after the second verse, his frantic run up the scale is answered by a suspicious snarl from trombone. After the verse with Sue's murder, there's an instrumental passage while McCaslin's creeping out of the room. He bores into the last verses, working against Bowie's voice, hounding him. Shifted to center-mix, McCaslin is the dominant voice of the closing section, the orchestra forming ranks around him as he plays in his altissimo range — getting higher-pitched notes from his tenor saxophone through different fingerings.

The lead actor has left the theater, McCaslin has to carry on. It's how their roles would play out in 2016.

Re-Sue

Bowie was interested in more collaborations, but Schneider couldn't spare the time due to her recording with her band, scheduled for the following month (*The Thompson Fields* (2015), cut with most of the "Sue" orchestra). She recommended that he use McCaslin's quartet instead (see "'Tis a Pity She Was a Whore").

Cut in the second set of *Blackstar* sessions, in early February 2015, a fresh arrangement for "Sue" (called "Re-Sue" in Bowie's notes for the album) proved difficult. "The new version of 'Sue' took the longest," McCaslin said. "Because the original we recorded with Maria is so specific, with all the orchestration." First he thought to cut a take with the band "just jamming, and there's David singing that first part. Then we'll all just cue the sections." It didn't work, although "we did one or two passes at that which were really wild." McCaslin went back to Schneider's score and slimmed the cast to saxophone, clarinet, and alto flute, all of which he played, while giving a greater role to Ben Monder.

"We'd get the roadmap [of songs] together and that took a while, especially on the arrangement for 'Sue', because it's kind of nebulous and floaty," added Tim Lefebvre, one of the musicians in the *Blackstar* sessions, along with keyboardist Jason Lindner, who hadn't played on Schneider's version. "We figured out where to change, because it's not an eight-bar groove kind of thing." There are no longer factions of instruments competing to be heard — the players move together at a gallop (Bowie gets through eight verses in roughly the length of the single edit). For the remake, Bowie "wanted a bit more edge, a bit more urgency," Guiliana said. "David encouraged us to really go for it... By the end, we really get to another gear. I have some Gregg Keplinger metal percussion on my ride cymbal on this take — you can that hear stuff bouncing around!"

Bowie's notes for "Re-Sue" emphasized "strong bass," which Lefebvre delivers: he opens with a funk riff distorted by a Pork Loin pedal, then later switches to an Octave pedal, with faster hand-picking, while using a Corona pedal for the sludgy passages — towards the close he plays what he called "EDM kind of stuff," working the top strings of his bass. Lefebvre described the breakdown after the sixth verse (3:07) as "they gave us eight bars to just *rage.*"

Monder had a similar role in the revised "Sue." At first doubling Lefebvre's bassline, he followed Bowie's request for

> really atmospheric stuff, so I did one pass with a lot of reverbed-out guitar... My go-to trick was turning the mix on my Lexicon LX-P 1 [an older half-rack reverb unit] all the way up, as well as putting the delay and decay all the way up — which makes this giant wash of sound and makes whatever note you play sound really good.

(He played the main riff on a hybrid Stratocaster, switching to his 1982 Ibanez AS-50 for harmonics.) Lindner, on two different Wurlitzer organs, takes over parts that horns and winds had played in the Schneider original, and also used "some extreme sounds in the drum and bass part, these huge sounds which are delayed; that's one of my Prophet keyboards. A lot of the watery reverb sounds used in 'Sue' are the Wurlys through pedals."

The stars of the original "Sue" — Bowie and McCaslin — are lesser figures in the remake, with McCaslin in particular a secondary voice: a wasp-like buzzing after the first verse; introducing the "Sue" motif on clarinet at 2:02. And while Bowie uses some phrasings from the original, he sings with less vibrato and his emphases are less stark — *you have a son* is as an aside that doesn't really matter (the clinic called again; the x-rays weren't good). The *Blackstar* "Sue" is less subtle (there's more intricacy in Guiliana's playing on the Schneider take) but packs a harder hit. Each "Sue" revises the other. Fittingly, Bowie gave the track two titles. It's a cusp song. There's nothing quite of its like in the Bowie catalog: one of his true oddities.

'Tis a Pity She Was a Whore

> *Recorded: (demo) ca. June 2014, Bowie home studio, 285 Lafayette St., New York City, or Woodstock, NY. Bowie: vocals, guitars, tenor saxophone, piano, synthesizer, Korg Trinity, drum machine; (remake) (backing tracks) 5 January*

2015, Magic Shop; (saxophone overdub) ca. April 2015; (vocals) 20, 22 April 2015, Human Worldwide. Bowie: lead and backing vocal; McCaslin: tenor saxophone; Lindner: Wurlitzer, Prophet '08, Prophet 12, Mopho X4; Lefebvre: bass; Guiliana: drums, Roland SPD-SX; Erin Tonkon: backing vocal. Produced: Bowie, Visconti; engineered: Killen, Visconti.

First release: *(demo) 17 November 2014, "Sue"; (remake) 8 January 2016,* **Blackstar**.

A man of property, believing his new wife virtuous, is deceived. She grows ill, though *the clinic called, the x-ray's fine*; she says she just ate some bad melons. The truth is soon inescapable: she's pregnant, by another man. Worse, by her brother. *I know you have a son!* He's persuaded to forgive her but plans revenge. *In a season of crime, none need atone.* Her brother skewers her heart on his dagger, murders her husband, is killed in turn. A cardinal gets the closing lines:

> *Car.*   Wee shall have time
> To talke at large of all ; but never yet
> Incest and murther have so strangely met.
> Of one so young, so rich in natures store,
> Who could not say, *'Tis pitty shee's a whoore?*

The last words of John Ford's 1633 play are its title, as well as the title of Bowie's 2014 single. Bowie transplanted Ford's Jacobean revenge tragedy into a film noir setting, with Ford's incestuous, doomed Annabella recast as Sue in the weeds. But wait, no, the single is called "Sue." Turn the disc over. There, the B-side has the title of Ford's play. But if "Sue" is actually *'Tis Pity She's a Whore* under an assumed name, what's *this* song?

WITNESS: FEMALE ASSAILANT HAD "MASCULINE" STRENGTH

It's a Sunday in the late Seventies. In downtown Santa Cruz, a jazz band plays in front of the Cooper House, a buff-brick grandeur that was once a courthouse and now holds shops, bars, and restaurants. It's the maypole around which downtown dances, as recalled Jason Hoppin, a Santa Cruz journalist. The band is called Warmth, a good name for a group that keeps shoppers and idlers company through the Californian afternoons. The bandleader hops from Wurlitzer to piano to marimba; the tie-dye-clad saxophonist rips into a solo. The tempo picks up. Warmth plays "Feel Like Making Love" and "Mustang Sally." Couples tipsy from white wine over lunch get up to dance. Right offstage, sitting in a chair, is a boy of ten or twelve, watching his father's band.

The kid is Donny McCaslin, born in 1966, a jazz musician built by postwar America: a public school with a top-notch jazz band; a community college with professional jazz instructors; a municipal infrastructure that supported weekly jazz concerts; a community center that hosted jazz seminars. When he was twelve, McCaslin made an "impulsive decision to switch out of a class in junior high into beginning orchestra," mostly because a friend was in the latter. Asked what he wanted to play, McCaslin chose tenor saxophone because of how cool he thought Warmth's saxophonist, Wesley Braxton, was ("I remember looking into the bell of his saxophone and it was like a pool of condensation and a cigarette butt floating in it").

He was a professional by college, playing in Gary Burton's band before graduating from Berklee in 1988. In New York, he did stints with the Gil Evans Project, Steps Ahead, Danilo Perez, Maria Schneider. He thrived in groups, saying that "it would be harder for me to live in a place where I was isolated and alone, and it was up to me in terms of my musical development." McCaslin is 6'3", a great presence on stage — his lungs seem as large as mainsails. Watching him play in 2007, Nate Chinen wrote of McCaslin "unfurling intricate lines as if they were streamers, in great gusts of exhalation." A melodically-dedicated improviser, he favors long crescendos that expire in rapid-fire sprays of notes.

In the early 2010s, he put together his current quartet. In Mark Guiliana, McCaslin found a brilliant drummer whose beats have the snap of electronic percussion — for example, Guiliana will vary the pitch of his snare hits by putting a bottom-hat cymbal on his snare head. ("My goal is not to always be machine-like but to know what that feels like," he said in 2013.) In Tim Lefebvre, he had a monster of a bassist who gets thunderclaps from his pedals. And Jason Lindner glides from washes produced by his collection of Moogs and Prophet synthesizers to playing a Wurlitzer groove suitable for mall dancers. The McCaslin Quartet often played the 55 Bar, a former speakeasy that's been on Christopher Street in Manhattan since the Red Scare. One set was on 1 June 2014. It wasn't a flawless performance, as Lefebvre struggled with his pedals at times ("the outlets there are janky"). During a break, a waitress came by to say there was a guy at one table who looked like an old David Bowie.

WAR DECLARED: RESERVISTS TO THE FRONT

McCaslin, though not his band, had known to expect Bowie. While they didn't meet that night, the two were soon exchanging emails. Not long after their correspondence began, Bowie sent him "'Tis a Pity She Was a Whore," a demo that he'd recorded at home, inspired by his night at the 55 Bar. "I sat there in stunned silence for a while," McCaslin said, recalling first hearing it.

Bowie thought of using McCaslin's group as he had Schneider's orchestra — a combo for a few other jazz-style compositions. Around the same time in summer 2014, Bowie was in the studio making full demos with Tony Visconti, Zachary Alford, and the pianist Jack Spann, and it's possible that Bowie could've shifted towards a new album of mostly rock-oriented songs seasoned with jazz or electronic pieces — *Black Tie White Noise* again. Yet by the end of the year, he'd decided to use McCaslin's quartet as his main backing. In the spirit of *Low* and *1. Outside*, he brought them into the studio without expectations, looking to see how songs would develop.

A sign of his adventurousness was to release his home demo of "'Tis a Pity She Was a Whore" as the B-side of "Sue," a track full of keyboard presets and distortion. "It was just kickass," Visconti said. "His production skills have gone up 5,000%." While he'd been recording demos at home since his teens (one Sixties bedroom studio set-up had different-sized stacks of books for tom and snare drums), he was a full-on home-studio indie rocker by 2010. Each *Blackstar* home demo was a near-complete performance, with guitar, saxophone, bass, and drum parts. "The demos he sent us were nuts: so different and quirky and awesome," Lefebvre said.

Having gone through McCaslin's back catalogue in preparation (Lefebvre: "usually it's the other way around — you research the guy who hired *you*"), Bowie centered on two pieces from McCaslin's *Casting for Gravity* (2012). One was a cover of Boards of Canada's "Alpha and Omega," in which a multi-tracked McCaslin plays a looped, phased melodic theme over variations driven by Guiliana and Lefebvre. And McCaslin's "Praia Grande," which builds to a maximalist sax solo full of waggled bass notes, surfing over waves of drums (loads of splash cymbal and tom fills) and synths.

Another starting point for "Tis a Pity" was possibly Nine Inch Nails' "Mr. Self Destruct," which also opens with a sonic barrage (there taken from the film *THX 1138*) and has a similar timbre. As the writer S. Alexander Reed noted, the demo sounds as if Bowie was going for a Steve Reich- style phasing, with acceleration and heightening. And as he seemed to have the Nineties on his mind at the time, "Mr. Self Destruct" gave him one rock-beat-driven template to use.

There's a fundamental instability in "'Tis a Pity," which hovers between F major and F minor, from its intro and solo sections (Fm-Bb-F) to its coda, where backing vocals move between A-flat and A notes, and so shading the underlying F chord from major to minor. Bowie's accelerando-rallentando saxophone moves in and out of phase with a plinking keyboard line — at times it sounds like a locomotive slowly building steam. When Bowie starts singing, his saxophone slows in tempo, only to increase its speed again, worrying the same notes; it's the song's propulsive, corrosive agent.

THEFT OF PURSE REPORTED, A DEXTEROUS CRIME

Bowie sits down to write a song based on John Ford's *'Tis Pity She's a Whore* and winds up with a song called "Sue." Having potted Ford's plot into "Sue," he now has an empty title where once there was a play. A scratch-space to fill. Sure, Ford's lustful and murderous players are still there in "'Tis a Pity," if hidden behind screens and made absurd. But Bowie's second line refers to the first sonnet in Robert Southey's 1797 sequence of poems condemning the slave trade, and whose opening lines are:

> HOLD your mad hands! for ever on your plain
> Must the gorged vulture clog his beak with blood?
> For ever must your Niger's tainted flood
> Roll to the ravenous shark his banquet slain?

The Southey quote, if pursued, could turn the song into the grotesque, pathetic confessions of a former slaver. There's also the inevitable biographical reading. Reportedly having suffered more heart attacks and possibly strokes in the 2000s, he now faces worse medical news. Hence the references to disease and theft, to the idea of life no longer being skirmishes but moving towards a final battle the singer knows he'll lose. (Time itself — punishing, emasculating, thieving — could be the real target of Bowie's scorn here.) "'Tis a Pity She Was a Whore" is a hub around which the grandest interpretations can wheel. Like the now-demolished Cooper House in Santa Cruz, it's a maypole.

Bowie's only public statement on the song was "if Vorticists wrote Rock Music, it might have sounded like this." The Vorticists, Britain's answer to the Futurists, had been on his mind for a while — they're creeping around *The Next Day,* and the Vorticist publication *BLAST* was another of his "Top 100 Books." Sitting in the 55 Bar that night, watching a jazz band blast away on stage, his brain being its usual warehouse, did he flash on a parallel? The Cave of the Golden Calf, the Vorticist cabaret of the early 1910s: a gay bar/avant-garde hobnobbing gallery. Thinking about mad nights in London before the Great War while he sat with polite jazz enthusiasts in a cramped club in New York at the end of the Obama years. The Vorticists wanted the future, a world of dynamism, machines, color and noise, and they got the war, which began the summer that the Cave of the Golden Calf went bankrupt. The Vorticist Wyndham Lewis was sent to the Western Front, put on patrol for the Royal Artillery, calling in artillery strikes. We say we want the future, but when it comes, it's always the war.

The Cave of the Golden Calf was at 9 Heddon Street, London. You can see the building in the background of the cover photo of *The Rise and Fall of Ziggy Stardust and the Spiders from Mars*, with Bowie posed up the street.

HEARTBROKEN MAN SAYS MEMBER IN LADYLOVE'S POSSESSION

Making a "proper" version of "'Tis a Pity" for *Blackstar* was a top order of business — it was one of the first tracks cut for the album, on 5 January 2015. "When we got together that first week, David said he wanted to re-record [it]," McCaslin said. "We were playing hard, going for it. That just happened in like ten minutes. That might have been the first take."

The *Blackstar* "'Tis a Pity" opens with two sharp intakes of breath, like a man readying himself to walk up another flight of stairs. Or, to be fair, like someone snorting a line of coke.

In the "'Tis a Pity" demo, Bowie's saxophone and piano lines work against a steady rhythmic base. "Compositionally the bass part has more of a rhythmic and less of a harmonic function," Lindner said. "It remains pretty much the same through the harmonic changes, with a couple of notes shifting to complement the progression." ("That's one where I was using a lot of Octave pedal," Lefebvre added.) The same was true for the drums. "The groove on the demo was a driving one-bar loop," Guiliana said. "The challenge was to play this repetitive part but stay in the moment and keep pushing the intensity." In overdubs, Guiliana used a Roland SPD-SX "full of 808 sounds," almost all of which were kept in the final mix (see the burst against "'tis my fate" at 3:33). As often on *Blackstar*, the sensation is of everyone moving at different speeds. In "'Tis a Pity," Guiliana is the repetitive centerline, while McCaslin and Lindner speed up and slow down around him (the composer Kevin Laskey likened it to a highway with Guiliana on cruise control while McCaslin and Lindner roar by him, then sharply brake).

The demo vocal is Bowie making strange asides in a corner of a room. His *Blackstar* performance is more gregarious: he has an audience now. Man, she punched me like a dude, he begins in a conspiratorial tone, as if trying to cadge a drink from a stranger. He rubs his cheek in wincing recollection. My curse, I suppose, in a tootling phrase; his four-note closing emphases — that-was-pa-trol —broken with a piping lift up an octave to a high F on "waaaaar." His tale and his voice grow murkier (maybe he got that drink): he cracks the hard "ks" of "kept my cock" like walnuts, he sings of her rattling speed with leadenly-sung notes, and crowns "whore" with another octave-jump. Each time he repeats the title phrase, he grows more absurd; in the last go-round, his voice seems to have crawled into his pocket: teeshapeetysheeewarseurhoooor.

On the demo, Bowie plays a continuo figure on saxophone, king of a whirlwind of noise. On *Blackstar*, McCaslin takes the part (he did overdubs months after the initial take). He enters with a slow dancing phrase after "my curse"; in the third verse, he arrives with Albert Ayler-esque trumpeting phrases. His overdubs replace Bowie's piano on the demo, creating an upspeed-downshift duet of stereo-scoped saxophones. And as McCaslin spirals outward into the coda, we hear Bowie in the studio, delighted, urging him on. A whoo!, then two shouts — *t*his is happening — and a yell like he's coming off a roller-coaster loop. Standing there, facing this miraculous band he'd found from out of nowhere, stepping back to watch them. It's the Vorticists' "separating, ungregarious British grin," or Jacobean incest-murder noir, or God's judgment on slave traders, or whatever weird jokes floated through his mind when he taped his demo. A bloody history of this broken world is within "'Tis a Pity She's a Whore," a latter-life masterpiece, with no top and no bottom.

LAZARUS

Recorded: (backing tracks) 3 January 2015, Magic Shop; (overdubs) ca. April 2015; (vocals) 23-24 April, 7 May 2015, Human Worldwide. Bowie: lead and backing vocal, guitar; McCaslin: tenor saxophone; Lindner: Wurlitzer; Monder: guitar; Lefebvre: bass; Guiliana: drums. Produced: Bowie, Visconti; engineered: Killen, Visconti.

First release: 18 December 2015 (MP3: 0886445656510, UK #45, US #40).

Walking into a performance of David Bowie's play *Lazarus* at the New York Theatre Workshop in December 2015, the first thing you noticed was a man lying on his back on stage. You might have recognized the play's lead actor, Michael C. Hall. If not, you might have thought it was someone playing a corpse, which would spark the drama once other characters came in. Hall didn't move, barely breathed; people taking their seats spoke in hushed tones. (At a post-Christmas performance I attended, my friend and I sat directly behind Duncan Jones. Something had come full circle.)

Lights dim. The alien Thomas Jerome Newton grudgingly resurrects. He stretches, stands, walks over to his bed. An old friend comes in, asks him if he remembers being the person he once was. That was before, Newton says. "There's nothing left of the past. It left. This is it now." Behind a glass wall upstage is a band. They've been onlookers: a minor audience to mirror the larger in the seats. Now a keyboard line begins, a call to attention on snare, guitar and saxophone riffs, and Newton starts to sing: *Look up here, I'm in heaven...*

Script (1)

He'd always wanted to write a musical. At twenty-one, Bowie drafted *Ernie Johnson*, a rock opera about a man throwing a suicide party. In 1971, he envisioned Ziggy Stardust as a hipper *Jesus Christ Superstar*: he'd originate the role; others would take it over for road productions. Two years later, he was doing a *Nineteen Eighty-Four* musical. He was "keen on writing in such a way that it would lead me into leading some kind of rock musical... I think I wanted to write a new kind of musical, and that's how I saw my future at the time." On it went: stated ambitions, nothing produced. To the *NY Daily News* in 1999, he described the play he was then writing, another *Ziggy Stardust* musical (see "Safe"): "I would do all the music but not the book. I would like to work with someone more skilled than I am... I do know my limitations. I would like to tour it around so it wouldn't have to have the context of Broadway to give it worth. There must be other things you can do on stage." His itch to move on stood at odds with the time and drudgery needed to write and stage a play. There was always another tour, another album to make. And then there wasn't.

Around 2006, Bowie was done with touring and ambivalent about making new albums. He'd acquired the rights to Walter Tevis' *The Man Who Fell to Earth*, the novel that the 1976 film was based on, and was looking for a collaborator to turn it into a musical. As per an article by novelist Michael Cunningham, published in *GQ* in 2017, Bowie reportedly contacted him about a collaboration, saying he "was intrigued by the idea of an alien marooned on Earth," and that he'd never been entirely happy with his work as Thomas Jerome Newton in Nicolas Roeg's film. What apparently drew Bowie to Cunningham was the latter's *Specimen Days* (2005), a trio of novellas set in a past, present, and future New York City, with Walt Whitman as a link. In particular, the future story, "Like Beauty," where an extraterrestrial refugee and a male cyborg meet a group planning to leave Earth in a spaceship and take their chances on an unknown planet. But the alien is old and dying, and she can't escape her exile.

Cunningham's essay (notably called a "story" in *GQ*) sheds light on a dim time but adds more shadow. There's enough evidence (a 2006 *Haaretz* article in which Cunningham is said to be "working on a musical with David Bowie" and a photograph of him attending the premiere of *Lazarus* in 2015, as he wrote that he had) to suggest the collaboration was real. But Cunningham's prose style, his caginess about certain details and odd specificity about others, makes the piece read as if he's recounting a long, bizarre dream, which is perhaps what collaboration with Bowie was like. Some things are off. Working on the script, Cunningham makes a big deal of presenting Bowie with a key plot point — Newton reveals his true alien form to the woman who loves him — that's perhaps the most-remembered scene of *The Man Who Fell to Earth* (Cunningham didn't recount Bowie's reaction, which perhaps was "so you watched the DVD, did you?"). There are also irregularities in the timeframe: though their collaboration was apparently in the mid-to-late 2000s, Cunningham writes of seeing Bowie's artifacts being readied to be shipped to the *David Bowie Is* exhibit, which wasn't happening until 2011 at the very earliest.

If the piece is to be believed, the musical's initial concept had it taking place in the future and having unrecorded Bob Dylan songs discovered after Dylan's death — Bowie would write these fake posthumous Dylan songs. He also told Cunningham the play should have mariachi music, which he thought was under-appreciated outside of Mexico. And according to Cunningham, Bowie wanted to use the name "Lazarus" in some way.

Sermon

Lazarus is a name with many stories within it. He's a double in the New Testament: two different men, with no relation to each other.

In the Gospel of Luke (16:19-31), Christ tells a parable. Lazarus is a beggar at a rich man's gate. Lazarus dies, ascends to heaven; the rich man dies, goes to hell. He cries out to "Father Abraham," asking for Lazarus to dip his finger in water and cool the rich man's burning tongue for a moment. Tough luck, Abraham says (imagine him in the voice of Dylan on "Highway 61 Revisited"). "Son, remember that thou in thy lifetime received thy good things, and likewise Lazarus evil things; but now he is comforted, and thou art tormented." Then the rich man asks for a resurrected Lazarus to go to his home to convince his family to change their ways. They already have the words of Moses and the prophets, don't they? Abraham says. If that's not good enough, well, a dead man at the door won't make a difference.

But in the Gospel of John (11), there's Lazarus of Bethany, a friend of Christ. Lazarus is dying of an illness, and his sisters ask Christ to intervene. Christ tarries; when he arrives, Lazarus is dead; Christ calls Lazarus forth from his tomb. Lazarus has no lines in the gospel. Waking up after four days of death, his body swathed in bandages, he intersects with the divine and is left behind. A resurrected alien, a man fated to die twice. There were plenty of favorite Bowie themes here — exile, doubles, death, resurrection, legend: the Biblical story is heard in the African-American folk song "Poor Lazarus," who's an outlaw left to die on a commissary table after asking his mother for a glass of water (Luke's parable is reversed — now it's Lazarus who asks for his thirst to be quenched).

Bowie also had another Lazarus in mind. With an eye towards his own posterity, he told Cunningham he'd been thinking about artists who had been popular in their time but lack critical appreciation today. In particular, Emma Lazarus, who wrote "The New Colossus," the poem that adorns the Statue of Liberty. Her words have been memorized by generations of Americans but she never got the type of critical apparatus that was built around a Whitman or Tennyson. ("The New Colossus" is reprinted at the end of the *Lazarus* script book.) Emma Lazarus, a lifelong New Yorker, would be the one piece of this early scenario to survive into later drafts. A character who falls in love with Newton and believes she's Emma Lazarus reincarnated would eventually become Newton's assistant Elly, played by Cristin Milioti in the first run of *Lazarus*.

Cunningham wrote that halfway through a first draft, Bowie's heart trouble returned and he needed immediate surgery. Their collaboration never resumed. Upon his recovery, Bowie focused on music, devoting much of 2011 and 2012 to *The Next Day*. But he didn't let his latest theatrical idea expire — he pressed on with it, growing more realistic. To get it staged in New York, he'd have to do a "jukebox musical." If people pay to see a David Bowie musical, sure, let them hear "Changes" and "All the Young Dudes" while they get buckets of weirdness hurled at them. Finding an established playwright collaborator was essential: two absolute beginners at musicals was too many. Bowie asked his producer Robert Fox for suggestions — who's a great contemporary playwright? Fox recommended Enda Walsh.

Script (2)

Walsh was born in Kilbarrack, a suburb northeast of Dublin, in 1967. Describing an early play *Misterman*, Walsh told the *Guardian*:

> I wanted it to be about a man and a building and for the audience to be asking from the off: "How did he end up there?" And: "What's he trying to tell us and why?" He's looking for some rest, but his guilt is overwhelming and, besides, he's existing on Fanta and Jammie Dodgers and cheap cheesecake, so there is no rest.

As this is *Lazarus* in a nutshell, it's no surprise that Bowie thought he'd found the right collaborator at last.

When Walsh first met Bowie in New York, in the autumn of 2014, he recalled entering "a secret lift [and] arriving in a completely grey corridor, with this huge ridiculous fucking door at the end of it." This led to a gallery, where he found Bowie, who embraced Walsh, saying "you've been in my head for three weeks." Naturally, he'd read every Walsh play, and peppered him for a time with questions about his work. Then Bowie slid four pages' worth of ideas across the table.

The two wrote for over a year, often by Skype: Bowie in New York, Walsh in London. "He had it mapped out for me," Walsh recalled. There was Thomas Jerome Newton; his savior, a dead girl; a woman ("Ellie Lazarus") "who over this short period has a mental breakdown;" and the psychotic murderer Valentine, "who just wants to fucking kill love!" There wouldn't be a narrative as much as events refracted through Newton's diseased mind: the perspective of a man who can't leave Earth and who can't die. "I said to him, 'Jesus, all we're doing is constructing weather — it's all atmospheres and rhythms clashing together'," Walsh recalled in 2017. The aim was to have a ninety-minute play seem like a Bowie song. "It's this dream piece, connecting sort of but not fully," he said. "We talked a lot about a man who effectively wants to die... can we make a piece that feels like it's been infused with morphine?"

When Walsh later learned that Bowie had cancer, he wondered how much his partner had been grappling with mortality while writing. "What must it be like to be David Bowie? [When you die,] are you truly dead?" As they were writing Newton's final speech, Walsh thought can you [imagine] the last moments of your life... to have that grief and fight with yourself, wanting to live, wanting to continue, but wanting rest. That's what we ended up making... having a silent conversation with each other without it being, "let's go down and have a pint"... how do you deal with the fact you're not going to be here in three months' time?

Caged in his apartment, Newton begins *Lazarus* as he'd been at the end of Roeg's film: drunk, isolated, bereft, numb, missing his home planet. He's the play's hollowed-out center, around whom livelier personalities circle. *Lazarus* was the reclusive sister of *Blackstar* — a messier, stranger, more hermetic work (until it was staged in the UK and Europe, the play had only been seen by a relative handful of people in New York). It was a glimpse into how Bowie's mind worked and was his opportunity to have new songs performed on stage that he would never sing live. And after January 2016, a deeper layer was revealed: a dying father was saying goodbye to his teenage daughter.

"Visionary crap," pronounced a man sitting behind me at the end of a preview performance.

Studio

At first Bowie planned to use catalog songs for *Lazarus*, but his producer Fox suggested that he write some new ones. By summer 2014, he had a sketch known as "Bluebird," which he proposed developing with Maria Schneider after writing "Sue." He also demoed the song (now called "The Hunger") in the studio. Renamed "Lazarus," it would be the first track recorded in the first *Blackstar* session in January 2015.

On *Blackstar*, "Lazarus" moves at a morphine-drip tempo (it takes a minute to get through sixteen bars — Mark Guiliana can fit four kick drum beats between each snare hit) and is harmonically sparse: the verse moves from the home chord of A minor ("I'm in") out to F major ("heaven") and slowly goes back home. Its regimentation — how the guitar (and later saxophone) fills close every Bowie phrase — is hit by turbulence in the bridge, which jolts from C major ("I was") through E-flat major ("looking for your") to land on D major ("ass"). One possible inspiration, in mood and tone, was the Cure's "The Big Hand" ("it traces back to the Cure and New Order," bassist Tim Lefebvre said of his opening bassline).

In the verse, Bowie's vocal line has a five-note range — he's mostly keeping to the root notes of chords, his closing phrases dragged across bars. He alters his phrasing in the bridge, singing declamatory phrases that sink a third to expire ("used up all-my-mon—ey") and keeps on with this phrasing while the chords resume the Am/F pairing. It conveys Newton's frustration at being stuck in limbo, and creates a structural tension — is this still a bridge? a new verse? an outro? The song winds down, unresolved.

The *Lazarus* performance needs to have Hall quickly bring the audience into Newton's state of mind, so the bridge is the dramatic peak (complete with backing singers), after which "Lazarus" is snuffed out to cut to a fresh scene. Compare the *Lazarus* version's quick-sweep keyboard intro to the opening of the *Blackstar* track: a chordal bass run by Lefebvre, improvised early in the session. "The intro didn't exist on his demo, but after the first take we kept playing, and Tim started playing this beautiful line with the pick, which David liked and thought would make for a nice intro," Guiliana said. Lefebvre plays eighth notes on his E string, moving up the neck, going so high at first (at his nineteenth fret) that it's often been mistaken for a guitar line. It began as an embellishment during the first take's outro. "I'm a big fan of this band Fink, and their guitar parts are like that, where they move roots around," Lefebvre said. "So I did it at the beginning, too, and it became the thing. Anybody that's heard my playing had heard me do that five billion times… I just improvised the high stuff."

McCaslin plays what were originally Bowie saxophone parts in the verse. Bowie wanted the song to linger, open up, build. "I remember that we played a really nice first take — everyone played very musically, but politely," Guiliana said. "David said something like, 'Great, but now let's *really* do it.' He was always pushing us. The version on the record is the next take, where we are all taking a few more chances."

There was a raw element needed — a clanging, distorted guitar to abrade the verses and outro. Though Ben Monder did guitar overdubs for most *Blackstar* tracks, "the bizarre shrapnel guitars in 'Lazarus' are all Bowie," Monder said. As Nicholas Pegg discovered, Bowie played the Fender Stratocaster that Marc Bolan had given him in 1977, weeks before Bolan's death. The power chords — three sliding stops down the neck — at first stand alone, tearing through the opening verse: scars that can't be seen but heard well enough. Later they align with McCaslin's saxophone.

Stage/Screen

McCaslin's roaring saxophone (at times thickened with overdubs and drenched in reverb) is urged on by Guiliana's drums and Lefebvre's rolling bassline. But when compared to some of his wilder moments on *Blackstar*, McCaslin seems held in check.

At a show in London in November 2016, McCaslin announced "Lazarus" with its three-chord banner. He played the verse melody somberly, then in a higher register. By the bridge, he lifted into the song, twisting through it while Guiliana detonated around him. Five minutes in, he was whirling, with higher and higher phrases, choking off notes. And in New York, in February 2017, he played "Lazarus" with Gail Ann Dorsey for a Bowie tribute. She captured the song with her first line. Done singing, she sat down onstage, letting McCaslin take her place in the relay. There's no warmup — he tears into his solo, running up and down scales, boiling and rolling while Dorsey nods along, her eyes closed. It's a seance where the spirit doesn't need to talk, where the living do the work.

Bowie had been selecting heirs, distributing properties. "Lazarus" became McCaslin's and Dorsey's song. It was Michael C. Hall's song, too — he first performed "Lazarus" to an audience, on stage and on the *Late Show* in December 2015. More inheritors will come. But its video, shot in November 2015, made it impossible for "Lazarus" to fully escape Bowie's orbit. A jovial *not so fast, loves*.

"I just thought of it as the Biblical tale of Lazarus rising from the bed. In hindsight, he obviously saw it as the tale of a person in his last nights," said Johan Renck, who directed the "Lazarus" video. Bowie plays two roles, already seen in Renck's earlier "Blackstar" video. A dying mortal with "button eyes" (his eyes blinded by swathes of bandages, with two black buttons for pupils), reaching out to heaven, his wasted body being tugged out of his hospital bed. And "Bowie": trickster daemon, still at work, plotting, wearing his *Station to Station* jumpsuit. In the video, Button Eyes takes the mournful verses and Bowie the bridge lines. "So British, the wit, like a guilt thing, making sure it's not coming across as too serious or pretentious — and yet that enhances the humanity of it," Renck said. The video even ends with "Bowie" packing off into a wardrobe, reportedly a suggestion from a crew member.

He'd kept cameras out of the studio when making *Blackstar*, when he was visibly affected by chemotherapy, so Button Eyes is his officially-approved

"Dying Bowie" for the tabloids to use. It's the act of dying as a pantomime, a caricature to entertain the young and healthy, as performed by "old age, calm, expanded, broad with the haughty breath of the universe," as Whitman wrote in "Song of the Open Road." "Old age, flowing free with the delicious near-by freedom of death."

In a sketch for the video, Bowie called his other role "the somnambulist." The name goes back to Conrad Veidt's character in *The Cabinet of Dr. Caligari*, a sleepwalker used by the title character to commit murders and robberies. The "Bowie" figure is the sleepwalking half of dying Button Eyes, but here devoted to work: scribbling away, thinking up new names, new costumes, albums, movies, musicals. *Nineteen Eighty-Four* at last! *2: Contamination*! A small residency with McCaslin in New York — it'll start at a comfortable hour, home by eleven. Always more. When he was twenty-six, Bowie sang a curse on time, making time pace in the wings like an antsy stage manager. A wanker, a puppet dancer. Time took the insults in stride. Watching Bowie work at the solitary candle's end, he's sympathetic, but really, we should be on by now.

Sing

The cast and crew of *Lazarus* didn't know if Bowie would make the play's opening night, on 7 December 2015. His declining health was still a secret held among Walsh, director Ivo van Hove, and a few others. But he was there. At the end of the performance, after taking a bow with the cast, Bowie "went around to everyone in the theater... he wanted to celebrate the stage managers and the doormen — he thanked everyone," Walsh said. Cunningham wrote that he and Bowie embraced for a moment, that he told Bowie he was happy the play had worked out. When Bowie left through the front door, out to his car on East 4th St., Walsh said he "knew that was going to be the last time I would see him."

A month or two earlier, Bowie is at an early run-through performance of *Lazarus*. The bandleader Henry Hey asks for his thoughts: "Is everything OK? Would you like anything else?" "Yes," he says. "I think I'd like a sing." A keyboard intro, a call to attention on the snare. David Bowie sings before an audience for the last time in his life. A performance that's the memory of a few actors, musicians, lighting techs, stage managers. He sings "Lazarus."

The song of a dying New Yorker, a pop poet of the downtrodden. A beggar in heaven, a twice-dead man, an outlaw. An exiled alien, living on Twinkies and gin. *Look up here*, Bowie begins, the musicians there to back him up. *I'm in heaven…*

WHEN I MET YOU

Recorded: (backing tracks) 3 January 2015, Magic Shop; (vocals) 5 May 2015, Human Worldwide. Bowie: lead and counterpart vocal; Monder: acoustic guitar, lead guitar; Lindner: Moog Voyager, Micromoog, Wurlitzer, Prophet '08, Prophet 12, Mopho X4; Lefebvre: bass; Guiliana: drums. Produced: Bowie, Visconti; engineered: Killen, Visconti.

First release: 21 October 2016, **Lazarus: The Original New York Cast** (Col 88985374912, UK #10, US #129).

At the end of *Lazarus*, Thomas Jerome Newton learns that the teenage girl ("Marley") he's been talking to throughout the play is dead. "Not properly dead," she notes. She's the Baby Grace Blue of *Lazarus* — her murderer is never caught; her death needs a ritual act to complete. Until then, she's condemned to wander the Earth (or at least Second Avenue) as a ghost. When Marley tells Newton he has to help her die properly, he says she's his last hope, so how can he kill that? Cue the duet "When I Met You," the play's penultimate song.

"When I Met You" isn't sung by Newton and Marley, as one might expect given the narrative — its performers were misidentified as such in a bootleg audio recording of an early *Lazarus* performance. Newton instead duets with the "First Teenage Girl" (Krystina Alabado, in the New York production), one of the play's (teenage) Greek chorus. It's a duet between a man and a voice in his broken mind — a dialogue on love, despair, and redemption. When Bowie recorded "When I Met You" in the *Blackstar* sessions, he took both parts, the interplay a wrestler-tumble, with his lead voice gaining ground, while his chorus vocals, shunted left and right in the mix, mount fevered responses. On the *Lazarus* cast recording, the distance between Hall and Alabado's voices is so great that they sound like they're in different rooms.

A composition that takes its time (the intro alone is thirty-two bars), "When I Met You" moves from Newton-sung verses to Newton/Teenage

Girl counterpoint/harmony refrains to a bridge where the home chord of G major is altered, diminished, augmented. It suggests the convulsions of Newton's mind, where nothing's solid anymore. "You knew just everything," Newton begins. "And nothing at all." (Bowie changed it to "but nothing at all" in his recording.) If Newton is a Lazarus, the girl in his head is Christ — she called him from the tomb, opened his eyes, let him speak.

"A scuzzier version of one of his grand ballads — imagine 'Word on a Wing' with three-day growth and hangover," as Alfred Soto wrote of it. A biographical reading is obvious: Bowie thanking his wife for saving him, for Coco Schwab for protecting him, for his children for letting him escape being "Bowie." "When I met you... the edge had become/the center of my world..." Yet whatever salvation he'd gotten is fading now. *It's all the same*, rescued and rescuer sing to each other. In *Lazarus*, Newton sings the final refrain as he prepares to kill Marley, stabbing her as the final notes sound. Death's release; no knowledge comes.

Bowie tackled "When I Met You" during the first *Blackstar* sessions in January 2015 — he was starting out with remakes ("'Tis a Pity She Was a Whore") and takes on *Lazarus* songs, as if to clear the ground. He made minor alterations to "When I Met You," cutting a line ("the dream of time") and switching lines around in later refrains. For the arrangement, he emailed Donny McCaslin that "the structure of 'When I Met You' is sound, but now we need to mess with it so we hear it from another angle. Put in a couple of passages in the corner (in darkness) and throw a small pen-light beam on the rest — like a P.I. scouting a motel room." ("He's never saying something like 'can I have a bass drum on 2 & 4'?" McCaslin said.) First appearing as a bonus on the *Lazarus* cast recording and later on the *No Plan* EP, Bowie's "When I Met You" lacks McCaslin's saxophone, whereas for *Lazarus* Henry Hey scored brass lines for refrains. Instead the track runs on skitterings (Jason Lindner's Prophets and Moogs in the intro and vocal breaks), pulses (a jaunty Lefebvre bassline) and jabs (an acoustic guitar with more bite than in the *Lazarus* cast recording), with "Hawaiian"-sounding lead lines (McCaslin heard "an African highlife thing") as a dreamy counterpoint to Bowie in the verses.

In the *Lazarus* duet, Alabado's chorus vocal is insistent, holding one note high over Hall's lower-pitched phrases — her final repeats of "when I met — when I met" are a distress call. Bowie's backing vocals have a broader emotional spectrum. Faced with lines like "the peck of a blackened eye" and "now the luminous dark," Hall unfurls them, stiffly at times. Bowie takes more pleasure: there's a grin in his phrasings. He always wrote his parts with one actor in mind.

No Plan

Recorded: (backing tracks, vocals) 7, 10 January 2015, Magic Shop; (overdubs? retake?) ca. March 2015, Magic Shop? Bowie: lead and backing vocal, lead guitar, rhythm guitar; McCaslin: tenor saxophone, clarinet, alto flute, C flute; Lindner: Wurlitzer, Prophet '08, Prophet 12, Mopho X4, Moog Voyager, Micromoog; Lefebvre: bass; Guiliana: drums. Produced: Bowie, Visconti; engineered: Killen, Visconti.

First release: 21 October 2016, **Lazarus: The Original New York Cast**.

When he dies, his spirit rises a meter. No music, but sound. Nowhere, but Second Avenue just out of sight. The pieces of his soul — memories, lusts and hates, ambitions, all his arable and barren selves — hold together but may soon drift apart. There's no recognizable street plan anymore. North could be west, Broadway could cross Avenue D. "This is no place," the spirit says. "But here I am." It steps aside into the not-quite-yet.

"No Plan" (called "Wistful (This Is Not Quite Yet)" in an early Bowie draft of the album sequence) was always intended for *Lazarus*, Donny McCaslin believed (Enda Walsh said Bowie asked him if he had any lyrical ideas for the song). It's the most "Broadway" of the *Blackstar*-era songs, its melody's wide intervals suggesting Leonard Bernstein's "Maria" or "Something's Coming." It's unknown if Bowie wrote the song with a woman's voice in mind, but by the time that *Lazarus* was being cast in summer 2015, he was looking for a young female singer for it. He found her in the then-fourteen-year old Sophia Anne Caruso, who once described "No Plan" as "a new song by David Bowie just for my character." Bowie sent her a card on *Lazarus'* opening night to say how much he appreciated her interpretations of his songs (in an act worthy of great karmic retribution, someone stole the card soon afterward).

In *Lazarus*, it's one of the spotlight songs for Caruso's character, Marley, known mostly in the play as The Girl, a not-quite-dead murder victim who becomes the guardian angel of the exiled Thomas Jerome Newton.

Singing "No Plan" is how she introduces herself, stating the terms of her confinement while Newton pours himself another drink.

McCaslin recalled of the Bowie version of "No Plan" that

there was more tinkering with the instrumentation than we did with the others, and more takes... It's a bit more like a show tune. In fact the second time we approached it, he sent a new demo. First time was David and guitar. This one had acoustic piano [Henry Hey] and a female singer, and she had a dramatic musical theater approach.

(Given the timing, the demo singer couldn't have been Caruso. McCaslin's recollection of remaking "No Plan" in March 2015 clashes with Nicholas Pegg's assertion that the track was recorded at the January 2015 sessions, including Bowie's full vocal; perhaps the March retake wound up being unused.)

Sparse in its harmonic structure — verses hold on a B-flat major seventh chord, with shifts to F# ("I'm *lost*" "nowhere *now*"); refrains move to E-flat minor, with shifts to F major ("without a *plan*" "here *I am*") — "No Plan" is subtly clever in its construction, having a five-bar phrase in the verses that, the next time around, extends to seven bars. "On this version I play a bunch of flutes and some clarinet and low-end tenor sax stuff," as McCaslin told *Mojo*.

As Bowie's humbled take on "No Plan" was cut well before Caruso's wide-eyed take, listening to the two tracks in their recording order reverses the progression of *Toy*, where Bowie remade his earliest songs as an older man, imposing the costs of age upon youth. It's a different degree of tragedy here — Bowie's "No Plan" assesses a full life at its end; Caruso's mourns one that was barely allowed to begin.

GIRL LOVES ME

Recorded: (backing tracks) 3 February 2015, Magic Shop; (overdubs, treatments) ca. March-April 2015; (vocals) 16 April, 17 May 2015, Human Worldwide. Bowie: lead and backing vocal; McCaslin: alto flute, C flute; Monder: guitar; Lindner: Wurlitzer, Prophet '08, Prophet 12, Mopho X4; Lefebvre: bass, guitar; Guiliana: drums; Murphy: treatments, percussion. Produced: Bowie, Visconti; engineered: Killen, Visconti.

First release: 8 January 2016, **Blackstar**.

The second round of *Blackstar* recording, in February 2015, began with revising "Sue." On the second day of the session, the Donny McCaslin quartet turned to a demo that Mark Guiliana recalled having "two loops on top of each other, creating a very dense groove, which I couldn't play all at once." There were synthesized string parts, some of which McCaslin would score for flute. Then there was the lyric. As Jason Lindner said, "when we first heard the demo, we said, 'what the hell? What are these words?'"

The opening line is *cheena so sound so titi up this **malchick** say!* and it goes on from there. Bowie sings "Girl Loves Me" in chunks of sound — his words packed together like bullets — and draws from two dialects, each the tongue of subcultures, outsiders, young toughs, criminals. Both connect to his youth.

Polari (or Palare), source of "titi" (pretty), "nanti" (no), "omees" (boys) and "dizzy" (flaky), is a spoken tongue derived from Italian or Shelta. As Ian Hancock wrote, it was "the language of the theater, the circus, show business, and... certain male homosexual communities, especially those with connections to show business and with life at sea." Bowie picked up Polari from the mid-Sixties BBC radio comedy *Round the Horne* and, more directly, from being a young man in the center of Sixties British gay life — the London-based theater and music scenes — and an intimate of the mime Lindsay Kemp and the composer Lionel Bart. "David uses [Polari] words like 'varda' and 'super' quite a lot," as Michael Watts wrote in his 1972 *Melody Maker* "Bowie comes out" article, and there's Polari in Bowie lyrics of the period (e.g., "traders" ("Bewlay Brothers"), "trolling" ("Looking For a Friend")).

The other tongue is fictional — Nadsat, a Russian pseudo-dialect created by Anthony Burgess for his novel *A Clockwork Orange* (the first verse of "Girl Loves Me" alone has "malchick" (boy), "cheena" (girl), "moodge" (man), "vellocet" (drugs) and "polly" (money)). In the Ziggy Stardust days, Bowie used Stanley Kubrick's film adaptation of *Clockwork Orange* as a sartorial guide for the Spiders from Mars, and put a touch of Nadsat in "Suffragette City." In 1993, he said "this kind of fake language... fitted in perfectly with what I was trying to do in creating this fake world or this world that hadn't happened yet. It was like trying to anticipate a society that hadn't happened."

In "Girl Loves Me," a single verse is chanted more than sung — Bowie harps on one note until the end of each phrase, when he moves up by a third ("this *mal-chik*") and ultimately an octave, yodeling the last note ("say-*ay*"), his vocal given heavy doses of echo. His verse lines have a tumbling consonance ("*po—po* blind to the *pol*-ly") and chase their short-held notes with longer ones. "As he was listening back, I could see him experimenting with different words," as McCaslin recalled of Bowie in the studio. He tweaked his Nadsat — "yarbles" (balls) became "garbles," "spatchka" (sleep) became "spatchko."

Droogs and queens, police and cheenas. Tacky things drive the gang wild; party now because we're out of drugs tomorrow. Set up the old men and take their cash; screw in the street, sleep it off in jail. It's the balls-out sequel to "Dirty Boys." Some of it came from Bowie's fandom for shows like *Peaky Blinders*, full of sharp young Birmingham toughs. Some came from books, as usual. And then a man with an unpromising diagnosis wonders where the time's gone. More succinctly: where the fuck did Monday go?

Its minimal harmonic movement (shifts between two chords for all but the bridge) is the work of keyboards or synthesized strings. The driving wheel is Guiliana's drum 'n' bass-inspired snare, kick, and cymbal figures. "I tried to capture the feeling of the halftime backbeat with the undercurrent of the busier sixteenth-note details," he said. "The ghost notes in the groove are heard through the close mic on the snare, but the backbeat is being captured through David's vocal mic. There was lots of bleed since we were all in the same room, which often led to very interesting sonic results. This, like many of the other songs, is a full drum take." Tim Lefebvre doubled his free bassline (as Lindner noted of his friend's performance, "the bass note is not representative of the key or the root — it's really coloristic") on guitar, borrowing one of Bowie's, along with a "little multi-effects pedal… it was a cheap little thing but it sounded great." McCaslin worked in the backline, tracking alto flute and C flutes for an interlude where the track lets in sunlight.

Sloosh to Polezny Murphy

The producer James Murphy struck up a friendship with Bowie in 2013 when, having retired his group LCD Soundsystem (very temporarily), he was recording Arcade Fire's *Reflektor*, for which Bowie cut a guest vocal. Upon Bowie's return to music that year, Murphy was talked up as a potential producer: he was a dance-rock classicist in obvious awe of Bowie's late-Seventies albums. After Bowie's death, Murphy revealed he'd indeed been slated to co-produce *Blackstar* but had backed out, feeling "overwhelmed."

"It takes a different kind of person than me to walk into that room and be like, I know exactly... I belong here, I should definitely insert myself in this relationship because they just can't manage to make a record without me," Murphy told Radio One in 2017. He'd prepped himself to be the Brian Eno of *Blackstar*, to the point of using an EMS Synthi AKS, Eno's weapon of choice on the "Berlin" albums. But he couldn't go the full Eno — he couldn't ask musicians to play random chords, or erase a half-finished track he felt wasn't working. "Eno is, I think, open, manipulative and confident. I'm shy and self-directed and controlling. I have to micromanage," Murphy told the *Guardian*. So he kept to the sidelines at the February sessions, filtering guitars and keyboards through the EMS on "Girl Loves Me" (see the burbling percussive line mixed left through much of the track). Murphy "was just in there hanging out," Lindner recalled. "They weren't clear on his role."

Murphy's legacy on *Blackstar* would be some treatments, percussion on "Girl Loves Me" and "Sue," a suggested chord change on one undisclosed song. "I thought, well, I just had a moment where there's this Bowie song and I suggested the chord change. I can go home happy now," he said. "It wasn't selfless of me to back out. I'm incapable of working in that situation. I'm not being inflexible, I'm not being stubborn, it's just not there. I can't produce. I think I'm done producing. I can't do it." (McCaslin did recall Murphy taking "Girl Loves Me" to his home studio and doing "this whole other thing with it," but that seems likely an as-yet-unreleased remix instead of the *Blackstar* track.) Murphy put his frustration and loss into "Black Screen," a song on his 2017 LCD Soundsystem album *American Dream*, where he honored Bowie ("you fell between/a friend and a father") and confessed that "I had fear in the room/So I stopped turning up."

It's easy to see how Murphy was intimidated — just listen to Bowie's vocal on "Girl Loves Me," tracked to a squadron in the verse, a cheering section in refrains (the wonderful GO! GO! GO! GO! GO! GO! GO! that starts at 1:26); doubled over an octave for the bridge; murmuring conspiratorial "hey cheena"s under his boasts that the girl loves him, reminiscent of the vocal arrangement on "No One Calls." Lefebvre recalled "the brilliance of that writing. How it's all dark gibberish and then it turns into this beautiful melody. The chords are very interesting — aggressive but at the same time very languid and soft." As often with Bowie, there was a disgraced ancestor. A song of dealers, druggies, and hustlers, whose semi-spoken, nasally-intoned verses spool into bounding refrains? It's "Shining Star (Makin' My Love)" for the 2010s. All that's missing is a Mickey Rourke rap.

The refrain stands outside the song. Bowie's line about sitting in the chestnut tree has bred a host of speculations. Is it the Chestnut Tree Cafe of Orwell's *Nineteen Eighty-Four*, and so suggesting a place of betrayal? (Orwell's novel was to Bowie what Bowie's Berlin albums were to Murphy.) Or, in an inspired suggestion by the writer Yanko Tsvetkov, a nod to Gabriel Garcia Márquez's *One Hundred Years of Solitude*? In that novel, the patriarch José Arcadio Buendía goes mad, trapped in a perpetual Monday, while for his family the week proceeds as usual. Raging, he starts to destroy his house. He's held down, bound, dragged "to the chestnut tree in the courtyard, where they left him tied up, barking in the strange language and giving off a green froth at the mouth."

Barking in the strange language. Bowie sings words quarried from lost pasts and lost futures, now mangled and chewed up, made into a cipher of lust and spite. "Girl Loves Me" should be done after two or so minutes but it won't stop. He's up in his tree (even if he's been left to rot in it), piling up what he can. The dirty boys and dirtier old men, the traders and droogs and crooked cops, sex, money, pills, schemes — the roil of life, a filthy tide sweeping out. Who the fuck's going to mess with him? Nobody.

DOLLAR DAYS

Recorded: (backing tracks) 6 February 2015, Magic Shop; (guitar overdubs) ca. late March 2015; (vocals) 27 April 2015, Human Worldwide. Bowie: lead and backing vocal; McCaslin: tenor saxophone; Monder: acoustic guitar, lead guitar; Lindner: Wurlitzer, piano, Prophet '08, Prophet 12, Mopho X4; Lefebvre: bass; Guiliana: drums. Produced: Bowie, Visconti; engineered: Killen, Visconti.

First release: 8 January 2016, **Blackstar**.

Among the last songs composed for *Blackstar*, "Dollar Days" was the only track on the album Bowie hadn't demoed beforehand. He came into the Magic Shop one February morning, sat down with an acoustic guitar and taught the song to his players, singing what lyrics he had, soon moving to work with Jason Lindner at the piano to establish chord progressions. Donny McCaslin sketched a lead sheet and the track was cut so quickly that McCaslin all but forgot it for a time ("it had just happened in a few hours in one day of recording"), as had Lindner, who said before *Blackstar*'s release: "I can't even recall in my head what song that is. I remember a couple of songs [Bowie] played us on the guitar. I think he said he wrote them this morning and we made something out of them."

Much of "Dollar Days" feels written on guitar — its verse melody rhythms sync to the guitar strums, with Bowie moving to sing eighth notes to match the faster strums that close out bars; how his notes work to support the underlying chord, with his vowel sounds — all those rich ees — mortaring the guitar's coalitions of notes. And there's a physicality to the chord changes: an E major half-diminished 7 ("got no enemies I'm") to an E-flat major 7 ("walking down"), a move on guitar done simply by shifting a finger while keeping a barre chord shape. Ben Monder played Bowie's acoustic lines in overdubs, in stereo-panned tracks for the verses. "I was just not hearing an acoustic part in my head. I didn't know what to do. I tried one thing after another and nothing was working," he said. Finally Tony Visconti told him to "'play what a rock guitar player would play.' So I just started strumming, and that ended up being the perfect idea."

"Dollar Days" moves by pushing and being pushed back (Tim Lefebvre: "I felt the incredible sadness of this song while we were recording it"), with its yearning and swooning key changes — the E minor bridges (which close with an F#7 chord to step "up" to the Eb major verse and its opening G minor chord); McCaslin's solo break, which stays in Em but has ambitions towards A major, and the outro sax and guitar solos, which fully move into the light of A major.

Some of "Dollar Days" is in the voice of the boaster of "Girl Loves Me" — Bowie's got no enemies, everyone caters to his needs. There's constancy and venom in the bridge ("don't believe for just one second I'm forgetting you — I'm *trying* to"), with its pun on "I'm dying to [forget you]/I'm dying, too." The urge to keep kicking against the pricks until the spirit snaps, then keep them guessing after death.

This barely-sublimated anger makes "Dollar Days" not quite the ashen "farewell to England" that it seems on first hearing. It's a song of exploitation, of people as beasts (oligarchs foam at the mouth like rabid dogs; bitches rip up magazines) who reduce others to less than beasts. Take the "cash girls" of Bowie's opening line. This was an occupation in American department stores of a century ago — young girls were called by "cash," not their names, and summoned by salesclerks to run a customer's money to a cashier. It was ruinous work: the labor leader Samuel Gompers to Congress in 1883 described the life of cash girls, testifying how "puny these poor children looked... All the children dropped off after a while." Elsewhere in the song is "survival sex": a term used to describe when the poor and exploited sell their bodies for the next day's meal or a night's lodging. Even "dollar days" is a shopkeeper's term — a bonanza sale, or a store's end days, when retail prices are cut below cost to move inventory. A life cut to meager wages, or a life at its close, a fire sale underway. The track opens with the sound of shuffling paper, whether stacks of cash or unpaid bills.

Against this, "Dollar Days" has the lushest arrangement on *Blackstar*. Lindner's keyboards and synthesizers purl through like fog, while he's also a counterweight to McCaslin's tenor saxophone in the solo break — his notes rising in pitch when McCaslin sinks to bass notes, later aligning with McCaslin's rising scales, and ending with a block of chords as McCaslin departs in his lower register. For a groove, Mark Guiliana struggled at first for the right feel in the verses until James Murphy suggested using toms instead of hi-hat to keep the pulse. (The gong-like cymbal crashes in the bridge sound like waves striking against rocks.)

The track's closing minute is Bowie repeating two lines, stressing each in the same way as if *this* time he'll make it clear, while his players act out his longings and rages. A fuzz guitar line, with clouds of synthesizers, invokes the coda of the Beatles' obsessive "I Want You (She's So Heavy)." McCaslin's last solo builds to a canyon-leap up two octaves into a spin of triplets, a spendthrift tearing through more and more notes until dancing out with a descending figure, like taking a staircase two steps at a time. Monder's closing guitar solo started as a Visconti suggestion "for a vague line going through that part of the tune, but he didn't have specific notes," Monder said. "He sort of had a contour of the line in mind and I came up with the notes. It was mapped out pretty well by the time we tracked it." Monder's closing note aligns with Lindner's closing four-octave figure, making a thick field of E notes.

What of the English evergreens that Bowie may never see again? Among his last public statements was months before the Scottish independence referendum of 2014: "Scotland, stay with us," a message delivered via Kate Moss at the Brit Awards. It infuriated some Scottish Bowie fans who supported independence and who found it galling that a notorious expatriate was asking a place he'd hardly known to "stay with" the country he had left. But considering himself still part of Britain, one particle of the "us," wasn't surprising. Though he'd lived most of his life away from it, with his daughter born an American citizen, it was as though he still held an undisclosed stake in the country.

He'd kept returning home, making expeditions to the source. After going to Marc Bolan's funeral in 1977, he had his driver take him to Haddon Hall, where he'd lived in the *Hunky Dory* era. In 1991, he asked Tin Machine's bus driver to do a detour through his birthplace, Brixton; two years later he did a tour of his Ziggy Stardust years for the benefit of *Rolling Stone*, concluding his interview on the stage of the Rainbow Theatre. While recording *1. Outside*, Bowie was nostalgic and sentimental about London, as per Kevin Armstrong, and was often out walking through Soho. And he spent years building a house on Gilston Road, Chelsea, with the designer Jonathan Reed. In a touch a novelist would scrap for being too on-the-nose, Bowie built his dream British home but would never live there, eventually selling it.

Towards the end of his life, he went back again — viewing the *David Bowie Is* exhibit in London (see "Blackstar"), riding the London Eye, bringing his daughter around the old haunts. On some morning or afternoon, a car pulls up to 4 Plaistow Grove in Bromley. An older man and a young woman get out to survey the two-story house where he'd lived long ago. Decades of owners have spruced it up, removed the lumps and ridges in the wallpaper, banished the dusty-brown paint with coats of sunnier colors. But the house has the same face: two bedroom windows above, two windows for the front-facing living room. The house where he first heard Little Richard, where he learned to play guitar, where his father died. He poses before it; she takes a shot of him on her phone. Look, he says, it's nothing to see.

I CAN'T GIVE EVERYTHING AWAY

Recorded: (drum loop, harmonica) Bowie home studio, ca. mid-late 2014; (backing tracks, vocals) 21 March 2015, Magic Shop; (guitar overdubs) ca. late March 2015; (vocals) 7 May 2015, Human Worldwide. Bowie: lead and backing vocal, harmonica, drum loop; McCaslin: tenor saxophone, alto flute; Monder: lead guitar; Lindner: Wurlitzer, Prophet '08, Prophet 12, Mopho X4, Moog Voyager, Micromoog; Lefebvre: bass; Guiliana: drums. Produced: Bowie, Visconti; engineered: Killen, Visconti.

First release: *8 January 2016,* **Blackstar**.

Cut in the final *Blackstar* sessions of March 2015, "I Can't Give Everything Away" was "trancelike," Jason Lindner said. "I just had this piano figure I played on the Wurlitzer that keeps going and stays consistent through the bass notes moving down. It keeps repeating and gets bigger and bigger." For *Blackstar*, Lindner translated what he heard on Bowie's demos into backdrops in the studio, converting many demo guitar parts into synthesizer lines, and he gave "I Can't Give Everything Away" overlapping, swirling layers of Moogs and Prophets:

> I would dial in a basic patch on my Prophet '08 as a sort of blank canvas sound... It has an organic quality and it matches incredibly well with acoustic instruments. The Prophet 12 produced some beautifully edgy, full pads with ringing metallic overtones that really fit the more intense moments.

(There's an odd mixing choice to abruptly cut off one of Lindner's high-pitched drones at 4:28.)

The drum loop that links the track to its *Blackstar* predecessor "Dollar Days" came from Bowie's home demo, as did his harmonica parts, unavoidably calling back to "A New Career in a New Town." As on much of the album, Mark Guiliana had to play a drum part that would hold true to Bowie's demo, to "accommodate this simple part but also interact with the rest of the guys and build the song in a spontaneous way." Guiliana's work was the fulfillment of what Bowie, Mark Plati, and Zachary Alford had done on *Earthling* (a favorite album of Guiliana's teenage years) — live drum tracks with the roll and rigor of synthetic ones, playing human variations on an electronic theme. On "I Can't Give Everything Away," Guiliana takes Bowie's drum loop and builds it out — laying off his snare in verses to play subtly-changing hi-hat patterns and kick beats, getting in sharp fills to round out refrains, quietly building in intensity and dynamics when responding to Donny McCaslin's solo.

647

Bowie starts out low in range, moving around the underlying F chord (there's a touch of Roy Orbison's vocal on "Blue Bayou"). He makes a quiet assertion, moving up a third ("thing's ve-") and down ("-ry wrong"), ending a tone higher than where he started. Two steps up, a step down. He makes the same movement, only going higher, when the chord changes. He keeps pushing upward until, with the plaintive "GIVE" that opens the refrain, he's on the peak, looking down at the valley. And in a breath, he tumbles down again ("ev-ry *thing*"). He does it again: striving, collapse. At last he reaches a compromise for "away," holding on a C note that's an octave up from where he'd started in the verse.

It's a small monologue, a surging lifeline against repetitions of drums and keyboards. But Bowie's refrain vocal freezes into a pattern. He's fallen into the song. No longer the lead actor, he slowly moves into the background, his refrain phrasing becoming another staggered loop, now working in support of his soloists. First McCaslin, who plays a melody to wreathe Bowie's "away" and then takes a journey that parallels Bowie's: lightly stepping up, sliding down, fixating on notes, urging himself onward, finding new pockets of melody as means to keep aloft; it's an aeronaut's solo.

Then Ben Monder. On *Blackstar* he's often the touch-up man, working in overdubs, the inker and colorist who moves in once pages have been penciled. But when he appears on "I Can't Give Everything Away" it's as if the whole song has been laid out for his benefit, to be raw materials for his coruscating, shredding solo. Monder is another force pushing upward, again and again moving to his highest two strings, peaking on a sky-high A note and then making a tumbling chromatic descent back into the atmosphere. As "I Can't Give Everything Away" moves into its outro, Monder plays a ritardando figure of alternating high notes, closing out broadly, no longer in tempo. Where the ear expects the song to close on its home F major chord, it instead ends on D minor, its vi chord, which aches to be resolved but never will.

This is the last song on the last album that David Bowie would release in his lifetime. And it's called "I Can't Give Everything Away." You can hear his mordant voice in the title — he could have called it "What Else Do You Want, Enough Already." Who is the "I," anyway? David Jones has brought back David Bowie by popular demand. It's a show that could go on for years, but he feels that it won't — the spells aren't holding, the bindings are cracking. Bowie's stunning lines in the second verse are his Prospero moment. An old magician drowns his books in the sea, makes amends for his witchcraft: "Now my charms are all o'erthrown/and what strength I have's mine own." But Bowie sings one last riddle. He saw more than he felt, he said no when he meant yes. "I Can't Give Everything Away" is the last scene of a mystery in which the detective reveals there's been no crime.

Here he stands in his deaths-head shoes, smiling and waving and looking so fine. The image to recall is one of Jimmy King's last photographs of Bowie, shot around September 2015. On a downtown New York street, before a grated door, dressed for a tea social, grinning from ear to ear, he looks ready to leap into the air.

KILLING A LITTLE TIME

Recorded: (backing tracks) 23 March 2015, Magic Shop; (overdubs) ca. April 2015; (vocals) 19 May 2015, Human Worldwide. Bowie: lead and backing vocal; McCaslin: tenor saxophone, alto flute, C flute, clarinet; Monder: guitar; Lindner: Wurlitzer, Prophet '08, Prophet 12, Mopho X4, Moog Voyager, Micromoog; Lefebvre: bass; Guiliana: drums. Produced: Bowie, Visconti; engineered: Killen, Visconti.

First release: 21 October 2016, **Lazarus: The Original New York Cast**.

Bowie's *Blackstar/Lazarus* songs accept death and dismiss it, regret having to leave and grumble about doing the packing. Then there's "Killing a Little Time," a rage at death in a would-be heavy metal/jazz fusion piece. Take its opening guitar riff, F and E notes played over E minor and A minor chords, with a descending A-G#-F tag. It's chest-puffed-out adolescent riffing, with another guitar line harmonized two steps up in a cheesy Eighties metal move. Donny McCaslin recalled that "it was always this angry, pissed off-song."

A labored-over composition, "Killing a Little Time" was first cut in either the January or February 2015 *Blackstar* sessions, its initial arrangement having prominent synthesizer parts. Recut in March, the instrumentation was simplified, with McCaslin writing new horn lines and "harmoniz[ing] them in this dark way." Its drumline was one of Mark Guiliana's master performances in the sessions. While technically in 4/4 (emphasized by his clanging cymbal pattern), Guiliana's doubling time on the third and fourth beat of every measure, which, along with Tim Lefebvre's heavily-syncopated bassline, makes "Killing a Little Time" feel punch-drunk — a close comparison, and a possible influence, is the similar time tricks of "If You Can See Me."

Bowie applied what he'd learned from watching Maria Schneider at work, as he and McCaslin drew from her "Sue" arrangement (see how McCaslin uses woodwinds in the verses of "Killing a Little Time") and, for organizational and tonal ideas, Bowie's favorite of her compositions, "Dance You Monster to My Soft Song" (1994), a piece McCaslin said helped him "get inside of ["Killing"] a little bit." (Henry Hey's arrangement for *Lazarus* kept close to Bowie/McCaslin's, with minor changes such as substituting horns for keyboard chord support in the intro, while the lead-up to the refrain lacks McCaslin's ascending woodwind line.)

Lyrically, the song also took a long path — Bowie kept revising lines, cutting his vocals at the tail end of the sessions. Tim Lefebvre said in 2018 that "Killing a Little Time" began as a song that originally was reported as an outtake, "Black Man of Moscow," whose title subject was a) an undisclosed medieval czar or b) the nineteenth-century Russian poet Pushkin, who had African ancestry. "I lay in bed/the monster fed/the body bled/I turned and said" isn't quite a Pushkin sonnet, though.

In *Lazarus*, Michael C. Hall sings "this tidal wave" like "thees tidal waaave," treats notes as if they've done him wrong. It's his most *Hedwig and the Angry Inch* moment in the play. In his version, Bowie hangs back, though he expectorates "*fuck* you over" and digs into his blood-sponge words ("sym-pho-n*eeee*," "*fyur*-ious-raaaain") with as much relish as Hall.

Not making the cut for *Blackstar* was understandable, given its similarities to "Sue" and the title track (its refrain is close to the "Blackstar" coda). "Killing a Little Time" wound up in *Lazarus* as a piece for Thomas Jerome Newton to sing when his deranged assistant Elly and the killer Valentine invade his apartment. Until the outtake "Blaze" is released, the track has Bowie's last studio vocal: a petulant rant whose core demand is that of his 1969 "Cygnet Committee" — *I want to live!* If he can't, he'll bring the house down with him.

BLACKSTAR

Recorded: (backing tracks) 20 March 2015, Magic Shop; (flute overdubs) ca. April 2015; (vocals) 2-3 April, 15 May 2015, Human Worldwide. Bowie: lead and backing vocal; McCaslin: tenor saxophone, alto flute, C flute; Monder: guitar; Lindner: Wurlitzer, Prophet '08, Prophet 12, Mopho X4, Moog Voyager, Micromoog, clavinet; Lefebvre: bass; Guiliana: drums; Visconti: strings. Produced: Bowie, Visconti; engineered: Killen, Visconti.

First release: 20 November 2015 (UK #61, US #78).

1.

The *David Bowie Is* exhibit opened in London in March 2013 and closed five years later, its last port of call the Brooklyn Museum in the spring and summer of 2018. To get to the Brooklyn Museum exhibit, you had to go through some of the permanent collection (Bowie would have approved — an *amuse-bouche* before the main course). Before reaching the *David Bowie Is* gallery, you saw a Gilbert Stuart portrait of George Washington, hung alone on a wall to give Washington command of the room, as if he stood atop a pitcher's mound. Children ran around the painting. For these kids, there wasn't a great difference between George Washington and David Bowie. Both live in museums, keeping company with tapestries, suits of armor, and uncomfortable wooden chairs.

There was something of the pharaoh's tomb to the Bowie exhibit, with its treasures under glass and ceremonial costumes fitted to mannequins, some of which had Bowie death-masks for faces. Walls with objects of obscure significance except to the initiated: a set of heavy keys, which looked as if they opened wine cellars and priest holes; an elegant hairpin-sized cocaine spoon. Paintings and preserved telegrams. Handwritten notes mounted like butterflies in cases that you had to shoulder through the crowd to see. After circling the overpacked rooms, you were pooled into the last, where the far wall had rows of screens with loops of performances — the Mick Rock "Space Oddity" video, the *Reality* tour "Heroes," the *Top of the Pops* "Starman." More costumed mannequins watched the show from state boxes.

Geoffrey Marsh, who co-curated the exhibit with Victoria Broackes, said that after all their work, he still had no idea who David Bowie really was. The man had escaped his memorial. There was close to nothing in the exhibit on Bowie's family, and his friends were only there in work they had done for him. Apart from a few photos, his youth's representatives were magazines, book jackets, film clips, LP covers; the first set piece was the Bromley bedroom where he'd dreamed up the life whose leavings would fill a museum wing. "It's an archive about a character," Marsh told Dylan Jones. "It's about this construction... I don't think I ever got to the heart of it, the reason he did what he did."

This was apparently Bowie's aim — he'd had concerns that an exhibit of his life would seem grandiose, and while he originally planned to help curate it, at some point he pulled back, making a public statement that he'd have no connection with *David Bowie Is* besides being a supplier of goods. (The truth of that statement is questionable: Marsh had the sense of Bowie orchestrating things from "behind a screen, like the Wizard of Oz.") He would be another visitor. Bowie and his family had a private viewing in London. Broackes handed him a pair of headphones and watched him walk around his life.

The Brooklyn exhibit had a unique section. The *Blackstar* case held two rows of loose-leaf papers and notebooks, all of it work: lyric sheets, tracklists, sketches for costumes, the "Blackstar" bible that Bowie wields in the video. This case was the last thing you saw before the exit. If you were distracted or exhausted, you could have missed it.

2.

The last three years of Bowie's life have a sextant's precision, from the surprise release of "Where Are We Now?" on his sixty-sixth birthday to that of *Blackstar* on his sixty-ninth, two days before his death, and as his play was running at the New York Theatre Workshop. The mind can't help but consider it a design. His Acts of the Apostles: resurrection, a time of last miracles and visitations, then a final farewell, with *Blackstar* as the Feast of the Ascension.

Tug at a thread, though, and the idea of a masterplan goodbye sequence frays apart. As per Jones, *Blackstar* was meant to come out in autumn 2015. Its release was in part delayed because its videos (particularly "Lazarus") weren't completed, and then to avoid being drowned out in the Christmas season, it was decided *Blackstar* would be released on his birthday. Nor was *Blackstar* meant as his last album: Bowie was working on writing the next one and even considering a post-*Lazarus* play. "I can't stop it. It's coming full force and I'm just creating and creating and creating," as he reportedly wrote in an email to Floria Sigismondi.

Blackstar was conceived as a wilder, funnier *Heathen* — another album that he'd make with Tony Visconti as a side-road adventure, a dark vacation from his standard rock, with a unifying concept of spiritual and bodily decay. Visconti recalled that in the early 2000s he and Bowie had kicked around ideas for albums to do after the *Reality* tour, including an "electronica" record where "he'd make up a group name. He wanted to have more fun and not have the pressure of releasing another David Bowie album for a while." Given that he'd started chemotherapy in late 2014, he wrote *Blackstar* as a hedge: this *could* be the last album, let's dress it as such, but I pray it's not going to be. Then it was. One of Bowie's "Last Albums" was finally the end. Even he couldn't keep rolling sevens.

3.

"Blackstar" was always conceived as being two sections ("a two-part suite rather than two different songs," as Jason Lindner recalled) that were to be married in the studio with a "freeform middle bit," as per Bowie's emails to the band. Ben Monder recalled to *DownBeat* Bowie's instructions: "'We're going to do a section and it's going to dissolve and morph into the next section,' which is more like a pop tune, 'then it's going to morph back into the original thing with a stronger beat'."

"Station to Station" has a three-part structure, where an ominous opening section leads to a manic middle part which bursts open to a romping finale. "Blackstar" is circular, ending as it had begun. "We looked at ["Blackstar"] sonically as a film," said Erin Tonkon, *Blackstar*'s assistant engineer. "The thread that ran through it all was David's backing vocals with reverbs and delays. It all sounds completely different, but it's a cohesive piece of music."

Bowie thoroughly demoed the opening section ("the first part of it, with all of the droning stuff, is sticking to David's plan," Tim Lefebvre said). Again Mark Guiliana approximated on his kit the beats Bowie had programmed ("I play some embellishments and some fills here and there, but the core groove is true to the demo"), using a tuned-down and dampened snare and a kick drum often overdubbed with Lindner's Moog Voyager, which makes kick beats sound like samples. While he stays within Bowie's structure, Guiliana's playing courses with energy, looking to break free. His internal tension is part of a wider dislocation in the opening section — everyone moves at their own speed, like ships of different sizes navigating a river. Monder's fingerpicked guitar lines are contemplative; McCaslin darts in and out, playing little shards of melodies. Lindner is the backdrop artist, contrasting the warmth of his Prophet '08 with colder, more industrial synth pads from his Prophet 12.

Into this coalescing world falls Bowie, in a chorale of himself, his two lead vocal lines with a fifth interval between them. It's his declamatory, liturgical voice, as on "Sue." We're hearing the opening of a mass. "In the villa of Allmen," as he originally wrote for his opening line. "Stands a solitary candle." He wails a wordless response, amen to Allmen. He changed the name to Ormen (though still singing it at times like "Allmen"), which prompted internet sleuths to unearth all known connections to Ormen, from a 1966 Swedish film (*The Serpent!*) to a village in Norway. But Ormen is also a response to, and a correction of, his first idea. The villa of all men is now a place where "men" is one choice, with the other half of the "or" conjunction hidden.

4.

McCaslin recalled Bowie once telling him "Blackstar" was about ISIS, and its recording coincided with ISIS' peak territorial gains in Iraq, Syria, and Libya and subsequent media attention (e.g., the March 2015 issue of the *Atlantic* had the cover line "What ISIS Really Wants"). Bowie never told this to anyone else involved in the sessions. He could have been having some interpretive fun ("here's another clue for you all/the Walrus was ISIS"), or talking through ideas he'd later discard.

But it's easy to imagine him being fascinated by the terrorist group — ISIS as a tentacled organization that lives in night and shadow until appearing at noon to conquer. It was something out of "Panic in Detroit," although much of the twenty-first century seems like a Bowie song from the Seventies. In his rough draft lyric, there are some scratched-out lines: "I'm not a christstar...

shia/I'm not a jewstar... sunni." The lines in "Blackstar" that most suggest the ISIS concept are in the second verse: the day of execution at the Villa of Ormen, where only the women kneel. An ISIS occupation of a town where the women smile when the axe falls.

It's Ormen as another incarnation of Georges Rodenbach's purgatorial Bruges, as in Bowie's "The Informer." "Bruges-la-Morte, the dead city," Rodenbach wrote in his novel. "A sensation of death emanated from the shuttered houses, from windows blurred like eyes in the throes of death." A cloistered city where passion is a clandestine act, where the streets are full of old women, where residents keep small mirrors on their window ledges: "little reflecting traps that, unbeknownst to passersby, capture their antics, their smiles and gestures... transmitting all of it to the interiors of houses where someone is always keeping watch."

The verses have the same cycling progressions, with chords changing on the last beat of every measure, again on the first beat of the next. The drum pattern shifts to center on the beat; more squiggles, zaps, and bleats are heard in the margins. McCaslin takes a generously melodic solo and the song seems poised to open up in his wake. Instead the opening ceremony loop returns, with Bowie locked into his invocations and amens. The band quiets down, as if falling to sleep.

5.

It's one of Bowie's greatest fake-outs. Until now, "Blackstar" has kept to the shadowy path of "Sue" and "Lazarus," and its preview appearance, in a fragment used in a *Last Panthers* TV trailer in October 2015 (see below), had prepared fans to expect it to sound like this. But now there's a key change, a "string" line on keyboards, and a gorgeous, fragile-sounding Bowie vocal, like a shaken sun coming out after a storm has passed.

The transition is roughly thirty seconds of guitar, bass, saxophone and vocals that sound as if they've been processed through a sandstorm, and drums murmuring and freefalling before a keyboard progression announces the new regime. It was improvised in a single take. The band was asked to "somehow dissolve this into the next section of the tune," Monder recalled, and "somehow we did that dissolution perfectly on the first attempt, and that's what you're hearing on the album — no punching-in or anything." Each player trails off in their own way, then come back together. It's as if the audience had gone out to the lobby and now resume their seats in time for the next act.

After a break (whether of a few hours or a day — by most accounts, it was the former), the band cut the second section, the "pop song" segment of "Blackstar." In F# major, it has Lefebvre playing a looser bassline ("some Sixties Serge Gainsbourg-inspired stuff and some Justin Meldal-Johnsen kinda busy pick-bass stuff") to complement Guiliana, who keeps to a simple pattern, building up reserves.

The last man in the villa has been put to the sword. His spirit leaves his body and someone takes his place: a sly cut-up who sneaks into the song. *Wait a sec, doc*, like Bugs Bunny breaking up a black mass. The sacrificial victim dusts himself off, laughs and points at the crowd. He tromps on the altar, knocks over the sacred relics. "I am large, I contain multitudes," Walt Whitman once wrote. To hell with that, the singer says. I'm one thing, and nothing else. Not the Thin White Duke. Not a Marvel star, not a pop star, not a film star, just one thing.

There's an army of reasons why Bowie chose the name "Blackstar" (see the list below). One is the term's astronomical sense. "We talked about black stars as a force that drives you out and drags you back in," as Jonathan Barnbrook recalled of an early conversation with Bowie about the album. Bowie had been fascinated by black holes for decades: the aliens who announced themselves to Ziggy Stardust were the "black hole jumpers," for instance.

But black holes have an event horizon beyond which nothing can escape their gravity. To get to that point they must collapse past a radius that's a sort of 'point of no return', where not even light escapes its pull. A black star is something else, a more recent theory: of a developing black hole that's stuck in a limbo in which the collapsing star never gets smaller than this radius, so that light can still escape and the black star never becomes enveloped in an event horizon. As scientists who theorized black stars in a 2009 *Scientific American* article wrote:

> The gravitational field around it is identical to that around a black hole, but the star's interior is full of matter and no event horizon forms... If a black star could be peeled layer by layer like an onion, at each stage the remaining core would be a smaller black star... The black star's collapse may one day stop just short of forming an event horizon.

Or a black star may continue to collapse at slower and slower and slower rates, inching ever closer to an event horizon but never forming one.

"I'm a blackstar," Bowie sings. I'm what lies between the promise and the reality, always changing, always collapsing, never arriving.

6.

Another trail to follow. On the sketch sheet of Bowie's "Blackstar" lyric, there's a parenthetical, "(Lucy)," on the margin of the first "villa of Allmen" stanza. Bowie was listening to Kendrick Lamar's *To Pimp a Butterfly* in the latter stages of *Blackstar*, while writing lyrics and cutting vocals. And on *Butterfly*, "Lucy" is a Lamar character, and his tormenter: Lucifer, voice of temptation and greed, as heard on Lamar's "For Sale?": "Lucy gon' fill your pockets/Lucy gon' move your mama out of Compton... Lucy just want your trust and loyalty." "I see it all around, man," Lamar told an interviewer. "It's not just the positive energy that speaks to me. It's the negative, too; it's the evils, too — Lucy is me coming to a realization of the evil." Later on *Butterfly*, at the end of his track "I," Lamar says "black stars can come and get me!"

The mid-section of "Blackstar" as Bowie playing with the idea of doing a Lamar-esque character. With "Lucy" as the forces being summoned in the opening section, and now in the circle is a no-fucks-given figure who stands there, mocking any wishes you ask him to fulfill. Some of Bowie's scrapped lines for this section were "I got no gas, I don't have coke... I'm not a no-show, I'm not a go-to... I'm not a black mark... I'm a blackstar on my way up." In the middle of the song, at the center of it all, "Blackstar" starts to groove. Also in rotation during its making was D'Angelo's *Black Messiah*, released at the tail end of 2014: this section of "Blackstar" seems most indebted to it. In the way Bowie sings "I-can't-an-swer-*why*" on one fat note that he makes sound like a roaming melody; in the looseness and snap of the rhythm section (Lefebvre has called D'Angelo's *Voodoo* as being key among his influences, as it has been for a generation of jazz musicians); in the way the ominous monk voices of the opening are now a call-and-response team. In Bowie's vocal, which has the feel of his work on *Young Americans*, that crowns the section.

Is he using "Blackstar" to reference the power and resilience of black music, from which his own music had taken for so many years? With a sixty-eight-year-old white Englishman singing lines like "I've got game" and "I'm a black star?" When "Blackstar" drifts into its final section, resuming the key of the opening section but now with a more swinging beat, it's the sound of a transformed music, of a revivified music. Lefebvre described his playing in the last part in various interviews as "sort of a Sly Stone or Pino Palladino mode, playing loose fills over the top of it... certain bars are pretty jagged but they kept it all... that humpy kind of eighth-note thing."

The ceremony begins again. The same lines are said, the same movements at the altar. It's loops and loops of motion, like the jittering dancers of the "Blackstar" video. But something is new. Something has gone and something else is there in its place. And "Blackstar" starts to crumble from within. Its last minute slows in tempo, with Monder using the shimmer effect on his Strymon blueSky Reverberator pedal ("it has that upper register sheen to it and all of those nice overtones"). McCaslin is a small flock of birds, his flute and clarinet and saxophone notes pecking and squawking. A synthesizer starts up in response, excitedly, making contact, but then there's a hard close. Project cancelled.

7.

There are other interpretations, of course.

"Blackstar" is an Elvis Presley homage. A 1960 Western directed by Don Siegel, *Flaming Star* was the post-Army Elvis' return to "serious" film acting, with Presley playing a half-Kiowan, half-Texan renegade (poster tagline: "The White Man's Song Was on His Lips... But an Indian War Cry Was in His Heart!"). Originally called *Black Star*, the film's title change meant Presley's August 1960 first recording of the theme song got scrapped: it was only available on bootlegs until the Nineties. "Black Star" was Presley's "Because I Could Not Stop for Death": a horseman spies doom in the sky and rides faster, trying to keep his black star behind him. "There's a lot of living I gotta do," he implores, but no one's listening. *Likelihood*: Bowie and Presley shared a birthday, he'd covered Presley before, the lyric has obvious resonances. If it was a subconscious reference, Bowie's subconscious deserves a posthumous award.

A black star is a cancerous lesion. "Black star" specifically applies to a lesion on the breast (also called a radial scar) that's generally benign or precancerous. Someone Googling on the morning of Bowie's death likely came upon it and eureka: Bowie was secretly telling his fans that he had cancer. *Likelihood*: Too inaccurate, too pat.

"Black star" is the name of Saturn for "ancient religions". "Saturn is referred to as Black Star in ancient Judaic belief," as per an unsourced line on Wikipedia that has spread throughout the internet like a norovirus. It's complete hooey, conflating all sorts of things, such as the belief that worshiping a black cube (such as the Kaaba in Mecca) is to worship the alchemical symbol for Saturn. *Likelihood*: Low. That said, this is the writer of "Station to Station" and "Loving the Alien" we're talking about.

"Blackstar" refers to a government space conspiracy. In March 2006, the reputable trade magazine *Aviation Week and Space Technology* published an article that claimed the US government was running a secret orbital spaceplane program known as Blackstar, a program yet to be verified or acknowledged in the twelve years since. *Likelihood*: Low. Though again, it's Bowie.

A black star refers to: Episode five of the first series of *Peaky Blinders* (2013) where gangster Tommy Shelby plans a "black star" day on which he'll eliminate his rival (almost certainly); Talib Kweli and Mos Def's hip-hop group, named after Marcus Garvey's shipping line, also the inspiration for a host of reggae songs including Fredlock's "Black Star Liner" and Culture's "Black Star Liner Must Come" (possible); a Greek anarchist terrorist group active around the turn of the twenty-first century (too random); the leadoff track of Avril Lavigne's 2011 *Goodbye Lullaby* **and** the name of her first fragrance (epic if so); a series of crime novels by Johnston McCulley from a century ago ("the Black Star had terrorized the city for the past four months. Whenever a master crime was committed a tiny black star had been found pasted on something at the scene of operations") (not random enough); a 1969 novel by Morton Cooper described by *The Crisis* as "a black girl's search for identity in a white world she cannot understand or control" (could be the Rosetta Stone to the whole album); "Chemosh, or black star, who was reputed God of the Moabites," as per *Iconography: A Tract for the Times*, an 1852 treatise by "Vigil" (Bowie probably did read this); a short-lived 1981 cartoon in which astronaut John Blackstar is swept through a black hole into another universe, where he becomes the champion of the "Trobbit" people in their fight against the cruel Overlord (another possible Rosetta Stone).

Villa of Ormen = "Lover of Iman." *Likelihood*: A sweet sentiment, but he would've done a proper anagram.

8.

Bowie had made promotional films as early as 1969, but there were no videos of real significance in the years after *'hours…'*. He said at the time that doing them was a waste of money, given that they wouldn't get played. But in 2013, with YouTube and his website as his personal MTV, he returned to video. As he no longer toured or gave interviews, his videos were now his music's only supplement.

Johan Renck directed the ten-minute "Blackstar" video, drawing from Bowie's sketches and ideas. For instance, having a trio of dancers wriggle and convulse came from Bowie noticing how in Max Fleischer cartoons of the Thirties (like *Popeye*), animators put marginal characters into loops of motion, repeating actions in the background of a scene for half a minute. The video also had a young woman with a tail (Renck recalled Bowie saying that he thought the idea of gender was changing; this was his attempt to symbolize it); a planetscape out of Georges Méliès' *A Trip to the Moon*; a jeweled skull in an astronaut's helmet, like a Fabergé saint's relic; an empty town that's basically the Goblin City of *Labyrinth*; a trio of crucified scarecrows who start bumping and grinding.

Bowie also played three characters. A blind, bandaged figure who sings the opening section, whom he dubbed "Button Eyes" (see "Lazarus") and whose look he'd designed anticipating that he could lose his hair via his medical treatments. Then an imposing figure, brandishing a blackstar bible like a country preacher, or posing as if he's in the vanguard of a Chinese Cultural Revolution propaganda poster: he's the rationalist/control element (he never sings). And finally a soft-shoe artist dancing up in the brain-attic (a set with a similar triangular design as the artist's loft in David Mallet's "Look Back In Anger" video), who takes the middle section. Cut the symbolism any way you'd like — say, the idea of "Bowie" severed in thirds: dying mortal, immortal scamp, dictatorial ego.

Some of the video was stunning and eerie, some of it was ridiculous (a coven summons a Lovecraftian demon out of Seventies *Doctor Who*; the demon attacks the scarecrows for the video's climax — you remember that this is the man who did the Glass Spider tour). The "Blackstar" video is the song's preset interpretations. Use what Bowie gives you, or break it up and rework it, or drag it into the recycle bin and start fresh.

9.

Blackstar was the digital version of Visconti's analog editing heroics on *Scary Monsters*. McCaslin's group said they were stunned upon hearing the album, finding that tracks they'd worked on had radically changed, that some tracks they expected to hear weren't there, while pieces apparently destined for the scrapheap instead had been polished into a lead riff or solo passage. The final mix of *Blackstar* drew on everything from Bowie's home demos to in-studio "mistakes" to late-in-the-day overdubs. As McCaslin said of the *Blackstar* sessions, "David and Tony were gathering information, laying it down, then the two of them would comb through everything."

Some of the title track's most striking instrumentation was owed to improvisations, such as McCaslin's flutes in the outro ("something I had added on an overdub day, when I was there just overdubbing flute parts") and Ben Monder's repetitive guitar line, which Bowie and Visconti promoted to a motif and Bowie used as a basis for his vocal melody.

With Bowie's vocals finished by the start of June 2015, Bowie and Visconti planned to mix the album at New York's Electric Lady but learned that the room they wanted was booked by British engineer Tom Elmhirst, mixing Adele's *25* and Frank Ocean's *blond* at the time. It was a final bit of serendipity — Bowie asked Elmhirst to mix *Blackstar*, with Bowie and Visconti showing up each afternoon for critiques. Elmhirst's work, done in about ten days, was a finishing coat, making the album's seven tracks flow sumptuously (he soldered "Blackstar" together and segued "Dollar Days" into "I Can't Give Everything Away") and creating a narrative in the mix, with its last two songs mixed softly, blurrier than the more dynamic Side One.

"Blackstar" itself kept changing. Like "Bring Me the Disco King," it debuted in a remixed form — a fragment used in the opening titles of *The Last Panthers*, a trailer for which aired a month before the single's release. For *Last Panthers*, Visconti and Bowie took a verse from the third section of "Blackstar" and added different guitar tracks and effects than on the album.

And upon learning that iTunes wouldn't allow "Blackstar" to be purchased individually if it was over ten minutes, Bowie whacked around a minute's worth of it to get the track to 9:57. "It's total bullshit," Visconti told *Rolling Stone*. "But David was adamant it be the single, and he didn't want both an album version and a single version, since that gets confusing." So "Blackstar" is both an intricately-designed piece of music and has an apparent edit at 9:00 and a few other possible tucks — e.g., the abrupt disappearance of McCaslin's saxophone at 7:42 — made in order to conform with Steve Jobs' edict for a pop single.

10.

Though most have heard *Blackstar* on CD, download, or streaming, the album's ideal form is its LP release, with its Barnbrook-designed five-point-star cutaway gatefold cover and a thick, glossy paper stock that loves fingerprints. According to McCaslin, Bowie originally wanted *Blackstar* to have a vinyl-only physical release, and a worksheet in the *David Bowie Is* exhibit has sequenced sides for a two-LP set (one provisional side: "Blaze" [see appendix] /"Lazarus"/"'Tis a Pity She Was a Whore"/"No Plan").

"I wanted to make it very much a physical object," Barnbrook said of the *Blackstar* LP in late 2015,

> Vinyl is in an interesting place at the moment, similar to letterpress where the craft and tactile quality of it is everything. So that's why the cover is cut away and you can see the physical record — the opposite of the digital download. I wanted to give it the feeling that it contained something quite threatening.

The LP is a souvenir book from the farewell tour that never happened. Solidly black, even its lettering a lighter shade of black, it's the paper and vinyl embodiment of the title track, as imposing as the monoliths of *2001: A Space Odyssey* — a dense light-absorbing square, an event horizon at 33 1/3 rpm (its CD cover has a white background with black images — the universe beyond). "The role of the LP cover is different today," Barnbrook said in a 2016 interview. "(It) has to complement all this, be robust on different technologies, quickly identifiable and stand up to all the noise around it."

On the LP's back cover, track times are as prominent as titles: each strip of time (9:57, 4:40, 6:22) is the price of a song. And there are the hideaways that Barnbrook worked into the LP sleeve and booklet: a photograph of Bowie overlaid with a matrix of lines Barnbrook said was the "depression a star makes in spacetime"; the starfield photograph in the inside gatefold with a constellation of a "starman" figure. Stars that appear when the gatefold is held to direct light. Using ultraviolet creates 3-D effects and, allegedly, Shroud of Turin-esque images of Bowie's face on the spinning vinyl.

Album and song title are officially ★ (Unicode +2605). Bowie thought future typography letterforms would become more like hieroglyphics, with the use of emoji in texts as a harbinger. "People [are] creating whole narratives out of them, as well as using them in everyday communication," Barnbrook recalled him saying of emojis. "Will there be a time when we use only these to express thought?"

His last album cover doesn't show his face or his name (or so it seems). It's a hard break with tradition. A Bowie album cover almost always has a photo or drawing of him, his name, and its title (almost always a song). *The Next Day* began the process by obscuring his face. On *Blackstar*, Bowie's the man who isn't there: you have to know how to look for him. B O W I E is spelled in star symbols. He's handed over his name to the future.

11.

To compare "Blackstar" to "Station to Station" is inevitable — he must have intended some correspondence, if only for his listeners, between two of his epic songs. Roughly the same length, they hold the same position on their respective albums.

"Station to Station" was the work of a worn-out, addicted, lonely man who was exiled in a city that he hated, who dreamed of transformation and escape while saying that it's too late. "Blackstar" was made by someone who the writer of "Station to Station" could never have imagined becoming: a family man whose circle was confined to people whom he loved and trusted. A man who could stand outside of the personae that he created, even take a walk around them in a museum. Look, there's the coke spoon, the koto, the wasp-waisted suits that even he can't imagine ever fitting into. "Blackstar" is the sort of song that the Thin White Duke Bowie could have conceived of but never could have made: there are too many jokes.

It's as if Bowie's covering a packed-up self, playing a Variation in the Style of Thomas Jerome Newton.

To chronicle the music of David Bowie from 1976 to his death forty years later is to chronicle a decline in rock music. *A* decline, because it's not *the* decline of rock by any means. There are great rock musicians today; there will be others when you and I are dead. But the centrality of a certain type of rock music, particularly one marketed to the working- and middle-class white youth in the late twentieth century, has fallen away. Rock music may well mean less to many young people today. The myths no longer have the same kick; recitations of the feats of (mostly male) heroes no longer bring crowds to the temples. Monoculture-era rock 'n' roll closed as many doors as it opened; it oppressed as much as it purported to liberate — we have only just begun to come to terms with how many people, particularly young femmes, were exploited in the age of the rock star. The subject of this book is one of many with an allegation of abusing their power and celebrity at the time. If young people today have passions stronger than their love of rock music, if they can see through the star-maker machinery, well, all power and strength to them.

With the end of rock as a centerpiece of youth culture, there are fewer chances of a "David Bowie" coming along again. He'd lived by tacking and weaving, going out to obscure corners of the map, returning to the center with what he'd picked up along the borders. Still, he'd needed the map. Perhaps we no longer do. David Bowie today is a language, a set of precepts and responses, a code that anyone with requisite amounts of style, guts, shamelessness, and weirdness can access. And unlike his music, it's in the public domain. Everywhere I look, I see musicians and artists who employ Bowie dialects: Annie Clark and Janelle Monáe come to mind.

So "Blackstar" is the dissolution of "David Bowie," a commercial enterprise created by an ambitious London suburbanite around 1965. Time to move on. Take your passport and shoes, he says. Get some pills for the plane. I'll take you there, but I'm not coming with you. In the Bowie tradition, "Blackstar" is sillier than it seems and more sublime than it should be. "I'm the great I Am," he sings, an audacious moment in a life of them. It's Bowie as Yahweh, god of the Israelites ("I AM THAT I AM," as Yahweh boomed at Moses), now an old swinger. He's cashed in his shares.

12.

Beyond *Blackstar, No Plan*, and the few outtakes from the *Blackstar* sessions, which Visconti said in 2016 he thought might appear in a deluxe set (see "When Things Go Bad" in the appendix), there remain five last songs. These are the demos that Bowie made at home, in his last months in New York (as per Visconti). No one but his family has heard them, perhaps not even them. The question is whether we, as an audience, should hear them one day.

There's the argument for history. If we found five last poems by Keats written before his death, should we not read them? An unburned Kafka story? A half-finished Woolf manuscript? The world grows rounder with new "lost" works; our knowledge of the artist broadens. Hasn't this book been a rummaging through a magician's cabinets, guessing what went into his tricks, where he stole from, which ones worked, which blew up in his face? To hear his last demos, to guess where Bowie planned to go next, to taste the music that he never made, would be invaluable.

There are the artist's intentions to consider. Bowie rarely made sketch work public, hardly ever released demos. If he was ailing and not up to par when he made these recordings, what good would it do for us to hear them? Shouldn't we remember him as he wanted us to — the creator of a strong, meticulously-designed album?

A final perspective. There are five new David Bowie songs, songs that we know nothing about, not even their names. We may never hear them, but we know that they exist. Let them be unheard. Let this be our gift to the future. There will never be a last David Bowie song if there are always five more to come. The end of the David Bowie story is that it doesn't end. There will always be another chapter to write. An old-time ambassador, may he forever keep pushing ahead.

APPENDIX: THE UNHEARD MUSIC

Compared to the list of "lost" Bowie songs in *Rebel Rebel*, this one is miniscule. After 1976, not only was Bowie more successful in preventing demos and outtakes from being bootlegged, with a few exceptions (*Leon*, the *Scary Monsters* roughs, *Toy*), but at times he seemed to have a chilling effect on his musicians even *talking* about outtakes. So there's likely a pile of tracks from the 1976-2016 period that we know nothing about. Will we ever? Bowie had little interest in releasing what he considered half-finished work. Maybe in the 2020s, his estate will open the vaults. Color me doubtful. Then again, I said in 2012 that he likely wouldn't release another album.

1976
"Iggy Pop Don't Stop." A reportedly "comedic" track cut during *The Idiot* sessions.

1977
The *Q: Are We Not Men?* sessions. As per Devo's Mark Mothersbaugh, the band was recording their debut album *Q: Are We Not Men? A: We Are Devo!* in Cologne, Germany, with Bowie visiting the studio. At one point they jammed with him, Eno, Can's Holger Czukay "and a couple other odd Germans that were electronic musicians that happened to be hanging out there," he said in 2017. Mothersbaugh added that Bowie cut backing vocals (unused) for the album proper.

1978
"Working Party," "Pope Brian," "Eno's Jungle Box," "Aztec." Outtakes from the *Lodger* sessions, as per Visconti. Unclear if Bowie did vocal tracks for them; "Pope Brian" was confirmed as being an instrumental by Nicholas Pegg.

1979

"Sabotage." Tragically unrecorded: Bowie sawing away at John Cale's viola during a Cale Carnegie Hall performance (see "Piano-La").

1981

"Death in the Woods." A poem in Bertolt Brecht's *Baal*, "Death in the Woods" was recorded for the *Baal* BBC film in the same session Bowie taped "The Drowned Girl" and "Baal's Hymn," on 12 August 1981. It's unknown whether, as with the other songs, Bowie sang to the off-screen banjo accompaniment or if he simply recited the poem. John Willett said that as Bowie "never securely mastered" the poem, the performance was scrapped.

"Ali," **"It's Alright**," **"Knowledge**." Copyrighted songs credited to Bowie and Queen, apparently from the same studio binge that produced "Under Pressure."

1988

"All Tomorrow's Parties," "Holy Spin," "Rashomon (Mellow Blue)." Bowie and Reeves Gabrels cut a number of still-unreleased songs as demos in the pre-Tin Machine 1988 sessions, including "Holy Spin" and "Rashomon (Mellow Blue)," written in the same period as "Baby Can Dance" and "Pretty Thing." Tin Machine also recorded the Velvet Underground classic "All Tomorrow's Parties" during the fall 1988 Montreux sessions.

1992

The Modern Farmer instrumentals. In a session in New York during the making of *Black Tie White Noise* (where the first version of "Strangers When We Meet" was cut), Bowie and Gabrels' band at the time, Modern Farmer, recorded two lengthy instrumental pieces. Tapes exist.

1998

The pre-'*hours...*' demos. During composing sessions at Reeves Gabrels' New York apartment, Bowie and Gabrels wrote five songs that have never been released. All are acoustic, in altered tunings, and exist today only on a Dictaphone mini-cassette.

2000

"Miss American High." A song mentioned in reports of the *Toy* sessions — possibly a working title for a released track.

2001

Untitled *Heathen* demo. The first song Bowie and Visconti recorded as a demo for *Heathen* "never made it to the final list. However, it was our starting point," Bowie wrote in a web journal entry. Possibly reworked for *Reality*.

2011-2012

"Chump." There are reportedly a handful of unreleased or half-finished *The Next Day* tracks, many not making it past the backing tracks stage. According to Pegg, one was titled "Chump." Zachary Alford recalled cutting a "straight-up country song," while another track was based on a blues riff but the players were told "not to make it sound like a blues" — whether these became full songs or were left unfinished is unknown.

2015

"When Things Go Bad," "Someday/Blaze." Though many outtakes described by Bowie's musicians in early *Blackstar* interviews were working names of released tracks ("Black Man In Moscow" allegedly became "Killing a Little Time," "Wistful" became "No Plan," "The Hunger" became "Lazarus"), there are still some unissued tracks from Bowie's last studio sessions. In a 2016 *Rolling Stone* interview, Visconti said there were five, apart from the three tracks that were issued on *No Plan*. One is apparently "When Things Go Bad," described by Tim Lefebvre as being a Seventies-style Bowie track in the vein of *Station to Station* (or *Hunky Dory*) ("a classic banger... thematically it wouldn't have fit"). One song, which no one has recalled the title of, was being considered as a duet piece with Lorde (quite possible this was "When I Met You"). And "Someday" ultimately became "Blaze," which Pegg has heard, describing it in his book as an uptempo rocker. Given that "Blaze" has Bowie's last-completed studio vocal, its eventual release seems inevitable. Should it be released before this book is published, and so making this book incomplete, that would not be surprising. As for Bowie's final home demos, see "Blackstar."

LIST OF SONGS

PARTIAL DISCOGRAPHY, 1977-2017

Low, January 1977. Speed of Life/Breaking Glass/What in the World/Sound and Vision/Always Crashing in the Same Car/Be My Wife/A New Career in a New Town/Warszawa/Art Decade/Weeping Wall/Subterraneans. [1991 Ryko: Some Are, All Saints, Sound and Vision (remix).]

Sound and Vision/A New Career in a New Town. February 1977 (RCA PB 0905, UK #3).

[Iggy Pop] *The Idiot*, March 1977. Sister Midnight/Nightclubbing/Funtime/Baby/China Girl/Dum Dum Boys/Tiny Girls/Mass Production.

Be My Wife/Speed of Life. June 1977 (RCA PB 1017).

[Iggy Pop] *Lust for Life*, August 1977. Lust for Life/Sixteen/Some Weird Sin/The Passenger/Tonight/Success/Turn Blue/Neighborhood Threat/Fall in Love with Me.

"Heroes"/V-2 Schneider. September 1977 (RCA PB 1121, UK #24).

"Heroes", October 1977. Beauty and the Beast/Joe the Lion/"Heroes"/Sons of the Silent Age/Blackout/V-2 Schneider/Sense of Doubt/Moss Garden/Neuköln/The Secret Life of Arabia. [1991 Ryko: Abdulmajid, Joe the Lion (remix)].

Beauty and the Beast/Sense of Doubt. January 1978 (RCA 1190, UK #39.)

Stage, September 1978. 2005 reissue sequencing: Warszawa/"Heroes"/What in the World/Be My Wife/Blackout/Sense of Doubt/Speed of Life/Breaking Glass/Beauty and the Beast/Fame/Five Years/Soul Love/Star/Hang Onto Yourself/Ziggy Stardust/Art Decade/Alabama Song/Station to Station/Stay/TVC 15 [2017 reissue added Jean Genie and Suffragette City.]

Breaking Glass (live)/Art Decade (live)/Ziggy Stardust (live). November 1978 (RCA BOW 1, UK #54.)

Boys Keep Swinging/Fantastic Voyage. April 1979 (RCA BOW 2, UK#7).

Lodger, May 1979. Fantastic Voyage/African Night Flight/Move On/Yassassin/ Red Sails/D.J./Look Back in Anger/Boys Keep Swinging/Repetition/Red Money. [1991 Ryko: I Pray, Olé, Look Back in Anger (1988 remake).]

D.J./Repetition. June 1979 (RCA BOW 3, UK #29.)

John, I'm Only Dancing (Again)/John, I'm Only Dancing. December 1979 (RCA BOW 4, UK #12.)

Alabama Song [studio version]/Space Oddity [remake]. February 1980 (RCA BOW 5, UK #23).

Ashes to Ashes/Move On. August 1980 (RCA BOW 6, UK #1.)

Scary Monsters, September 1980. It's No Game (Pt. 1)/Up the Hill Backwards/ Scary Monsters (and Super Creeps)/Ashes to Ashes/Fashion/Teenage Wildlife/Scream Like a Baby/Kingdom Come/Because You're Young/It's No Game (Pt. 2). [1992 Ryko: Space Oddity (remake)/Panic in Detroit (remake)/Crystal Japan/Alabama Song.]

Fashion/Scream Like a Baby. October 1980 (RCA BOW 7, UK #5.)

Scary Monsters (And Super Creeps)/Because You're Young. January 1981 (RCA BOW 8, UK #20.)

Up the Hill Backwards/Crystal Japan. March 1981 (RCA BOW 9, UK #32.)

[Bowie and Queen] Under Pressure/Soul Brother [Queen]. November 1981 (EMI 5250, UK #1, US #29.)

Wild Is the Wind/Golden Years. November 1981 (RCA BOW 10, UK #24.)

David Bowie in Bertolt Brecht's Baal, March 1982.

Baal's Hymn/Remembering Marie A./Ballad of the Adventurers/The Drowned Girl/Dirty Song.

Cat People (Putting out Fire)/Paul's Theme (Jogging Chase). March 1982 (MCA 770, UK #26.)

Peace on Earth/Little Drummer Boy [Bowie and Bing Crosby]/Fantastic Voyage. November 1982 (RCA BOW 12, UK #3.)

Let's Dance/Cat People [remake]. March 1983 (EMI America EA 152, UK #1, US #1.)

Let's Dance, April 1983. Modern Love/China Girl/Let's Dance/Without You/Ricochet/Criminal World/Cat People/Shake It. [1995 reissue: Under Pressure.]

China Girl/Shake It. May 1983 (EMI America EA 157, UK #2, US #10.)

Modern Love/(live). September 1983 (EMI America EA 158, UK #2, US #14.)

Without You/Criminal World. November 1983 (EMI America B8190, US #73.)

Blue Jean/Dancing with the Big Boys. September 1984 (EMI America EA 181, UK #6, US #8.)

Tonight, September 1984. Loving the Alien/Don't Look Down/God Only Knows/Tonight/Neighborhood Threat/Blue Jean/Tumble and Twirl/I Keep Forgettin'/Dancing with the Big Boys. [1995 reissue: This Is Not America/ As the World Falls Down/Absolute Beginners.]

Tonight/Tumble and Twirl. November 1984 (EMI America EA 187, UK #53, US #53.)

[Bowie and Pat Metheny Group] This Is Not America/(instrumental). February 1985 (EMI America EA 190, UK #14, US #32.)

Loving the Alien (remix)/Don't Look Down (remix). May 1985 (EMI America EA 195, UK #19.)

[Bowie and Mick Jagger] Dancing in the Street/(dub). August 1985 (EMI America EA 204, UK #1, US #7.)

Absolute Beginners/(dub). March 1986 (Virgin VS 838, UK #2.)

Underground/(instrumental). June 1986 (EMI America EA 216, UK #21.)

Labyrinth, June 1986. Opening Titles (inc. Underground)*/Into the Labyrinth*/Magic Dance/Sarah*/Chilly Down/Hallucination*/As the World Falls Down/The Goblin Battle*/Within You/Thirteen O'Clock*/Home At Last*/Underground. (* = Trevor Jones.)

[Iggy Pop] *Blah-Blah-Blah*, October 1986. Real Wild Child/Baby, It Can't Fall/Shades/Fire Girl/Isolation/Cry For Love/Blah-Blah-Blah/Hideaway/ Winners and Losers/Little Miss Emperor [CD only].

When the Wind Blows/(instrumental). November 1986 (Virgin VS 906, UK #44.)

Day-In Day-Out/Julie. March 1987 (EMI America EA 230, UK #17, US #21.)

Never Let Me Down, April 1987. Day-In Day-Out/Time Will Crawl/Beat of Your Drum/Never Let Me Down/Zeroes/Glass Spider/Shining Star (Makin' My Love)/New York's in Love/'87 and Cry/Too Dizzy/Bang Bang. [1995 reissue: Julie/Girls/When the Wind Blows.]

Time Will Crawl/Girls. June 1987 (EMI America EA 237, UK #33.)

Never Let Me Down/'87 and Cry. August 1987 (EMI America EA 239, UK #34, US #27.)

Tin Machine, May 1989. Heaven's in Here/Tin Machine/Prisoner of Love/ Crack City/I Can't Read/Under the God/Amazing/Working Class Hero/Bus Stop/Pretty Thing/Video Crime/Run [CD/cassette only]/Sacrifice Yourself [CD/cassette only]/Baby Can Dance. [1995 reissue: Country Bus Stop.]

Under the God/Sacrifice Yourself. June 1989 (EMI USA MT 68, UK #51.)

Tin Machine/Maggie's Farm (live). September 1989 (EMI USA MT 73, UK #48.)

Prisoner of Love/Baby Can Dance (live). October 1989 (EMI USA MT 76.)

Fame '90 (Gass mix)/Fame '90 (Queen Latifah's Rap Version). March 1990 (EMI FAME 90, UK #28.)

[Bowie and Adrian Belew] Pretty Pink Rose/Heartbeat [Belew]. May 1990 (Atlantic A7904.)

You Belong in Rock n' Roll/Amlapura (Indonesian version)/Stateside/ Hammerhead. August 1991 (London LONCD 305, UK #33.)

Tin Machine II, September 1991. Baby Universal/One Shot/You Belong in Rock n' Roll/If There Is Something/Amlapura/Betty Wrong/You Can't Talk/Stateside/Shopping for Girls/A Big Hurt/Sorry/Goodbye Mr. Ed/ Hammerhead.

Baby Universal/Stateside (BBC)/If There Is Something (BBC)/Heaven's in Here (BBC). October 1991 (London LOCDT 310, UK #48).

Tin Machine Live: Oy Vey Baby, July 1992. If There Is Something/Amazing/I Can't Read/Stateside/Under the God/Goodbye Mr. Ed/Heaven's in Here/ You Belong in Rock n' Roll.

Real Cool World/(instrumental). August 1992 (Warner W0127, UK #53.)

Jump They Say/Pallas Athena (Don't Stop Praying Mix). March 1993 (Arista 74321 139424, UK #9.)

Black Tie White Noise, April 1993. The Wedding/You've Been Around/I Feel Free/Black Tie White Noise/Jump They Say/Nite Flights/Pallas Athena/ Miracle Goodnight/Don't Let Me Down and Down/Looking for Lester/I Know It's Gonna Happen Someday/The Wedding Song/Lucy Can't Dance (CD bonus). [2003 reissue: Real Cool World/Lucy Can't Dance/Jump They Say (Rock Mix)/Black Tie White Noise (3rd Floor US Radio Mix)/Don't Let Me Down & Down (Indonesian vocal)/You've Been Around (Dangers 12" Remix)/Jump They Say (Brothers In Rhythm 12" Remix)/Black Tie White Noise (Here Come Da Jazz)/Pallas Athena (Don't Stop Praying Remix)/Nite Flights (Moodswings Back to Basics Remix)/Jump They Say (Dub Oddity).]

Black Tie White Noise/You've Been Around (Dangers Remix). June 1993 (Arista 74321 148682, UK #36.)

Miracle Goodnight/Looking for Lester. October 1993 (Arista 74321 162267, UK #40.)

The Buddha of Suburbia/Dead Against It. November 1993 (Arista 74321 177057, UK #35.)

The Buddha of Suburbia, November 1993. The Buddha of Suburbia/Sex and the Church/South Horizon/The Mysteries/Bleed Like a Craze, Dad/ Strangers When We Meet/Dead Against It/Untitled No. 1/Ian Fish, U.K. Heir/Buddha of Suburbia (rock mix).

The Hearts Filthy Lesson/I Am with Name. September 1995 (RCA 74321 307031, UK #35.) [US equivalent had Nothing to Be Desired.]

1. Outside, September 1995. Leon Takes Us Outside/Outside/The Hearts Filthy Lesson/A Small Plot of Land/Segue: Baby Grace (A Horrid Cassette)/ Hallo Spaceboy/The Motel/I Have Not Been to Oxford Town/No Control/ Segue: Algeria Touchshriek/The Voyeur of Utter Destruction (As Beauty)/ Segue: Ramona A. Stone — I Am with Name/Wishful Beginnings/We Prick You/Segue: Nathan Adler/I'm Deranged/Thru' These Architects Eyes/Segue: Nathan Adler/Strangers When We Meet. [2004 reissue: Hearts Filthy Lesson (Trent Reznor Alternative Mix)/(Rubber Mix)/(Simple Test Mix)/(Filthy Mix)/(Good Karma Mix)/A Small Plot of Land (*Basquiat* version)/Hallo

Spaceboy (12″ remix)/(Double Click Mix)/(Instrumental)/(Lost In Space Mix)/I Am with Name (album version)/I'm Deranged (Jungle Mix)/Get Real/Nothing to Be Desired.]

Strangers When We Meet/The Man Who Sold the World (live)/Get Real. November 1995 (RCA 74321 329407, UK #39.)

Hallo Spaceboy (Remix)/The Hearts Filthy Lesson. February 1996 (BMG/ RCA 74321 353847, UK #12.)

Telling Lies (Feelgood Mix)/(Paradox Mix)/(Adam F Mix). November 1996 (RCA 74321 39712, UK #76.)

Little Wonder/(Ambient Junior Mix)/(Club Dub Junior Mix)/(4/4 Junior Mix)/(instrumental). January 1997 (RCA 74321 452072, UK #14.)

Earthling, February 1997. Little Wonder/Looking for Satellites/Battle for Britain (The Letter)/Seven Years in Tibet/Dead Man Walking/Telling Lies/The Last Thing You Should Do/I'm Afraid of Americans/Law (Earthlings on Fire). [2004 reissue: Little Wonder (censored video edit)/(Junior Vasquez Club Mix)/(Danny Saber Dance Mix)/Seven Years in Tibet (Mandarin Version)/ Dead Man Walking (Moby Mix 1)/(Moby Mix 2)/Telling Lies (Feelgood Mix)/(Paradox Mix)/I'm Afraid of Americans (*Showgirls* version)/(Nine Inch Nails V1 Mix)/(Clean Edit)/V-2 Schneider (Tao Jones Index)/Pallas Athena (Tao Jones Index).]

Dead Man Walking/I'm Deranged (Jungle Mix)/Hearts Filthy Lesson (Good Karma Mix). April 1997 (RCA 74321 475842, UK #32.)

Seven Years in Tibet/(Mandarin version). August 1997 (RCA 74321 512547, UK #61.)

I'm Afraid of Americans (V1)/(V2)/(V3)/(V4)/(V5)/(V6). October 1997 (Virgin 73438 3861828, US #66.)

I Can't Read(remake)/This Is Not America. February 1998 (Velvel ZYX 87578, UK #73.)

Thursday's Child/We All Go Through/No One Calls [CD-ROM version also has We Shall Go to Town/1917]. September 1999 (Virgin VSCDT 1753, UK #16.)

'hours... ,' September 1999. Thursday's Child/Something in the Air/Survive/ If I'm Dreaming My Life/Seven/What's Really Happening?/The Pretty Things Are Going to Hell/New Angels of Promise/Brilliant Adventure/The Dreamers. [2004 reissue: Thursday's Child (rock mix)/(*Omikron: the Nomad Soul* Slower Version)/Something in the Air (*American Psycho* Remix)/Survive (Marius de Vries Mix)/Seven (demo version)/(Marius de Vries Mix)/(Beck Mix #1)/ (Beck Mix #2)/The Pretty Things Are Going to Hell (edit)/(*Stigmata* Film Version)/(*Stigmata* Film Only Version)/New Angels of Promise (*Omikron* Version/The Dreamers (*Omikron* Longer Version)/1917/We Shall Go to Town/We All Go Through/No One Calls.]

Survive (Marius de Vries Mix)/(album version)/The Pretty Things Are Going to Hell (*Stigmata* version). January 2000 (Virgin VSCDT 1767, UK #28.)

Seven (Marius de Vries)/(Beck remix)/(demo). July 2000 (Virgin VSCDT 1776, UK #32.)

Heathen, June 2002. Sunday/Cactus/Slip Away/Slow Burn/Afraid/I've Been Waiting for You/I Would Be Your Slave/I Took a Trip on a Gemini Spaceship/5:15 the Angels Have Gone/Everyone Says 'Hi'/A Better Future/ Heathen (the Rays). [bonus disc: Sunday (Moby remix)/A Better Future (Air remix)/Conversation Piece (*Toy* remake)/Panic in Detroit (remake). SACD version: When the Boys Come Marching Home/Wood Jackson/ Conversation Piece/Safe.]

Slow Burn/Wood Jackson/Shadow Man (*Toy*)/When the Boys Come Marching Home/You've Got a Habit of Leaving (*Toy*). June 2002 (ISO/ Columbia 6727442, UK #94.)

Everyone Says 'Hi'/Safe/Wood Jackson. September 2002 (Columbia 6731 34 3, UK #20). [Other versions inc.: When the Boys Come Marching Home/ Shadow Man/Baby Loves That Way (*Toy*)/You've Got a Habit of Leaving.]

New Killer Star/Love Missile F1-F11. September 2003.

Reality, September 2003. New Killer Star/Pablo Picasso/Never Get Old/ The Loneliest Guy/Looking for Water/She'll Drive the Big Car/Days/Fall Dog Bombs the Moon/Try Some, Buy Some/Reality/Bring Me the Disco King. [bonus disc: Fly/Queen of All the Tarts (Overture)/Rebel Rebel (2003 remake); tour edition: Waterloo Sunset.]

Arcade Fire and David Bowie Live at Fashion Rocks, November 2005. Life on Mars?/Five Years/Wake Up.

Where Are We Now? January 2013, UK #6.

The Stars (Are out Tonight). February 2013, UK #102.

The Next Day, March 2013. The Next Day/Dirty Boys/The Stars (Are out Tonight)/Love Is Lost/Where Are We Now?/Valentine's Day/If You Can See Me/I'd Rather Be High/Boss of Me/Dancing out in Space/How Does the Grass Grow?/(You Will) Set the World on Fire/You Feel So Lonely You Could Die/Heat. [deluxe edition: So She, Plan, I'll Take You There; Japanese deluxe edition: God Bless the Girl.]

The Next Day. June 2013.

Valentine's Day/Plan. August 2013, (Col/Sony 88883756667.)

The Next Day Extra, November 2013. Disc 2: Atomica/Love Is Lost (Hello Steve Reich Mix)/Plan/The Informer/I'd Rather Be High (Venetian Mix)/Like a Rocket Man/Born in a UFO/I'll Take You There/God Bless the Girl/So She.

Sue (In a Season of Crime)/Tis a Pity She Was a Whore. November 2014 (Parlophone 1ORDB2014, UK #81.)

Blackstar. November 2015, UK #61.

Lazarus. December 2015, UK #45, US #40.

Blackstar, January 2016. Blackstar/'Tis a Pity She Was a Whore/Lazarus/ Sue (Or In a Season of Crime)/Girl Loves Me/Dollar Days/I Can't Give Everything Away.

No Plan, January 2017. Lazarus/No Plan/Killing a Little Time/When I Met You.

Subsequently-issued live recordings of the 1976-2016 period. Date of recording in brackets.

Liveandwell.com, September 2000 [1997]. I'm Afraid of Americans/The Hearts Filthy Lesson/I'm Deranged/Hallo Spaceboy/Telling Lies/The Motel/ The Voyeur Of Utter Destruction/Battle For Britain/Seven Years in Tibet/ Little Wonder/Fun (Dillinja Mix)/Little Wonder (Danny Saber Dance Mix)/ Dead Man Walking (Moby Mix 1)/Telling Lies (Paradox Mix).

Bowie at the Beeb, September 2000 [Disc 3, rec. 27 June 2000]. Wild Is the Wind/Ashes to Ashes/Seven/This Is Not America/Absolute Beginners/ Always Crashing in the Same Car/Survive/Little Wonder/The Man Who Sold the World/Fame/Stay/Hallo Spaceboy/Cracked Actor/I'm Afraid of Americans/Let's Dance.

Glass Spider, June 2007 [1987]. Up The Hill Backwards/Glass Spider/Day-In Day-Out/Bang Bang/Absolute Beginners/Loving the Alien/China Girl/ Rebel Rebel/Fashion/Scary Monsters (And Super Creeps)/All The Madmen/ Never Let Me Down/Big Brother/'87 and Cry/"Heroes"/Sons of the Silent Age/Time Will Crawl /Young Americans/Beat of Your Drum/Jean Genie/ Let's Dance/Fame/Time/Blue Jean/Modern Love.

A Reality Tour, January 2010 [2003]. Rebel Rebel/New Killer Star/Reality/ Fame/Cactus/Sister Midnight/Afraid/All the Young Dudes/Be My Wife The Loneliest Guy/The Man Who Sold the World/Fantastic Voyage/Hallo Spaceboy/Sunday/Under Pressure/Life on Mars?/Battle for Britain/Ashes to Ashes/The Motel/Loving the Alien/Never Get Old/Changes/I'm Afraid of Americans/"Heroes"/Bring Me the Disco King/Slip Away/Heathen (the Rays)/Five Years/Hang on to Yourself/Ziggy Stardust/Fall Dog Bombs the Moon/Breaking Glass/China Girl/5:15 the Angels Have Gone [download only bonus]/Days [download-only bonus].

Live Nassau Coliseum '76, September 2010 [1976]. Station to Station/ Suffragette City/Fame/Word on a Wing/Stay/Waiting For the Man/Queen Bitch/Life on Mars?/Five Years/Panic in Detroit/Changes/TVC 15/Diamond Dogs/Rebel Rebel/Jean Genie.

Live in Berlin, March 2018 [1978]. "Heroes"/Be My Wife/Blackout/Sense of Doubt/Breaking Glass/Fame/Alabama Song/Rebel Rebel.

Welcome To the Blackout, April 2018 [1978]. Warszawa/"Heroes"/What in the World/Be My Wife/Jean Genie/Blackout/Sense of Doubt/Speed of Life/ Sound and Vision/Breaking Glass/Fame/Beauty and the Beast/Five Years/ Soul Love/Star/Hang on to Yourself/Ziggy Stardust/Suffragette City/Art Decade/Alabama Song/Station to Station/TVC 15/Stay/Rebel Rebel.

Serious Moonlight, October 2018 [1983]. Look Back In Anger/"Heroes"/ What in the World/ Golden Years/Fashion/Let's Dance/Breaking Glass/ Life on Mars?/Sorrow/Cat People/China Girl/Scary Monsters (And Super Creeps)/Rebel Rebel/White Light-White Heat/Station to Station/Cracked Actor/Ashes to Ashes/Space Oddity/Young Americans/Fame/ Modern Love.

Glastonbury 2000, November 2018 [2000]. Introduction (Greensleeves)/ Wild Is the Wind/China Girl/Changes/Stay/Life on Mars?/Absolute Beginners/Ashes to Ashes/Rebel Rebel/Little Wonder/Golden Years/Fame/ All the Young Dudes/The Man Who Sold the World/Station to Station/ Starman/Hallo Spaceboy/Under Pressure/Ziggy Stardust/"Heroes"/Let's Dance/I'm Afraid of Americans.

BIBLIOGRAPHY

Bowie: Life, Music, Collaborators

Adams, Richard, *The Complete Iggy Pop*. Reynolds & Hearn: 2006.

Banks, Bradley, "Iggy Pop's The Idiot," (http://idiotlust.blogspot.com/).

Bell, Edward, *Unmade Up: Recollections of a Friendship with David Bowie*. Unicorn: 2017.

Block, Paula M. and Terry J. Erdmann, *Jim Henson's Labyrinth: The Ultimate Visual History*. Insight Editions: 2016.

Bowie, David, "Sailor's Journals: 1998-2006." (Privately-assembled collection.)

Bowie, David and Enda Walsh, *Lazarus: The Complete Book and Lyrics*. Nick Hern Books: 2016.

Broackes, Victoria and Geoffrey Marsh, eds., *David Bowie Is*. V&A Publishing: 2013.

Brooker, Will, *Forever Stardust: David Bowie Across the Universe*. I.B. Tauris & Co.: 2017.

Buckley, David, *Strange Fascination: David Bowie: The Definitive Story*. Virgin Books: 2005.

Cann, Kevin, *David Bowie: A Chronology*. Hutchinson Publishing Group: 1983.

Carr, Roy and Charles Shaar Murray, *Bowie: An Illustrated Record*. Eel Pie Publishing: 1981.

Currie, David, ed., *David Bowie: The Starzone Interviews*. Omnibus Press: 1985.

Dayal, Geeta, *Another Green World*. Continuum International: 2009.

De la Parra, Pimm Jal, *David Bowie: The Concert Tapes*. PJ Publishing: 1985.

Devereux, Eoin, Aileen Dillane and Martin Power, eds., *David Bowie: Critical Perspectives*. Routledge: 2015.

Duffy, Chris and Kevin Cann, *Duffy Bowie: Five Sessions*. ACC Editions: 2014.

Edwards, Henry and Tony Zanetta, *Stardust: The David Bowie Story*. Bantam: 1986.

Egan, Sean, ed., *Bowie on Bowie: Interviews and Encounters with David Bowie*. Chicago Review Press: 2017.

Eno, Brian, *A Year with Swollen Appendices: Brian Eno's Diary*. Faber & Faber: 1996.

Flippo, Chet, *David Bowie's Serious Moonlight*. Doubleday: 1984.

Frederiksen, Peter, *Return of the Spiderman: David Bowie's Glass Spider Tour*. Private press: 1992 (2nd ed.).

Frederiksen, Peter and Sean Doherty, *The Sound + Vision Tour Book*. Private press: 1991.

Gillman, Peter and Leni, *Alias David Bowie*. Henry Holt & Co.: 1987.

Greco, Nicholas P., *David Bowie in Darkness: A Study of 1. Outside and the Late Career*. McFarland: 2015.

Griffin, Roger, *David Bowie: The Golden Years*. Overlook-Omnibus: 2016.

Helibo Seyoman (various authors). Bec Zmiana: 2016.

Hopkins, Jerry, *Bowie*. Elm Tree Books: 1985.

Jones, Dylan, *David Bowie: A Life*. Crown Archetype: 2017.

Juby, Kerry, ed., *In Other Words, David Bowie*. Omnibus Press: 1986.

LeRoy, Dan, *The Greatest Music Never Sold: Secrets of Legendary Lost Albums by David Bowie* [et al]. Backbeat Music: 2007.

MacCormack, Geoff, *From Station to Station: Travels with Bowie 1973–1976*. Genesis: 2007.

Matthew-Walker, Robert, *David Bowie: Theatre of Music*. The Kensal Press: 1985.

Mayes, Sean, *We Can Be Heroes: Life on Tour with David Bowie*. Independent Music Press: 1999.

Miles, Barry, ed., *In His Own Words... David Bowie*. Omnibus Press: 1980.

Paytress, Mark and Steve Pafford, *Bowiestyle*. Omnibus Press: 2000.

Pegg, Nicholas, *The Complete David Bowie* (7th edition). Reynolds & Hearn Ltd.: 2016.

Perone, James, *The Words and Music of David Bowie*. Praeger: 2007.

Pop, Iggy with Anne Wehrer, *I Need More*. Karz-Cohl: 1982.

Rodgers, Nile, *Le Freak: An Upside-Down Story of Family, Disco, and Destiny*. Spiegel & Grau: 2011.

Rüther, Tobias, *David Bowie and Berlin* (Anthony Mathews: trans.).
  Reaktion: 2014 (2008).

Sandford, Christopher, *Loving the Alien*. Da Capo: 1996.

Santos-Kayda, Myriam, *David Bowie: Live in New York*. PowerHouse
  Books: 2003.

Seabrook, Thomas Jerome, *Bowie in Berlin: A New Career in a New Town*.
  Jawbone Press: 2008.

Sheffield, Rob, *On Bowie*. Dey Street Books: 2016.

Sheppard, David, *On Some Faraway Beach: The Life and Times of Brian Eno*.
  Orion: 2008.

Slapper, Clifford, *Bowie's Piano Man: The Life of Mike Garson* (2nd edition).
  Backbeat Books: 2018.

Spitz, Marc, *Bowie*. Crown Publishers: 2009.

Thompson, Dave, *Hallo Spaceboy: The Rebirth of David Bowie*. ECW Press:
  2006.

---. *David Bowie: Moonage Daydream*. Plexus: 1987.

Thomson, Elizabeth and David Gutman, eds., *The Bowie Companion*. Da
  Capo Press: 1996.

Tremlett, George, *David Bowie: Living on the Brink*. Carol & Graff: 1997.

Trynka, Paul, *Iggy Pop: Open Up and Bleed*. Broadway Books: 2007.

---. *Starman*. Sphere: 2010.

Visconti, Tony, *Bowie, Bolan and the Brooklyn Boy*. Harper-Collins: 2007.

Wilcken, Hugo, *Low*. Continuum: 2005.

Art, History, Popular Music, Culture

*The following contributed to this book or provided a backdrop for periods
  discussed.*

Abish, Walter, *Alphabetical Africa*. New Directions: 1973.

---. *How German Is It*. New Directions: 1980.

Ackroyd, Peter, *Hawksmoor*. Hamish Hamilton: 1985.

Addison, Paul, *No Turning Back: The Peacetime Revolutions of Postwar Britain*.
  Oxford University Press: 2010.

Albiez, Sean and David Pattie, eds., *Kraftwerk: Music Non-Stop*.
  Continuum: 2011.

Albright, Daniel, *Untwisting the Serpent: Modernism in Music, Literature and Other Arts*. University of Chicago Press: 2000.

Amis, Martin, *Money*. Jonathan Cape: 1984.

Ballard, J.G., *Crash*. Jonathan Cape: 1973.

Barker, Hugh and Yuval Taylor, *Faking It: The Quest for Authenticity in Popular Music*. W.W. Norton: 2007.

Barker, Paul, *The Freedoms of Suburbia*. Frances Lincoln: 2009.

Barnes, Julian, *Flaubert's Parrot*. Jonathan Cape: 1984.

Bauman, Zygmunt, *Liquid Love: On the Frailty of Human Bonds*. Polity: 2003.

Beckett, Andy, *Promised You a Miracle: UK 80-82*. Allen Lane: 2015.

---. *When The Lights Went Out: Britain in the Seventies*. Faber and Faber: 2009.

Berkoff, Steven, *Steven Berkoff: Plays 1*. Faber & Faber: 2000.

Binkley, Sam, *Getting Loose: Lifestyle Consumption in the '70s*. Duke University Press: 2009.

Birk, Dennis L. and David R. Gress, *A History of West Germany: Democracy and Its Discontents: 1963-1988*. Basil Blackwell: 1989.

Blake, Mark, *Is This the Real Life?: The Untold Story of Queen*. Da Capo: 2011.

Bloom, Harold, *Omens of Millennium: The Gnosis of Angels, Dreams, and Resurrection*. Riverhead: 1996.

Brecht, Bertolt, *Collected Plays 1* (Ralph Manheim, John Willett, eds.). Methuen: 1970.

---. *Poems: 1913-1956* (Manheim, Willett, eds.). Eyre Methuen: 1976.

Broyard, Anatole, *Kafka Was the Rage: A Greenwich Village Memoir*. Carol Southern: 1996.

Bockris, Victor, *Transformer: The Lou Reed Story*. Simon & Schuster: 1995.

Bolaño, Robert, *Nazi Literature in the Americas* (Chris Andrews, trans.). New Directions: 2008 (1996).

Booker, Christopher, *The Seventies: The Decade That Changed the Future*. Stein & Day: 1980.

Boy George, with Spencer Bright, *Take It Like a Man: The Autobiography of Boy George*. Sidgwick & Jackson: 1995.

Boyd, William, *Nat Tate: An American Artist 1928–1960*. Edition Stemmle: 1998.

Buckley, David, *The Thrill of It All: The Story of Bryan Ferry and Roxy Music*. Carlton Books: 2004.

Buckley, David with Nigel Forrest, *Kraftwerk: Publikation*. Omnibus Press: 2012.

Burgess, Anthony, *1985*. Little, Brown & Co.: 1978.

Burroughs, William S., *The Ticket That Exploded*. Grove Press: 1967 (1962).

---. *Nova Express*. Grove Press: 1964.

Byrne, David, *Bicycle Diaries*. Viking Penguin: 2009.

Cale, John with Victor Bockris, *What's Welsh for Zen: The Autobiography of John Cale*. Bloomsbury USA: 2000.

Canetti, Elias, *The Torch in My Ear*. Farrar, Straus and Giroux: 1982.

Cardinal, Roger, *Outsider Art*. Praeger: 1972.

Carlin, Marcello and Lena Friesen, "Then Play Long." (http://nobilliards. blogspot.com).

Carr, C., *On Edge: Performance at the End of the 20th Century*. University Press of New England: 1993.

Chambers, Iain, *Urban Rhythms: Pop Music and Popular Culture*. Basinstoke: 1985.

Chatwin, Bruce, *The Songlines*. Franklin Press: 1987.

Christgau, Robert, *Rock Albums of the '70s: A Critical Guide*. Da Capo: 1981.

---. *Christgau's Record Guide: The '80s*. Pantheon: 1990.

Chusid, Irwin, *Songs in the Key of Z: The Curious Universe of Outsider Music*. Chicago Review Press: 2000.

Clay Large, David, *Berlin*. Basic Books: 2000.

Clover, Joshua, *1989: Bob Dylan Didn't Have This to Sing About*. University of California Press: 2009.

Conrad, Peter, *Modern Times, Modern Places*. Alfred A. Knopf: 1999.

Cork, Richard, *David Bomberg*. Tate Publishing: 1988.

Crary, Jonathan, *24/7: Late Capitalism and the Ends of Sleep*. Verso: 2013.

Crowley, John, *Dæmonomania*. Bantam: 2000.

Davidson, Telly, *Culture War: How the '90s Made Us What We Are Today*. McFarland & Co. 2016.

Davies, Paul, *God and the New Physics*. J.M. Dent & Sons: 1983.

Davies, Ray, *X-Ray*. Overlook Duckworth: 1994.

DeCurtis, Anthony, James Henke with Holly George-Warren, eds., *The Rolling Stone Illustrated History of Rock & Roll*. Random House: 1992.

De Groot, Gerard, *The Seventies Unplugged: A Kaleidoscopic History of a Violent Decade*. Macmillan: 2010.

Demetz, Peter, *After the Fires: Recent Writings in the Germanies, Austria and Switzerland*. Harcourt Brace Jovanovich: 1986.

Dick, Philip K., *Dr. Bloodmoney*. Ace: 1965.

---. *A Scanner Darkly*. Doubleday: 1977.

Di Pirajno, Alberto Denti, *A Grave for a Dolphin*. Andre Deutsch: 1956.

Doyle, Jennifer, *Hold It Against Me: Difficulty and Emotion in Contemporary Art*. Duke University Press: 2013.

Drabble, Margaret, *The Ice Age*. Weidenfeld & Nicolson: 1977.

Duncan, Robert, *The Noise: Notes from a Rock 'n' Roll Era*. Ticknor & Fields: 1984.

Elms, Robert, *The Way We Wore: A Life in Threads*. Indie: 2014.

Emerson, Ken, *Always Magic in the Air: The Bomp and Brilliance of the Brill Building Era*. Penguin: 2005.

Erdman, Paul E., *The Crash of '79*. Pocket Books: 1976.

Ewing, Tom, "Popular." (http://freakytrigger.co.uk).

Farren, Mick, *Elvis Died For Somebody's Sins But Not Mine: A Lifetime's Collected Writing*. Headpress: 2013.

Fisher, Mark, *Capitalist Realism: Is There No Alternative?* Zer0: 2009.

---. *Ghosts of My Life: Writings on Depression, Hauntology, and Lost Futures*. Zer0: 2014.

---. *The Weird and the Eerie*. Repeater: 2016.

Forster, Robert, *Grant & I: Inside and Outside the Go-Betweens*. Hamish Hamilton: 2016.

Fraction, Matt and Gabriel Ba, *Casanova: Avaritia*. Image: 2012.

Freud, Sigmund, *The Interpretation of Dreams: The Complete and Definitive Text* (trans. James Strachey). Basic Books: 1955 (1900).

Friedrich, Otto, *Before the Deluge: A Portrait of Berlin in the 1920s*. HarperPerennial: 1995 (1972).

Frith, Simon, *Music for Pleasure*. Routledge: 1988.

Fuegi, John, *Brecht and Company: Sex, Politics, and the Making of the Modern Drama*. Grove Press: 1994.

Gay, Peter, *Weimar Culture: The Outsider As Insider*. Harper & Row: 1968.

Giddins, Gary, *Weather Bird: Jazz at the Dawn of Its Second Century*. Oxford University Press: 2004.

Gill, John, *Queer Noises: Male and Female Homosexuality in Twentieth Century Music*. University of Minnesota Press: 1995.

Gillen, Kieron and Jamie McKelvie, *Phonogram*. Image: 2007-2016.

---. *The Wicked + the Divine*. Image: 2013-2019.

Gracyk, Theodore, *Rhythm and Noise: An Aesthetics of Rock*. I.B. Tauris & Co. Ltd.: 1996.

Grossman, Lev, *The Magicians*. Viking: 2009.

Haines, Luke, *Bad Vibes: Britpop and My Part in Its Downfall*. Windmill: 2009.

Harris, John, *Britpop! Cool Britannia and the Spectacular Demise of English Rock*. Da Capo: 2004.

Hatherley, Owen, *A New Kind of Bleak: Journeys Through Urban Britain*. Verso: 2012.

---. *Uncommon: An Essay on Pulp*. Zer0: 2011.

Haxthausen, Charles W. and Heidrun Suhr, eds., *Berlin: Culture and Metropolis*. University of Minnesota Press: 1990.

Hebdidge, Dick, *Subculture: The Meaning of Style*. Methuen: 1979.

Hepworth, David, *Uncommon People: The Rise and Fall of Rock Stars*. Henry Holt: 2017.

Hermann, Kai and Horst Rieck, *Christiane F.: Autobiography of a Girl of the Streets [Wir Kinder vom Bahnhof Zoo]* (Susanne Flatauer, trans.). Bantam: 1982 (1979).

Heylin, Clinton, *Bob Dylan: Behind the Shades: The 20th Anniversary Edition*. Faber and Faber: 2011.

---. *Still on the Road: The Songs of Bob Dylan Vol. 2: 1974-2008*. Constable & Robinson: 2011.

Hirst, Damien and Gordon Burn, *On the Way to Work*. Other Criteria: 2016.

Hollander, John, *Reflections on Espionage*. Yale University Press: 1999 (1974).

Huber, David Miles and Robert E. Runstein, *Modern Recording Techniques*. Focal Press: 2001.

Huyssen, Andreas, *Twilight Memories: Marking Time in a Culture of Amnesia*. Routledge: 1995.

Isherwood, Christopher, *The Berlin Stories*. New Directions: 1945.

Jaynes, Julian, *The Origin of Consciousness in the Breakdown of the Bicameral Mind*. Houghton Mifflin: 1976.

Judt, Tony, *Postwar: A History of Europe Since 1945*. Penguin Press: 2005.

Kael, Pauline, *For Keeps*. Dutton: 1994.

Kelly, Richard, ed., *Alan Clarke*. Faber: 1998.

Kemp, Gary, *I Know This Much: From Soho to Spandau*. Fourth Estate: 2009.

Kent, Nick, *Apathy For the Devil: A Seventies Memoir*. Da Capo: 2010.

Kerouac, Jack, *The Subterraneans*. Grove Press: 1958.

Kureishi, Hanif, *The Buddha of Suburbia*. Viking Penguin: 1990.

Kureishi, Hanif and Jon Savage, eds., *The Faber Book of Pop*. Faber & Faber: 1995.

Lacquer, Walter, *Weimar: A Cultural History: 1918-1933*. Weidenfeld and Nicolson: 1974.

Ladd, Brian, *The Ghosts of Berlin: Confronting German History In the Urban Landscape*. University of Chicago Press: 1997.

Lasch, Christopher, *The Culture of Narcissism: American Life in an Age of Diminishing Expectations*. W.W. Norton & Co.: 1978.

Lawrence, Tim, *Life and Death on the New York Dance Floor: 1980-1983*. Duke University Press: 2016.

---. *Love Saves the Day: A History of American Dance Music Culture, 1970-1979*. Duke University Press: 2003.

Leng, Simon, *The Music of George Harrison: All Things Must Pass*. Firefly: 2003.

Lyon, James K. and Hans-Peter Breuer, eds., *Brecht Unbound*. University of Delaware Press: 1995.

MacDonald, Ian, *The People's Music*. Pimlico: 2003.

MacInnes, Colin, *Absolute Beginners*. MacGibbon & Kee: 1959.

Marcus, Greil, *Lipstick Traces: A Secret History of the Twentieth Century*. Harvard University Press: 1989.

---. *Ranters and Crowd Pleasers: Punk in Pop Music, 1977-92*. Doubleday: 1993.

Martin, Bernice, *A Sociology of Contemporary Cultural Change*. Blackwell: 1981.

Matos, Michaelangelo, *The Underground Is Massive*. HarperCollins: 2015.

McNeil, Legs and Gillian McCain, *Please Kill Me: The Uncensored Oral History of Punk* (20th Anniversary Edition). Grove Press: 2016 (1996).

Merrill, James, *The Changing Light at Sandover*. Atheneum: 1982.

Middles, Mick, *The Smiths: The Complete Story*. Omnibus Press: 1988.

Miles, Lawrence and Tat Wood, *About Time 4*. Mad Norwegian Press: 2004.

---. *About Time 5*. Mad Norwegian Press: 2005.

Milner, Greg, *Perfecting Sound Forever: An Aural History of Recorded Music*. FSG: 2009.

Mishima, Yukio, *The Decay of the Angel* (Edward G. Seidensticker, trans.). Alfred A. Knopf: 1974 (1971).

---. *Runaway Horses* (Michael Gallagher, trans.). Alfred A. Knopf: 1973 (1969).

---. *The Sailor Who Fell from Grace with the Sea* (John Nathan, trans.). Alfred A. Knopf: 1965 (1963).

---. *Spring Snow* (Gallagher). Alfred A. Knopf: 1972 (1968).

---. *Sun and Steel*. Kodansha International: 1970 (1968).

Mitford, Jessica, *The American Way of Death*. Simon & Schuster: 1963.

Moore, Alan and Gabriel Andrade, *Crossed + 100*. Avatar: 2015.

Moore, Alan and Eddie Campbell, *From Hell*. Eddie Campbell Comics: 1999.

Morley, Paul, *Ask: The Chatter of Pop*. Faber & Faber: 1986.

Morrissey, *Autobiography*. Penguin Classics (sic): 2013.

Nabokov, Vladimir, *Pale Fire*. G.P. Putnam's Sons: 1962.

Nairn, Tom, *The Enchanted Glass: Britain and Its Monarchy* (2nd edition). Verso: 2011.

Nathan, John, *Mishima: A Biography*. Da Capo: 1974, 2000.

Neate, Wilson, *Read & Burn: A Book About Wire*. Jawbone: 2013.

Norman, Howard, *The Bird Artist*. Farrar, Straus and Giroux: 1994.

O'Brien, Geoffrey, *Sonata for Jukebox*. Counterpoint: 2004.

Pagels, Elaine, *The Gnostic Gospels*. Random House: 1979.

Palmer, Robert, *Deep Blues*. Viking Penguin: 1981.

Pelly, Jenn, *The Raincoats*. Bloomsbury Academic: 2017.

Penman, Ian, *Vital Signs: Music, Movies and Other Manias*. Serpent's Tail: 1998.

Perlstein, Rick, *The Invisible Bridge*. Scribner: 2014.

Piekut, Benjamin, *Experimentalism Otherwise: The New York Avant-Garde and Its Limits*. University of California Press: 2011.

Plagenhoef, Scott and Ryan Schreiber, eds., *The Pitchfork 500*. Fireside: 2008.

Prikryl, Jana, *The After Party*. Tim Duggan Books: 2016.

Pyzik, Agata, *Poor But Sexy*. Zer0: 2014.

Raban, Jonathan, *Soft City*. Hamish Hamilton Ltd.: 1974.

Reed, S. Alexander, *Assimilate: A Critical History of Industrial Music*. Oxford University Press: 2013.

Reed, S. Alexander and Elizabeth Sandifer, *Flood*. Bloomsbury Academic: 2014.

Reich, Steve, *Writings on Music: 1965-2000*. Oxford University Press: 2002.

Reynolds, Anthony, *The Impossible Dream: The Story of Scott Walker and the Walker Brothers*. Jawbone: 2009.

Reynolds, Simon, *Retromania: Pop Culture's Addiction to Its Own Past*. Faber & Faber: 2011.

---. *Rip It Up and Start Again: Postpunk 1978-1984*. Faber & Faber: 2005.

---. *Shock and Awe*. Faber & Faber: 2016.

Richie, Alexandra, *Faust's Metropolis: A History of Berlin*. Carroll & Graf: 1998.

Rimmer, Dave, *Like Punk Never Happened: Culture Club and the New Pop* (rev. edition). Faber and Faber: 2011 (1985).

Rodden, John, *Repainting the Little Red Schoolhouse: A History of Eastern German Education*. Oxford University Press: 2002.

Rodenbach, Georges, *Bruges-La-Morte* (Philip Mosley, trans.). University of Scranton Press: 2007 (1892).

Ross, Alex, *Listen to This*. Farrar, Straus and Giroux: 2010.

Russ, Joanna, *The Female Man*. Bantam: 1975.

Sandbrook, Dominic, *Seasons in the Sun: The Battle for Britain, 1974-1979*. Allen Lane: 2012.

Sandifer, Elizabeth, *TARDIS Eruditorum: An Unofficial Critical History of Doctor Who, Volume 5*. Eruditorum Press: 2014.

---. *TARDIS Eruditorum, Volume 6*. Eruditorum Press: 2015.

Savage, Jon, *England's Dreaming: Anarchy, Sex Pistols, Punk Rock, and Beyond* (revised edition). Faber & Faber: 2001 (1991).

---. *Teenage: The Creation of Youth Culture*. Viking: 2007.

Schneider, Peter, *Couplings* (Philip Boehm, trans.). Farrar, Straus and Giroux: 1996.

---. *The Wall Jumper* (Leigh Hafrey, trans.). Pantheon: 1984.

Sharp, Ken, *Starting Over: The Making of John Lennon and Yoko Ono's Double Fantasy*. Gallery Books: 2010.

Shears, Jake, *Boys Keep Swinging: A Memoir*. Atria Books: 2018.

Sheffield, Rob, *Dreaming the Beatles*. Dey Street Books: 2017.

Sinfield, Alan, *Literature, Politics, and Culture in Postwar Britain*. University of California Press: 1989.

Sisario, Ben, *Doolittle*. Continuum: 2006.

Smith, Andrew, *Totally Wired: The Wild Rise and the Crazy Fall of the First Dotcom Dream*. Simon & Schuster: 2012.

Stanley, Bob, *Yeah Yeah Yeah*. Faber & Faber: 2013.

Steiner, George, *In Bluebeard's Castle: Some Notes Towards the Re-definition of Culture*. Faber & Faber: 1971.

---. *Real Presences*. Faber & Faber: 1989.

Stoppard, Tom, *The Coast of Utopia*. Grove Press: 2007.

Strange, Steve, *Blitzed! The Autobiography of Steve Strange*. Orion: 2002.

Stubbs, David, *1996 and the End Of History*. Repeater: 2016.

---. *Future Days: Krautrock and the Building of Modern Germany*. Faber & Faber: 2014.

Tannenbaum, Rob and Craig Marks, *I Want My MTV: The Uncensored Story of the Music Video Revolution*. Dutton: 2011.

Taylor, Ronald, *Berlin and Its Culture*. Yale University Press: 1997.

Tevis, Walter, *The Man Who Fell to Earth*. Gold Medal Books: 1963.

Thomson, David, *Have You Seen...?: A Personal Introduction to 1,000 Films*. Alfred A. Knopf: 2008.

Thurlow, Richard, *Fascism in Britain: A History, 1918-1985*. Olympic: 1987.

Townshend, Pete, *Who I Am: An Autobiography*. Harper: 2012.

Trow, George W.S., *My Pilgrim's Progress: Media Studies: 1950-1998*. Pantheon: 1999.

---. *Within the Context of No Context*. Atlantic Monthly Press: 1997 (1981).

Tuchman, Maurice and Carol S. Eliel, *Parallel Visions: Modern Artists and Outsider Art*. Princeton University Press: 1993.

Valentine, Gary, *New York Rocker: My Life in the Blank Generation with Blondie, Iggy Pop, and Others, 1974-1981*. Da Capo: 2006.

Volker, Klaus, *Brecht: A Biography* (John Nowell, trans.). Seabury Press: 1978 (1976).

Weisbard, Eric, *Top 40 Democracy: The Rival Mainstreams Of American Music*. University of Chicago Press: 2014.

Weitz, Eric D., *Weimar Germany: Promises and Tragedy*. Princeton University Press: 2007.

Weschler, Lawrence, *Mr. Wilson's Cabinet of Wonder*. Pantheon: 1995.

Whitehead, Phillip, *The Writing on the Wall: Britain in the Seventies*. Michael Joseph: 1985.

Willett, John, *Brecht in Context*. Methuen: 1998.

Wolf, Christa, *The Quest for Christa T* (Christopher Middleton, trans.) Farrar, Straus and Giroux: 1971 (1968).

Young, Rob, ed., *No Regrets: Writings on Scott Walker*. Orion Books: 2012.

Essential Bowie Websites

Bowie Wonderworld (http://www.bowiewonderworld.com).

David Bowie (http://www.davidbowie.com).

David Bowie Blackstar (https://www.davidbowieblackstar.it/).

David Bowie News (https://davidbowienews.com).

David Bowie World (http://www.davidbowieworld.nl/).

Golden Years (http://www.bowiegoldenyears.com).

Helden (http://www.helden.org.uk).

Illustrated DB Discography (http://www.illustrated-db-discography.nl).

Teenage Wildlife (http://www.teenagewildlife.com).

The Young American (http://www.theyoungamerican.co.uk).

Film/Radio/TV Interviews/Documentaries

Absolute Beginners. Dir: Julien Temple. Goldcrest/Virgin: 1986.

"Arena," (Series 11, Ep. 5, "The Strange Case of Yukio Mishima"). Dir: Michael McIntyre: 1985.

Arena Rock. Dir: Alan Yentob. BBC 2: 1978.

August. Dir.: Austin Chick. Original Media/57th & Irving Prods./Periscope Ent.: 2008.

Baal. Dir: Alan Clarke. BBC 1: 1982.

Basquiat. Dir: Julian Schnabel. Guild/Eleventh St./Miramax: 1996.

The Buddha of Suburbia. Dir: Roger Michell. BBC: 1993.

"Changes at Fifty." Dir: Yentob. BBC 2: 1997.

Christiane F. — Wir Kinder vom Bahnhof Zoo. Dir: Ulrich Edel. Solaris Film: 1981.

David Bowie: A Reality Tour. Dir: Marcus Viner. Blink: 2004.

David Bowie: An Earthling at Fifty. Dir: Stephen Lock. Big Eye Film &
   Television Ltd.: 1997.

David Bowie: Five Years. Dir: Francis Whately. BBC: 2013.

David Bowie: Serious Moonlight. Dir: David Mallet. Concert Productions
   International: 1984.

David Bowie: The Last Five Years. Dir: Whately. BBC: 2017.

"The David Bowie Story." BBC Radio One (Stuart Grundy): 1976,
   updated 1993 (Paul Gambaccini, John Tobler).

Everybody Loves Sunshine (aka *B.U.S.T.E.D.*). Dir: Andrew Goth. BV Films/
   Gothic/IAC: 1999.

"Extras" (Series 2, Ep. 2, "David Bowie"). Dir: Gervais/Merchant. 2006.

The Falcon and the Snowman. Dir: John Schlesinger. Hemdale: 1985.

"Golden Years: The David Bowie Story," BBC Radio 2 (Mark Goodier):
   2000.

The Hunger. Dir: Tony Scott. MGM: 1983.

"The Hunger." (Season 2, 1999-2000).

I'm Not There. Dir: Todd Haynes. Endgame/Killer/John Goldwyn/John
   Wells: 2007.

Il Mio West. Dir: Giovanni Veronesi. Cecci Gori Group/Pacific Pictures:
   1998.

Inside the Labyrinth. Dir.: Desmond Saunders. Jim Henson Television
   Prod.: 1986.

Inspirations. Dir: Michael Apted. Argo/Clear Blue Sky: 1997.

Into the Night. Dir: John Landis. Universal: 1985.

Jazzin' For Blue Jean. Dir: Temple. Nitrate Films: 1984.

Just a Gigolo (*Schöner Gigolo — Armer Gigolo*). Dir: David Hemmings.
   Bayerischer Rundfunk/Leguan Film Berlin/Sender Freies Berlin: 1978.

Labyrinth. Dir: Jim Henson. Henson Assocs./Lucasfilm: 1986.

The Last Temptation of Christ. Dir: Martin Scorsese. Cineplex Odeon: 1988.

Lazarus: The Motion Picture. Dir: Ivo van Hove. 2018.

"Legends: David Bowie." Produced: Mary Wharton. VH1: 1998.

The Linguini Incident. Dir: Richard Shepard. Isolar: 1991.

The Man Who Fell to Earth. Dir: Nicolas Roeg. British Lion Films: 1976.

Merry Christmas, Mr. Lawrence. Dir: Nagisa Oshima. Recorded Picture/
   Oshima Prod.: 1983.

Moon. Dir: Duncan Jones. Liberty Films/Xingu Films/Limelight/Lunar
Industries: 2009.

Mr. Rice's Secret. Dir.: Nicholas Kendall. New City Prod./Panorama Ent.:
1999.

The Prestige. Dir: Christopher Nolan. Touchstone/Newmarket/Syncopy:
2006.

Ricochet. Dir.: Gerry Troyna. Maya Vision International: 1984.

"Rock and Roll" (ep. 7, "The Wild Side," dir.: Hugh Thompson). BBC/
WGBH: 1995.

Scott Walker: 30 Century Man. Dir: Stephen Kijak. BBC/Verve: 2006.

Tin Machine: Oy Vey Baby. Dir.: Hannes Rossacher, Rudy Dolezal.
PolyGram: 1992.

Twin Peaks: Fire Walk with Me. Dir: David Lynch. CIBY Pictures: 1992.

Velvet Goldmine. Dir: Haynes. Killer Films/Channel 4/Newmarket Capital/
Goldwyn: 1998.

"VH1 Storytellers," (Season 4, Ep. 7, "David Bowie)." 1999.

When the Wind Blows. Dir: Jimmy Murakami. Meltdown Prod./British
Screen Prod./Film Four: 1986.

ACKNOWLEDGEMENTS

Books are the work of a great many people other than the person whose name is on the spine.

Manuscript readers and friends: Mairead Case (whose kindness and support helped me to finish this book), Stephen Thomas Erlewine, Alfred Soto, Ian McDuffie, Michaelangelo Matos, Elizabeth Sandifer, Ned Raggett, Kate Izquierdo, Alex Reed, Jack Womack. Special thanks to: Ryan Faulds, who volunteered to edit early drafts; Nicholas Currie, aka Momus, who provided theories and quotes, as in the previous book; Stephen Ryan; Owen Hatherley; Agata Pyzik, guide to Warszawa; Greg Smith, guide to Bowie's chord progressions; Nigel "Nacho" Marshall, who should be the Bowie estate's film archivist. A few collaborators of Bowie's have clarified stories over the years. In particular I'd like to thank Reeves Gabrels (and Susan Gabrels), Dave Gutter, Mark Plati, and Maria Schneider.

Old friends and favorite locals: Morgan and Corey Griffin (and Ada and Alice), Mike Slezak and Iyassu Sebhat, Kristen and Joe Holmgren, Christopher and Susan George, Bill and Jess Madden-Fuoco, Mark Leccese, Dan Costello and Brittany Shahmehri, Alex Abramovich, Michael Dumiak, Adam Zucker and Heather Abel, Zack Lesser and Taije Silverman, Burns Maxey and Matt Medeiros, Seth Lepore, Sharon Esdale. To my mother and father, Don and Barbara O'Leary, and to the rest of my family. And to dear Lucy.

I've made many friends because of this project, by far its greatest reward: Rahawa Haile, Andy Zax, Lisa Jane Persky, Douglas Wolk, Tom Ewing, Dave Depper, Matt Fraction, Kate Koliha, Nikola Tamindzic, Alison Jean Baker, Jonathan Bogart, Brendan Byrne, Deanna Kerry, Sylvia Korman, Thomas Inskeep, Keith Harris, Michael Daddino, Jody Beth LaFosse, Annie Zaleski, Matt Wardlaw, Mike Heyliger, Caryn Rose, Maura Johnston, Chris

Molanphy, Liz Carlson, Kathy Fennessy, Norman Be, Evan "Funk" Davies, Christian Finnegan, Mike Duquette, Nate Patrin, Rob Sheffield, David Cantwell, Charles Hughes.

To Nicholas Pegg, whose *Complete David Bowie* is the essential Bowie tome and who has been gracious regarding my esoteric takes on an artist he knows far more about. To Tariq Goddard, who kindly endured my delays in finishing the previous book as well my fresh set of delays for this one.

I'm often asked if David Bowie read the blog or the earlier book. No idea. I never got a single indication that he did. He was internet-savvy enough that I feel he must have been aware that the blog existed, at least. If he did read it, I hope he got a kick out of it, though I imagine he more likely cracked up about how completely wrong I got something. The world is a lesser place without him.

Chris O'Leary
Easthampton, 2018

"That's the message that I sent."

Repeater Books

is dedicated to the creation of a new reality. The landscape of twenty-first-century arts and letters is faded and inert, riven by fashionable cynicism, egotistical self-reference and a nostalgia for the recent past. Repeater intends to add its voice to those movements that wish to enter history and assert control over its currents, gathering together scattered and isolated voices with those who have already called for an escape from Capitalist Realism. Our desire is to publish in every sphere and genre, combining vigorous dissent and a pragmatic willingness to succeed where messianic abstraction and quiescent co-option have stalled: abstention is not an option: we are alive and we don't agree.